The Author

Tony Beesley lives in Rotherham South Yorkshire with his fiancée, one of his two sons and their cat.

Our Generation

The Punk and Mod children

of Sheffield, Rotherham and Doncaster

1976 - 1985

Tony Beesley

Printed on FSC approved paper by

FASTPRINT GOLD PUBLISHING

PETERBOROUGH, ENGLAND

Our Generation
Copyright © Tony Beesley 2009

All publishing rights and copyright owned by the author Tony Beesley
'Days like Tomorrow' Books

ISBN 9781844266180

First Published 2009 by 'Days like Tomorrow books'

Printed by
FASTPRINT GOLD PUBLISHING
Peterborough, England.

Cover designed by Dave Spencer

www.printondemand-worldwide.com

Our Generation

Contents

Foreword

Dave Spencer

I first met the author, Tony Beesley in 1983. I was rehearsing with a band in a classroom at Rawmarsh Comprehensive School. So was Tony.

The first thing that made an impression on me about Tony was his shirt. It was identical to one that Joe Strummer had worn in 1977.

It turned out that a "punk rocker" by the name of Bryan Bell had been to see the Clash one night back in 1977 and swapped shirts with Clash singer Joe Strummer. Bryan wore it for a couple of years before eventually giving the shirt to Tony.

By 1983 I had been into the old "punk rock" for about 5 or 6 years. I had seen some great gigs. I had been toughened up by "punk rock". I had been attacked, not necessarily because I looked particularly different but because I looked different *enough* for people to know I was into "punk rock". So had Tony.

So what was strange was that although we had been into the same music, been to many of the same gigs and even shared the same friends, we had never met before. It made me see that it wasn't just me, then, that had been touched and changed by this music. If there were two people on opposite sides of a town as small as Rotherham who had been influenced as much as we had been by punk, but whose paths had never crossed, then there could be thousands of us. A generation defined as much by what we weren't as by what we were.

In the 1970s, in Rotherham, time stood still and the clocks had stopped at different times for different people. At the Dickens on Westgate it was 1970, Led Zeppelin, Deep Purple, Black Sabbath. Joe Cocker had played there, or so they say.... Oh, wow!

7

At the County Borough, on Bridgegate - Rotherham, it was still 1956. Teddy Boys stood outside, endlessly combing and re-combing their quiffs waiting for Elvis!

The ordinary people; the bus drivers; the shop assistants; the teachers; the butchers; the bakers and the candelabra swingers wore flares, long hair and moustaches just like The Beatles in 1968.

And parents looked like their parents and so on and so on and so on.

The past towered over us all and there was no future.

In 1976, the present crept into town, and the locals didn't like it. Not one bit. For the first time in a generation, it meant that to be a part of the new order, we had to reject the old. This time around though, old orders were here there and everywhere, left right and centre. This time we rejected everything.

This, I think, is what pissed people off more than the raucous music, more than the outspoken punk rock 'stars' and more than the clothes. What pissed the public off more than anything else was that punk rock made every previous movement/rebellion pitifully tame in comparison, because it challenged the way people thought.

Tony Beesley's book is about the rise and fall of punk in South Yorkshire. It's about the people who took the first faltering steps out of the shadows and how we were liberated by punk rock and how we were restricted by punk rock.

It's about 'Our Generation'.

Introduction

It is now almost 33 years since the words 'Punk Rock' first appeared firmly fixed on the nations lips. Everyone from sherbet and fudge-devouring school kids, TV obliterating lorry drivers to their Murray mint-sucking grandparents were introduced - via the ever dependable tabloids - to the 'Filth and the Fury' of those foul mouthed yobs the Sex pistols and their 'so called' spitting, swearing and subversive followers. Through the infamous Bill Grundy v Sex Pistols interview and its ensuing headlines of outrage, Punk rock swept the nation like a tidal wave of misunderstood, misinformed and widely held condemnation. From that day of infamy in December 1976, the image of the Punk Rock phenomenon was firmly set in stone and for the next few years would never fully recover from that very sensationalism that would also result in the disintegration of the Pistols themselves a little over a year later.

However, that's not the whole picture at all; there are many versions of the real story to be told from that era and even more individual stories from within them. Up here in Sheffield and within the steel city and its 'sibling urchin twins' Rotherham and Doncaster, there is a very different tale to be told. One that effectively began six months before 'the filth and the fury' at a pub-rock venue that was at the end of its illustrious career but still held one more momentous occasion up its sleeve in order to affirm its legendary status before its own passing.

In July 1976, the Sex pistols played at the Black Swan supported by the newly formed Clash performing their very first live set to a poorly attended but 'of the moment' audience. A few months later, the Pistols played to an almost empty Doncaster Outlook club a mere few weeks before the Punk outrage blew up into the nation's consciousness. The effects, however, of both these and other events were not lost on a small proportion of the local inquisitive youth, who would then spread the word and fan the flames of the new sounds and scene amongst our midst.

Almost immediately the main protagonists were racing from the starting point first with- Sheffield's very own Punk fanzine Gun-rubber, and then its own roster of Punk influenced groups... all inspired by Punk's 'Do It Yourself' aesthetic and its call to arms. The call, for a short while throughout the era was *anyone can do it'*, but more importantly there would be lessons to be learned from Johnny Rotten's own declaration of 'Lesson 1; Do it yourself – Lesson 2; Do it properly'.

From this self-created Punk ideology evolved Sheffield's own Punk-inspired musicians, the majority of whom would set out from Punk but take a separate route altogether from its accepted path. Local scenester Paul Bower, along with Gun-Rubber and his own hard working Punk three piece band 2.3, would be instrumental in helping to push the Human League on to the Post-Punk map from where they - along with Vice Versa (later ABC) - would kick-start their own diverse careers into the Thatcherite 80's and beyond.

However, the effect that punk had on the region and its youth is the real story of this book. The life defining experiences as told by the local youth, teenagers and young adults who embraced the new order changing their lives, attitude and outlook forever. This is the story of Sheffield, Rotherham and Doncaster's own Punk generation and the journeys taken from the starting point that is often mythically referred to as the year zero!

Told in autobiographical memoir form and based around myself (the author's) personal experiences, along with those of well over a hundred and fifty other local participants of the scene and beyond, this is a story told with many and varying viewpoints and insights. Here to read and absorb in this almost 'coming of age' story...are recollections of pure clarity and realisation, obsession, loss of faith, grabs for identity and a sense of belonging to a scene that existed for a short while, but managed to influence and inform many right up until the present day.

Within these pages, there are tales of unprovoked violence and jealous indifference amongst the pure innocence, frustration and naivety of being a young teenager during the late 1970's to early 80's. Stories also jump in from time to time of Punk and Post- Punk local groups formed and broken, along with musicians and fans reminiscing some of the many classic (and not so classic) gigs and music performed in the many venues in the area back in the day.

Accounts are recalled of meeting Punk generation figureheads such as Sid Vicious, Joe Strummer and Paul Weller and show new insights from local music fans' perspectives. Also, there are sure to be a fair share of moments when the readers will find themselves laughing aloud at some of the accounts, probably relating to their own experiences or recognising the long forgotten feeling of being young and often getting things wrong in a very much right kind of way. This is a very human story – warts and all – from a time when being young could have meant swapping boredom, frustration, long hair, flares – and for younger contributors (including myself) Airfix kits and chopper bikes for something called Punk Rock.

The euphoria, excitement and originality of the local Punk scene and its offspring movements is told by its participants with a mixture of often almost uncontrollable enthusiasm but at times unexpected disappointments, whilst recognising both the positive and negative infallibilities of our own generation. The Punk scene from beginning to end, along with the Mod revival and Post-Punk futurism, told from these viewpoints are all dealt with a refreshing honesty and clear focus that brings the era back to life.

The changes within the subject's northern boundaries are seen to be clearly as provocative and profound as those encountered further south in its original birthplace. As one contributor stated recently *'It says a lot for our local youth that they were willing to suffer the consequences of being different and dressing to the despised Punk style'*. Or as another voice featured within these pages adds *'I lived in a Yorkshire pit town and the locals did not take too kindly to anything different let alone Punks or New Romantics plastered with make up'*.

This local Punk generation does have a truly individual story to tell. One that spans almost two decades... from the words of aspiring local Punk Rockers and musicians, sharp suited Mods and 2-tone-loving Punks and skinheads, along with lipstick-smudged and floppy-fringed New Romantics. A representation of part of a local generation that within its midst of restless, misled, excitable, often exceptionally receptive 'bored out of their heads' kids is the story of 'Our Generation'. It is now being told for the very first time. It starts here - before Punk Rock - back in the mid to early 70's, back then and almost 40 years ago. Let the journey begin!

Notes

Before we start the Punk Rock journey, just a few notes explaining how the work is set out, and a little helping hand in getting to grips with its style and sequencing. The work, as you will have probably guessed is a biographical account of the era, including as much as I can recall myself that I consider will be of interest. With all speaking characters in the work, I have introduced them with where they are/were from at the time and any relevant facts i.e. musician, DJ, Doncaster Punk Rocker, Rotherham Mod etc. Each time that they re-appear they will only be referred to by their name only, but for extra reference, I have included a so-called 'cast list' following these notes, just in case you get stuck guys! As for my own words, first I will introduce myself as Tony Beesley in my first passage and then every passage afterwards will be just Tony. Simple ain't it?

This work covers roughly a period of 25 years (from 1970 to 1976, and far more extensively 1976 through to the mid 80's). I have tried to steer the work, as much as possible in a basic chronological order, though I have had to make some concessions to this. For instance, the Post-Punk period chapter of 'They must be Tourists' starts after the main bulk of the book that is the Punk Rock period of 76-81. The two chapters that cover the local Mod scene follow this and although this does digress back to 1978-79, I felt that it worked much better, arriving as it does, straight after the Post-Punk chapter. On that subject the term Post-Punk it should be noted, was not an actual style of music, but more of a Punk inspired attitude pushing out the musical boundaries of the Punk period and beyond.

Also, during parts of the Punk chapters, the story may jump back and forth slightly to accommodate the differing themes of the story. The 'Trouble with Punk' chapter has stories from within the whole Punk period, and is then followed by the next chapter, which continues in its correct time-line. However, the whole work does fall into place in mostly chronological order, with only slight steps sideways every now and again, in order to tell the story most effectively.

Finally, in order to capture the period and give the story some character and colour, I have used various experiences of my own that tie in with the stories theme, whilst also injecting a dose of humour that reflects how things were back then, and more importantly how profound our experiences were. Little did we realise, though, that we would be recounting them 30 years later. On that point, let's make a start!

The Punk and Mod Cast
(In order of appearance)

David McKendry ... (70's Rock fan and Sheffield Punk)
Tony Beesley ... (The Author)
Wilo ... (Sheffield Suede head)
Mikey ... (early 70's Sheffield Top Rank goer)
Bryan Bell ... (Rotherham 70's Rock fan and Punk Rocker)
Jo Callis ... (Rezillos/Human League musician and one time Rotherham resident)
Steve Haythorne ... (Sheffield Northern Soul/Glam Rock/Punk fan)
Paul Utley ... (Singer with Mexborough New Wave group the Diks)
Lynne Freeman ... (Sheffield Glam fan/Punkette)
Timothy Green ... (Rotherham Rock fan/Punk Rocker)
Steve Lloyd ... (Doncaster Rock fan/Punk Rocker/Outlook club staff member)
Simon Eyre ... (Sheffield Rock fan)
Paul Bower ... (Sheffield 70's rock fan/Gun rubber Punk fanzine writer/2.3 singer + guitarist/music writer)
Joe Strummer ... (101er's/the Clash singer + guitarist)
Morg ... (Doncaster Punk Rocker)
Graham Torr ... (Rotherham Punk musician/Cute Pubes)
Richard Chatterton ... (Rotherham Punk Rocker/Post-Punk fan)
Gary Gillott (Chippie) ... (Rotherham Musician – Vision – and Punk Rocker)
Rob Saripo ... (Rotherham Rock fan)
Duncan Payne ... (Northern Soul fan and Post-Punk fan and one time Sheffield resident)
Anthony Cronshaw ... (Sheffield Punk/skinhead and football author)
John D.Ellis ... (Sheffield Punk Rocker)
Mick Jones ... (Clash guitarist/songwriter)
Barrie Masters ... (Eddie and the Hot Rods singer)
Dave Berry ... (Sheffield musician/singer)
Bob Gray ... (Original Jam keyboard player)
Patrick Tierney ... (Doncaster Punk fan)
Nicky Booth ... (Rotherham Punk and Post-Punk fan)
Dave Spencer ... (Rotherham Punk/singer + guitarist with PVC/Cute Pubes/Springheel'd-Jack)
Paul Clarkson ... (Rotherham Punk Rocker/New Romantic scenester)
Phillip Wright ... (Sheffield Punk Rocker/Mod)
Joanne Orgil ... (Rotherham Punkette)
Sue Lowday ... (Sheffield Punkette)
Richard Kirk ... (Sheffield musician with Cabaret Voltaire)
Andy Blade ... (Singer with Eater)
Dave Vanian ... (Singer with the Damned)
Barry Bartle ... (Sheffield Punk rocker)
Pete Cooper ... (Rotherham Punk Rocker/musician)

John Harrison ... (Rotherham Punk Rocker/Mod/Bass player with the Way)
Paul Kelly ... (Sheffield Punk)
Chiz ... (Chesterfield Punk Rocker/Riot Squad singer)
Phil Oakey ... (Singer with Human League)
Phil Tasker ... (Doncaster Punk Rocker/Vice Squad singer)
Phil Udell ... (Rotherham Rock fan)
Tom Cleary... (Sheffield Punk Rocker)
Stuart Bates... (Rotherham Punk Rocker)
Jet ... (Doncaster Punk Rocker)
Pete Weston ... (Rotherham Punk Rocker)
TV Smith ... (Adverts singer/songwriter and solo artist)
Polystyrene ... (X-Ray Spex singer)
Ian Clayton ... (TV Presenter/author)
Simon Currie ... (Rotherham Punk fan)
Gary Robinson ... (Rotherham Punk Rocker)
Dean Stables (Beanz) ... (Rotherham Punk Rocker)
Paul White (Sugar) ... (Rotherham Punk Rocker)
Ivor Hillman ... (Rotherham Punk Rocker/New Romantic/My Pierrot Dolls singer)
Andy Goulty ... (Rotherham Punk Rocker)
Margaret ... (Sound of Music record shop sales assistant)
Honest John Plain ... (The Boys guitarist)
Pete' Esso' Haynes... (Lurkers drummer)
Joe Elliott ... (Def Leppard singer)
Arturo Bassick ... (Lurkers/Pinpoint/999)
Steve Marshall ... (Sheffield Punk Rocker/Top Rank roadie)
Tony Parsons ... (NME Punk journalist/author)
Stephen Singleton ... (Vice Versa/ABC)
Phil Taylor ... (X-Rippers bass player and Barnsley Punk Rocker)
Gill Frost ... (Rotherham Punk fan)
Dave Parsons ... (Sham 69 guitarist)
Helen McLaughlin ... (Rotherham Punkette)
Steven Doidge ... (Rotherham Punk Rocker)
Andrew Morton ... (Rotherham Punk fan)
Pete Roddis ... (Rotherham Punk Rocker/New Romantic)
Paul Clarke... (Rotherham Punk Rocker)
Andy Lee... (Sheffield/Dronfield Punk/Marples gig organiser)
Tracy Stanley ... (Rotherham Punkette/New Romantic)
Lynne Haythorne ... (Rotherham Punk/New Wave fan)
Simon ... (Sheffield Punk Rocker)
Julian Jones ... (Rotherham Punk Rocker/Musician/Songwriter with Alternative Route, Lazy Dollies and solo artist)
Michael Day ... (Sheffield Punk Rocker)
Martin Clarke ... (Sheffield Punk and Rock fan)
Deano ... (Sheffield Limit club goer)
Ian Robertson ... (Sheffield Punk Rocker)

Dave Burkinshaw ... (Rotherham Punk Rocker)
Anon ... (Sheffield Limit club goer)
Andrea Berry ... (Sheffield Punkette)
Chelle ... (Sheffield Limit club goer)
Brian Pearson ... (Guitarist with the Prams)
The Shapes ... (Post – Punk group)
Rob 'Dingo' Dowling ... (Sheffield Punk Rocker/Limit club goer)
Julie Turton ... (Sheffield Limit club goer)
Ric Robson ... (Sheffield Limit club goer)
Chris Lee ... (Sheffield Limit club goer)
Nick Orme ... (Sheffield Punk Rocker/Mod)
Knox ... (Vibrators singer/Guitarist)
Ian Marsh ... (Human League synthesiser player)
Steve Wright ... (Huddersfield Punk fan)
Howard Wall ... (Lurkers singer)
Martin Gordon ... (Radio Stars bass player)
Steve Mardy ... (Manchester musician – the Hoax – Punk Rocker)
Mark Senior ... (Sheffield Punk Rocker)
Martin C ... (Sheffield Punk Rocker)
Darren Twynam ... (Rotherham Punk fan)
Jim Darnill ... (Singer with Sheffield group Disease)
June Graham ... (Rotherham Punkette)
Dale ... (Mexborough Punk fan)
Michael Hill ... (Rock fan/Local music promoter)
Charlie Harper ... (UK Subs singer)
Shaun Angell ... (Rotherham Punk/New Wave/New Romantic fan)
Tony Atkins ... (Rotherham Punk Rocker)
Barry Thurman ... (Rotherham Punk fan/Bass player with My Pierrot Dolls)
Andrea Deakin ... (Rotherham Punkette)
Jeff Turner ... (Cockney Rejects singer)
Martin Hickman ... (Rotherham Punk fan)
Wayne Kenyon ... (Doncaster Punk/skinhead/musician)
Paul Smith ... (Sheffield Punk Rocker)
Jill Agar ... (Rotherham Punkette)
Claire ... (Sheffield Marples goer)
Valerie Garvey ... (Sheffield Punkette)
Gary Bushell ... (Sounds magazine writer/journalist)
Paul Moxon ... (Rotherham Punk Rocker/Marples gig goer)
Martin ... (Sheffield Punk Rocker/Marples gig goer)
Marcus Featherby – in his absence ... (Sheffield Marples gig organiser/promoter)
Martin Fry ... (Vice Versa/ABC singer)
Jarvis Cocker ... (Pulp singer/Sheffield gig goer)
Martin Dust ... (Sheffield Punk Rocker)
Dave Frost ... (Rotherham Punk Rocker)
Chris Sheridan ... (Chesterfield Punk Rocker)

Mark Barnet – in his absence ... (Rotherham Punk Rocker)
Simon Bird ... (Rotherham musician/Drummer with Cute Pubes/Springheel'd Jack)
Spencer Summers ... (UK Subs/Bad Manners roadie)
Cheryl ... (Sheffield Human League fan)
Steve Cowens ... (Sheffield New Romantic/football author)
Simon Hinkler ... (Artery)
Timo ... (Sheffield Limit club goer)
Gary Davies ... (Rotherham musician)
Katrine ... (Rotherham 60's Mod)
Ian Brown ... (Stone Roses singer/Rotherham + Doncaster Mod night's goer)
Paul Weller ... (Singer/guitarist/songwriter with the Jam/Style Council/Solo artist)
Steve Orridge ... (Barnsley Mod/Quadrophenia extra)
Kevin Lawn ... (Barnsley Mod/Quadrophenia extra)
Steve Parlett ... (Rotherham Mod)
Stewart Hardman ... (Barnsley Mod)
Darren Gray ... (Sheffield Mod)
Bob Manton ... (Purple Hearts singer)
Russ Weaver ... (Rotherham Mod/Guitarist with Revolver)
Lynne Rollinson ... (Rotherham Mod/ska fan)
Jimmy Mathison ... (Rotherham skinhead)
Julian McKenzie ... (Sheffield 2-tone fan/author)
Steve Emmerson ... (Chesterfield Mod)
Martin Ridgeway ... (Rotherham Mod)
Ian Deakin ... (Mexborough Punk fan/Mod/Drummer with The Way)
Mark Ellis ... (Leeds Mod DJ/Rotherham Mod event goer)
Andy Bull ... (Chesterfield Mod/Immediate Reaction fanzine editor)
David ... (Sheffield Mod)
Dave Gooderham ... (Rotherham Mod/skinhead)
Jamie Kennedy ... (Swinton near Rotherham Skinhead + Mod fan)
Gary ... (Rotherham scooter scene/Mod fan)
Vanessa Sorrell ... (Rotherham scooter scene goer)

Hey Ho Let's Go

Back in the 1970's and 80's 'The Falstaff' pub in Rotherham Town centre was dog rough. Not quite as rough as the old 'County Borough' but rough enough. Punters would always make sure they wore their six shooters and the place had an air of Dodge City about it. Wyatt Earp would have trod carefully if he had ventured in there. Some of the fellas in there were rough diamonds and if you were ok with them, they would leave you well alone. Unfortunately, not all the clients were that tolerant and some would get tanked up and go looking for trouble, either on the premises or around town. A red-hot summer's day many years ago I discovered this ritual first hand.

There were these two burly 30 something brutish Teds - the type that hated Punk Rockers and I happened to cross their path - worse luck... We were minding our own business on a sunny afternoon walking through Rotherham town centre. There was myself and my mate Gary, Joanne (who later joined Sheffield's answer to The Slits... Debar) with her purple spikes poking the sky and a guy called Chippie who later played in a local band called Vision.

The doors of the old Rotherham boozer Falstaff opened up and out came Eddie Vincent and Shakin' Cock-rum; who were both as pissed as a pair of barmaids' blouses and straight away they caught a glimpse of us and the array of colour we displayed. "*Oi! Punks hold on there,*" they shouted. We carried on walking, quickening the pace - as we could sense what was about to come. We could hear the drunken shouting and the abuse following us like a pair of bloodhounds who thought we had taken their favourite bones. We managed to get to the doors at the market and - I first felt a fist and then a kick, I could now smell their breath. Bang! a smack to the back of my head whilst at the same time a blue suede shoe attached to a drainpipe leg twisted round my ankle- giving me a push, twist and a kick to the floor. My face hit the rock hard floor. I looked up and Gary – though looking to give me a helping hand - was being pulled into the market by Chippie and then Joanne - whilst two heaps of rock n' roll hate and anger were laying into me thick and fast. Old ladies were 'ooohhh ing' and 'aaaaaarrr ing', the Teds were swearing and kicking me in the face and everywhere else, and I kept trying to get up. It seemed like ages but probably wasn't. I eventually managed to stand up and my arm felt limp, as it had been twisted round my back. My other arm managed to lift a stern two fingers up and my mouth also managed to say something that was anything but thanks for my summer afternoon's performance of '*How a Ted shows his punk enemy how to kiss the floor with a blue suede shoe in his face*'. Anyway I took it and was the only one who got hurt (cheers guys) - my faith in Edwardian gents forever tainted, covered in bruises and cuts. Still I always had that evening's youth club to go to and show off my wounds. That night I went to the youth club with a blue suede shoe imprinted on to the side of my face and I am not kidding either. That was what it could be like being a Punk Rocker in Rotherham back then!

Chapter one

Something Better Change

"The seventies were an ever-changing decade and time never seemed to stay still for long." **(The author)**

The 1970's - The Decade that style forgot! Or so they say. Thursday nights; Top of the Pops and Tomorrow's world...School holidays with The Beachcombers, Banana Splits, Robinson Crusoe and Flashing Blade on the mid morning telly. Chopper bikes, Scalextric, the three-day week and power cuts. Abba, Queen, Bowie, T- Rex, and the Supersonic pop show...Glam Rock, Prog Rock, Pub Rock, Disco, Philly Soul, Long hair, beards and bell bottom jeans, velvet jackets, high heeled platform shoes, cheesecloth shirts and dodgy tank tops. Ahh the 70's... and then there was Punk Rock!!!

Rotherham, Sheffield and Doncaster...the mid 1970's! Were they dull and grey towns? Were they the picture of boredom, unrest and social stagnation as is often typically depicted in most retrospective accounts of the UK - during the pre-Punk era?

David McKendry (70's Rock fan and future Punk) ..."Space dust, oral XXX, and losing my virginity to the lass behind the bar at the Penthouse. Oxford Bags, Star Jumpers, 5 Button High-waisters, ginormous shirt collars, Watney's Party Beer Cans, Colt 45, Long Life: and all this before I left school."

Evidently, not all accounts of the 1970's were exactly dull then?

Tony Beesley (the author - and in all following quotes referred to as Tony) … "For me personally the 70's were quite colourful. The North I knew was not so dull and grey and all those clichéd things. However, I myself was in the midst of the last couple of years of being a pre-teenager. My surroundings of Rotherham and my local area were not viewed as the history book version of mid 1970's England that we often accept as gospel. I remember those days as exciting, funny and often hard - I lived in a council house with no fridge, a coal fire for central heating and no colour TV - but life was colourful and my perception of my surroundings from that time will always be balanced with those images.

It's hard to remember it all, but I certainly remember the emergence of Punk Rock. Its idealism and approach to everything would remain with me steadfast from then on."

However, how did this anti-social, publicly detested and back to basics music get under the skin of us - the Punk generation of the area? In the UK, London had witnessed the birth of the Punk rock explosion closely followed, especially enthusiasm and originality wise, by Manchester. As soon as the word spread throughout the suburbs, however, the scene was no longer provincial. Truly anyone, it seemed, could have a go now and this could well be applied to Sheffield and Rotherham's youth as much as anywhere else in the country. Punk would soon become a starting point for a whole generation.

Until this unfolding of history had taken place - we up north and in and around Rotherham, Sheffield and the other towns and suburbs of the area - were left to put up with whatever was on offer oblivious to the rumblings further south.

Even so, totally independent of any of the capital's influence, brave and unique attempts were made to push things along in Sheffield amongst the city's underground scene when future members of Sheffield bands formed their own pre-punk shock ensemble Musical Vomit. The other important underground Sheffield group were Cabaret Voltaire, who pre-dated Punk by a good few years. Cabaret Voltaire member Richard Kirk, who was an ex-skinhead, was known to dress in a style that resembled the Punk look a good couple of years before the movement even kicked off, whilst their sound and musical approach was certainly no risk-free zone.

Before Punk hit the region there was a myriad of varying styles of music being played at a handful of licensed venues and hundreds of local youth clubs. The Top Rank venue in Sheffield would later be an integral stop-off point for the Punk groups. During the early 70's the venue held many popular nights, one of which was the Tuesday night disco that those who attended have fond memories of, speaking of a time when *'We looked good in our crombies, Ben Sherman shirts, sta-prest trousers and dockers or oxford brogue boots'*. A typical night at the venue in 1970 would see teenagers dressed in this post –Mod skinhead/suede head style and dancing to Blue beat, reggae, Amen Corner and Desmond Dekker. Things go round in circles don't they?

Wilo (from Sheffield) remembers … "One night in 1970, attired in crombie, Ben Sherman, Levi sta-prest and my pride and joy 'Oxford Brogue' boots (also known as granddad boots); well, they wouldn't let me in there because I had boots on. I was gutted, they had cost me about 6 weeks wages and the last thing on my mind was kicking someone and then spoiling them."

Those Tuesday nights at the Top Rank would soon reflect the changing sounds and styles of the decade with Glam Rock and its associated music being prevalent on the set list.

Mikey … "We used to go every week and loved it, apart from the occasional mugging outside! We listened to Slade, Roxy Music and all that disco nonsense. There were the collars, flares, segs, tank-tops, and the cardboard hankie in the pocket, levis, Ben Sherman's and the monkey boots for the girls."

Also, let us not forget those small 7-inch plates of plastic!

Bryan Bell (70's Rock fan) ... "The first record that I bought, I think it would have been 'School's out' by Alice Cooper."

Tony ... "Almost every Saturday afternoon, following the Rotherham footie game, my brother would arrive home with 2 or 3 new singles in a 'Sound of Music'(Record shop) bag. T- Rex, the Sweet, Bowie, Slade, 10cc, Mott the Hoople; the music would be playing as I came back from town with my latest Airfix set. I would be more interested in the labels of those records than the music in the grooves. Time though, would allow for giant leaps forward in my interest in the contents of those shiny black grooves."

Future Rezillo guitarist and Human League member Jo Callis had spent his early years living in Rotherham, inbetween moving around the world with his family due to his father's RAF postings. Jo recalls those days in the town during the mid 1960's to 1970's and also his early musical influences – revealing the many varied sounds that would later help feed The Rezillos musical vision.

Jo Callis (future Rezillo/Human League)... "My first days in Rotherham... I was born to parents who had just returned to Blighty from Singapore (My father had served in WW2 and Malaya in the RAF), and we lived in a two up two down in Wortley Road. As a keen cricketer, my father had wished me to be born in Yorkshire so I would be eligible to play for the Yorkshire County Cricket club once I had grown up. At this time one had to be Yorkshire born to 'play fer't team tha knows'. Unfortunately, for father's ambitions, a cricket bat to me was little but a badly balanced air guitar, I was rubbish at cricket.

After several years of being dragged up and down the country and a posting in Cyprus, which was another adventure for me as I combined my interests in James Bond, comedy and films with my growing taste in popular music. This then led to my first group, which we called the Cockroaches. It was really just a sketch which I had wrote for the end of term concert and consisted of me and three mates singing Beatles numbers whilst silently banging away at home made cardboard guitars and drums; the whole thing climaxing in a free for all band punch up. Needless to say, it was the highlight of the concert and for the next day or so, we were treated like pop stars at school – a career defining moment you might say.

Returning to Rotherham, whilst my father stayed in Cyprus defending the sovereign front line (the family had been evacuated from Cyprus due to the civil war that had broke out between the Greek and Turkish Cypriots), we stayed with Grandma at 252 Wortley Road. Britain was in the throes of the swinging sixties by now and I would watch 'Look North' that would always feature a performance from one of the new Beat groups at the end of the show, such as the Hollies, Dave Clarke Five or Sheffield's own Dave Berry. The most exciting part of an evening was when the immortal words 'The Weekend Starts Here' emanated from the puny old small b&w TV speakers, heralding the start of the groundbreaking and totally hip Ready Steady Go! All the top acts would appear on Ready Steady Go, now I could see all the things I'd only heard on the radio or seen grainy newspaper photo's of whilst in Cyprus. I loved the Beatles of course and the Stones, The Hollies and the Pretty Things who were the scruffiest longest haired blokes I'd ever seen fascinated me. They made the Stones look conservative by the standards of the day! I was also becoming interested in many of the black soul artists who were brought over from the USA by Ready Steady Go; I guess I loved it all really. It was a very culturally stimulating era for a daft wee lad whose only dream in life was to own a real electric guitar, and for Airfix to bring out a kit of The Bren Gun Carrier!

Eventually, after a few months, which seem like an eternity at twelve years old, Father returned from his tour of duty in Cyprus and soon it was time to move on again, just as I was getting settled. The difference between the grimy industrial Rotherham of the time and Aphrodite's sun-blessed paradise of Cyprus couldn't have been more marked, but I had always found a perverse and fascinating beauty in the northern industrial cities of my parent's birth. I liked the smoke the bustle and the noise, I was and still am quite enamoured of the moments when the dusk begins to set in and the street lamps and neon signs switch on, commanding their colourful presence over the previously grey urbanity. I liked buses and lorries and trains, the Rotherham indoor market and the toy stores with their tantalising displays of Airfix models and Dalek merchandise (the whole country was also in the midst of Dalekmania at this time) and the thought that somewhere lurking about some street corner there might be a little gang of Teds or Rockers, each with a fag hanging out of his mouth and a flicknife in his pocket. It was vibrant, stimulating and a bit scary, and lets face it Rock and Roll wasn't ever going to have been invented in some idyllic holiday location. Grim up North? Well, maybe you can take the boy out of Yorkshire but you can't take Yorkshire out of the boy.

I continued to be shunted around the country as our family moved from station to station ending up in Scotland and discovering The Kinks, the work of Gerry Anderson, the Small Faces, Mods and Rockers, Geno Washington, Jimi Hendrix, Deep Purple and more along the way. Other than the occasional visit 'up north', or 'down south' as it would come to be known whilst in Scotland, either to visit the Grannies or do the odd punk gig, I was not to spend any length of time in South Yorks. Until that is, my involvement in the Sheffield New Romantic scene of the early eighties through my work with the arty but wacky Human League."

The early seventies were not yet set in the stale and redundant state that would be prevalent a few years later. Glam Rock was fast becoming a colourful alternative to the grown-up rock sounds of the sixties generation. Just about everywhere, Bowie was always popular, and despite the effeminate image of Bowie and glam, was popular with many of the local football hooligan lads. Walls graffitied with Bowie, Mott the Hoople and Slade were commonplace. Another Glam act Marc Bolan and T-Rex played an open-air concert in Rotherham Town's Clifton Park on the 28th August 1971.

Steve Haythorne from Sheffield and originally from Rotherham remembers ... "I saw Marc Bolan and T-Rex aT the City Hall, it must have been about 1972; Marc made a big entrance on a big star that seemed to appear from out of the stage or something. Mickey Finn was throwing these plastic tambourines into the audience causing small scraps to break out here and there."

Paul Hutley who would later form Mexborough New Wave group the Diks reminisces about his earliest influences during the 1970's ... "My biggest early influence was Marc

Bolan; I had every single, every album, every poster etc. I considered myself a true fan. Other influences were always the bands that had great stage presence- Alex Harvey Band, Heavy Metal Kids. We used to travel miles to see Heavy Metal Kids. I also enjoyed Heavy Metal music."

Punk was a couple of years away still, but for some local teenagers the appeal of Glam rock was also a starting point for the later Punk rebellion.

Lynne Freeman (Sheffield Glam fan and future Punkette) ... "Well, my drinking days started long before any 18th birthday was celebrated! I was always a rebel, not in a loud and brash way, but in a way that meant I felt I didn't quite fit in. For instance at the age of thirteen, we had to wear uniform at school, blazer, shirt and tie etc, I really railed against having to dress the same as everyone else. I had just discovered David Bowie and thought he was wonderful with his ever-changing characters, and slightly dodgy lyrics for a girl of 12/13 to listen to. One day, at school, I took a black marker pen, took my blazer off and emblazoned the back of it with 'BOWIE' and the traditional lightening flash. From then on, my blazer was different, I was different, and my little fight with establishment had begun!!"

Saturday afternoons, for the region's teenagers would be either spent watching their favourite local football teams, or buying records from the many record shops that were to be found in the area.

Many of these teenagers also loved Roxy Music. The group played quite regularly in Sheffield and lots of local fans would make the gigs a kind of celebration. Phil Oakey and Martyn Ware (who later would form the Human league), and Richard Kirk and Simon Mallinder of Cabaret Voltaire were all massive fans.

Above: Rotherham's epitome of fashion and jeans wear

Steve Haythorne ... "I was a massive fan of Roxy Music and saw them play quite a few times, including a couple of times at the City Hall. My very first gig was Roxy Music at the City Hall. I remember thinking at the time that they were the coolest group ever. They looked so cool, in particular Bryan Ferry. At one of these gigs, they were using a see through violin. I would follow Roxy around and saw them play five nights in a row on one tour. I knew every song that they ever played. 'Man alive' I paid a quid to see them at the City Hall. I used to buy the NME and check for release dates of their records and then go and buy them from the Sound of Music record shop in Rotherham. I had every single and album and... wow they were the coolest group ever for me at the time."

At this time, Sheffield clubs like the Crazy Daisy were becoming popular with the city's more flamboyant music fans, where they could express their fashion sense more freely.

Lynne Freeman ... "I started to frequent the Crazy Daisy club on High Street in Sheffield. A girl at school went with her (much older) boyfriend, and asked me if I wanted to go with them. I got there and it was a revelation, loads of loud music and of course Bowie look-alikes. I drank and danced and met loads of people and really enjoyed myself."

While the teenagers were digging the pop music of Glam and disco, their older brothers and sisters would be getting off on the over-indulgent sounds of progressive Rock. Adult saturated Prog Rock would be one of the biggest contributory factors to the aching need for something like Punk Rock to come along.

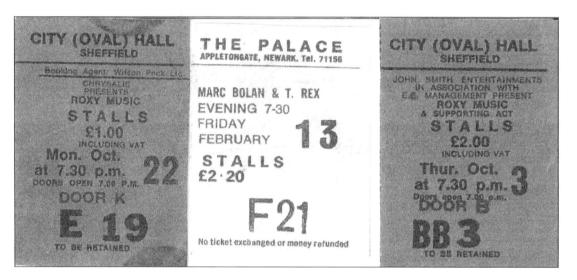

Roxy Music and Marc Bolan tickets from Steve Haythorne's collection

Tony ... "One of the main things I remember of that time in the mid 70's, and this also contributed to my distaste towards grown up music- so to speak was 'Tubular Bells' by Mike Oldfield. It was everywhere at the time and it really did drive me crackers. It was so boring and over-indulgent. I hated it with a passion and I still do. My brother had it on his 8-track tape player in the car and all we heard on our trips to the coast was that rotten sound of 'Tubular Bells'."

Timothy Green (Rotherham Rock fan/future Punk) ... "In 1975 music was boring, apart from the Sensational Alex Harvey Band's sense of theatre and Dr. Feelgood's short, fast songs that were played with some real aggression. I do remember getting enthused reading about the scene in New York in the NME, though."

Steve Lloyd (from Doncaster) ... "I went to see Barclay James Harvest at Sheffield Top Rank. I was about 15 years old and this was 1975 and the music was just so far removed. It was ok for rich rock stars but for kids like me, we couldn't give a toss. This was like the music equivalent of Jurassic Park."

Tony ... "When I think back to the mid 70's music scene I always think of beards and long hair and all those groups that were so unreachable. That's why the Glam music was so appealing to us young kids because it was not as serious and was more down to earth even if it was dressed up in a sugar coating. It was simple pop I suppose. I did like Queen for quite a while though. My brother had their 'Sheer Heart Attack' LP and that was really good. I bought a few of their LP's just before Punk, but I didn't really have any musical heroes as such; my heroes were Alf Tupper out of the Victor Comic, George Best, Tony Curtis, Steve McQueen and Barry Sheene."

Steve Haythorne ... "As for all the prog rock of the time, I did like early Genesis when they had Peter Gabriel in them. This was a time when I would go to Virgin records at the bottom of the Moor in Sheffield and buy records taking a risk on them. I spent hours in there."

While the music and fashion of the mid 70's was far less than inspiring for many of the youth of the local area – likewise throughout most of the country – some Sheffield music fans found the live scene to be continuing to deliver the goods.

Rock fan **Simon Eyre** ... "The Sheffield music scene in the mid to late 70s was incredibly diverse and there seemed to be room for every type of band. I was a guitar player, mainly playing with Jazz Rock bands Plastic Max and Double Life, and also the short-lived Clayton Eyre Band with keyboardist Dave Clayton but that never got past the rehearsal stage. Any night of the week, though, if you wanted to see a band, you could, there was live music venues everywhere back then."

Steve Haythorne ... "When we used to go to the City Hall, we would always buy the cheapest tickets, knowing that when the groups came on everyone would make for the front of the stage. We might have been on the balcony, but as soon as the group appeared on stage we would make our way to get as close to the front as we could."

Despite the healthy and varied music scene in Sheffield, and to a far lesser extent its local towns and suburbs, the mid 1970's soon became the most jaded and washed out period of Rock n' Roll's whole history so far. The Faces were past their prime, with Rod Stewart chasing his solo career, stadium gigs, Brit Ekland and ultimately disco music, Glam Rock was becoming almost passé and Pop music, along with its more grown up album orientated spouse 'Rock' was in dire need of a kick up the backside. The Doobie Brothers, Eagles et al and their Californian sun soaked sounds of M.O.R mediocre laid-back sounds may have been great if you had a beach home, an unlimited personal bar, a host of models on call and a bank account to fund all of these. But for the UK's bored and restless teenage population in places like Northern suburban towns such as Rotherham, Doncaster, Barnsley and Sheffield's many reaches, this music and its affiliations were simply not relevant nor exciting. The kids at local comprehensive schools and the ones who were just starting their apprenticeships on their way to a life of adulthood – they needed something much more immediate, real and down to earth. Something like Punk Rock!

Thankfully, during the pre-punk period of the early to mid 70's there was an alternative to the overindulgent rock scene and the over-commercialised Glam rock of the charts. This music was mainly played in a live setting and mostly around the London area and was loosely termed 'Pub Rock'. Groups varied between the country blues of Brinsley Schwartz to the 'back to the roots' rhythm n' blues of - perhaps its greatest exponent and its direct link to punk - Dr Feelgood. Dr Feelgood's guitarist was Wilko Johnson and is often considered to be one of the key influences on many of the first wave of Punk group's guitarists, most notably Paul Weller of the Jam. Though the pub rock scene was most prevalent down south, Dr Feelgood was very popular closer to home and recorded a full side of their 'Stupidity' album at Sheffield's city hall. The recording being taken from a gig at the City Hall on May 23rd 1975.

Paul Bower (2.3 Vocalist/Guitarist and Gun Rubber fanzine) … "One of the groups around that time that I liked was Dr Feelgood who were a great R&B band. Also, there was Kilburn and the High Roads. These would play the Black Swan venue in Sheffield and if you could get in, this was the place to be. I was around 20 at the time, but some of my friends were under age and couldn't get in."

Another visiting Pub Rock group to play Sheffield were the 101'ers. Their singer was future Clash singer Joe Strummer. **Joe Strummer** later remembered those gigs in an interview with Sheffield Punk fanzine 'Gun Rubber'… "I can remember when we (the 101'ers) played Sheffield and the P.A was live, so I said to the audience *'Well the P.A is live, so if I touch the guitar and the mike at the same time I will die before your very eyes.'* And you know what, they all burst out laughing. They thought I was joking. So everything else I said that night they laughed at. The next time the 101'ers played Sheffield people turned up thinking we were a comedy act."

Not quite a comedy act; AC/DC also played the same venue. But then they did have guitarist Angus Young on hand with his insane schoolboy nerd impersonation.

Paul Bower … "I actually saw AC/DC at the Black Swan venue when their original singer Bon Scott was with them. I surprisingly quite enjoyed them. Their songs were short and although it was hard Rock and 12 bar blues, they weren't 20 minute guitar solos and all that we would later be rebelling against."

Tony … "I wasn't that crazy about pop music when I was really young. Much as I came to love the Beatles in later years, they got on my nerves as a young lad. I can just about remember the Beatles splitting up and I am sure that I thought at the time *'Thank God for that'.* I know this may sound sacrilegious now but so what! My older brothers were more into music: The eldest one being 18 when I was born so he was into the sixties stuff and rock n' roll too.

Later on, I would sneak a listen to my other brother's Glam records, and I started liking Marc Bolan, Bowie and Slade...but I hardly ever bought any records. These would be amongst the very few records from the pre-punk era that me and my mate Pete didn't smash up or use as Frisbees a few years later. One record I did love, that my brother bought and that was the Osmonds' 'Crazy Horses'. What were they on when they recorded that one? Another one that I would always play was 'Children of the Revolution' by T-Rex. That song could have been written about our generation.

One of my mates (Andy Goulty) used to buy lots of singles and we would go to Rotherham on a Saturday for the latest pop hits from the 'Sound of Music' record shop. We would be listening to stuff like David Essex, Sparks, and Suzi Quatro. 'Can the Can' was a big one for us... He was really well ahead of me in appreciating pop music at that time, and I picked up on a lot of pop music through knocking about with him.

He also used to buy the pop mags like 'Supersonic' and one was called 'Disco 45' or something similar? I just used to let him buy the records and I had the ones my brother had too, so between us we had the makings of a decent record Collection.

Above: Who ticket (Steve Haythorne)

I started buying my own records about 1975- 1976, building up an assortment of 7 inch singles with no sleeves on; all racked up on one of those aluminium record racks; Typical 1970's tack!"

Throughout this period, some 1970's music fans did have an eclectic taste in music that would later reflect their open mindedness to music during the punk period itself.

Paul Bower ... "The music I was listening to before punk?: A mixture of stuff ranging from Bowie and Mott the Hoople to the Sensational Alex Harvey band, early Roxy Music, Doctor Feelgood , Family, Free and early T-Rex. I was and still am a big fan of Leonard Cohen. I just loved his independent bohemian spirit. I would lie in my bed in my Sheffield terrace and dream about lying around the Greek islands drinking Ouzo and strumming a guitar. Other kids dreamed of being George Best. I wanted to be Leonard Cohen'. Martyn Ware, who would later form the Human League, introduced me to the joys of pure 3-minute pop. He was a big fan of Sweet and Brian Eno and convinced me that just because a track was very long and had a long guitar solo in it did not mean it was in any way intellectual and in any way deep. Writing a great short pop song was actually much harder."

It was also clear back then that there was a cultural difference between music fans that either lived in the Rotherham area or just up the road in Sheffield.

Paul Bower continues … "As a Sheffielder I only went to Rotherham to visit my sister who lived somewhere on the outskirts, or on one occasion when I worked nights at a warehouse in Kimberworth. In 1976 the only reason you would go to Rotherham was to work. Kids from Rotherham thought that Sheffield was pretentious, or as one kid said to me Sheffield… *'Went theer once… Dint like it…full of puffs and weirdoes'.*"

Even so, Rotherham did also have its music fans with taste that did not depend on that week's Top of the Pops.

Future Punk Rocker Bryan Bell from the Rotherham area, for instance, was also quite eclectic in his taste in music during the pre-Punk period of the 70's.

Bryan Bell … "About 73-74 time I was what you could call a hippy… with the long hair and flares etc. I was into Frank Zappa and the Mothers of Invention, Be Bop Deluxe, Bowie, obviously, and Lou Reed and the Velvet Underground: Dr Feelgood who kind of bridged the gap between the old style of music and Punk. Also, Captain Beefheart and his magic band. Not all of his stuff as some of it was a bit too weird.

I used to go to the Parkgate 'Miners' club (a local youth club between Rawmarsh and Rotherham), and kids used to bring all their LP's down with them. We used to sit down and listen to them. Some nights it might have been soul music and others it would be all heavy Rock. It seemed at the time that a lot of people were into all the Glam stuff like Sweet and Slade but I liked all the weirder stuff. I liked Alice Cooper too. It was my mother that had introduced me to him (laughs) she was a big fan."

Morg from Doncaster was a young teenager during the mid 1970's and before Punk his taste in music was totally focussed on one group in particular, A group that was almost universally popular with lads of a certain age. He recalls -

Morg … "I was born in 1962 and being brought up by parents, whose record collection consisted mainly of stuff like Cliff Richard or brass bands, music never played a major role in my life as a child. This changed for me in the early 70's when I discovered Slade; with their basic but catchy anthems, coupled with Noddy Holder's gruff vocals. I became a big Slade fan. I was somewhat single-minded in my taste though, with Slade being the only band I would listen to."

Tony ... "Most lads did like Slade I suppose. They were very much a lad's band...A bit like a 70's type of Oasis really. I can remember Slade getting played a lot at the Xmas school party. I got my first guitar, which was only a poor looking acoustic type, the Xmas that 'Merry Xmas everybody' was out. I used to mime along to it in my mum's front room, what a plonker."

Graham Torr (Rotherham music fan and future Punk musician) ... "I'm pretty sure I always wanted to be a musician. I just knew I wanted 'some of that there attention'. So inevitably, my parents bought me a 'B – Classico' guitar (Spanish acoustic ... God forbid)...which of course never really cut it but the die was likely set from there on. So from miming to the Sweet on 'Top of the Pops' on a Thursday night or sitting in the bath listening to the Top Twenty Countdown on Sunday nights...I was in like Flynn."

Richard Chatterton (From Brinsworth near Rotherham) ... "Musically before Punk I had been in the doldrums for years. I was fond of Slade, Bowie and T-Rex in my later primary school years. Slade's 'Gudbuy to Jane' had been my first single but this enthusiasm soon waned."

Gary Gillott (Chippie) (Rotherham musician) ... "Before Punk, I was listening to and playing totally across the board stuff; honky tonk piano and Wurlitzer stuff, a bit of Pink Floyd, all sorts of weird shit as well as E.L.O with Roy Wood's influence and the pop stuff like Mud etc."

Sheffield, Rotherham and the surrounding areas were also very much a breeding ground for club acts. Working men's clubs were probably just at their peak at the beginning of the 70's (if not just passing that point), but that didn't stop the smoke-filled concert rooms getting packed out when regular groups on the club circuit such as Bitter Suite played. Throughout the 70's, time almost stood still in the clubs of Rotherham and to a point in the clubs of the neighbouring areas. Sheffield was also a long way off from the heady days of the Punk explosion and the city's homegrown Post-Punk scene. Club land aside and strangely ominous, an early taste of Sheffield's pre-emptive outlook to music and future things to come was displayed with the previously mentioned band Musical Vomit...

Paul Bower ... "Sheffield was very quiet in 1976. Earlier in 73 – 74, we had all been involved in a youth arts workshop called Meatwhistle. We formed a band called Musical Vomit where we dressed in blood-splattered leotards and simulated throwing up on stage. We played numbers such as 'Laxative Lament', 'Self Abuse' and 'I was a Teenage Necrophiliac."

Indeed Musical Vomit was an early precursor of the more 'shock and offend' style of Punk if ever there was one. Although, hardly even heard of outside Sheffield, their reputation and proto-punk approach did manage to reach and impress Marion Elliot alias Polystyrene and future singer of X-Ray Spex, who witnessed a performance in Bath and acknowledged that their style was a part of her inspiration to be involved in Punk the year afterwards. Sadly when asked about this experience she unfortunately cannot remember.

One group who, along with Pub Rock, managed to bridge the gap between Glam Rock and the forthcoming Punk Rock style was Doctors of Madness. They would later play gigs to the Sheffield Punk crowd and be associated with the 'New Wave'; bringing along Punk bands as support and at one time, for a short while in-between Damned line ups, included Damned singer Dave Vanian in their line up. Future Punks would be getting a glimpse of what would soon be on the way on the music scene.

David McKendry …"I seemed to see 'em (Doctors of Madness) more than any other band from 1975 - 79 ish. I had first noticed them supporting Be-Bop Deluxe at the City Hall (still got the silver flexi-disc promo they gave out), then they seemed to be at the Top Rank every couple of months! Really enjoyed them, in a pre-punk post-Glam way."

Back in the 1970's the country, never mind the world, was a lot smaller- in a sense of where you went, the speed of communication, how far your travelling distance was, and even how limited your local travel was.

Tony … "I had only been to Sheffield city centre maybe once or twice before the Punk era. I can remember going up there sometime during the early Seventies and being a little in awe at how much bigger and noisier Sheffield was compared to Rotherham. I did go on a few trips to the Attercliffe part of Sheffield. It was quite a busy and interesting place back then with name stores etc, but I can't remember any record shops."

Paul Bower … "Back in those days I only went to Rotherham out of sufferance."

The Seventies in the region may not have been tainted with a fifties shade of grey - but the adult approach to music was certainly breeding boredom, even amongst the younger generation of the area! Gradually though, there was an air of change that would see music fans take up more challenging sounds than the pop music of the time and also a more basic style and approach to Rock n' Roll. The roads leading to the approaching Punk explosion were now being explored and discovered. Over in the states, the shape of things to come had been visible ever since Iggy Pop and his Stooges had first taken to the stage in the late 60's and Punk pioneers the Velvet Underground, MC5, Patti Smith and more recently the New York Dolls followed by the Ramones, Neon Boys (soon to be Television) and the NYC scene had began their individual attacks on the musical template.
But it was only a minority of tuned in music fans in the UK that were picking up on this new wave. Most of those that did, would largely provide the cast for the soon to come UK Punk explosion. One of Rotherham's born and occasionally residing music fans – soon to be a part of that Punk scene – was Jo Callis.

Jo Callis ... "I suppose I came across punk before the word was much more than American vernacular, when it was first applied to the New York Dolls, who I'd heard doing 'Jet Boy' on Radio One, and read a little about in the NME. By this time, I was still listening to the Stones and things like the Pink Fairies and Alice Cooper but was becoming heavily into Bowie and Roxy Music and all things loud, trashy and Glam, 'the Dolls' were right up my street. It was now the mid seventies and I was an art student in Edinburgh along with Eugene (Reynolds), we had started in the same year and I made a point of getting to know him because he was the maddest most hyperactive lunatic I'd ever seen. He'd be wearing the skinniest trousers possible, the biggest shoes, an Afghan coat turned inside out, and likely as not a leather WW2 flying helmet over shoulder length hair and wispy D'Artagnan beard and tash. I'm sure I probably looked equally ridiculous. Eugene played the drums a bit at that time and we began forming bands at college, mostly of the cod 'prog rock' variety, though we secretly wanted to be the Sweet.

With our Glam Rock aspirations never quite materialising we eventually began to start more light hearted side projects, the first of these being the Knutsford Dominators, playing a bizarre hybrid of 'ruff and ready' Sixties garage and Fifties Rock n' Roll covers. The Doms, as we called ourselves, became a sort of blueprint for the Rezillos, which we probably had on the drawing board at around the same time. The Rezillos took the Dominator concept a stage or two further but in a less 'casual' fashion and this time, for better or worse, involving girls. Fay (Fife) who was also at our college and had brief involvement singing with our most recent prog rock effort was roped in as backing singer along with friend Gayle (Warning) and with Eugene deciding that he would now like to be a lead vocalist, we had to poach Ali (Angel) Paterson, another college friend who had been drumming with some of the more successful bands on the local folk rock scene, to thump the skins. College pal and former Dominators roadie Mark 'Hi-Fi' Harris was drafted in on second guitar and with a guy Eugene had found called Dr. D.K Smythe (a real Doctor of Marine Geology) on bass, the Rezillos were born.

We played mostly sixties pop hits and the tried and tested crowd-pleasing rock n' roll standards, with the idea of trying to sound like a twisted r n' b beat group and look like an explosion in Andy Warhol's art factory. At the time we had no aim in mind other than to wind up the local gig-going populace and provoke some kind of reaction from them, whether that be positive or negative we just didn't care. However, after our first handful of gigs we found ourselves becoming surprisingly popular, and realising that this was really more 'our kind of thing', the prog rock was promptly ditched!"

During the middle of the 70's, as Glam Rock was slowly reaching its end some of its stars would return to their roots. Marc Bolan had started out (after his pioneering Mod phase) as a contemporary folk artist playing to Hippies at Festivals during the late 60's before going electric at the start of the new decade and spearheading the Glam revolution, along with Bowie. Now he could be seen playing acoustic sets once more, but his audience were no longer hippies.

Steve Haythorne ... "A mate asked me to go along to see Marc at a venue in Newark so I bought a ticket and went along. This was around the time that his star was just starting to wane. Anyway, he did an acoustic set, which was very informal; he was sat cross-legged playing his guitar and chatting to us, the audience, between songs. At this time, he also had quite a large skinhead following as well and they were at this gig. There was no trouble from them though. They were just there for the music."

A couple of years later Marc Bolan would be revitalised by the Punk explosion, championing the scene and many of its bands (taking along The Damned as support for his 'Dandy in the Underworld' tour). His career would once more seem to be on the up; but that prospect would be cut short prematurely.

Marc Bolan and T-Rex would be one of the few 1970's artists that the coming Punk generation would still hold with respect. His influence would be evident in many of the early Punk band's sets. Now in the mid 70's there was a scattering of seminal groups and sounds that would appear to be blueprinting the prototype sound and approach of Punk; most of the musicians involved doing so unwittingly.

Rob Saripo (Rotherham rock fan) ... "I once saw a band in 1973 called the Pink Fairies. Although they were 3 years before the punk scene and very Heavy Metal, 'City Kids' from the album 'Kings of Oblivion' would have held up to any audience if performed by a punk band."

The other popular style of music in the region was 'Northern Soul'. Commonly popular at the local discos of the time as well as having its very own insular and 'word of mouth' scene, the Northern scene attracted many who had been too young for the original Mod and Soul scene of the sixties. This mid-seventies generation were fervently addicted to the pulsating sound of rare up-tempo soul and 'Tamla' pastiche R&B preferably played at all-nighters like the Wigan Casino, The Torch and Blackpool's Mecca.

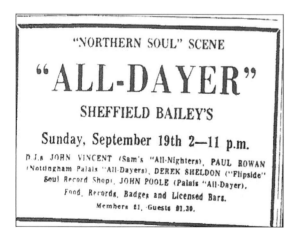

Above: Northern Soul in Sheffield

Truly, a Northern genre in name, and mostly in location, there would be a proportion of these Pre-Punk scenesters who would be revolutionised by the forthcoming Punk explosion and the inevitable Post-Punk scene.

Steve Haythorne ... "Apart from Glam Rock and other Rock groups, my greatest love in music then was Northern Soul. Typically, it all started at the local youth club and hearing the Northern records.

This would be about 1972 and I would be listening to Northern Soul and buying the records from a little record shop in Mexborough, which was near the 'South Yorkshireman' pub. That shop was crammed with records. Some of my favourites are 'Emperor of my baby's heart by Kurt Harris, Chuck Wood's 'Seven days too long' and my all time fave which is Timmy Yuro's 'Never be over for me'; that's a breathtaking record.

32

Some of the kids would manage to get to the Wigan casino, though how they ever got in I do not know, we were that young. I would go to 'Samantha's' and Rotherham Clifton Hall. At this time I had moved from Rawmarsh to Swinton and lived in the Patios up there; not a very desirable place to live even then."

Duncan Payne (Northern Soul fan) … "From the age of 10 I had been heavily into Soul music. While my mates at school were digging Glam Rock, I was into the O'Jays and Harold Melvin and the Blue notes."

Anthony Cronshaw (football author and future Punk and Skinhead) … "Back in say, mid 1976, I was listening to a lot of soul music amongst other stuff. At this time we would be going to discos and places like 'Samantha's' and we would be still dancing to Tina Charles records. That would all soon change later on in the year."

Even if some of the Northern Soul fans did turn to Punk Rock for kicks during the next couple of years, many would stay faithfull to their first love in music and keep the torch burning for many years to come. Theirs is a story to be told in a different time and place.

During mid 1976 at the start of the famous red hot summer - while the 'Northern Soulies' were giving it their all at the Wigan casino or the local youth club's 'Northern' spot, and the young pop fans were dancing to 'Tiger Feet' at the youth club - something was happening just a short bus ride away from the town centre of Rotherham and a mere walking distance away from Sheffield's city centre.

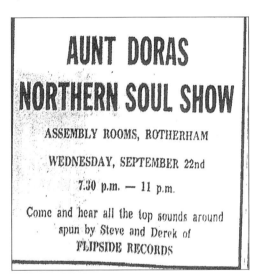

Northern Soul at Rotherham

Inside a Sheffield pub called the Black Swan on July 4th 1976; two bands had set up their gear and played their sets to an audience of mixed taste and opinion. Playing their first ever gig supporting the (as yet almost unknown - especially out of London) - Sex Pistols were the Clash. Richard Kirk of Sheffield group Cabaret Voltaire was at the gig and noted with a curious precursory view to the future Punk style "The Pistols are ok and great catalysts but if you listen to the music it is really just heavy metal speeded up a bit."

Still Richard did like the band, or at least their front-man, stating in local fanzine 'Gun Rubber' some months later that – *There was a lot of raw energy and Rotten is a good performer, but I don't think much of the rest of the band. Yeah I enjoyed them a lot, but really, 'Johnny Rotten' is the 'Sex Pistols'.*

At the gig Punk Rocker **John D.Ellis** recalled … "*Rotten asked 'put your hands up if you bought Patti Smith's Horses album.' I, like a fool, did, along with a few others. 'You've all* *been cheated'* he retorted. A few people walked out when they started 'Substitute'. By the time the Sex Pistols got to 'Whatcha' gonna do about it', there were about ten people left.

John also spoke to Clash singer Joe Strummer and asked him if they would be playing Them's 'Gloria', which was a song Strummer used to perform with his previous group the 101er's (who coincidentally also played the Black Swan about a year before). Joe's reply was '*Nah, don't do all that anymore'.* **(Quotes from 'Beats working for a living' by Martin Lilleker)**

Also at the gig was Adi Newton who would later form Sheffield band Clock dva; supposedly that night Adi and Richard engaged in a spitting battle with members of The Sex Pistols. Punk antics aside it was clear that the idea of Punk excited many of the Sheffield crowd but more than being just a 'back to basics of rock n' roll' approach, some saw it as an opening for something almost completely new, and that did not necessarily mean guitars.

Paul Bower ... "The Black Swan gig was a classic one where several million people claimed to have been there, which of course they weren't. Richard Kirk and Mal from Cabaret Voltaire were there and I remember them talking to me at the time and they said there was around 30 to 40 people there. The same when the 101er's had played there previously, everyone saying they went."

Despite mythical numbers of people who now say they attended the gig, the actual attendance being reported by various sources as being somewhere in-between 50 to 200, there were clear positive signs that something was about to happen and change was only around the corner. Clash guitarist **Mick Jones** noted at the time that '*Even though some of the early punk fans had got it wrong in their idea of punk dress, in a way you couldn't get it wrong as it wasn't yet formed.*'

It is often over-looked how much the early punk fans adopted clothes in a non-informed way. There really was no real guideline as such and the uniformed accepted punk look was still a long way off the agenda. Mick himself describes their look at the Black swan gig as being- black and white shirts with suits, which were ripped, and tight fitting. The look was still clearly being developed.

Joe Strummer ... The lead singer and guitarist of the Clash did note- and was impressed by the prototype punk kids that seemingly came out of nowhere to come and check the two groups out. Strummer is quoted as saying of the Black Swan gig - "*It was really good because we were in Sheffield on a Sunday afternoon and all these people came out of the woodwork looking like punk types: they were obviously ex-Roxy Music fans and wore leopard-skin trousers and stuff. But we noticed that they were searching and looking for the next thing. Lots of make up and hair were clearly beginning to go berserk. There was a great audience there, and it gave us a lot of heart and inspiration. We also started to realise that this nationwide 'punk' thing was soon about to explode.*"

Joe Strummer acknowledged that these must have been the kids from the area who were listening to the MC5, New York Dolls etc and like a few other wise kids that were very thin on the ground at that time, could sense a change in the air. Not quite sure what and who would be the exact catalysts but something was starting to happen.

The Black Swan venue had played a pivotal part in establishing a local live music scene and saw many of Pub Rock's pioneering groups play raw and energetic sets to an often packed and sweat soaked audience. The venue, situated on the corner of Snig Hill and Bank Street – close to the city centre – began its musical career back in 1965. Managed by Terry Steeples, who had previously been the manager of Rotherham's Empire Cinema, the Black Swan put on gigs from Timebox, Sweet, Mud, Average White Band, Genesis, the 101'ers, Ian Dury's band Kilburn and the High Roads and legendary Pub Rockers Brinsley Schwarz (featuring Nick Lowe) as well as occasional appearances from local acts such as Joe Cocker. Ultimately ironic though, considering that it was the two bands that were part of a scene that the Black Swan's manager couldn't stomach and found revolting that would – in future years - hold the venue's flag of fame. The Sex Pistols would soon be on their way to infamy and the Punk explosion's fuse was soon to be set alight.

The Clash had now begun their career-spanning love of Sheffield as a place to play, whilst the Black Swan closed and eventually became The Boardwalk. Certainly, back in mid summer 1976, Sheffield had been part of one of Punk's first main acts. The Mucky Duck's much-loved Pub Rock genre was coming to an end and Punk was sneaking in through the back door...but not as yet through the nation's television sets. Ironically, it was at the legendary Black Swan gig, that Clash guitarist Keith Levene spoke - between sets with Rotten - and said *If our groups don't make it we will form a group together'*. Less than two years later Levene and Rotten (then Lydon) had formed Public Image ltd.
The Black Swan received a nasty little present from the Luftwaffe during the war, when the pub's top floor was blown clear off. Now it had received the Sex Pistols and the Clash and the impact would be just as explosive!

Earlier in the year, in February, the two main protagonists of Pub Rock and what would become Punk Rock (a term actually tagged onto the new garage music by music journalists in homage to the American garage Punk groups of the mid to late 1960's), Eddie and the Hot Rods and Sex Pistols had played together. The Pistols had supported the Hot Rods and gained notorious attention in the music press by putting on their 'manager-incited acts of indifference' to the Hot Rods, who they believed were a symbol of the old to be replaced by themselves (the new). In fact, the Hot Rods had not been around as a recognised professional act that much longer than the Pistols.

Barrie Masters (Eddie and the Hot Rods singer) ... "Yeah, I remember that night pretty clearly. The Pistols were totally controlled by Malcolm Mclaren. The actual incident was actually over nothing really. They were showing off and smashing up the stage gear – which wasn't even ours anyway – so I told Johnny Rotten that the next time they played with other bands it may be wiser not to try and wreck their gear. I then gave him a sort of gentle slap, as if to say naughty- naughty behave yourself, and the next thing after he had ran off and told Malcolm that's when they had got their heads together and a bit of a ruckus kicked off. It was all hype and a put-on. After that there was a bit of a war of words between both of our groups but they never turned up to sort it out; but there you go."

Whilst The Sex Pistols and the Clash had been playing to Sheffield's proto-type punks and curios, most teenagers in the local area were still mostly asleep to the idea of punk. True, there was a small core of enlightened fans in the Sheffield area who clearly saw the change in the air, but it would take a more media focussed outlook to inform most of the future punk generation of the area. For the rest of 1976 things would remain pretty quiet on the punk front in Sheffield, with only Sex Pistols actually playing a gig in the area at Doncaster Outlook in September. Within the next year though, Punk and 'New Wave' groups would be playing more and more regularly in Sheffield and Doncaster. Rotherham too would soon be well and truly on the punk map and would play host to one of the best 'New Wave' venues around at the time.

The Sex Pistols had formed a couple of years earlier and were pieced together by Malcolm Mclaren, who had previously managed the New York Dolls in the States for a while. Their manifesto was *'We're not into music; we're into chaos'.*

The Clash had come together from the ashes of the legendary non-gig playing London S.S, who saw most of the future London punk scene pass through its ranks. Its members (guitarist Mick Jones and new to the Bass Paul Simenon) had been picked up on by a friend of Malcolm Mclaren's called Bernie Rhodes, an ex – mod friend of his from the sixties who was looking to start a new movement in which he could manage a key group. Soon after being introduced to the 101er's singer/guitarist Joe Strummer, they became the Clash... ready to take on the music scene at any cost. Punk Rock, which as yet had not been officially named so, now had its two prime movers.

Another 'sixties' connection arose when Sheffield's Dave Berry was playing a gig just outside London and came into contact with the fledgling Punk movement. Dave, who is largely known for his 'Crying Game' hit was also a pioneering R&B exponent – covering Chuck Berry and the like before R&B even caught on nationwide in the early 1960's – and had also committed some quality R&B sides to his hits' flip sides; one of which 'Don't Gimme No lip child' had recently been part of the early Sex Pistols live set. Dave Berry recalls the experience –

Dave Berry ... "It (Punk) was a bonus for me. When it all started, I was doing a gig on the outskirts of London. There were lots of different age groups that I was pulling in at the time, but there were these 17 and 18 year olds coming along. At first, I thought they were taking the piss, 'cos they were stood at the front of the stage. Then some of them came in the dressing room and told me that the Sex Pistols were doing 'Don't Gimme No Lip Child', which was the b-side of 'Crying Game', and they were also doing 'This Strange Effect'. Siouxsie Sioux was also a fan and somebody else was also doing a couple of other things, so they liked me. Then in the late Seventies, I was invited to do three or four shows with Adam and the Ants when they were really into their heavy Punk thing. And I went to see the Monochrome Set and they did 'Little things'. **(From 'Not like a Proper Job' by John Firminger and Martin Lilleker)**

Add to this, along with the major Punk landmark event of the Black Swan gig, the often forgotten Chris Spedding connection. He of 'Motorbikin' fame and a born and bred Sheffielder who produced the early Pistols demos and even appeared at the 100 Club Punk festival with the Vibrators as well as sharing a single 'Pogo Dancing' with them, and the Sheffield placement on the early Punk map is confidently sealed.

However, in late 1976, Sheffield had no Punk venue at all, with only the City Hall and the University being remotely suitable to host Rock events or if the situation arose Punk Rock concerts. Doncaster had the Outlook venue, where the Sex Pistols would soon be on their way to perform the first of two dates they would play there during their short but illustrious career.

Nearby Rotherham was firmly off the Punk Rock tour guide and the very small handful of Punk Rockers that lived there, were just about starved of anything exciting to happen on the Punk front.   Meanwhile throughout the rest of that red-hot Indian summer of 1976, the small but growing punk scene in London would attract more interest from the music press and a scattering of groups and gigs would soon be linked together and recognised as a movement. Many of the music fans who attended those early Sex Pistols gigs would soon be forming bands themselves.

Back in March Johnny Rotten had stated in an interview that he wished to see more bands like themselves to form. This would later annoy Rotten but one thing was for sure, the kids had been taking notice and soon Sheffield itself would see a change in the musical climate.

Chapter Two

Johnny Rotten's staring at me

"Around early 1976, there were the new groups like Eddie and the Hot Rods coming through and there was a sense that things were heating up. I had just about given up on music really at that point but now things were getting more exciting" – **Steve Lloyd (Doncaster Punk Rocker)**

Tony ... "I started at comprehensive school in September 1976 and I suppose this is when I and my mates all started to listen to music properly and think about the clothes we should wear. We went to the Rawmarsh Comp's disco, which was held most weekday nights, and we had some great times there. The music was a mix of Disco and Pop stuff from the charts and some oldies and there would be a Northern Soul and Heavy Rock spot as well. At the end of the night, the DJ would put two or three slow records on that we would call smoochies; we would look forward to this as we would try and get a smooch with the lasses enabling us to hug and get our arms round them getting close to them for at least 3 minutes. Happy times, but the smoochies would eventually be replaced by the Pogo.

During this period I was still listening to all the chart crap at the time and our gang's clothes attire was very 70's.The Music was the Real Thing, Hot Chocolate, Tina Charles; typical 70's disco and soul along with all those 70's rock n' roll revivalists like Showaddywaddy and Mud. The Clothes were flared pin-stripe trousers, brogues, cheesecloth shirts and Brutus tops.

Above: Punk Rock begins to be noticed by the media

There were Leo Sayer and David Essex look-alikes at the local disco and no sign of Punk at all. Ah but we still thought we looked cool. Everyone had long hair. I can't think of anyone with short hair at all at that time."

But, unbeknown to the author (and the majority of the public) there was something happening, to start with in London, but also for a rare minority of music fans starting to tune in further North. The whole music scene was ready to change and along with it fashion and culture itself; and it did involve short hair.

Timothy Green (Rotherham Punk Rocker) ... "When Eddie and the Hot Rods released their EP 'Live at the Marquee' virtually everyone I knew in Rotherham appeared to buy it. It was now 1976 and I heard the Ramones & Patti Smith on the John Peel show. Around this time, I started wearing drainpipe jeans and a leather jacket and got accused of being a teddy boy? I went to the London Roundhouse to see Patti Smith (supported by a band I instantly hated: the Stranglers) followed a little later by the Ramones at the same venue, which was on American bicentennial day. The Ramones came on ...Dee Dee shouted '1234' into his mike, but we couldn't hear anything, so they went off until it was fixed! They did a fabulous twenty-minute set and went off. Sadly, the support band were once again the vile Stranglers but the main band the Flamin' Groovies weren't too bad. Afterwards we were given a flyer advertising a Sex Pistols gig at the 100 Club on Monday, but I had to leave London."

Timothy would fortunately grab his chance to see Punk in the making a little closer to home a few months later. Meanwhile, some local music fans were becoming tired of the same old adult controlled rock and its boring diet of virtuosity and safety.

Bryan Bell ... "In 76 I used to watch the 'Old Grey Whistle Test' with old whispering Bob Harris...I wasn't very impressed with the music on at that time. Something had to happen."

Jo Callis ... "During our very early days we were finding the work of contemporary groups like Dr. Feelgood and Eddie And The Hot Rods quite inspirational to our cause, and with these sort of bands already paving the way for what would become the new wave and the first tremors of the approaching Punk earthquake being felt on the Richter scale, it seemed there may be a current relevance for our new band. But in order for us to move on we really needed to develop our own original material, so Mark (Hi-Fi) and myself thought we'd give this a go, and see what we could come up with. Mark was a real vinyl enthusiast, he not only had a proper Hi-Fi system, but also a treasured collection of American blues and R n' B records which he'd built up over the years. Mark also had his finger very much on the pulse of what was upcoming and crucial on the underground music scene in both the UK and the US. I hung out with Mark quite a lot then, either disturbing his domestic peace with girlfriend Frances when we'd play his records and then listen to the John Peel show, or accompanying him on his record hunting jaunts around the many independent record shops in town. Between John Peel and Mark, I was discovering acts like Nick Lowe, Motorhead, Television, The 101er's (featuring a pre-Clash Joe Strummer) Larry Wallis -still keeping 'Kings of Oblivion' and the Pink Fairies alive, and many more.

One cannot underestimate the importance of John Peel not only as a champion of the movement in question, but as a mentor to our, and subsequent music loving generations, many a band or artist destined for greatness or legendary status were given their first airings on one of John Peel's shows, indeed just to perform on one of his famous BBC studio sessions was the Holy Grail of many an aspiring young musician. John's integrity and honesty also earned him the undying respect of not only his 'protégé's' but established figures alike, a rare and envious position for a radio DJ to find themselves in at that time.

Above: The Rezillos in 1976 with Rotherham's Jo Callis at far left (copyright Karl Heideken)

This I'm sure, along with John Peel's open minded affability, led some of the more mainstream Radio One DJ's to up their game a little by slipping in a few new things they'd heard, or something they thought perhaps a little risqué for their predominantly die-hard Rock or 'grown up' audiences. Through listening to these shows which were aired in the evening or at weekends, and picking up the odd snippet of information from the music press and the word on the street, one sensed that a storm might be brewing."

By late summer 1976, the new music, now being termed 'Punk Rock' by the music weeklies, was starting to gain a foothold on the live gig circuit. The Sex Pistols had played a few gigs up north at places like the previously mentioned Sheffield gig, Scarborough, Manchester and Northallerton and were starting to play London more frequently.

Above: late 1976 Daily papers 'Punk' reportage

More groups were starting to form in and around London but also up in Manchester and Newcastle. The Ramones had made a massive impact on the burgeoning Punk scene. With the release of their first LP (which influenced most of the groups to speed up their songs), they played gigs at the Roundhouse and Dingwalls where most of the whole punk scene also turned up (the Clash and Pistols being in Sheffield for the first one but attending the second). In July, Mark Perry launched the first Punk fanzine 'Sniffin' Glue' that would catalogue, praise, criticise and just about bookend the initial first year of punk.

Following the legendary 'Screen on the Green' Punk night in Islington in August, the next important date on the Punk calendar was the '100 Club' Punk festival in London. This took place across the 2 nights of September 20th and 21st with the Pistols, Clash, Buzzcocks (From Manchester), Damned, Vibrators, Subway Sect, Stinky Toys and an improvised set from the fledgling Siouxsie and the Banshees (with Sid Vicious on drums). Music fans like Gaye Advert and TV Smith (just on the verge of forming The Adverts), Paul Weller (who had already seen the Pistols and the Clash and was inspired enough to use their influences in his songs and approach to music) and future Nips and Pogues singer Shane McGowan were there – amongst many who would soon form the nucleus of the early Punk scene. Heavily Mod influenced the Jam would play an early support slot to the Sex Pistols, and even from this early period, there was clear signs of both a Punk influence, but also an indication of where the real blueprint for the future lay: both in Paul Weller's work and a proportion of the Punk generation that would in 2 or 3 years time join in with the Mod cause.

Bob Gray (original Jam keyboard player) … "I had just come back from Canada to get my work visa, when Bruce Foxton asked me to join the Jam. We drove up to Dunstable in the back of a Bedford van with Paul, Bruce, Rick and a pal of mine. Paul's Dad John was driving. Paul was reading the Melody Maker and on the front cover was a picture of the Pistols. Bruce told me that they were the band we were opening for. So I figured that they must be good if they are on the front page.

I remember the Pistols coming in for a sound check and I could not believe how much great gear they had. I recall them using scope tuners for the guitars and Steve Jones not even getting close to tuning it. I thought '*This guy is either too stoned or just has no idea?*' Johnny Rotten came out and started shouting and spitting everywhere. I didn't know who he was trying to impress because no one was there, just the road crews, which as far as the Jam were concerned was us and John. The only sane one who played in tune was the bass player Glen Matlock. Of course, I came to understand John Lydon a little better and actually enjoyed some of their music, not a lot, but some of it. Like Paul, I loved the old Stax and Motown Soul music.

Coming over from Canada, I didn't really get where the Pistols or the Jam were coming from. I do not know how much Paul was influenced by the Pistols, I can only guess. I do remember thinking how much he was copying the Who, even down to the poster that his Dad showed me of the guys playing at the Greyhound. It was like looking at a Who poster. Then when we played the 100 club, Paul finished off the gig by kicking over the amps and Rick kicked over the drums. I thought I was in a 'Who' time warp!"

By late 76 and quick signings, the first UK Punk records New Rose by the Damned, the poor 'We Vibrate' (flipped with the far superior 'Whips and Furs') by The Vibrators and Sex Pistols 'Anarchy in the UK' were soon in the shops but not many but the chosen few, so to speak had yet heard of any of these groups or 'Punk Rock' for that matter...

Anthony Cronshaw … " While the Sex Pistols and the Heartdrops (soon to be renamed the Clash), were playing the Black Swan(also known as 'The Mucky Duck') - which the Sheffield Star had labelled as a Heavy Rock night on Sunday 4th of July 1976, I was getting totally plastered in some suburban Sheffield 12. The DJ would be blasting out the likes of Abba and Tina Charles plus the rest of the dross we had to listen to most weekends when we ventured to the local nightspots such as 'Genevieve's'.

I would be dressed to the nines in my Birmingham Bags and a ghastly white shirt that was adorned with loads of little men with bowler hats on. A few months down the line and it was the same old song that was being churned out most weekends, unless I had enough money left to enjoy the 'Crazy Daisy' who held a Roxy night mid-week."

Locals who happened to be in London at the time were lucky enough to witness Punk first.

Paul Bower (of Sheffield Punk band '2.3') ... "I briefly lived in London in 1976 and was running a junk shop in Kings Cross with a mate of mine, which was a madcap adventure and why we ever thought we could make it work, I have no idea as we had no money and no car and no experience. I moved into a flat in Croydon in the middle of nowhere.

The Sex Pistols were never a major influence at all to me and many kids in Sheffield. The main issue was the energy of youth, creativity and a feeling that the bloated super ego bands with 10-minute drum solos were being swept away. Philosophically we were rejecting rubbish like Yes's 'Tales of Topographic Oceans' LP and the cult of pseudo virtuosity.

We loved the idea that with Punk you could get up there and just do something exciting on stage. We had done something similar with Musical Vomit in 73/74 although we were derivative of Alice Cooper at that time.

I passed on the opportunity of going to the two 'big' Summer of Punk gigs. I went to the pub with my mate Ian Reddington (Tricky Dicky of Eastenders and more recently Vernon in Coronation Street) who had just got a place at 'RADA', instead. Another friend Nick Dawson (The Extras drummer) went to both nights at the 100 club and loved Punk. What really turned me on to Punk was when Ian Marsh played me the first Ramones album. We played 'Blitzkrieg Bop'10 times on the trot. I could have cried. It was a celebration of youth and a dagger in the heart of Yes and ELP. Later listening to The Clash energised me, particularly in their uncompromising stand against racism."

Steve Lloyd ... "I was in London in 1976 and went to see the Damned at the Nashville and this was something amazing and more real than anything I had seen or heard before. I know it's a cliché of the time, but this really felt like year zero. I had long hair with split knee jeans but I then got my hair cut short and it all changed. Not long afterwards, I went back to Doncaster and I was the first Punk in that area. There were very few people who had picked up on Punk in Doncaster at that time. I would walk through the market and the stall holders would be throwing their vegetables at me and shouting, for some stupid reason *'Rock on Tommy'*; which was a catch phrase of comedians 'Cannon and Ball' at the time. The only other Punk I knew early on was a girl called Kathy from Rotherham. She was a very early Punk."

Timothy Green ... "The Sex Pistols played Donny Outlook. There was about thirty of us there - Paul Cook wore an 'I hate Pink Floyd' t-shirt, which reminded me of my own 'Yes are crap' shirt that I had made at the Reading Festival in 1975 (when Yes were headlining); Good set, but disappointing. Soon afterwards, I bought a copy of 'New Rose' by the Damned while I was in Newcastle and then in Sheffield 'Anarchy in the UK' on the day it came out."

Doncaster Rock fan Patrick Tierney was turning onto Punk by the time The Sex Pistols played their first Doncaster Outlook date; but the Punk look had not filtered through to the early Pistols gigs up North and the standard seventies long hair was still much more common than a short spiky cut.

Patrick Tierney (Doncaster Punk fan) ... "At the first Sex Pistols Outlook gig in 1976, I went with a school mate, Gav Gee from Harworth.The gig was sparsely attended, and we stood about 10 yards from the stage on the left hand side. The crowd did seem to have a largely negative attitude. Musically, the band was alright, but nothing special. Matlock seemed to be the only one trying, but this opinion may have been influenced by what I had previously read. The one thing that does stick in my mind is that Johnny Rotten started to stare at Gav and held the stare. Gav always maintained that he out-stared Johnny Rotten. I wondered if this was to do with our appearance, as we both had very long hair. Maybe Johnny thought we shouldn't be part of their crowd."

Punk fans in the provinces and places like Sheffield, Rotherham and Doncaster during those days of late 1976 were fairly scarce. True, there was the odd scattering of kids who were excited by the prospect of this new attitude and a return to basics of the new music, but they were almost out on their own and any resemblance of a scene was just not yet happening. Then something happened that brought 'Punk Rock' and its followers into the media spotlight and straight on to the front pages of the daily papers- the infamous Bill Grundy interview!

The daily papers had been running inquisitive and uninformed articles on the Punk scene for a few weeks previously. They were asking *'Who are these Punks?'* and were attempting to describe and categorise their clothes, look and music... almost always embarrassingly wrongly. It was obvious that they needed some serious headlines and outrage to sell their version of what Punk was. Punk, being unconsciously honest, naïve and open would inevitably send the gutter press the present they were wanting for Christmas.

In December super group Queen pulled out of an interview for 'Today' programme and the Sex Pistols were invited along as a quick replacement. The group arrived and were soon taking advantage of the free drinks in the bar. Grundy who himself was part drunk, quickly tore into the assembled crowd of the Pistols and their 'Bromley Contingent' followers- goading them into a provoked response of verbal expletives that were plainly everyday language for the interviewees. Soon Steve Jones gladly gave Grundy exactly what he was hoping for with his hilarious and legendary retort of *'You dirty bastard'*.... *'You dirty Fucker'*... *'What a Fucking Rotter'*. The plugs were pulled, the programme's credits came up and Punk Rock's future, reputation and infamy were now sealed in sensationalist tabloid fervour. 'The Filth and the Fury' was now born and the media had its darling of outrage to play with at its own will. The headlines were typical and the public's reaction also as predictable (as could be expected). What was not expected was the catalytic explosion of New groups, teenage music fans and clued in writers, that would take the initiative and do something with their lives – inspired by the idea that 'Anyone can have a go'. The whole country was now gripped by the excitement, disgust and outrage of Punk Rock. After the 'Grundy' spectacle, there can hardly have been a person from comprehensive outsider kids to everyone's grandma, who had not heard of the Sex Pistols and Punk Rock.

Anthony Cronshaw ... "Like a bolt from the heavens, the Sex Pistols gave poor old Bill Grundy a right fucking gob full, and with this being tea-time viewing the media launched head on into these foul mouthed Punks. With it being shown on Granada, the youth of South Yorkshire missed it, but on grabbing my morning paper while dragging myself off to work, it was there for all to see in all its glory. Punk had hit the headlines and boy did we reach out and grab it with open arms."

Not so easily accessible for the younger lot of kids who would later become a part of the Punk generation.

Tony ... "I can remember buying an issue of 'Melody Maker' that was a few weeks old from the little paper shop down the road and it had something about the Sex Pistols in it. I didn't have a clue who they were or what they were about, even though some of us were buying the NME and Record Mirror now and again. I was still listening to bleeding Showaddywaddy I'm embarrassed to say, anyway 'Under the moon of love' at that time, did more for my pubescent hormones than 'Anarchy in the UK' could ever have done even if I had heard it. Then I saw all the papers with all the headlines about Punk being the disgusting new fashion and all the swearing and sick things punk fans did etc. I never gave it much thought really after that, but that tabloid idea of what Punk was about was firmly implanted in my consciousness - which was really a load of Bollocks!"

Nicky Booth (Rotherham Punk) ... "Punk came along at the perfect time. I was in my early teens when it really started to take off. The first thing I remember of it was seeing articles in the tabloid press accompanied by pictures of youths in torn clothes and covered in safety pins. The tone was almost hysterical – it was the end of civilisation – and to be honest I was a bit freaked out too."

Future Punk musician Dave Spencer, who coincidentally was born on the exact same day as the author, recalls those early days when Prog Rock still ruled and Punk had yet to have any measurable impact on the local youth.

Dave Spencer (musician/songwriter from Rotherham) … "My big brother, Peter, is five years older than me, and in 1976, he was sixteen and I was eleven. Peter had already nailed his musical colours to the mast - his passion was prog-rock; Genesis, a bit of Pink Floyd, but most of all, Yes. Every Thursday he bought the Melody Maker to find out the amazing adventures of mysterious space/time travellers who sang tales of topographic oceans and whose singer claimed '*Nous somme du soleil*' which I think is French for "we are from the sun", when actually he came from Accrington. The Melody Maker was always laying about the house, and I'd glance at it from time to time and the cover would say things like Eric Clapton to play at the blah blah blah. Led Zep - say that - blah, blah, blah. On page three it would say stuff like the Stranglers banned from blah, blah, and blah - the Clash - Blah. Sex Pistols. BLAH!

To me, at eleven, in Rotherham it was seemed like blah, blah, and blah. If I wanted time travel, there was Doctor Who. If I wanted music, we'd got records – three Beatles albums. 'Please, Please Me', 'Help' and 'Sergeant Pepper'. That was it. I wasn't fed up or pissed off about the musical state of the nation or anything in particular. I just wasn't particular interested in anything either. My family had just moved back to Rotherham after living in Scotland, for four and a half years, and I didn't really know anyone so all that was important to me was trying to fit in.

I would be lying if I said I remember the Grundy incident, or the Anarchy tour, but slowly something about a vile, vicious, revolting new movement started to seep into the public consciousness.; Punk Rock. At first, absolutely everyone I knew hated it. - Absolutely everyone. It was nearly impossible to find anything positive written about it anywhere. There were snippets in the beloved Melody Maker, but I read these articles out of curiosity more than genuine interest."

Richard Chatterton - was initially unconvinced of the merits of the fledgling Punk scene … "I first heard about Punk Rock around 1976, when it was dominating the tabloids and getting lots of headlines. I can remember, a little later on, reading ridiculous articles such as the one about a guy who was a bank clerk by day and pierced his cheek with a pitch fork at night. Another headline was about the new Phenomenon called 'Puke Rock'! I think the press at the time, couldn't deal with it yet they profited from it by making up outlandish stories and fuelling public ridicule, scorn and often hatred.

Most of my fellow students in the sixth form were still listening to Yes, Led Zeppelin and dressing in cheesecloth shirts and kaftans, long hair flowing.

Once, when the deputy Head at my school, came into my English lesson - he was laughing about how the Punk bands were using shock tactics to get attention and I can remember thinking that I agreed with him. Brinsworth Comprehensive (they had removed the cooler sounding High school bit in 1975), wasn't exactly a hot bed of Punk activity; but then, it was slow to get to the provinces. The seeds in my head must have been sown, however- I can remember a lad in my year showing me some clippings of Punk band the Cortinas that he had cut out of a magazine. There were also a couple of lads in my year and the year above, who were starting to go and see Punk bands."

Punk was now starting to inspire the young generation who were tired of Rock in general.

Steve Lloyd (Doncaster Punk) … "Before Punk, there had been a large gap and I had been away from music for a couple of years. Now this new music made me feel totally alive and it was new and the way forward."

Paul Clarkson (Rotherham Punk) … "I was sick of all the crap music and hated all the Hippy Led Zeppelin and Yes stuff and all the clothes that were around. I got into Punk and it was like aliens had landed and said *'Come up to our planet for a while'.* Brilliant!"

Also, Punk was even impressing rock fans who had not lost faith in the old guard.

Rob Saripo from Rotherham was a Rock fan but felt the impact of the first throes of Punk Rock and the Sex Pistols … "I was never really fully into the Punk scene. I had been to the Lincoln Festival (still have the programme), which had David Bowie and the Spiders from Mars, Hawkwind with Lemmy from Motorhead singing 'Silver Machine' and amongst others Queen. So I did not really have a Punk pedigree.

However, one day on the radio in late 1976, I heard the most amazing opening guitar riff ever put to a record. That record was 'Anarchy in the UK' by the Sex Pistols and it still sounds as fresh today as it did back then.

At the time, I was working in Brighouse over in West Yorkshire. When I got off the bus on my way to work, I used to call into a shop to buy a paper and a packet of fags. They also used to sell records. In those days the singles that did not sell or had just gone out of the charts, they would be put in the bargain bin. One morning I was looking through this and I came across two copies of 'Anarchy in the UK' on the E.M.I label, price 20p, each of which I purchased. As I said 'Anarchy in the UK' still holds its head high today, and will not be surpassed by most of the so-called guitar bands of today. That record is the reason that I became aware that there was more to Punk music than safety pins; in some cases anyway."

But the lines had not been clearly drawn yet – between old and new as Rezillo Jo Callis observed -

Jo Callis … "I think at first, the rock orientated DJ's weren't quite sure what might or might not constitute a Punk band, and would play some relatively new unheard of band's track, then make some vague reference to this new underground punk scene which was springing up. They were reserving their judgement of course, and wisely, so, they wouldn't want to potentially alienate their audience anymore than they wanted to be left behind in the wake of a phenomenon. I think it was these things I was hearing first which aroused my curiosity."

The Anarchy in the UK Punk package tour which featured the Pistols supported by the Clash, the Damned, Johnny Thunders and the Heartbreakers (who had recently arrived from the U.S.A with hair freshly cropped at Malcolm's request)…was booked for 19 dates nationwide. Following the outrage and 'the Filth and the Fury' sparked up by the Bill Grundy affair the bands managed to play 5 dates. (The Damned were thrown off after they supposedly agreed to play the Derby gig without the Pistols; though this is all open to misinterpretation).On Friday December 17th the frustrated entourage arrived in Sheffield but weren't allowed to play.

Timothy Green … "I remember getting pissed off as the 'Anarchy' tour by the Pistols fell to pieces and got almost nowhere near us."

Over in Leeds, the tour arrived at the City's University and the show went ahead. That night, with the Damned still in tow for the time being, the Clash opened up at the bottom of the bill, while most of the audience were still in the bar. The atmosphere from the sightseeing, jeering Punk Rock hating crowd soon turned to an air of pervading violence and following the Heartbreakers set, during which Johnny Thunders asked if there were any junkies in Leeds after failing to make a hit in the city throughout the day, the Pistols finally arrived on stage.

Rotten's first comment was *'Your not wrecking the place enough, the News of the World will be disappointed'* and the 'public enemy number ones' were met with a barrage of abuse, beer cans, bottles, spit and intense hostility.

Above: Anarchy tour ticket

As was clear almost everywhere else throughout the country at the time, empathy with the Punk scene was in short supply that night, with anyone showing allegiance being subjected to threats and pushed around. Even so, there were some in the hall that night that had been there for the right reasons: amongst them future members of Gang of Four.

Down in Wales for the tour's Caerphilly date, Hell's angels and religious choirs turned up to show their distaste towards the evils of Punk rock. A local priest even proclaiming *'God can forgive anyone, anyone except Punk Rockers, they are the devil's children.*

Anthony Cronshaw …"As we headed towards the end of 1976, the authorities in their wisdom started banning Punk concerts right, left and centre, including our illustrious City Hall where they stopped the Sex Pistols from playing on the Anarchy tour..

The live version of Punk was thriving in the Capital and we up here in Sheffield were gagging for some of what those down south were experiencing. With money in short supply, a trip down south to see a gig was off the menu - the only time we ventured towards London being for the football."

The media, social think tanks, school teachers, the clergy, local councils and your Mum, Dad and least favourite Uncle...what did they all have in common? They all hated and despised Punk Rock! What better reason, excuse and validity for the disenchanted, bored or merely impressionable youths of the region to show more than a passing interest in the new phenomenon?

Phillip Wright (Sheffield Punk) ... "The first time I saw any mention of punk was on the front page of a Sunday newspaper, it would have been 1976 and they had pictures of early punks on the front page with some headline saying how outrageous it all was. I felt excited by what little I had read and the next day at school (Gleadless Valley) me and my mates, Tim, John and Mark, talked about it. At that time we were all into the Who and Dr Feelgood. Luckily for us, the school library had the NME delivered and we soon read about the bands that were part of this new scene. A few weeks later, the Anarchy tour was announced, with a 'who's who' of the whole punk scene on the bill. Headline band was the Sex Pistols, the Damned, the Clash and I think Johnny Thunders as support.

Within a few days, the Pistols had sworn on TV, there was more national outrage, and news of the tour being cancelled. In fact a few venues did host the tour, about four or five, the nearest was Leeds but we never got there. Sheffield City council ordered the City Hall to ban it I think. But that was it; Punk was all we talked about, even though at that point we had heard nothing!"

Joanne Orgill (Rotherham Punkette) ... "My first memory of punk rock arriving in Rotherham was when we were sitting down as a family eating our tea in our lovely pine-clad kitchen at the pine table (It was all the rage, apparently!). A news item came on – possibly 'Nationwide' - talking about the Sex Pistols and what a disgrace they were for swearing on telly. Mum was probably tut-tut ting and Dad was saying how disgusting and talent less they were. (No music could ever compare to my Dad's beloved 50's Rock n' Roll) My older brother, Antony and I were trying not to choke on our fish fingers – we thought it was hilarious and the perfect vehicle for two soon to be rebellious teenagers."

By the end of the year, new groups were forming all over the country- some of them had been playing for a few years even and simply took Punk as the way forward. Groups like the Jam, Stranglers, Vibrators and others spurred on by the new music and its manifesto would quickly become favourites amongst the Punk kids, whilst never being accepted by the Punk elite. Punk bands like the Adverts, Eater, Subway Sect, X-Ray Spex, the Lurkers and Buzzcocks and Generation X (formed from the ashes of Chelsea) sprung up directly as a result of the first ripples of the burgeoning new scene spawned by the Pistols. Sheffield itself now had its own Punk Rock fans and some of them were already starting to form their own groups - all with their own varying ideas of what Punk meant to them. Meanwhile, the outrage aimed at Punk Rock continued unabated!

"Punk Rock… It's disgusting, degrading, ghastly, sleazy, prurient, voyeuristic and nauseating. Most of these groups would be vastly improved by sudden death." **Bernard Brook Partridge'** – Greater London Council Christmas 1976

Phillip Wright … "I was only about 13 when our first Punk experience had occurred, but as 1976 became 1977 things started moving fast. My brother came home one night from the local pub, The John O'Gaunt, which had a Wednesday night disco, saying that the DJ had played the Sex Pistols song that was all over the NME, 'Anarchy in the UK'. It had nearly caused a riot as local middle aged blokes had threatened to hit the DJ for offending them (Gleadless Valley estate and the John O'Gaunt area in particular was a tough place, full of hard nuts), but the DJ would not back down. The following week, me and a few mates crowded outside the fire doors with our ears pressed to the wood, trying to make out what songs he was playing …waiting to hear more Punk Rock."

Chapter Three

Sheffield's Burning

"One of the members of our gang was called Will and he was the first of us to discover punk when he ventured into a London club, and came back with stories of pogoing and mayhem" – **Sue Lowday (Sheffield Punk girl)**

1977 arrives and the Clash brought in the New Year playing at the Roxy club and soon afterwards signing to C.B.S records. The Sex Pistols continued courting controversy and outrage wherever they went, resulting in record contracts being terminated and the group seemingly being unable to play any proper dates in the UK.

When Glen Matlock was ousted early in the year he was replaced by 'Pistols' camp follower and original 'Banshees' drummer Sid Vicious. To many the group would never be the same. Punk and 'New Wave' groups were now forming all over the country, the Boys being amongst the first to get a real Record Company contract, but soon the Jam, the Clash, Eater and others would be ready to record their first records for their newly signed labels. Many musicians and bands simply jumped on the bandwagon. Not so for some of Sheffield's new music fans.

Above: Early 1977 Punk Rockers

Fans of the New Wave (or at least the spirit of the movement) such as Phil Oakey (later of the Human league), were certainly swept along with the excitement and D.I.Y approach to music and dress style of punk, but, like a lot of the Sheffield crowd, didn't really look to the new sounds of Sex Pistols, Clash etc to display the blueprint of what they were looking for in starting up musically. Even so the excitement of this new style was, for the moment, influencing how they looked. Phil Oakey was reputed to have owned the first zip shirt in Sheffield, which was an home made one and seeing as Punk fashion clothes were virtually invisible at that time in Sheffield, this is almost sure to be true.

Oakey and his friends always saw Punk as a next step forward from the Glam period, Ian Craig Marsh exemplifying the new style when he turned up in his own expression of what the Punk style was. Super tight drain pipe jeans, with a leather crotch, a pair of tights with holes and rips everywhere making do for a t-shirt and 2 baked beans tins worn across each wrists as a D.I.Y bracelet. It's clear by this evidence that the innovative style of London punk was not without its northern competitors. In fact throughout the Punk era Sheffield and by proxy of location - the surrounding area - would hold on to its own individuality regardless of what was in or within the trendy crowds of down south. The influences and instigation may have been from the London art school crowd but Sheffield certainly had a style of its own.

Whilst there was still no sign of Punk Rock appearing on the Sheffield live circuit at the beginning of 1977, in January Sheffield produced its very first Punk fanzine Gun Rubber. The fanzine (Sheffield's first Punk inspired one) aimed at the new music being produced and interviewing the punk groups that would eventually play around the area. It also did its very best to focus on the local groups that were starting to spring up around here too.

Most of these locals, groups and fans alike, were influenced and instigated by Punk's energy and fresh approach, but almost to a man were determined to offer something more interesting and left field than the standard one chord wonders of a lot of the London bands.

'Gun-Rubber' was created by Adi Newton and Paul Bower and ran from January to December of 1977. During its heyday it was recognised by 'Sounds' magazine as being more open minded than a lot of the other fanzines and more 'rough, snotty and spirited'.

In the February issue of the fanzine, Sheffield group Cabaret Voltaire were interviewed and when asked what they thought of the punk scene they gave the following answers -

Richard Kirk ... *"I bought the Ramones album as soon as it came out. It gets most of my playing time. Any change is good news. We saw the Damned in Leeds last week and they were great .I was very impressed. They have improved a lot since the first time I saw them in London."*

Fellow band member Malcolm (real name Stephen 'Mal' Mallinder) also showed enthusiasm saying *"I like the punks a lot. The only band I haven't seen yet is The Stranglers. I like their ideas. It's fresh and exciting. But I'm not sure. Their ability is way beyond their ideas."*

The writers of Gun-Rubber fanzine were regularly on the scene, interviewing which ever groups were in town. Paul Bower wrote under the name of Ronny Clocks. In March, he took a trip to London to check out the Punk Mecca 'The Roxy' club where he found himself brushing shoulders with various members of the Punk scene such as Billy Idol, Siouxsie Sioux, Steve Severin and Eater's Andy Blade. Interviewing Andy, he was told that

"*If Punk stays in London it will die. We'd like to tread up North where the kids are fresh. We'd like to play in Sheffield but we've been banned twice by the police. The only places to play are licensed and since we are all under age and our drummer's only 15 they don't like it*."

Paul Bower… "I can remember doing an interview with Joe Strummer whilst down in London. I was leaning over him asking questions about the Punk scene."

Ronny Clocks alias Paul Bower also managed to chat with Damned singer Dave Vanian, though at first he was told that he wasn't he but just an unfortunate look-alike. This was at the time that the Damned was still being partly ostracised for their 'Anarchy' tour misdemeanours, and it was evident that they still felt like outsiders within a scene that they helped to create.

Paul - "Hello you look a lot like Dave Vanian. Are you him?"

Him - "No actually I'm not. It's an unfortunate resemblance."

Paul - "Unfortunate? Why unfortunate? I think the Damned are great."

Him - "Oh really have you seen 'em?"

Paul - "No. They've never played Sheffield. But friends saw them in Leeds and they said they were brilliant."

Him - "Oh really? I think they're crap. I'm a Pistols fan."

After watching Wayne County and the Electric Chairs play their set and chatting to Eater, Paul was told that it was really Dave Vanian who he had been talking to.

Paul - "I felt like a right mug, so I went up to him and asked him if the Damned would be playing Sheffield soon?"

Dave Vanian - "yeah we hope so, as soon as possible."

Paul - "I help some mates run a magazine in Sheffield. We think you could do with some support. The Pistols seem to get all the publicity."

Dave Vanian - "Sounds good; Send me a copy at Stiff records- I'm sure the rest of the group would be interested in reading it."

Ending the Roxy review, the fanzine recommends that if you do go to the club 'Drink before you go in' and 'Go mid-week when there's more room to pogo'. Summing up the Roxy as an interesting place with good management and groups, the piece ends with a quote from a Roxy goer Punk fan from Harlesden who is named as 'A.F.Wanker for his quote of ...*The Gun Rubber? I didn't know Punk had got as far as Sheffield*'. That London Punk would have been right say six months ago. But now the tide had changed. Punk Rock was now a nation wide scene and Sheffield was slowly starting to play its own part in it.

Summing up his visit to London and the Roxy club, **Paul Bower** recalls ... "I was kind of disappointed with that whole Roxy scene, other than the Clash, who weren't really a part of it as they from west London. I thought that it was very pretentious, very posey and very fashion orientated. People were sucking their cheeks in trying to look cool and not actually doing anything. It had that kind of fake cynicism. So part of that motivation from that experience for me was doing Gun-Rubber and then starting '2.3'. It was partly in reaction to what a lot of the London Punk scene was like. I have to say though, that we were always great fans of the Clash and the Ramones."

Above: flyer for Roxy Punk club (most of the above Punk groups listed would soon be appearing at Rotherham's Windmill club and Doncaster's Outlook)

Another local Punk managed to venture further a field to witness the early Punk gigs -

Timothy Green ... "Early 1977 and I went up to Newcastle to watch Iggy Pop and the Vibrators at the City Hall. I found out that one of my mates had written a fanzine so I sold it for him. On another visit to Newcastle, I saw The Damned supporting T-Rex. Selling the fanzine, I bumped into Captain Sensible of the Damned and ended up going backstage."

Punk Rock was now sweeping the country by storm. Headlines, mostly fabricated or exaggerated, in the dailies of disgusting and violent acts from Punk groups and fans were common place. Punk Rock really gave Fleet street something to chew on and throughout the year this media version of what Punk was supposed to be, led to a lot of miss-informed punk fans playing up to that very misconception . Even so, to the kids affected by it, the new scene gave them a purpose and a new outlook to their lives. Surprisingly to begin with, there were very few Punk records, then as the year progressed along came a sudden influx of records.

Anthony Cronshaw ... "I went down to Revolution records at the Castle Market and bought the Ramones' 'Blitzkrieg Bop' and that was it - I was hooked. Most Fridays I would fly into town while ripping open my wage packet and I would climb the stairs that led to the Gallery above Castle Market and I would be there in 'Revolution Records' so aptly named as this was our musical revolution and I was loving every minute of it. In there I would gaze at the list of ever increasing Punk singles that was stuck on the wall by the doorway as you walked in."

 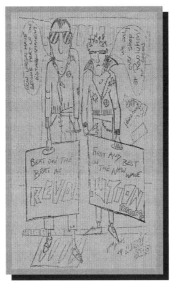

Jo Callis ... "Grip by the Stranglers came out, which I think was one of the first records I heard classified as being Punk Rock, I liked it, and the Stranglers, and its echoes of the Doors and Deep Purple certainly made it rock friendly compared to what was to come. I think I was expecting something a little more radical, and I wouldn't be disappointed. Soon Mark had found 'Spiral Scratch' by the Buzzcocks, then another week he'd play me the thunderous quasi-gothic -

Above: Ripped and torn fanzine No.2 & advert for Sheffield's finest Punk and New Wave records shop Revolution Records'(from Gun-Rubber fanzine no.3 March 1977)

- cacophony of catchy hooks and blitzing riffs that was 'New Rose' by the Damned, this was bliss! (And still one of my all time favourite records) it owed as much to the girl groups of the sixties as it did to the Stooges and the Dolls.

I think Mark was first in line outside his favourite record store in Cockburn Street Edinburgh, when 'Anarchy in the UK' came out, the EMI pressing of course. Then out came the Clash with 'White Riot'? Yeah, I was beginning to get in the mood for a bit of a riot of my own by this time. Then that was it, we knew it was all going to change, we lived in a Britain of Industrial Dispute, economic recession, power cuts, over a million unemployed and IRA bomb threats. The music of the day was at last beginning to reflect the state of the nation, and the discontent of its population. But I knew that we were now rebels with a bit of a cause, and my song writing, and to a certain extent Mark's, would start to reflect that, as my Bowie hairstyle became spikier, and my bomber jacket became a leather one."

Lynne Freeman … "After I had left school, this thing called punk had just started. My Dad had a paper, I think it was the News of the World or something, and it reported on this new band that had said stuff about the Queen and had done a gig that was revolting. That was it, I was hooked. Who were these people, where did they play? and the rest as they say, is history."

Phillip Wright … "One night at the Wednesday night disco, the DJ played a new song 'God Save The Queen', cue more threats and stuff, but by now the 'Gaunt' pub was attracting a lot of Bikers on a Wednesday, so the DJ played more Punk along with traditional rock stuff. Soon after that, a local lad, Robert 'Dingo' Dowling, turned up at Herdings Youth Club with a brand new LP, 'Damned, Damned, Damned' by the Damned. A few minutes after hearing 'New Rose' for the first time, I was hooked. Over the next few weeks, we almost wore that LP out at the Youth club, as it was on continual rotation along with 'Stupidity' by Dr. Feelgood.

Above: The Clash in classic 1977 pose in this Punk Special feature – which I came across by chance during an art lesson at school

I also remember watching the Tony Wilson show called 'So It Goes', recorded live in Manchester, he had Eddie and The Hot Rods on one week playing 'Teenage Depression', and although they were not strictly punks, they looked sort of punkish and sounded like a speeded up version of Dr. Feelgood."

Paul Clarkson … "I had bought 'Anarchy' the year before. Then it was Buzzcocks 'Spiral Scratch', and all the others. I can remember spring bank holiday 1977; it was hot and sunny; I had just bought 'Remote Control' by the Clash. I played it to death on the small

58

cream and red Dansette record player that we had. Then came 'God Save the Queen' not long after. Then there seemed to be new ones out every week. Me and my flat mate, used to buy two of every single. The idea was, one to play, and one to keep, don't ask me why, but that was the idea…it never really worked because at the end of term, we would sell 'em 'cos we were skint (grant had run out, therefore it was a question of lager and food or save a single - the singles lost out usually). Or it would sometimes be '*Wow look at those trousers…I'll buy 'em"*. 'Anyone wanna buy some records?"

Phillip Wright … "A great record shop was located on The Gallery, above the Castle Markets, called 'Revolution Records', the lads who worked in there played in bands and dressed in home made shirts with slogans sprayed on them in spray paint, just like the early pictures of the Clash."

Some young music fans felt the impact of Punk almost head on.

Paul Clarkson … "Punk made me feel different, but also part of a tribe maybe: an unusual and slightly menacing tribe - seen as very menacing if you lived in Rotherham. I had always been a non-conformist and suddenly there were others too. There was a healthy dollop of social exclusion involved."

However, other local teenagers were attracted to this new thing called 'Punk Rock' but, were often coming from a musical diet of 70's takeaways that were far removed from this new brash and immediate 'in yer face' rock sound. Some Punks had been fans of prog rock and Heavy Rock amongst other styles before Punk.

Barry Bartle … "Before Punk came along I had been into Heavy Rock. I had been too young to catch the original Mod era and the following Hippy scene, so when I found out about Punk, I thought *I am having some of this*. I started to go to the Crazy Daisy where there was a healthy mix of the Bowie crowd and Punks."

Bryan Bell … "I had seen the Pistols at the Mucky Duck (Black Swan), but wasn't that impressed. To begin with I wasn't quite sure which way I was gonna go. I then started buying the singles when they were being released- 'Anarchy in the UK', 'New Rose', and then later on 'In the City' by the Jam, the Clash with 'White Riot' and 'One Chord Wonders' by the Adverts.

To start with, I had no what you could call Punk clothes as such. There was nowhere in Sheffield or Rotherham to buy Punk clothes. It was a case of 'Do it yourself'. Around this time I started to bleach my hair as well as making up my own kind of Punk style with odds and ends of what I had hanging around. My Dad didn't recognise me and the rest of my family did not approve at all. People would walk the other side of the road to avoid me and people who had known me for years refused to speak to me. They all got used to me eventually."

In Sheffield, during the early days the Punk attitude was adopted by a handful of music fans and musicians, but almost all of them carried a different interpretation of what the

Punk ideal meant. It is fair to say that the Sheffield Punk scene was much less orthodox than most places and the regular style of Punk group were pretty thin on the ground.

Perhaps the earliest so called Punk group in Sheffield was Reactor, formed in 1976, and whose songs included titles such as 'Don't wanna live in no steel city', 'Born to Hate' and 'Pretty soon there's gonna be some change'. Led by singer Gary Warburton, they were championed by Sheffield's 'Home Groan' fanzine.

Next up were the Extras who, whilst not strictly a punk group, were caught up with the mood of the time and enjoyed the best part of a year being the Sheffield group everyone went to see and talked about. It was almost a foregone conclusion that they were going to hit the big time, but bad luck, mistiming and an ill fated move to London would decide their fate.

The Extras started out as a Roxy Music influenced group fronted by singer John Lake and could actually play their instruments proficiently. They never really succumbed to the punk fashion and scene as such, but were for a short time the one group in Sheffield who were seen to be a part of the new music scene. Caught between Glam and punk they would have probably been more comfortable being classed as 'New Wave'. Their style would certainly have been more suited to the later New Wave style that was a watered down version of Punk and would regularly dent the charts a year or two later.

For a while, the Extras were known under the more traditionally Punk sounding name Abattoir, playing for three nights at the 'Crazy Daisy' (Sheffield's in place at the time). They Xeroxed posters for gigs and took them to places like 'Rare and Racy' record shop. They donned Abattoir hats and retained the name for about a month, before becoming the Extras and playing their first gig under the new name in April 1977.

The line up was now John Lake: vocals, Simon Anderson: guitar, Robin Allen: bass guitar, Robin Markin: keyboards, Andy Quick: saxophone, Nick Dawson: drums. They played support slots for many of the visiting Punk bands including Boomtown Rats, Slaughter and the Dogs and Siouxsie and the Banshees. Their audience at the time would include most of the musicians to be of the Sheffield scene, such as Martin Fry, Phil Oakey, Martyn Ware, Jarvis Cocker and working musician Simon Eyre.

Simon Eyre ... "I'd seen Abattoir at the Broadfield a few times and thought they were fantastic, then my flatmate, Mark Anderson joined them on drums they were called The Extras by that time and he really turned them into something special. We went to see them at a Sheffield Uni gig and you couldn't get near the stage, it was heaving and they sounded amazing!"

The Extras were the band most likely to make it and helped to push the Sheffield scene into focus. Their decision to follow an invite from record label Phonogram to move to London proved to be their nemesis. They managed to play venues such as 'Hope and Anchor', 'The Music Machine' and 'The Marquee', but after the initial boom of interest faded and record companies lost enthusiasm, they decided to move back to Sheffield.

However when they arrived back in the city, the fledgling Sheffield scene had moved up a few gears and the Human League, Cabaret Voltaire etc had started to gain their much earned recognition. The Sheffield music scene had evolved and sadly, there was no gap left for the Extras to fill. They continued until late 1979 before calling it a day. In June 2003, a tragic ending to the Extras story occurred when singer John Lake drowned whilst on holiday in Malaysia.

As well as writing and working on Gun Rubber fanzine, Paul Bower and Adi Newton had now formed their own Punk band, initially called 2.3 Children - but later shortened to just 2.3. Guitarist Paul Bower talks about the group's formation and early days.

Paul Bower …"It was tied in with Gun Rubber fanzine, me and Adi Newton being the writers. I put an ad in Gun Rubber for a bass player, which Paul Sharp replied to, and I also went down to the Crazy Daisy with an advert for 'Drummer wanted' pinned to the back of my shirt and it was from that that Hayden joined the group. From that, things happened very quickly. We were playing our first gig about 2 and half weeks from the three of us having our first rehearsal at the work shops on Devonshire Lane in Sheffield. It was a kind of a desire to stop talking about it and actually doing it. Bands seemed to be forming every other day during that period of May/June 1977. Everything happened very quickly.

We played our first gig, which was a benefit for strikers at 'Bachelors' food factory at the Sheffield Penthouse supporting the Extras, who were popular at the time. From there we managed to get a whole series of gigs."

Above: Sheffield Punk Fanzine Gun-Rubber No.3 (Paul Bower)

The creativity of Punk was something largely dismissed at the time but something that could not be ignored. From the early Punk ethos of D.I.Y attitude came a new approach to music, song writing, poetry (see John Cooper Clarke), art and unavoidably fashion and clothes…

Paul Clarkson … "Yes Punk had informed my life up to this point. I was now studying graphic design at Poly and the whole Punk movement opened up a massive channel for creative risk taking and in this followed through the new processes in typography, photography and image making. It certainly did so for fashion (Vivien Westwood etc and to a lesser admired degree Zandra Rhodes). I was also aware how it had affected film makers like Derek Jarman and later on Julien Temple.

It was a great time, because, as students of graphics and design, we had a new kind of freedom, we could be more challenging and not just accept what the designers of the time were offering us. I remember being involved in designing a poster to advertise a band that was playing at some club/Punk venue. Well my mate was in the band as well as a guy from the photography course and we got a picture from a gay porn mag, which was of a gay bloke in full biker gear with his cock hanging out, full frontal! We blew it up to A4 size and screen-printed it and it looked fucking brill; we put the pub name and details on and stuck 'em up all around college and some around town. As a result they all got ripped down within a few hours and we got 'done' off the college head – who threatened us all with expulsion. *'We were a disgrace'* he said. The cleaners were shocked and refused to clean the student common room. We got a proper telling off 'obscenity lecture etc', the band played crap but the pub was packed but hey who gave a fuck!"

By the middle of 1977, as Punk groups that had been signed up started to release their first and second singles, some of them began to appear on BBC's Top of the Pops, gaining even more publicity and often giving a young generation, still listening to chart fodder, their first sighting of Punk Rock. Also, while many local punk fans had been eagerly awaiting the first punk rock on vinyl, there would be many uninitiated young music fans that would come across their first Punk records by chance.

Pete Cooper (Rotherham Punk Rocker) ... "I was 15 in 1977 and living in Rotherham. I had heard 'Anarchy in the UK' in the 5th form common room at school, where we were allowed a record player. Wow!! It blew me away. That was my first life changing experience. That weekend, with my paper round money I went into Rotherham to the record shop 'Sound of Music' and tried to locate this single. Unfortunately, they didn't have it in stock, but not letting this deter me, I instead purchased a single by the Stranglers 'Peaches'/Go Buddy go'. That was it. Each week I could be found buying every possible Punk record that I could lay my hands on. The majority I still have today."

Paul Kelly remembers buying his first Punk single ... "My first Punk single was 'London Lady/Grip' by the Stranglers and it was purely by chance that I bought it and from the most unlikely place. For some reason I was in Debenhams in Sheffield on the Moor, which used to have a rather large record department downstairs. In there, were a couple of wooden boxes where they sold off old singles for 20p (I think a single was about 70p back then). Looking through the box, I came across the Stranglers single in a picture bag and there were about 10 copies of it. I just liked the look of it and thought to myself *'I'll have one of them'.* I remember when I got home, I left it around and my Mum said *'By, they look a rough lot.'*

Anyway I played it immediately and ran across to my mate Howard's house, and after he'd heard it, we jumped on the number 52 bus to town (2p to anywhere back then), and he invested 20p in a copy himself."

Bryan Bell ... "To begin with there weren't that many decent punk records around. At a lot of the early gigs a lot of reggae would be played."

Anthony Cronshaw ... "Try as I may, our local DJ did not share our enthusiasm for Punk, and even though I'd stand by his decks all night - clutching my latest Punk vinyl acquisition - would he fuck play it. He would say *'It's only charts and disco at weekends'.* I'll be fair to him though, he would give us six minutes of heaven playing our stuff on a Tuesday night, but that was it."

The new Punk generation were now starting to have their own individual favourites amongst the 'New Wave'.

Phillip Wright ... "In 1977, Top of the Pops started featuring a few punk bands, and I remember me and my mates seeing the Jam play 'In The City' for the first time, that was it, this band became a big part of my life, they sounded like a Punk version of the Who and (instead of the standard Punk attire of the time) dressed like Mods."

Paul Bower ... "The Clash was (for us) always the greatest band. Ramones were also special and I liked the Adverts because they had a very different take on life. 'One Chord Wonders 'and 'Gary Gilmore's eyes' are classic records. I did always feel that Generation X were fabricated by their management. I also regarded Lou Reed and the Velvet Underground as the godfathers of Punk."

Timothy Green... "I saw the Clash's White Riot tour in Leeds and Newcastle (wearing my home-made Clash t-shirt)...Fantastic."

Whilst many would totally embrace Punk Rock, there would be some music fans that would be happier to sample certain bands and records, with much of Punk leaving them cold.

Steve Haythorne ... "For me, a lot of Punk was not that great. I just couldn't get my head around all the shouting and screaming of a lot of it. I have always considered that the music is always the most important. I don't fully go in for the cult thing and the fashion; it's the music I am interested in. I bought the Clash first album when that came out and enjoyed that; their cover of 'Police and Thieves' was fantastic. I never became a mad fan of the Clash but did like a lot of their album tracks."

And the innocence and feeling of discovering something new in music was often tainted by the Media's perceptions – if only for the short term.

Dave Spencer ... "These days, when instant global communication is pretty much taken for granted, it is hard to imagine how hard it was to even know how to hear Punk Rock, especially considering that every record shop in the land supposedly refused to stock anything by the Sex Pistols. I clearly remember a rumour going round school about someone who had actually heard 'God Save The Queen'. They said that in the song the

Sex Pistols sang about killing the Queen's corgis! I can only think now that I must have assumed that the grown ups were right. My first real interest in the 'New Wave' was in a chap who went by the quirky moniker of Elvis Costello. I can't remember how I first could have heard him, but I did buy his 'My Aim is true' on the day it came out. It sounded so fresh and bright and shiny and different."

Tony ... "I really had no idea at all of what Punk was all about during those first six months of 1977. It was something that was in all the daily papers, all the outrage and stuff. My parents weren't the type to be disgusted at it all anyway, so it never really became a topical issue. At the time, I had this stupid idea that the Sex Pistols were some sort of biker band. How wrong could I have been?"

Punk Rocker **John Harrison** from Rotherham remembers his first experience of hearing The Sex Pistols etc ... "My brother had bought 'God Save the Queen' and I can remember looking at the cover and wondering 'What's this'. I instantly related to it. It sounded amazing. For me, Punk was like a massive release of all those emotions that were pent up, all the teenage stuff that had built up, and suddenly I had this outlet. That's why I latched onto it straight away. The next one I heard was the Jam's 'In the City'. I followed them all the way through after hearing that record."

Life-defining 'first time experiences' of Punk Rock were becoming more frequent.

Chiz lived in Chesterfield during the late 1970's but would later travel to Punk gigs in Sheffield and now fronts Punk group Riot Squad. His initiation to Punk Rock is quite typical of young teenagers at the time ... "I completely missed out on the Punk Rock explosion of 1976, due to not living in a major city and only being 12 years old at the time. However, one night on the way home from my Aunties, in the back of my Dad's car- I heard something that was to change and shape my life forever. 'Peaches' by the Stranglers came on the radio and I was blown away. The heavy bass line was unlike anything I'd heard before and the 'puke sounding solo' made me realise this must be 'Punk Rock'! I decided there and then to find out more. My parents thought it was a phase, as I am sure most young Punks' folks did, but all my pocket money went on Punk vinyl, as did a lot of my wages once I turned 16 and began working on building sites."

Paul Clarkson who had been living - and discovering Punk Rock - in Rotherham in 1976 then became a student in Nottingham. Whilst on a student trip from Nottingham to London early in 1977, Paul came across his first real experience of 'live Punk Rock' close up... "This was my first time away from home and also my first time in London. I went down the King's Road and into the 'Chelsea Potter' pub, had a pint and noticed a poster up in the pub, which said there was a band on tonight coincidentally called Chelsea. In a back room, we heard some music – the bands were doing a sound check whilst waiting for their singer.

In the toilets downstairs, I came across their singer who was, shall we say, 'very much the worse for wear'. I leg it back upstairs to the other lads I'm with, and while the band are still playing, we go back down to check on their singer. I was shocked and scared stiff (he looked that bad). Anyway, we realised who he really was when we got chatting to the band at the bar. We tell 'em their singer, who is called Gene October we are now told, is crashed out downstairs! This is all in the afternoon. They were rehearsing for a gig that evening. They invited us to come back down at 8pm, which we did. Chelsea took to the stage some time later and played a half hour set - my first taste of Punk played live. They played to a crowd of London townies, tourists, Rod Stewart fans and hippies. They got booed and heckled. One of the members of the band told them all to fuck off! There was a bit of a scuffle and then end of the gig. I thought *'this is great, who are they? They look different'.* I heard someone say *'Punk Rockers'* with a disgusted reply."

Above: Sheffield fanzine Gun Rubber No. 4 (Paul Bower)

Lynne Freeman … "I hot footed it with my mate down to London to see what was happening. A load of funky shops had sprung up and the place was full of punks. I had to have some of this action. I bought some clothes there and then and bought a fab bag in a sale on the King's road. It was completely see through."

Whilst the young teenage generation were starting to turn onto this new Punk experience, the older, more demanding - and often more easily bored - music fans were, along with being excited by the new creativity and shifts in attitude that Punk offered, also becoming objective in their opinions of what Punk could inspire for Sheffield itself.

Phil Oakey (Human League) … "I don't think the Second World War finished until Punk came along. Punk changed peoples attitudes, they realised they didn't have to do what their parents did. I was just excited by Punk. It was great. But Sheffield was different to the rest of the country. In Sheffield Punk was just Roxy Music taken a few stages on, with added zips and safety pins." **(From 'Beats Working for a Living' by Martin Lilleker)**

Nevertheless, there were still some last acts of 'Punk style chaotic expression' to be displayed before the new collective of Sheffield musicians would take their own individual different paths. In mid 1977, the 3 members of Cabaret Voltaire, along with 2.3 drummer Hayden Boyes-Weston, Martyn Ware, Glenn Gregory (of future Heaven 17), Adi Newton and Ian Craig Marsh all played a gig as a punk spoof-type group, which they named The Studs. Supporting Manchester Punk group the Drones they played improvised versions of 'Louie Louie', Lou Reed's 'Vicious' and a version of the Dr Who theme. Whilst they played their set, friends of this 'one day only punk group' threw pigs ears into the audience to catch at their own will. The audience were neither impressed by the 'pork catchings' nor the first home grown attempt at archetypal Punk Rock.

However, feeling an ever growing disenchantment with the conventional idea of what a punk/new wave group should be, and after struggling to become friends with the six strings of a guitar and its resulting sore fingers, the core members of the Sheffield punk crowd turned to a different music in a different room altogether. By late summer punk was almost past its interesting phase for many forward looking music fans. Hearing Donna Summer's 'I feel love' and then Kraftwerk's 'Trans-Europe Express' LP at a party held by Richard Kirk of Cabaret Voltaire, Ian Craig Marsh, Martyn Ware, and Adi Newton saw their own vision of the future of music. Guitars were out of the window and in came the synthesiser. Which is another story in itself.

Meanwhile in Mexborough, in March, Punk group Hobbies of Today were formed. Their line up of Kevin Hobbi: vocals and guitar, Stuart Holie: bass guitar and David Exciting: drums did actually record a single called 'RUI2' B-SIDE 'Piss on you'. After problems in getting the record made, resulting in its release being cancelled, the group split up - later resurfacing as a Post-Punk synthesiser band a couple of years later.

It cannot be denied that Sheffield was quite late to regularly promote Punk and 'New Wave' gigs, with only sporadic gigs by the likes of pub rock band Little Bob Story at the Polytechnic. Soon however, signs were evident of the city catching up with the times. The Crazy Daisy had started to have Punk nights (which were a start) but these first forays into putting Punk started in the steel city were not always held in high respect.

Gun Rubber fanzine issue no.4 (spring 1977) in a rant against the fickle Punk fans stated that...'*Daisy's getting' on my tits as well. How many people who go down on a Wednesday actually do anything except think that they're real cool. How many bands are coming out of it? How many mags? Not a lot. Well piss on them' cos at least I write a bit and me and some of me mates are getting a band. So if you're one of those silly cunts who thinks all there is to the New Wave is a blank expression, a mohair jumper, tight trousers and knowing which end of the Kings Road is where it's at...fuck off!!'*

In the same issue (that also included interviews with The Damned, Joe Strummer, Kid Strange, a live review of Generation X and a visit to ' Seditionaries' in London), the Drones gig at the Crazy Daisy on 6th May is briefly reviewed... '*The Drones played two sets that night, but again it was the Punks themselves who received the worst review when they are criticised for being 'posing twats' and not being able to commit themselves to either liking or disliking the band, for fear of getting it wrong.'*

The first name New wave group to play Sheffield that year was Ultravox who played at the Top Rank suite on Sunday the 3rd of April 1977. They opened with 'Wide Boys' followed by 'Saturday Night in the City of the Dead' to a pogoing crowd of Punks with John Foxx announcing before one song *'This is called the city doesn't care.'* A pogoing John Foxx and his band were consequently given a roasting in 'Gun Rubber' fanzine.

In the Rotherham Advertiser of 20th May 1977, Mark Whiting; who went on to say 'Ultravox's sound takes on a more powerful and menacing quality at a live show reviewed Ultravox's gig at Doncaster Outlook. *John Foxx trips and stalks around the stage as he dominates the events that follow and his automation pose is strikingly magnified under stabs of strobe lighting'.'*

In the next few months the Stranglers, Johnny Thunders and the Heartbreakers, Boomtown Rats, Penetration, Slaughter and the Dogs and the Jam would play the same venue whilst The Damned would play the university, Wayne County and the Electric Chairs, Television (supported by Blondie) played the City Hall and at Doncaster's Outlook - club the Ramones played a legendary and energetic classic Punk gig on Monday 23rd May.

Above: John Foxx of Ultravox at Sheffield Top Rank April 3rd 1977

Paul Bower ... "The Ramones gig was unbelievable. I had seen them the night before at the Electric Circus in Manchester and they were fantastic. I interviewed them and they were really nice people, very friendly and down to earth. At the Outlook, they came on and the crowd went bananas; Encores? They did so many I can't remember how many? It was perfect."

Anthony Cronshaw ... "We were now well into 1977 so it was now time to see some of the Punk music played live for the first time. Time to see the Ramones. I was still eking out a living at the 'arse slapping' supermarket I was exiled out to in fucking Rotherham, so I knocked off early, telling my Boss I was going to the dentist and then I dashed back to the Steel City. Once there, I rendezvoused with the lads in the local boozer...I bloody looked the biz- baseball boots, ripped jeans and a bin liner that I used for a shirt. I had attacked an old jacket with a Stanley knife and it looked a mess, Punk style mess that is.

My Mother had given me a puzzled look as I had bolted through the door and strutted through our Council estate on my way to the boozer. In the pub, my mate Martin walked in.

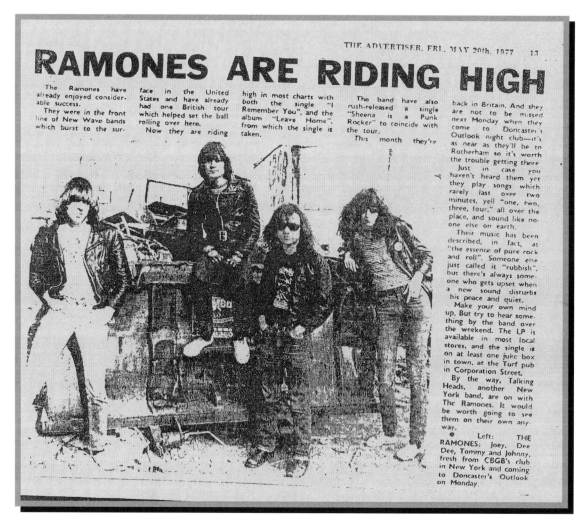

THE ADVERTISER, FRI. MAY 20th, 1977   13

RAMONES ARE RIDING HIGH

The Ramones have already enjoyed considerable success.

They were in the front line of New Wave bands which burst to the sur-

face in the United States and have already had one British tour which helped set the ball rolling over here.

Now they are riding

high in most charts with both the single "I Remember You", and the album "Leave Home", from which the single is taken.

The band have also rush-released a single "Sheena is a Punk Rocker" to coincide with the tour.

This month they're

back in Britain. And they are not to be missed next Monday when they come to Doncaster's Outlook night club—it's as near as they'll be to Rotherham so it's worth the trouble getting there

Just in case you haven't heard them yet they play songs which rarely last over two minutes, yell "one, two, three, four," all over the place, and sound like no-one else on earth.

Their music has been described, in fact, as "the essence of pure rock and roll". Someone else just called it "rubbish", but there's always someone who gets upset when a new sound disturbs his peace and quiet.

Make your own mind up. But try to hear something by the band over the weekend. The LP is available in most local stores, and the single is on at least one juke box in town, at the Turf pub in Corporation Street.

By the way, Talking Heads, another New York band, are on with The Ramones. It would be worth going to see them on their own anyway.

● Left: THE RAMONES: Joey, Dee Dee, Tommy and Johnny, fresh from CBGB's club in New York and coming to Doncaster's Outlook on Monday.

Above: Ramones feature in Rotherham Advertiser 20th May 1977

He looked cool in his sheepskin trousers that were about four sizes too big for him- looking like a bag of shit which was a compliment in that sense. It was Andy, though, who stole the show with a bin liner on and a noose around his neck and topped off with a mop of red fucking hair that he'd emptied two full bottles of cake dye onto his bonce to get the effect. We jumped into the car and we were off to Doncaster Outlook club - our mates we'd left behind pissing themselves at the state of us, but did we give a fuck?.We had arrived!

At the Outlook, we paid our 75p - yes 75 bloody pence - and we climbed the stairs and entered one of the smallest clubs I had ever been in. It was heaving and as we fought our way to the bar, the place was buzz, buzz, buzzing. Talking Heads were playing support but we'd come to see the Ramones and boy was this a sledgehammer of a set- the place was literally bouncing and how we didn't finish up in the basement I'll never know.

I looked around and it was electric- this was something I'd never experienced in my life, the adrenalin was shaking my body and what a feeling this was. It even beat my other passion in life and that was fighting at the football matches. This was simply the biz. Andy was bouncing his hefty frame like some kind of demented Ballerina, but his face was covered in the red cake dye. It was so hot, that when he was wandering round the place the red food colouring in his hair was dripping all over his face and the bouncers were thinking he had been glassed in the face or something. We were sweating and steaming that much moisture that it was rising off our saturated bodies.

But it was over far too quickly; mind you, they must have played their entire record catalogue of the two LP'S and the singles. It was one song done with and then a quick 1-2-3-4 and off they'd go again. You never had time to draw breath- it was amazing. As we descended the stairs and out into the chill of the evening, we were piss wet through. I didn't get this wet in the fucking bath. I was on such a high that I could not wait for my next fix- there wouldn't be too long to wait to get that fix."

The Ramones Outlook gig was also reviewed in Rotherham Advertiser (which at the time was surprisingly quite on the ball with the local Punk scene and especially the live circuit). In the issue dated 27th May 1977, the reviewer recounts *'The club was hot and steamy. The atmosphere was tense and the Ramones were due on any minute. Talking Heads had set the scene. They had played songs that no one had heard before and had been called back on for more. But they finally cleared the stage and tightly packed bodies pushed forward. People stood on chairs and The Ramones appeared.*

As the first two minute song was unleashed, the mass up front began bouncing up and down, jostling and pushing against each other. And from then on, through nearly 30 numbers, the high level of excitement and energy never dropped. It was exhausting, it was magnificent. 'Gabba Gabba Hey! is all there is to say.'

Patrick Tierney ... "The epochal Ramones/Talking Heads gig. That was one of the biggest crowds I ever saw at The Outlook. It was Life-changing and still in my top 5 gigs of all time. Madly enough, I remember the sweat marks under Tina Weymouth's arms when the Heads finished. *'Wow'*, I thought, she's human."

The Punk Rock gigs were now arriving at the region's doorstep a little more regularly.

Timothy Green ... "On consecutive nights I saw Talking Heads and the Ramones at Donny Outlook, Blondie and Television at Sheffield City Hall and then the Adverts and the Damned at Sheffield Poly."

The same Ramones tour stopped off at legendary Manchester Punk venue the Electric Circus and a gang of Sheffield Punk fans decided to make the trip to see the gig.

Sue Lowday ... "The clan at Kites (the wine bar where I worked) loved Talking Heads and the Ramones and so it was a must to go and see them live. Mini Robertson, Ted Gush, George Slater, Will, Annie Cole, Chris Thompson and Terry amongst others squeezed into cars and drove over to Manchester via the Snake Pass, music blaring. Will met up with Punk friends from Manchester, and decided it was best to see the gig from the balcony. It was packed, no room to move and it was a slow walk up to the balcony level because of the numbers of people, mostly wearing black. Bare stone steps with water pouring down from a blocked sink or loo. I was desperate for the loo, (must have been the drinking on the way) but there were no doors and it was shared men's and ladies... everybody going up the stairs were looking straight into the loos. The choice was of peeing in the sink or the loo, all cubicles busy. What do you do for cover, should you care, this is anarchy after all. I cared, so I got cover.

Eventually getting onto the balcony, it was very dark, no seats, standing room only, metal bar to lean on. Our priority is getting the drinks in and with a massive queue; it was two pints each in plastic glasses. In the place, there were egg boxes on the walls, but I don't think they could have done much to deaden the deafening sound of the gig. Talking Heads were a bit of a disappointment, I think it was the wrong venue for them. The Ramones, though, were pure energy and the audience was alive with one mass of movement. We were looking down into the heaving crowd. A few of the Kites mob went to join in the fray, but I was happy to watch from above. My ears were ringing for days after."

Back in Sheffield, the Punk rush was speeding up.

Anthony Cronshaw ... "My next fix came just two days after the Ramones gig and this time, we had the pleasure of the company of the Damned at the Sheffield University. We headed up to the gig on the bus and the driver must have thought that all the loonies had been let out for the evening. But Andy had toned down his appearance a little and the red hair had gone. Martin had also ditched his gigantic trousers and my bin liner had hit the bin.

We stumped up the cash on the door and strolled up to the bar, with beers in hand and standing around going over what a great night we'd had in Doncaster the other night. What amused us, was that the Damned were also hitting the beer and Captain Sensible was such a larger than life character. We chatted to him and he signed a £1 note - adding a beret to our dear majesty the Queen.

Again the set was awesome and the place was bouncing, it was the spitting that I took offence to and when one bastard hit me instead of the band, that was it, my terrace instincts took over and I lamped the bastard. It was now a free for all and the bouncers waded in, but luckily, I was not ejected, that would have been a right downer. The band was covered in spit, and if I'd been them- well I'd have lost it completely. The kid I had hit was covered in claret, but he still pogoed and spat like a trooper, but his spittle was now a nice crimson colour.

Yet again, it was all over too quickly, and off we trudged into the night, and again I was piss wet through. We finished off the evening in the Daisy after the bouncers reluctantly let us in. It was during this period that the Roxy night was binned and Punk took its place. The Damned already had their debut album in the charts for two months, but it would be another two years before they breached the top fifty in the singles chart."

The Damned played Sheffield University, first with the Adverts supporting in May, and then returning to the venue less than a month later on June 13th. Later in the year, following a quick to develop 'Damned' backlash that had kicked in throughout the music press and one that had sadly spread to the fans themselves, they played with USA Punk band the Dead Boys at the Top Rank to a poorly attended audience. The Damned split early in 1978, but reformed later that year and consequently would play many dates in and around Sheffield throughout the ensuing years.

How lucky could you get? As when gaining employment right at the centre of one of the region's greatest 'New Wave's' venues -

Steve Lloyd … "I started working at the Doncaster Outlook in May 77. My first night was the Damned and Adverts gig. This was probably my all time favourite Punk gig too. I was really impressed with both bands and managed to meet them both. Gaye Advert appeared shy but I had a long and interesting conversation with singer TV Smith.
    The Punks that night were now in full force. I remember being really impressed with this one guy who was wearing a jacket made out of polythene plastic type of material and inside it was loads of Punk newspaper headlines. I thought it was incredibly inventive."

Timothy Green … "The Damned/Adverts gig was next at Sheffield Poly. It was the same day as Liverpool winning the European Cup for the first time, but no-one was bothered with that. I liked the Adverts; 'One Chord Wonders' is still one of my favourite singles. The Damned were fine, but I've never bothered with them since. The last thing I bought of theirs was 'Neat, Neat, Neat'."

One of the first big major Punk tours by a signed band was the Jam's 'In the City' tour, which took in both Doncaster outlook and Sheffield Top Rank in the summer of 1977.

Anthony Cronshaw … "Back at the Outlook in Donny we went to see the Jam. These boys wore suits and looked like a throwback to the swinging sixties, but wow they could play. They were amazing and again the gig was so good it took your breath away. If my memory is correct, I think that the Punks toned down the gobbing at this gig."

Steve Lloyd… "The Jam at the Outlook were very tight and you could tell that they could really play. They went through their set really fast with hardly any gaps between songs. They were maybe a bit too Modish for myself but they were good. There were some Punks who were dressed a bit like the band. I think they had come up with the band."

Phil Tasker (Doncaster Punk and Vice Squad singer) … "I thought that the Jam gig at the Outlook was really crap, the sound was awful and they didn't seem to give a shit about the audience, perhaps it was beneath them ? I don't know, but it was before they were famous."

Bryan Bell … "I saw the Jam at Sheffield Top Rank on the 'In the City' tour. That was amongst the first ones I went to. I suppose it was also one of the first of what you could call big Punk gigs in Sheffield. There had not been that many up until then, although I had seen the Clash on the 'White Riot' tour, the Damned at the University and a couple of other groups. From what I can remember of the Jam gig there were a lot of Punks there but even then there were a few who were trying to dress like the Jam with the black suit jackets and skinny ties look. This was halfway through 1977 and the Punk look was still developing, but not fully formed as yet.

Punk was storming the whole country but the thing is there still wasn't anywhere to buy the punk clothes at this time, not around here anyway. It was all in London really. So it was a case of making do and amending the clothes you had to suit. It might have been an old leather jacket you would dig out and punk it up. After a while all the painting of groups on the back of the leather jackets started."

Patrick Tierney … "The Stranglers also played The Outlook. I had read (in the NME) that during one song, Hugh Cornwell threw up. I was mightily disappointed when it was more like a heavy gob.

Above: Spot the 2 Punk singles in this Top 20 provided by 'Sound of music' shop

I do distinctly remember their obvious musical skill, with JJ blowing me away with his bass playing. They were definitely 'Other' and had an almost sinister presence. I didn't see the Jam at this time as I wasn't a great fan. I did however, go into the dressing room the week after they played and saw an ornate felt tip crest that Bruce Foxton had drawn on the back of the door.

I think the Drones replaced the cancelled Boomtown Rats. I don't think they had been going for long, and it showed. No substitute for Bob & co. The head bouncer at the Outlook was called Tom Higgins. What a great man. Even under severe provocation (e.g.: drunkenly slurring *'I pay your wages'*) he never got heavy or held anything against me. Many years later, when he was a sweet seller, I was able to apologise. Around this time too, there was a lunatic who always turned up to the gigs in a frogman suit and did his frenzied thing on the small dance floor at the right hand side of the stage."

The 'New Wave' was now starting to kick down the doors of numerous venues in the steel city and the region…even colleges now succumbing to the lure of Punk's offerings.

Sue Lowday ... "I was in my second year at Art College then and we had Thursday nights at the college where there was a band or DJ. One of the most memorable was Wreckless Eric. I think we had hoped he would be a bit more reckless than he was. It was a good laugh though...and I think he threw a few instruments around at the end of the gig."

The Extras by Pete Hill

Paul Bower of 2.3 by Pete hill

Cabaret Voltaire by Pete Hill

Above: Sheffield's mid 1977 Punk roster – from top left The Extras, Paul Bower of 2.3, Cabaret Voltaire and a Punk night poster

Sheffield's Punk scene was now starting to kick in with the help of a variety of Punk inspired groups; most of which would support the visiting Punk and 'New Wave' groups now playing more regularly in the city. Meanwhile, as the local Punk generation were discovering the joys and excitement of this new Punk Rock phenomenon and its new fledgling music scene, another new Punk Rock arrival was on its way from across the other side of the Atlantic.

Above: 'New Wave' gear of mid 1977 now available from the back pages of the music weeklies

Those early few months of summer saw American 'New Wave' pioneers Television release their seminal album 'Marquee Moon' to wide acclaim from the music press. Along with Talking Heads, they represented the intellectual side of the 'New Wave', with Johnny Thunder's Heartbreakers taking the trashy rock n' roll Punk style as their template. Richard Hell and his Voidoids would soon be releasing their classic '77' Punk album 'Blank Generation' that would inspire many Punk musicians to at least try to achieve some level of musicianship... not that the local Punk fans showed any appreciation towards the group or Punk Rock's first iconic figurehead 'Hell' who had seen his make-do D.IY Punk look be imitated by countless UK Punk Rockers. When they did end up visiting the UK later in the year, they were treated to a barrage of bottles, spit, beer, abuse and any other missiles at hand; their Sheffield Top Rank gig with the Clash being no exception. But it would be a future female pin-up and sex icon that would bridge the middle ground between the no-mans land of American Punk Rock.

American Punk with a 'sixties garage buzz' Blondie arrived in the steel city in May 1977 along with New York's early 'New Wave' pioneers Television. Of Blondie, Rotherham Advertiser gave a one lined report stating that 'Blondie's set was, unfortunately a bit of a flop. They didn't seem to cope with the big hall venue'.

Barry Bartle … "Television played Marquee Moon early on in their set resulting in them being booed at. They then played it again at the end and we were shouting for Blondie to come back on."

Deborah Harry, of Blondie, pictured during their Sheffield City Hall concert last week.

Blondie's set was, unfortunately, a bit of a flop. They didn't seem to cope with the big hall venue.

Their good time, fun-loving approach hit the floor between the stage and the first row of seats and never recovered.

Television did much better. The two groups were a bad mix. Their styles were totally different and Television had all the help.

As soon as the band took the stage there was a rush to the front, but if the supporters were hoping to dance they were disappointed.

Tom Verlaine's music was excellent listening but it was nothing to bounce up and down to.

The band showed that their New Wave tag hangs very loosely. They are on their own, playing a unique brand of music and they demand our attention. (Picture by Dave Muscroft).

Timothy Green … "Blondie supported Television at Sheffield City Hall. Blondie were good, but Television was, in hindsight, as dull as I'd expected them to be. I would probably bracket them with The Stranglers (and later on, Dire Straits) as a 'safe' band for people who were a bit scared by punk, but wanted to seem 'with it'."

Sue Lowday … "Another memorable gig was Blondie at the University, she was really good in hindsight but I think that we were quite blasé about them at the time."

One of Johnny Rotten's favourite groups at the time was Shakin' Stevens and the Sunsets who performed at Rotherham Clifton Hall on June 5th 1977. Later in the year Shakin' Stevens would be lined up to participate in the ill fated and cancelled Punks and Teds get together gigs with Johnny Thunders and the Heartbreakers. When strong rumours circulated that a major confrontation was on the cards, the events were pulled.

One cannot help but speculate with wonder, if the gigs had been given the go ahead and a date had been pencilled in for Rotherham's Clifton Hall…would the gig have been allowed to go ahead and what would the outcome have been considering the violent climate of the time.

Above: Blondie featured in Rotherham Advertiser in May 1977

Anthony Cronshaw … "After seeing the Ramones, the Damned and the Jam we went to see loads of groups all over the place. It had taken a while for the Punk scene to take off in Sheffield, up to then most of the venues had seemed to deliberately steer clear of

Punk, but by mid 77, there were starting to be plenty of gigs. You could now go to see a decent Punk group most days of the week and if it wasn't in Sheffield it would be Retford Porterhouse, Manchester Rafters, Rotherham Windmill and Doncaster Outlook. I remember me and my mates went to Manchester Apollo in June to see Eddie and the Hot Rods. Gigs were coming thick and fast, Stranglers, 999, Slaughter and the Dogs, the Adverts to name but a few."

1977 was also the year of the Queen's silver jubilee; A time remembered by most of street parties and a public holiday. But there was also an alternative side to the Jubilee. The Sex Pistols famously held their own alternative celebration, which involved their own Thames cruise private party which resulted in arrests and yet more media publicity the following day. Young teenagers may or may not have shown much interest in the nationwide celebrations and Jubilee parties, but Punk Rock and The Sex Pistols were definitely now on the agenda.

Above: Jubilee News

Paul Clarkson ... "Whilst being a student I shared a flat in Nott's with some others. The street where we lived in-Hucknall- was all decorated for a Jubilee street party by the residents and the only ones who didn't get invited were us (the punks) and the 2 or 3 hookers that used to live/work nearby (they would stand and talk to us sometimes 'between clients'!). We were obviously not the types you would want at a neighbourhood street party, fancy being in the same social category as hookers! So, the street party... what did we care about the queen, or the fucking Jubilee, apart from playing the pistols records, getting a day (or 2?) off college and abusing her image aka Jamie Reid? So off we went as usual to the local pub (the Newcastle arms) near the college -

- we always went there as normally none of the locals wanted to fight. It was near the town centre, so we got drunk as usual, watched a bit of the Jubilee on TV in the pub, which was all trimmed up for it. We saw the Thames boat/pistols/coppers on the news and thought *'yeah, nice one Pistols'* (when I moved to London I later met a guy called Roger, he lived in London and was on the boat, or getting thrown off it, on that very night – small world eh!)

Anyway after kicking out time we went into the town centre to find somewhere else to drink (they shut the pubs those days about 10.30? but I think there was an extension that night?) more time to get legless! So off we went in search of something, anything to prolong a night's activities, maybe gatecrash a party or something? We couldn't always get in to the more traditional nightclubs (dress code!) but I remember we went to one club, *'in you go lads' - great* we thought till we got in seeing about 30 people! It was a very NORMAL type club, we spent the rest of the night drinking, pogoing, drinking, and also pogoing to some very straight music, anyway with enough booze inside us, it was a riot! Later on, we went back to the flat and on the way saw the remnants of the street party, some paper plates scattered about, ripped down bunting, etc."

Ones that get away

There has been a rush of single releases recently that will probably never be heard on radio, television or in discos.

For example: THE SEX PISTOLS have a remarkable record, topically entitled "God Save The Queen", on sale at the moment. It's a great rock and roll song.

In fact, the Sex Pistols are a special case. Their release has smashed into the charts nationally and has come in at number seven in our chart. But even that is without extensive airplay.

THE HEARTBREAKERS (nothing to do with Tom Petty) have released "Chinese Rocks" on Track. The song was jointly composed by Johnny Thunders and Jerry Nolan (the group's drummer) and special guests

Richard Hell and Dee Dee Ramone.

CLASH have taken "Remote Control" from their album on C.B.S. and have released it to keep the fires burning during their extensive tour. The track isn't one of the best on the album and you really should have that anyway.

NICK LOWE has made a silly dig at David Bowie by caling his E.P. on Stiff "Bowi", following Mr. Bowie's album "Low". Apart from that the four tracks inside, "Mary Provost", "Shake That Rat", "Endless Sleep" and "Born A Woman" are quite sensible.

Finally, without mentioning "I Don't Care" by THE BOYS on Nems, and "One Chord Wonders" by THE ADVERTS on Stiff, which have been out for a couple of weeks now, I'll come onto my favourite new release.

VIBRATORS' "Baby Baby" on Epic is a classic It's charmingly simple and very effective. The guitar is sharp and the drumming is very neat.

Crow puts lenty of material on the folk scene are

Above: Rotherham Advertiser regularly reviewed the new Punk vinyl offerings

Tony ... "That day, the Queen's Jubilee day, we had the day off school. I can remember during the morning it was all over the bleedin' telly and it was absolutely boring. I went to some kind of youth camp kind of thing at my old junior school and there were a couple of lads I vaguely knew, who were the same age as me, and they had arrived dressed as punks- all covered in safety pins and the like. I think they were only doing it for a joke, which was quite funny I suppose cos the teachers were not at all impressed which must have been a good thing. Anyway later on me and my mate Robbo we were going out with these two lasses (Hello Denise and June if you are reading this) so we biked it down to their Jubilee party. One of the lads down there had the Sex Pistols 'God save the Queen' single blaring out, and in the street these two lads had started squaring up to each other; one seriously stating, with fists raised to -

- Queensbury rules height, *'I'm not a fighting lad but I shall't have thee'*. This was spoken in damn good Yorkshire fighting chatter and was absolutely hilarious...two mothers started wacking each other with their dust brooms as well...that's the closest I saw of anarchy on my Jubilee day."

Anthony Cronshaw ... "It was the Queens Jubilee and the Sex Pistols had reached number two in the charts with 'God Save the Queen'. I personally thought that the establishment stopped it making the top spot."

Graham Torr (Rotherham Punk and musician) ... "Imagine a kid who's sucking all this shit up and trying to emulate one artist after another with all the curiosity and admiration of a little brother (even though I was the classic example of an only child) finally approaching the rebellious puberty years...when one night they get to the number one spot on the countdown and... (Wait for it) they refuse to play the song! Well tell a kid the shit is banned and he can't listen to it and what do they expect?? The law of adolescence demands that you simply have to get a copy and insist to the world, you like it (whether you do or not)...so how cool would it be if you actually did like it? Instant Karma!! Well tell me someone under 18 who doesn't get a kick out of 'God Save The Queen' the first time they hear it and I'll show you a lying bastard."

Nicky Booth ... "When I first heard the Sex Pistols' 'God Save the Queen' I wasn't sure what to think because at the time we were being fed a diet of soft rock and other overblown nonsense. By the time 'Pretty Vacant' turned up I couldn't say that I definitely liked what I was hearing, but I was certainly intrigued by it. I had grown up thinking nothing of stupid stage names like Alvin Stardust, but now we had Sid Vicious and Johnny Rotten – I don't think people now can quite appreciate just how shocking that sort of thing was at the time."

Some Punk purists consider that the movement had reached its high tide around the time of the Silver Jubilee (others swear it had reached its peak even earlier and others considerably later on)...one thing is clear though, even around Rotherham and Sheffield, the appeal of Punk had started to lose its shine for some local Punk Rockers.

Sue Lowday's Kites wine bar 'New Wave' friends. Back row: Julia Stanley, Ché, And John...Front row: Marie Collier and Libby

Timothy Green ... "Around this time - mid 77 - I had just started a full-time job in Rotherham as a (printer/type-setter), and I saw the Jam at Sheffield Top Rank and realised that punk was dead, and this was confirmed for me when prog-loving mates returned from university and they all said that they liked The Stranglers."

78

'God Save the Queen' managed to get banned by WH. Smith (*'we don't sell that kind of thing'*), Woolworths (Who refused to acknowledge its very existence) and Boots the chemist (*'do they wear make up then?'*). With a fix on the chart return shops, the record was outlawed by every aspect of respectable society with only John Peel being brave enough to play it on the radio and only Punks and the curious committing to buying the record. It still sold 200,000 copies...

Deprived of its rightly earned number one spot, which coincidentally now belonged to Rod Stewart, 'God Save the Queen' only served to prove just how much of a threat to the powers that be and the establishment Punk Rock actually was!

    Whilst local Punk Rockers such as John Harrison, Paul Clarkson, Bryan Bell, Phillip Wright, Tony Cronshaw and others were spinning the disc on their mono dansette record players and 'groovy' seventies music centres, the Sex Pistols and a posse of followers, hangers on and friends were taking a Jubilee boat trip - with the Pistols playing on board - up and down the Thames. It would not take long for the river boat police to arrive and break up the party and arrest all they could get their hands on.

Punk Rock had possibly reached its zenith by mid 1977, despite the summer of hate and many of the best group's most memorable moments on vinyl yet to come. It would take a good few years for the shock of Punk Rock to wind down: before it would be integrated into the many different facets of popular culture. As for Sheffield and the region's Punk Rock generation, the fun had only just begun!

Chapter Four

Summer of Hate

"During 76 and early 77, I was always getting chased through Rotherham by the local knuckleheads" – **Paul Clarkson (Rotherham Punk Rocker)**

During the turbulent months of the summer of 1977, there were few places for the local Punk fans to go and socialise except perhaps (and age depending) their local youth club. The Crazy Daisy in Sheffield, as already mentioned, did hold Punk and 'New Wave' nights on weekday nights, but often the atmosphere could be precarious to say the least. Unfortunately the arrival of Punk had also coincided with a revival of Rock n' Roll and the Teddy boy fashion that went along with it.

Sheffield, Rotherham and the local area had its fair share of Teddy Boys and these type of rock n' roll fans were never going to accept the new music or its fans. The Crazy Daisy would often see the place being divided in two with Teds on one side and Punks on the other. The DJ would cautiously try to ease the tension by playing a punk record followed by a rock n' roll one; the atmosphere at the club was subsequently quite often tense.

Anthony Cronshaw ... "There was the Roxy night at the Crazy Daisy, and there were still all the Bowie types going there; when Punk kicked in. Also, there would be still Soulies with their long leathers around as well.

Some of 'em were a bit resentful of Punk coming in and taking over. It did take a while for Punk to get across properly .Eventually we had our own Punk night there, which kind of pissed off the old school, but who gave a fuck."

Phillip Wright ... "The 'In-crowd' in Sheffield, just before punk exploded, went down to a club called the Crazy Daisy on a Wednesday night, which was called Roxy Night and the

DJ played mainly Roxy Music and David Bowie stuff. You would see people from that scene walking around town on Fargate on a Saturday afternoon. Some of these people became the early punks, as they were always looking for a way to stand out from the crowd. I remember seeing some lads in bright blue mohair jumpers stood at the top of Fargate near the town hall. They had cheap sunglasses on and spiky hair, the first punks I had seen. Soon after that the trouble started. Teddy Boys would go drinking in the Barley Corn pub on Cambridge Street on a Saturday afternoon and then go looking for punks. Punks were well outnumbered and had no choice but to run, so this ritual of Teddy Boys chasing Punks up and down the Moor and Fargate became a regular occurrence."

The summer of 1977 was not termed the summer of hate for no justifiable reason. Amongst the many widespread incidents of violence directed at Punk Rockers that summer were attacks on the Damned in Penzance, and assaults on TV Smith of the Adverts, Kid Reid of the Boys, Heartbreakers manager Lee Childs, Bob Geldof...notable violence involving the Stranglers in Cleethorpes and the more famous attacks on Johnny Rotten and Paul Cook of the Sex Pistols. The NME ran a centre page spread on the subject of punk and Violence and on 2nd July a front page on the Murder at Punk festival incident. These were mainly attacks on known Punk group members, but the average Punk kid himself could usually expect similar or worse. Sheffield was no exception in displaying this kind of indifference towards the Punk generation.

On July 28th 1977 a gang of boozed up straights and beer boys decided to go to the Crazy Daisy in Sheffield city centre and throw their weight around, bashing punks who were pogoing on the dance floor. Many bloody noses and bruised faces were the result of this misdirected and senseless violence and even after the bouncers tried to get between the thugs and the punk kids, another attack started up. The trouble really kicked off and the Police and an ambulance were called for to help the injured punk kids. Still, the situation was dangerous for anyone looking slightly New Wave-ish. The manager of the club offered protection for the punks, but only if they all left together as the trouble makers were still hanging around waiting for the ones and twos to dwindle out of the venue.

Barry Bartle ... "I was there that night. I seem to remember it was a lot of the Northern Soulies that had it in for us Punks. They came along and there was some right scrapping."

Around this time, another outburst of violence occurred at the Slaughter and the Dogs concert at Sheffield Top Rank. Punk bashing straights were already gathering at the Claymore pub just below the venue and were abusing and threatening the punks as they passed by on their way to the gig. Once inside the venue, the kids who had come to see the groups were met with ongoing unprovoked attacks from the mindless punk hating straights who had followed them into the place. The violence continued throughout the gig despite many efforts to sustain it and calm it down.

This was now at the height of the Punk bashing period that followed the Jubilee 'God Save the Queen' spectacle and the general media sensationalising that would more often than not result in anyone with short hair and tight jeans being subjected to verbal and physical abuse for looking different. This attitude would continue on and off for the next few years all the way through the Punk era and sometimes beyond. Being a Punk Rocker, expressing yourself clothes wise and just being different were not easy pasttimes in Sheffield and the locality back then.

Anthony Cronshaw ... "It was now open hunting season on Punks and one or two were getting battered in and around Sheffield, but our motley crew also did football and we could look after one another. On one occasion we just happened to be passing the Top Rank at kicking out time (the venue also held many disco nights and Punk gigs were only just starting to get bookings there), anyway outside the rank a coach full of disco boys thought it would be fun to have a bit of Punk baiting. They set about one of the Punk girls with us at first and they weren't playing about either, so that wound us up to start with. Even though we were numbered about a dozen we were outnumbered about 4 – 1, but we loved every bloody minute. For the next ten minutes, we were back on the terraces, kicking and punching anything that moved. We scattered the bastards all over Arundel Gate. The coach driver pissed off and the disco lot all ended up getting on their coach, all bruised and battered with no one to drive them back to where they had come from. For us, this had brought a very enjoyable day to a very enjoyable conclusion."

This was evidently one occasion that the 'white shirt beer guzzling numb brains' had not got the upper hand when taking on a bit of Punk bashing for their night's entertainment.

Anthony Cronshaw ... "We always seemed to be fighting the Teds when we went to the Rotherham Windmill."

The Rotherham Windmill club (later called The Tivoli), was a night club that was part of the Rotherham United football team's ground in Masborough and back in the 1970's held discos, the occasional Northern Soul night and concerts from local M.O.R style rock bands. Nothing too out of the ordinary really and virtually untouched by Punk.

In August 1977, towards the end of what the music press were calling 'The summer of hate', one of the first Punk nights was booked for Thursday August 18th with Doctors of Madness supported by Newcastle's finest Punk group Penetration.

BAN ON PUNK

Punk rock has seen its last days at the Grange Disco.

A good mixture of dance music can usually be heard at the disco, which is held at the Grange Park Golf Clubhouse.

But a DJ there recently declared a ban on punk after a group of pogo dancers started jumping into one another with pints of beer in their hands, taking a mouthful of beer and spitting it across the dance floor—much to the annoyance of people who happened to be standing in the way.

The offending record was taken off and that was the end of punk sounds at the Grange.

Rotherham area Disco Bans Punk

Fronted by vocalist Pauline Murray the band were early fans of The Sex Pistols and had first seen them play in May 1976 at Scarborough Penthouse. Being impressed by the new attitude and music of the fledgling Pistols they were motivated to form their own Punk band taking their name from the last track on side one of Iggy Pop's 'Raw Power' album. Yet without a record contract they were playing regularly, including 3 dates around the Rotherham area in a matter of days (Doncaster Outlook club the previous Monday, and Sheffield top rank the following Saturday). A more suitable band to kick off the Thursday 'New Wave' nights at Rotherham Windmill could not have been found.

Interestingly the 'New Wave' nights were being advertised as 'Heavy Rock' nights for the first few weeks. This was perhaps a little cleverness in the part of the organisers who may have been treading water to see how the bands would be received. Also at the time a lot of Punk gigs were being cancelled, groups being banned etc. So this also may have been the reason for the Heavy rock tag.

Timothy Green … "I went to the first ever Punk gig at the Windmill (outside Millmoor-Rotherham United's old ground) to see Penetration (supporting Doctors of Madness). We were the first to arrive so we got a free single ('Strawberry Letter 23' by Brothers Johnson). We left before Doctors of Madness came on."

Rob Saripo attended this gig … "Actually, Penetration didn't go down very well, because most of the audience there were supporters of the rather M.O.R (at that time) Heavy Metal sounds of Black Sabbath, Deep Purple, AC/DC and Thin Lizzy. Only about 25% of the audience were Punks who had come to see Penetration, and the other 75% were definitely not impressed and created a bad atmosphere. They did not like the way the audience at the front were spitting at the band, and some pogoing action was going on, and in the same way that a football Derby can go wrong, the two factions in the crowd became quite violent towards the end."

Left: Pauline Murray of Penetration at Sheffield Top Rank August 20th 1977

Phil Udell went along with Rob to see the same gig and recalls … "We stood at the back, as we tended to do anyway, and we were actually quite intimidated by the Punk scene ourselves that evening. We weren't used to seeing young girls using kettles as handbags and taking fags and lighters out of them and also using safety pins in various parts of the face."

Rob Saripo … "At that time, live music was not massively available in Rotherham, so any time a gig was advertised, we all went along to see what we would be getting. I don't really know why we went to see Doctors of Madness except to hear how they sounded and what they looked like. Having heard the best Heavy Metal riff ever in 'Anarchy in the UK', we were very interested to hear and see what Punk had to offer. Well, we did like the Doctors of Madness, and we went into the dressing room after the gig to meet up with them and one of them was sitting in his underpants. He apologised for this, and I said- '*Don't worry- I'm not proud*.' They were far nicer than they came across on stage, and I treasure the poster they signed for me and still have it after all those years. The lead singer Kid Strange signed the poster – To Rob with optimism xx."

Two days later at Sheffield's Top Rank the same line up played to an enthusiastic crowd of - this time - predominantly Punk Rockers. Pauline dressed in a parachute jacket and zip covered trousers gave an impressive performance and the group won over the audience. Doctors of Madness were also given a warm response, despite not being in effect a Punk band as such.

Doctors of Madness singer **Kid Strange** was interviewed by Gun-Rubber fanzine a little earlier in the year and gave some interesting opinions about the Punk scene and on its relation to Sheffield he noted... "*It's funny, 19 months ago* (which would be more like mid 76 time), *when we were touring with Be-Bop Deluxe, this was about a year before this whole Punk circus blew up, I was talking to some of the audience in Sheffield and when I saw the plastic gear that they were wearing, I thought 'Yeah!, this is gonna be next year's big thing.'* Very perceptive of Kid Strange but also a solid indication that the Punk scene had reached further north and up to Sheffield much earlier than is often recognised. But to keep in realistic context, these kids who were being described, although certainly very much being almost proto-type Punks, were just as sure to have been a very rare exception to the norm in Sheffield at the time

Tom Cleary (Sheffield Punk) ... "Penetration; they were an unbelievable band, great looking singer and very powerful."

Penetration's set at the Outlook in Doncaster was well received, but it would be the group who had kick-started the whole Punk phenomenon off... that would be the talk of Doncaster during that same month.

The Sex Pistols gig at the Doncaster Outlook club on August 24th and the remaining secret gigs they played...has since become a part of Punk folklore with varying accounts of the actual performances. The Outlook gig was part of their 'S.p.o.t.s' tour (Sex Pistols on tour secretly) and they played under the banner of 'The Tax Exiles'. Rumours had been circulating for a few weeks throughout the local punk crowd. They had already played an earlier gig at the Outlook a couple of months prior to the 'Grundy' affair, but this one was at the height of Punk and perhaps their most significant northern date played yet. As for the local Punk fans...If you were persistent and lucky, you may just happen to be in the right place and at the right time.

Punk Rocker **Stuart Bates** from Wickersley (Rotherham) ... "We used to visit the Doncaster Outlook club in 77 and one night we managed to get in to the Sex Pistols gig after many phone calls of *'Is it on ?...Is it off ?* .We just had to turn up on the night and luckily it was on. And very memorable, if only for us all being covered in beer and spit!

We had heard a rumour that The Sex Pistols might be putting in an appearance but it was only speculation. We decided to phone the club and ask but after 2 or 3 calls, the staff always said *'Sorry they're not appearing'*... Then, after another call we asked who were going to be playing on the Thursday Punk night as we normally did. The girl at the other end said some band called the Spots... we then knew it was the Sex Pistols as this was one of the names they were using as an alter ego to avoid unwanted publicity. Sex

Pistols on Tour secretly! As you can imagine we were chuffed. We decided to go to the concert on my mate's lambretta! Very un-punk...ha ha!

Sex Pistols as the Tax Exiles Live at the Doncaster Outlook August 1977

When we arrived at the Outlook, the queue wasn't that big, we were actually quite near the front. As we stood in the queue we noticed a mini-bus slowing down by the side of us. We looked and noticed the band was in there and they were waving at us as they passed, except for Sid who was frantically giving the V sign out of the rear window.

Once inside, we made for the bar and were surprised to find the Pistols all stood there talking to fans and looking at photos, except Sid again, who was sat on a sofa at the side. He was wearing a pair of Doc Marten boots, stripy pyjama bottoms, and vest and leather jacket. He looked, as usual, totally out of it!

When the band hit the stage to the opening bars of 'Pretty Vacant', the place erupted, beer and spit was flying everywhere. Can't remember the exact set they played. It was all a blur after the opening song because fights started as people were trying to take photos and some of the road crew were trying to stop them. I remember one of them throwing beer all over one guy's camera to stop him taking photos.

Johnny then threw the mike down and told people to stop. He then said '*Right we're just gonna' treat this as a fucking recording session*'. He walked back on looking his usual manic self. Sid tried to hit someone with his guitar and slipped off the stage, but it was

86

only a low stage so he got back up and carried on playing and snarling. We were tossed about and hurled all over the place throughout the set. I told my work mates about it the next day and none of them believed me. They said *'Why would a band like the Pistols want to turn up at Donny?'* But I can say *'Been there, seen that, had the bruises to prove it!'"*

Steve Haythorne ... "I remember the buzz going around about the S.P.O.T.S tour. Some of the lads in the boozer (The Gate in Swinton) were talking about it and a few of them managed to get to the gig. I didn't go myself."

Jet (Punk Rocker from Doncaster) ... "I went to the Sex Pistols gig at the Outlook and they were bloody awful."

Timothy Green ... "I heard about the news of the secret Sex Pistols tour and managed to get to see them at Donny Outlook; the first time they had played - the September before - was empty just about but this time it was rammed. I wore a homemade anti-fascist t -shirt and got a bit of grief for wearing it. The atmosphere was quite heavy, but I thought the band were fine."

Steve Lloyd ... "I remember at the Pistols gig, they fell out with their roadie 'Rodent' and he was throwing and smashing bottles about. I think he was aiming for Nancy. Being totally honest though, for me, the Pistols weren't that good really."

Phil Tasker ... "The first time the Pistols played the Outlook it must have been late 76 but I didn't go to see them then, luck would have it that I saw them second time around, but to be honest I can't remember much about the gig, apart from it was packed."

Steve Lloyd ... "The Sex Pistols were awkward that night, and Sid Vicious was a completely nasty piece of work. I asked him *'so Sid, are you as vicious as they say that you are'* to which he replied nastily *'what's it Fucking look like'*. Nancy Spungen was there and I think he was showing off in front of her. She was just sprawled all over the front of the stage most of the time that they were in there. They were setting out conditions that they would only have kids so close to the stage etc and then when they played they were encouraging them to get on stage and the bouncers were giving the kids a few kickings."

Patrick Tierney ... "By the second Donny gig (The SPOTS one), The Pistols were much better known and the interest was much higher. I can't remember who I went with, but I know we went to The White Swan in Frenchgate first. This was par for the course. Go to The Swan and fill up with cheap Wards beer rather than pay silly Outlook prices. The Outlook was only over the road, anyway.

The queue was the first thing you noticed. It was right round to the bus station. When we finally got inside it was busy. This time I was further back and only slightly left of centre. The first thing you noticed was the musical improvement (even with Sid), but this also could have been more familiarity with the songs. There was some unfamiliar material and I found out afterwards (possibly in The Evening Post) that this was the first live outing for 'Holidays in the Sun'. True or not, when released as a single, it got heavy airplay at The Outlook.

My abiding memory of the second gig was that some people were there who had been so negative at the first one back in 76. Now they were cheering and raving about the band. Hypocrites I thought. One of these was in the year above me at school. I could name him now, but I won't as he later died in unfortunate circumstances. And that wouldn't be right."

Meanwhile over in Rotherham, the Windmill club was starting to gain a foothold with its Thursday 'New Wave' nights. Following the Doctors of Madness and Penetration gig - over the coming weeks and months - the venue managed to put on gigs by Generation X, Ultravox, the Adverts, X-Ray Spex, Buzzcocks, the Motors, the Saints (Australia's top Punk band), the Pirates (then going through a revival of sorts and coasting the edge of the New Wave), the legendary Wayne County and the Electric Chairs, XTC, Skunks, the Stukas, Satan's Rats and reggae group Steel Pulse who were one of the reggae/Punk cultural crossover groups that was very much prevalent at the time. Unfortunately, both Slaughter and the Dogs and Radio Stars had to cancel their bookings at the venue.

Paul Bower ... "I can't really remember how we got to playing The Windmill. I think it kind of happened when someone approached us, cos they'd heard about us and how we were building up a following quite quickly. There was hardly anywhere to play in Sheffield. The Penthouse rarely put gigs on, as it was so high up and you had to lug all yer gear up all the way. That club was sort of the first place we had gone to when we were about 17... our first kind of under age drinking place. So it was actually better to go out of Sheffield to play gigs at the Outlook in Doncaster and of course the Windmill which was the social club for Rotherham United. The management started booking Punk bands as they saw that it was basically a good business opportunity. You know, everyone wanted to see the Pistols, the Damned or Johnny Thunders and the Heartbreakers. So when the big kind of early Punk explosion of bands like Generation X played the Windmill we supported them. We just by accident sort of became the regular support band at the Windmill and also the Outlook. We would get forty quid, which thinking about it was a lot of money back then. We'd be getting to bed about 3 or 4 o'clock in the morning and then be up for work in a couple of hours as we all worked as well as playing in the band."

Timothy Green ... "All I can remember about the Generation X gig at the Windmill is a feeling of exhilaration at seeing such a brilliant band in such a small space. The gig was absolutely rammed, but, if I recall correctly, never turned nasty."

Following the Generation X gig at the Windmill the Rotherham Advertiser newspaper reported *"Surely after the '2.3' and Generation X concert yesterday week, the Windmill club in Masbrough will become the best New Wave venue in South Yorkshire"*. It continued with *"Both groups yesterday week got an almost unqualified enthusiastic welcome from the locals, especially Generation X who recently released their first single, but perhaps more attention should have been paid to '2.3' a band from Sheffield who seem to have more power and energy held in reserve than Generation X displayed in their whole act."*

Paul Bower … "The audience at the Windmill would be a mixture of people who had kind of become Punks last week and people who were wearing high waisted bags and platform shoes. But they were always an energetic audience. At that time, we were very provincial and aggressive and I remember some of our fans were booing Generation X off stage. It was like, '*get out you London poseurs, we want 2.3 back.*'

Above: A Rare flyer advertising Ultravox unconfirmed gig at Rotherham Windmill's 'New Wave' night 22nd September 1977

We always got a massive amount of support from the audience - which could have been because we were local and played all our own songs and also because we looked different. We weren't trying to be like the Pistols or the Clash. Our name was not one like the Vomits or the Shits or something either. The original idea of the group's name 2.3 Children was kind of tongue in cheek really. It was not like the other group names.
It is actually not a great name and quite forgettable, but there you go. We would support The Saints, Doctors of Madness, Adverts and Generation X etc."

The Windmill's 'New Wave' nights had an average audience attendance of around 300. Inside an issue of 'The Rotherham Advertiser' manager of the Windmill venue at the time Dave Gill had heard some feedback from fans that said they had to miss the last bus home in order for them to be able to see the headline groups full set or otherwise watch half the set and rush for the last bus. As a good proportion of the Windmill's audience were travelling from Sheffield, a double Decker bus was laid on to leave at 12.15am for the journey back to Sheffield bus station. This allowed the fans enough time to catch the whole show.

In the Rotherham Advertiser, manager Dave Gill also spoke of the typical audience to frequent the new wave nights. *"People have stopped coming just to gawp at one another or to see the band throw abuse or spit at the audience. They just don't do that any more, and you don't see many people with safety pins either. The majority of our Thursday night customers are intelligent, well behaved and polite people. You get the occasional idiot and those who come just to poke fun and criticise. Some stupid people think because they don't understand it they should knock it."*

Punk Rock seemed to be a fairly regular subject in the Rotherham Advertiser during that late summer to early autumn weeks of 1977. There was even a piece on Rotherham's 'First Punk Rocker Rotherbird'. A girl called Pat Bentley from Arren Hill Thrybergh was the chosen star. In the article Pat gives her taste in 'New Wave' music as The Jam and the Stranglers but also, and bravely so for the times (this was year zero remember) also admits to liking funky music like James Brown and also David Bowie. Good on yer Pat. Her taste in clothes state string vests, straight leg trousers and baggy jumpers and her taste in boyfriends indicate that she has a thing about blonde hair (bleached blonde as well we can safely presume). Interested applicants should share her interest in the 'New Wave'...I wonder if Pat managed to find her perfect Billy Idol?

Phillip Wright ... "Punk was a DIY fashion and me and my mates started to go to the old army surplus stores and buy ex-army trousers, which looked the part for a few quid; Lots of straps and pockets on them. I asked my mum to sew zips into perfectly good shirts and began wearing a leather bike jacket. We all still wore Doc Martin boots most days, as we always had for school."

Two Punk Rockers who were regulars at the Rotherham Windmill club were the sisters who would only be referred to as 'Repulsive Plug' and 'Superior'. Wearing the standard Punk attire of safety pins, torn clothing, school ties and cheap plastic gimmicky glasses etc, they stated at the time *'Punk is different... For people like us it gives us something to do – better than the dole queue'*. Going on to criticise the punks who spend all their money on punk clothes - *'those who spend £10 or more are just poseurs -* they confessed that *'My dad would kill me if he saw me coming out dressed like this'*. Another Punk girl called Sharon wore a jacket covered in zips that Clash singer Joe Strummer had given her. The only down side of it was that Sharon was suspended from her job for wearing the Clash shirt, as the management said it was turning customers away.

Other Punks going to the Rotherham Windmill wore various versions of punk dress; one Punk from Herringthorpe in Rotherham even turning up with beer mats and empty crisp packets attached to his jacket. The local Punk fans were certainly creating their own idea of what Punk was and even though it may have been naïve and innocent in its looks and improvisation, it was showing itself to be a more genuine youth movement than in the more so called trendy places down south and elsewhere.

The Advertiser's entertainment page reviewed the Adverts who played at the Windmill on September 15th 1977 and who were currently enjoying chart success with their classic single 'Gary Gilmore's eyes'. The article reports…"*The Adverts attracted a large crowd at the Windmill, Rotherham, yesterday week*" and also showed a photo of TV Smith (the singer/songwriter) and bass player Gaye Advert playing to a tightly packed crowd. They were favourably reviewed by the local paper who stated that - "*The Adverts are well worth seeing and their album promises to be good… The group have improved a lot since their early London concerts, with a well rehearsed set and improved playing.*"

Rotherham Punk Rocker **Stuart Bates** was at this gig … "One gig that does stand out was 'The Adverts' gig - due to the fact that I fancied Gaye Advert (the female bass player who was quickly becoming Punk's first girl pin up star). Also, I had just bought 'Gary Gilmore's eyes', so as you can imagine, I was buzzing when I heard that they were on.

When we arrived at the place, it was packed, but as I remember you always had a decent view of the stage. The gig seemed to pass in a blur, but I recall TV Smith having chains hanging from his mike stand and a rope with a headless Action Man hanging from it! The place erupted into a pogoing frenzy when 'Gary Gilmore's eyes' was played. I also remember going to the toilet later on and seeing a guy I thought had been in a fight.

His head was pouring with blood and it was all running down his face. I asked if he was ok and he said '*Yes mate, it's not as bad as it looks, I dyed my hair with red food colouring and all this sweating and dancing has made it run!!*'"

Above: Rotherham Windmill poster advertising the Thursday New Wave nights from summer 1977

During those red-hot summer days of 1977 the Rotherham Windmill was the only venue, apart from The Outlook in Doncaster that was holding regular weekly 'New Wave' nights. The other venues like Sheffield's Top Rank were putting on irregular Punk gigs (often marred by violence from the Punk hating straights who tagged along to see what all the fuss with Punk was about), but that venue and similar ones could not capture the atmosphere of small venues such as Rotherham Windmill.

Adverts Singer TV Smith only vaguely recalls playing the venue with little memory of the actual night. In fact until I myself reminded him, he had totally forgotten they had even played the venue at all. A lot of gigs and years have passed since then so this is hardly surprising...

TV Smith ..."I can't really recall playing at the Rotherham Windmill venue, apart from being interviewed by the guys from Sheffield Punk fanzine 'Gun-Rubber.'"

Due to the archive status of the above Photograph, quality is low, but the shot remains a crucial and rare document of the time

The Adverts also played Doncaster outlook club on numerous occasions ... almost always to an energetic and receptive crowd. TV shares his memories...

TV Smith ... "I do have a few more memories of Doncaster outlook as we played there a few times. It was more of a regular on the circuit. I remember it as a dark, sweaty, low ceiling-ed pit that would have certainly been a disco when it wasn't hosting Punk rock bands. It was very loud, claustrophobic, and almost-

**Above: The Adverts live on stage at Rotherham Windmill
September 15th 1977 (Advertiser)**

- impossible to move in there when it was packed with people. Low stage, people right in front of us as we played, tiny dressing room behind the stage. Excitable and lively audience and bottles of 'Newcastle Brown Ale' behind the bar-something of a treat in the days of Colt 45 and Breaker."

Stuart Bates ..."The Outlook was only a small club and the Punk room was upstairs and really quite small and as I remember we were always able to get very close to the bands."

92

Bryan Bell recalls going to see the Adverts at the Doncaster Outlook in 1977 and also other gigs at the time - and we can assume that the security at the venue had improved some since their last visit back in September ... "I went to see The Adverts at the Outlook with Christine (a punk lass mate) and my other mate Martin. I was sat on the stage at the front and I can remember in between songs TV Smith was chatting to me. He was asking me if I was going to any more dates on the tour and stuff. At a later Adverts gig at the Sheffield Top Rank we got talking to Gaye Advert - Gaye the bass player was so named by the Stranglers after she was always on their guest list at gigs. They did not know her surname so she became Gaye Advert; anyway, she was having a birthday party in Portsmouth or somewhere. I think it was the following day and she invited us down for it. Course with working it wasn't always possible. I think I was on an afters shift at Hatfield's steel works in Sheffield the next day so that was out of the window."

Fans in Doncaster remember their own Punk scene and the all too human shortcomings of Punk musicians, as well as making their own first journeys into Punk Rock.

Jet (from Doncaster) ... "I saw the Damned at the Outlook on their first tour. They were really good and better than I expected. After the gig, I went backstage, which was very tiny. I was talking to various punks and Damned drummer Rat Scabies' girlfriend, she kissed me on the cheek or something and 'Rat' saw it and started to come over all heavy and nasty. He was giving me the stare and eventually I faced him out and told him if he wanted some I was ready for it. He was ok after that. You got more respect that way."

Doncaster Punk Rocker Phil Tasker, also to be a member of his own Punk band Vice Squad (not the later Beki Bondage fronted version from Bristol), came across two well known Punks in the audience at the Outlook.

Phil Tasker ... " I remember seeing loads of bands during the 77 period, mainly at the Doncaster Outlook, including the Ramones supported by Talking Heads, the Stranglers when Jean Jacques Burnel made a hole in the stage, the Sex Pistols, Magazine, Wire, Generation X, Buzzcocks, the Jam, Siouxsie and the Banshees and more. There was one notable time, however, when we went to see the Kursaal Flyers and Joe Strummer and Mick Jones of the Clash were there at The Outlook in the audience. They must have known the group or something, as they had come up on the train especially for the gig. I asked for Joe Strummer's autograph and he wrote it in block capitals, which taught me a lesson! I used to paint T shirts at the time and Joe gave me a compliment on the one I was wearing, Both Joe and Mick were really friendly."

Morg (from Doncaster) remembers his first introduction to Punk and then the Outlook club ... "In 1977 a life changing experience happened for me, and one I would never regret. I don't remember the exact date as it was over 30 years ago, but early in '77' I started hearing about a music called Punk Rock. I was very sceptical to liking it, as I had only ever listened to one band, but later I was told about a club in Doncaster that had Punk bands playing on a weekly basis. So me and a few friends decided to check one of these gigs out to see what all the fuss was about. Although only 15 years old at the time, and the club being an over 18 venue, I wasn't worried about getting past the door staff as I always looked old (laughs)."

In fact Morg's example must be one of many similar ones at the time, due to the turning of a blind eye almost continuously by door staff and security at punk gigs nationwide. Most Punk kids were well under age when first starting to attend Punk gigs regularly. Ironically by the time a lot of them were at legal age most of them had stopped going to punk gigs anyway.

Morg continues ... "I had seen pictures in magazines and also watched news items on TV about punk rockers so knew roughly what type of clothes they wore, but I turned up that first night at the Outlook in some of my bright coloured flares with a T- shirt and smart jacket, same as I usually wore. I can remember clearly walking up the stairs into the Outlook club and being amazed at the sight in front of me. There were people doing some weird kind of dance on the dance floor, which I was told later was the 'Johnny Rotten walk'. They basically looked as though they were crippled and trying to shuffle across the dance floor – then occasionally would go into a kind of spasm, come fit.

There was spiked hair, ripped clothes, safety pins and zips a plenty, youths walking into the toilets and coming back out with stars drawn around their eyes, or safety pins stuck through their noses or ears. It all seemed very weird to me, but in the background the music being played was simple, but with an excitement to it, and the words were not all about love and shit like that. People were actually singing about other things going on in life. There was a lot of reggae played as well, which I hadn't heard much of at the time, but I grew to like this music style as well.

After downing a few pints of Stones bitter, I got a bit brave and got into the mood by getting up and copying the dances being done, this was not at all complicated so I learnt quickly. By the time the first band played I was having a real good time, even though I felt a bit of an odd one out with the way I was dressed. Nobody said anything to me about this. In fact everybody was really friendly and talking, telling me which bands to listen out for etc. I never jumped about to the support band, but stood at the back watching and feeling unsure. I think they were called the Jermz or something. The headlining band that night though I do remember, it was the Adverts.

After the gig, when walking the 7 miles home back to Rossington, I and my friends couldn't stop talking about the night we had just had. The next night, after school, I took a trip to the barbers and had my nice long hair cut short, spiked it up, and much to the dismay of my parents, set about writing on T-shirts with marker pens and ripping them and safety pinning them etc."

Members of the Punk groups who played the venue could be equally as affected by their experiences, in one way or another... X-Ray Spex singer **Polystyrene** says ... "I can't really remember that much it was so long ago. I know we got a lively reception and then after the show I saw a U.F.O from my hotel window. It really made me think about what I was doing and where I was going and it seemed a bad omen at the time."

Patrick Tierney ... "After the Outlook gigs everyone would be waiting for the DJ to play the Table's 'Do the Standing Still' and then would be...standing still."

Ian Clayton (TV Presenter and author)... "I used to go to the old Outlook club in Doncaster a lot; I guess it would have been around 1977 or thereabouts. There were quite a few of us who used to travel down from Pontefract to see the punk bands that played there. I remember seeing all sorts – the Clash, Patrik Fitzgerald and Slaughter and the Dogs. Loads of bands... Sadly I didn't see the Sex Pistols when they played there - I don't know why I didn't go - I think I might have secretly sneaked off to see a Wishbone Ash concert that night!. I'm 48 so I sort of fell between two stools - I loved punk, but I still had a penchant for some of the older bands like Wishbone Ash. Mind you, if I did go to see them I don't imagine I told any of my punk mates about it!" **(From 'Bringing it all back home' by Ian Clayton)**

As well as the visiting Punk bands, the region's local Punk offerings were picking up the pace.

Phil Tasker ... "The whole reason why I formed a band – mine being called Vice Squad - was because of the punk thing, the idea that you could do it yourself and write your own songs."

As previously mentioned a regular support band at the Outlook club were Sheffield band '2.3'. When they played as support to Scottish 'New Wave' group the Rezillos at the Doncaster Outlook club later in the year, they were approached by Bob Last who secured them a deal with his record label 'Fast Records', thus becoming the first of the new Sheffield bands to be signed up. Their single 'All time low'/'Where to now' was released in February 1978. Guitarist and vocalist Paul Bower remembers the Outlook gigs and the singles release.

Paul Bower ... "A lot of people would actually travel out to Rotherham and Doncaster, because this was before the Limit opened and venues in Sheffield would not book anything Punk or different. At the Outlook, you went on stage a lot later on. We would support bands like Siouxsie and the Banshees, Ultravox, XTC (who were a pain in the arse), and also Steel Pulse who were great. We also supported the Rezillos where we met 'Fast Records' Bob Last who asked us if we wanted to make a record. The record sold about 4 or 5 thousand copies. By the time it was released, Paul and I had fallen out very badly, and the band weren't really doing anything for a few months, so we didn't really capitalise on it. We never did another record, even though we did demos. It never really happened. We were going to record an e.p for Zigzag magazine as they really liked us, they always did. But then Zigzag went into receivership and had no money left so that never came out."

The communal spirit of the Punk movement, that was rapidly being abandoned further south, could often be still experienced intact up here.

Paul Bower ... "The Stranglers were very friendly and helpful. We played with them at the Top Rank. I just turned up with 'Gun Rubber', which interestingly actually had an article that was slagging the Stranglers off, which I ripped out of the magazine as I didn't want Jean Jacques Burnel seeing it (him being quite handy at Martial Arts). They were very helpful - We just sort of showed up and said '*we wanna support you*'. I talked to Jean briefly and he says '*Are you any good*' to which we said '*Yeah of course*'. He had a word with the tour manager to which he came back with '*ok then*'. I don't think you could do that nowadays. It's a lot more complicated now with bands having to pay to get a support slot and it being so much more formulised."

Steve Lloyd ... "2.3 were different from all the other Punk bands. They came across as being quite thoughtful in their approach."

Due to the archive status of the above Photograph, quality is low, but the shot remains a crucial and rare Document of the time

Surprisingly, given the nationwide hate campaign against anything remotely connected to the so called 'Punk Rock' fad, the local press were noticeably far more ambivalent and tolerant towards the Punk being seen on its own doorstep, if not being fans of it, at least managing to have the foresight to understand its relevance for the young generation. Sheffield Star gave the local scene some positive coverage and reviewed numerous visits to the city by the Punk groups, as well as keeping an eye on what the local Punk inspired kids were up to.

Above: Paul Shaft and Paul Bower of Sheffield Punk group 2.3 at Doncaster Outlook in 1977 (Rotherham Advertiser 1977)

In an issue of 'Rotherham Advertiser' at the time a feature entitled 'Give punk a chance' was included that tried to balance the opinions of punk that summer of 1977. In the piece it states "*I'm fed up of hearing rubbish on the subject of punk rockers and I reckon it's about time that someone put this new craze into perspective. Let's get this straight. 'New Wave' followers are not some breed of aggressive moron. They are ordinary people caught up in a new trend.*" In the piece, it continues to draw parallels between punk and previous fashions that were once considered outrageous and dangerous; Although the features author was not personally a fan of punk music, describing it as "*Raw, rather - tuneless, very simple and usually loud. Personally I think it is awful*;" on a positive note, he goes on to show admiration for the D.I.Y side of punk fashion "*As for 'New Wave' clothes you could say they are sensible in the sense that they are cheap. A typical outfit is*

96

a pair of old plimsolls, trousers with holes in the knees and a badly ripped shirt with paint on it."

The summer of 1977, Punk's very own 'Summer of Hate' also affected a new generation of younger kids who were not quite sure about what Punk was really meant to represent and what it was all about, but could not help being interested in its appeal.

Tony ... "I can remember seeing the odd few 'Punk' looking type of kids around Rotherham town centre. There would be one or two who hung around the old 'Ring o ' Bells' café near the old bus station and I can recall some of them getting chased around town, probably by jealous straights. There was one girl with multi coloured hair around our end called Sharon. I later found out that she was really just a biker bird. The first proper Punk I spoke to was Bryan Bell who I saw surrounded by a gang of kids who were mesmerised with Bryan's bleached blonde hair that was stuck up in spikes and his coloured trousers, bondage jacket and leopard skin t-shirt. I can't remember what we said at the time as it's so long since but he certainly made an impression on us all. This would be about mid summer 1977."

Bryan Bell ... "The Teds would hang around the Ring o' Bells café and would often be ready to give chase to us Punks if we showed our faces. In Sheffield around the middle of 77, a couple of us got into some bother with some Teds. They came gunning for us and one of the big un's set about my mate and there were two others aiming for me...I looked at 'em, sized 'em up and took my chances on the smaller of the two and he ended up being the toughest of the whole bunch. Bang! He stuck one straight on me and we ended up having a right scrap. There was no real remorse though...I would see this guy for a couple of years afterwards and he would kinda give me the nod."

Timothy Green ... "The Teds in Rotherham weren't too bad some of the time, but occasionally you'd come across some half-wit, usually from Worksop or somewhere, who believed all the shit that he read in The Sun, and he would try to start an argument. They were easy to ignore."

Pete Weston ... "The thing is - me and my mates already knew the Rotherham Teds, so we were ok and got on fine. I can't imagine any other Punks who didn't know 'em would get away without a scrap or getting chased though!"

Nicky Booth ... "And then I heard the Stranglers. They were older than most of the other bands at the time, but they still looked like they would kick your teeth in. They were accomplished musicians too which I guess was a bit out of step with the 3 chord wonders that were rising through the ranks, but it was something to do with their ability to find a balance between melody and aggression that sucked me in. By the time 'Something Better Change' came out, that was it, I was totally hooked. Until then I had just observed what was going on in the world of punk, but now I was avidly buying the records and starting to assume a dishevelled look much to my parents' horror."

As young Punk fans in the school playground were starting to find out about the new music being made, the older local Punk Rockers (while dodging angry local Teddy boys) were finding that, although the accessibility to Punk was easier, there could be a downside to being of school leaving age.

Bryan Bell ... "I missed the Stiff tour cos of work and I really wanted to see that one. There was Wreckless Eric, Ian Dury, and Elvis Costello all on the same bill so it was good value for money but I missed it so I would have to go and see them separate at some time. (This concert was the one where the Sheffield Polytechnic rugby team decided to go Punk bashing)."

But when the shifts allowed there was time to make up on lost chances of Punk events.

Bryan Bell ... "But I saw Wayne County and the Electric Chairs or Jayne County whichever you want to call him/her. They were crap. The other groups I can remember seeing around the 77 time were the Stranglers, Generation X (quite a few times as they always seemed to be around the area), and the Clash on their 77 tour. I'm sure it was on one of those dates that I swiped Joe Strummer's shirt. I were always getting the groups t-shirts or something."

Rotherham held a Folk Festival while the local Punk Rockers went out to 'The Sound of Music' record shop to buy their choice of Punk singles. Around this time Johnny Rotten featured on Capitol Radio with his choice of Desert Island Discs. Surprisingly, amongst his choices were tracks from Captain Beefheart, Can, Tim Buckley, Neil Young, the Chieftains and not surprisingly a selection of Reggae.

Rotten's disdain for the majority of Punk groups is well known, with only X-Ray Spex and The Buzzcocks gaining approval, and this indifference was also present with other notable Punk speakers such as the Clash and Paul Weller. The splintering of the Punk scene, at least amongst the groups themselves was now very clear. The Punks of our story never really took that much notice of this kind of chain of thought. Many were still very much in awe of the new sounds that were confronting them and often still trying to shake off the old guard in music.

Richard Chatterton ... "The Stranglers !...A fret less bass played by J.J Burnel, and the scowl of singer Hugh Cornwell as they played 'Go Buddy Go' on Top of the Pops. It was the directness, the stripped down honesty and no nonsense attitude that grabbed me."

Phillip Wright ... "By making just a few changes to what you wore would be enough to get other people into the scene coming up and talking to you. At gigs, on the streets, or at school Punk became the common bond that drew us together. We would chat about bands and gigs and occasionally a 'one off special' magazine would come out which was all about the new punk scene with pictures and articles about new bands."

Tony ... "Emerson Lake and Palmer with 'Fanfare for the Common Man': that was out around this time. I hated it with a passion and I reckon that record helped push me towards Punk. What a pompous horrible load of crap that was."

Dave Spencer ... "The only window on the musical world at that time, for me, was BBC1's Top of the Pops. It had everything you could possibly want, and less - Disco (yawn), Rock, (yawn) and as far as I can remember, hundreds of novelty records. I started to notice more and more of this new music on Top of the Pops. One day they had *the actual* Sex Pistols doing 'Pretty Vacant'. They looked terrifying, but - sounded, much to my surprise, pretty catchy in a weird way. That's how I remember my initial reaction; Weird. Nobody stood up to switch it off and my dad didn't kick the telly in. It was tolerated. But by the next day I got in to trouble from my mum just for singing it around the house. Then I remember the Stranglers 'Something Better Change' -It must have been on towards the end of its run in the charts, because when I went, with my best mate Adrian 'Cav' Carver, to buy it, upstairs at Boots on the High Street, They didn't have any left, but they did have their new single 'No More Heroes'. I was a bit disappointed but, having been fired up enough to actually think of parting with my hard-saved pocket money on one Stranglers record I just thought 'OK' and bought the new one instead. It was fantastic! I listened to it again and again for hours on end. I even made a cassette with just 'No more Heroes' and its B-side, 'In the Shadows' over and over for the whole C60! Next, in November, Top of the Pops had Elvis Costello on; My Elvis Costello singing 'Watching the Detectives'. I didn't find out until years later that he'd been on before doing '(The Angels Wanna Wear My) Red Shoes', but this time he seemed to catch everyone's attention. The next day at school I asked my mates if they'd seen him the night before. *'Yeah what a load of crap'...* was the unified response. Oh..."

Steve Haythorne ... "I would still go and see the much hated, at the time, Pink Floyd and some others like Bowie and Rod Stewart right in the middle of Punk. I had kind of grown up with their music and along with Northern Soul, I would still listen to them. It's all about the quality in music and there was some of that in Punk; but I have never subscribed to the theory that anybody can play. You have to be able to play for longevity. Some of the Punk bands clearly could not play, whereas the Clash clearly could and the Jam as well. Paul Weller was and is a true genius – the John Lennon of our generation."

Tony ... "Liking Rod Stewart's nothing to be ashamed of. I was still buying Wings singles in mid 1977. Can't remember the exact month though, but I can recall Pete Roddis buying 'Pretty Vacant' by the Pistols and an older kid down the street used to play it all the time. We would walk by his house and listen to it and the tune started to get into my head. The Punk year zero attitude was a fair way off for me but the path was already being laid."

The Punk kids in Sheffield, Doncaster and Rotherham were now gaining their confidence and identity, utilising whatever means that they could to express themselves.

Anthony Cronshaw ... "Early on in the year I had a go at the Punk D.I.Y style. I had an old blazer and cut off both of the arms. I then put 'em back on but now attached with safety pins. I would buy army trousers from the army stores and cut the collars off my old shirts. I can remember my mum saying to me *'Wait until the neighbours are out before you go out like that'.* I wasn't into the Punk fashion thing for that long really. It was the music that was the most important for me."

Pete Cooper … "We used to scour through second hand shops for old granddad shirts. I would have my jeans taken in and after spiking my hair I was generally becoming a Punk Rocker. The only local place in Rotherham where you could possibly listen to any Punk, for us anyway, was at South Grove School. Even so there was only a few of us strange looking punk rockers. But at least you could pogo away quite happily in-between all the rock and soul records. There was a group of about 4 or 5 of us and we would walk the streets getting strange looks from everyone we met. But we didn't encounter any aggression; maybe it was the way we looked that put people off. Once when we were walking through Sheffield, we were stopped and asked if we could be photographed which we duly obliged as we were definitely not what you could call the norm at the time."

Phil Tasker … " The clothes worn by most punks were straight jeans, old jackets, leather jackets, mohair jumpers were popular, baseball boots or plimsoll type shoes, Cuban heeled pointy winkle pickers were worn by some and these were favoured by our own Punk group Vice Squad. Not many brothel creepers, bondage trousers and Mohicans in Donny but brightly coloured straight trousers were popular with cap sleeve t shirts or t shirts that were torn and painted up. I used to do t-shirts and jackets with car paint as well.

Doc Martens were popular but no coloured ones were available, I don't remember loads of piercing, the odd ear ring but no face piercing. Safety pins and chains were popular pinned on jackets and stuff. Most kids could not afford the stuff from punk clothes shops. I didn't get any stuff until I was working but I do remember getting some vinyl trousers on mail order from the NME, and a mohair jumper from X Clothes in Leeds."

Steve Haythorne … "I remember wearing those cheap plastic glasses, we were at a gig and everyone was going into this shop and buying them - They seemed to be the thing at that point. I also wore a red hoop t –shirt, a big white Mac, always had both ears pierced anyway and have never had long hair- always had skinhead just about, a suede head style I suppose."

Phil Tasker … "Skinny ties were quite popular and quite a few hippies who would wear ties and jackets before fully embracing the punk lifestyle were now getting their hair cut etc, Clive and Roger were long haired hippies when they joined the band but eventually realised that they needed to conform to punk!"

Paul Clarkson … "The problem was, when I lived in Rotherham and I wanted to buy some Punk clothes there was nowhere so I had to go to Manchester, London or Nott's where I went to college to really search out something different. My brother used to go

100

out with a girl who was studying fashion at Trent Poly in Nott's so she would make clothes for me."

Simon Currie (Rotherham Punk fan) … "I went to see the Jam and I wore my old fella's black blazer, skin tight jeans, white shirt and a long thin tie."

Gary Robinson (Punk Rocker from Greasborough near Rotherham) … "I had the bondage trousers, zips, PVC trousers, big mohair jumpers; the whole lot. The full on Punk look."

Stuart Bates went to see most of the Punk groups who would play around Sheffield and Doncaster … "Back in the day, we used to meet up on Thursday nights in the 'Three Horseshoes' pub in Wickersley. Myself, my brother Steve, Mick Roe, and Paul Ricket (who is now the sports editor at Rotherham Advertiser); we would go to The Windmill most Thursdays to the 'New Wave' nights.

Above: typical newspaper reportage with their guide on how to be a Punk Rocker

The most memorable gigs there were Generation X, the Adverts and X-Ray Spex. We also used to go to the Sheffield Top Rank. We saw the Clash, the Jam, Boomtown Rats, Slaughter and the dogs, Richard Hell and the Voidoids to name but a few…Happy Days!!!"

Phil Tasker … "I remember most kids just wore drainpipe jeans and charity shop jackets or leathers, short hair and docs or cheap baseball boots from army stores and a few dog collars bought from pet shops. Plastic Macs were also popular. As regards hair, it was mainly quite short, perhaps spiked up, but not shaved, some colouring was evident but mainly with the girls, you did get some blokes who had moustaches and hair stuck up in spikes with a bit of eye liner and a dog collar, but actually dressed quite straight, some were even still wearing flares!"

Steve Lloyd … "The Punk look for me was sort of an adapted thing; black blazer, usual spiky hair and boot polish in my hair which would run down my face when hot. I got barred from a pub when I walked in with a condom through my ear. I went to Rotherham

Windmill club with a Sex pistols badge piercing my ear. That got some looks, though it was a reggae gig and the crowd there weren't as rough and ready as usual."

Phil Tasker ... "It was a great time to meet up with kindred spirits and I look at it as one of the best times I've ever had. The down side was that Doncaster was so backward thinking that you used to get a lot of stick from people for not being that particularly outrageous and maybe just wearing straight jeans and a tie!"

The few Punk concerts that were held in Sheffield during the Summer of Hate of 1977 could assuredly live up to the public reputation that Punk held; a fact rammed home by the moronic few who could not rest for fear of the young Punk generation being allowed to enjoy themselves. Despite the indifference shown by the Punk hating element, they did not always get away with their ignorance- especially when meeting more than their match in football terrace initiated Punk fans like Anthony Cronshaw.

Anthony Cronshaw ... "The Boomtown Rats gig at the Top Rank; I think it was around the end of August. Well I went to that one and it lasted all of about ten minutes as some idiot threw a bottle at Bob Geldof and it hit him on the head and cut him. The place was full of straights and curiosity seekers.

Above: Advertisers Windmill club feature from late summer 1977

There were some Punks but the idiot who wasn't one ruined it for us all. The crowd were not Punk friendly at all. It was the disco types who were causing all the trouble. Well if it was trouble they were after they had come to the right place. As we approached the bar, there was a group of bastards who thought what had happened was amusing. One of the lads asked the tossers what they were laughing at; to which one replied '*Not very hard these Punks are they?* ' To this my mate nutted him and the rest of the lads set about doing what they do best, that is giving grief to those who deserve it."

Meanwhile early Punk memories were being created by a younger generation, not yet old enough to be a part of the big Punk Picture.

Tony ... "That summer there was stuff in the papers and music weeklies all the time about Punk and Violence and the like. It's obvious who it was that was causing the trouble and it wasn't the short spiky haired lot. Around this time I can remember the

'Total Punk' poster magazine came out. It cost 30p and it was an all colour mag crammed full of all the Punk bands at the time. There was the Clash, the Jam, Buzzcocks, Ramones, 999, the Saints: everybody really and it folded out into a massive Johnny Rotten poster. I hadn't even heard of, never-mind, listened to most of the Punk groups listed in the mag. Predictably I later cut mine up to put in my Punk scrapbook. I ended up making loads of Punk scrapbooks and in the end they chronicled the whole Punk to Post-Punk era from late summer 77 to 1985. I sold them all on eBay eventually and Black Flag singer Henry Rollins bid and bought all the 1977 to 1978 ones."

Above: Total Punk Poster magazine ad from summer 1977

Gary Gillott (Chippie) … "Punk for me wasn't really a thing of particularly rebelling or either tagging on to it…it just seemed to fit into who I was at the time."

Teenagers were still coming across the Punk groups by sheer chance, but once heard- never forgotten. Often there was no way of avoiding Punk…in 1977 it could appear anywhere.

Dean Stables (from Rawmarsh Rotherham) … "I got into punk music by some of our 'bird watching' friends from Wath Ings. (Dean was and still is an avid nature studier and is a strong believer in animal rights). They used to play Slaughter and the Dogs and Eater on their car stereos. I thought hey, what the fuck is this? This stuff has attitude, just like me in a way. Music to fit my personality; and I'm still the same 30 years on."

Paul White (Sugar) (Rotherham Punk) ... "I used to go bird watching around 77/78 time and the older lads had seen the Pistols, Slaughter and the Dogs etc and they introduced me to Punk groups like Eater and the Drones and the rest."
But the indifference towards anyone remotely Punk still continued at many of Punks live outings in the Steel City and in Rotherham suburbs that were mostly of a straight – laced and strictly traditionally (un)cultured nature.

Anthony Cronshaw ... "A few of us went to see 999 and The Runaways at the University. I wasn't too keen on The Runaways, but I liked 999. Anyway the place was full of students and when 999 were playing they all just turned their backs on them. They obviously had no time whatsoever for 999 and showed their distaste by choosing to ignore the group, as though they didn't exist. Me and my mates were so pissed off with this, we just looked at each other and all at once we just steamed into them. That's how we let them know what we thought of them. Later on we got talking to 999 and they were great fellas."

Ivor Hillman (Rotherham Punk and later New Romantic and My Pierrot Dolls singer) ... "During 1977 to 1978 I was working at Butlins and I would get some stick for wearing my pyjamas when going out on my nights off. Back home, being from a mining town, wearing pyjamas and having red hair wasn't always the most popular thing to do. I would get a taxi to Rotherham and then up to Sheffield on the no.69 bus."

The gig-going Punk rockers knew which path they had chosen to take and were enjoying every minute of it, despite the constant threat of ominous danger. Meanwhile, young music fans such as the author were still trying to catch up with the changing times.

Tony ... "Throughout that summer of 77(during which the local youth club's DJ's records all melted as it was that hot), I was still listening to lots of chart pop stuff. I loved Donna Summer's 'I Feel Love' and quite a lot of the disco/soul that was around at the time and getting played at the youth club. I knew a little about Punk Rock and had heard 'Pretty Vacant' by the Pistols that Pete Roddis had bought (I even had it on one of those dodgy 'Top Of the Pops' compilation LP's that we all bought for the front sleeves?) Also there were Vibrators 'Baby Baby' and some other records like 'Peaches' by the Stranglers. Initially any Punk I heard was from a chart kind of view. I did hear of the Damned but to be perfectly honest I never actually heard their records until they re-formed a couple of years later. I had noticed though, that Paul Weller wore a Damned badge on the front cover of the Jam's 'In the City' LP.
　　Not long afterwards, me and my mate Andy Goulty heard and liked 'Looking after number one' by the Boomtown Rats when that was released. That and Eddie and the Hot Rods 'Do anything you wanna do'. They were perhaps the only 'New Wave' records that got played at the youth club that late summer time. Another one I liked was 'Gary Gilmore's eyes' by the Adverts. I managed to scrounge that single off Ian Hillman who was later in My Pierrot Dolls a little later on. I started buying the Stranglers singles around this time too, but the one group who really grabbed my attention were the Jam who I saw perform 'All around the world' on the Marc show. I dug their energy and the fact that

they didn't seem all that much older than us at school. But also Paul Weller even then stood out and looked so cool... Much more than say - the Stranglers who looked older than our teacher's dads. Also I dug Weller's hairstyle and that suppressed aggression he displayed. That summer I pulled out the centre page poster of The Jam out of the 'Look in' comic and backed my c3 studies school book with it. The Picture was of the Jam stood at the side of a black car in some kind of park or something.

After that, even though I still bought plenty of crap records, it was a gradual thing of buying more and more so called New Wave records. I know with a lot of the Punks back then, it seems that Punk sort of hit them between the eyes and it was a life changing moment there and then. It was like the old kids programme we used to watch 'Mr Benn'...they would walk in looking like a member of Status Quo and re-emerge looking like one of the Clash. I suppose it did affect lots of kids a bit in yer face but being the age me and the couple of other enlightened ones were, it was a lot more of a gradual thing; having said that; I was one of the first at our school to get my hair cut fairly short. I finally ended up getting my classic seventies shoulder length hair lobbed off and cut into a sort of bog brush looking version of Paul Weller's short spiky cut. Me and Andy Goulty now started having our hair cut short, to begin with; looking a bit crap but we adapted eventually.

August 1977- I remember going on a family day trip to Scarborough and there was John Harrison, who was a big Jam and Punk fan at the time, he was on the back of the coach pissing about. One of the lads he was knocking about with later got killed while on his bike as he was being chased by the police. Me and John weren't mates at that point, but we would give each other the nod in respect of what we were into. We both had those larger sized 'In the city' Jam badges. Mine I think was the red logo one and John's was the blue one.

When we got back from that day trip my dad, who was seriously ill with emphysema, was waiting for us at the Pub. He should have been at home in bed in his condition, but he was a proud bloke and he somehow managed to get up there to meet us in his black suit. My Mum went crackers with him.

Right: Me on a day trip to Scarborough late summer 1977

A little earlier he had once noticed that I had put some plastic ear ring on my ear - my kind of subtle Punk homage- and he was laughing at me calling me a Punk Rocker. He did say, though, that if I wanted my ears piercing he would let me. Don't know if he would have agreed if I had said I would have my nose done instead. Sadly my Dad passed away early in the following year of 1978.

Also during the school holidays of 77, I can remember it as clear as yesterday the day Elvis Presley died. It was pissing it down all day long. I suppose this was the day that the old order died and withered away and the new order was now manning the barricades for sure – and only time would tell if that was a good thing or not."

Andy Goulty (Rotherham Punk Rocker) … "There was one or two of us young 'un's starting to get into the Punk thing. It's strange cos the year below at school, there was absolutely no one into it. I suppose we can't have made that much of an impression on them. But then a year at that age is a lot of difference."

During the last few weeks of the summer, following a comeback that warmly embraced Punk (including a tour with the Damned), Marc Bolan re-emerged, rejuvenated with a new half hour music show simply called Marc. The show would showcase Marc Bolan songs but also gave open hearted creedence to the Punk scene with its weekly Punk groups live spots.

Phillip Wright … "Marc Bolan also had his own TV show on at 4.25pm on a Tuesday afternoon on ITV. He seemed to like the Punk movement and had bands playing live in the studio, including Generation X and the Jam playing their second single 'All around the World.'"

Tony … "The Marc show was broadcast on ITV around 4pm(ish) and I can remember rushing home from school to make sure I saw every bit. I did like Marc Bolan and still played all my brother's old T-Rex singles, but it would be these unknown groups that he would introduce that would have the most lasting impressions. There was Radio Stars who performed 'No Russians in Russia', Generation X with 'Your Generation' and Eddie and the Hot Rods with 'Do anything you wanna do'. Most importantly for me, the previously mentioned Jam - whose performance would eventually lead me on to a more exciting path than the one at the time that was being sound-tracked by Hot Chocolate's 'So you win again', the Rah Band's 'The Crunch' and Space trying to be futuristic with 'Magic Fly'?. No the future was here in the Modern World!"

In September Marc Bolan was tragically killed whilst driving his mini. Punk's most honest celebrity fan was no longer with us and another era was at an end.

Chapter Five

Vinyl Pleasure and Punk Rock comes to town

"Richard Hell and the Voidoids supporting The Clash at the Top Rank in 77 ...Oh! How those glasses and ashtrays flew through the air. But the Clash...their energy ripped through you" – **David Mckendry (Sheffield Punk Rocker)**

Record shops were now starting to stock Punk and 'New Wave' records without question; only the Sex Pistols retaining the notoriety of being banned from time to time. Local record shops now had a whole new influx of brand new sounds to stock, display and sell.

many others to follow. Paul Bower played there with his band 2.3, supporting Generation X: "We ple that come here who spend £10 and more on punk stuff. They're just posers. It's completely

Above: Sheffield Star newspaper's feature on the Punk scene at Rotherham's Windmill club in 1977

Tony ... "The 'Sound of Music' record shop was really good with the Punk and 'New Wave' records. They used to put all the picture covers of the singles in a plastic sleeve attached to 12" sized card. It was great to go through the singles available in this way. The record sleeves of most of the 'New Wave' ones were mostly quite eye catching and colourful. I would spend many hours in there just staring at the first Clash LP cover.

My mate Andy bought the Jam 'Modern World' single after he had seen 'em on Top of the Pops the night before. I saw them but wasn't that keen on that one on first hearing, but after two or three plays I had to have it off him. I ended up swapping it with him for a Queen single."

Bryan Bell ... "Yes I think 'Sound of Music' record shop was the main place in Rotherham that you could buy all the Punk records back then. The other shops would sell them if they were in the charts but 'Sound of Music' had most of the punk records. They had a separate section for it all. The first punk records I bought, and there weren't that many out to start with, were the Sex Pistols ones, the Adverts 'One Chord Wonders', the Clash 'White Riot' and then a little later Buzzcocks 'Orgasm Addict'. The first Clash LP too. That was one of the first LP's I bought. I also used to buy imports out of the back pages of the NME. Some would be different singles not out over here or have a different b-side."

Tony ... "I was talking to one of the lasses who used to work in 'The Sound of Music' a few years back and she didn't look hardly any older, but she did remember us Punk kids as being a pain in the arse."

Margaret (Sound of Music assistant) ... "Whenever people talk to me about it (Sound of Music), the first thing they all say is '*What about those sound booths*'...they always seem to trigger something with them. As for the Punk records, we weren't a chart return shop so we basically stocked whatever we wanted and if people asked for something we would try and get it for them. We always stocked most of the Punk records. The picture sleeves started with Punk. There weren't many at all before Punk came in with all the colourful picture covers

It was my Mum and Dad's shop... and I think it opened about 1969 as far as I can remember. I worked there from about 1970 and all the way through the Punk era. The thing is when the shop was sold the next owners thought it would be easy to run, but it wasn't. We all worked hard to keep the shop running... those days were really special and we will not see the like of them again."

Pete Weston ... "They knew me at the Sound of Music, and any Punk sounding record that came in, they would save for me. I spent a fortune on records in there when I look back and think on it. Some great Punk records though."

Gary Robinson ... "The record shop 'Sound of Music' was fantastic. I would buy loads of the Punk records from there and you could listen to them too. It's now a clothes shop but if you go in there you can still see the sound booths in there."

Tony ... "It was a fantastic experience being able to scour through all these unknown and weird sounding records and then listen to them in the sound booths in the Rotherham 'Sound of Music' shop; far more exciting and more real than downloading music today."

Timothy Green … "I soon became known in the Sound Of Music record shop in Rotherham as someone who buys anything punkish or 'New Wave'. I'd go in there either straight from work on a Friday or on a Saturday afternoon if I wasn't watching the Millers. I would ask about the latest releases that I'd read about in NME. Sometimes they had got them in, or I would order stuff. They got to know me, and would suggest stuff that they thought that I'd like. They were usually wrong, mind."

Paul Clarkson … "In October 77 a girlfriend at the time, bought me an 'Orgasm Addict' for my birthday… the Buzzcocks record that is."

Apart from the visual and listening pleasure of discovering new sounds and groups, the music weeklies were now open to discovery, where if you skipped the pages of bearded keyboard wizards and serious looking rockers, you may find enthusiastic reviews on some of the groups and sounds you may have heard in the Record shop's sound booth the weekend before; The cynical and elitist attitudes within the pages going straight over the young fan's heads.

Tony …"I used to buy the NME and Sounds mags - usually a few weeks later in a bargain bundle from the newsagent on Bridgegate in town. It would be say, 15p for a batch of a few weeks old music papers bound together with an elastic band. It didn't take long to build up a pile of em. The news would be a little old but I would read about these strange sounding groups like Slaughter and the dogs, Penetration and Cocksparrer and wonder what they sounded like. Ian Hillman (at school) would relay what a lot of them were like from their Ivor, who was well into Punk at that time. We would chat about these weirdly named groups in boring Maths lessons, but often it would be a while before I actually got to hear a lot of them."

Above: Mark Perry's Punk alternative to the music weeklies

From midyear 1977, Doncaster's Outlook club had been putting on an increasing amount of Punk gigs, and the venue was swiftly becoming a key entry of most Punk and 'New Wave' group's tour listings. Generation X played there regularly, as did the Adverts, along with all the best that the 'New Wave' had to offer including a Punky R&B band called The Boys…who were always warmly received by the Outlook's hardcore Punk crowd.

Honest John Plain (The Boys) … "Coming from Leeds, I always enjoyed returning to Yorkshire to play with The Boys and I have fond memories of playing Doncaster Outlook – twice in 1977 and 1978. The audience were fantastic on both occasions."

Phil Tasker … "I was at Art School at Doncaster college during the Punk era and I liked bands like Magazine and Wire, I had started going to the Outlook around the time that Be Bop Deluxe were playing that type of venue in about 76.

The year after and it was the Punk groups I was going to see there; I remember talking to Pete Shelley after the Buzzcocks gig and he was saying how much he liked Lou Reed and Velvet Underground. It was a great time when you could talk to the band members after the gig. There were no barriers as they were just like us. Of course some of them went on to have long careers in music but it brought everything down to ground level in order to make a new start."

Doncaster's very own Punk group Sublimal Cuts featured singer Russ Carlin who was sometimes likened to Billy Idol. The rest of the group consisted of Kevin Pass on guitar, Dave Linnel on bass guitar and a drummer only known as Col. They played at the Outlook club playing covers of 'Waiting for my man', 'Gloria' and sixties garage classic and proto-type Punk record 'Louie Louie'. They added an element of comedy to their set with the singer often admitting that he'd forgotten the words and pulling out a piece of paper to recite from and also departing the stage while he 'went for a piss'.

Siouxsie and the Banshees also played the Outlook and their gig was reviewed in The Rotherham Advertiser in which Siouxsie describes one of their first unwelcoming receptions afforded them whilst playing the local venues.

Right: Siouxsie at Doncaster Outlook In 1977 (Rotherham Advertiser)

In the piece, it tells of how The Banshees abruptly ended their set after being constantly heckled by a large section of the audience. The group described the Doncaster audience that night as *'The worst we have ever had'* and Siouxsie labelling them as *'A pretty sorry crowd'*. And continuing *"You can't play 'as well as you can to an audience like that. There were a lot of morons out there. I don't really care though. It was much better the last time we played here and it will probably be much better if we come again."*

Whilst hostile Punk audiences up North could sometimes antagonise the visiting Punk groups, the Punk kids themselves were often still very wary of their common foe: and if the media were to be believed that was the Teddy Boys.

110

Morg ... "As everywhere at the time there was a lot of problems in Doncaster with the older Teddy Boys who were generally in their late 30's through to mid forties. They were attacking and beating up young Punks who were an average age of 14 to 20. One gig at the Outlook was when Wayne County and the Electric chairs played there on their 'Eddie and Sheena' tour (This was one of their singles that lyrically and musically told the story of a Punk girl and Ted boy becoming an item).They had a rockabilly band support them on the tour and this was supposed to bring Teds and Punks together for the gig.

However, us young punkers were bricking ourselves in case the older Teddy Boys came to the gig. Due to this the crowd was not a big one. In the end no Teds turned up, but I for one was still nervous when leaving the club after the gig."

Anthony Cronshaw ... "I used to work at the Asda store in Rotherham back then. Once when I had finished my shift I got on the bus to go home and went upstairs and it was rammed full with Teds. I expected the worst, but I think cos I was alone they just left me be. I remember buying a pair of Brothel creepers. I used to really like them plus it used to annoy the Teds as well."

Steve Lloyd ... "The Lurkers were a great Punk band and at the time their roadie was Dave Tregena. One night, after a gig at the Outlook, he was so pissed that he ended up missing the truck back to the next venue and ended up stopping at my mate's house. We kept contact with him after that and he ended up playing bass guitar for Sham 69."

The Northern 'Make yourself at home' hospitality ideology could often amuse band members who were playing the local venues!

Pete 'Esso' Haynes (drummer with the Lurkers who played regularly at the Outlook club) ... "Now the Outlook club in Doncaster; I remember it for being an unforgiving place-it was rough. I remember a bloke walking behind the bar, dropping his trousers and having a piss in the empty bottle cart thing. This big bouncer bloke came up behind him, grabbed the back of his collar and pulled him backwards, dragging him along and out of the bar, his trousers and pants down. The girls behind the bar were laughing, some faking embarrassment."

Even so, these earthy and colourful venues would consistently make a lasting impression on many of those young Punks who frequented them.

Morg ... "The Outlook club was my regular haunt, seeing bands such as the Cortinas, X-Ray Spex, Siouxsie and the Banshees, Sham 69, Eater, Blitzkrieg Bop, Slaughter and the Dogs, the Lurkers and lots more. I can also remember seeing Ultravox play there with their original singer (John Foxx) when they still played good fast songs. It was a sad day when the Outlook closed down, but by this time there were punk rockers everywhere.

Doncaster had a huge scene with local bands popping up all over the place. We also had gigs to go to at places like Retford Porterhouse and in Sheffield the Limit club and the Top Rank. Netherthess, I will always look back on the Doncaster Outlook days as the most important and special days of my life."

Phil Tasker ...” I spoke to Billy Idol before the Generation X gig at the Outlook and he put a Vice Squad badge (which I had made at college) on his trousers, it was so crap that it fell off as soon as he started gyrating around, good gig though!”

Steve Lloyd ... ”Working at the Outlook, I saw just about every Punk band that was around and there were so many new ones appearing all the time. The Stranglers were great live and so were Wire, 999, Damned, Adverts, the Jam and lots more. The Management were ok and the bouncers were fine with us but they could be a bit hard with the punters, kicking them as they queued up outside etc.”

Punk groups could also be found playing the area on tours supporting groups that were not Punk at all, but would often be loosely associated or partially accepted by the Punk fans. Radiators from Space supported Thin Lizzy at the City Hall,(The Vipers another Irish band would also play that venue with the same group a couple of year later) and in October 1977 Australian hard rock band AC/DC played Sheffield Polytechnic supported by Suburban Studs.

Paul Kelly went to that gig and recalls ...”Gigs at the Poly back then were up on the eighth floor in the student bar-you had to get a lift up there. Anyway this gig was when AC/DC were only playing small venues and the support was Suburban Studs. Some of the student dick heads had gone along to the gig thinking AC/DC was Punk. They had been used to listening to Genesis and Rick Wakeman and all that bollocks.

On came the Studs and halfway through the opening song someone gobbed on Eddy Zipps who was right at the front of the stage. Well Ed just kicks him straight in the head, no questions asked- as the bloke was just on the right level-the stage was about 4 foot high. Then all hell breaks loose with fists flying all over the place. They were very close to pulling Ed into the crowd, but luckily the bouncers arrived in time and just managed to save him from a right kicking.

Once things had calmed down, the crowd were warned *‘Anyone spits on AC/DC and they will refuse to play’-* obviously they didn’t and AC/DC played a full set, and I have to say they were brilliant, but I was pissed off ‘cos the Studs didn’t finish their set. I never got the chance to see ‘em again.

I bet Ed was well pissed off, had it been a bigger venue in London or Manchester, it may have given them some much needed bad press. I don’t recall seeing a review of AC/DC of this gig anywhere, but back then they were just some little known Aussie band with a sense of humour. In those days things were moving so fast. Kids were turning on to the punk thing and many changing their outlook and look overnight. The excitement was captivating.”

The anti-fascist stance taken by some of the local Punks would sometimes clash with the shock tactic stylings of swastika-wearing groups such as Siouxsie and the Banshees who played a short set supporting Johnny Thunders and the Heartbreakers late in 1977 at Sheffield’s Top Rank.

Timothy Green ... "At that gig I ended up having an argument with Siouxsie about her fascist salute. The Banshees used to do a version of the Lord's Prayer, during which, for some reason, she used to do a Nazi salute. When Johnny Thunders and the Heartbreakers were on, (they were the headliners) Siouxsie came out to have a drink. As part of the punk ethos was that you could mix with the bands, I went up to her and remonstrated about her doing the Nazi salute. I was never happy about that very early punk/Nazi symbol crossover and tried to combat it wherever I could and luckily all that shit died out pretty quickly."

The love/hate relationship with the Banshees would continue into the next decade. Meanwhile Punk fans too young to see the gigs (at least for now) were absorbing the Punk phenomenon...

John Harrison remembers ... "It seems such a long time ago now, but I can always remember the feeling I got from Punk. It was so exciting and I had to be a part of it. I was 14 years old and the energy and attitude of Punk was exactly what I wanted at that time."

Tony ... "To begin with, I fell for the whole clichéd idea of what Punk was. Me and my mate used to see the groups on Top of the Pops and then we would buy the records and play 'em and mimic and exaggerate them. It was funny though. After a while you start to realise that the groups were (mostly anyway) serious about their music. The Stranglers were hard to find funny and the Jam and the Clash meant what they were doing."

Gary Robinson ... "There was me, Bryan Bell, Alison, Mandy and a few others into the Punk scene. We would go to all the Top Rank gigs: Penetration, the Clash, the Stranglers, and the Adverts we saw them all. Those days were fantastic times."

Ivor Hillman ... "One of the best gigs I saw was the Adverts, just after 'Gary Gilmore's Eyes' was out. After the gig we decided on a cheap night home and the plan was I would pretend to be dying and we'd get a free ambulance ride home. Unfortunately the plan backfired and we ended up further away at the Hallamshire Hospital and then ended up walking back into Sheffield city centre right back where we started."

Surprisingly, considering Punk's across the board general avoidance of black music (The Jam, Clash, The Boys, the Saints and a handful of others being the exceptions), using the metallic blueprint of the Stooges, sleazy rock n' roll of New York Dolls etc for the staple 3 minute standard Punk song... the influence of reggae was considered very cool. The presence of reggae and dub sounds had been there almost from the beginning with Roxy DJ Don Letts spinning hip 45's when there was hardly any Punk vinyl to play. As explored in much greater detail in other sources Reggae soon became a massive and profound influence on many of Punk's prime movers including the Clash and the Slits. Young Punk fans who themselves were only just getting to grips with the Punk scene itself were also quick to appreciate the Jamaican sound.

Tony ... "Late 77 and Andy Goulty bought Bob Marley's 'Jamming' single and the b-side was 'Punky Reggae Party' which we discovered was a tribute to the Clash, the Jam, Damned etc. I bought Althea and Donna's 'Uptown Top Rankin' really as a chart single. Soon Andy would be listening to Bob Marley more avidly and later on, a few years later, I would start listening to the more obscure reggae stuff from the likes of Mighty Diamonds, Burning Spear, Junior Murvin, U-Roy and the legendary Steel Pulse."

Steel Pulse actually played at one of the Rotherham Windmill New Wave nights at the end of the year and also very soon afterwards at Doncaster's Outlook club.

Steve Lloyd ... "Yeah, I went to the Steel Pulse one at the Windmill. It was well attended by the Punk kids."

Interestingly, Steel Pulse compared the Punks and how they had embraced their music and reggae with the same vigour the 60's Mods had checked out Stax and Tamla Motown.

Steve Haythorne ... "I got turned onto a lot of reggae through the Punk bands. I liked Black Uhuru, Burning Spear and lots of that stuff, though I was never that keen on the commercial stuff. Not being that bothered about Bob Marley even."

Patrick Tierney ... "That's another thing Punk can be credited with - helping reggae into wider acceptance. For a lot of people, 'Police & Thieves' on the first Clash album will have been their first exposure to reggae. And most of the punk bands (and John Peel) championed reggae in some way, but mainly the Clash. Maybe this made it O.K to like it. People of my age had been listening to ska/rocksteady/reggae for years without realising it was a particular genre. I remember, as a very small child, loving 'My Boy Lollipop' by Little Millie, then later 'Israelites' by Desmond Dekker, and later still Dandy Livingston's 'Suzanne Beware of the Devil' To me it was just great music, but punk's affinity to reggae made me dig a bit deeper."

The Damned, meanwhile, were coming to the end of their first Punk phase. Their 'Music for Pleasure' LP had brought in Pink Floyd's Nick Mason on production duties and Lol Coxhill on saxophone. Punk's great eccentrics appeared to be taking things seriously.

Barry Bartle ... "I saw the Damned on that tour at the Top Rank. There must only have been 200 in there that night. When they played MFP track 'You know' with the sax break at the end, I can tell you what! Black Sabbath couldn't have sounded any heavier."

October 1977 and 'Never Mind the Bollocks' the first and only real Sex Pistols album was released. In-depth analysis could go on for ever regarding its importance, with many declaring it the greatest Punk album of all time, while some Pistols fans – Paul Weller for example – declared it a Greatest Hits LP, due to all of their singles being included. Others classing it as an over produced poor relation to the 'Spunk' demo's version. One thing is for sure, and clearly so in this region, the record did manage to inspire and excite; and in some cases resulting in a Punk sound of their own.

Graham Torr ... "Listen to anything on 'Never Mind the bollocks' and compare it with 'Love Gun' the album from Kiss (the biggest band in the world back then) released at the same time and the production just pisses all over the Kiss sound. So the buzz quickly gets round school and before long, a few like minded 'erberts decide that that's where it's at and talk of a band ensues."

John Harrison ... "That was the big Punk record really...we all had to hear it and it did deliver the goods. I still have a copy on CD now and play it from time to time."

Above: 'New Wave' kid Andy Goulty Christmas 1977

Tony ... "I can remember my mate Andy Goulty buying the Sex Pistols 'Never mind the Bollocks' LP around Christmas time, which was shortly after it was released. He was well into the Pistols and not that long afterwards the Buzzcocks, Patti Smith, Stranglers and others. He also bought Ian Dury's 'New Boots and Panties' LP around that time and we would listen to that record a hell of a lot. We were just starting to discover and dig a lot deeper into the 'New Wave' sounds... but we were still buying lots of Pop crap as well. No one ever told us that to be into Punk you had to get rid of everything else. There simply was no year zero for us at all.

A lot of the time, we used to buy different records so that we had the chance to hear more music. I was buying Boomtown Rats, Tom Robinson Band, Elvis Costello and the Jam. I got a real bargain when I picked up The Jam LP 'This is the Modern world' for 75p from Brittain's record dept about this time. It was released in November and by Christmas it was in the bargain section. I quickly became immersed in the record and my life long Jam obsession was well in swing."

The Jam first played Sheffield on their first tour earlier in the year at the Top Rank and this was followed with another date on their 'Modern World' tour; where they played an energetic and well-received set at the same venue.

Paul Kelly remembers the Jam finding time to pay a visit to meet fans at the local Punk record shop 'Revolution' at the Haymarket in Sheffield earlier in the year ..."I can't actually remember the name of the bloke who ran the record shop, but he did look after the regulars. I don't know how he got the Jam down there, but it was the day after they played the Roxy (then known as Sheffield Top Rank).

Basically the shop owner had told me and my mate Howard to come into the shop on the Monday morning following the gig. *'Don't tell anyone, but bring your LP covers 'cos there will be opportunities to get autographs*' he said. I took the first LP and the first 2 singles sleeves along. About 11am that day, he cracked open a bottle of wine, there could have only been a dozen or so people there, and in strolled the three members of the Jam in their stage gear. There was another bloke with the Jam who could have been Paul's dad, but I'm not sure. He didn't really say anything. Now had that been a Saturday in 1977, I don't think they would have been able to just casually stroll along the gallery. At this time there was always hundreds of West Indians hanging around there once the Crazy Daisy had shut and it was always quite intimidating passing by them.

Anyway, the Jam: they just hung around for a while but didn't have a drink. Paul and Rick were talking to everyone, but the thing I remember most was that Bruce was so quiet and shy. He hardly said a word. I remember thinking to myself' '*These lads aren't much older than me, they're only kids.*' They signed autographs for everyone, I got my records sleeves signed, and then off they went on their way."

Above: The Jam in typical punk poses around the time that they visited Sheffield's Punk record shop Revolution

Phillip Wright ... "The big venue was Steelys (Top Rank) which became Roxys and is now the Carling Academy. It was a good size venue and the Jam played there in 1977 on their first UK tour, the 'In the City' tour. It was a great gig, on a Sunday night. Also on their 'Modern World' tour, if my memory serves me right, the support was a band called New Hearts, who went on to become Secret Affair."

While Punk and 'New Wave' groups such as the Jam were playing at Sheffield venues, young Punk fans were picking up on their records; and relating their music to the events of the time.

Dave Spencer... "Apart from Punk, 1976 to 1978 was just about knocking about with my mate Cav, whether playing on skateboards or going to watch Rotherham United. I can remember Cav buying the Jam's album, 'This Is the Modern World' when it came out and he put up with my marathon 'No More Heroes' sessions. We were fascinated by what was happening but it all seemed a world away from us. All the bands seemed to come from elsewhere (usually London). All the music press ever seemed to mention were the London gigs. Little did we know that there was a venue above the Tivoli end of Rotherham United's Millmoor ground called the Windmill which was putting on bands every Thursday night?"

116

In November 1977, the Clash returned to Sheffield to play their first gig there since making their live debut in the city almost a year and a half since. This was their biggest tour yet and was named the 'Get out Of Control' tour. They played at the Top Rank and were eagerly anticipated by many of the local Punk fans. Unfortunately, the reception given to support bands Richard Hell and the Voidoids and the Lous was not at all to their benefit.

David Mckendry ... "Outside the Top Rank, there were hundreds queuing and the most unbelievable sights you could ever see. Punk girls wearing bin liners and not much else."

By the end of their set, Richard Hell and the Voidoids were covered in beer and spit with more than a few cuts and bruises to add insult to injury. The stage had to be cleared of pint-pots, belts, tab ends and assortments of clothing for The Clash to appear. The Clash came on stage with a greeting from Mick Jones *'Alright, how you doing'* followed by Joe Strummer's angry plea for the spitting to stop *'When I want to gob I gob on the floor, right!'* They then kicked into a raging version of 'London's Burning' and then straight into their recent single 'Complete Control' and a set that included '1977', 'Jail Guitar Doors', 'Clash City Rockers', 'Police and Thieves' and 'Protex Blue' which Mick introduces with *'This is the first one we did last time we were here at the Black Swan'."*

Martin Clarke (Sheffield Punk fan) ... "That first night that I saw the Clash, I was wearing what I thought were really trendy clogs... flared jeans and a bomber jacket. I soon had to trade those in for tight straight leg jeans and winkle picker shoes."

Bryan Bell remembers this gig ... "With the Clash playing live it was all about the energy. They had so much power and energy to give and watching them play live was a real experience."

Def Leppard singer **Joe Elliott**, although a Heavy Metal fan, was also an admirer of some of the original Punk groups and attended this 'Clash 'gig. He recalls ... "I remember seeing the Clash at Sheffield Top Rank in 1977 and thinking Wow!!!- compared to what was usually on at the Top Rank they couldn't really play (in the sense of what was the norm back then) but the excitement that came off the stage was phenomenal!!! **(Sheffield History site)**

Punk Rocker Paul Clarkson went to the gig with 3 friends. The 4 of them were dressed in an assortment of 'Bondage trousers, WW2 flying suit, biker jackets, leopard skin jacket, doc Martins, red skin-tight rubber trousers topped off with brothel creepers and pink socks'. The two girls with shocking pink hair and loads of black make up. On the way they were refused to be allowed on the bus; the driver saying *'We don't have your kind ont' bus, we dunt want any trouble'.* After being refused to be served in the pubs in Rotherham they manage to get the train from Masbrough to Sheffield.

Paul Clarkson ..."We went to the Stonehouse pub in Sheffield for a pint and we get *'Soz mate you freaks aren't coming in, fuck off back to the fucking circus.'* After protesting the reply was *'Fuck off before we give you a slap, you fucking queer'.* 10 minutes inside the Top Rank and a group of 8 – 10 skinheads surrounded us. You know the Jam song with the lines *'I first felt a fist and then a kick, I could now smell their breath', they smelt of pubs and wormwood scrubs'* etc.

Well this is what happened here. I got up - bloodied and bruised. The Clash came on and everything was now fine .They were great as usual. We knew most of the set by now, so started to pogo.

After the gig, we had a few beers and decided to go home, but no- one would let us get in their taxi! So, cunning plan, get one of the girls with us to charm the cabbie. We got a black cab outside the rail station, she gets in, we all pile in and he asks. *'Have you all been to a fancy dress then?'*

Anthony Cronshaw … "Towards the end of the year my gig count was increasing by the day almost, but the two premier bands of the movement had eluded me. I had not yet seen the Clash or the Sex Pistols. On the 1st of November the Clash played the rank and they blew us away. They became, and still remain, my greatest group of the era. We had met in the Claymore pub before the show and in there was a mixture of Blades fans and us Wednesday fans too. You could tell this was not a football night. Our rivals had also come along to see the Clash and witness the youth revolution that was Punk - just like us."

David McKendry … "The Top Rank was the main venue as the Sheffield students union was a complete twat to get into (if you weren't a student that is). Punk bands at the Top Rank were always value for money, short sets but you got several support bands (mainly crap - but Jesus, there was Siouxsie Banshee to be seen 'strutting her stuff' supporting the Heartbreakers). Within months the majority of these support bands would have an NME single of the week to their names!"

Over at Doncaster's Outlook club, Lurkers bassist Arturo Bassick noticed the trendy Punk look being displayed by a future 'Hollywood' star!!

Arturo Bassick … "We played Doncaster Outlook club with Pink Military, who had Holly Johnson, later of Frankie goes to Hollywood on bass. Me and him had a row because he had bondage gear on and we, the band, thought it was overpriced rubbish from those two tailors in the Kings Road. We hated the Punk elite and expensive shops – we thought Punk should be charity shop clobber customised to peoples own taste and styles." **(From 'Fat Bloke, Thin Book' by Arturo Bassick)**

Those fun loving Beat Punks the Rezillos played at Doncaster's Outlook club late that year (also returning to the venue in 1978). However, this date would prove to be a pivotal moment for the unmapped future of the local music scene... and would, in a twist of fate, provide a future job opportunity for one Rezillo a few years later, guitarist Jo Callis recalls.

Jo Callis … "I remember The Outlook in Donny, it backed on to the Railway station. As I recall it was a last minute booking. The Banshees were originally meant to be playing the Outlook that night, but had to cancel for some reason and we ended up filling the spot, I think we were touring round England at the time and were able to fit it in. This turned out to be quite a seminal engagement, particularly in how it affected my future.

Our roadie/road manager at the time was Bob Last, who would go on to manage the Human League, Scritti Politi etc and subsequently ourselves. I knew Bob from a stint working in The Traverse Theatre in Edinburgh, where Bob was Assistant Stage Manager; - in fact nearly all our original crew were poached from The Traverse. At the time, Bob, inspired by the exciting contemporary cultural developments, was just starting his own independent label 'Fast Product'. He'd already found his first signing in the Mekons who had been our support act a few weeks earlier at the F Club in Leeds, and we all loved them.

When we got to The Outlook our support that night were 2.3, a politically motivated band from Sheffield led by the enigmatic Paul Bower. Bob was suitably impressed and approached Paul with a view to make 2.3 his next signing. This duly happened resulting in 'All Time Low' cw 'Where to Now'. But Paul, - ever the champion of causes seemed more concerned that his mates from Sheffield the Human League' (possibly still then called The Future) should not go overlooked, than he was with the fortunes of his own band. Paul struck up a very good rapport with Bob, and was soon bombarding him with Human League demo cassettes and other material. So The League owe it all to Paul, and those events subsequently shaping my own future. Funny how it all comes full circle back to more or less your hometown, it's like Yorkshire's still looking after you. You might leave Yorkshire but it never leaves you behind."

1977, the year almost universally considered the high tide of the Punk explosion and Sheffield and the locality had finally caught up on the Punk Rock gig front. Whilst the music journalists were already looking for the next big thing to follow Punk (Wire, Siouxsie and the Banshees, Magazine and others already being termed as 'New Musick') there was a whole new generation of local young people who had turned onto Punk and as long as there were venues to go and see the groups, the Punk scene of the region would remain alive and kicking. Local Groups such as They Must be Russians (starting their career covering 'Rebel Rebel' and 'Virginia Plain'), Reactor (who played at Rotherham Windmill club in December), and Stranger than Fiction (Ultravox influenced Barnsley band) were forming... joining the small but impressive roster of existing Punk and New Wave bands of the area; all encompassing a 'style and identity of their own'. There were also now plenty of gigs to attend in the area. How long would the scene last before the bubble burst?

Christmas 1977; The Sex Pistols played their last ever UK gigs including a Christmas day one at Huddersfield 'Ivanhoe's' for the local kids of firemen who were on strike at the time. According to many who attended, this gig was one of the most enjoyable and genuine performances the band had ever played.

Steve Marshall (Sheffield Punk) … "I was just turned 17 when I went to see the Sex Pistols at Huddersfield Ivanhoe's. I went with my sister Deb and I think there were 3 others in her small orange mini clubman. This was Christmas day 1977 and it turned out to be the Sex Pistols last ever gig in the UK - with that line up anyway.

I was amazed and a bit freaked out too. I was at a young age and standing next to Sid Vicious at the bar, and me not daring to talk to him in case he hit me or something! Rotten was amazing though, with his stage presence. I don't have any of my ticket stubs, but I did have some of those rare Sex Pistols *banned* posters, from the concert. Years later in, 2003, I sold them at 'Christies' pop memorabilia auction in London for a fair bit of capitalist money."

Timothy Green … "The Sex Pistols last ever UK gig was in Huddersfield on Christmas Day. I had tickets, but, in the end, no means of getting there. Fucking annoying it was."

Anthony Cronshaw … "1977 was topped off with seeing the Sex Pistols on Christmas day at Huddersfield. I remember you had to go and see the Rich Kids- who I was never a fan of - to obtain your Pistols tickets.

That was one hell of a concert. They'd done a charity gig in the afternoon for the striking firemen and had given out presents to their kids- one of whom after witnessing the matinee show had said '*I can't see what all the fuss is about*'- now it was our turn. When all the afternoon lot had cleared off, our lot were let in and once inside we headed for the bar. With beers in hand, we took up our positions near the front. The Pistols came on- Rotten was wearing a white hunter's hat- he introduced 'God Save the Queen' and the place went mental. It was an unbelievable experience and how were we going to follow that. We had done it all and as we moved into 1978, we were wondering what delights were to be on the horizon?"

Soon afterwards at the beginning of 1978 the Sex Pistols played their first U.S tour and imploded. This was to some the end of Punk! It was now left to the Clash to carry the heavy burden of being the UK's leading punk band.

Chapter Six

'New Wave' Daze

"Of course we were all madly in Love with Debbie Harry!" – **Paul Bower (2.3 singer/guitarist)**

Tony ... "The Clash were quite close to being my favourite Punk group. It was always between them and the Jam and still is in a way. I went out and bought all their singles that had been released up until that time. 'White Riot', 'Complete control', 'Remote Control' and 'Clash City Rockers'. They were never off my record player for ages. To me the Clash beat the Pistols hands down. I couldn't wait to get the chance to see them play live. That run of Clash singles from 'White Riot' to 'London Calling' were superb... a classic run of quality rock n' roll. After that, the Clash continued to make great and interesting singles, a lot of the time really breaking the mould and annoying the narrow minded punk crowd, but for me they never matched that first couple of years for sheer intensity. They certainly peaked with the 'London Calling' LP."

Above: Doncaster Outlook 'New Wave' stars performing at the venue in 1978. From the left Wayne Barrett (Slaughter and the Dogs), Jimmy Pursey (Sham 69) and Cherry Vanilla.

Steve Lloyd ... "When a certain Punk band played the Outlook club (they later became very well known), their singer was so full of himself and acting really vain. He sent for

Kathy, a Punk girl from Rotherham that I was friends with, and she went into the backstage dressing room and there he was; he had dropped his trousers and was asking for a blow-job. Not surprisingly, she told him where to get off."

Tony Parsons on reviewing Sheffield band 2.3 and their just released single 'All time low'/ 'Where to now' in the NME unwittingly (or not) complimented them with the following review comment ... "2.3 'All time Low' sounds like an out – take from the annals of the 'Nuggets' album...quintessential listening during a nervous breakdown."

Jo Callis (also known as 'Luke Warm') Rezillos guitarist; when asked what do the Rezillos stand for? Replied – "I dunno...we don't even stand for the National anthem."

The first Punk fatalities, apart from the Radiators from Space gig-stabbing the previous summer and the unfortunate Henry Bowles who was beaten to death by bouncers at a Punk disco in October of 77, occurred in 1978. The year had barely began when Punk 'also rans' the Dead lost their singer Tone Deaf in a hit and run car accident in Paris. In May, well known on the Sex Pistols scene, the beautiful and much loved Tracie O' Keefe died of bone marrow cancer after a short illness. Within the next couple of years there would be more unexpected casualties amongst the Punk fraternity.

1978 also saw the 'New Wave' movement split off into many other different sub- genres and styles. Many reckoned that the term New Wave was just a watering down of the original Punk sound and although this was partly true, it's fair to say that many of the new groups at the time were clearly not Punk rockers in the strictest sense or if at all, but were very clearly part of something new and as such were what you could term close relatives of the Punk scene. 'New Wave' was a label thrown at groups like Squeeze, Elvis Costello and the Attractions, the Police, Ian Dury and the Blockheads and often the Jam. Also at the beginning of the year the term 'Power Pop' was being bandied around when describing music from the likes of Rich Kids, the Pleasers and Tonight etc.

Following a great performance on Top of the Pops, Tonight were booked to play Rotherham's Windmill club on January 26th, though this was actually the week after the venue had officially announced they had ended their 'New Wave' nights. The venue had slowly decreased their Punk and 'New Wave' nights during the first few months of 1978, officially ending with the Rich Kids gig but still putting on gigs by Cocksparrer and the Stukas. Violence was now becoming more common at the venue and last orders were sounded out for good not long afterwards.

Tony ... "Me and Andy Goulty loved all that Power Pop stuff at the start of 78. Records like Tonight's 'Drummer man', Radio Stars 'Nervous Wreck', 'Rich Kids' by Rich Kids were all super 45's. He would buy Record Mirror every week and we would pore over it, checking out all the new singles every Thursday."

John Harrison ... "I bought the Rich Kids single on red vinyl. It was the only one of theirs that really got played by the Punk kids at the time."

Rich Kids were 'ousted' Pistols bass player/songwriter Glen Matlock's new band and also included in their ranks 'Pistols singing duties refuser'... Slik's Midge Ure. They never hit the heights expected of them, disintegrating in the early spring of 1979 following a brave attempt at creating a new vision of Pop from the ashes of Punk.

Young Punk fans : me and Andy Goulty: Blackpool 1978

They played a series of local gigs around the region in early 1978; firstly the one at the Rotherham Windmill on January 19th and then at the Sheffield Top Rank on February 26th and the Doncaster Outlook on the following day. At a later date Malcolm Mclaren spoke some wise words when he came up with his own version of why Rich Kids did not become bigger, citing the reason being they arrived too quickly following Punk's first wave. In truth as Matlock himself agreed *'When we play gigs up north* (Sheffield, Doncaster etc), *the Punks seem to think that we are taking it (Punk) away from them."*

Timothy Green ... "I went to the Rich Kids one at the Windmill and enjoyed it. Yet again, the place was rammed. I was really disappointed and pissed off when they closed it down for Punk gigs."

Tony ... "Me and Andy were so naïve and young it's beyond belief. We had not really developed the 'New Wave' look that well. We would get our hair cut at Sweeny Todd hairdressers in town and after getting a spiky hair do, it would all fall flat within a few days. It was a nightmare trying to keep it stuck up at all. We would also dive around the room and mime along to Tonight's 'Drummer man' and Boomtown Rats 'Mary of the Fourth Form' singles that we had bought from Sound of Music shop and seen on Top of the Pops. It was fun but I am glad there were no camcorders around back then."

The year also saw the beginnings of a more rowdier street wise style of Punk emerge, which was also accompanied by the re-emergence of the skinhead movement that had been gradually gaining convertees since the middle of 1977 with Punk turned Skinhead bands like Skrewdriver. Howeve, it would be a London Punk group that would soon be a firm favourite with this new kind of updated skinhead movement.

Anthony Cronshaw ... "We were on a return visit to Doncaster Outlook and a new band was making their South Yorkshire debut - Sham 69 was their name and they had been gaining rave reviews. The first thing they did was give us a freebie in the shape of their record 'What have we got?' Their set was enlightening to say the least, as one thing that had changed- and that was the audience. Punks were now being joined by Skinheads and rumours surrounding this band were abounded. Some lads said that the name Sham 69 was short for 'Skin-Heads at Margate 69', but we were later to find out the truth- which was that it had come from some faded toilet graffiti that originally worded Hersham 69.

Some five days later I had ditched my Punk image and given myself the old crew cut and donned the old bovver boots and braces. This also fitted in with the terrace culture that was sweeping through Football.

Sham 69 were playing at the Polytechnic, and after returning from the football, we headed for the venue. There had already been trouble in the concert with some skins battling with the Punks and the students, but our crowd was not involved.

Above: Rich Kids sound the final death knoll for the 70's Rotherham Live Punk scene

This did not stop the police singling us all out and making us line up in a kind of identity parade for the security to pick out all the trouble causers. That night literally kicked off; Slaughter and the Dogs were on the bill and Sham played to a very appreciative audience with trouble never far away."

Steve Lloyd … "Sham 69 played the Outlook a few times. The first couple went great but the third one was when the skinheads started to come along and they ruined it. Jimmy Pursey was pissed off with them but there was nothing he could do really."

Phil Tasker … "When we (Vice Squad) supported Sham 69, we came back in to the dressing room after the gig and Jimmy Pursey was sat on a chair in a massive mohair jumper reading Moby Dick, he looked at us as if we were scum!"

Patrick Tierney … "I only saw Sham 69 once…I made sure that I got my free single 'What 'ave we got' though."

Sheffield band Vice Versa played their first gig supporting Wire at the Doncaster Outlook. Stepping in as support at the last minute, they were subjected to a hail of abuse and disdain from the mostly hardcore Punk crowd who had come along to see Wire – themselves never to be considered as the archetypall Punk band. Both these groups were attempting to broaden the horizons of the musical landscape, but unsurprisingly finding it hard to do so within the Punk climate. Wire were brought back on for two encores- Vice Versa were not. It would be a little longer before the local Punk generation would start to stretch their minds and taste in music past the confines of the average 3 minute Punk songs.

Stephen Singleton (Vice Versa/ABC) ... "We got shouted at and abused, but it was really good. We loved it because we really got up the noses of the people in Doncaster. We thought if we could do that then we were really onto something. It was just totally obscure stuff we'd written the week before. We'd got a gig and we said we'd do a 50 minute set so we wrote this music that meant something to us but nothing to anyone else, peppered with cover versions such as New York City by T-Rex. We were supposed to be getting paid £11 at the end of the gig but the club owner disappeared."
(From 'Beats working for a living' by Martin Lilleker)

Not long after that particular gig, a pre-fame Adam and the Ants also played the same venue. They were joined onstage by *known on the scene* Punkette and 'Sex' shop conspirator Jordan: who was at that time co-managing them and also performed vocals on their number 'Lou'. Again, the audience consisted of the hardcore Punk crowd, many of whom were around the 12 to 13 year old mark, and who exuberantly hurled themselves about and pogoed like there was no tomorrow. The typical Punk audience at the Outlook certainly knew how to have a good time and their reaction to live music was very much indicative of the time, but they were not yet ready for the progressive music of tomorrow from much of the Post-Punk groups of the time.

Another notable Punk performance at Doncaster Outlook in early 1978 was by Slaughter and the Dogs, during which gig, singer Wayne Barrett jumped into the audience and pogoed along with the kids resulting in an upstairs private party continuously sending down their middle class guests to view the 'shocking and outrageous vile antics' of 'real in the flesh' Punk Rockers.

Steve Lloyd ... "Ultravox were much punkier when they played the Outlook. I remember a group called The Secret playing there and they were a sort of bog standard Punk band and were getting spat at all the time. They started to spit back and everyone ended up getting absolutely drenched... Wayne County and the Electric chairs were good too and I have to say that Wayne was a really pleasant guy and really into the music. He would be dancing along to all the Punk music being played. Great guy, probably a hardcore tart though.

The Rezillos were great fun on and off stage and Magazine were a great band but Howard Devoto was difficult to talk to and very intense and it was hard to get used to that haircut. I was never a fan of the Buzzcocks though. Another group I enjoyed seeing there was Big in Japan."

The sound of American Punk had already been seen at the Outlook the previous summer with the Ramones and also Johnny Thunders and the Heartbreakers playing memorable gigs there; now it was the turn for the notorious rock n' roll sleazy rock of Cherry Vanilla to try and woo the Punks at the venue.

Starting the set with 'I know how to Hook' followed by 'Great big grown up girls', 'Foxy Bitch' and 'The Punk' the band played a musically proficient set with Cherry teasing the young Punks with *'All you dirty little boys at the front'* to which they responded by attempting to drag her from the stage. The bouncers did their usual stuff in dealing with the over excited Punks.

While one Punk fan had now had enough of the scene... others were only just becoming at one with its increasingly wider accessibility.

Steve Lloyd ..."I think that in Doncaster the Punk thing was a bit of a fad really. It came and it went. In early 1978 I moved to London and it was all over for me. I lost touch with Punk and when it became thrashier I wasn't interested anymore. I did like a lot of the Post-Punk that was coming through like the Mekons and Gang of Four."

Tony ... "I can remember almost all of the punk groups that played on Top Of the Pops as it were always a ritual to watch the show, whether at home or at the youth club or round at a mate's house. There was lots of punk and 'New Wave' singles coming out every week and our collections were rapidly growing. I know Punk had been and gone down in London by 1978, but it had taken it well into 1977 to make an impact in Sheffield and for kids like myself it was really 1978 that Punk broke through. There really was something special about that year for me. And this was when I was buying loads of records and not caring if they were hip or not with the hard core punk crowd. That attitude, around my surroundings anyway, would come about a little later when some of the punk kids were setting the rules about what you were supposed to like and not like. That eventually was part of what ruined it for me."

Timothy Green ... "At the Sound of Music record shop, I gradually started buying old soul and pop singles from those boxes at the back, rather than all the latest Punk and 'New Wave' sounds."

Varying opinions, by the local Punks themselves, were to be heard about the groups and music of 1978.

Bryan Bell ... "A lot of the Punk music was, to be honest, a load of crap. Some of it you had to wonder why on earth they had even bothered to put it down on vinyl."

Steve Haythorne ... "I didn't like the Tom Robinson Band; they were too much of a sing- along type of band for me. One of my favourite records at that time was Jonathan Richman's 'Morning of our Lives'."

David McKendry ... "The Stranglers always seemed strange, their age and musicianship made them seem somewhat false (as in them being Punk rock) and their fans started to look more skinhead/thug than punk."

Steve Haythorne ... "I loved the Stranglers LP's and was I desperate to like them live, but to be honest they were the worst group I ever saw play live. I Went to see them at Bingley Hall in Stafford in early 1978 and was so disappointed by them. It was just a wall of noise and I so much wanted to enjoy them. I saw them again, including when they supported The Who and they were still the same."

Paul Clarkson ... "Buzzcocks were great and always seemed to be more musically proficient than a lot of the groups."

Another new group from Manchester who had sprung from Punk were called The Fall and were fronted by enigmatic lead singer Mark E.Smith. As the standard Punky New Wavers were either splitting up, changing their image and direction and starting to dent the charts -

Right: Stranglers ticket (Steve Haythorne)

Harvey Goldsmith Entertainments presents
Ticket
Price
£3.00
THE STRANGLERS
in concert
(IN ASSOCIATION WITH ALBION MANAGEMENT AND THE DAILY MIRROR POP CLUB)
TUESDAY 30th MAY 1978 at 7.30 pm
BINGLEY HALL, STAFFORD
No re-admission for conditions see reverse to be retained and produced on demand.
Scot Auto Edin
Nº 24278

- (bringing with that very act a new generation of young Punk fans), original Punks were becoming more excited by Punk's bastard offsprings; a title that could never suit a band more aptly than The Fall who would play many gigs local gigs at various venues.

Timothy Green ... "I had seen the Fall the year before, first supporting Penetration at Liverpool Eric's and then with the Buzzcocks and Siouxsie and the Banshees at Manchester's Belle Vue. I had created my own 'Fall' badges and later on seeing the band support Buzzcocks at Sheffield Top Rank, I was wearing one with 'I like drugs' on and Mark E.Smith was after it but I wouldn't give it to him. Not long after, I finally joined the Anti-Nazi league, going along to my first rally in London; and also around this time, my musical tastes started to really change."

Patrick Tierney ... "The Fall. Saw them a few times; Once at Retford Porterhouse. Even their most fervent fan couldn't keep up with their line-up changes. They were great, though."

Steve Haythorne ... "I went to the City Hall gig with Eddie and the Hot Rods, Squeeze and Radio Stars on the same night. Never that bothered about the Hot Rods and Squeeze; they were too middle of the road for me, but Radio Stars were good. I bought some of their records after seeing them there. Around this time I saw Elvis Costello and the Attraction's at the City Hall and they were really good. They came on and it was a case of '*Hello! We are Elvis Costello and the Attractions and this is our music*'... no in between songs interruptions or anything, it was bang...*lets get on with it, its all about the* *music we are playing*. This was on the 'This Years Model' tour and I think it sold out. I loved it and returned to see them again at the same venue the year after."

Bryan Bell ... "I used to go to see punk groups all over the place. X-Ray Spex were great as were lots of others but surprisingly some of the ones you wouldn't expect to be that good were actually quite good. The Fly's I saw them play in Bradford and I enjoyed them. Mind you they played at some pub and when me and my mate went in we realised that it was a bikers' pub. My mate, not being the most tactful kind of guy says *'Fuckin' hell it's full of hairy Bastards!'* They were Hells angels too. They didn't take us on but we were lucky."

Anthony Cronshaw ... "The next visit to the Poly would come a month after seeing Sham 69 play there and this time it was the group 'Bethnal' that was making our boots move. They played a tremendous set and had the auditorium rocking to their version of 'Baba O' Reilly' by the Who."

Steve Haythorne ... "I liked John Cooper Clarke. He was one of the first of my generation to do that kind of poetry to music thing. He was a big influence on me."

Bryan Bell ... "To begin with Generation X weren't that hot but they improved as they went on. I saw them quite a few times, though I never got on with Billy Idol's style. It was like he was trying to be the punk version of Cliff Richard or something."

Tom Cleary ..."Generation X' were probably a lot better than anything Billy Idol did since, the first album was probably one of the best debuts of that time."

Paul Clarkson ... "I went to a very early Generation X gig at a club in Notts. Good old Billy's haircut! There were people there with moustaches, dodgy mullets and flares and they were shocked by our look and Billy Idol's."

Tony ... "The first Generation X LP (which I remember buying from a large record store on Chapel Walk, Sheffield's answer to Carnaby Street – where you could listen to the records on the shop's PA before buying) ...well I think that is a fantastic record, marred only by the over indulgent ramblings of the last half of 'Youth Youth Youth'. The second and third LP's were ok but nowhere near as good as the first one. I really regret never actually seeing Generation X play live. I almost got to see 'em once when they played the Limit club but got let down at the last minute by the kid I was going to see 'em with."

Pete Cooper ... "Generation X - I personally thought they played the worst gig I ever saw."

Anthony Cronshaw ... "I could never work out why hardly anyone liked Generation X, as far as I was concerned, they were a damn good band."

Generation X were Punks first Pin ups and as early as mid 1977 could be found in Day-Glo colour and gracing their coloured hair on the back page posters of teen girl mags such as Jackie whilst also appearing on the Marc Bolan show, Top of the Pops and Supersonic. Never over popular with the hard core Punk elite and certainly not purveyors of lyrical social realism, Generation X did manage to produce one classic debut album and an handful of quality Punk/Bubble gum 45's, perhaps their most anthemic being their answer to The Who's 'My Generation' which was now re-titled 'Your Generation'.

Despite their apparent call for the sixties generation to be cast aside, within a few months they would be championing the swinging sixties scene with Punk power pop single 'Ready Steady Go'. The NME were starting to lay odds on which New wave group would be the first to be top Mod group between Generation X and the Jam.

If Billy Idol was Punk's most easily recognisable Male pin up, then there is no doubt as to who was the 'New Wave's Female Pin up!

Left: Steve Haythorne's tickets

Tony … "I can remember going in Sound of music shop and asking for the new Blondie single 'I am always touched by your presence dear' and being asked if I wanted the normal 7" single or the 12" version. That was the first time I had heard of the 12" format so I bought it.

Debbie Harry! She was The Punk generation's Marilyn Monroe. Well when you are a teenager what better poster could you hope to have on your bedroom wall? Ok the Bionic Woman poster was fine to keep your Six Million Dollar Man annual company, but Blondie and Debbie Harry were so damn hot in 1978!"

Blondie's Sheffield university gig in February saw fans getting over zealous, groping and reaching for Debbie Harry as she held out and touched the overstretched hands whilst the group performed 'In the Flesh'. Debbie wore a mini skirt and vest with thigh length boots!

Simon Currie … "I can't remember too much from that night, we were too drunk but I remember that the place was heaving and me and my mate Tubby Everington were pogoing to something; Tubby got off with a Blondie look-alike (or so he thought),

129

bleached hair with black trim and she wore a black ripped all in one, there was lots of students and kids like us but that is all I can remember really."

Tony ... "There was a period during 1978, that Blondie were just perfect. Their style of 'New Wave' crossed over, obviously helped in great lengths by Debbie Harry's sex appeal. I bought their first two LP's and the first run of singles and they were one of my fave so-called Punk groups for a while."

There was, however, another contender for Punk's sexiest female pin up. Adverts bass player Gaye Advert was the first choice for many teenage Punk kids back in those days and finally does almost triumph in the end.

Paul Clarkson ..."Gaye Advert, yeah what a babe."

Stuart Bates ... "One of the reasons I was so excited about going to see the Adverts was 'cos I really fancied bass player Gaye Advert."

Phil Taylor (X – Rippers from Barnsley) ... "I met Gaye Advert back then and she was well fit. Saw her at one of the Punk festivals we played recently and she is still very tidy."

Paul Hutley singer of the Diks... "We supported the Adverts at the Top Rank and we were eventually evicted from backstage by the Adverts minders. I was being a nuisance and trying to cop off with Gaye Advert. I was drunk and was tormenting her- apparently I kept saying to her '*I want to kiss your lips a thousand times*."

Above: Debbie Harry at Sheffield University February 1978

Tony ... "I had a fantastic large poster of Gaye Advert on my bedroom wall. She was so sultry and far more down to earth sexy than the escapist and untouchable sexy-ness of Debbie Harry. Gaye was like the girl down the street but so much more gorgeous."

John Harrison ... "Gaye Advert? She was gorgeous all right. I remember telling a lad that I really fancied Gaye Advert and he looked at me strangely thinking I meant I had been fancying some advert for gay people or something. When I saw The Adverts live, I couldn't take my eyes off Gaye Advert. Bryan Bell and another of my mates grabbed me and threw me right onto the stage. I looked up and Gaye was there, looking down playing her Bass, looking luscious and gorgeous. "

Punk Rocker Phillip Wright didn't need to fantasise about Punk's favourite Pin-up. He met her and even received some flirtstious teasing from her.

Phillip Wright ... "Marcus Featherby put together a benefit gig (can't remember in aid of what?) at the Top Rank/Steelys, which featured local bands (from memory) the Deaf Aids, Artery and the Negatives (who I once opened for as DJ for their gig at KGB's on Abbey dale road)..Cherry Vanilla (a female singer who was part of the early New York punk scene, and hung out with Andy Warhol in the early 70's, plus Bowie, etc.) was also there with of course the Adverts.

Above: Punk pin up Gaye Advert

The Adverts were still well known but had not had a hit for a while. Most of the blokes in the audience were, of course, only interested in Gaye Advert... dressed all in black as always. After the gig I got backstage with a few people. Gaye Advert nudged a girl in our crowd and said *'your boyfriend is quite dishy!'* pointing at me! She said, *'oh he's not my boyfriend'*, so Gaye said something like *'come and sit here next to me young man'*... in a sort of spider catching a fly voice. She was a good laugh and she asked what music I liked and stuff and we had a few free drinks. She seemed very exotic and needless to say I was smitten, I seem to think she kissed my cheek as I left but that may be wishful thinking and old age blurring my memory.

Cherry Vanilla gave me one of her albums as I left and she seemed quite jolly and a good laugh too. She was of course much older than every body else, probably early to mid 30's at that time I would guess."

Aside from inciting anger from local Punks, Siouxsie's misconceived and inflammatory fascist iconism, which was now being gradually dropped, didn't halt young Punks' admiration; the first signs of becoming a female punk figurehead being just around the corner...whilst the new wave itself held other attractions!

Tom Cleary ... "I fell in love with Siouxsie and tried to date as many girls who looked like her until I found out why they wore all that makeup!"

The 'New Wave' and Punk singles were coming out thick and fast by the middle of 1978. Not surprisingly, the music press had long since kick started their anti-punk stance and were always on the prowl for the next thing to emerge from the Post-Punk fall out. Nethertheless to the young teenage kids who lived in the suburbs of Sheffield, Doncaster and Rotherham, the energy and appeal of Punk and its 'New Wave' cousin was still as exciting as ever. To a new generation of 13 to 16 year old school kids the stance of Punk was just what they needed to feed the restless growing pains of being young.

Above: me during late Summer 1978

Rotherham Punk Paul White whose nickname was 'Sugar' was one of a small crowd of younger Punk fans in Rawmarsh who were rapidly getting to hear the Punk and 'New Wave' LP's. His brother worked for Virgin Records and would send him the latest LP's through to listen to.

Paul White (Sugar) ... "Yeah, it was great having my brother being able to get a hold of all of the albums. I had the first LP's from Magazine', Rich Kids, 999 and others. They were all promo ones. Later on my record collection was what you would class as hard core Punk."

Tony ..."We could hardly afford to buy LP's. They used to cost £3.49 at r.r.p, which was a lot of money for us kids back then. Most of the New Wave LP's I bought were usually bought when they had gone cheap.

I can remember one Christmas all I got for presents was a load of punk albums. I reckon I got about 25 LP's and they were all out of the bargain section of the 'Sound of music' record shop costing a quid, or less, each. All I did that Christmas was to listen to all these records. The main exception to this rule for me was with the Jam. I had to have them on release day; Also likewise with the Clash. A school friend sold me his brother's 'Give em enough Rope' LP a few weeks after it came out. Apparently, his brother was a Heavy Metal fan and bought the record cos of Sandy Pearlman producing it. I managed to buy every Clash record straight away after that. Andy Goulty was big on The Ramones and in 1978 was starting to buy their records beginning with the singles and then the 'Road to Ruin' LP."

Andy Goulty ... "I bought the Ramones 'It's Alive' LP too. It was never off the turntable... classic record that one."

132

Tony … "I liked 'Sheena is a Punk Rocker' and some of their stuff but I wasn't that up on the Ramones to begin with…The first one I bought was the first LP followed by all the rest of their stuff…but in 1978, I was too obsessed with the Jam and the Clash to give them the time on my record player that they deserved. I love that b-side at the time though 'I don't want you'. Andy was always playing that one.

That Spring and Summer of 1978 was soundtracked by Boomtown Rats, Stranglers, Buzzcocks, Tom Robinson Band, the Lurkers, Rezillos, Ian Dury and the Blockheads, Siouxsie and the Banshees, the Motors, The Clash and of course the Jam. It was a time of going along to the fun fair in Rotherham – where Tescos supermarket now stands – of hanging around the Park with our mates and getting chased by the cops. I went to Great Yarmouth for my hols that summer and I missed the Jam playing there by a matter of a day. That was a right downer. I did catch a glimpse of who I thought were The Rezillos playing at a pub near the seafront. The door was open and I popped my head in to see who was playing and yeah there they were (or so I thought…it turns out it was some club band playing 'Top of the Pops'). My brother soon back tracked and pulled me out of there. Anyway I did have the consolation of coming home from that holiday with the Clash 'White Man in Hammersmith Palais' single. That summer was also a time of the massive music centres that were all the rage and the records that we were playing on them was the stuff of Our Generation."

Richard Chatterton … "In 1978 I had started to try and listen to everything in Punk. I watched Revolver on TV, acquainted myself with the Vibrators and The Buzzcocks, saw Devo and 999 on the Whistle Test, bought the NME and so on. I borrowed a tape off a friend and took it on holiday with me with all the three chord Punk classics on.

I couldn't afford many singles or albums so I bought ex- juke box singles. 'Love You more'/ 'Noise Annoys' by Buzzcocks, 'Hong Kong Garden' by Siouxsie, Stranglers 'Grip' and when I could afford them, I bought 'Never Mind the Bollocks', Damned Damned Damned and the Jam and Clash first albums. I remember one of my friend's cousin was called Iggy – who as well as having a cool Punk name - had been along to see Siouxsie and the Banshees at the Limit club."

Timothy Green … "By early to mid 1978, I was starting to lose interest in Punk; I still ensured that my trousers didn't go out at the bottom though and I bizarrely got some grief from some Teds (Pillocks!) in Rotherham town centre."

As the Punk and 'New Wave' groups were breaking through and denting the charts, and in turn bringing Punk to the attention of the nation's young teenage music fans, there was a new wave of what would be termed Post-Punk groups starting to come through. Mostly signed up by the independent labels that had sprung up out of the Punk explosion, these new groups were inspired by Punk but were aiming for something different- taking their influences from a whole array of different styles of music. Groups such as The Mekons, Scritti Politti, Gang of Four, the Raincoats, Au-Pairs and as previously mentioned Manchester's the Fall (who, in 1978 were blessed with Bass player Johnny Brown from Rotherham being with the group for all of three weeks - not bad going in 'Fall' terms).

Sheffield also saw its own Post-Punk groups emerging who – unlike their contemporaries The Human League who would manage to break through a couple of years later during the Punk fall out – these groups, like a lot of the Punk ones before them, would have a limited life span.

Above: Home grown Sheffield Fanzines

Long since forgotten groups like Vena Cava (who would play gigs around Sheffield and one at Rotherham Arts centre), Used Toys (who only managed a few gigs throughout their short career), TV Product (who recorded a single 'Nowheres safe' for Marcus Featherby's Limited Edition Records label and also included future Artery member Simon Hinkler) and Ashmore's Brain. It must also be recognised... the importance and massive influence of Cabaret Voltaire who had already been working steadfastly in creating their own musical vision: one in fruition long before Punk had burst onto the region's map.

Not far behind the Post-Punk groups were Sheffield's fanzine explosion. 'Gun-Rubber' had been the very first, followed by 'Home Groan', future ABC star Martin Fry's 'Modern Drugs' and in no particular order 'Tigers on t'moor', 'Proper Gander', 'Bath Banker', 'Grey Matter, 'Pink Flag' and one of the most enduring of the era 'NMX' which was run by They Must be Russians member Martin Lacey. These 'Steel City' fanzines would cover all the newly formed and gigging groups of the Sheffield area and beyond. Almost universally throughout, and not surprisingly, the zines had an industrial look and feel to them. The grey zerox look and lay out would mirror the greyness and smog of the city. Meanwhile, the new generation of local Punk influenced teenagers were still absorbing the initial shock waves of punk and keen to find their own identity.

Tony ... "Punk for me personally, was always meant to be for the kids. It was probably the only music scene to so obviously appeal to kids aged from 12 year old to 17. It was dangerous and I got more excitement and euphoria out of Punk at the age of 13 to 15 than at any other time. It was the perfect sound track to those teenage years.

I had been buying Punk and so called 'New Wave' records for quite a while by the middle of 1978 but when the Jam released 'All Mod Cons' that was a major event for me...I bought it from Boots in Rotherham town centre (from their old High street store when they sold records upstairs).

Above: Doncaster Punks - 1978

It was supposed to be a Christmas present, but I would sneak plays on it every single day from its release until I could officially (re- open) it as a present. I had been playing it on my old dansette record player upstairs and now knew every single lyric on the whole LP. What a classic it was too... I ended 1978 eager to fully embrace the 'New Wave' and become a part of it all. At that age I was bored and restless and really wasn't that interested in anything else but having a good time and listening to music. I suppose that without Punk I would have become a completely different person. Up until then I wasn't that sure of whom I was anyway? Lots of the young Punk kids became so involved in the music to find out who they really were. It was an Identity thing, though we didn't realise this at the time."

135

Chapter Seven

'Identity it's the Crisis can't you see'

"For me Punk was like a Television being turned on for the first time and seeing everything in Technicolor, and that was just the hair. It was great to stand out and be noticed" – **Tracy Stanley (Rotherham Punkette)**

Above: Local Punkettes Helen and Joanne

Tony … "The first time I heard the first Clash LP was when I began to take music seriously. Before hearing that record it had all been about the energy, the laughs, the venting of my frustration through fast and raw rock n' roll. Now I wanted to change things and I started to feel differently about my surroundings. I no longer felt the need to hear the 'mostly worthless teachings' at school. I wanted to decide for myself what was important. There is not a single bad track on the Clash and for over thirty years or so since hearing it I have never once begun to tire of it. My copy is battered, the cover is a right state and it crackles like hell, but it still sounds like the finest and most important rock n' roll record ever made."

Paul Clarkson … "Most of the teenagers and early 20's kids in Rotherham and Sheffield were a bit behind in the Punk fashion/music stakes in those days. Those that were into it usually appeared to be less extreme."

Old school blazers, drain pipe trousers and jeans, skinny ties, narrow lapels, mohair jumpers, ripped t-shirts, plastic trousers, tennis shoes and hair all over the place. This was a typical Punk's clothes requirement. Sheffield and Rotherham were much less fashion orientated and outrage concerned than the London Kings Road lot. But then it could be said that the music was always far more important to the lads up this neck of the woods.

Tony … "One of my favourite singles of the whole Punk era is 'Up against the wall' by Tom Robinson Band. I know they weren't classed as Punk as such, more of a protest - rock group, but that record is a classic. The lyrics are fantastic too *'Dark haired dangerous school kids, vicious suspicious sixteens'* what an opening line for a song. It just mirrors the danger of being a teenager at the time and it could have been written for my own generation; the second wave of Punk Rock kids. I bought the first T.R.B LP too in May 1978. It came with a free T.R.B fist stencil and a little later on me and a mate- Stephen Doidge- we sprayed it on the wall of a local snicket. It stayed there for years afterwards. In fact it could still be there 30 odd years later."

At one time, students in Sheffield had been almost all rock fans and hippy types; protesting vainly at the wave of new music that was threatening their established rules and music. Now, things were beginning to change and the spirit of Punk was spreading through the common rooms of the Polytechnics and universities.

Tom Cleary … "The hope and the buzz of possibility were tangible. And yet; we were unwelcome or somehow 'other', even from the guys who were helped by the change, like steelworkers or whatever. They seemed to go out of their way to pick on us. There was very little appreciation of the enormity of it all, but plenty of eyes on the 'main chance'. Even then, there was a kind of disbelief that the sincerity of the bands could survive the experience of wealth. But everyone wanted to try. I was a 'freshly peeled' kid (in both the raw prawn and John Peel sense) and was looking to get away from home to somewhere I felt comfortable, somewhere…tangible, and Sheffield fit the bill. I dropped into a group of people who were all prepared to give life a go and took to it with gusto."

Tony … "Around this time there were a handful of like minded kids at our school that were listening to Punk and New Wave. Apart from myself Andy Goulty and Pete Roddis, there was Nicky Booth (he was well into The Stranglers) and two lads who were more hard core punks (Sugar and his mate Paul Maiden) who were into Slaughter and the Dogs, Eater, Drones etc. Dean Stables was starting to like a lot of the Punk stuff too…and Andy Morton was listening to 999 etc. Together we were all picking up on the Punk scene quite quickly by now. If we had been born maybe two years earlier we may have been going to see the Sex Pistols on the ill fated Anarchy tour; well the dates that got played anyway."

Punk and 'New Wave' was now crossing over to an even younger generation.

Gill Frost (Young Punk fan from Rotherham) … "It was my older brother's fault. There I was, happily listening to my Abba records, when he brought home the Sex Pistols 'Never

Mind the Bollocks' album. I have no idea why I loved it so much; I certainly wasn't pretending to like it to be 'cool', as I was only about ten years old and wouldn't have been clever enough to do that. But I couldn't get enough of it. I do remember not having the usual taste when it came to music, as I thought most of what was in the charts at the time was a load of old rubbish (apart from Abba, of course).

Try as I might I couldn't get my friends to share my new-found enthusiasm. I remember forcing one friend in particular to listen to the Sex Pistols every time she came round and I just couldn't understand why her eyes would start to glaze over."

Whilst the local young teenagers were getting to grips with Punk and picking up on the attitude of groups such as Sham 69 - who along with Boomtown Rats and the Jam were inarguably responsible for many youngsters' first real taste of Punk - meanwhile older and more seasoned Punk fans ,who were becoming skinheads, were also taking the opportunity to get to know their heroes first hand.

Anthony Cronshaw ... "Sham 69 was now taking up a lot of our time as we travelled across the Pennines to Manchester to see them play at the Rafters venue. Again, there was trouble, but this had nothing to do with Sham; the support band just happened to be scousers and the Mancs lot hated them. Sham played a terrific set that night, but after they had finished we hung back a bit as the trouble had spilled out onto the streets.

In the meantime, we got talking to 'Sham' bass player Dave Treganna discussing their music etc. Then we pissed off back to Yorkshire - leaving Lancashire's troubles behind, as they were still slugging it out on the streets outside the venue.

Soon Sham would be back in Sheffield and the Top Rank was the venue this time. I was still earning a crust at my job in Rotherham, and once my shift was done, I headed for town to meet the lads. I'd just got off the bus and was making my way to the Claymore, when my mate Malc stuck his head out of a mini-bus and shouted me over. It turned out that they had been in town all afternoon and him and Shaun had been helping with the gear, and in return they were invited back to the band's hotel for a beer.

We ended up tagging along and were soon rubbing shoulders with Pursey (Sham singer) and co at this nice hotel in Nether Edge. Before long, we were back on the bus and heading for the gig with the good news that we were all now classed as being part of the band as unofficial roadies. When we got in to the Rank, I helped myself to a beer backstage, before taking up my position at the side of the stage. I looked down into the audience and could see some of the football boys thinking to themselves *'What's that bastard doing up there?'* When the set was over we staggered off stage and sat back enjoying a beer in the comfort of the dressing room. The crowds had long gone and we gave Neil and Albie a hand with the gear. All of Sham's equipment fitted in a transit van and as the last piece of gear was being slotted in, Shaun asked Albie if we could join them on tour. He pissed off to ask the band and returned saying that they had said ok to the idea.

Back at the hotel, we hit the booze - that was the tradition - but disappointingly, no TV's were thrown through the Hotel window. But then this was Sham 69 not the Who or The Stones. Looking at the tour dates there was Glasgow, Edinburgh, and Sunderland and then back to the Outlook in Doncaster again. Looking in my pockets I had the princely sum of £3. I pissed off home and told Shaun (who stopped with the band), that I would be back in the morning. Malc was gutted because he'd got his City and Guilds to do and pass on Friday, so he was out of the equation for going on tour."

During Sham 69's set at Doncaster Outlook, a solitary fan jumped on stage and after singing at the side of Jimmy Pursey, he then grabbed the mike out of Pursey's hand and yelled 'Wednesdays'. After a few songs the stage was full of fans and they were told by Pursey to take no notice of the bouncers who were trying to clear the stage. Dave Parsons from Sham 69 recalls one of their 1978 era gigs in Sheffield.

Dave Parsons (Sham 69) … "I remember one gig where the bouncers were really fucking with the kids, letting some in and not others, even some who had pre - bought tickets, and then Jimmy saying something to the bouncers whilst we were playing. After the gig while sitting in the dressing room the bouncers appeared in the doorway and told every one to get out. At first we didn't realize they were talking to the band as well, but things started to get a bit heavy and it all became very clear that none of us were welcome - I seem to remember a very quick exit and at one point one of the bouncers pushing one of our fans headfirst down some escalators."

Whereas a year previously it had been the Sex Pistols who were inspiring the young Punks of the area, now, for many, it would be Sham 69 for a few exciting months during the summer of 1978.

Tony … "I can remember when my mate Andy first had the skinhead. This was around the time Sham 69 were breaking through with 'Angels with dirty faces', I had seen 'em play this on Top of the Pops and gone straight out to buy it. I also began to realise that a lot of skins were moving onto punk. It was also around this time, about mid 1978, that me and Andy went to Blackpool. We saw our first proper mod there, though at the time we looked at him and saw him as a Jam fan. At this time I had a kind of vaguely mod type of hairstyle based on Weller's, but it was always falling flat. We never used stuff like hair gel back then. Most of the other kids at school still had longish hair. There was still probably only a handful that was into Punk and 'New Wave' at that time."

Meanwhile Sheffield lad Anthony Cronshaw was still having the time of his life with Sham 69.

Anthony Cronshaw …"Well that was it I was going on tour with Sham 69. Tony, their tour manager was driving the mini-bus up to Scotland with me and Shaun, while the roadies were bringing up the van. The band were travelling up by train and meeting up with us in Glasgow.

We stopped off in Carlisle for dinner and as I slumped into my chair, I asked Shaun how much cash he had got on him. He answered that he had a couple of quid. We scoured the menu and tucked right at the bottom was chips and egg, I budgeted that we could have that and half a beer each, while Albie and the rest of them were knocking back the ale and tucking into the finest fucking steak dinner the Scottish had on offer.

140

We'd sat there nearly an hour before I pushed our money towards them to settle our part of the bill. Albie turned and uttered the words *'What yer facking doing it's all for free on the road, Polydor- Shams label- pick up the tab'.* Well I was gutted; we had sat there with half a beer each when we could have been chucking it down the neck!

We arrived in Glasgow to find that the concert venue was up nine flights of stairs and there was no lift; it was called Satellite City and was in the Apollo complex. With the job eventually done, it was time to go back to the B&B for something to eat, before returning to the venue for the gig. Sham was excellent, as always. My mate Malc managed to join us in Edinburgh and by the time we'd camped up in Sunderland another half a dozen lads had joined us.

It was in Sunderland that we met the Londoners who followed Sham, this included Vince Riordon who would later play with the Cockney Rejects, but in the meantime we were the Sham army, as the music press had labelled us.

It was at this gig that trouble reared again, but ironically it was the students who caused the bother this time. We'd finished setting up the gear and decided to find a boozer to wet our whistle. On leaving the venue one of the students had a stamp in his hand and before he could stamp anybody, Vince snatched it and planted it on his forehead with a few fine choice words to show he meant business. We all fell about laughing as this kid had a blue square on his bonce.

When we returned to the venue for the gig we could see loads of kids outside and Jimmy Pursey was going mental. It turned out that the security students were not letting anybody in unless they had a ticket or a student card. Most of the kids had travelled from all over the North East to see Sham; but would they fuck let them in. As a result it was one of the most poorly attended Sham 69 gigs I'd witnessed; there seemed to be more outside than in the place. The students' security lot tried to get a bit heavy handed as well so us lot and the cockneys evened it up a bit and backed the loppy bastards out of the venue. Sunderland was soon behind us and after a free day with us all on the lash- courtesy of Polydor- we were heading back to Doncaster.

After the Doncaster gig, I left the tour to return to work, but Malc and Shaun carried on to London with Sham. While we were watching Top of the Pops in our local, who should appear on the box but those two, as Sham belted out 'Angels with Dirty Faces'. The group had made the charts and by the time we joined them on our travels again, they had ditched the transit and B&B's for executive travel and proper hotel accommodation. That summer of 1978 would see the lads follow Sham across the country and as those times were; trouble was never far away."

Tony ... "Back then I felt so angry and frustrated. My dad had passed away at the very start of 1978 and I felt really pissed off about that, but at the same time it gave me so much more freedom to do what I wanted. I don't know how much of a Punk I would have been if my dad had still been around but I could never accept the authority of school. I was always ready to rebel against the ones who were telling me what to do. Punk perfectly reflected how I felt back then and its energy just completely took me over."

The idea of how a punk looked was a new one. The look had only been created just over a year ago and so the classic uniformed Punk look was not yet that prevalent. Many young teenage Punk fans were approaching the style and image with a mix of uninformed naivety and the Media's version of what a Punk should look like. With this cheap and quick approach, the Punk kids around the area started to create their own version of Punk attire.

Helen McLaughlin (Rotherham Punkette) ... "I can't exactly remember the exact moment it (getting into Punk) happened although I do recall opening the huge broadsheet 'News of the World' and reading about Sid Vicious, Johnny Rotten et al and all the nasty things they had been up to and how they and their followers would be the downfall of 'Great' Britain etc..."

Above: Joanne Orgill and Helen McLaughlin 'New Wave' 1978 style

Nicky Booth ... "I had always been a bit creative, so I learned how to use my mum's sewing machine and began converting flared trousers into drainpipes. Over the next year or two everything changed. X Clothes opened in Leeds selling punk gear, but I could never afford it so I went to jumble sales and converted clothes instead. I made bum flaps (I never understood what that was all about but they looked great) and being a bit arty I started painting punk t-shirts for myself (and for friends at £5 a go). I was a regular customer at the pet stall on Rotherham market where you could get dog clips – just the job for finishing off home made bondage trousers."

Tony ... "The first time I decided I was going to deliberately dress up like a Punk was a bit crazy really. I suppose looking back it's a bit daft and typifies the kind of image that some of us younger less informed kids thought would make us look Punk. Anyway I decided to tear bits out of my white t-shirt and emblazon it with punk groups logos...then as a coincidence the bad tooth I had at the time started bleeding again so I spit the blood out and smeared it on my t-shirt... '*Sid Vicious would surely have been proud*' I thought. Then I tore up my school blazer, chalked The Clash across the back and put some badges on it. My jeans were an old pair of Brutus ones that were now too small for me but still flared out at the knees, so I stuck some safety pins in 'em to make 'em straight leg. I scrunched up my hair with Vaseline and in my head I looked the part. I walked the streets like I bloody owned them hoping to get plenty of weird looks and jealous comments. I went to the shop and around the block a few times but nothing...no outrage no disgust no threats...Christ what's wrong it's not like Rawmarsh was full of Punks was it. Oh well it seemed a good idea at the time. Later on with the dyed hair and stuff I did get noticed...but not in a way to my liking."

Steven Doidge (Rotherham Punk Rocker) ... "My Mum has never forgotten me going out with my pyjamas on, just to be different."

Paul Clarkson ... "I had a Mohawk like Travis Bickle (Robert De Niro's character in 'Taxi Driver') at one point."

John Harrison ... "We would wear plastic trousers, mohair jumpers, string vests and always used to wear baseball boots. The Jam used to wear them and I always used to make a point of wearing them. Spiky hair was a must. Some of the kids used to call me 'Sid Vicious' (laughs). I used to rip my clothes, my jeans and stuff. Now they bloody buy em already like that (laughs)."

Bryan Bell ... "We would to go to X-Clothes in Leeds- it later on also opened up a shop in Sheffield which wasn't anything special really."

Gary Gillott (Chippie) ... "I used to go to X-Clothes in Leeds and Sheffield. We would buy the crazy colour for our hair from there."

Tony ... "I painted my Doc Martin boots yellow! I must have looked like something out of a sci-fi film. You wouldn't have got knocked over by a car with them on, that's for sure. I also always used to wear my Dads old scarf that he had worn to go to work down the pit. That is one thing that I still have from those days."

Andrew Morton (Rotherham Punk fan) ... "I would sometimes buy Punk t-shirts from a Punk t-shirt shop on Howard Street in Sheffield. It was only there for a couple of months and I reckon the t-shirts were dodgy. They had racks of them for £3 each but I don't think that they were official ones – they must have screen printed them in the back of the shop or something."

Tony ... "Punk clothes were great for a while I suppose. They mirrored how you felt at the time. I never really went in for that typical Punk look for that long. I would go through phases. Sometimes it would be gear like PVC trousers, mohair jumpers, coloured jeans and the obligatory tennis shoes. Clash style combat trousers were great. Me and my mates went to X Clothes in Leeds a few times but hardly ever bought anything. The only thing I can remember buying from there was a pair of bus conductor trousers with the thin red line down the side of each legs and that was as much for the fact that they were the only pair of black straight legged trousers I had set my eye on all that year. The D.I.Y look was my favourite Punk style with zips all over the place at first; then less of them. Black denim shirts washed loads of times to get that faded Clash style look. Then I would have patches of the Clash first LP sewn on the pockets and a couple of zips down the front. Also a pvc jacket and hair like I had been dragged through the bush backwards, sideways and back again."

Stuart Bates … "We were not your archetypical punks. We didn't go for the leather jackets and bondage trousers. We wore tight jeans, pointed toed shoes, ripped and pinned t- shirts. Most of the shirts we made ourselves – just plain tees which we splashed or ripped and I made stencils on a machine at work, which we then spray painted through onto the shirts things like 'Anarchy', 'Destroy', 'The Clash', 'White Riot' etc. We also made our own badges from pictures in the Melody Maker and NME."

Tony … "Funnily enough, I did the home made badge thing as well. I did a great Clash one with a Joe Strummer picture that I cut out of an observer Punk supplement. I did this during an art lesson at school. I covered it with sellotape."

Pete Roddis (Rotherham Punk Rocker) … "We would go to Rotherham market and buy a load of those big zips they had for sale and then I would go and ask my Mum to sew 'em all over my jeans. She would look at me 'gone out', as if to say *'is he serious or what'*. The other Punk clothes were army combat trousers with the pockets on the side of the leg, like The Clash used to wear. We used to wear Donkey jackets and then I had the coloured trousers and some red bondage trousers. Once I had to try and run with them on, to get away from someone. I didn't get very far. We would also go to X-Clothes in Leeds, but we didn't often buy much."

Tony … "Bryan Bell had managed to acquire Joe Strummers shirt at a Clash gig. It was one of those 'White Riot' tour style ones with the epaulettes and tower block patches, zips and pockets and the like. When I saw him wearing that round at the local shops round Thorogate I was so envious. He sold it to me for £3 eventually and I wore it with pride. It looked so much better than my home-made 'Clash' style shirts. Some years later I reminded Joe about the shirt and he remembered it. I believe it's now in a New York museum as part of a Punk memorabilia tribute or something."

Paul Clarke was a young teenager from Rotherham who had started to tune into Punk music towards the end of 1978 … "I can't remember what exactly got me into Punk. I do know I missed the early days. I have a Damned record sleeve autographed as Dave Vanian 1979, which I remember I got signed when I saw the Damned at the Top Rank. I had been into Punk a while before then. I was knocking about with lads who were buying these records and the vinyl was appearing in yellow, green, pink and gold etc. The music was actually good, not just because it was a change from the usual radio drone. It was different. My dad was into the Beatles (no shame in that), but my mum had been into Cliff Richard and Gene Pitney (ouch!). So when I had Top of the Pops on and the likes of Generation X were on, it was like *'Come and watch my music old people! It rules."*

Richard Chatterton … "The floodgates were opened wide- I spiked and dyed my hair, bought mail order bondage trousers and my Mum made me two more pairs; one leopard skin and one tartan. My dad was bemused when I pulled out a pair of his never worn straight leg jeans from the airing cupboard. *'About a year ago you would have laughed at them trousers'* he said .My appearance drastically changed from daring to wear a mohair jumper and straight leg jeans and sticking my hair up with soap at the school disco to wearing eye liner and a dog collar I bought in Chesterfield- where I would start to go to the 'Fusion' club every Friday night. A girl at school said I had really gone wild."

Above: Richard Chatterton

Paul Clarke ... "I was drawn into putting loads of zips on jeans and taking a marker pen to plain t-shirts, sounds daft now, but for me at the time it gave me that bit of Identity. It made me feel a part of something and the zips etc was the badge that stated I was a Punk Rocker. It felt good and I also felt like the old apron strings were finally off and I was out into the big wide world."

Phillip Wright ... "As 1977 became 1978, a few specialist clothes shops started selling 'New Wave' clothes, drainpipe or peg trousers, thin ties, small collar shirts, and Rebina Shoes sold thin, pointed shoes and black and white 'Jam' shoes, just like The Jam wore. This meant you could get into pubs and clubs and still look like you were different."

Tony ... "We had so many laughs back then and Punk was our soundtrack. I can remember many times when we would be crying with laughter and have those absolute belly aching laughs. It was usually at someone else's expense but we never meant any real harm."

Pete Roddis ... "I think back now, and I wonder how we got back from all those gigs. How did we get home afterwards, I mean me and Tony were only 13 to 15 and we were hanging around and going to see gigs in Sheffield. We would go to see 999, the Damned, Undertones (who were a tremendous band to see live, unbelievable).

Also we saw the Jam, Stiff Little Fingers, Devo, Siouxsie and the Banshees and the Clash. Amazing times; I think, also that, considering our age, we were very much ahead of ourselves and most of the other kids our age."

Tony ... "Andy Goulty was the first of our lot to buy that Wayne County 'Fuck off' e.p in 1978 and we used to play it really loud in my Mum's front room. You should have seen the faces on the 'old codgers' walking by when they heard it...Oh man the laughs we had were unbelievable."

Chiz … "Punk clothes are great for the girls because they are the sexiest clothes ever. I did however, in my teens, have a pair of furry leopard skin trousers which I wore till they were almost bald! I came off my motorbike once while wearing them and they ended up looking like road kill. I had blonde Billy Idol hair at that time as well so girls used to ask if they could stroke my trousers. Shallow I know… but I wasn't complaining."

Steven Doidge … "I have got some fantastic memories of our younger days; of sex drugs and rock and roll. Well maybe our punk days were not quite like that - although they were enjoyable. I do remember the first time I got up to pogo to a Sex Pistols song at our school youth club. After the song had finished I was fucking knackered. I could not believe what hard work it was. I later went back to my girlfriend at the time - Sharon - with sweat running underneath my stripy mohair jumper and she told me I stunk. I only went to a few concerts but I remember the Clash walking off stage for a short while due to being covered in spit. Also there was the time I went to a 999 concert with green food colouring in my hair which looked quite good until it started raining on the way there and it all ran down my face. And then there were the record collections, fantastic; I wish I still had some of those picture discs and coloured vinyl singles. I would not swap those times."

Andy Lee (Dronfield/Sheffield Punk) … "I became a Punk whilst still at school, listening to the Sex Pistols and the Stranglers. I grew up in Dronfield and there was a band called Repulsive Alien, who were on the 'Bouquet of Steel' compilation LP put out by Marcus Featherby. Repulsive Alien became my friends as I moved more towards Punk and I started hanging out with a couple of them at school and saw less and less of my old friends. They practised at the village Hall in Holmesfield, so a load of fans used to go and watch them practise. The group had a hardcore of about 6 fans that went to every practice and every single gig that they played. Some of these fans, including myself, tried to form a band called The Epsilons; we were great at graffiti, but we never got round to gigging. I soon started going to gigs at the Top Rank seeing the Skids, Ruts, Stranglers, the Damned etc - in-between watching Repulsive Alien playing Holmesfield and around Sheffield."

But the image for young New wave kids was still a hybrid of many different styles.

Joanne Orgill … "Up until that point (getting into Punk), I'd been pretty much the perfect daughter – fairly quiet-ish, worked hard at school and I was in the Girl Guide band. My parents were quite horrified by how I changed over the next few years as I became more interested in punk music (and punk boys!)."

Helen McLaughlin … "The transformation was almost overnight I had all my hair cut off and spiked in a little hairdressers in Mansfield Road, Rotherham and dyed it black at home. My mum altered mine and Joanne Orgil's jeans so they were skin tight.
My mum was handy on the old sewing machine as Joanne also recalls and made and altered me various items of clothing including leather and p.v.c. mini skirts and knitted me some massive holey jumpers."

146

Tony ... "About that time, we really didn't know how to look cool really. It was a mix of all sorts really; Jam shoes, mohair type jumpers, combat trousers, tight fitting Adidas sports shirts, Doc Martin boots, donkey jackets, old denim jackets, cheap plastic imitation leather jackets, pin stripe trousers taken in from the knee, plain white t-shirts with groups' names written all over, tennis shoes and fly away spiky hair that would hardly ever stick up. The proper Punks in the cities and especially down south would have pissed themselves at us lot, but we were having fun. This was the summer of Jilted John, Plastic Bertrand's 'Ca Plane pour Moi'(also a favourite of 'Joe Strummer's at the time), Rezillos - 'Top of the Pops', Blondie, the Jam's 'David Watts', Clash - 'White Man' single, Patti Smith, X-Ray Spex 'Identity', Siouxsie and the Banshees 'Hong Kong Garden', Ian Dury 'What a Waste', Stranglers - 'Black and White' LP, Buzzcocks and the Sid Vicious version of 'My Way'. It was a great summer."

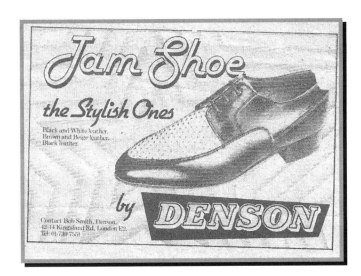

Above: the classic 'Jam' shoe as available on Rotherham outdoor market in 1978

The expression of dressing Punk was not always scorned upon by the older generation.

Helen McLaughlin ... "I don't think I realised so much at the time how really cool my Mum was about it. Joanne's parents and grandparents, I think, thought I was leading her down the path to hell, especially her grandma who lived across the road from my family and I

- don't think they were all that keen on us being such good friends as before all this she had been a 'good girl', although saying that, so was I. We were, however, inseparable and are still good friends."

Joanne Orgill (Rotherham Punkette) ... "Helen McLaughlin and myself considered ourselves to be the only proper female punk rockers in our school! Our transition into the full regalia was a cautious one. Just wearing a tie and huge badges was radical enough for us in the early days but we became more and more daring. For me, it wasn't a matter of wanting to shock but just wanting to look a bit different – and quirky really!

I remember Helen's Mum being really cool about it all to the point of running up a bum flap for her on her sewing machine. Looking back, it's interesting to recall how some parents reacted to the whole thing. Some just put it down to a phase in their children's lives and didn't appear to get too hung up about it all. Others (including my own, to a degree) were horrified by the whole scene and thought that it was turning us into

147

monsters! I remember getting on the bus one day with full Siouxsie Sioux make up on and possibly green hair. I got the usual stares but expected a friendlier reaction when I saw my Grandma with my young cousin, Scott. So I was quite flabbergasted when she refused to acknowledge me and told Scott to do the same! I was very close to my grandparents so felt quite bewildered that they chose to ignore me because of my appearance. Perhaps I was naïve about the impact that Rotherham's punk rockers were having on its gentle town folk!"

Tracy Stanley (Rotherham Punk Rocker) ... "The Punk look?, I remember it started with my parents' disgust; as their precious daughter turned into a rebellious, strange looking teenager, who died her hair red with 'cochineal' food colouring and went out in black bin bags fastened together with safety pins. I was about 15 at the time, so it was quite radical.

I listened to Siouxsie and the Banshees, the Damned, Joy Division (a particular favourite), the Clash and every parent's worst nightmare – The Sex Pistols. I also had hardcore friends like Fiona Palmer, Tony Beesley, Nicky Booth and Lynne Haythorne.

Above: Helen McLaughlin and Joanne Orgill's Punk transformation

I used to spike my hair with a mixture of sugar and water, which gave very large spikes and I loved to wear heavy make up and fishnet tights. At the time my boyfriend – Pete Roddis, his brother David and myself decided to try to form a band, which we named Scattered Remains. I was lead singer, while Pete played air guitar and David played drums on a collection of kitchen stools; we thought we were up there with the best. That's what that era did, it let you use your imagination and get totally lost in it. We used to go to gigs at the Top Rank in Sheffield and everything was exciting, new and vibrant.

I used to love buying singles on vinyl from 'The Sound of Music' record shop in Rotherham, but mostly from the Virgin shop at the bottom of the Moor in Sheffield. It was always full of weird and wonderful characters. I would particularly love all the coloured vinyl, picture discs and limited edition records."

Helen McLaughlin ... "School (Oakwood Comprehensive on Moorgate) weren't too keen on the new us. I was sent home on numerous occasions for having coloured hair. They

148

sat me in the headmaster's office and told me I couldn't have coloured hair at school. I asked where it said that and they read me the rule about not allowing offensive hats in school. I pointed out that my hair was not a hat but they said it was the same. In the end I gave in and dyed it black. They said it was blue and sent me home again."

School could, however provide local Punk kids somewhere to hang out... especially for the younger 2nd generation kids.

Nicky Booth ... "Still being quite young at the time, there was no real outlet for all this so the school disco had to do. We used to go along dressed in our gear and ask for our favourite punk singles so we could leap about the place – but the DJs were still trapped in a mire of mindless and bland middle of the road pop rubbish. They would play a few singles if we pestered for long enough, but they weren't keen. It was like what was going on at the BBC but in miniature, what with all these aging poptastic DJs who were clearly horrified that their cosy world was being given a good kicking. These days the marketing men are right on top of any trend or fashions, but back then they were caught with their pants down."

And 'New Wave' style clothes to wear to the youth club had to be found no matter what!

Lynne Haythorne (Rotherham Punk and New Wave fan) ... "Around 1979, and we were all desperate for getting our hands on some winkle picker shoes and also any items of interesting clothing that we could buy...Like fingerless lace gloves etc. We wanted to get some good Punk gear without paying the expensive costs of X-Clothes in Leeds and Ribena shoes in Sheffield. On Greasbrough Road in Parkgate (near Rotherham) we discovered a scruffy little shop called Pembertons... which was like stepping back in time and so were the prices. Just what we needed!"

Local Punks would occasionally experience the London Punk scene.

Paul Clarkson ... "Whilst In London I went shopping in 'SEX' down on the Kings Road for some clothes. I felt a bit apprehensive and the place felt quite odd. There were about eight Punks in there, and four of those were the assistants; I think Jordan was one of them. They had some very Loud Punk music playing. I bought a 'Destroy' Johnny Rotten style long sleeved shirt thing with some sort of webbing overlay. I wish I still had it! Anyway, it wasn't a very friendly shopping experience at the time and it seemed very extreme. That's how I felt about it at the time anyway."

Bryan Bell ... "I went to London now and again as well. Me and my mate Martin would save up some of our wages and as soon as we had some time off work we would go down to London and buy some new Punk gear. They were spoilt down there - absolutely spoiled for choice."

The exuberance of the times was overwhelming and the energy would sometimes be so intense that it simply had to be released.

Tony ... "Once; me and Pete decided to pogo all the way up to a mate's house. We jumped up and down all the way, laughing our heads off as we pogoed. At a party, we persuaded one of the lasses to put some of our Jam singles on. We started to dive up and down to 'All around the World' and Pete went up so high he smashed the posh crystal lampshade that was hanging from the ceiling. All the lasses were searching for some superglue to fix it – which they did manage to do. I often wondered how long it took the parents to find out.

Another party that Pete and me went to, it was one that was put on by a straight lass who used to fancy me, but to be honest, I wasn't really bothered about. She bought me a gigantic Valentines card and I was so embarrassed by it I tore it up – anyway the usual bottles of cider were getting guzzled down and after a while me and Pete managed to get the Jam's 'In the City' LP played. We ended up piling out on to the street and furiously pogoing to 'Art School', 'Slow Down', 'In the City' and the rest of the songs. All the neighbours were at the windows, curtains twitching. We didn't get invited to the next party she held. I also recall two of the lads Clarkey and Doidgy turning up at the youth club chained together... that was part of the euphoria of the times."

Above: Punkette Cheryl Harding (Steve Marshall's photo)

Simon (Punk fan from Mosborough near Sheffield)... "I remember a remarkable 'Punk party' in leafy Fulwood one Saturday night, held in my mate's house while his parents were out. Neighbours were definitely not impressed by the sight of numerous 15-18 year olds dressed in torn clothes and black bin bags vomiting profusely over their manicured grass verges."

That summer of 1978, a new programme shown late on Saturday nights would be the talking point and a must see for most New Wave minded teenagers, especially those that were still too young to see the bands that they were listening to.

Tony ... "The big TV programme back then for us was 'Revolver' on 'ITV' late on Saturday nights. Despite it being an old school attempt at getting in on the 'New Wave', some great bands were on there and it was a great show. I remember the Jam playing 'David Watts' on there and that was the first time I had heard it as it wasn't out on vinyl yet. Also on there were the Lurkers with 'I don't need to tell her', Boomtown Rats, Rich Kids, X-Ray Spex, The Motors, Stranglers, Buzzcocks and loads more great bands as well as reggae bands like Hi-Tension. It was a fantastic show and we used to look forward to it every week; it was the big thing on the telly that summer. We never got 'So it goes' around our area so Revolver was the only thing we had apart from the Thursday night ritual of Top of the Pops which most weeks would have at least one punk or new wave band on. If we were at the youthy we would always converge around the portable TV in the telly room to watch Top of the Pops."

Chiz ... "I was mad on 'Chelsea 77' by the Maniacs, and still am. I also had THE MANIACS painted on the back of my leather jacket for years until someone smashed every window in my old Morris Marina and nicked it...Bastards!"

Tony ... "Later on, I got sick of the bog standard Punk look. After listening to the Clash obsessively, I went for that kind of Mick Jones and Mark Laff of Generation X look; the longer straggly unkempt hair, Chelsea boots, quarter length Donkey jacket, Clash t-shirt and punk group the Boys badge. I kept that style for about a year, but got fed up with that and had my hair cut really short again. I started to dye my hair. First a crazy colour green but soon a jet black colour that went purple, then proper black followed by all shades of browns and blondes and sometimes a mix of them all. Once Bryan Bell, dyed my hair bleached blonde and when we went round to my house, my Mum nearly had a fit she thought: I was a burglar and screamed and shouted-bless her. Bryan was off like a shot."

Above: Helen McLaughlin's friend ...Ricky Thorogood outside Seditionairies in London

Graham Torr ... "So it's all over then...the clothes, straps, painting Slaughter & the Dogs on my leather, the gigs (getting suspended from school for fucking off for 2 days to see the Banshees in Leeds or Clash in Derby), the meetings in the 'Hole In The Road' (up Sheff) every Saturday for the ceremonial walk down The Moor. God I felt like a rock star and could barely play a note...in fact I'm getting chills just remembering that shit...all of it.."

Paul Clarke ... "Tony had got a coat like the ones Strummer and Jonesey wore. It was cool and I used to call it his 'Not bovered coat' (laughs)...cos at that time Tony didn't seem to let anything bother him. I had to get one and get one I did. Right...I got the similar coat but I had to have something different painted on the back! I opted for a band who were close to being one of my fave bands at that time. I painted the name of the

151

band across the back of the coat in thick white paint. On wearing it for the first time my mother spotted it and was disgusted and my dad thought it was quite funny for some reason. I didn't realise why my mum was disgusted or what was amusing my dad until later when the penny dropped. I had PENETRATION splashed all over my back (doh!)."

Tony … "Another big thing at the time was bloody badges. Heaps of em were flooding the shops in Rotherham and Sheffield. Badges of your fave punk groups were essential. They started out as the big door knocker size but then we realised that these really did not look very cool so we moved on to the button sized ones. I had loads of badges but it only looked good if you wore just a few and swapped em around next time you came out to hang around. We would also swap them with each other much the same as we did with the records.

   The same thing applied with group t-shirts. The Clash were always gonna be cool on a t-shirt for me, but generally the more obscure the group on your t-shirt was it would raise your punk credentials considerably. I suppose all this sounds like inverted snobbery and like there were rules to follow but what you have to remember is the age we were at. We were only kids still at 13 and 14 and we didn't yet have that kind of suss that some of the older kids had. Also the whole intellectualising of the punk scene was only really something that seemed to happen years later with all the retro pieces done by journalists. I suppose the first real damning put down of the punk scene was the book 'The Boy looked at Johnny' written by Tony Parsons and Julie Burchill but I never read that and still haven't. Besides, to begin with all we were into was the energy and excitement of punk. It was rebellious and fast and straight to the point. Also there weren't any beards. Not that we could have grown any if there had have been."

Paul Clarke … "Badges were cool back in those days and were essential accessories to a good Punk jacket. The best place to get them from was Pandora's Box which was a small shop up Wellgate in Rotherham. (It later moved to the small kiosk in Rotherham Market that now sells newspapers)."

David McKendry … "One of my most prized possessions was a Clash 'Complete Control' badge that a Roadie gave me, until some cunt at a party 'borrowed' it and fucked off to Europe with it ! I know it was you Hague-ey, and I still miss the bloody thing."

Punk still had the power to shock; badges with expletives, or worse than that …the notorious swastika, obscene slogans painted on the back of jackets, torn t-shirts, coloured hair- even short hair and straight trousers were still getting the attention of Punk hating neanderthals that were still very much at large around Sheffield and especially Rotherham.

Bryan Bell … "I had some great t-shirts; Penetration, X-Ray Specs, the Clash and one of my favourite ones was the stiff label one with the slogan *'If it ain't stiff it ain't worth a fuck'*. I also had an original 'Anarchy' t –shirt with all the straps on and the instructions on how to make a bomb. Imagine trying to get away with wearing that nowadays."

Punk lyrics also reflected the way the local Punk kids felt. This was a time when bad language in songs was very rare. A far cry from the 'expletive littered lyrics' of the gangsta rap records of the 21st century.

John Harrison ... "The thing is people used to say to me *'why is all the swearing in Punk records so necessary'*. So I would say *'Well that's how we express ourselves, I mean you can't exactly write angry lyrics and call someone an old dear and say 'would you please move out of my way'* or something. It was more like *'I think it's Time for Truth so why don't you just fuck off!!'*"

Tony ... "Paul Weller's lyrics in the Jam were the ones I took the most notice of. The most disappointing thing though, was when he changed the line in 'The Modern World' single... *'Don't give two fucks about yer review'* to *'don't give a damn about your review'*?...then there was the stuff that the Clash were writing about that really made me think about my surroundings and all the bullshit around me, especially the teachers and their rules. The words meant a lot to me back then."

Not all of the best Punk singles were of an angry and rebellious stance.

Tony ... "I bought the Saints' 'Know your Product' single from Revolution records shop in Sheffield. I loved that one and there was something different about it. It was clearly a punk record but with something else added to it. It was only later on that I realised it was that Stax label type of Soul sound, with the brass on it. We bought the 'Eternally yours' LP from Revolution a couple of weeks later for a quid or something but I never got to hear all their other stuff until much later on. Another great LP was the Jolt one. Me and Pete got that one out of the cheap box from Revolution as well, along with many others."

Bryan Bell ... "I would buy Ian Dury and the Blockheads records but no way was it Punk. At that time everything and anything got tied in with punk. If you had a short punk sounding group name or had shortish hair that was it you were punk. This was the music press really. But us punks we would decide what was cool or not and it wasn't always straight forward punk stuff. Mind you, I saw them at the City Hall and they were really good live."

Tony ... "It's important to remember how big Ian Dury's 'New Boots and Panties' LP was on the punk scene, even though it was never a punk record as such. My mate Andy bought that when it first came out and almost everyone else seemed to have it after a while. I had the gold vinyl edition for a while but it went in a swapping session one Sunday afternoon. It was usually poor old Ian Dury or Elvis Costello who suffered the most in those swapping sessions."

Ian Dury and the Blockheads' had recently made an appearance at the Sheffield Top Rank when they played a pre-Christmas gig with a party theme. They played to a mixed audience of hippies, students, soldiers on leave and inevitably an assortment of Punk Rockers, who were more than happy to show their enthusiasm for Ian Dury and co without the usual array of spit and missile throwing. The Punks were met with typical Dury sarcasm and put down banter between songs. Ian Dury and the Blockheads were now part of the ever increasing, and often diverse, play list of Punk and 'New Wave-related music that the local fans were listening to, along with the help of John Peel's late night radio show and its diverse new music coming through.

Steve Haythorne … "Ian Dury and the Blockheads at the City Hall were amazing. They played so tight and Ian had so much energy. It was funny though, cos this being at the time of the world cup, Ian had a telly at the left of the stage, which he kept checking on, for the scores of the Scotland match in-between songs and he was shouting out the score to us all. He had such great stage presence. There was a mix of all sorts of people there at that gig; Punks, straights, long hairs everyone really."

Pete Roddis … "As far as I can remember- what got me really serious about listening to Punk was when me and Tony would pick up on all the stuff that John Peel was playing. Tony would record his show and then the next day we would both listen to it. We found out about lots of groups that way."

Julian Jones (Rotherham Punk fan/musician) … "I can remember coming round to Tony's house and he had loads and loads of cassettes from the John Peel sessions."

Dave Spencer … "So, over the next year, I bought stuff but kept it to myself, venturing out on a Saturday morning to go to The Sound of Music near the market. Money must have been tight, because I must have only bought about three or four records, that whole year. Although I did win the second Elvis Costello album, 'This Year's Model' in a Rotherham Advertiser competition, simply for knowing that Elvis Costello's new record label was Radar. When I went to collect it, the woman on the desk said, *'Ooooh, you must be the youngest Elvis Costello fan in the world'*."

Paul Clarkson … "I guess the main groups I liked were the Clash, Sex Pistols, the Jam (early on with their raw power) and Generation X. I also liked Iggy Pop."

Tony … "I bought the first two Boomtown Rats LP's. They were really good Punky pop dance records. I think a lot of the younger Punks did get into Punk through the Rats. Lots of Punk kids did look down on them though, but we had hours of fun miming to the 'Tonic for the Troops LP."

154

Andy Goulty … "Yes, 'Tonic for the Troops' and 'Black and White' by the Stranglers were two of the big ones for me about midway through 1978!"

Andrew Morton … "The first so called Punk LP I bought was 'Tonic for the Troops' by Boomtown Rats."

Bryan Bell … "I thought the Boomtown Rats were crap. They were rubbish live and I never really liked any of their records."

In the late seventies record shops were plentiful and by 1978 it was easy enough to go and buy most of the 'New Wave' records that were being released endlessly each week. Rotherham had Circles and Sound of Music and both of these carried a good stock of Punk especially the latter. Woolworths and Brittain's would stock mainly chart stock, but could often be depended upon to get a bargain New Wave LP that had failed to sell its anticipated amount.

Doncaster and Mexborough had Track records, while Sheffield had a whole array of record shops to choose from, starting at the bottom of the moor with Virgin records and its obnoxious hippy sales assistants

Above: Back page ads designed to appeal to gullible young Punk kids such as me… I bought a pair of PVC's and a pair of Jam trousers

and continuing with K and D in the hole in the road (fantastic for 49p New Wave cheapies), Curtis Records on Fargate, Rare and Racy (with its free form Jazz on constant play), and always at least two open on Chapel Walk (which was once known as Sheffield's own Carnaby Street). A great record shop - in a visual sense as well - was Impulse records situated across from Cole Brothers. Impulse was set out like a cavern inside and its walls were plastered with all the many different and vividly colourful 'New Wave' singles sleeves. There was also a scattering of second hand record shops (including one that specialised in rock n' roll behind the Moor called Violet Mays), but the very finest record shop for buying Punk Rock had to be Revolution Records up on the top balcony near the castle market.

Tony … "Me and my mates would come home every Saturday with a bag full of new Punk and 'New Wave' singles each from the cheap boxes. I started 1978 with maybe 20 or so

155

singles (apart from the old ones of my brothers and the chart throwaway singles).By the middle of the year my 'New Wave' box was full and I had a handful of LP's.

By the end of the year, me Pete and Andy had gone into the hundreds each and were buying more and more all the time. Andy bought the Undertones 'Teenage Kicks' e.p when it was first released. As soon as he played it for me that was it; I was hooked. We never stopped playing it for weeks. I managed to swap it with him a couple of weeks later. I would always love The Undertones. When I went to see them live it was fantastic. They were one of the very best groups I ever saw during the punk era – come to think from any era. There was such a great atmosphere at the Undertones gigs. I never felt any of that violent tension that was in the air at most Punk gigs. The energy they had was amazing. A shirtless Feargal and his jumble sale clothed side-kicks with their Irish brogue accents were loved and welcomed by all of the Top Rank crowd. Fantastic group and I still bloody love them now."

Pete Roddis ... "Me and Tony would spend hours and hours going up to Sheffield and buying loads of records, usually cheap ones. We'd buy all sorts of different stuff. Back then, music was everything to us. It took over our lives."

Patrick Tierney ... "My friends and acquaintances were into a fairly wide variety of music, (mostly of the classic rock sort) but punk and 'New wave' was generally accepted. There was a cross-pollination thing going on. You could love Bob Dylan and the Clash. Music was music. To give an example, I remember going to a pal's house - Michael 'Scrote' Coning - to listen to his new records.

Above: Richard Chatterton's back garden guitar practice

They were: Jilted John/Jilted John single, 'American Stars and Bars' by Neil Young and 'Bat out Of Hell' by Meatloaf. He also later played Suicide's album. We had to wait until his Mam went out, because she had lost a parent to a heart attack, and could not bear to listen to music with a heart beat rhythm. This sort of thing was common. People mixed and matched. Some artists were acceptable across the board. Hawkwind and Gong were O.K. for punk purists to like. To me they were the epitome of Hippy music (not necessarily a bad thing), but perhaps their anti-establishment stance helped. Even the most Stalinist of my friends - (Dave Brown of York Road, Scawsby - for whom 1976 was year zero) still liked The Who and Tim Buckley."

156

Tony … "Some time after 'Bollocks' came out, there was a rumour going around that 'Sound of music' was selling some 'Spunk' from under the counter… eh?. So me and Andy Goulty went there and, hiding our embarrassment, we asked if it was true that they were selling 'Spunk' from behind the counter. We got a suspicious and uneasy look – which was unusual as the staff there were quite good with paying customers – then realising that we must be genuine, they pulled out a copy of Sex Pistols 'Spunk' LP… the rare and unofficial demos version of the only Pistols LP 'Never mind the Bollocks'. They weren't supposed to be selling them but they knew that they could sell plenty. Where they got them from no one knew but we wanted it no matter what. Me and Andy came out with a copy each in the plain white sleeve…another top slice of vinyl each for the collections."

Another unique vinyl find occurred in the most unusual of places to imagine coming across any rare Punk vinyl.

Tony … "Rawmarsh hill in Parkgate… there was a really small family run, old fashioned record shop. Two old people who seemed to have been there forever ran it. As was our compulsive duty back then, if it sold records we had to know about it and check it out.

Andy Goulty and me used to rummage through their stock on say a monthly basis to see, if they had anything decent in… which was extremely rare. It was really a chart return shop and almost every one of their records came minus the picture sleeve, which was sacrilege for us… I think I bought some Motors singles from there when they were just dropping out of the charts and Andy bought Skids 'Sweet Suburbia' and 'Saints are coming' the day after their Top of the Pops appearance with the latter song. That was it as far as I can remember…

Above: Indecent Exposure Bootleg: we didn't find that one but we managed to stock up on Spunk!

Then one day just before Christmas 1978, Andy comes back with this novelty Punk single called 'White Christmas' by a group called Slush. No picture sleeve of course. It was kinda good in a trashy sort of way…so bad it's good really. We played it that Christmas of 1978 and never thought any more about it afterwards. As time goes on I found out that the record was never actually given an official release and had been withdrawn straight away. It's now fairly collectable as is most of the obscure 'New Wave' stuff from the time. Priced at £70 in the last Record Collector rare records guide. But how did it make its way to the most out of town, obscurest hidden away record shop this side of Juke box jury? That's a question that we will never get answered."

Lynne Freeman ... "Gradually we took over the pubs on High Street in Sheffield, and their juke boxes, if anything too smooth or trendy was selected by someone else, a riot would ensue, beer would be thrown and everyone would chant and someone would nudge the jukebox so that the needle would skeeter across the record and make a horrid sound. Then something like the Clash would come on and everyone would leap around. Anyway, one night especially I felt like the bees knees. I walked down the steps into the cave of a club I thought of as home. Steve the manager greeted me at the door, he called me by my name, but the other bouncers had their own name for me, they used to call me something that rhymes with 'Fits' cos I was quite well endowed. Still, it was punk, so I couldn't be offended! I was wearing a pair of bright red, leather, winkle picker boots that clashed with my maroon, skin tight, leopard skin trousers, on top I wore a baggy, mohair, purple sparkly fluffy jumper with holes and tears and stitches dropped, and round my neck a bandana type scarf made of the same material as my trousers. On my hands, my nails were painted with different coloured spots, long before nail bars and manicures and nail transfers became the norm! I wore several earrings; my hair was dyed red and spiky and clashed with my boots and trousers!"

Dave Spencer ..."Laughable as it seems now, just by saying we were punks, made us punks. At first, there were a mere handful of us in our year, Dom, Graham, Lawrence, Dave (Diddy) Eastburn, Helen McLaughlin, Joanne Orgill and myself. Within a matter of weeks the numbers would swell to about 40.

The music coming in to our ears, though somehow sounded different to the music we made. We made a racket, but the music that we heard was all bright and exciting. New records seemed to be appearing every day from the likes of Buzzcocks, Undertones, Stiff Little Fingers, Public Image Limited and many, many more.

Above: Punk spreads into the classroom in this school artwork of mine

We all listened to John Peel and shared what we knew and what we loved. Dominic was particularly obsessed by the Stranglers. Graham, I recall, was more into the Damned & the Clash. I still hadn't deserted Elvis Costello, although, he now seemed extremely tame at the side of the 'proper' punk bands."

As the local Punks were picking up on the latest new Punk sounds through the John Peel show along with the local record shops that were stocking the new sounds of Punk and its offspring 45's, there would be somewhere needed to spin these 7 inch plates of coloured
158

gems wrapped in Day-Glo picture bags. As well as after-school (or work if you were old enough or inclined to participate in that pastime), and Punk vinyl sessions in the front rooms and bedrooms of Punk's chosen followers, there would be other places where so called normal people socialised. Punk rockers were not genetically designed to be ignored and would find a way of creating and adapting their own scene wherever possible! And what better place to start than at the Christmas youth club disco!

Tony ... "The Christmas disco at our school (Rawmarsh Comprehensive) in 1978; we were all ready to screw things up Punk style for all the straights and disco types. There were about five or six of us Punk kids; me, Steven Doidge, Pete Roddis, Clarkey and I think Andy Goulty. Anyway we were waiting for our Punk spot to arrive, wasting time laughing at the lasses grooving away to the Bee Gees and the Nolans. We requested Sid's 'My way' from the pile of records that we had brought along. The DJ began to spin the record and in a last minute decision, we put our plan into action. All the other lads laid all over the floor as if they were dead, whilst I remained stood up.

I sang along, swaying and lip curling 'Sid Vicious style' to the opening slow section of the song. All the kids stopped in their tracks and it being the Christmas disco some of the teachers were there too, with all eyes fixed upon us. Then when the guitars, bass and drums kick in and the song speeds along like an express train, all the lads suddenly sprung to life, and as if awoke from the dead, leapt up and started diving around, pogoing furiously in fits and spasms like demented loonies. The teacher's mouths were a gasp with shock. Were these young upstarts the very same young pupils that they were teaching by day? You bet they were SIR! The disco kids were almost crying with their Christmas disco spoilt whilst some -

Above: Sheffield Punk Rocker Steve Marshall's best 'Sid Vicious' impression ... which would have been most welcome at our Xmas disco

- of the others clearly thought it was funny and a good laugh. That 3 minutes of festive Punk fun belonged to us and we had our 15 minutes of Warhol comprehensive fame. That was one Christmas that we did things our way!"

Chapter Eight

Take me to the Limit

"At the Limit club a bloke came up to me and asked 'Are you the Lurkers?' I told him that we were – 'You're shite' was his reply; happy days in Yorkshire" - **Pete 'Esso' Haynes (The Lurkers drummer)**

The Limit club in Sheffield is often credited mostly to its pioneering support for the burgeoning electro scene that was starting to show itself in 1978 and which would be a major part of Sheffield's musical pedigree from then and onwards into the 80's.

It was also, however, a regular starting off point for punk groups and many of the New Wave groups that followed the initial explosion of 1977. In fact The Limit club's doors were almost always open to anything new, underground and struggling to gain a foothold on the ladder to success.

The Limit club on West Street had previously been the basement of an old jeans factory and opened on March 30th 1978 (although stated as March 22nd in some sources). Owned by ex Policeman Kevan Johnson and George Webster, during the next 20 odd years it would play host to hundreds of upcoming groups including then little knowns U2, Human League, Bow Wow Wow, Adam and the Ants and many more including a momentous Joy Division date in July 1979.

Left: The entrance to the depths of Sheffield's most legendary Punk era club

Throughout 1978 - 79, groups such as Subway Sect, the Adverts, Siouxsie and the Banshees, the Lurkers, the Dickies, Penetration, Chelsea, The Police, Generation X, the Members, Tourists, Gang of Four, Revillos, Specials, The Fall and many others would play there; usually starting their sets well after midnight in the small and claustrophobic heat

161

of this 'Sheffield' equivalent to the cavern with its extremely low roof, stink of blow and soaking beer drenched and sticky carpeted floor. The first group to play there, though, was decidedly very non Punk and that was Bitter Suite, a popular Sheffield rock band better known on the club circuit.

Above: Wire at the Limit Club 1978

Phillip Wright … "It was the best club Sheffield ever had. It opened on the same night as a rock gig at the City Hall and the club was virtually empty. A mate of mine from Gleadless Valley, Ian Williams was walking into the club when the owner, George Webster said to him, *'If you and your mate go and give out these flyers to people walking out of the City Hall you can come in for free'*, so he did and by the time he got back, The Limit was full. George Webster gave Ian Williams a VIP card, which said 'Limit for Life' on it, and gave Ian free entry for the rest of his life. Ian was a regular character in there; openly gay, very effeminate acting but actually as hard as nails and from a very tough family.

He had helped out with Sheffield's first home made music paper, called (I think) Home Groan and had interviewed Pete Shelley from the Buzzcocks, who he kept in touch with. He had a fascination with Blondie, Ultravox (John Foxx days, not Midge Ure) and a band called Dead Fingers Talk, who I think he hung around with for a time. He had been one of the first people I ever saw dressed in Punk clothing, home made stuff and old charity shop stuff and he dyed his hair bright orange. He went on to run the Human League fan club in the early days, but died young. He was a regular fixture of the early punk scene, always at gigs and the Limit and a really nice lad.

A few weeks after the Limit opened I finally went down into the actual venue for the first time. I was 16 but because I was tall at 6ft 2", I looked old enough to get in (just!). Even at my size I was actually the smallest of my crowd, so hats off to Jon Oxley, Mark Parsons and Neil Kitson who all towered over me and made it so that none of us ever got turned away at the door."

Sheffield Punk Michael Day was a regular at the Limit club and recalls the clothes worn around West Street at the time that Punk was still an healthy and invigorating scene to be a part of.

162

Michael Day (Sheffield Punk Rocker)... "I think everyone wore different clothes and while some of them mirrored the classic punk attire there was a lot of DIY stuff going on and I used to wear some old suits and shirts that my dad had in the 50's. I remember the Clash crowd – Trigger, John Hancock et al. and they all wore the zip pants and had that first Clash album look. I occasionally could be seen sporting a pair of tartan bondage trousers and a green mohair sweater which for a time was the defacto garment for everyone to wear. After the initial rush everything seemed to settle down and the groundswell of Sheffield bands began to infuse the local scene. It was at this point that the Limit became the last stop on the scene after running up West St and stopping at the all important Hallamshire hotel to see which bands were on at the time."

Lynne Freeman ... "The Limit opened and after a while, became my haven. We were like a huge family, all kids, fed up of the establishment, fed up of Thatcher's Britain, expecting more and never getting it, all these things brought us together like nothing else.

   I walked into the Limit one night after drinking and imbibing of smokes and stuff starting at the Blue Bell on High Street, and working our way up West Street. In those days you could go to town completely on your own, cos the very first pub you walked into would have someone you knew in it."

The Limit club always seemed to create a story to be remembered.

Phillip Wright ... "The first band I saw at the limit was called Bethnal from Bethnal Green in London. They were dressed sort of like punks but sounded like the Who with an electric violinist, if you can imagine that. The night that Bethnal played, a lad from our estate, Alan Clark, escaped from Borstal and came to the Limit. A few plain clothes policemen were in the Limit that night, looking for underage drinkers (let's face it in those days, plain clothes policemen stuck out like a sore thumb) so we asked the Limit DJ (the legendary Paul 'Legs' Unwin) to play a Sham 69 song called 'Borstal Breakout', which he did, we were all dancing about and laughing and everyone who knew Alan Clark started cheering, but of course the boys in blue didn't know why!"

Lynne Freeman ... "When it was time to go to the loo, the ladies was always full, and if they weren't going to the loo, applying vast quantities of make up etc, then they were gathered around various substances. So, I would calmly walk into the mens. The stink was unbelievable and I'm sure the piss on the floor rotted my boots. I would go in a cubicle to the embarrassed shouts of some men who weren't used to the Limit *'Oi, you're in the wrong toilet'...* I used to peep round the cubicle while they resumed peeing, and say *SO?!* That always put them off their stroke and I bet many a shiny shoe was ruined there!!"

Bryan Bell remembers going to the Limit club... "I would go and see Generation X, The Adverts, Undertones, Penetration and X-Ray Specs at the Limit. They were all really good and we had some superb times there. One of the times after going to see Generation X, we decided to walk back home, as we often did back then, and we set off down the parkway route. About halfway down one of the lads, who had got left behind, went past the rest of us on a coach he had hitched a lift from. He got the coach to stop so that he could get to us and he was full of it...Laughing and whatever...whilst in the meantime the coach pulled off leaving the lot of us to continue our walkies. '*What the hell are you playing at*' we said to him '*we could have all got on the bleeding coach instead of walking you pillock*'. His reply was '*Well I was so glad to see you lot that I forgot to tell the driver to wait for us all*'. Whack! He got a belt around the lughole for that."

Arturo Bassick (Pinpoint vocalist/ bass player – now fronts the Lurkers and plays bass in 999) ... "All I can remember of playing the Limit club was my mate Colin – he was sitting on the edge of the stage puking into his Harrington, then he got up to pogo with it dripping all over the place."

Tony ... "The very first time I ever set eyes on the Limit club was in the summer of 1978, when I was up West street with my brother. He used to get some car spare parts from a shop somewhere around there and I can remember him pointing over to the Limit club over the road and saying '*Look, that's where all the Punk groups that you like play*'. There was a Dickies poster stuck at the side of the door, but at that point I had never heard them, only heard of 'em."

Above: Limit club flyers from 1978

Lynne Freeman ... "We danced, laughed, and loved. There was always some scandal of who was going out with whom, who robbed something, who got kicked out of their bed-sit and who had been to court. I got really blasted one particular night and one of the bouncers threw me over his shoulder to carry me out. As I was upside down and my head was spinning, I pleaded with him to stop, you see all my precious make up, my weird eyeliners and black lipstick had fallen out of my pocket and was rolling around on the floor, loads of lads rushed forward, not to rescue me but to nick my make up!!"

Martin Clarke (Sheffield Punk fan) ... "At the Limit, one of the great things was the support bands... I saw Subway Sect, Neon Hearts, Spizz Oil, Chelsea. Everything was so new and the energy levels were awesome. Generation X; we were stood on chairs so we could see them play on the low stage."

164

Sue Lowday ... "I used to have a pass for the Limit. I worked occasionally for Mr Kites when it was the first wine bar in Sheffield. One of the perks was our pass - which we used on Saturday nights after Kites closed and we piled down there to get some bevvies down and have a bop. I have a feeling that the pass was quickly withdrawn when we used it a bit too often!"

Deano (Sheffield limit club goer) ... "I virtually lived in the Limit seven days a week. I knew most of the Faces. I used to love going up West Street even prior to the Limit opening. Everyone knew everyone else, like a big cool family. We started going to the Limit when they had tablecloths and flowers on the tables...Yes really! We soon kicked that into touch!!" **(Sheffield Forum site)**

Lynne Freeman ... "After the Limit, someone always had a party, every weekend, it didn't matter if you didn't know them, cos you always knew someone who did!!Fab!! I recently had contact with someone on Sheffield Forum who used to be part of our punk family. I reminded him of going to someone's party one night and we ran out of booze. The party was in a second storey flat next door to an off licence. This kid in the group, I shall call him 'Bubbles' decided the best way to get beer was to smash the offy door, and just walk in and take stuff. He did just that and appeared with four large party sevens, these were big cans that held seven pints. We rolled around on the floor laughing. There was a knock on the door and it was the cops, we quickly hid the cans in the wardrobe, but they came in and said ... *'who broke into the off - licence?'* We were all dying to laugh, but Bubbles stood up and said *'I did'*! We couldn't believe it, he wasn't even accused and he admitted it, God we were peeing ourselves with laughter as he was carted away!!"

The Limit club managed to book countless bands of the Punk and Post-Punk era. Wire played a prototype Post-Punk era defining set in May 1978 with the best part of their recent 'Pink Flag' LP forming the nucleus of the set. The following couple of months of 1978 saw memorable gigs from the likes of Penetration (June 23rd), a double treat of the Lurkers and the Dickies on 13th July and one of Generation X's handful of gigs they performed at the venue which took place on Saturday August 15th. Another Punk band to play the venue was 999.

Pete Cooper ... "999 were playing the Limit and it was an afternoon one. We queued for around two hours in the snow to be then informed that the band couldn't get to the venue. But we were told that we could still get in to the Punk disco! We re-joined the line at the front to suddenly be confronted by Nick Cash and Jon Watson of 999. They said if we helped them unload their gear, we could get in for free. Fantastic, it turned into a brilliant gig. They were full of energy and it was great to meet the band who were all regular blokes."

Young Punk fan **Ian Robertson** from Sheffield was also at the same 999 matinee performance. He recalls ... "999 were one of my favourite 'New Wave' bands and they were good musicians and a tight band. At this Matinee gig (We went to quite a few matinee gigs at the Limit, but at the late ones the bouncers would usually turn us away), anyway there was a petrol shortage and the band were a couple of hours late for the matinee performance. I remember all the kids lined up on West Street waiting for the band to arrive. When they arrived late, the PA announcer asked for volunteers to go outside and unload the bands gear into the venue. So off I went with my mate Sid. I carried a snare drum in its case on to the stage, but the highlight was when a roadie gave me this guitar and I was told to carry it into the dressing room. In there; 999 singer Nick Cash asked me to open the case and then hand him his guitar. He explained to us why they were late and he thanked us for helping with the equipment.

We watched the roadies furiously set up and there was an almighty roar when the band took to the stage. 999 were excellent live and it was a great gig- no backstage passes no corporate hospitality, no glossy programmes, no 10 yard gaps between stage and audience just fantastic Rock n' Roll."

Phillip Wright ... "The next band I saw at the Limit were 999, a sort of Punk/New Wave band, who were actually really good live, this was in the old days when the stage was next to the DJ box. It was tough getting home on the late night bus and then getting up for school, but we used to do it all the time. We even got a lift home from one of our teachers one night! He said something like, *'you don't tell anyone you saw me here and I won't tell anyone I saw you lot'*, which was cool, his name escaped me but he looked like Jason King from off the telly and wore flares and a velvet jacket at school, he was probably quite young but seemed old to us at the time. The list of bands that played at the Limit, before they became famous, is incredible, I saw The Undertones there, the B52's (their first ever UK gig I think, the place was packed, well over safety limits!), the Skids, the Lurkers, Gang of Four, the Revillos, the Barracudas and loads more."

Above: Flyer advertising UK Subs at the Limit club in 1979

John Harrison ... "I went to the Limit club a few times. Once we went to see Squeeze but they didn't turn up and this other group played instead. I think they were called Liquid Stone or something. They weren't a punk band by a long shot. They played all sorts. This was the first time I had been proper drunk and after drinking rum and blacks, I went outside and saw double. I was sick as a dog. Later on I went to see the UK Subs there. This time it was absolutely packed full. I was right at the front and the stage at the Limit was only small. I was getting pushed and getting crushed right up against it, it was red hot too, and I almost fainted and had to be pulled out of the crowd by the security blokes. They took me into the dressing room. Good gig though."

Dave Burkinshaw (Rotherham Punk) ... "The UK Subs at the Limit was the first punk concert I went to. I had dyed my hair red and must have looked a right twat (but I felt good at the time). I had severe sunburn on my back and there I was trying to do the pogo and in agony with the sunburn and getting knocked all over...but it was one of the best days of my life. I've still got the autograph of Charlie Harper from that gig too."

Bryan Bell ... "Me and a couple of the Punk lasses (Gill and Christine) used to go to the Reggae nights at the Limit. We had some great nights and often we would be the only white faces in there apart from the bouncers and the bar staff. One of those nights Black Uhuru had been playing at the City Hall and afterwards – I think it was their singer – came over to the Limit and did a bit of a set; singing over the reggae records with the original vocals dubbed out. We had some great times. We never got any hassle at all on those nights."

Left: Toyah at an early Limit club Gig (Courtesy of Sheffield History site)

Ian Robertson ... "The Skids I saw at the Limit. We could not understand a word the singer said or even sung! They played 'Into the Valley' two or three times in the set. However, we all came away in awe of lead guitarist Stuart Adamson- God rest his soul."

Anon (Limit Club regular) ... "I remember a Francis Rossi(Status Quo singer/guitarist) look-alike who used to fly down the stairs, attack a few Punks, get 7 bells of shit knocked out of him, cause a near riot, get slung out of the door by Egor, then repeat the act the week after...Happy days." **(Sheffield History site)**

Sue Lowday ... "One of my mates (Libby) was famed for drinking rather too much. One night at the Limit and deciding she could drive a friend's car (not having learned to drive) she ran straight into the back of a Rolls Royce."

Andrea Berry (Sheffield Punkette) ... "My first visit to The Limit was in 1979 - I was THIRTEEN YEARS OLD! I don't know how I got in but my brother took me to see John Cooper Clarke there. It stank of stale beer, I didn't understand a thing J.C.C was on about only that he used a lot of swear words and I laughed because everyone else did. I drank half a pint of Stella and felt blind drunk, perhaps the reason I couldn't walk properly was because of the sticky carpet though!"

Chelle (from Sheffield) ... "I went to the Limit a few times. I always enjoyed it. One time I was tapped on the shoulder by a massive mean looking kid with an enormous Mohican. I though, *'Oh Eck, I hope I haven't spilled his pint'*. It turned out he was a little lad I'd been friendly at school with. He'd grown."**(Sheffield Forum site)**

Anthony Cronshaw ... "We went to see Wayne County and the Electric Chairs at the Limit club and then later on it was Jayne County (following his sex change). Well we just couldn't handle that one and one of us threw a pint of piss at him/her."

TV Smith (The Adverts) ... "We played the Limit club fairly often, and I remember it as always being a good venue for us."

Brian Pearson (guitarist with Rotherham Punk band The Prams) ... "I played guitar in a band called the Prams from Rotherham. We played a few gigs around South Yorkshire and had a single released plus a few tracks on a compilation album along with other bands from around Yorkshire. We supported the Adverts at the Limit club but they didn't seem to warm to us and spent most of the day avoiding us."

Limit club free pass from Phillip Wright's collection

Post-Punk group The Shapes recall one of their experiences of playing the Limit club whilst supporting the then little known the Cure ..."On to Sheffield where we support the Cure at the awful Limit club. They have just signed to Polydor, and their single 'Killing An Arab' is doing rather well. We arrive to find that the Cure are there and although a three piece with minimal equipment, they take up the whole stage and refuse to move so much as a plectrum to allow us on. The drummer in particular is a complete git, complaining that we shouldn't even get a dressing room. I get on all right with the bass player, and Dave works out a compromise with the Cure's drummer.

Their drummer will move his kit back enough so that Dave can fit his on the

stage, and in return, Dave won't hammer the Cure's drummer to an unrecognizable paste. This seems to be an acceptable solution to both parties, and we go on only to find that the Cure's crew have sabotaged the lighting rig and we are forced to play under the minimal house lights. We'd done a lot worse in the past, so we got on with it and did really well with the crowd.

We load the van, and just before the Cure go on, Dave suddenly remembers he has to do something. He disappears back inside and re-emerges a little while later looking somewhat flushed and suggests that we make our regress with all due speed. Apparently, he had reneged on his part of the agreement with the Cure's drummer, so the chances of further outings with them were minimal to say the least. We were just disappointed that we were not asked to join in. We did however; have a nice fight with each other on the way home, so the evening wasn't without its little share of excitement."

Anon ..."I went to the Limit Club from 1978 to 1986. I spent most of my time at the small bar drinking Holsten on tap. The girl that worked behind the bar was called Judy, I think. Wednesday night was student and nurses night. I had that same pass for many a year. There was one guy who used to carry a Teddy and always wore a kilt and always with a group of women - Happy times."

Rob (Dingo) Dowling (Sheffield Limit club goer) ... "I practically lived there and once fell asleep in the bog and had to let myself out of the fire escape at 6am...I was so wasted one night I went to see Simple Minds and came round just as they were going off."

Tony ... "Once, when I went to the Limit club – I can't remember who it was I had gone to see – anyway, I kept feeling something prodding my leather jacket on my back. I didn't really think that much about it (this was the Limit wasn't it?), and carried on watching the group. When I took my leather off later on it had been slashed with a knife!"

Julie Turton (Sheffield Limit goer) ... "People seemed to think it was a dive but loads of quite normal people went there. Everybody and we mean EVERYBODY got on the dance floor. Still got bruises from 'Into the Valley'. Lots of male pushing & jumping in a circle dances (The pre runner to the modern day Mosh pit)."

 **Michael Day** ... "The limit club was really the place to be if you were a punk or one of the marginalized groups in Sheffield, so if you were different, Gay or had reggae leanings that was where you went to meet like minded people and to listen to some great music and see awesome live bands."

Martin Clarke ... "I saw Simple Minds at the Limit twice. One of those times, I was talking to their bass player Derek Forbes. I remember asking him if Simple Minds would make it big. He answered confidently '*Oh yes*'. A few years later they were enormous...what did I know?"

Ric Hobson (from Sheffield) ... "I remember being deafened when Ultravox did their 'Systems of Romance' tour there. I shouldn't have stood right in front of the speaker stack I suppose!!"

Phillip Wright ... "The Revillos arrived at the Limit in a big old American car - Cadillac I think - it had arrows that lit up instead of normal indicators, to signal left or right. There was a video game cabinet at the back of the Limit, like an early space invaders era system, with a game on called Caterpillar. Revillos singer Fay Fife was fascinated by it and spent ages playing on it."

Chris Lee (Sheffield Limit goer) ... "Wednesday night was the best. I saw some great bands there. Bill Nelson from Be Bop Deluxe (Yorkshires very own and finest), Cabaret Voltaire and Nigel Renshaw and the Stunt kites...Also the mad Pyschobillies and the dance they did where it was basically just crashing into each other. The awful kebabs they used to sell outside the club. After the Limit, we used to go roof walking on top of Cole Brothers and mess around with the search light they had up there. We would abuse the cops and then run away over the rooftops like bloody Spiderman." **(Sheffield Forum site)**

Anthony Cronshaw ... "The Undertones...they were one of my favourites of the Punk era. We very nearly missed seeing them play at the Limit after we had thrown the pint of piss over Jayne County and got banned for it. Fortunately, the management kindly consented to us attending the afternoon matinee with all the screaming school kids, but at least we saw the band."

Bryan Bell ... "Two things I remember about the place were the plastic glasses and how late the groups came on. You were stuffed if you were on early days. I seem to remember them moving the stage around as well."

Dave Spencer ... "In 1979 one of the big records to have an impact on me and the mates was POP PUNK CLASSIC, 'Into the Valley' by Dunfermline's Skids. Dominic bought the entire available back catalogue, i.e. singles 'Sweet Suburbia' and the 'Saints are coming' EP. We all promptly digested every last minute of 'em. I don't know what the actual date was, but around this time we went to see Skids at the Limit Club on West Street in Sheffield.

Skids did two shows that night. One for the kids, and one for the grown ups. Richard Druce's dad dropped us off at some ridiculous time like 6:30pm and we went into this amazing subterranean venue called the Limit Club. I was wearing a jacket with chains safety pinned to it, that were so heavy that when the doorman insisted I took it off, I stood up straight for the only time all night. Walking into the club opposite the cloakroom was a revelation. At the bar as we walked in, stood a couple of the band, I think it was the bass player and the drummer, but I'm not sure. More important than them, in a way, was the perfect setting – low ceiling, low stage probably only about 3 feet high and the rest of the local juvenile punks. Everyone looked a lot fiercer than I felt, but no less excited. They also looked a lot more colourful than what the crowds would become before long. The band came on and was met by an immediate onslaught of wave after wave of under eighteen punks falling and crashing onto the tiny stage. There were bouncers holding us back and they were struggling. I can't remember with much detail exactly what they played, but I do recall them coming back again and again to play 'Into the Valley'. Diddy Eastburn reckons it was four times & I have read on the internet that it was seven times, but I can say, without fear of contradiction, that it was 'A Lot'. My first ever punk gig, and in some ways the best - there were bigger, perhaps more 'important' bands, but the overall experience was never bettered. Fun... Energy... Great tunes...Albert Tatlock!"

Phillip Wright ... "The Skids played to a packed house (of course) and one of their songs was all about TV characters, with the whole audience joining in the chorus of 'Albert Tatlock!'. The Limit eventually stopped playing 'Into the Valley' on a Saturday night as the crowd would get out of control, pogoing wildly and drinks flying everywhere."

Sheffield's Cabaret Voltaire came across threats from Skinheads at one Limit club gig they played in 1978 and later on they were plagued by skinheads of a fascist nature due to their single 'Do the Mussolini (head kick)'. The Limit club's warm and friendly homeliness (that often came with a punch and a booting out), would have been more welcoming than the reception that the 'Cab's received when playing with Buzzcocks at London's Lyceum. They were spat on and almost bottled off, but withstood the barrage and came away to tell the tale; fit to return to Sheffield and its much loved Limit club.

The Limit club crowd could also shower the stage with a kind of applause and appreciation, that while not quite rivalling Cabaret Voltaire's London reception, was still an unwelcome hindrance to such professional performers of the 'New Wave' as Joe Jackson who played at least twice at the venue in 1979 once in June, but first of all on February 15th 1979.

Nick Orme (Sheffield Punk) ... "I went to the Limit club quite a few times, though not always to see just Punk bands. One of the gigs that is clear in my mind is the first Joe Jackson gig there. It was his first real tour and he was playing all of the 'Look Sharp' LP. It was a great show, fantastic musicians and a great crowd. There was a sprinkling of Punks there and they started gobbing at Joe Jackson. As you can imagine, if anyone who ever went there they would recall the place was so small, so when they were gobbing the people straight in front were getting covered in it too. I thought, at the time, why are they spitting on this group as they weren't really Punk as such. Anyway Joe Jackson took it on the chin basically. He did protest a couple of times but he was in good humour that night. This was his first tour and he was happy soaking up the exciting atmosphere and, unfortunately the spit as well."

Chapter Nine

Uptown Top Rankin'

"Patrik Fitzgerald came on and then the Dickies followed by the Jam. One thing I remember was that the venue was packed and John and I were getting crushed against the stage in front of Bruce Foxton, I honestly thought I was going to die at some points as I could not breathe and I kept having to put my hands on stage and push back, like doing a press up. But it was worth it of course" – **Phillip Wright (Sheffield Punk/Mod)**

Sheffield in the late 70's was now an important date for the ever increasing 'New Wave' tours. Most of the established Punk groups would play at the Top Rank, whilst the remainder would play late night sets at the Limit club or occasionally the University or Polytechnic. The Top Rank, also commonly known as 'Steely's', held many memorable concerts from mid 1977 through to the first two years of the next decade.

Above: Sham 69 at Sheffield Top Rank 1978 (Anthony Cronshaw)

Brian Pearson (Prams guitarist) … "I saw loads of bands mainly at the Top Rank and Sheffield University. I went to see the Clash twice at the Top Rank and even spoke a few words to Joe and Mick as we waited outside the venue."

Ian Robertson … "If you could walk, they would let you in to the Top Rank."

Tony … "Yeah I would vouch for that."

173

But there was the odd exception to that ruling as we will see in parts of some of these accounts; when some unusual or rigid decisions on entry were decided upon...

Knox (**Vibrators -** singer/guitarist) ... "I don't remember very much about the band's early time as we were gigging such a lot during this period, and now it's so long ago that it all becomes a bit of a blur. The one thing that does stick out in my mind, though, is that we turned up to play at Sheffield Top Rank (I think it was this venue !), and after we had done our sound check, we found out that the club wasn't going to be letting any Punks into the venue. We thought *'It's no use playing if they're not letting our audience in'*, so we packed up our gear and went back to London. This must have been around the time of what I'd call 'Punk paranoia', which was fuelled by the press's usual sensationalising of everything to do with Punks and violence.

We always used to get enthusiastic audiences in Sheffield and Doncaster, but then everyone did at that time. We'd be playing round there in those days with the band's original line up of myself, John Ellis, Pat Collier and Eddie. Pat was then replaced by Gary Tibbs."

Bryan Bell ... "I can remember going to see The Stranglers at Sheffield Top Rank and Human League were supporting that night. They had a see through protective plastic surround type thing around the keyboard player. That's what I can remember and I am sure it was to protect them from all the bottles and missiles flying through the air being aimed at them."

This Human League defence system invention became known as modern music's first Riot Shield.

Ian Marsh (Human League synthesiser player) ... "When you're faced with the prospect of three years working the night shift to pay off the HP on £1,500 worth of wires and knobs, the last thing you want to see is the well aimed pint glass of some ignoramus flying towards it." **(Taken from NME September 9TH 1978)**

The group's fears were certainly influenced by the reception that synth/avante garde group Suicide had received earlier in the year at the same Sheffield venue when supporting the Clash. Fortunately, with the League, the audience reacted more with a show of bemusement, than aggression or projectile throwing, but the group were taking no chances anyway. The idea had come about at an earlier jaunt they had made to play the Music Machine in London supporting The Rezillos whose guitarist was Jo Callis a semi – native of Rotherham and a future 'League' member.

Steve Wright (Huddersfield Punk fan) was a Stranglers fan and also saw Human League at this gig ... "Five of us from work went to the gig and I remember going for a few beers beforehand at a pub not too far away from the Top Rank. When we got in, support band The Human League had just come on stage. I was quite impressed with them and thought the two TV's they had set up at each side of the stage, possibly on the P.A speakers, showing stills of 'Thunderbirds', 'Fireball XL5', and possibly 'Captain Scarlet' characters, was superb. A few days later I went out and bought their debut single 'Being Boiled' even though it was in mono.

The Stranglers were as good as I expected them to be and everyone was into their songs. I spent a lot of the gig on my mate's shoulders, Richard Sullivan. Sadly he is no longer with us anymore. He was a big fan and whenever I think of him I always think of this gig. Whenever I went to a gig, if the band had tour programmes, I always used to pick one up. The only thing I could find that resembled a tour programme at this gig was a fanzine called 'Strangled', which I purchased. I had far too much to drink on this occasion. That is probably why I ended up on my mate's shoulders!"

The Human League continued working hard playing gigs amongst a gob drenched Perspex protected Punk Rock climate; eventually coming out the other end all in one piece only to split into two different factions. The Stranglers would play many more gigs in the city...not always converting everyone they played to or heard their records.

Paul Clarkson ... "Never liked the Stranglers; I saw 'em once at a university somewhere in North London, maybe Holloway Road? And they were crap! I hated 'Peaches' and all that 'No more Heroes' LP."

John Harrison ... "I saw the Stranglers at the Top Rank, but I have to say I wasn't that impressed by their performance, in as much as they hardly played any of our favourite songs. They came on with some of their good stuff and that was it really, all album tracks after that just about."

Perhaps the prospect of playing the local venues was also a yardstick to measure success within the Punk live music scene.

Howard Wall (The Lurkers' singer) ... "We'll keep plugging on. We're The Lurkers. We're on the outside looking in.....everyone's playing the Hammersmith Odeon and we're still doing the Doncaster Outlook." **(NME October 28th 1978)**

Tours and gigs came thick and fast during the Punk era, so it is hard for many of the musicians (and often fans), to recall exact gigs and anything of note from individual performances. Radio Stars bassist Martin Gordon did keep a diary of his experiences and recalls his gigs up North and in particular one that he played at Sheffield City Hall in March 1978. Here Martin takes a humorous approach to his reflections.

Martin Gordon (Radio Stars Bass player)... "Generally speaking, the gigs in the Midlands were the most fun of all gigs in the UK. Go too far south and the people were more reserved, or perhaps overburdened with choice. Too far north and things became indescribably violent or extreme – fans in Scotland once showed us how they injected boot polish and whisky, on one occasion. At the Apollo in Glasgow, the stairs on each side of the stage were covered with aluminium to stop disgruntled fans from taking it out on the group that was currently disgruntling them. It was never Radio Stars, of course – we had a rapport that transcended geography but still, it was nice to know that we were protected should it all adopt the form of a pear.

It was with Eddie and the Hot Rods that we played at Sheffield city Hall on March 8th 1978. According to my diary, it was a great gig, and I got pissed afterwards. Nothing unusual there, often I got pissed before as well. On this occasion, however, we were visited by our champion at the NME, Monty Smith. He had endured ridicule and scorn at the hands of his colleagues for daring to proclaim his love for Radio Stars. Well, we weren't terribly serious, you see, which clearly appealed to him, and evidently didn't to his rather po-faced colleagues, who felt that a spot more social commentary and a lot less electroencephalograph(eh ?) would improve the thing vastly. Monty quoted '*Radio Stars stick out from the fetid morass of garage bands on fly- by – night labels like Nureyev's whatsit through his leotard*', and he would know.

The Sheffield audience agreed with him. The sound crew were on good form this evening. They had recorded our version of 'Arthur is dead boring' the previous night and, a split second before we counted it off, it burst out of the PA. Look, no hands! We caught on instantly, and spent an energetic two and a half minutes miming perfectly to ourselves. Nobody noticed, and we were awarded two encores that night. Apparently, we then went back to the hotel and had a big row about plagiarism, according to my diary. Philosophical discussion was not usually so high on the Radio Stars agenda, but this time it was clearly in honour of our guest from London. In fact, the discussion became so animated that we were thrown out of the hotel, being described as 'undesirables' by the night manager. We left to seek other accommodation.

Above: Martin Gordon (Radio Stars)

Perhaps the reason for this was – the staged fight in the foyer. When we arrived back from the gig, drummer Jamie Crompton and I wanted to kidnap the hotel notice board, in order to rearrange the letters in a form more pleasing to us. Head roadie Danny Goodwin organised a kind of Wild West brawl, with people falling over potted plants and waving fists ineffectively at each other, while Jamie and I nabbed the board and stashed it in the lift. It was later reinstated in the foyer: '*Bugger off you dumb Germans*', read one announcement, and '*Atom Bomb at 10.00*', which amused us no end. Possibly it was '*Hot and cold running rats*' that caught the manager's eye. Anyway, Jamie and I were summoned to his office, told off like naughty schoolboys and were asked to restore it. Which we did, but to no avail, as we were then all chucked out. A teetotal member of the crew asked for '*an iced coffee*'. '*Oh, don't say that, dear, they're all nice!* Came the response. Oh, well, can't win 'em all. Sometimes you can't win any of 'em."

Steve Wright (who now runs the Radio Stars website) was from nearby Huddersfield but went to see Radio Stars (and other punk groups in Sheffield). He was at the Sheffield Top Rank gig of October 25th 1978... "Having seen my favourite band a few times on the Radio Stars Holiday tour during the autumn of 1978, I booked two days off work to go to Sheffield as I wasn't sure where I would be spending the night. Things like this never came into my mind back then. You just went to the gig and took things from there!

Thanks to the tour manager Danny Goodwin, I met the band backstage after they played in Huddersfield the month before. I also met up with the band the day after at the George Hotel and we all had lunch together. From there, and for future gigs, I thought it would be a good idea to turn up at venues for the sound check as I could chat to the band hoping they would remember me. It was always nice when they said they did!!.

At the Top Rank during the sound check, I remember whizzing a Frisbee around the venue with the girl who was doing the merchandise on the tour. The gig went very well and the venue was packed. Support band for the tour was called the Reaction. The singer went on to form Talk Talk and had a lot of success. After the gig I went backstage to chat with the band, as I always did, and somehow ended up going back to the 'Rutland Hotel' with them. So I booked a room for the night.

The following morning when everyone met up, Martin introduced me to, his then girlfriend top model Kelly St John who is on the sleeve for the 'Dirty Pictures' single and also appeared with the band on Top of the Pops. She had also been on page 3 of the Sun a couple of times.

The next day Andy gave me his address and phone number so I could keep in touch with him. A great friendship developed between us and we have been the best of mates over the three decades that has passed. It was also nice to meet up with Kelly again, this time nearly 30 years later, when Radio Stars played a 31st anniversary gig at the 'Blow up Metro club' in London."

Midway through 1978 the Clash returned to the Sheffield Top Rank for the second of their four gigs that they played there between late 1977 to Jan 1980 and were supported by work horse Punk Band Chelsea (who ritually suffered the avalanche of saliva yet again). Americans Suicide also suffered greatly at the venue on this occasion and so inciting Cabaret Voltaire's 'Paul Smith' to decide that he had seen enough of Punks mindlessness - observing that the Punk audience now seemed to more increasingly consist of one taking on 'the fad rather than the real culture'.

The Clash played a set – to the backdrop of a Messerschmitt 110 montage – that showcased a selection of their new numbers including new single 'White Man in Hammersmith Palais', which had been part of their set-list since the previous summer. As usual 'Complete Control'(their first song played) drove the local Punk fans into a frenzy of pogoing mania and the group played a storming set for the Sheffield crowd that ended with an encore of 'I'm so bored with the U.S.A', 'Janie Jones' and the expectant 'White Riot'. An early incarnation of the Specials also played at the bottom of the bill at this gig. The Clash would return to the venue again during November of the same year.

There were some other classic double bill dates to appear at venues in Sheffield during 1978. Amongst these were Penetration supported by Subway Sect (Limit club -Friday June 23rd), Buzzcocks and the Slits (Top Rank – Tuesday 14th March) Buzzcocks and Subway Sect (Top Rank Sunday 15th October), The Jam supported by the Dickies and Patrik

Fitzgerald at the Polytechnic (Friday 10th November); but the worst scenario must have been for Generation X and Adverts fans when both bands played Sheffield on Friday 8th December at Polytechnic and Limit club respectively.

TV Smith (The Adverts) ... "I can remember a gig we played at the Top Rank. Howard (Adverts guitarist), was in hospital at the time and we had three gigs booked so I had to quickly learn to play the guitar parts myself- I'd written all the songs on the guitar, but it was the first time I'd ever played guitar on stage so I was pretty nervous. We'd just got Tim Cross in on keyboards, so that helped cover some of my worst playing!"

Above: The Clash onstage at Sheffield Top Rank 1978

Punk Rocker **John Harrison** was a regular at the Top Rank venue during the late 70's, seeing groups play there such as the Vibrators, the Adverts, Penetration, Stranglers, the Damned, Ruts, The Police, 999, Siouxsie and the Banshees, Undertones and the Jam. He recalls his Punk era days watching Punk groups at the Top Rank ... "We used to go in the Claymore pub before the gigs...It was almost always the Top Rank. the Adverts; they were very good. The support bands were usually great too. I always loved the Adverts stuff...obviously 'Gary Gilmore's eyes' being one of my favourites. As much as I always loved the Jam, I have got to say the best group I ever saw, and I saw them 3 times, was the Undertones. They were fantastic. The atmosphere at their gigs was terrific."

The Polytechnic was a venue not so easy to get into back then due to the rule of having to be signed in by a student. Still – it did hold some memorable gigs and experiences, often helped out by members of the groups themselves.

Simon (Punk fan from Mosborough area of Sheffield) … "I remember Slaughter and the Dogs not turning up at Sheffield Polytechnic leaving their support act Sham 69 to put on the rawest Punk performance I ever witnessed."

Phillip Wright … "Sheffield Polytechnic (now Sheffield Hallam University) had bands playing in the old exam hall, near The Globe pub. Sham 69 played their first Sheffield gig there, with two local bands as support, Reactor and the Tornadoes (although they might have been called 'The?'). Reactor were (from memory) from Greenhill area of Sheffield, the singer dressed like Malcolm McDowell in 'A Clockwork Orange'. The Tornadoes were the early nucleus of legendary band Artery. They sang songs that were very political; one was about the Sun newspaper, called 'The Sun Says'. Sham 69 were great back then, before they went on to become a sort of cartoon version of themselves.

The Nelson Mandela building in Pond Street also hosted gigs, I saw the Jam there in 1978, although I had no ticket. The venue was sold out so me and my mate, Big Jon just went for a drink in the students' bar (which is on ground level and the venue being upstairs). It was 22p for a pint of Stones, I remember that. I had been working away (trainee telephone engineer) and then arrived late at the venue and the place was sold out. We were having a pint to drown our sorrows at the bar when Paul Weller came and stood next to us, fag in hand and ordered a drink, lager I think. I can't work out why he would come into the bar when they must have had cans of beer backstage, but he did (when I first met Big Country in later years it was the same thing) anyway Weller was wearing a dark, bottle green three button jacket, grey trousers and I think a white Ben Sherman, shoes were the black and white ones from memory. This was not what he wore on stage so he looked the part even when he was dressed casual - living the part so to speak. I fumbled around in my pockets and pulled out my Granville College Students card (I was on day release doing electrical and electronic engineering) and said something like *'I know you just want a quiet drink but would you sign this?'* and he said *'sure, no problem'*. I think he liked being recognised because the vast majority of students there were still long haired and wearing flares and just had no clue who Paul was. He said something like *'looking forward to the gig then?'* and that's when I explained that we had no tickets. We both wore three button jackets (Mine was an original from the late 60's in mint condition that my sister in law's brother gave me) and Ben Shermans. We also wore two or three Jam badges on the lapels so he knew we were telling the truth. He asked our names and if it was just the two of us or anyone else turning up? *'Just us two'*, so he said *'come with me'*. We walked to the bottom of the stairs where the desk was for collecting tickets and he said casually *'Phil and John, on the guest list'* and nodded towards us and just carried on walking up the stairs as we followed. The security bloke was looking up and down the names on a clip board but obviously never saw ours but never said anything either.

As we walked into the venue, it was empty, just Rick and Bruce on stage in street clothes (still quite mod-ish) playing a few bars of a song and then stopping, so that the sound engineers could change settings and levels and stuff. Paul Weller turned to us and said, *'don't go back out or you won't get back in, just stay in here and you'll be ok'* so we sat on a table and watched the sound check. Then the band went off we just stood around for about 20 minutes looking like spare parts until the public started coming in. We were literally at the front of the stage. After Patrik Fitzgerald and the Dickies, the Jam came on to play a blinding set. Stand out tracks were 'All around the world', 'Modern World', etc., 'Butterfly Collector' (probably the first time I can ever recall a 'B' side getting the reception that an 'A' side would get) was probably the highlight, with the lights going down and Paul Weller bathed in a coloured spot light, red I think.

   'David Watts' (the whole crowd jumping up and down in time to it) was another highlight and so was 'News of The World' with a strobe light effect for the lead guitar break. The crowd was still mainly punk, but a few other mod faces were appearing and these were the lads I would always nod at and say hi. Never knew most of their names but they were always at the Jam gigs."

Andy Goulty ... "At one Stiff Little Fingers gig at the Poly I spent the whole of their set in one of their speaker stacks with a lass I had got with. I could hardly hear a thing after that for a few days."

Patrick Tierney ... "I saw Stiff Little Fingers supporting T.R.B at Sheffield City Hall. They absolutely blew me away. Tom and his band were very good but I was much more impressed with Jake and the boys. I still play 'Inflammable Material' regularly. I have it on CD, but this album must be heard on vinyl. I saw them shortly after when they were headlining, possibly at Sheffield Poly. Terrific band."

Nick Orme ... "I saw Devo twice at the City Hall. The first time was in 1979 and they had The Members supporting them. I loved The Members and had their 'Chelsea Nightclub' LP, so I enjoyed them. Singer Nicky Tesco was running up and down the aisles trying to get some response from the slightly indifferent audience who were mainly there to see Devo. They got a luke-warm reception from a half full City Hall and couldn't get things livened up, not for a matter of not trying."

Local Punks who had been too young to have seen the first wave of Punk gigs in the area back in 1977, were now eager to catch the vibes of a real Punk Rock gig. The 70's would soon be drawing to a close but the enthusiasm towards Punk was not yet lost for many of the 2nd generation.

Richard Chatterton ... "I had no one to go to a gig with, but finally got myself enough courage to sample this music live. I went to see the Undertones at Sheffield Top Rank in June 1979. I was wearing a sleeveless t-shirt and jeans which bordered on flares. On the way, I was excited but nervous and on arriving at the gig some spiky haired youth commented on my appearance and this made me feel really inadequate. Inside the venue it was dark and exciting- youths in bin liners and one Punk in a tartan suit kissing his girlfriend at the back of the venue. There was a curly haired freak wearing 'Devo' overalls and he was pogoing to the disco beforehand.

The first band on were the Deaf Aids from Sheffield. I experienced a feeling of sweaty ecstasy at the front of the stage, inside a whirling mass of youth and I remember being mesmerised by a shirtless Feargal Sharkey the front man for the boys from Derry. I was well and truly hooked.

I still have a list of the bands I saw after that first brilliant evening- the Undertones, the Damned, Ruts, Buzzcocks, Skids, Siouxsie and the Banshees, the Clash, Ramones, Magazine, Adam and the Ants. Also the local bands Artery, Human League, the Diks, the Spasms, Xero, the Negatives, Cabaret Voltaire, Spiral Vision and later on Pulp. I would average about 2 to 3 concerts a week at the Top Rank, Sheffield Poly, Rotherham Art Centre, and Chesterfield Fusion. I saw the Specials (again a sound I had never heard before- but with Punk sensibilities)."

As well as forming his very own Punk band, local Punk enthusiast Dave Spencer was now more than ready to taste a piece of the action and see some live Punk gigs.

Dave Spencer… "My brother, Peter had taken me to my first ever gig to see Elvis Costello and the Attractions at Sheffield City Hall on 18 January 1979, supported by John Cooper Clarke and Richard Hell and the Voidoids. John Cooper Clarke was very funny. Richard Hell seemed to be there to attract as much Sheffield phlegm as possible and even though I knew he was supposed to be one of the founding fathers of punk rock he just looked a bit rubbish. Elvis Costello, wearing a lime green suit, looked less like the angry young man of eighteen months previously and more the pop star he was about to become. I had just bought 'Armed Forces', his third album and he I'm sure he played loads of stuff from it and I'm sure I loved every minute of it, but it would be about 15 years before I bought another album of his and 15 years before I saw him again (at the very same venue).

After the Elvis Costello and Skids gigs …next up was the Stiff Little Fingers gig at the Sheffield Top Rank. Every night out like this required intense negotiation with mum, understandably being the protective mother. I was still not quite fourteen years old and was already becoming a Punk Rocker! The SLF gig was sometime around the end of May/early June 1979.

I'd managed to convince my Mum and Dad (who was usually working in Scotland, so could only assert his authority by telephone) that this punk rock malarkey was a load of overblown exaggerated nonsense. I never mentioned how mental it had been at the Skids gig and I wasn't interrogated for detailed information, so I kept schtum. I almost blew it though, when I insisted that we all sit down on Sunday 27 May to watch a documentary about Rough Trade records in case Stiff Little Fingers were on; Big Mistake. They were on, and the live scenes were crazy. Like my limited 'Limit' experience, but bigger and wilder. I bullshitted my mum that they whipped up the crowds for the cameras and that it wasn't really like that, whilst all the time hoping it would be.

By the time of the gig, my mother was beginning to come to terms with my "lifestyle choice" even if she couldn't quite get to grips with the terminology. On the afternoon of the show I overheard her telling Mrs Sneath from across the road, *'David's going to a punk rock concert tonight to see the Little Stiff Fingers'*. The Top Rank seemed enormous after the Limit Club and we had to queue for what seemed like ages on the steps outside before puffing ourselves up to look like we were eighteen.

Even more than the Limit, what really impressed me was the crowd, especially the guy with a butcher's coat on which was covered in (fake?) blood and the kid who was Turquoise! Hair, Suit, and Shoes everything - Turquoise. He looked amazing! SLF were supported by the (very poppy) Starjets who later morphed into the Adventures who during the late eighties had hits with something I can't remember.

Stiff Little Fingers looked good and sounded very thrashy and a little bit Clashy. This was their first ever headlining tour, having just completed a tour supporting The Tom Robinson Band. They, quite rightly, complained about being gobbed on and played what I knew from John Peel's championing of their music. They encored with '78 Revolutions Per Minute' (obviously endebted to the Clash's '1977') and Mud's 'Tiger Feet'. Oh Yes."

Meanwhile, Punk was still attracting more new gig goers to the scene and finally, it was now the chance for young Punk fans see the Punk groups play live all those records that they had been buying. Pete Roddis was a fan of hard Rock group Thin Lizzy- who were one of the few old school groups that many of the local Punk generation still had respect for, due to their uncompromising street credible boys own Rock style. Liking Punk (as well as Thin Lizzy) it was now time to see an example of both styles of rock n' roll played live. Pete attended a Thin Lizzy Sheffield City Hall gig where they were supported by Irish Punk band the Vipers. This time the old school won. Pete carried on digging the 'Lizzy' but recalls nothing of the Punk supporters.

Pete Roddis ... "Thin Lizzy must have been one of the very first gigs I went to. I was about 13 or 14 at the time and enjoyed the gig, but I can't really remember if the Vipers were any good really. Not long after that we went to see the Damned for the first of many times. They were superb. I can still see Dave Vanian slipping all over on stage with all the gob."

The excitement and anticipation of going to a first Punk concert was still being experienced by the second generation of Punk teenagers.

Tony ... "For fuck's sake Punk will be over by the time we all reach 18. Somethings got to be done about that we thought. I know, let's con our parents into selling a valuable household item for the £3 it costs to see one of these groups, gang up together and that will make us look older. Then, lets set off to the Top Rank, lie about our ages and get the fuck in there. What could go wrong?"

Chiz ... "At the age of 15 I went to my first gig with my brother Mick and, two mates from school- Hawkey and Malc (the first line up of our band The Septic Psychos). We were ecstatic when we heard our favourite Punk band the Dickies were coming to the Top Rank in Sheffield. My Dad said we couldn't go at first but changed his mind reluctantly when we assured him that Hawkey's Dad was going as well and that he would be with us all night to keep us out of trouble. I can still picture my Dad's face when this 40-year-old businessman turned up at our house to pick us up in his flash red jag with plastic yellow glasses, badges and safety pins all over him. Hawkey also had plastic glasses, a pyjama jacket and a big yellow plastic chain wrapped around him. I felt like my life had now begun. I knew the Dickies would be good but I was totally unprepared for the intense power of their opening track 'Hideous', and I was in awe of their whole sound and stage presence. I couldn't wait for my next gig."

Tony ... "We had been listening to Punk long enough now and were hearing about all these Punk concerts at Sheffield Top Rank. Even though we were all still young, we just had to see some of these groups. It was unthinkable to consider missing out on the live Punk experience.

Some of us decided to go and see the Stranglers at the Top Rank. The tickets were about £3.75 or something and I remember my Mum sold one of her posh dining room pieces of furniture so that I could afford to buy a ticket – bless her. There was me, Andy Goulty, Lynne Haythorne and her boyfriend Nicky Booth, who was massive on The Stranglers. We went to the gig and the atmosphere was intoxicating. The place was full of Punks in all sorts of different Punk clothes. We felt so insignificant but despite this we all felt a part of it. It was like coming home for us. The DJ played a mix of Reggae and Punk and 'New Wave' stuff and after the support group, on came the Stranglers with 'Five Minutes'. The place erupted and we got swept along with the pogoing mass.

A Rare 'Siouxsie and the Banshees' poster for a date at Sheffield Top Rank in 1978

I can remember seeing John (Harrison) and his mate Shane diving straight through to the front. The spitting was rampant to begin with but calmed down when Hugh Cornwell got pissed off.

We bought programmes and after the gig we went over the road to wait for our lift home. We were saturated with sweat and high as kites. We sat on the steps on Arundel Gate, just below the Crucible and were all chatting and looking at each other. It seemed that we had all changed within those 3 hours or so of that Stranglers gig and nothing would be the same ever again. I don't think the four of us were ever together again after that, but for me, I just had to have some more of this."

Nicky Booth ... "There was no way I was going to miss this one so 3 or 4 of us got tickets at £3 each which seemed like a lot at the time. I remember rolling up on the evening and feeling intimidated by the hordes of enormous punks congregating on the venue. We had existed as punks in and around school up until that point, but here we were in the big bad world at last.

The doors opened and I made for the front of the stage – I might have been younger than most of the people there, but I was the number 1 fan so had to be in pole position. The atmosphere was rowdy, with the crowd surging back and forth and beer being spilled and thrown about in plastic pint pots. Then the lights went down and the crowd heaved forward, pinning me against the stage – but I didn't care about that because I could see the band walking on stage in the gloom. The familiar intro to '5 Minutes' filled the air, momentum building, and as it reached the point of no return and the beat kicked in the crowd leapt into the air and jumped up and down as one. Volleys of spit and phlegm flew overhead, but the band didn't seem to care, they just kept on hammering it out. All my free time was spent listening to their music and here they were, bashing out all my favourite songs just for me – sensory overload!"

Helen McLaughlin ... "We went to loads of gigs at the Top Rank in Sheffield. For some reason The Top Rank was called Steely's on Sunday nights and you had to be over 21 and have a membership card to get in. Joanne and I were members of the Steely's over 21's Club for 2 years, when we were 15 and 16!!"

Richard Chatterton ... "After the gigs at the Top Rank I would come out into the cool night air sweating and when I got home I would peel off my skin tight plastic trousers and stick on the Punk records on the turntable for an hour or so before going to bed."

Above: Rotherham Punkette Helen McLaughlin Getting ready for a 'Punk Rock' night out

Punk pioneer Iggy Pop often referred to as the Godfather of Punk(though that title has also been given to other influential musicians) played at Sheffield Top Rank in April 1979. Not surprisingly there was a heavy presence of Punk rockers attending that night; all eager to see one of their most respected Punk originators.

David McKendry …"I was a big Stooges fan, so couldn't wait to see Iggy at the Top Rank (April 79). The Igg was wasted, clung to the mike stand, and murmured through the 1st couple of numbers but by the 3rd or 4th song he looked into the audience and was taken aback - taking it as a personal affront to see the bar was still serving drinks during his performance. So off came his shoes and socks - that were then aimed at the distant bar staff. Of course not being in top athletic form, the footwear only made it to the rear of the pogoing crowd, where they were fought over as prize trophies…Iggy watched the goings on then emptied his pockets of money, which was then chucked into the throng…he found it very amusing. After the Iggy gig, Glen Matlock (he was bass player on that tour) came and talked to the fans in the club, it was the first time that most of us had come close to seeing a Pistol as not many had been around to witness the band a few years earlier at the Mucky Duck."

Phillip Wright … "One night when The Undertones were playing at Steely's, we called in the Marples for a pre-gig pint, and a few minutes later The Undertones walked in, minus Feargal Sharkey, and they joined us at our table and were a great bunch of lads."

John Harrison … "Yes, they were a friendly lot. After their May 79 gig Mickey Bradley of the Undertones was just strolling around and mingling with all the Punks. He wore a parka and I can remember him chatting to us about the gig and where we were from etc."

Dave Spencer … "There were so many great records coming out and so many bands touring we were literally spoilt for choice. With our limited pocket money we had to decide carefully which gigs to go to and those to ignore. It was a gamble. We had planned to see The Undertones but changed our minds at the last minute to see Stiff Little Fingers instead. I wish we'd gone to see the Undertones.

The next gig was the Damned and the Ruts and Sheffield band, Artery. It would be really cool right here to say how much I enjoyed Artery, what with them being an almost legendary missing link in the history of Sheffield bands, but the truth is I can't remember a thing about them. They were just in the way. I wanted to see the Ruts. The Ruts came on slowly, Malcolm Owen appearing after what seemed ages, complaining that he was just about to go for a shit when someone said *'You're on'*.

Despite any discomfort he might have been feeling, the band was great. I think The Damned might have been fucking about at the back of the stage, Dave Vanian might have even sung with them. I dunno.

The Damned were chaotic and fun, but there was something about the gig that seemed more like I'd imagined a punk gig to be. It was heavier somehow - harder. Once back at school, the next day I knew that it was certainly louder. I couldn't hear a word anyone was saying."

John Harrison …"Also I think it was at the Damned concert. I am sure there were 3 groups on. I know one of them was the Ruts, as 'Babylon's burning' had just come out, but I think the first one on stage that night was Def Leppard. They were playing just as people were still coming in, but all the punks were booing them for being heavy rock or whatever. It is hard to remember which gigs were which sometimes. I can't remember which group I saw first at all."

The Damned had just re-formed and this night at the Top Rank on June 11th 1979, they played a blinding set to an enthusiastic Punk crowd. Their set kicked off with 'Jet boy Jet girl' followed by 'Teenage Dream', 'Stretcher Case', 'Ballroom Blitz', 'Second Time around', 'Burglar', 'Born to Kill', 'Looking at You', 'Melody Lee', 'New Rose', 'Help', 'Noise Noise Noise', 'Do Messed up', 'Love Song', 'Neat Neat Neat', 'Pretty Vacant', 'I feel Alright', 'Overkill', 'All the Young Dudes', 'I'm so Bored' and a reprise of the Stooges 'I feel Alright'.

Chiz … "It wasn't long before the Damned came to The Top Rank and this time we went on the train, meeting quite a lot of Chesterfield punks (and future partners in crime) on the way. I noticed a big difference in the people attending this gig to the previous one with the Dickies. Most people looked meaner and a lot of fights were breaking out. I moved back a bit to get out of the way and found myself stood in front of Tiny. He was an enormous punk from Sheffield who I observed chasing other punks around most of the time. He had horrible black teeth if I remember correctly. He crunched a load of crisps in his mouth, took a big swig of his beer and then pulled my sweaty t shirt away at the back and gobbed the whole lot down my back! You can imagine how that felt later on the way to the train station as it was all drying up in the night air."

Pete Cooper … "The Damned had recently reformed and I was mad for it. I saw them at the Top Rank in Sheffield and then a few days later at Retford Porterhouse. There I had a drink with Damned bassist Algy Ward. Now the Porterhouse could be a dodgy place, I never got into any trouble there but I saw plenty! I saw them again a few months later at the Top Rank again and after fighting my way to the front I was rewarded by getting a face full of Dave Vanian's boot as he slipped on something on the stage. Ouch!!!"

Tony … "Funny that, as I can remember myself and a couple of my mates laughing at Dave Vanian slipping down on stage, but we didn't see the boot in the face that happened to someone as we were a little further back."

Pete Cooper … "On quite a few occasions the Damned were supported by the Ruts and I remember once while they were playing the Damned appearing behind them and proceeding to remove their amps and drum kit. It was highly amusing to see."

Tony … "The Damned were always fun to go and see. They would taunt the punks and get up to allsorts of onstage mischief. Captain Sensible would often end up naked except for his guitar and Rat Scabies would sometimes be offering to fight someone and at the end of their set he would kick his drum kit over or smash it up. I can remember one of the times I saw the Damned...the 'Machine Gun Etiquette' tour in 1979 when Slaughter and the Dogs didn't turn up for support, queuing up outside the Sheffield Top Rank Dave Vanian and Captain Sensible walked up the ramp past us. I remember thinking *'Christ how the hell did they get away with walking round Sheffield dressed like the original Count Dracula and the Captain in a multi coloured - walking monkey suit.*

Those first few gigs we went to at the Top Rank; there were some very original looking Punk kids there. We were so young and were in awe of the way these kids were dressing. They were wearing military tunics, bandsmen's jackets, Clash style combat gear like the first tour image, bleached hair and some of the lads wore make up, Johnny Thunders look-alikes, brothel creepers... the girls in ripped fish nets and see through tops, Pauline Penetration panda eyes make up, tartan, zips, straps and plastic Macs. And there was me thinking I looked cool in my Buzzcocks t-shirt and plastic trousers."

Not all of the Punk gigs left a positive impression on the local Punk Rockers.

John Harrison ..."The Police; to me were the worst group I ever put my hand in my pocket to pay and see. This was around the time 'Roxanne' was out, and I was looking forward to seeing them. They were crap. Me and Bryan Bell (my mate) and our girlfriends we basically spent the night just walking around bored all through their set with our pints of cider. I can't remember anyone getting over excited in the crowd, to be honest. No one was making a big deal of them at all."

The Police had played an earlier gig at the Limit club on Tuesday 28th November 1978 and also one at the Top Rank in December on the very same tour (Their first in the city was back in May 1977 at the City Hall). Their days of playing large arenas for re-union tours were not yet at their door step.

Pete Cooper ... "I persuaded a good friend of mine, Shaun to see the Police who were supported by 'The Cramps' and that was a brilliant gig, especially as the Police had yet to make an impact on the charts. Shaun was converted too."

Two varying opinions of the Police a group who were, by and large, mostly held with more than a little mistrust amongst the Punk scene; Playing in Sheffield was no exception.

Bryan Bell ... "The support group was the Cramps and they were better than the Police that night."

Throughout the late 70's Punk era, most young Punks had their own particular favourites. To some it was the Stranglers or the Damned and admiration for the Clash was certainly well up there; but Paul Weller and the Jam were also many young Punks' first choice and finally getting to see them was quite an experience.

John Harrison ... "Seeing the Jam, finally after listening to them from 1977, was an awe inspiring thing for me. I can remember being totally mesmerised with them on stage. I remember that during 'Down in the Tube Station at Midnight' in the middle bit where the song then speeds up , 'Weller' yanked all of his strings off of his guitar in that unmistakable anger he was so good at. The roadies just passed him one they had ready earlier. I had managed to get in to the Top Rank that afternoon for the sound check and Weller was hanging around. Him and Bruce and Rick were chatting to the fans, but Paul always had that presence about him."

Simon Currie ... "I used to hang out with some of the older lads and follow them up to the gigs at Sheffield Top Rank. I saw Rich Kids there and also the Jam. They were fun times."

Steve Haythorne ... "Joe Jackson on the 'Look Sharp' tour was fantastic. They did an acoustic version of 'Is She Really going out with him', all harmonies and barber shop style and really striking to hear."

Ivor Hillman ... "An obvious influence at the time was my cousin Richard Jobson, who at the time was enjoying great success with Scottish Punk band the Skids. I saw a great Skids gig at the Top Rank and afterwards went back to the hotel they were stopping in and we drank and drank and drank."

Above: Skids flyer and ticket (from my collection)

Rob Saripo ... "We saw the Jam at the Top Rank in Sheffield. It must have been the early eighties, as 'Start' was their latest single which they played. I think it was number one in the charts at the time. The Jam Were Fantastic. Such raw power and energy on stage from one guitarist, one bass player and one drummer. Without doing a breakdown of individual songs, for me the Jam were masters at creating a rolling wall of sound. The all powerful guitar, the bass that ran up and down the fret board and the drums, always there; To me what made the Jam special was the punctuation between these three musicians. Check out the intro of 'Eton Rifles'. Need I say more?"

Nicky Booth ... "After seeing the Stranglers gig we went to see lots of bands. The Rezillos, Stiff Little Fingers, the Clash (they were bloody brilliant, definitely one of the best live acts), Siouxsie and the Banshees (she got quite grumpy about the spitting, and quite frankly who can blame her), Adam and the Ants (when he was a cult hero, before the pop success), Toyah (got a few albums signed by her before she made it big) and of course, the Stranglers every time they came to Sheffield. On one occasion I managed to get several record sleeves signed at the stage door. I still have them."

Gary Robinson ... "I went to see Eddie and the Hot Rods at the Top Rank in early 1979 on the 'Thriller' LP tour. This was when lead singer Barrie Masters had a row with a Punkette about Sid Vicious in the middle of their set."

Barrie Masters (Eddie and the Hot Rods singer) ... "I can't remember that at all, but then we played so many gigs it's so hard to remember them all. I know we did some great ones in Sheffield but it's so long ago they all merge into one really. Mind you, Sid Vicious did ruin the Sex Pistols. They were never the same after they kicked Glen Matlock out of the band."

Gary Robinson ... "I saw the Members five times. They were fantastic...loved The Members...what a group and they played some fantastic sets. Still love 'em now."

Steve Mardy from Manchester came through to Sheffield to see Manchester group's double bill Buzzcocks and Joy Division play at the Top Rank. The date was 21st October 1979. He recalls ... "We drove over from Tameside Manchester, where we were living at the time, up the A57- the route to all evils! We arrived in our Ford 8cwt in the steel city and parked up round the back of the Civic Hall, then made our way to the Top Rank venue. I saw the gig as a double blow to South Yorkshire in that two contingencies from Manchester were arriving to play there in one night.

Above: Pauline Murray of Penetration at Sheffield Top Rank May 1979 (Steve Marshall's collection)

Back then, shows were not for all ages so why I brought along my 12-year-old brother that night was an adventurous oversight on my part. My friends entered the venue and paid on the door, whilst I was firmly stopped by the doorman and told that he, the 'little un' wasn't coming in.

My mind went into overtime thinking how I could somehow smuggle him in without the doorman knowing. My thoughts ranged from bribes on the door to scaling a wall and entering a toilet window. We'd come too far to turn back and leaving him outside would have amounted to a visit from the social services the next morning. Joy Division were now on stage and about two songs in to their set. Ah well, I thought, they rehearsed in the same building as my band The Hoax so I could always catch 'em another night.

I came to a decision that we would have to both wait attentively and miserable on the steps outside the Top Rank until the end of the whole gig, then go home having learnt a horrible lesson, having developed a hatred towards the doorman who could have just turned a blind eye to us two weary travellers. Desperation turns to desperate measures and these were needed urgently. Looking down towards the Arundel Gate main road, I saw a red-headed Richard Boon accompanied by Steve Diggle with his girlfriend and also

Pete Shelley of the Buzzcocks. They were hastening towards the main door entrance where we were now standing. In a very un-rehearsed and impromptu act, much in the spirit of Punk, I said, *'Pete, we've come over from Manchester tonight to see you and I can't get him past the doorman because of his age'.* Unaware of the doorman seeing this or my actions in general, Pete Shelley looked at Richard and on the spur of the moment they took my brother back down the steps and entered the venue via the car park entrance and to my relief that was the problem solved.

By the time I got into the gig itself, Joy Division were two songs from completing their set. The gig was absolutely rammed and I couldn't get near the stage until Joy Division had finished their set. Amid the hustle & bustle, sweat and downing a few pints, I was able to make my way to the front of the stage by the time that the lights dimmed again for the Buzzcocks to come on stage. This moment also coincided with Peter Hook and Steven Morrison sweeping by me- making their way through the audience and out of the venue. I can also recall Ian Curtis passing by with a glamorous looking woman, who I guess was Annick: They were both being pursued by autograph hunters. I made my way to the front of the PA stack, which was on some kind of scaffolding, and I crouched down to see if my brother was there or looking around to meet me.

There he was, in some kind of an open space pit area in front of the stage- beaming away as Pete Shelley opened up with 'Real World'. My brother stayed in the ringside viewing area for the whole of the gig and from the age of twelve until this very day, he has remained a devotee of Buzzcocks music. I will forever be indebted to them for their attitude in taking care of the music and what ever comes with it."

Mark Senior (Sheffield Punk) ... "Around this time I attended my first punk gig (Buzzcocks with Joy Division at the Top Rank). I'd never heard of Joy Division and when this bloke came past us on the steps and said hello my mate told me that it was Ian Curtis, the vocalist. I met a girl from college called Dawn at the gig and ended up snogging at the bar, clutching my bag of badges, 'Different kind of tension' t-shirt and poster and banging down snakebites."

Gary Robinson ... "Yeah I went to that gig; Joy Division supporting Buzzcocks what a double bill that was. Another good one was Magazine at the Top Rank supported by Simple Minds. I can remember Simple Minds playing 'Life in a Day' loads of times, or so it seemed."

Martin C (Sheffield Punk) ... "I remember at one Damned gig at the Top Rank, me and my mate thought it would be a good idea to get backstage (I don't know why). Anyway we sneaked through a door to the right of the stage to be met with the sight of Damned singer Dave Vanian stood in a coffin. Needless to say we decided this was a bit weird and beat a hasty retreat!"

Paul Clarkson ... "My girlfriend knew Dave Vanian's wife quite well. So we used to look after their two pet rats 'Edgar' and 'Allen' when they went on tour."

Darren Twynham (Rotherham Punk fan) ... "Going to the Top Rank to see the Punk groups, we would neck a few pints down when we got there and head straight to the front of the stage to get a good view and be in the thick of it and then dive about when the groups came on."

Sham 69 at Sheffield Top Rank in 1978 (Anthony Cronshaw's - collection)

Martin Clarke ... "XTC at the Poly playing Hendrix's 'All along the watchtower' and their own 'Radios in Motion were amazing. Also one band that I always wanted to see were Talking Heads. I loved their 1977 album. We went along to the lower refectory when they were playing, but when we got there only one ticket was left. We tried to pay the door man to let us in but he wasn't having any of it. It was winter and freezing cold. We could see the support band through the window as clear as anything. They were just some pub rock band and nothing special at all. The following year Dire Straits were superstars. Never would have imagined that it would have happened for them. The night got colder and colder, the windows steamed up so much we couldn't see anything so we went home...would have loved to have seen em though."

Tony ... "After seeing the Stranglers I wanted to get and see as many Punk groups as I could and with a variety of different mates I set about seeing The Damned, The Clash, 999, Undertones, Siouxsie And the Banshees, Stiff Little Fingers and many many more. Because of our young age we had certainly missed some good ones but fortunately made up for them with some real classic gigs."

In addition to the vast selection of Punk groups, gigs and even the ever increasing amount of local 'garage and front room formed bands', there was also another lesser known aspect to the local Punk revolution that inspired new and refreshingly raw talent...Punk poetry.

The most well known exponent (nationally at least) was Manchester's John Cooper Clarke... who himself ventured to Rotherham in the mid 80's to perform his blend of Punk cutting edge poetry at, of all places Tiffany's nightclub...even staying at a fan's house in Rotherham after the gig... (Sham 69 also played there around that time as well)....But the lure of putting pogo pen to paper would most often come from the classroom.

Tony ... "I would spend hours at school and instead of doing my work I would be writing poems that reflected my anger and frustration. Some of the work would pass into the songs I would later write, but a lot of it was as trashy as shit really."

Another fellow Punk who vented much of his teenage anti-authoritarian anger in poetic verse was John Harrison (later adding his talents to some of the lyrics of Mod bands Reaction and The Way) but it would be a Sheffield 'New Wave' ranter called Mark Miwurdz who became most recognisable as the face of local Punk poetic commentary ...taking his talents along on tours with the Jam amongst others and earning a regular spot on the early shows of channel 4's new music programme of 1982 The Tube.

Tony ... "Before I could afford a proper electric guitar... the only way to express how I felt about the system and all that shit... was by writing it down on paper in poetic form. If all those Punk musicians could write all those lyrics, then why couldn't I? But for the time being it would be watching the bands play, rather than be a part of one, that would have to suffice. But as the weeks went by and I saw all the gig listings in Sounds and NME of my favourite Punk groups playing in Sheffield, I desperately wanted to go and see them all play. Very soon I would be going to see loads of the Punk groups play in Sheffield, Doncaster, Manchester and later on in Rotherham, when Punk made a welcome but unexpected return."

Chapter Ten

The Trouble with Punk

"Talk about the knife culture nowadays, which is very scary I must admit, but we experienced that kind of thing many years ago during the Punk era" – **Andy Goulty (Rotherham Punk Rocker)**

The prospect of violence and confrontation in Sheffield and the area was never far away during the turbulent times of the Punk era.

Anthony Cronshaw ... "We had a right old scrap with the Teds one Saturday afternoon. There were loads of 'em and they started on us – as they always did with any of the Punk crowd – but they got a right good reception back from us and the bottom of the Moor in Sheffield was strewn with Teddy boys laid out all over after the scrap."

Gary Robinson ... "One time at the height of all the Punk hating fury in 1977, I went into Virgin Records at the bottom of the Moor in Sheffield and I got hammered by Teddy Boys in there. They knocked me all over the place, records flying all over and everything. The Teds never had any time for us Punks."

Above: Anthony Cronshaw- Sheffield Punk fan, skinhead and Sham 69 roadie

Tony ... "One of the worst things about the punk era was the violence. Not so much at gigs - though I did see quite a bit from time to time- but my problem was from either straights (or the white shirt brigade as I called em), or rotten bloody Teddy boys. I apologise to any peaceful and gracefully growing old Teddy boys who never even looked at the cat the wrong way, but my experiences of Teddy boys back then were less than favourable. The worst incident with Teds for myself I have already mentioned but we would often run into them and sometimes they would be pretty hostile towards us to say the least."

Dave Spencer ... "On one occasion Cav, Dom and I went to Doncaster. We had a pretty uneventful shopping trip. Cav bought 'Teenage Warning' by the Angelic Upstarts and Dom and I clubbed together to get the Clash songbook. We had decided it was time to head back to the railway station and grab the train back to Rotherham, but just as we were leaving the Arndale Centre a lad approached us and said he was a Ted. I can clearly remember thinking, *'he doesn't look like much of a Ted to me'* as I looked him up and down. Whether this guy was older than us or not, I'm not sure, but he was definitely bigger. None of us was tough, and we probably didn't look it either, but Cav looked a bit bigger than Dom or myself so the 'Ted' zeroed in on him. *'Let's hurry up or we'll miss the train'...* I cheerily announced, but the 'Ted' was determined to slow us down. As we walked down to the underpass that runs from the back of the Arndale to the station the 'Ted' managed to stop Cav before Dom or I realised. He said to Cav, *'Do you know what Teds do to Punks?'* Unfortunately, Cav knew the answer to this one and volunteered, *'Beat them up?'* As soon as I heard this over my shoulder, I turned round to see 'Ted' kicking Cav in the head. Dom and I went back to help Cav and 'Ted' ran off back into the Arndale. We had to dash to get the train and as we sat down we guiltily consoled Cav. We were just starting to celebrate our scaring off the 'Ted', when he suddenly appeared at the train window with three or four other unconvincing teddy-boys. *'We're dead.'* I thought, but I was wrong, because just as the 'Teds' were about to open the carriage door, the train started moving and we escaped; Hurray for British Rail – friend of the punks!"

Paul Clarkson ... "I got chased by some skins, just managed to scramble over a fence to escape, those fucking bondage trousers meant you could never run away properly; legs tied together and all that."

Tony ... "Not much would go off inside the venues - not often at the Top Rank anyway - cos the bouncers would have kicked ten shades of shit out of anyone kicking off. They used to lay the boot in for nothing half the time to start with. They were not to be messed with that's for sure. I can remember after a Jam gig at Sheffield Top Rank. Me and my mates were getting our tickets signed by the band and trying to get a few words with em when a couple of skinheads charged through the fire exit that must have been open for some reason. They had broken bottles in their hands and ran in shouting and brandishing their weapons around offering to fight anyone who wanted a go. The bouncers soon made em turn tail and run. Weller never even looked up at all. Cool cat.

At another gig one skinhead was pissed and throwing his weight around threatening all of us. He was only a big mouth but he had a right gang behind him cracking their knuckles and just anticipating the promise of a scrap where they could outnumber the opposition. That night he didn't get what he was after and we managed to get out in one piece - only to get some aggro from another lot of idiots outside when we were walking up past Pond Street bus station. We just carried on walking and as I glanced around my mate Clarkey got a punch straight in the nose from behind. The blood just splattered

194

everywhere and he half went down. There was about 5 of us and maybe 15-20 or more of them with probably plenty more in the shadows. I waited for Clarkey to catch up and we stayed calm and carried on just as if nothing had happened with him holding his blood splattered nose. Soon we were safe on the number 69 bus and the gang would be starting on some other poor suckers.

He never had much luck old Clarkey poor lad. Another time we were waiting for a bus in Rotherham town centre bus station and we were laughing at something or other between us. These older blokes about twenty years old were pissed and one of them looks round says *'What you laughing at?'* and then just wacked Clarkey knocking him straight over the bus rails. Then a few weeks later the two of us were up Sheffield and a gang came and pummelled him into 'Our Price' records store window. Like I said he didn't have much luck in that sense. But it never got him down."

Paul Clarke … "I once got cracked by some skins while I was flipping through punk singles on a market stall on the Moor in Sheffield."

Helen McLaughlin … "I remember my mum telling me she had got on the bus to Rotherham town one day and went to sit upstairs so she could have a fag. The only room was with all the skinheads at the back of the bus so she sat with them. One of them said that no-one ever sat with them and wasn't she scared and she proudly said '*no, my daughter is a punk rocker'*, then they happily shared fags and sat together on the bus on numerous occasions afterwards."

Paul Bower … "The Good Mood club in Halifax was probably the most violent place we ever played in and we had pint pots thrown at us by the local Townies."

Jim Darnill (singer/guitarist 'Disease') … "We played in Wath and people were just scrapping with each other. The whole town seemed to be scrapping. I was giving them the evil eye. When we walked off stage this lad came up to me and said, *'what you looking at?'* He then squidged beer all down the front of me; I went barmy. He ended up roaring. He was supposed to be the local hard case. The bouncers chucked him out. We got outside and there was this big gang waiting for us. But they came up and said *'that was great, we want more bands playing here'.* I couldn't recommend it to anybody."**(From 'Beats working' for a living' by Martin Lilleker)**

Richard Chatterton … "I once got arrested for kicking and breaking a window in the door of the Adam and Eve nightclub in Rotherham market. The bouncers had wound me up for some reason during the college end of term do, and I unwisely threatened them. They slapped me around and I ended up spending the night in the Police cells. I didn't tell my parents but a guy from the CID called by when I was doing my art college homework. I got a £10 fine and £60 damages but they never fixed the window."

The inevitable dodging of school was not exempt with young Punk kids.

Pete Roddis … "I was wagging school one day and ended up in Rotherham Town centre. I was wearing a Stiff Little Fingers shirt with the two fingers V sign on. Some older lads came up to me and they said *'Oh right then, so you are telling us to fuck off then?'* and then they gave me a right hiding. I never forgave those guys for that."

Tony … "Me, Pete and Beanz (Dean Stables) went for a stroll one sunny summer's day. We ventured over to Abdey, which was kind of in the middle of nowhere. As we turned a corner near to where the old DC Cook house used to be, we walked past a bunch of about 7 or 8 older lads who looked like typical Punk hating fellas. They looked us up and down with sarcastic grins on their faces… the usual disgusted look we always used to get and carried on walking past us. Pure instinct told me that no way were they gonna leave it at that and as they were a few yards away I turned around and saw them stop, take a look at us, mutter a few words to each other and taking a few first steps forward, start to sprint towards us. *'C'mon lads lets get the fuck out of here'* me and the lads decided and off we scarpered with the gang chasing us.

We ran like bastards… it's amazing how fast you can run when you are outnumbered. It seemed like eternity though as we were speeding through the countryside and leaping over fences and gates with our pursuers gaining on us more and more. They were shouting allsorts of Punk abuse at us and we all knew that if they caught us they would give us a right hiding. The three of us were 14 to 15 years old and this lot were almost blokes… probably 18 to 20 year olds.

As we approached one of the countryside gates and tried to leap over it, Pete got his t-shirt stuck on the barbed wire at the top of it. He was stuck and it looked like we were now in for it. I stopped, turned around and saw Pete trying to pull himself free. I tried to help him, keeping a wide eye on the fast approaching gang of scurvy inflicted anti-Punk cutthroats who could now see Pete's disposition and knew that they were going to get their chance to punish us for having the nerve to be different. Time seemed to stand still for a few moments but then with one last tug, we pulled Pete's t-shirt free and continued our retreat with our last remaining ounces of sprinting energy. The distance between us increased and the twats finally had to give up as we got close to the end of the fields and almost to the main road over the hill. Too many fags and lard burgers hindered their chances of catching us little Punk waifs without an ounce of fat between us. If they had have caught us they would have got a shock too as Pete would have knocked at least a couple out and I reckon me and Beanz would have kicked a couple of bollocks for free… but ultimately we would have ended up laid out on the green grass of some South Yorkshire foreign field that would remain forever Punk land!. Oh well we got away and lived to tell the tale with Pete's t-shirt being the only injury. His t-shirt was his Stiff Little Fingers one with the V sign. Perhaps that was what inflamed the wrath of those out of date Punk haters. I mean we hadn't really told 'em to fuck off had we?"

Punk haunts in the Rotherham town centre were not always exclusive to their own crowd.

Gary Gillott (Chippie) … "Some Maltby skinheads came over one day to the Charters Arms pub where we used to hang out. One of them was going *'C'mon do yer want some'* – so I nutted him."

196

Meanwhile in the steel city, the violence was more methodical and to get to certain venues and pubs, Punks had to run the gauntlet.

Chiz … "Trouble used to flare up with the Sheffield skinheads who used to hang around the top of the escalators outside the Showboat amusements. They would bully young Punks into handing over their money, but all that stopped when the gigs moved to The Limit, Dingwalls and The Leadmill."

Over in neighbouring Doncaster, trouble could often find a home at the actual Punk gigs.

Tony …"I went to Doncaster to see the Damned and the punks were scrapping all over the place and hanging off the balcony and all sorts…It was kicking off all night for some reason. The Punks in Donny always seemed a lot more hardcore than the other places.

Another time in Doncaster we went to some sort of punk festival just outside of town. The Angelic Upstarts were playing and they always had a fair sized skinhead following. The tension was so noticeable in the air. You could literally taste the impending violence. Some other groups, the Uncool dance Band etc… well they did their sets and then not that long into the Upstarts set the fighting kicked off. It spread all over the park and kids were getting thrown into the nearby moat and all sorts. We luckily came away unscathed.

This all may sound like all the skinheads were bad lads but I met quite a few who were sound blokes and didn't cause us any hassle at all. I think it was just the image that they had and a lot of them always felt that they needed to live up to it and felt compelled to start a ruckus.

The very worst time I ever saw fighting and trouble at a gig has got to be at Manchester's Mayflower venue where once again we went to see the Damned. The fighting that night was unbelievable and there didn't seem to be any security at all. Well no one stopped it anyway. I can see this kid now with a completely shaved head and he had been bottled on the dance-floor and his head was cracked and blood just streaming down his head. He stood for a while and then just crumbled onto the dance floor. After the gigs at the Mayflower you wouldn't dare walk back into the city centre to catch the early morning train home or you would get a pasting off the local 'Perrys'.These were casuals and usually Manchester city fans. We used to get a taxi past there to the train station and we could see the gangs looming about.

Some of us used to go to Manchester regularly on a Saturday to see punk groups. There would be always myself and Andy Goulty and sometimes other mates like Andy Morton. We would skive a free ride on the national coach from Sheffield on a Saturday afternoon, arrive in the city an hour or so later, go to a café for a bite to eat and then hang around the city centre until early evening. Then we would catch the bus to the Mayflower and go and watch the groups. Often it would be about 5am on Sunday morning when we arrived back home. Other times we would go to the matinee show.

During one of these ventures over the Pennines me and my mate Andy were in the Arndale centre and suddenly aroused the attention of quite a few of the members from a mixed gang. We knew they were after something, even though they were coming up to us trying to appear friendly. More and more of them started to follow us. We saw a copper and had a word with him telling him we thought we were going to get a hiding off the gang who were now numbering around 20.

Above: Damned Mayflower club flyer

The policeman simply did not want to get involved and just told us to move on, which we did with our newly acquired friends along with us. Outside we were getting worried. The gang were drifting back a lot but still tailing us and pointing. We managed to get near Piccadilly station and thought they would let us go, when this coloured guy with a Michael Jackson afro caught up to us and started chatting to us- asking where we were going and what group we were there to see etc.

He seemed ok that lad – until he pulled a knife on us and demanded all of our money. His attitude changed and he threatened to stab us if we didn't comply. Me and Andy looked at each other and understood what the other must be thinking. We both knew we were not going to give him all our cash. We could see his mates watching and time seemed to stand still. Then at once I said *'Look mate this is all we have got'* and we both lobbed a pocketful of Penny's each at him. Then we scarpered while the fella just stood there amazed at our cheek. We heard him shout his mates and we think that they pursued us for a while as we sneaked in to the bus station and hid in the travel and enquiries place. We had had some good times in Manchester and some great laughs but this was not one of them and we never went again. After that experience – walking home from a gig and going through the gauntlet of beer boys in Parkgate shouting abuse and threats whilst stood outside after kicking out time from their pubs. Well that seemed like nothing from then on."

John Harrison … "The thing is, as far as I can remember, there was hardly ever any fighting at the actual Punk gigs- certainly not between the Punks; maybe the skinheads and the straights, but not between us lot. Mostly everyone went out to have a good time and that's what we had; A bloody good time too."

June Graham (Rotherham Punkette) … "Yes there were some scuffles here and there, but mostly we all were out for a good time. Nothing was ever intended malicious or anything… and there was not the stabbings going on like nowadays. I met some great people by going to Punk gigs and we all got on great."

Phil Tasker ... "I don't remember any specific violent incidents, but some gigs were packed and could be dangerous when people were pogoing freely and bashing in to each other. Some gigs were pretty dangerous if you were at the front, I remember the Clash gig at Sheffield Top Rank, there was a massive crush at the front and people were pushed against the stage."

The Punk scene also had another setting. It had now spread to the football terraces, and Sheffield's two football teams 'Sheffield Utd' and 'Sheffield Wednesday' both saw the appearance of Punk Rock in their grounds and amongst their fans. As previously stated both sets of these rival fans were attending Punk gigs in the city, where for a few euphoric hours, they forgot about their differences. Sometimes- due to mere coincidence- the presence of football could infiltrate the culture of Punk in often funny scenarios.

Paul Clarke ... "Me and Tony were on our way to Sheffield one Saturday afternoon. We were on the old number 69 bus but got fed up with being stuck in traffic, which wasn't moving as it was mostly heading for the football match in Sheffield. We got halfway there and decided to get off and walk the rest of the way; Bad idea. As soon as we started walking, the football fans in the cars started winding their windows down and shouting obscenities at us. Why? Well Tony had the punk band's name Chelsea painted on the back of his leather jacket and the football fans were 'Spurs' fans on their way to a cup match. Tony put two fingers up to them, saying *Fuck off! It's a punk band!'*... Me? Well I was shitting myself (laughs)."

Tracy Stanley ... "Once there was me, Tony and Pete Roddis in Sheffield. I think we had been to see Adam and the Ants or Siouxsie and we were chased by the skinheads - God it was scary - and we just managed to jump on the number 69 bus before they got us. We were so lucky cos they would have killed us, there were loads of them and they looked much older. Someone was looking over us that day."

Jo Callis (Rezillos guitarist) ... "We in the Rezillos took a great pride (and still do) in the fact that we try to encourage an audience who want to have a good time and discourage any violent element, but I guess there's always going to be the odd nutter. If anything does kick off, we'll try to nip it in the bud, we'll just stop playing until it's sorted. It's just not tolerated and thankfully those instances were rare, you'd see more violence on the stage than in the audience at one of our gigs, and that's the way (the way, the way) we like it, uh huh, uh huh!"

Mark Senior (Sheffield Punk) ... "Some of the gigs could be violent; I remember getting in a fight at the Sham 69 one at the Rank, all hell broke loose. The Adam and the Ants gig was heavy too with the Sheffield lads banging at it with the Londoners all night."

Tony ... "I suppose the other common occurrence at Punk gigs that always got blown out of proportion by the dailies was the spitting lark. Well I don't suppose it was a lie at all really. It did happen a lot. I know the Clash despised it and when I saw them at the Sheffield Top Rank they made it perfectly clear that they would not tolerate it and the gobbing just about stopped. The Jam didn't get much spitting and always demanded respect from the crowd. Siouxsie and the Banshees were spat on at their Sheffield Top Rank gig and vowed never to come back to Sheffield again."

Martin Clarke ... "One of the things that startled me was the spitting! I never got used to that. I can remember Steve Severin of Siouxsie and the banshees walking onstage and the first thing that he said was *'Stop fucking spitting ok?'* My first Punk gig had been The Clash. Richard Hell was the support and he was on his knees a couple of feet away from the throbbing crowd who were pouring drinks and gob all over him. He never complained at all.

The Damned on their November 1977 tour got spat on. They had an old jazz musician Lol Coxhill on stage with them playing saxophone. He just stood there playing there in his duffel coat and as he was getting spat all over he never moved or showed any reaction either. The Dead Boys were also on the bill and a can of beer hit singer Stiv Bators on the head and he never even flinched."

Phil Tasker (left) ... "And then of course there was the spitting, when we (Vice Squad) supported Sham 69 at the Outlook there was loads of spitting and it would fall like rain highlighted against the coloured lights."

John Harrison ... "At one of the Undertones concerts I went to in 1979 some of the punks started spitting at them and I remember Feargal Sharkey saying that if it didn't stop they were going off. It stopped after that."

Tony ..."Me and Pete went to see 999 a couple of times and at one of the gigs we were there quite early on before the place had started to fill up so we decided to get a place at the very front of the stage leaning right up against it.

The groups 999 and Pinpoint were great that night, and we got bruised which was to be expected. One thing we had forgotten though was the spitting. 999 went down so well that all the punks showed their appreciation with their mouth contents. We couldn't get out of the way if we had tried to. Me and Pete came out of that gig completely covered in gob and it was not pleasant at all. But it didn't phase us. Just have to make sure we got a better place next time."

Pete Roddis ... "I remember at some of the gigs at the Top Rank, there was this Hippy fella who used to fill in between the groups and he would play these tunes on an acoustic guitar, getting absolutely covered in spit. That 999 gig …I got a drum stick when their drummer threw it over. I shoved it down my trouser leg as some of the other lads were after it as well."

Phil Tasker … "I don't remember much in the way of drugs being about, mainly a bit of dope, but you didn't see that much smoking going on maybe a few poppers being passed around."

John Harrison … "Drugs? I never bothered with 'em. To be honest I don't think there was that much knocking about on the scene. Now, later on with the Mods there were certainly more drugs floating about when I was into the Mod scene, than during my Punk days."

Above: Sham 69 onstage in Sheffield at the Top Rank (Anthony Cronshaw's collection)

Tony … "I did see a little drugs being passed around, but not like you would have imagined going on compared to what the media was saying. Obviously, the glue sniffing did go on and cider was a popular drink with Punks. Later on some of the lads I hung about with; they started taking drugs, but I never asked them what it was or wished to get involved at all. There were needles being passed around, I do know that. Some others may have had a bit of blow every now and again, but that was a hippy drug really. Quite suitable for Crass I suppose. Personally the only stuff I did during the Punk era was amyl nitrate once (which made me feel like my head was gonna bust), and the obligatory pints of cider or lager."

Another ominous sign of the times back in the late seventies and this coincided exactly with the emergence of the Punk scene, and that was The National Front. They were to be seen campaigning around the Rotherham area, in particular.

Tony … "I can remember the National Front and the Anti-Nazi League both being visible in Rotherham Town Centre around mid 1978. There would be each one of them set up near each other, trying to put their cause across. I was pretty naïve at the time about politics but went for the Anti- Nazi League for three reasons. First cos the yellow badge they gave me looked the most cool, second because I had heard some connection between them and the Clash, and third because I came from a generation of World War two obsessed kids who naturally hated the Nazis. I had two Uncles that served in WW2, one of whom had been ambushed and then captured by the Germans who then turned their guns on him and his mates and bayoneted all of the survivors… my Uncle managed to survive to tell the tale, and he became an atheist after the war. So no way was I gonna give my support to a party that had respect for the Nazis."

John Harrison … "I kind of designed a badge for the Anti-Nazi League, which came about by accident really. I was in Rotherham town centre, where they used to set up regularly, and I had this badge on that I had made myself; it was one with the pig with a policeman's helmet on and I added 'Who killed Liddle Towers' on it and sellotaped over it. Anyway the ANL saw it and when I told them I had made it myself, they asked me if they could use it for themselves as well, so I let them use it."

Paul Bower … "At the time The National Front was really active- mainly coming down from Leeds. We used to do a song called 'Fuck the National Front', which at gigs once or twice caused huge fights, which thankfully resulted in the Front getting beaten up cos there was more of us than there were of them. It was quite a tense time."

Chapter Eleven

Groups, gigs and gig goers

"Gigs in Yorkshire were sometimes a little scary at times due to football rivalry. The band played at the Windmill Club Rotherham in 1979, and as we were carrying our gear out down the steps... Rotherham's finest were raining blows down at us and throwing bottles from the balcony above" – **Phil Taylor (X- Rippers from Barnsley)**

For a period of around four years - spurred on by Punk - Sheffield's live music scene thrived and a genuine music fan could most likely go and see a good live band most nights of the week. The gigs themselves would enable young Punk fans to socialise and meet other music fans (Sometimes forming their own bands together) ... people who, otherwise, they would never have come into contact with.

Above: Punk fans at Sheffield City Hall

Richard Chatterton ... "In Sheffield, I got to know most of the local Punk Glitterati. A couple of older guys at the Top Rank, I was told had been there right at the very start of Punk. They had chiselled features, spiky hair and wore shades. Compared to me they seemed statuesque. I never got to know them well but I think one of them was called Tank. I did get to know big John, a loveable six foot seven Sid Vicious look-alike from Malin Bridge who spent most of his time falling in love and then being dumped, getting into odd situations with handcuffs, police stations and gelignite. He had, and still has, a slight stutter and a number of catch phrases like *'Anarchy or what!* , *'You dog'* and *'Two pints of lager and a packet of c-c crisps'.* Everyone loved him and he truly was a gentle giant. He used to tell me he wasn't going to live past 21 but he is still around. He would take fellow Punks on mystery trips in his dad's bakers van. I once went to Manchester airport with him just so he could see the runway on which he was going to fly to New York from during the following week.

The other Sheffield Punks I can remember were Eileen (the vicar's daughter), and Jane. They used to follow bands around and were kind of groupies I guess. There was a Punk girl called Sarah who used to hang around with the Damned, following their motto of 'Anarchy and Chaos' to such an extent that they ended up having to throw her off their tours. Sarah was briefly in Sheffield Punk band Debar. There were two lads from Brinsworth who were briefly on the scene. I think they were called Smith and Stu. I have to admit that I was a little jealous at first as I wanted to keep this exciting new scene to myself and I was a little jealous of Stu's looks. Anyway they didn't hang around the scene for too long. I think Stu's dad told him to cut his hair and smarten up his image. There was one lad from Rotherham who also hung around Sheffield and he also knew Big John and partook in his mystery trips. He was called Derek Morley and he wore black bondage gear and had blond locks when I first met him."

Above: A rare original Clash tour poster from a 1978 date at the Top Rank (Courtesy of punkrockposters site)

Steve Marshall ..."I got a temporary job at the Top Rank as a Humper, which was humping/unloading all the band's amps and stuff into the Top Rank from those big trucks and up the steps and ramp and onto the stage. We got free entry into all the gigs, extra tickets for our mates (guest lists stuff too), free food from the kitchens AND they paid us about £14 a day. As well as this we got credits to play on the space invader machines which were big at the time... Excellent - would you believe it?

I did work for all the Punk groups- The Clash, Damned, Buzzcocks, Police, Stiff Little Fingers, Undertones, Skids, Joy Division and some reggae stuff too. Brilliant times. I had some really good mates back then."

Richard Chatterton ... "I remember all of the venues around the area; one of them was the Polytechnic where you had to get a student to sign you in. I remember carrying some gear for the Magazine road crew and I got in to the gig for free to see one of the gigs of the decade- Magazine with Bauhaus supporting. I bumped into Pete Murphy of Bauhaus on the spiral staircase. I instantly saw him and decided on my own new look."

Gary Gillott (Chippie) ... "My tastes in Punk were not like just one group or anything. Like some kids would follow a particular Punk group like you would follow a football team. With me, a good song is a good song. You can't hold a good song down so it was straight across the whole thing really, picking up good stuff from it all. I did like Magazine, Ultravox with John Foxx in, the Stranglers, the Pistols – obviously – and early Cure."

Although the Sheffield Top Rank and the other few venues in Sheffield and Doncaster were the main focal point for gigs, many young Punk fans would go further afield to catch their favourite groups in action.

Paul White (Sugar) ... "After seeing my first Punk gigs in Sheffield and also UK Subs in Barnsley, I would go all over the place to see bands; London, Manchester, Nottingham, Derby, Leeds, all over the country. We would also end up doing a bit of roadie work too, shifting the gear about for the groups and then we would get in to the gigs for free."

Martin Clarke ... "I saw the Adverts at Retford Porterhouse and the ceiling was so low that Howard Pickup (their guitarist) couldn't stand up straight as he was so tall. We talked to TV Smith at the bar for a while and he was great fun."

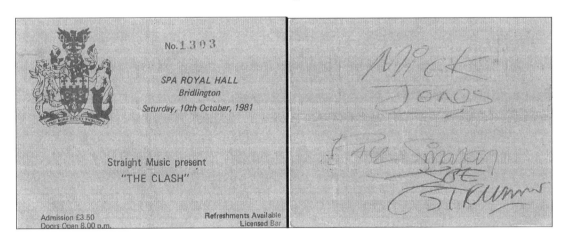

Above: 'Clash' ticket and autographs- from Punk fan 'Andrew Morton's collection

Andrew Morton ..."I saw Tony (the author) at school with the Clash LP 'Give 'em enough Rope' under his arm. He also had the Clash chalked on the back of his school blazer. It got me interested and I managed to get that LP, from of all places, Grattons catalogue. I always liked the Clash and still love 'em to death even now.

Later on I went to see them at Bridlington Spa. The Clash were fantastic and it was a really memorable gig. Afterwards I got to meet the group. Joe Strummer was really friendly as was Topper. Paul Simonon was too, but he was a lot quieter. I don't think Jonesy came out to chat at all. At the gig we had met an old school friend who had just moved to Brid. He offered to put me and my mate Chris up for the night round at his place, so after the gig we went with him, heading for his place. He told us to wait outside and he went in to the house. Lights went out and he never came back out. Cheers, we thought and off we went to sleep it rough for the night. I have never felt as cold in my life, as I did that night. I woke myself up with my own teeth chattering. But it was all worth it to see the Clash. The next night I went to see them play in Sheffield."

Bryan Bell … "I used to go to places like Nottingham Sandpipers to see Punk groups. Also I would go to Retford Porterhouse. I went to see Adam and the Ants there and they talked about cancelling the gig after they saw how small the venue was."

Over in nearby Chesterfield there was also a Punk scene developing and it would sometimes attract punk visitors from Sheffield.

Richard Chatterton … "I met a girl called Lisa at the front of the stage at a Skids concert at the Top Rank. She was from Chesterfield and she told me about this venue in Chesterfield called Fusion that she had been to. I had read about it when the Sheffield Star was raving on about it so I was determined to go. I went there on my own one Thursday night on the train. I was nervous as hell. The venue was as good as I had imagined it would be. As I arrived there were two girls in monochrome Sixties dresses dancing to Blondie, Talking Heads and Squeeze records. I later bumped into Lisa and her friends on my third visit.

One of the times I ended up missing the train and stayed with a peroxide blonde youth called Chris Kneller. He put me up a few times and also introduced me to the sound of Punk band Eater, New York Dolls and The Rocky Horror Picture Show as well as advising me on my fledgling love life.

Above: Richard Chatterton – Punk Rocker from Brinsworth (Rotherham)

The Fusion was the best club I ever went to – it had none of the pretentiousness of Sheffield, the music would rotate (an hour of Heavy Metal, then Soul followed by Punk and 'New Wave') and there was never any trouble. Everybody seemed to know each other and there were plenty of people who would help you out. I remember some of their names – Chris, Simon Charity, Mark Adams, Mick, Pez, Dawn, Steve, Julie Kerry, Bev, the guys in the band 'Yah- boo!' and 'Foot rot' Dave, John etc."

And the Chesterfield Punks certainly knew how to have fun.

Chiz (Chesterfield Punk) … "We mostly drank in The Buck Inn across from the Crooked Spire in the town centre. One of the more colourful characters who we hung around with was a punk called Bernie. There was never a dull moment when he was around. I remember once in The Buck Inn he read a label under his stool and pronounced it was a 'Japanese Hover stool' but the instructions were in Japanese so he couldn't understand them. The next thing we new he was running around the pub with the stool firmly attached to his back side, crashing into tables and chairs, even cascading behind the bar where the landlord proceeded to chase him with a baseball bat. At this point most people would stop and apologise but not Bernie, he ran up the road, still attached to the Japanese Hover stool with the landlord chasing him with the baseball bat. Then we saw his head come past the windows and he ran back in the pub, did a somersault and landed on a couch with the stool. He told the landlord the stool had stopped and he could calm down. Just as the landlord got back behind the bar Bernie shouted *'It's starting again!!'* and the whole comical episode was repeated!

I could go on forever about the antics of this one man who got us barred from most town centre pubs at one time or another: but one more that springs to mind is upstairs in the Trap 7 bar above The Greyhound pub next to the Crooked Spire (now a coffee shop after it got trashed in a brawl with a party on a stag night). Someone touched one of Bernie's badges on his leather jacket and asked him what it was for. He replied *'That puts me into Batman mode!'* and jumped straight out of the upstairs window. When we looked out we could see him laid on his back on the pavement with his leg broken. He shouted *'Chiz! Are you in your car? Can you nip me to hospital'* I said *'Yes, it's in the car park over the road. Start crawling and I'll be there when I've supped my pint!'* The next few months he had a pot up the whole of his leg and used to come into town wearing his sister's mini-skirt and fishnet tights."

Richard Chatterton … "One drunken Sunday night me and the Chesterfield Punks (Seven of us and one girl I think), well we went for a midnight jog, me in my underpants. Me and a guy called Mick were separated from the others after seeing a squad car but we all made it back to safety. The experience was exhilarating though."

Tony … "On the way back from a gig in Manchester there was me and Andy Goulty and Andy Morton (we would catch the early morning train about 4am ish), we had a piss about on the train as there was no guard on and hardly anyone on there except the driver. We left a right mess on there when we got off in Sheffield and one of the two Andy's nearly missed the stop and just managed to get off in time, otherwise it would have been next stop Retford. From Sheffield we would walk it home and get in about 5am.

Another time me and Andy Goulty were on the way to Manchester on one of our Saturday afternoon jaunts…well I had been feeling unwell before we set off and wasn't really feeling up for going but Andy talked me into it. Anyway, we got our snap packed up and set off to Sheffield to catch the National coach and sneak on for free as usual.

Halfway to Manchester and I was feeling like shit - I must have looked as green as the fuckin' Pennine fields we were passing - well in a frantic rush out came the sandwiches and food from my carrier bag, just split seconds before I heaved my guts up into the bag. Talk about coming prepared. The other passengers were looking at us as if to say 'Disgusting Punk Rockers' and shaking their heads. Andy looked a bit squeamish and I couldn't really blame him. When we arrived into Manchester bus station he went and puked his guts up too. Yes that's what you call Punk unity."

Andy Goulty ... "How we managed to get away with going to the Manchester gigs, I have no idea. It was a case of telling our parents we were off to Sheffield for the day and then sneaking onto the national coach for free and off to Manchester to the Mayflower club. That was a rough joint. Unbelievable."

Sheffield and the local region's Punks now ritually met up for Saturday afternoon parades down the Moor.

Above: Local Punk gig goers

Gary Gillott (Chippie) ... "Saturday afternoons; it would be a 2 o'clock meeting up at the fish bowl in the hole in the road (in Sheffield city centre), and then we would parade ourselves down the Moor and head for Virgin Records at the bottom. There would often be about 100 of us Punks and the grannies would be running around trying to get out of our way."

Bryan Bell ... "I remember the trips down the Moor on Saturdays. It would usually end up with some trouble kicking off, especially later on when the skinheads came about and the Teds had always been around anyway and when there were enough of them trouble would usually flare up."

So, there were the Punks in the region and the many styles of Punk to listen to on vinyl...with a good selection of the groups now playing local venues regularly. Not a week went by (between the years 1978 to 1980) when there wasn't at least three or four Punk gigs going on; But what were the local Punk influenced groups getting up to amidst a small but developing local music scene?

Patrick Tierney ... "Mention should also be made of our local bands. I think all music fans in Donny at that time will have seen the Shy Tots and the Uncool Dance band at least once. I saw both a number of times. The Shy Tots drummer was Colin Rocks and he was a real powerhouse of a drummer who could really take on diverse influences. I rehearsed with him once in a brick practice area behind The Sun Inn. I was playing bass in an aspiring band (which never really came to anything, although we nearly supported the Mekons) and I was terrible. Colin sat in and played drums. He wove patterns around my bass parts and actually made me sound passable. What a drummer.

Above: Doncaster's Shy Tots

The Uncools (Uncool Dance band) were a good, tight band with some good material. The original singer was called Chris Bottrell and he was a nice bloke, but unfortunately he died very prematurely (leukaemia, I think).The band carried on and the gig of theirs I particularly remember was an open-air concert at Sandhall Park. Can't remember who else was on the bill, but I think the Uncools may have headlined (it was the Angelic Upstarts who headlined) they were brilliant anyway. There were other local groups, like Rotherham's The Prams - singers of the immortal 'Is It Love (Or Is It Indigestion)?' And Mexborough's Eyes at Risk and many more that fell by the wayside."

Although Sheffield had by this period quite a few of its own groups to emerge around the time of the punk era, there were still not really that many that could be termed Punk Rock groups. For a while the Stunt kites were probably Sheffield's only real punk group in the conventional sense; if that's not too lazy a description to use.

The Stunt kites were formed at the height of Punk Rock in 1977 and were Sheffield's most enduring band of their kind. The original founder members were John Allen on vocals, Steve Chapman on guitar and they were joined by Nigel 'Reg' Renshaw also on guitar, Mick Greening on bass guitar and Brent Sharp on drums. Their name was chosen after a TV advert for, you guessed it, Stunt-kites. After playing a first gig in July 1978 for handicapped children and a few other low key ones, they played their first serious gig at the Penthouse on the Tuesday Punk night. Other groups playing that night were Clock Dva, Vice Versa and Used Toys.

Subsequently the Stunt Kites played gigs all over the Sheffield and surrounding area. They played in Wath upon Dearne, Barnsley, Retford and just about every venue in the

Sheffield city centre. They were always very popular with the 14 year old Punk kids who were just getting into the scene.

Tony ... "I can remember walking around Sheffield at the time and it seemed that every where you went, there would be gig posters of the Stunt Kites knocking around(band members John Alan and Nigel Renshaw were both fined for putting posters up at one point). I first heard them on the John Peel show and thought they were great. I can't remember which song it was but I had it on tape for ages. I saw the Stunt Kites a couple of times in pubs in Sheffield. One of the times was a bit later on and when they were supposed to be playing with the UK Subs at the Marples. Well they didn't play as such. They were actually a play; some kind of Christmas play or something?"

Above: the Stunt Kites playing at Sheffield Marples (Steve Marshall's collection)

John Harrison ... "I liked the Stunt Kites. I saw them play a few times; usually in some pub on the outskirts of the city centre, but also when they supported the Adverts at the Top Rank. I took my girl friend at the time to see them and we both thought they were great. They brought out a couple of decent singles too."

Highly critical of some of the other Sheffield groups and especially the Bryan Ferry look-alikes who went to the Crazy Daisy and Limit club, the Stunt kites once made a list of all

210

the Sheffield band members in their audience at a particular gig. They read them all out and then proceeded to pull to pieces the local groups who were not in attendance. The Stunt Kites split up in mid 1980, after releasing a track on an E.P with other Sheffield groups. Their track was called 'Beautiful people'. They soon re-formed with a slightly changed line up. Guitarist Steve Chapman and Drummer Brent Sharp left and Tony Armitage and Andrew Young joined on drums and bass respectively. The new Stunt Kites were of a more post-punk musical approach and were admired by John Peel amongst others... They released a 12" e.p 'Lebensraum' on the Pax label and a further single 'Leonora/Hail to the Roots'. They performed at a 25 years anniversary gig in 2003 at the Memorial Hall in Sheffield, alongside long time fan Jarvis Cocker.

Late 1978 and the first and second wave of local Punks were starting to lose a gradually increasing amount of their favourite groups. Eater, Slaughter and the Dogs, Depressions, Damned, Heartbreakers, Vibrators and many more bit the new wave multi - coloured dust that year...most of them returning to fight the Punk Rock cause another day. Another one to part their ways was the Rezillos who had played a handful of memorable gigs at the local venues of the region.

Jo Callis ... "Oh God, that was a difficult time, the Rezillos split has been covered here and there, the usual stuff; Differing opinions on direction, hotheads, power struggles, ego's, the bloody mindedness of youth."

But for ex Rezillo Jo, that was not the end of it as far as performing live was concerned and Sheffield along with good old Donny had not seen the last of his many ventures.

Jo Callis ... "After The split I formed SHAKE with Ali (Angle) and Simon (Templar) from the Rezillos, along with Troy Tate (later of Teardrop Explodes fame). We released a couple of records (10" EP SHAKE; Culture Shock, Glasshouse, Dream On, (But) Not Mine. and 7" single 'Invasion Of The Gamma Men') and gigged around, in fact we definitely played The Limit club in Sheffield, and The Top Rank (I think it was) supporting The Undertones.
     We played Donny as well, can't remember the name of the gig, but was in a really tacky seventies disco type place, with the fixtures decorated in denim. After SHAKE came 'Boots For Dancing', a local Edinburgh band I joined which was out of Bob Last's current stable of Post Punk Indie hopeful's! I loved that Band and Ali (Angle Paterson) was in it for a while too."

Jo was to return to the Sheffield scene yet again not too far down the line; though without the high energy and sci-fi injected fun of the Rezillos and in a different setting altogether...but still performing on the steel city's stages...The Sheffield live scene was stepping up a few paces by the late 70's and the new set of local musicians who were rising through the ranks often inspired Punk fans to take note and sometimes have a go themselves.

Michael Day ... "I had always been into the usual stuff that seemed to lead people towards punk, David Bowie, T.Rex and the Sweet but really got into the scene when I started to meet some local bands that were playing around. I had been to see a number of punk bands playing at venues in Sheffield and knew some people who were really into the early scene such as Ian Williams from Gleadless Valley who was always around town and knew bands like the Buzzcocks extremely well. I went to a party and met The Negatives who had just released a couple of tracks on 'New Wave from the Heart' LP so I finally knew someone in a band. This propelled me headlong into the scene and at that time everyone was in a band and so I started one too. We were called Short Circuit and we played a few gigs with The Negatives and also with The Stunt kites."

Other Punk inspired groups to emerge in the Sheffield and surrounding area at this time were Low Life (from Bakewell), Repulsive Alien, a Punk group from Dronfield who formed after meeting at a Clash gig in Sheffield while still at school and after encouragement from local fanzines and line up changes, eventually split in 1980. Then there was Shattered Life (who later merged into Debar), The Ultimate(who played punked up first generation rock n' roll), Jam influenced band Difficult Decision from Dronfield, the X-Rippers from Barnsley and early skinhead band Molodoy.

Molodoy were popular with the Punk crowd and were influenced musically by Wire with singer Gary Warburton visually influenced by 'Clockwork Orange'. They wrote Post-Punk sounding songs with questionable titles such as 'Children of the Third Reich'.

Perhaps one of the most 'Punk' in attitude was a Sheffield group simply called 'The', who would later become Artery. Led by charismatic front man and singer Mark Goldthorpe 'The' played a supporting slot for Sham 69 at Sheffield Polytechnic after Slaughter and the Dogs failed to turn up for the gig (yet again!). The gig started badly after technical problems, but after a few numbers they won over the Punk audience.

Their songs such as 'Change it all' and 'You on the street' were compared to the Clash by local fanzine 'Home Groan' and the next time Sham 69 played Sheffield (this time at the Top Rank) Jimmy Pursey asked for the group to support them again.

By this time, Sham 69 had acquired their infamous east end skinhead following who had come along for the tour, along with local skinhead Sham fans. The first song was dedicated to the Anti-Nazi League, which was unsurprisingly not appreciated by some elements of the crowd. An onslaught of glass throwing, abuse and threats was the response from the skins. Singer Goldthorpe offered to take them on and the night erupted into a continuous succession of fight after fight. Not long after the gig 'The' threw out guitarist Paul Bellamy and had a line up change and switch in direction, becoming Post- Punk group Artery.

In July 1978 Sheffield's 2.3 were featured in 'Zigzag' magazine, where they were given a firm thumbs up from writer Chris Westwood. Under a headline of '2.3 The Birth of Sheff Rock', the band talk about Politics, line up changes and their single released earlier that year. Asked if they thought that Punk was a fading dying thing'... Paul replies *'No, not really. It's just that much of it has become too clichéd. It did provide an incentive. I think it's been good in directing attention away from the Rock dinosaurs.'*

2.3 songs mentioned are titles like 'summer of 69' (about mindless football thugs), 'The Beats are back', and 'Bright lights over Europe'. The writer proclaims that *'2.3 have 'A whole lot more credibility than any bloated BOF you care to name' and that 'Paul Bower is one of the most sincere committed, no- bull out and out straight guys you're ever likely to cross paths with.'*

Above: Sheffield's 2.3 in 1978 and at right members of Doncaster's Vice Squad Punk group backstage at Retford Porterhouse

As much as there was an enthusiastic local Punk audience keen to hear what the region's live scene had to offer, most of the groups themselves were by and large unwilling to follow the typical Punk path of playing three chord energetic pogo offerings. Sheffield always had its own slant on the notion of what Punk represented in relation to the live scene. As such, it has often been quoted that the steel city was more interested in taking up the challenge of the synthesiser as its torch of Punk rebellion!

The early work of the Human League did retain the initial spirit of adventure that Punk had encouraged, as did other Sheffield Synth hopefuls Vice Versa amongst others. But the sound of Punk Rock guitars being tuned (or de-tuned) was still to be heard along the dotted boundaries of Sheffield and the locality's suburbs as a further core of Punk influenced combos began to hear their voices heard. As well as Sheffield's Stuntkites and others previously mentioned...during the middle of 1978 there were still plenty of those incisive power chords waiting to be heard. For a short while, the local Punk scene was alive and well... but time was running out!

In Doncaster there was the aforementioned Sublimal Cuts and Shattered Life but the town also offered the handcuffs and ID cards of Vice Squad; fronted by Doncaster Punk Phil Tasker who had formed the group in 1977.

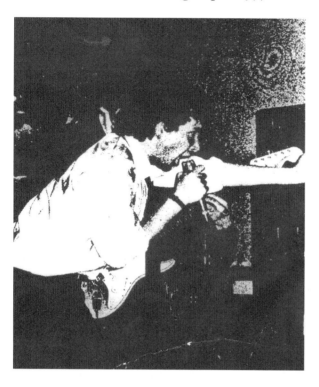

Above: Vice Squad's Phil Tasker at Their first gig (March 1978)

Phil Tasker … "We started as three kids just out of school, there was me on guitar and vocals, Chris Bedford on bass and a guitarist called Ray Campbell. I had been writing stuff for a while and we started writing together and rehearsing at a place in Woodlands. We decided to form a band because we were excited by bands that we'd seen, mainly at the Outlook, such as the Boys, Generation X, Buzzcocks, Stranglers and many more. Early influences were the Stooges, Velvet Underground, Lou Reed, Roxy Music and Bowie, also more locally, Be Bop Deluxe. The main problem that we had was we had no drummer, and without a drummer there was no drive behind the music.

Eventually we heard about Roger Jackson and Clive Brooks, they were still at school and had long hair but were keen to join a band, so we got together and things seemed to gel. We started rehearsing at a youth centre near a cemetery in Balby and worked on original material with the odd Velvets track and a punked up version of 'Can't Buy Me Love' by the Beatles. We were all from the Intake area and had a Green Transit van called 'The Green Bomber'.

The first gig was at The Woolpack in Doncaster in March 78 and had a good turn out, mainly because people were so curious about these 'punk rockers'. It went pretty well, there were no major incidents although we were very nervous, especially as we were playing our own stuff and most people were used to bands doing covers. I had moved to just doing vocals now that we had two guitarists and we kept working on new material. Not long after, we played at the Outlook supporting Sham 69, it had been snowing and the van was playing up, I remember we had to push it quite a lot, sliding about in winkle pickers! The gig was packed to the roof and we were extremely nervous, I felt like I wanted to throw up, especially as I was the front man. Of course, everyone had come to see Sham 69; I think they had been on Top of the Pops -

- with one of their famous tracks and we really felt like we were second class citizens. I remember Jimmy Pursey not being particularly friendly, I think he thought we were just hicks from the sticks. The gig itself didn't seem too bad but it all went by in a blur, I remember we were gobbed on copiously, but that came with the territory really, all bands whoever they were got gobbed on in those days. Of course, we relied on friends to help hump the gear about, a bloke called Andy Fountain used to drive the van and roadie for us. People were always asking for freebie ties as we wore skinny ties sometimes as if they were some kind of sales gimmick. We did a 4 week residency at Lincoln AJ's which was also very strange but we needed the money, talk about the city of the dead!"

Photo by Paul Sharpe

Above: Doncaster Punk group Vice Squad' from left Chris Bedford; Bass guitar –
Phil Tasker; Vocals and Clive Brooks; Guitar – seen here playing a
'Rock against Racism' gig at First aid youth centre Doncaster

Eventually we had enough material for a demo tape, and we managed to find a recording studio at Heckmondwyke, can't remember the name of it, I think Be Bop Deluxe had recorded there. We recorded five or six tracks, live in the studio, no overdubs, and it was ok really, we were quite proud of it. Not long after recording the demo, Ray decided to leave the band, and the master tape disappeared with him, never to be seen again! We continued to rehearse and did some hideous gigs at Thurnscoe Hotel and somewhere else I can't quite remember. Working men's clubs venues were not a good idea especially after the Bill Grundy debacle with the Pistols.

There was a constant threat of violence and when one venue had guard dogs roaming about, we were out of there quicker than you could say Johnny Rotten!

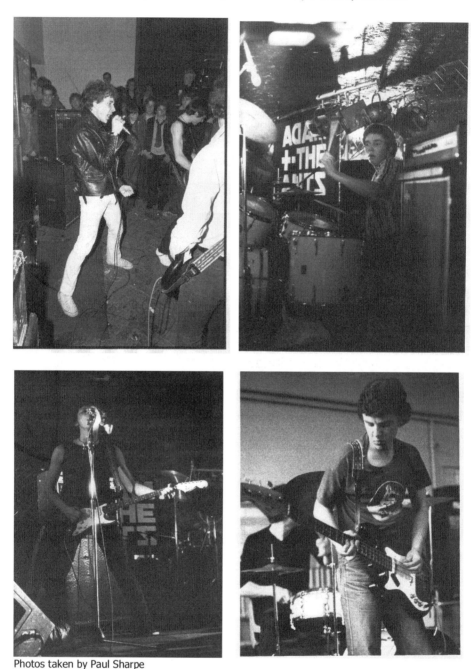

Photos taken by Paul Sharpe

Vice Squad Live – including a support slot at Retford Porterhouse with Adam and the Ants in early 1979

The Adam and the Ants gig we did was early on in 79 and Adam was conspicuous by his absence, we never saw him in the dressing room, I think we saw him once off stage, he

216

was wearing a see through rain coat and national health glasses at that particular time, and of course the Ant followers used to have those angular lines drawn on their faces with eye liner. I don't think we actually spoke to Adam at all, and he didn't talk to us! Perhaps he stayed in a hotel; I remember it was really cold and snowy that night, more pushing the van in the snow!

Later that year we recorded two tracks for the 'New Wave from the Heart' LP, I remember we recorded the tracks live in some guy's garage studio with overdubs for guitar and backing vocals. The record was recorded locally, with the tracks 'Prison Girls' and 'Words and Pictures'. Not brilliant, but a product of the minds of four teenagers at the time! We never met any of the other bands but we had some weird rivalry with Subliminal Cuts for some reason.

At our last gig it was packed out with kids and there was a really good atmosphere, everyone seemed to really enjoy the whole experience and it felt good to end on a high. It was a shame to have to end it really, it had been a really creative time and we had produced some quite valid music for the short period that punk actually existed in its true form."

Sue Lowday ... "The Kites owners Ted Gush, Mini (Richard I think), and George were all keen devotees of the new musical era as we all were. Ted managed a punk band called the Push who memorably did a gig at the University. Still have the single 'Cambridge Stomp' on 'Sticky Label'. The reverse is 'Front Room Revolution'. Written and performed by Ray Ashcroft plus pals. Ray was part of the gang that hung out at Kites. He went on to become an actor in the Guinness ads and then The Bill."

Gary Robinson ... "We would go and see all the local Punk groups like the Negatives, Stuntkites, 2.3. There was a great local scene out there."

Nearby Rotherham was also showing signs of a local band scene spurred on by Punk; attracting young musicians of the area who now saw the opening that had been created by the Punk explosion.

Gary Gillott (Chippie) ... "I was 12 to 13 years old and playing drums in bands around 1977 - 1978. The first one was called Frequency who were kind of new wave(ish) and had many line ups. Amongst these line ups were Bob Yeardel who looked like Bob Geldof, Andy Stevenson on keyboards, Pete Cooper on guitar and Pete Davies and myself. We would play the obvious youth clubs etc. Also there was Blonde Bombshell who used to rehearse in Bob's garage and was a proper garage band. The main places that bands would rehearse at were the White Lion pub on Westgate in Rotherham, the Dusty Miller ('*Turn that music down*') and The Effingham also in Rotherham."

Richard Chatterton ... "I became a great fan of local bands and saw Artery, The Human League, the Negatives, Hobbies of Today, Cabaret Voltaire, the Spasms, Xero and the Diks."

Dale (Mexborough Punk fan) … "The first real Punk looking types that I saw around my end, were the ones who were going round and watching the Diks; they were looking like Devo and Ultravox Punks- very original."

The Diks were another local group that were caught up with the local punk scene, though being more of a Power Pop/New Wave style. Formed in Mexborough they became famous for managing to get on the Sunday Mirror front page after allegedly dedicating songs to the Yorkshire Ripper (who was very much still at large at the time).

Diks singer **Paul Hutley** takes up the story … "We were a bit late getting onto the Punk scene and our first proper live appearance was at The Eagle and Child pub in Conisbrough on Friday August 4th 1978. We had a half page feature in 'South Yorkshire Times' paper headed Dik Rock- Power Pop or Punk?' to launch the first gig. We had to hire a PA system from Ben Page Music shop in Doncaster but it was only about 100 watts and totally useless. Another band Weazel was in the pub whilst we were doing our sound check and it was so bad they let us borrow their PA which they had out in the van.

It was difficult to get gigs in those days. Most of the time, our only chance to get gigs was to hire a hall and sell tickets on the door. Some of the best we did were Wath Montgomery Hall and Rotherham Arts centre and also Doncaster's Romeo & Juliet's. One of those gigs at Romeo's was where we hired the club on a Monday night. The bouncers still refused to let anyone in who were not smartly dressed so as you can imagine it was a disaster.

Gary Holton and the Heavy Metal Kids were also a big influence on us.

Above: Mexborough New Wave group the Diks

We used to travel for miles to see them play. We would also hire them to play a gig, which knocked us back £450, just so that we could support them. In fact The Diks is an anagram of the Kids – that's how we got our name. Course my new name became Dik. We used to spend a lot of time with Gary Holton until one night in Nottingham The Heavy Metal Kids played a gig at the Nottingham Boat club. After the gig, Holton wanted to go out on the town. We took him to Nottingham Sandpipers the late music venue. Holton and the band didn't know where they were going so they went along with us. When we got there Holton and his band all got free entry – the doorman asked who

218

we were and were we with them (so as to get us free entry as well). He turned round and said *'Never seen 'em before'* and strolled into the venue. We were poor ourselves so couldn't afford to get in. So we took revenge and smashed up their car and punctured the tyres. That was naughty.

We also used to support main line groups at Retford Porterhouse. We played with Starjets (from Belfast) and Slaughter and the Dogs. The audience at the Porterhouse were always on the same level as the stage so they were right in your face. They used to give you swigs of their beer and snacks etc. I was once given a bite of a kid's burger which actually didn't contain any burger but pure shit!"

On the subject of that infamous 'Sunday Mirror' Yorkshire Ripper article Paul says... "The Sunday Mirror claimed we were dedicating songs to the Ripper. We did have a song about a pervert we called 'Ernie Cringeworthy' – but our message to the girls- *'If you're going out alone take extra care in case you bump into a similar character'*. I might have dedicated it to the Yorkshire Ripper, but it was meant in a way to warn and deter and not to glorify as they claimed.

Above: The now almost Legendary Collectors item 'New Wave from the heart' LP

We didn't really mix with any of the other bands. We were too far up our own arses. We also had a reputation of not paying our support acts. We once asked local band Eyes at Risk to support us and we would pay them a fiver. For months after, every time we saw them about they would say *'Have you got that fiver?'*

We played a gig at Rawmarsh Cricket club on 12th September 1979. We got paid £25 plus the door money which was £12.20. Can't have been many people there!. Our support act that night was The Flying Alfonsos. Can't remember anything about the actual gig so I don't think it was anything spectacular."

The Diks were featured on two local Post-Punk compilation LP's 'New Wave from the heart' and 'Logical Steps'. These are now highly collectable sought after albums.

Paul Hutley himself sold two of the 'From the heart' records on eBay for £160 to an American. They are also on many wants lists of Japanese collectors. A long way from those days as Paul recalls... "We used to have to pay to record the songs and then try and sell the albums ourselves. We would often do that by going from door to door on the streets."

Tony ... "I used to pick up the 'New Wave From the heart' LP in 'Sound of Music' record shop in Rotherham Town Centre. I had it in my hands numerous times and always used to wonder if it was any good?"

Paul Hutley ... "It was all a great hobby. We did feel like rock stars for a while. Our last gig was at the 'Thurnscoe Hotel' about July 1980. The landlord there was always good to us. I think they called him Fred Powney. We were called The Villains now after numerous line up changes. Our sound man walked out on us, and I had to have the day off work to go and set up in the afternoon. The gig was a disaster with no sound man. We got paid up, which was a very hard thing to do at the Thurnscoe Hotel. It was embarrassing. I decided there and then it was the end. In fact I started selling stuff off on that same night."

Backtracking to the late summer days of 1978, local teenage Punk Dave Spencer was starting to feel the confidence to make his own Punk Rock racket. Here he recounts his school days during the middle of the Punk era and also trying to get a band together.

Dave Spencer ... "Maybe it was the Sex Pistols splitting up at the beginning of the year, but 1978 saw the hysteria calm down, and the whole Punk Rock thing seemed less threatening, and to be honest, apart from Elvis Costello the memories of that year are all a blank to me up until September.

Back at school after the summer holiday, during which our family had holidayed in Great Yarmouth, with beautiful oil-drenched beaches, courtesy of the Amoco Cadiz, I moved into the third year at Oakwood Comprehensive. My world changed because I started taking sandwiches to school instead of opting for the daily gruel.

The tables in the school dinner hall were set out so that three quarters were available to children who ate school dinners and the rest were for us sandwich eaters. On the sandwich tables everyday I ate alongside an intelligent, outspoken, cricket-loving, reluctant swot, Dominic Wood and the rougher, tougher Graham Torr. I think, Dom and Graham may have been friends since Sitwell Junior School, but all I knew was that the only thing they seemed to have in common was a love of punk. I sat opposite Dom and Graham everyday, excited that there were other people taking interest in what was happening. I seemed to remember Public Image Limited by Public Image Limited was the one song that we all loved. Then one day, they mentioned that they had a band....

It was probably that fact alone that made me grasp the future (and hold on to it for thirty years!). Once I realised that I could make punk music rather than just listen to it, I was truly converted.

I spent the next couple of weeks worming my way in with them so I could somehow join their band. I had had a guitar for a couple of years, but I'd only learnt four chords and had just about given up on it. I must have mentioned it to Dom, because one fateful Friday afternoon as I sat watching Dom and Graham arguing about whom they should have in their band, my chance came. Graham was insisting that Stephen Kidd, who was even more nerdy than me, should be invited to join, because, as his mother was a singer on the clubs, he had access to a MICROPHONE! Dom countered by saying, '*well if we're after people to join why don't we have Spencer* (nobody called me Dave, or David) *because he's got a guitar.'* Graham spun round to me, *'Have you?'...'Err, yeah.'* So, that was it, next morning I found myself walking the half mile from my house to Dom's, for a rehearsal. I was absolutely terrified, because I only knew four chords, but as it turned out, it was four more than the rest of them put together. They had already written a song though, called 'Operation'.

'Terry's had a crash on his Honda plastic
I've seen it all and I've just been sick
There was blood and giblets everywhere
He needs an operation...Oh Yeah!'

Fucking fantastic! And it only used up two of my chords. They were all playing single notes - Graham on a Bontempi organ, Dominic (I think on 'cheap as chips' electric guitar) and another kid called Richard Druce on a Red Hofner Colorama guitar that might have been his dad's. I was immediately 'IN'.

We rehearsed all day every Saturday at Dom's house, because his mum worked at Peck's in Rotherham and therefore, we had the place to ourselves. Over the next months we started to take it more seriously, Dom became the bass player, Graham and I played guitar and Richard Druce sang. Dom fought my corner, saying that since I was the only one that could even half play the guitar, I should be the main guitarist and he stepped aside and, in his view (at first), stepped *down* by opting to play the bass. He gave me a hard time for not standing up for myself, which I more than made up for in the next year or so in re-organisation, recruitments and to be frank, sackings, in pursuit of the perfect band. Eventually, we got another lad in called Lawrence Major to play the drums, mainly because he had a set of drums.

We got a lot out of the Clash songbook. Obviously, we learnt how to play Clash songs for a start, but also a street cred lesson in 'The Work Ethic'. In the songbook there were some interviews with the band. In particular, one in which Paul Simonon describes his adolescence. He claimed that he had to cook his Dad's breakfast then do a paper round then go to school, then come back and cook his dad's dinner before doing another paper round and so on and so forth. I think he was trying to tell us that he'd had a tough upbringing. Either that or that he was a good cook."

Graham Torr (guitarist) ... "Now I have vague memories (maybe) of us making do with fake guitars for a while but where the pocket is weak, the spirit is willing and before long we had real guitars from the Swap-Shop down Wellgate, a drummer and everything! There were obviously a few line-up and name changes but I don't think it was that long before we were The Cute Pubes. Fuck! – the first time you get through a song with everyone reasonably tight is like butter!...(and still is, right kids??). Even the acoustic stuff we played while staying up all night, eating toast and working on 'White Man in Hammersmith Palais' when my Mum had fucked off to Spain for a fortnight."

Dave Spencer ... "Our band was fired up but it wasn't long before Graham Torr was fired. I can't remember why, but one minute he was in, the next he was out. He started a new band called the Blur (what a ridiculous name!) and I think around this time we became PVC. We listened to everything that we could and I must have virtually moved out of the family home because my memories of this time are just sitting around at other peoples houses (particularly Dom's) listening to and learning from his ever growing record collection."

Barnsley too, had its very own Punk band... the X-Rippers.

Phil Taylor (Bass player) ... "The Legendary X-Rippers were founded in the fall of 1978 from the ashes of the Maingate Rippers. The band's original line up was Brent Stables aka Freddy Red vocals, David Youel aka Munk guitar, Gavin Brain aka Brainy drums, and myself Philip Taylor aka Rots on bass.

Above: 3 Barnsley X-Rippers

The rivalry with The Restricted another Barnsley punk band became almost anarchic. The Restricted consisted of Gary Reece: vocals Paul Brookes: guitar, Gary Bower: Bass, Terry Naylor (Ex Maingate Rippers) guitar and Paul Gilmartin: drums...who became The Dance Society's drummer. Both bands used to play on the same bill in Barnsley and had a grudging respect for each other but didn't really get on.

The first gig the X-Rippers played was at the Portcullis in Barnsley Nov 1978 without Brent due to a foot of snow being down so it was an instrumental affair. The first set list consisted of 'Magnet Blues', 'Rippers Lament', 'Belfast', 'Nasty Nazis', 'Who's the Restricted', 'Sunshine' and a couple of rip off songs.

The gigs came thick and fast over the first year and the X-Rippers were slowly building up a reputation that they could hold their own amongst the so called big boys. The song writing continued and after a gig at the F Club in Leeds with the Drones, a write up by a man called Worrall from the Melody Maker inspired the song 'Tedious'. Other songs...'Jimmy Kelly', 'Sex Life', 'In Death', 'What we want', 'Terry', 'You don't like us' and '4 inch' were added and the X-Rippers had a solid 45 minute set."

Meanwhile, Dave Spencer was following Paul Simenon's work ethic example as read in the Clash songbook.

Dave Spencer ... "As our band, PVC, was getting better; it became apparent that we'd need proper equipment. So, I got a paper round and saved up to buy a cheap Kimbara semi-acoustic electric guitar. Then I needed an amplifier, so I got a second paper round. I was out of the house at 6:30am doing my first round, and then starting my second by

7:45am. My schoolwork went down the pan; I got detention for being repeatedly late; but I saved up and bought an amplifier. We were almost ready to face an audience.

We'd spent much of the year rehearsing punk rock classics, ripping 'em off and writing our own songs. Song titles I remember were 'Have You Got Enough Money?' 'Man O' War' and one about band politics called 'One's Got To Go'.

Lawrence Major's mate, Rob Galloway had started turning up at rehearsals and occasionally asking for a go on the kit. It wasn't long before it became obvious that although it was Lawrence's drum kit, Rob was a drummer - a 'Natural', simple as that. So, we gave Rob the drum sticks and we gave Lawrence a guitar, a couple of rudimentary lessons and turned him down, Sid Vicious style.

The other 'Major' problem was that Richard Druce had got a Saturday job, working on a fruit and veg stall on Rotherham market. Absolutely nothing wrong in that, but it meant he missed every all day Saturday rehearsal. It caused a simmering resentment amongst the rest of us until Richard's dad came up with the solution. We could use the social club bar where he worked at Swindon Laboratories, on Moorgate Road on *Sunday* afternoons.

Swindon Labs was a scientific research plant owned by British Steel and it must have been funny seeing these tiny baby-punks wheel their amps in to make the most awful noise. My strongest recollection is of one of the kids from school, Stephen Kidd messing about behind the bar whilst we were trying to concentrate on rehearsing.

He was fiddling about with pumps for ages, and we kept shouting at him to leave them alone or we'd get chucked out. After about ten minutes he walked out holding a near perfect pint. Clang! Bang! Clatter! All the guitars dropped to the floor as we legged it for the free booze and promptly got spannered. We all had to stifle drunken giggles when Richard's dad came to pick us up at the end of the afternoon.

When we finally decided we were ready to play, we hired St Barnabas church hall in Broom Valley, just down the road from our school, Oakwood Comprehensive, one Saturday night towards the end of October 1979. We picked up the keys from the caretaker, a sweet old lady who lived on Moorgate Road, the night before the gig, and told her that we were putting on a 'disco'. She must have thought we were very enterprising. As we were – we knew that if we had told her we were putting on a punk rock gig, we wouldn't have got the keys. So we paid our 18 quid deposit and spent the next day setting up and sound checking.

We had sold about a hundred tickets. Graham Torr's new band was supporting us. As they went on we all cowered at the dressing room door, terrified, waiting for the crowd's reaction. They started with 'God Save The Queen' and the reaction was a massive roar of approval, and a massive relief to us. This quickly changed when the singer, Daryl Huggup, apparently leapt in the air in an extremely, inelegant, girlie kind of way and the roar of approval changed to howls of laughter. Our mood changed to one of panic.

Half an hour later we were on. I don't know what we opened with, but I am pretty sure we played 'Pretty Vacant', 'Anarchy in the UK', 'White Riot' and maybe even 'Clash City Rockers' as well as our own home grown classics (!). The audience didn't care. They'd paid their money (some as much as 30p!) to watch and spit. Within seconds of going on stage, we were drenched in a hail of 'gob'. It was during either 'White Riot' or 'Clash City Rockers' that Richard Druce froze. I don't know if it was due to the number of rehearsals he'd missed out on, or if it was just plain stage fright, but he just stood there staring at the floor, until I walked over, fired up by adrenaline, and kicked him up the arse. He gave me a kick up the arse back. It wasn't a wise move on my part, as he was built like a brick-shithouse and I, well, wasn't. How it didn't escalate into a full blown scrap, I will never know, but within seconds he'd remembered what he was supposed to be singing, and within minutes we'd finished. We stared at the crowd and they stared back. We'd done our full set and we'd only been on stage about 15 minutes. During the months of rehearsals, we'd never actually timed it! So, we went back to the beginning and started the whole set again. Half an hour, that's more like it. We were just about to start the set for a third time when a brick came through the window. My first thought was, *'Thank God, we can get off now'*. My second was *'what about the 18 quid deposit!'* We all ran outside trying to catch the culprit. Lawrence's brother, Alexis was standing near the window, laughing, saying the guy who'd thrown the brick had run off *'that way'* and we all ran after him. Never found him though."

5 Barnsley X-Rippers

Phil Taylor (X-Rippers) ... "Most gigs we did, the band played for 20 pounds or free beer - usually the latter - and at times the gigs were a bit of a blur. In Bradford at the Royal Standard 1979 the band played to a bunch of fans and a group of hells angels called the Southport Survivors (on their way back from a convention in Epping Forest) where hell broke loose and two from other chapters were blown away...one from the Windsor Chapter I think. The Southport Survivors were a mean looking bunch some with hooks or balls instead of hands and they took offence to our song 'Nasty Nazis' and consequently Rots was cut with a knife on the chest not a bad cut just a warning.

(Ironically going to Halifax Sept. 2008 on our way to a gig the chapter passed us on the motorway). Due to the beer and occasional violence, the X-Rippers started to get bad press at venues and had to play under the names of The Storm troopers over Moscow and The Young Criminals. Venues were slow to click on because at times we recruited another guitarist Stuart Sikes aka Spike or Stu'd Onions. This also gave the band a fuller sound and it was easier to cover up mistakes."

Meanwhile over at Dave Spencer's Punk Rock camp.

Dave Spencer (PVC Vocalist/guitarist) ..."Back at school, the post mortem began and we talked about it all week. On Friday morning, I suggested we get rid of Richard Druce and get Graham Torr back in. On Saturday I was fired. I narrowly escaped a beating from the understandably aggrieved Mr Druce.

I spent the next six months in purgatory hanging about with the rockers in our year, having been ostracised by all the punks apart from Cav. I even went to see Saxon and I can honestly put my hand on my heart and say it was awful. Having by this time seen the Damned twice and the wonderful Penetration at the Top Rank I knew what was good and what wasn't. It was absolutely Fucking Awful.

Eventually, being in the same classrooms together we started to talk again and somehow around the end of the school year, Dom, Graham and I got together and something clicked. Other people drifted in and out, for the next couple of months and eventually we got some proper songs together. We were listening to more bands too, like 999 and Chelsea. In the time that we'd all been apart, we'd all leant to play a bit better, with Graham having become particularly accomplished on the guitar. We started out with Rob Galloway in on drums, but by the time we were back at school for our final year he had traded in his sticks for a pair of Farah's jeans, as he had discovered the Charade nightclub and just wasn't interested in playing music anymore. Rob didn't last long. We got Ramones freak, Neil Moxon to replace him. Neil was a couple of years older than us and played heavy!"

Continuing the X-Rippers story-

Phil Taylor (X-Rippers) ... "Gav our drummer is still the baby of our band now a mere 45 years of age. But Gav used to play at holiday camps and we were at times without him with Paul Gilmartin standing in for him. One particular gig in Hull 1980 we were that desperate for a drummer we actually went to the holiday camp Gav was playing at and politely persuaded him to join us to the gig. Basically it was an organised kidnap and Gav didn't know what hit him until we were far enough away from the camp so that he was unable to walk back and reluctantly then agreed to play. The gig was a great success and we got our foot in the door playing with bands like the Angelic Upstarts and the Cockney Rejects at bigger venues like the Winter Gardens in Cleethorpes (still putting on bands today).

We had a hardcore fan base and some of them are still good friends today. David Ralph Edward Harding (a bit of a posh lad) came to every gig and acted as security and at one gig in Millhouse Green Youth club got a beating trying to protect us and I can still remember the Doc Martin sole imprint embedded down the side of his face. Billy Haimes was the poor punk who came to all our gigs hardly ever having a penny in his pocket. That's why we used to play for free beer. The cheap hair dye... well when it rained it usually washed all the dye out making Billy look like one of the black and white minstrels.

The biggest mistake was getting a so called manager Malc 'something or another'... he got us the gigs, free beer and a little money - a lot for Malc but he started to look at the bigger picture and decided that some of the band were not up to scratch and maybe another member would get us further. Therefore the bitching and back biting started and rows broke out between the band that 20 years on we were not very proud of. So the writing was on the wall and after a gig at the Centenary Rooms at Barnsley Civic Hall in 1981 and yet another argument the X-Rippers finally called it a day; probably a sad day for us all but for the best."

Sadly, for local 'New Wave' groups like the Diks, the Prams, 2.3 and Vice Squad, X-Rippers, PVC (and many others) the hard work would never be rewarded with a major record contract and nationwide recognition. But, like many of the Punk era groups, in later years their recorded work would be sought after and finally help to achieve some recognition of their achievements from a time when the doors had been kicked open giving these 'young angelic quick - starters' of the region a chance to make their mark in the Punk explosion.

Above: Doncaster's Rock Festival of October 1978 included Rotherham's The Prams on the bill

It was now well into 1979 and Punk was no longer the new thing, the Mod Revival was just around the corner and the end of the decade was close. Changes were once more in the air and the Sheffield and Rotherham Punk scene would end the 70's splintered and - though still impassioned with the spirit and energy of Punk - would be welcoming the new decade with open but increasingly directionless arms.

Chapter Twelve

The Modern World

"I remember the Ivanhoe's gig in Huddersfield on Christmas Day 1977... I must have only been 17 years old. Before the gig, I was standing at the crowded bar trying to get a drink and found myself standing right next to Sid Vicious, can you believe it. I was startled, amazed and a little afraid too, what with his reputation of aggression and all!! I didn't' speak to him or anything, but it was an amazing gig/night" - **Steve Marshall (Sheffield-Punk Rocker)**

Tony ... "At my brother's wedding in June 1979 a couple of his mates at the disco that night; they offered me pints of beer to encourage me to pogo to some punk music. Well I knocked the pints back and after about 4 pints I was ready to do my bit to the Skids 'Into the Valley'. My nephew Dave was up for it as well so we dived about to please the straights...err I mean the family and friends.

This was the first time I ever got pissed on proper beer; we only really drank at parties back then...bottle of cider etc.We would have the odd few pints at the Top Rank but it was the music we were there for. You wouldn't get served with a bleeding shandy now without your I.D card."

Punk may have been on its last legs nationally, but there was still plenty of enthusiasm left up north and the local Punks were ready for plenty of any action that was left to get their teeth into.

Right: Joanne Orgill – still up for a Punk party

Tony ... "1979 and the youth club Punk days were in full swing. At the start of the year there had been a right load of great Punk singles and we would get them played at the local youth clubs. I seem to remember some of us going to 'Track records' in Mexborough quite a lot back then. A couple of singles that we bought there that spring to mind are the

Wall's 'Exchange' (*'go on Doidgey – my mate - buy it it'll be good'* I was saying)...and also The Outcasts 'Just another Teenage Rebel'. It was still a really exciting time for us lot."

Darren Twynham ... "I met Tony through mutual Punk-loving friends and I would go up to his house and we would play all the records and go to gigs together. That front room at his Mother's old house was fantastic. It would be full of Punk kids all of the time and we would be swapping Punk records, swap sessions were usually on a Sunday afternoon for some reason, the room was like a Punk commune but his Mother never once complained. The music would be banging out all of the time. We had some superb times. The best days of my life really!"

The much dreaded fear of leaving school and college and taking on responsibilities now loomed.

Pete Cooper ... "In 1979 I left college and got the dreaded job with the suit and tie but I was still a Punk. The one good thing about the job was that I now had more money to fund my record collection and get to more gigs. It was now time to sell my old Sweet records and invest in a guitar. Having witnessed a local band called the Prams who were made up of students; I decided I wanted to be a Punk musician as well. The Prams were brilliant performing cover versions of Pistols, Clash and early Cure. Unfortunately there weren't many Punks at their Rotherham Clifton Hall gig. Rotherham was still mostly into heavy monotonous rock."

On February 2nd Punk icon and former Sex Pistol Sid Vicious died of an overdose whilst on bail for the alleged murder of girlfriend Nancy Spungen. To many 'Vicious' personified the Punk look and style and although it cannot be denied that he was an embodiment of the Punk lifestyle, in many ways, it was also true that he was a victim of its media overkill and took the lifestyle to its extreme. Opinions of Sid from the local Punks were varied.

Tony ... "I can remember clearly the day that Sid died. I found out on the late news and I remember my brother was saying it served him right etc. I didn't bite as to be honest-even though I was a fan in a sense - Sid was never someone that I had ever truly related to. Of course, being 14 at the time, I was still into that Sid Vicious myth. In truth, I suppose he was his own worst enemy... live fast die young... was there ever any other way for him to live his short life? Ultimately, he did leave a lasting iconic Punk image and he wouldn't have to worry about being an ageing old Punk though... would he?"

Bryan Bell ... "Sid Vicious? Well he was an idiot really. I much preferred Glen Matlock being in the Pistols. At least he could write songs. I mean all that crap about 'Sid Sings' and the Sid doll in the coffin. It was all just a total cash in scheme. I can't say I was that bothered when he died."

Dave Spencer ... "Oh yeah poor old Sid... I had almost forgotten about him."

Not surprisingly, it was not long before the 'cash from demise' cold sell followed in the wake of John Simon Ritchie's premature death at the age of 21. The most commonly known single, Swindle spin off 45's 'Something else' and 'C'mon Everybody' aside, was the April 79 release of the Cash Pussies record '99% is shit'. Sleeved in a classic 'Sid' photograph of him complete with bleeding nose... the shameful cash-in opened its grooves with Sid mumbling about how the general public were mostly scum - then merging into a backing track played by ATV's Alex Ferguson and members of Throbbing Gristle leaving the single itself to bleed the listener dry. Supposedly released as an attack on the music industry itself, the record managed to manipulate a proportion of Sex Pistols schoolboy fans to part with their paper rounds hard earned pennies.

The other lesser known 'Sid' cash in, although probably meant in more earnest intentions, was the March 79 issue of 'Pistol boy' by Militant Barry produced by reggae maestros Tapper Zukie and Keith Hudson. And then there was the rest of Virgin's post Pistols discography releases... continuing with the 'Some Product' interviews and radio jingles long player and the year ending 'Sid Sings' LP. However, all this consumerism is over-rode by local Punks and their own personal memories and vision of what Sid meant and represented.

Tony ... "Sid pushed everything to the limit, and as a teenage Punk, I can't say I didn't follow his example every now and again."

Above: Sid Vicious 'Punk Rock icon'

Michael Day ... "Anyone who heard the Pistols had to be amazed by the sheer energy of the songs and the audacious content for the time, and then there was Sid who became the face of punk to all the scared grannies out there. Although playing bass was clearly not one of his major assets he had a magnetic appeal that transcended the genre. Sadly he fell under the spell of hard drugs with the influence of some dodgy people around him but he will always have a place – albeit posthumously, in people's hearts that identify with those times and ironically has now become a legend for a whole new generation of punks growing up."

Tom Cleary ... "Sid was kind of a zeitgeist of punk. He was the essence of 'wannabee made good', but foundered on the rock of skag because he bought the hype.
   We all had a soft spot for Sid; he fed the voyeuristic thirst for the outrageous we all felt and was plainly 'one of us' (in fact that was true of all the Pistols...). But it was still a tragedy that the scruffy kid with attitude was downed by 'the man', fucked over by 'the

229

management' and that he couldn't get it together enough to survive. In the end, it fed our sense of frustration and oppression because the story was still *'you can't beat the system'.* Not that we had much faith in anything they did anyway, because they were like us – 'the common man', flawed and alone."

Steve Marshall …"I used to buy both NME and Sounds magazine weekly in those days and, when I read that Sid had died, I wore a black armband on my jacket for a day or two…and remember the bus driver saying to me at Shirecliffe, *'Is that for Sid then?!'"*

Phillip Wright … "Sid - I always thought the name was great, no one was called Sid our age, unless it was a nickname, and 'Vicious' just sounded great. The fact that he was about nine stone wet through made the whole thing seem really funny. He looked the part; skinny, black spiky hair, pale skin, biker jacket, and looking permanently stoned in the 'Pretty Vacant' video. He couldn't really play of course, Steve Jones taught Sid enough so he could muddle through live gigs. His solo artist persona was pretty good though, the singles all charted in the top 10. The two Eddie Cochran covers 'Something else' and 'C'mon everybody' were played at the Limit a lot and his version of 'My Way' was pretty good, a sort of two fingers up at the world.

Sid always seemed like a little boy lost in the big world to me, not sure why. I was shocked when he died because it meant that the Pistols could not get back together (although they later made up with Glen Matlock) and I just thought*, 'This is it, punk is dead'* and I guess for me it was. Sid was and still is a Punk icon."

Sid Vicious left a lasting legacy with the Sex Pistols. Although, barely playing on their work, it is Sid's image that is associated with the band as much anyone else. Sid remains one of Punk's iconic images and his image continues to be worn on t-shirts to this day.

Growing up in the late 1970's to the early 80's did not have the benefits of today's mass media availability or the 21st century's politically correct right-on attitude. Teenage crime was usually petty and often harmless and fun could be had without virtual reality.

Tony … "Me and Pete Roddis were big mates at this time. He was one of the hard kids at school and never failed to have a girl on the go. We would take our separate paper rounds out in one go, talking about music all the way round. I would wake up every morning excited about Punk Rock and it was running all the way through my system…I was that crazy about it and it was fantastic to be able to share it with my best mate.

Sheffield was on our jaunts at least once or twice a week for the record shops. Sometimes we would go to Doncaster as well. We were buying records all the time and going to as many gigs as we could afford to get to. We would hang around and just be stupid a lot of the time. We had allsorts of daft things to keep us amused. Often we would be in some sort of trouble but nothing major. I always smile when I think of those days. You really never get them back again and it was such a great time to be alive."

Pete Roddis ... "We would be forever bus-in it somewhere. We would always be laughing at people as we passed 'em on the bus - we had this thing of spotting look-alikes- war criminals we would call them."

Tony ... "When the first Undertones LP came out we scrounged some promo posters and sleeves from the Sound of Music record shop. I can remember walking around Rotherham town centre with the LP sleeve on my head: God knows why? We were so daft in those days."

The 'New Wave' style did strangely emerge in unusual places on very rare occasions.

Tony ... "The local fruit case in and around Rotherham in 1978 and beyond, was the Bionic Man. He was complete nuts and talked to himself, supposedly carried an axe in his jacket at one point and fought many dangerous missions in various global conflicts – or so he thought. Once in Rotherham bus station in the summer of 1978 me and Andy Goulty got off the bus and couldn't believe our eyes. There he was the Bionic man in a smart three-buttoned suit and a Jam David Watts badge. *'What you up to'* we said to him. To which he replied *'I am off to meet Bryan Ferry and we are going to check out some Punk groups together!'*... It could only have happened in Rotherham."

There were still kids out there who were only just picking up on what was happening. However, they soon managed to tune in.

Julian Jones ... "I had been turned on to Punk music by a tape my brother had been given by a friend. The tape had Clash, Sex Pistols and Buzzcocks tracks on it and got me interested. Being a Punk, if having badges too big and zips in the wrong places and not knowing which the right groups to like were, then I definitely fitted the bill on that count.
    In 1979, there was no one I knew at my school who was into Punk, so I only knew what I had heard from my older brother. I went up to the Rawmarsh youth club with safety pins all over my blazer and my dad says *'Where you going dressed like that'* so I took them all off and put 'em back on before I got up to the youthie. It was there that I met the handful of Punks that were around, Tony Beesley, Pete Roddis and a couple of others. Around this time, there were lots of Mods and Rockers there and when it was our turn, we would clear the dance floor. It was always 'My Way' by Sid Vicious and we would all lay on the floor doing the squirm at the slow bit and then leap up and pogo all over when the fast bit comes on. The Mods and the rest would be laughing at us, but at the time, we thought we were the best. Being so few of us, it was something kind of special."

Tony ... "I had known Julian back at junior school but had not really seen him for a few years, even though he only lived round the corner from where I lived. He ended up going to Swinton Comprehensive as I had gone to Rawmarsh Comp the year before him. Anyway, I can remember he turned up at the Rawmarsh youth club one night and he was covered in Sex Pistols and Clash badges and was clearly attempting to be a punk rocker. He was naïve, exuberant and wanting to be in on the scene. We were laughing at how he looked and this must have been how the older punk kids had been seeing us a couple of years earlier. He soon fitted in with us. In fact, for a while he ended up as daft as us - humour wise. We went to Doncaster a few times and I can remember us both buying Clash t-shirts with the first LP cover on. I think one of us also bought a leather jacket too. This was from this back street Punk clothes shop."

John Peel, it will be forever understood, contributed to the discovery of new music (most notably during the Punk and Post-Punk period) than anyone else. His influence could be as profound as the actual Punk groups themselves; especially to young and impressionable over exuberant teenage Punks.

Tony ... "I can remember Julian Jones coming around and laughing at me and Pete Roddis. We were that engrossed in John Peel's show and his legendary sessions that we started doing our own show in the front room. We set the old music centre up surrounded by all our records and we had a mike to plug in to the centre. We did our own sessions...4 tracks each from a punk group just like 'Peely' did. I can't believe how excited we were about Punk around that time. We also started writing our own lyrics, punk poetry and they were very teenage, and naïve to the extreme but they were funny. But one day I got embarrassed about them and threw them onto my mum's coal fire."

Julian Jones ... "Tony and Pete Roddis would be doing their own version of the John Peel show with their own sessions. Then one day, Tony and Beanz (Dean Stables) let me have a go at doing my own show, we would do them at each other's house and this was my turn. I didn't even have enough Punk records but managed to put some Stiff Little Fingers and Angelic Upstarts on and some tracks off the 'Give em enough Rope' LP, I had a couple of Sex Pistols records but they weren't trendy at all at that point. I then put Simon and Garfunkel on and that was it, they were pissing themselves at me. They were going *'What's that? this is not Punk!* So I was saying *'yeah but this is pre-Punk and what Punks were influenced by'* (laughs)...They were great times though and loads of laughs, and I have to say that I learnt a lot about Punk from knocking about with that lot."

However, it did not have to be 'Homeward Bound' that would sometimes get up the noses of the hardcore Punks.

Tony ... "I got stick from a couple of the hard core punk kids for liking the Jam and the Undertones. Don't get me wrong I have Eater, Drones and Slaughter and the Dogs LP's in my collection too, but for me punk didn't begin and end with the fast nihilistic stuff. I even had the 'Vortex' live compilation at one time, but I still loved The Jam no matter what."

In addition, some music fans of 'Our Generation' simply did not want to take sides.

Michael Hill (Band promoter/DJ) ... "I was 14 – 15 at the latter part of the 70's and I just remember the Mods v Rockers v Punks thing at school and how you would only listen to either rock or Punk etc. Now you realise what a great variety of music there was and is to listen to and how people get on now instead of being rivals like in the late 70s and the early 80s."

Paul Clarke was inspired by Punk rock and after briefly trying out the punk look, settled down to just being a fan of the music: taking on board a lot of its attitude ... "I think that young teenagers have always felt a need to fit into some gang, or to follow a certain trend. They always have and probably always will. It's an identity thing. It is being noticed, sometimes it can be competition, but kids don't want to hang around on their own do they? They will find something to follow be it good or bad. In my case it happened to be these kids who were listening to this music called punk."

Tony ... "We used to go somewhere nearly every single night, usually a youth club like our own at Rawmarsh comp (back then simply known as Haugh Road); this was open Monday to Friday. Or we would go to the 'Miners' in Parkgate or the Wednesday night discos at Rawmarsh Cricket club. Wherever we went, we would take a selection of punk singles to get played. Sometimes there would be trouble kick off but most of the time it was ok. From 1978 to 1980, I lived and breathed Punk Rock. It was my whole life and nothing else mattered, nothing at all."

Mark Senior ... "I used to knock around with Big John in Sheffield a lot, I remember the police constantly telling him to remove his bullet belt! I just loved being a punk in Sheffield."

Punk Confessions –

Bryan Bell ... "I fancied the blonde bird out of 'The Runaways'. I remember when they were in the papers and there were features of 'em and the theme was *'Are these girls going to be allowed to corrupt our youth with their raunchy image etc.'* Well when I had seen the pictures of them in suspenders and the like I thought to myself *'I'm having some of this. They can corrupt me any time'.* I went to their gig at the Sheffield City Hall in 1977 and they were great. 999 supported them that night and you would have needed to call that number if some of the crowd had got their hands on 'em (laughs)."

Tony ... "I did have a thing for Gaye Advert and later on Pauline Murray of Penetration. However, didn't we all back then? Around late 79, I used to go out with this 'Northern Soul' lass. She was 18 and I was 14. We would go to the youth clubs together; all the local ones and the always-welcoming Rawmarsh Comp one. She would have a dance during the Northern Soul spot – to the Tams 'Be Young be Foolish be Happy' and Derek and Ray's 'Interplay' etc and then I would have my turn when the Punk records came on. I would dive about instead of dancing though. Then we would sit at the edge of the stage with our arms around each other. The other lasses used to call me Sid. Can't think why for the life of me? Perhaps they meant Sid Little? I wonder what she did with her life.

I really liked the 'New Wave' punk style for girls (rather than the hardcore look). That 'New Wave' look was kind of something like this: Straight legged jeans (faded), a baggy knitted jumper (preferably a mohair one), shortish hair, though not necessarily spiky, a bit of black eye liner, training shoes and one or two of those big Punk badges worn on the jumper. To be honest the best way to describe this version of the female punk style would be Jackie magazine's guide to how a girl should dress 'New Wave'. Leslie Ash would have looked the bizz like this.

I got chatting to a Clare Grogan look-alike at one of the early Marples gigs. We just cuddled in the corner, sat on the floor, while most of the punks sniffed glue, threw pints all over and pogoed to the groups. She was from a rough area of the city that had a large feature of flats and I have to say I am glad I never got a date with her on her own turf. My favourite girl though, throughout all that time, was Sarah and she was very 'New Wave' and into Devo, Undertones, the Jam and most of all stiff Little Fingers. She had a big crush on their drummer Jim Reilly."

Bryan Bell ... "I hung around with UK Subs for a while and nicked Charlie Harper's Iggy Pop 'Metallic k.o' t-shirt. Well I did leave him mine in exchange for it."

Charlie Harper (UK Subs singer) ... "Nicked my shirt? (Laughs)Yeah that did happen quite a lot in those days."

Tony ... "Me and my mates Pete Roddis and Andy Goulty, we were always up Sheffield and on one of these trips we went in WH.Smith on Fargate on one of our usual record hunts. We ended up eye-balling a £20 note on the floor. That was a hell of a lot of money back then, so it was as if all our Christmas's had come at once. We picked it up and scarpered. Later on Andy told his dad about it and he wanted to hand it in somewhere saying it could have belonged to some poor old age pensioner. Eventually, what happened was Andy took us to Sheffield and bought us £6.33 worth of vinyl each. I went to Revolution Records and bought the first UK Subs LP that had come out that very week and a bagful of cheap Punk 45's from the record shop in the hole in the road. Can't remember what Pete got.

Above: Richard Chatterton in 1979

On another jaunt to Sheffield, me and Pete went in Marks and Spencer's and we saw a massive opened bag of chipsticks. We loved our crisp so couldn't resist them. Grabbing mouthfuls and laughing our heads off we turned around and saw a bloke in a uniform heading towards us. We were still grabbing the loot when the security guy grabbed hold of us both and frogmarched us both out of the store - us still with gobs full of salt and vinegar chipsticks and laughing our heads off. The guy's face was so serious and was making us laugh even more. Anyway, the chipsticks were already open so we didn't think we were doing anything wrong. Besides, he never grabbed the collar of the o.a.p who also sampled them at the same time. Could it have been the way we were dressed: Nah! Surely not.

We also used to go in Circles record shop and change the stickers around on the albums so we would come out with stuff like the Siouxsie and the Banshees first LP for a quid and the guy who ran it - he'd be looking at the record with a puzzled look when he saw the price. He was such a nice guy too, but he was from the old 70's pre-punk lot so we justified ripping the shop off. The staff there were really quite friendly and would try their best to get you a record if not in stock. So if you are reading this- sorry! We were only kids."

Paul Clarkson ... "My room mate had 'Don't Fear the Reaper' by Blue Oyster Cult and he kept on playing it non stop on and on and on."

Tony ... "That's not so bad; I bleedin' bought the bastard record. It's actually a great record but not one that you would admit to at the time, especially after the Jam had such a hard time supporting them in the states at the time."

Steve Haythorne ... "I went to see Pink Floyd in 1977; Punk's year Zero."

Chiz ... "Before punk I was a big fan of Sweet and bought all their singles and must admit to looking over my shoulder to make sure nobody had spotted me when I bought 'Love is like Oxygen' due to the fact it sounded more like Queen!"

Joanne Orgill (Left) ... "I became an avid follower (hanger-on!) of the Cute Pubes – the school punk rock band. They were all in my year at school – David Spencer, Graham Torr, Dominic Wood and the drummer – I never could remember his name! I had Cute Pubes painted in bright yellow on the back of a green jacket with 'Pubic Fan No. 1' along the waistband. It got a bit of a crease in it and ended up looking like 'Public Flan'."

Julian Jones ... "Apart from Simon and Garfunkel, I liked Bob Dylan who was definitely not the in thing around the Punk era and afterwards."

Tony ... "I also liked the Korgis...ouch that hurt my Punk credentials, but I can do much better than that. During the whole Punk period, I bought LP's by ELO, Rod Stewart and wait for it the Darts LP. Wish I still had them as well!!"

Paul Hutley singer with the Diks ... "I enjoyed Heavy Metal. I used to knock around with the guys from local band Saxon and was one of their roadies whilst still at school in 1976. They would pick me up outside the school gates and I'd get home around 3am."

Tony ... "The Dickies LP was hilarious. It was fast, catchy, short songs and it was on yellow or blue vinyl. The songs 'Mental Ward', 'Poodle Party' etc were great. I know it was a bit sort of 'cheesy American Punk', but it had real energy and was catchy as hell and when that LP came out in early 79 it was massive for me for a few months."

Darren Twynham ... "It seemed like almost all of the Punk records coming out were on coloured vinyl at the time. X-Ray Spex and UK Subs records were all on different coloured vinyl. One record I was always after and Tony had it, was Buzzcocks 'I believe'. It was an American issue and could I get it from anywhere? Could I fuck? I used to hate Tony for having that, the bastard (laughs). But I am now pleased to say I have finally got the damned thing."

Julian Jones ... "My first Punk clothes were a blazer with a massive Clash patch on the back that my Nan had sewed on and it was all bubbled up and didn't look right so I took it off."

Tony ... "I had a pair of Clash style zip trousers. They were proper ones with big 'heavy duty' zips on them. One of the zips went all the way down the side of the leg and they opened up and unlike the zip trousers that we made ourselves these were straight through. At a Damned gig, I was stood near the front waiting for them to come on and this Punk bird undid the long zip and stuck her hand in there. What more could you ask for...teenage bliss or what."

Charlie Harper ... "Before Punk I used to like Aretha Franklin and R&B as well as sixties American garage bands. 'Woolly Bully' that was a great record!"

Tony ... "I suppose it was uncool to like The Motors, and Squeeze but I thought they were great. I can't remember even once pogoing to any of their records though!"

End of Punk Confessions

By the end of the 1970's and 1980, it is true to say that the original Punk spirit had been dwindling nationally. It was closing in on itself and had long been sold out to the media and the old school music industry. Only groups such as the Clash, the Jam, Wire, Magazine, Siouxsie and the Banshees and a few choice others were successfully attaining a fine balance between still openly embracing their roots and fan base whilst moving forward.

Even so, there was a new generation of groups that were waiting to follow in Punks old guard's shadow making their own classic Punk sound. These new punk groups, many of whom had been around since the early days but had only recently been offered record deals etc, were the Members, UK Subs, Angelic Upstarts, the Ruts, and Stiff Little Fingers (who managed to get their first LP 'Inflammable material' banned at WH.Smith's for being offensive? One can only wonder why?). And there was also The Skids.

Tony ... "Back in early 1978 or maybe even earlier, a lad at school Ian Hillman (later of My Pierrot Dolls) who was in my class told me about his cousin Richard who was in a punk group up in Scotland. The group was the Skids, who I did become a great fan of after seeing them perform 'The Saints are coming' on Top of the Pops. A year or so later his cousin Richard Jobson did visit his relatives in the Rotherham area. Also local Skids fan Shaun Angell (and a friend of Ian's and mine) managed to get an invite to see the Skids play in Doncaster and meet Richard, Stuart and the rest of the group."

Shaun Angell (Rotherham Punk/New Wave fan) ... "Yeah, I got my 'Days in Europa' LP sleeve signed by all of The Skids. I also went to see them at Doncaster Rotters; long since gone, but a top venue in its day. The Skids were playing there and one of the lads is the cousin of lead singer Richard Jobson, so off we went. The gig was brilliant, the songs, the new fashions, the atmosphere and everything about that night was fantastic. To top it all off we managed to get backstage after the gig and meet the band members – that just wouldn't happen nowadays, but for us it made the ten mile walk back home from Doncaster to Rotherham all the more bearable."

Tony ... "I went to see the Skids that following night in Sheffield. They were fantastic. The musicianship was spot on and they still had the energy and speed of Punk; but they wrote better songs than most of the other so called punk groups. I can remember it was red hot that night, as it often was at punk gigs - we would only ever wear t-shirts as it was so hot down at the front near the stage - and the kid I had dragged along to see them play that night called Richard nearly collapsed cause of the heat. In addition, there were still a few kids who wanted to spit at them and the Skids were having none of it.

Above: Rotherham Punk fans Paul and Denise

Stuart Adamson the guitarist (who is sadly no longer with us), he was going crackers at the gobbers; Giving it his all in the very best Scottish tongue-lashing he could muster. For me, this night was like a cross roads really between Punk and the new decade that was looming. Now the 80's were upon us and these days and times would soon be a thing of the past."

Darren Twynham ... "I saw the Skids and they were fantastic. After the gig, I managed to get the chance to meet them and they were great with us. I chatted to Stuart

Adamson. What a shame it was when many years later he took his own life. Such a talent and a massive loss."

Steve Haythorne … "I liked Stiff Little Fingers a lot. 'Alternative Ulster' was a classic single and 'Johnny Was' (their reggae cover on their album) was superb. I did like a lot of that cross-over stuff that came along, especially the reggae stuff."

The Punk scene was now throwing up a different creed of Punk group and most of these, if not all, would play in the area.

   Sunderland Punk group Angelic Upstarts, who had formed after seeing the Clash on the 'White Riot tour' but were only just coming to the fore, were regulars to play in and around the area, playing gigs at Sheffield Penthouse, the Limit club, Marples and also in Manchester.

Bryan Bell … "We ended up going on tour with the Upstarts early in 1979. I saw them in Manchester and I got quite friendly with them, resulting in them asking me along for the rest of the tour. I can remember ringing my dad up and he says '*Where are yer?*' and I goes '*I'm in Aberdeen where do yer think!* From there I saw them play in Sunderland, Dundee and Glasgow, and I am sure that one of the next ones that they played was their Sheffield date. After that gig, the Upstarts came back to my dads place and they all kipped on the floor. Next morning the drummer rang up Jimmy Pursey from Sham 69 who wanted them to come and record their first LP. I went round to the local shops with the Upstarts, which was Thorogate shops Rawmarsh and there used to be GT News there and when we went in we got some right funny looks."

Tony … "Yeah, my mate Andy's Mum worked in there and when she finished her shift she told us that The Angelic Upstarts had been in to the shop. We were like '*Yeah, sure, what ever!!*', but it was true. This was around the time we had just heard 'I'm an Upstart' on the John Peel show and we couldn't believe it."

Sheffield Punk Tom Cleary recalls an encounter with Punk group The Members.

Tom Cleary … "Well, my mates used to think I was a prat for working for my tickets - they'd all just lig in, as was the punk thing to do. But when the Members were playing, my mate John said he'd join in with the Ents committee, so I spoke up for him to the management, got him a badge etc. etc. and all went well until the band turned up and dropped off their stuff before the sound check. John shouts out '*Oi, Nick'* (turns out he and Nick Tesco were mates) and he's off backstage with the band getting smashed and I'm doing twice as much work and getting earache for allowing him to let the side down. Talk about wet behind the ears, eh?"

A slightly different meeting with an associate of a 'New Wave' star as recounted by Joanne Orgill and Helen McLaughlin.

Joanne Orgill ... "Another abiding memory that has stuck with me over the years has probably done so because it was so bizarre. Helen and I were big fans of Elvis Costello. For me, it was the geekiness that did it – Yes, I fancied him like mad! The music speaks for itself. We bought Smash Hits one week and there was a letter from Elvis Costello's Dad – Ross McManus, with his address printed at the bottom. We decided to write a letter to his Dad (Jim'll Fix it style) to ask if we could meet Elvis. He replied to us and even sent photos of Elvis with his first wife celebrating Christmas at his Dad's, and signed photos of himself – he was a club crooner at the time. Over the next year or so, we wrote to each other quite regularly and then we had a bit of a surprise. We were out on our paper round delivering the Rotherham Record (many of which ended up in the bin). When we got back to Helen's, there was Ross McManus sitting in Helen's living room! I can only imagine he was gigging in the area and decided to pop in on the two girls who had been writing to him for so long in desperation to meet his son. As I said – it was all pretty bizarre really! Eventually the correspondence dried up as, like normal fickle teenagers, we moved onto something else."

Helen McLaughlin ... "I remember coming home from school and Elvis Costello's dad was in our living room! My dad met me on the front path and told me and I didn't want to go in. Joanne had gone home, I rang her up to make her come up to our house, and she kept refusing. Eventually she gave in and came but it was so embarrassing. We couldn't think of anything to say and we were so relived when he left. I think the correspondence ended there!!! My dad was an 'older' dad and Irish and I really don't know what he made of it all. My mum, as usual, was fine and thought he was lovely."

Tony... "A lot of people say Punk was dead in 1979, and I can see that may be partly true in some ways, but there were some fantastic records out that year. The Banshees were only just coming into their own, the Jam were sounding on top form and there was -

"This is Rotherham... close by to Sheffield steel"

- some top class 45's during that year. In the first few months there was fantastic singles from The Members, Skids, Generation X, Buzzcocks, Stiff Little Fingers, Doll by Doll, the Clash, Damned, Elvis Costello etc...There was the Lurkers e.p and from that 'Cyanide' was a big one that we would pogo to at the youth club, looking like we had swallowed cyanide pills. I suppose at that point the Punk kids at my age were still excited about Punk and were really getting a kick out of it. The energy we had was never ending."

Although, Punk and its original ideology had been very much diluted by 1979, that year was still a particularly healthy one for music. The Punk generation of Sheffield etc were, much like the rest of the country, starting to move into different directions. The more musically demanding would be digging the many variations of the Post-Punk groups, some of them opting for the synthesiser sounds of The Human League etc. Other Punk fans were now becoming bored of the confines of the Punk scene and, inspired by the Jam and a burgeoning Mod scene starting in the south, were trading their leather jackets and bondage trousers for a pair of sta-prest trousers and a Ben Sherman button down shirt.

However, some decided that they could listen to and be part of all these diverging scenes and sounds. For a while in 1979, it seemed that there were no limitations to the amount of thriving youth scenes and new music being made.

Nicky Booth ... "I thought 1979 was one of the best years for punk. It had really found its feet by that point with some bands such as the Stranglers already on their fourth album. It was also the year I started going to gigs regularly so for me it was the heyday. Maybe things reached their peak in London earlier, but in Yorkshire, punk was at the height of its powers. A lot of bands had lost their initial venom by this point in favour of a more mature sound, which I, for one, preferred. For example, 1979 was the year that the Clash released the brilliant 'London Calling' and the year that I saw them at the Top Rank in Sheffield which was a truly memorable night."

Some local Punks were also beginning to tire of the straitjacket rules and regulations of the Punk manifesto and rulebook.

Tony Atkins (Rotherham Punk) ... "I remember being in a club with a bunch of like minded Punk fans, and a Disco track came on. My mate was a proper Punk and he shook his head and muttered *'Hate this crap. You can't dance to it'*. I was just about to laugh out loud, thinking he was being ironic, when all the others shook their heads too and joined in saying *'Yeah, know what you mean mate'*. To be honest I quite liked the Disco track, but what did I do? I shook my head and added '*Yeah, Disco sucks, can't dance to it at all! -*

Above: Used Punk gig tickets (from my collection)

I remember the day that I decided to revolt! One of my mates asked me what my favourite track was from the newly released Sex Pistols 'Great Rock n' Roll Swindle' album; I thought long and hard about it before admitting that my favourite was actually the 'Black Arabs' medley. Anyone who remembers that track will know why it was a brave call."

'The Great Rock n' Roll Swindle' double album contained some vintage Pistols tracks, all the recent hit singles and most of the b-sides, as well as a menagerie of Pistols songs re-vamped with a new approach and style. 'The Black Arabs' Medley was one of these. It was a Disco/funk medley of Sex pistols songs such as 'Pretty Vacant' and 'God Save the Queen'. Not exactly pogo friendly versions!

Some displaced teenage Punks would find their resolve by getting directly and actively involved in the local Punk gig scene; Andy Lee was a young teenage Punk who found an unlikely partner by sheer chance.

Andy Lee ... "I was in Sheffield one day with the bass player Simon from Repulsive Alien and we happened to go to Marcus Featherby's house around the time he was bringing out the 'Bouquet of Steel' album. Marcus was bringing out the album but in actual fact, he was skint. He had just about enough for a tin of cat food, so I gave him some money (I worked on a milk round every morning before school so I earned a few pounds). Marcus and I became friends. Some months later my parents, who were both alcoholics, kicked me out of my home. I turned up on Marcus's doorstep with two carrier bags and he just said *'I wondered how long it would be'*. So I moved in- I was about 17 by that time. Together we immediately started organising and putting on gigs and putting out more records."

Meanwhile, the ever-evolving experiences of young Punks could occur anyway, anyhow and anywhere... and at any time of the day!

Tony ... "Pete Roddis and me both had paper rounds about this time (1979) and we would merge both of our separate rounds into just one. Our boss was always giving us grief for doing this but we never took notice. His face was hilarious when we turned up one morning at 6am with our dog 'Sheena the Punk Rocker' in our bag... her head popping out of the top. We would tear pics of the Punk groups out of Sounds mag which got delivered to a heavy rocker so he wouldn't have minded anyway would he?

One morning Pete turned up with his parka hood up and when he pulled it down he had bleached one side of his hair. Great stuff...I got the sack from the paper round eventually. So I threw the paper bag at the newsagent manager...minus the dog of course."

The initiation to the Punk live experience still managed to set Punk kids off on their Punk Rock journeys.

Mark Senior ... "I went to see the Stranglers at Manchester Apollo and that night changed my life. From the off I thought Burnel was God. Since then I have followed them all over Britain, I did most of the gigs on the 'La Folie' tour, all of the 'Feline' tour and many more. I've also seen them all over Europe, Zurich, Hamburg, Munich, Geneva, Paris (Twice) being only a few of them. I still love them to this day. I also had a few good parties with the band over the years too."

1979 was a year of change. For Sheffield, the industrial greyness of the city would soon be met with the prospect of a new decade. But for the time being, for some at least, the sun was still shining.

Tony ... "There was a classic episode of Top of the Pops that summer of 79 when the Undertones 'Here comes the summer', Buzzcocks 'Harmony in my Head', Specials 'Gangsters', P.I.L with 'Death Disco' and Siouxsie and the Banshees 'Playground Twist' were all on. That day was red hot and my heart was still racing with the sounds of Punk Rock."

Late that summer the Jam released what many of their fans consider their ultimate Youth anthem; the timeless and pulsating sounds of the Punk Generation personified 45 'When Your Young'.

Tony ... "That was it! 'When you're Young' managed to capture it all in its lyrics and its crashing wall of 'New Wave' sound. 'No Corporations for the New Wave sons' (actually new age sons! But who cared). Indeed! Whenever I hear that song and listen to the words, I am fourteen year old again. It will forever remain timeless for me."

Whilst The Jam released one of their last in a clutch of classic 'Jam sound' singles ('Eton Rifles' and 'Going Underground' would complete the collection) that summer saw the underground Mod Revival become more noticeable. The excitement was in the air for those last few weeks of summer and into the early autumn. Then the bubble burst. It was with the first 2-Tone singles and the cinema release of 'Quadrophenia' that it attracted an unhealthy dose of its fashion victims. Yet again, the media and music press were allowed to mould and control another youth movement. Although, starting out as a smart and healthy antidote to the hardcore Punk scene, and giving many teenagers their first taste of authentic black music with an alternative lifestyle, this time the new movement termed the Mod revival would last little more than a year, before disappearing back to its underground roots.

Tony ... "We always got on with the Mod lads. It was only the posy sort of mod who ever had a problem with us and then we could usually put them straight if they wanted to argue about music. I mean a lot of the time, some of us didn't look that much different to the Mods. I had my hair like Paul Weller a lot of the time, wore Jam shoes and a blazer with Jam badges on. The skinheads, though, would beat the Mod revivalists up at any given chance. I saw loads of Mods get hammered by skins. They were ruthless.

That end of summer period of 79 was a great one. We had so many fantastic nights at the youth club. The music we were getting put on and pogoing to was Angelic Upstarts 'Teenage Warning', Buzzcocks 'Harmony in my head', Dickies, 'Paranoid', all The Clash singles and punk fan Sugar was bringing singles along like Eater's 'Thinking' of the USA', Drones 'Bone Idol' and Slaughter and the Dogs 'Cranked up really high'.

The DJ at the youth club once tried to throw me off the stage due to my hassling him to put on more of our music. We really did have some great fun and the future never seemed brighter. We had all found ourselves at last. Here we were the last of the Punk Rockers; or so we thought!"

A few weeks later and 2-Tone really hit in and lots of the lads at the many local youth club Discos were dancing to the Specials, Selecter and the Beat and Secret Affair's 'Time for Action' (which proudly proclaimed *'we hate the punk elite'*). Meanwhile the last bastions of the original first wave of Punk Rock were coming to a musical crossroads and change was also in the air with the very best of these groups too.

The Clash had started 1979 as the leading Punk Rock group. Their sound was still firmly rooted in classic rock n' roll Punk. They were, however, subtly changing their image throughout the year (which began with the group having a *'Thank you for giving us enough rope – from Joe, Topper, Paul and Mick'* full page ad in Sounds magazine), and were now utilising many of the American influences that they had assimilated whilst on tour over in the states. Their last record had been back in May; the classic 'Cost of Living' E.P, which included their version of Bobby Fullers 'I Fought the law', and an updated meatier take on their earlier Punk garage track 'Capital Radio'. In July 1979 they came back with a totally new look and approach to rock n' roll; Gone was the spiky Punk Rock hair and clothes along with the speed-driven rock n' roll of classic Clash.

Above: NMX Sheffield fanzine (From Phillip Wright's collection)

Here was a new Clash that was exploring a whole new array of diverse musical styles. From R&B, ska, rockabilly to jazz, soul and blues, the Clash were now at their most openly creative and were ready and confident enough to take on the world. Their Punk Rock fans were almost all shocked and up North around Rotherham was no exception.

243

Tony ... "At that time the Clash were the last hopes of the original Punk Rock explosion. Everything they had done, played and said had been mostly respected and taken on board by the Punk kids. True there had even been some who had given up on them a long time before, because of the U.S.A tours and 'Give 'em enough Rope's HM production etc. Now though, they really had broken away. Well, when Pete and me went and bought the 'London Calling' LP, it was quite a shock really.

We had read the reviews but still expected to hear about half of the record sounding like the Clash that we knew and loved. To be honest when we played it through, we found it hard to take in. We played it again and then once more. A few days later we both agreed that it was a fantastic record. It really opened our eyes and our minds to other music. We couldn't stop playing it all through Christmas. 'London Calling' is truly a classic Rock n' Roll LP. After hearing that, the other Punk groups started to sound a bit boring."

Julian Jones ... "One of my biggest regrets was not getting the chance to see the Clash."

Pete Roddis ... "Yes 'London Calling' was a massively important record back then and still is. I can remember me and Tony both went out and bought it as soon as it came out. The first time we played it we were like *'hold on a minute what's this?'* - Then after one or two plays, it really grew on us and it just went from there. There really was nothing else like it. The Clash were so ahead with that one, and it was the same the following year with 'Sandinista'."

Helen McLaughlin ... "We were offered £20.00 per ticket for our Clash London Calling Tour tickets outside the Top Rank. £20.00 was a hell of a lot of money then. Needless to say we refused!"

Above: Clash Sheffield Top Rank ticket

Patrick Tierney ... "The Clash I saw at Sheffield Top Rank on the '16 Tons' tour. I think they were past the real glory days. It was a bit cabaret-ish. *'Here's one off our latest album'* and so on, but they did play 'Complete Control' which was, and still is, my favourite song of theirs. I bought the single on the day of release at Bradley's Records at the entrance to The Arndale and played it first thing every morning and last thing at night. I still don't really know the words, but it's more of an attitude than a song."

Mark Senior ... "The Clash on the '16 tons' tour were amazing."

Tony ... "I went to see the Clash at Sheffield Top Rank on the 'London Calling' (16 tons) tour. There was me. Pete Roddis and another lad called Steven Doidge. He had been into the Punk scene for a while and had built up a fantastic collection of records, sticking the picture sleeves to his bedroom wall in homage to 'Impulse' records shop in Sheffield.

The Clash that night were absolutely out of this world. The atmosphere before they came on was of an unbelievable air of excitement and anticipation. Mikey Dread, who has since passed away, was support and he came back on again doing his reggae toasting stuff. Then we could see a few dark figures, collars raised and wearing crombies and trilbies, they were dancing rude boy style on stage. Some didn't realise at first who they were; we figured out it was The Clash. Then after a while - they picked up their guitars, Topper retiring to the drums and the first chords of 'Clash City Rockers' blasted out.

Whoaa! If I never feel that way again, which I probably won't, it will do me for life. The adrenalin was astounding. A massive rush of teenage thrills came rushing through my body and soul as the Clash raced through 'Protex Blue', 'Safe European Home', 'Complete Control', 'I Fought the Law', 'White Man', 'Capital Radio', 'Brand New Cadillac', 'London Calling', 'Police and thieves' and encored with 'English Civil War' and 'Garageland'.

Above: Me and John Harrison- 'Under age drinking in Sheffield'

This was the gig where Joe Strummer whacked Mick Jones because Jonesy didn't want to play 'White Riot'- which everyone was shouting out for. Me and Pete saw some bits of what was happening- Joe told Mick to *'fuck off!'* and then we could see that there was some sort of commotion going on at the side of the speaker stacks. Apparently, Joe hit Mick twice and after a little sulking from Mick the matter was forgotten. Afterwards Mick got drunk silly back at the Leeds Hotel they were staying at after the gig. That night at the Sheffield Top Rank, we pogoed and dived all over: We sweated extremely and were over-heating but on cloud nine! Dripping wet, we filed out of the venue...the Clash playing a post gig 'Armageddon Times'.

Two mean hard-core punk birds were eyeing up my very own 'Armageddon Times'. They ripped the back cover off Steven Doidge's copy but I made sure they did not get mine. It was tatty from all the sweating (I had it tucked under my t-shirt all night), but it stayed in one piece. Coming out of there, we were totally high from the gig. What a fantastic experience. It is hard to describe in words how I felt... The euphoria was tremendous. Imagine going to school the next day after that!"

Barry Thurman (Rotherham Punk and My Pierrot Dolls bass player) ... "At this particular Clash gig, there was so many in there that, by the time I got in there, the bouncers wouldn't let us go through into the hall. So we had to listen to The Clash play from near the doors. It was absolutely heaving that night."

John Harrison ... "Yes, I would have loved to have seen the Clash. That is one of my biggest regrets of the Punk era, as I was a big fan of them but somehow fate decided that it was not to be. But there you go!"

Tony ... "I feel so lucky to have been there that night on the 'London Calling' tour at the Top Rank. For me it was one of those massive moments in life that I will never forget. I can still visualise it after all those years and if I play their records; sometimes I can travel back to that night. What an event!"

Pete Roddis ... "That Clash gig was really the high point for me with Punk. It was an amazing experience and something changed with me somehow. It kind of opened up my eyes and ears to other types of music and made me realise that Punk was not the be all and end all of it. We would still listen to Punk- but it was never really the same after that. This was the way forward now."

Chapter Thirteen

Under the Floorboards

"A lot of the people I hung around with were a little blinkered, just being into three chord thrash Punk, which although I loved, I thought was getting a little limited after a while. I admit I always had to wrestle with these dilemmas" – **Richard Chatterton (Rotherham Punk)**

Julian Jones ... "Even by late 1979 – early 1980, being into Punk, we were the minority really."

Left: Rotherham Punks Helen McLaughlin, Joanne Orgill, Dave Spencer, Graham Torr and Dominic Wood

Tony ... "I rescued the Adverts LP 'Cast of Thousands' from destruction. My mate Pete had bought it from Brittain's store in the January sales (the record had only been released a few weeks back in November 1979(ish) but had sold very poorly; not helped by the group splitting on its release). Pete was not impressed at all by it and decided to break it, bending it into almost half its size, but it wouldn't break. He tried once more and as he was doing so, I said *'Don't smash it I'll give you 10p for it'... 'Ok then here you are its yours'.* I came to really dig that LP and begrudgingly Pete did as well. We got to know all the songs on it and to -

- this day I am proud to say that I saved the Adverts...though I didn't manage to save Wire's 'Outdoor Miner' single from Pete's vinyl smashing wrath, nor him likewise with some of mine like Fingerprintz and others that I smashed up."

At the start of the new decade the Sheffield Top Rank played host to a superb double bill of The Ramones supported by the Boys. The gig was the stuff that legends are made of.

Andrew Goulty … "The Ramones were tremendous live. I saw them at the Top Rank supported by the Boys and what a gig that was."

Patrick Tierney … "I went to the Ramones at the Sheffield Top Rank. This was the Marky incarnation, rather than the Tommy one as it had been at The Outlook. Still great; although the Outlook gig was the real thing for me."

Honest John Plain (The Boys) … "I have always been a fan of The Ramones and to support them on their 1980 UK tour was a great honour. We played Sheffield Top Rank towards the end of the tour and I remember it being one of the best shows on that tour."

Andrew Morton … "My first gig was at the Sheffield Top Rank to see 999. There were about 3 or 4 gigs on that week, including the Clash and the Ramones and I had to choose one so I went for 999. Not sure why, probably cos they were the cheapest. Anyway, they were really good. After that I went to loads of gigs. There always seemed to be someone playing. I think one of the next ones I went to was Sham 69. That was a scary one. All the skinheads had come up with them from down south and they were mean. I can still see em all, with their tattoos. There was a lot of fighting that night inside the Top Rank. Some of it was between them too. Thing is, the support group were crap so they were getting bored and that didn't help. It got them fighting even more. Jimmy Pursey was doing his usual banter, trying to calm it all down."

Bryan Bell … "I was at that gig too, and yes it was a right riot. I had seen Sham 69 at the Top Rank once before too and both gigs were violent. The skinheads would kick off and all hell would break loose. I can remember looking round and it was as though they were coming out of the woodwork. They were just appearing out of nowhere – loads of them."

Tony … "I was meant to be going to the Sham 69 gig – until one of the local skinheads pulled me and Pete to one side at the youth club a day or so before. He said if we went to the gig he and his mates would throw us off the balcony. He really meant it as well. We didn't fancy learning how to fly; so we gave it a miss."

This gig from Sham 69, which saw them make their stage entrance after a '2001 a space odyssey' intro and chants of *'there's only one Jimmy Pursey'* was ill received by some of the audience that night. Some thought that Jimmy Pursey was naïve in his vision and if he didn't get his act together could soon end up being a Punk parody singing 'Hersham Boys' at the end of the seaside pier in true cabaret style.

1980; and attitudes were starting to change for many local kids of the Punk generation. It was now time to begin broadening the musical boundaries and discover other musical styles as well as Punk Rock.

Anthony Cronshaw … "Around the 79-80 period, the Clash were back in the city and once again they proved that they were the Kings of Punk. Whilst this was happening, we saw the Mod and Ska revival kick in and a lot of the boys made for the Top Rank to see The Specials, Madness and Selecter introduce the Steel City to 2-tone."

Tony … "One of the times at Rawmarsh Youth club - this would be right at the start of 1980 - me and Pete decided to do something a little bit different for a change. Instead of doing our usual punk dance, we thought why don't we do a Rude Boy kind of dance to The Clash 'White man in Hammersmith Palais'. So we asked the DJ to put the record on and we borrowed a trilby each off a couple of the Mods (these were some of the earliest Mod kids around the area and they were suited up; not the 2-tone parka lot). Anyway me and Pete already had our clash style coats on, which were kind of crombie like. We stood our collars up and when the record came on, we were straight on the dance floor, just us two. The spotlight went on us and all the other kids started to take notice, as we did our Ska dance. The couple of Mod lads were well impressed and started moving in closer and were encouraging us. I don't know to this day what made us decide to do this (probably influenced by the Clash themselves at the Top Rank) and it might seem quite trivial nowadays -

Above: myself wearing Clash badges and my dad's old pit scarf

- especially to those who weren't around in those times. But to us it felt so good. It felt like we were shaking off the shackles of the straitjacket of Punk Rock. It certainly felt liberating and yes it was fun. The other punk kids just laughed at us and carried on talking (probably about the next UK Subs record due out or something).

We started to listen to reggae and ska a lot more after that and really began to appreciate the rude boys and respect the Mod kids, well the proper Mod kids. I never had much time for all those sheep following kids who thought being a mod was buying the Specials LP and wearing a target on the back of their parka. That night all those years ago will always be a clear memory. When we met up many years later at a Buzzcocks concert, and this was 26 years later, the first thing, just about, that we both remembered was that rude boy dance to the Clash. Yeah for me it was quite a life defining moment and it indicated where I would eventually be going next."

Pete Roddis … "I will never forget that night either; when me and Tony did that dance. Can't really say what made us do it. It was probably a result of us seeing the Clash quite recently and we were very much affected by how they looked at that point. We were really out on our own with that one. All the other kids all kind of stopped what they were doing and were all stood around watching us- wondering what the hell we were up to."

Tony ... "Yeah! it still gives me goose bumps when I think back to that night. That was what being young was all about for me - expressing ourselves and having fun."

Julian Jones ... "Around this time I would always be borrowing Tony's Damned 'Machine gun Etiquette' LP and another one that I would get Tony to play was the X-Ray Specs LP. I loved that one. It was all about getting to hear as much music as possible."

Even though, the second generation of Punk teenagers were still very much keen to hear their music fast, loud and with plenty of energy and aggression, there was an increasing amount of different sounds being introduced to their record collections.

Tony ..."Me and Pete always took a selection of new punk records we would have bought recently, when we went to the youth club. I can remember the first time we took Joy Divisions 'Transmission' single and we got the DJ to put that on and the b-side 'Novelty'...We made a new dance to this one...it wasn't Punk, it was something like it but different and although I never became a big fan of Joy Division I always had respect for them. The first time I had heard of them was when I saw them on BBC's Youth/Punk show 'Something else' during the late summer of 1979. It was the same programme that the Jam were on doing 'Eton Rifles' and 'When You're Young' and I taped the music of both groups on my cassette player using an old mike I had. There was something mesmerising about Ian Curtis. A couple of months later I was with a couple of my mates outside the Sheffield Top Rank. The Buzzcocks were playing that night and we had run out of money so couldn't afford tickets to get in, but for some bizarre reason we ended up going up there for a laugh and to hang around really. We could hear Joy Division play their supporting set and one of us remarked that we would have to make sure we got to see them play next time they come to Sheffield. Fate was never going to allow that to happen, unfortunately."

The Punk gigs around this time were becoming actual major events for the local Punks and the Top Rank venue was probably at its peak for popularity on the gig circuit. Sunday nights in Sheffield couldn't be any better spent than at the Top Rank.

Tony ..."We went to see Stiff Little Fingers quite a few times. The first time I saw them was when they were still the original line up at the Top Rank and I still have my 'Alternative Ulster' single signed by all four members from that gig. They would play the rank on the next tour but the last couple of times I saw them it was at the polytechnic and then Sheffield Lyceum. They were always good live and I suppose for a while back then, they were really 'flying the flag' - to quote one of their-

- song titles - for the last bastions of Punk. Also, as it said on one of their labels, *'Punk is dead but we are still dying'.* That was certainly true and it seemed a worthy cause for a while. They released a fantastic run of singles and a couple of near classic LP's. I had met up with a great girlfriend called Sarah at a 'Fingers' gig who lived in Brinsworth. I ended up seeing her for a while, almost getting quite serious if I hadn't been so selfish and put my mates first, or would it have been selfish to put my mates second best ? I don't know? At that age all that matters are yer mates and music.

On the 'Nobody's Heroes' tour in March 1980 S.L.F were supported by Another Pretty Face - a punk group with some traditional rock n' roll leanings. Their leader and singer was future Waterboys singer Mike Scott. At this gig the group received a lot of hassle from the hardcore punk crowd, including spitting. I can remember feeling sorry for the group as they were trying really hard to get their music across. Mike Scott was coming back with jibes like *'you lot still think its 1977, why don't you realise we've all grown up a lot since then'.* Funnily enough, I recall the Stranglers Hugh Cornwell saying almost the exact same thing, just about at an earlier gig. Some of those support bands on the punk tours didn't half take some stick, but they almost all took it straight on the chin - often literally from a flying bottle.

Often a lot of the support groups were really good and it was great to catch some of them when they were only just starting out. Groups like The Moondogs, Pinpoint (who released a classic punk 45 'Richmond), Victim, Rudi, Vic Godard and Subway Sect, the Straps, UK Decay, Altered Images (they supported Siouxsie and the Banshees during their early Punk/Banshees guise) and later on Theatre of Hate. I saw all of these bands play fantastic support sets."

In 1980, the opposing youth cults were always evident and young Punks would take any measures at their hands to look after number one.

Julian Jones ... "Knocking about with the Punk lads, Tony, Beanz, Pete Roddis, I would go up Sheffield with them. They would want to go to Revolution Records up at the Castle market area, which was always full of skinheads. They would use me as a scout and send me around the corner to see if there were any skinheads around and see if it was safe or not to go ahead."

Above: SLF and Sham 69 ticket stubs (Andy Morton)

In March 1980, one of the last great Punk singles was released: the Ruts 'Staring at the Rude Boys'. Lead singer Malcolm Owen had very little time left before he would succumb to a Heroin overdose in July. How long did Punk itself have left until its own rapidly self-destructing path was at an end?

Tony ... "1980...I was also going to see groups at this time that were breaking out of the confines of Punk. Me and Pete went to see Devo at the City Hall and we really enjoyed

251

them. They were totally different to any of the groups I had seen before. And as everyone knows Devo did look; let's say a little strange dress wise. Anyway their music sounded great that night and we went out and bought all their records that we didn't have shortly afterwards. We had to hide behind a wall on Pond Street across from the old bus station after the gig, when a horde of skinheads were heading towards us."

Pete Roddis ... "Yeah Devo; that gig we went to was phenomenal. They had no support, but a film short instead. It was so different to all the other gigs."

Richard Chatterton ... "At this time I was averaging 2-3 concerts a week at venues like the Top Rank, Sheffield Poly, Limit club, Chesterfields Fusion club, The Saddle and also at Rotherham's Arts Centre. The Arts Centre was a great venue and a place where I could just chill and forget the big city whilst enjoying the bands in a relaxed environment. I remember Pulp playing an early gig there but I missed it as I had gone to see a different gig in Sheffield. My younger brother Phil(from Phil Murray and the Boys from Bury)did manage to go- he was two years younger than me and I really resented him going to gigs, especially after he saw the Damned at the Top Rank not long after I had seen my first gig at the same venue. Yet again I had wanted the music and its scene to be mine only, but I soon grew out of this and often we would go to gigs together."

Tony ... "Some of the most memorable gigs I can remember are not always the obvious ones. I went to see the Photos at the Limit club up on West Street and they were fantastic. Wendy Wu was absolutely gorgeous and the group played faultless. Sod off to that old malarkey that was going around at the time that the Photos were the poor man's Blondie. They deserved a heck of a lot more credit than they got and a lot less criticism too. Another group who I saw were the Vibrators. That night they played a blinding set and sounded so much better than the LP's I had of them, which always sounded too sort of conventional rock sounding to my ears.

    The only trouble at the Limit was not how old you looked, but the doorman wouldn't let you in with Doc Martens boots on. I can remember going all way up there one night, in the pissing rain too, and it was to see the Ruts and we got turned away cos of the dockers. Another night me and a mate Ian Cooper went up to the Top Rank to see the Skids and they didn't turn up. I think that the date got changed or something? It was pissing it down that night as well. I still have the flyer."

One Punk influenced group starting to achieve more recognition were Toyah; lead singer Toyah Wilcox had featured in the 1978 Punk spirited film 'Jubilee', along with Adam Ant.

Bryan Bell ... "I was a Toyah fan and I knew a lass called Mandy (who also played in a group called Shattered Life), she was from Doncaster and she was a massive fan of Toyah. Anyway she had ended up getting to know Toyah and had her telephone number etc. One day she told me she was playing in Sheffield so I went to the gig. I went back to the hotel afterwards for the party. I ended up being a fan as well. This was around the time the 'Sheep Farming in Barnet' e.p was out. Originally she still looked a lot like when

252

she played Mad' in the 'Jubilee' film, but she changed over the next year or so. Later on I saw her at the Top Rank. That was a good one. A year later and she was all over the place."

Andy Morton ... "Toyah was great on the 'Shoestring' programme. For a while there seemed to be token Punks popping up on the telly in TV series and stuff."

Above: Toyah at Sheffield Limit club (courtesy of Sheffield History site) and ticket from Andy Goulty's collection

Tony ... "I was never a big fan of Toyah really, though I knew a few who were. I had the 'Sheep Farming in Barnet' LP that was ok, 'Neon Womb' was good, but mostly it didn't rock my boat that much. I did really enjoy the Shoestring show that she was on though.

Anyway, I had heard that she was supposed to be quite good live in concert, so I decided to rope a pal in to go and see her play at the Sheffield Polytechnic. This was one of those stupid gigs where, in order to gain entrance, you had to get a student of the place to sign you in. Well, we couldn't quite manage that, but this fella a couple of years older than us called Bob, or so he said. He says *'Do you two want to buy some tickets?'* Course we did, that's why we are freezing our 'Never mind the bollocks'off. So he manages to persuade us to part with 3 quid each and says he was going to go and get the tickets from his mate at the bar. Fair enough, we thought. Surely he won't rip us off that easy. I mean he's only a few yards away and we could grass him up to the door guys anyway if he did. What happens? He rips us off, we never see him again, and the door guys aren't the least bit interested in our story.

A year or two later me and my ripped off Toyah gig goer mate had a fall out. We had been friends on and off since junior school but he tried to rip me off, by swapping me his brother's leather jacket for a Lurkers LP of mine, and then he was demanding the jacket back. We had a bit of a scrap in Rotherham bus station and I never saw him again."

Andrew Goulty ... "I saw Toyah play at the Top Rank in early 1980 and then again the following year. Fantastic gigs...I saw Toyah perform recently and met her; I told her I had seen her back then and she was so surprised and saying *'I don't believe it you saw me all those years ago and you are still coming to my gigs'.*"

Tony ... "There was a rumour at the time that one of the Punk kids from our end had a pair of Toyah's knickers."

Above: Local Punk fans Fiona Palmer, Nicky Booth and Paul Maiden.
And in the photo at the right Paul Maiden and Lynne Haythorne

Lynne Haythorne ... "When Toyah played 'Danced' at the Top Rank she lay down on the stage, whilst singing the song. The crowd were fighting to grab her with their hands grabbing all over... I ended up getting pushed down but got pulled back up."

Toyah played at the Sheffield Limit club, Top Rank and in January 1980 played their first gig in Doncaster. The energetic set fronted by a sexually over-toned performance from Toyah herself, included Neon Womb, Victims of the Riddle, Insects, Tribal Look and the current single Bird in Flight. She was dressed in extremely tight bright red trousers and the Punk kids at the front of the stage were more than appreciative of the attire.

Toyah was now at her best musically and was rapidly gaining a good following around Doncaster and Sheffield. Within a year, though, she had ditched her original band and was promoting herself as a solo artist and appealing to a bubblegum mainstream pop audience. As Toyah, herself, was now beginning to achieve pop star status, some local Punk fans also took her colourful 'peacock' Punk persona as an influence. Whereas fairly recently it had been out of the ordinary to see straight legged trousers and short hair... it was now not so uncommon to bump into a multi-coloured Punk Rocker on the way to the local paper shop.

Sheffield Top Rank's regular Punk and 'New Wave' gigs were now reaching their peak. Sometimes, though, things didn't always work out as anticipated.

Andrew Morton ... "A load of us went up to see the Angelic Upstarts at the Top Rank and they ended up not even playing. That was an anti-climax."

Steve Smardy ... "My group the Hoax were a Post-Punk Manchester based band, originally a four piece , but later settling down to being a three piece combo featuring Andy Farley on guitar and vocals, myself on bass and vocals and (future Smiths drummer) Mike Joyce on drums. We supported the Diagram Brothers, Cockney Rejects and then we got a gig supporting the Angelic Upstarts at the Sheffield Top Rank. I still have the backstage pass, which says 'Ana kissed promotions – permit The Hoax to the backstage area, concert – Angelic Upstarts Mon 30th June 1980."

Tony ... "I went to that gig as well and I do not have one single memory of being there at all. Like some of those gigs back then, it has been totally erased from my memory. I only find out about going to some of them when my mates remind me and the Angelic Upstarts (or not) at the Top Rank is one of them."

Steve Mardy ... "The Upstarts gig proved to be both rewarding and hysterically frightening at the same time. We got to do a proper sound-check and to top it all we got to enjoy full backstage hospitality consisting of beer and sandwiches for the bands and crews...any of the rothe

Well, 'we'd landed in heaven'. There were two support bands, including us. Our sound-check was a real treat when the PA desk not only got our sound balance as we'd never heard before, but they also commented on how they liked what we were playing. Those moments you treasure because someone is actually listening. The vastness of the venue had escaped me during the sound-check, but it was when I put my head through the curtain during the first support act, that I noticed the

Above: Local 'Punk' gig photographer?? With Julie Lee, Darren Twynham and friend at a Toyah gig in Sheffield

place filling up and realised that there might be quite a few in that night. Around 8.30-ish, we took to the stage and the capacity audience had arrived in their two thousand mass. The Hoax did a thirty minute set. 15 songs in 30 minutes are what they got. Historically, support acts are there to warm up the audience and hopefully give them a flavour of what's to come next, and I personally think that on the night, despite the nervousness of playing to an away crowd and a big one at that, they got their pound of flesh; plus for a further pound in cash at the door they could buy a copy of our 7″ e.p single 'Only the blind can see in the dark'.

My lack of knowledge of the Upstarts had led me to believe that they were a London band, but now, through the intensity of the atmosphere, there was a clear sound of Northumbrian voices. The Upstarts were blokes. We were fledgling late teens to early twenties and they'd seen life from a much older perspective. Here was a band who had the mental maturity and personal political awareness to write a song like 'Who killed Liddle Towers'.

What I do remember is singer Thomas Mensforth being quite humble and supportive of our performance, saying *'Thank you'* and offering us more sandwiches with one hand while trying to throttle the promotions manager with the other. He was outraged. Just to stay on 'Mensi's good side was enough for me so I tried to ignore what was going on. A little later I found out that the full cash promised to the Upstarts prior to the gig was not going to materialise.

What followed within minutes was the Upstarts deciding to quit the gig and leave immediately via the underground car park. In the ensuing minutes, the audience also got wind that the Upstarts were not going to appear and were asking for their money back. We, The Hoax had also decided to leave. In Andy's words *'We were not welcome anymore'* -

The five yards distance from back stage to the front of the stage was no small distance to cross with a case of insurrection from a crowd that size. Our guitars, amps and drums were packed away double quick, despite the narrow metal staircase that led to the lower ground car park. The two things I remember were seeing the beige coloured MK 1 Jag the Upstarts had arrived in, winding its way out of the Top Rank car parking facilities and away from the escalating noise from inside the venue. I guess that the crowd would have bounced the Jag and its occupants out of town had they got the opportunity.

We left in a hurry, shortly afterwards; just as well in case the angry crowd wanted to take their revenge out on us instead. I would love to hear exactly what any members of the audience that night can still remember about those events as they unfolded on the inside of the Sheffield Top Rank."

Three Great Punk Films

Tony ... "The three main punk films that came to the cinema at the time (apart from Jubilee back in 1978) were the Clash film 'Rude Boy', which me and my mate Dean went to see at the old classic cinema in Rotherham – there was only myself, Dean and an old fella in there who must have mistaken the film's title to have been for a Porn movie. Where were all the Clash fans? Then there was 'The Great Rock n' roll Swindle' which was a bit busier at the 'Scala' cinema (now Ritz bingo hall). A couple of kids started dancing down the aisles during the Sid Vicious version of 'My Way'. Then there was 'Breaking Glass', the Hazel O'Connor one. That played at the Scala too."

Gill Frost ... "I carried on with my obsession with the Sex Pistols until, one day, they brought out a film: the 'Great Rock 'n' Roll Swindle'. I was overjoyed and went to see it with my brother, even though it was an 18 certificate and I was only about twelve and my brother fifteen. Luckily, we're a tall family and we managed to get in! We saw it at the Scala Cinema on Corporation Street – now a bingo hall. I loved the film, although I got pretty embarrassed by the rude bits, but it was nearly over for the Sex Pistols as a recording act after that, so our musical taste started to move on."

That year (1980) was a sad year for the punk generation. Malcolm Owen of the Ruts died of a heroin overdose in May, followed in July with the suicide of Ian Curtis of Joy Division. Both groups were at the premise of something special and seemed very likely to be on the way to achieving much more.

Tony ... "I can remember when I heard Malcolm Owen had died. I think I heard it on the radio in the morning. By lunch time kids who didn't like Punk were taking the piss and being really cruel, laughing at our loss. The same thing happened when Ian Curtis died as well. They were both a sad loss to the music scene and who knows what they would have achieved if they had chosen to live?"

Above: In 1980 I was trying to hang on to the last few surges of Punk Rock whilst keeping an eye on much of the Post–Punk music that was around

Andrew Morton ... "I would go to see Punk groups at the Top Rank and it was obviously an over 18's policy. In those days they were so much more relaxed about it though. One night the bouncer at the door asked how old I was. He didn't believe I was 18, or 17, or 16. He says *'tell me the truth and I will let you in.'* So I told him I was fourteen and he says *'Go on then get yer self fuckin' in then'.* Yes I was in the Top Rank to see a Punk band. It felt fantastic."

Tony … "I was a full time club member of 18's only Top Rank club. Still have one of my membership cards, which is signed by some of the Punk groups. It cost a quid and had to be renewed yearly. I never went near the place after I was 18."

Meanwhile other groups such as Adam and the Ants, who had never been darlings of the press, by any means, were on the verge of breaking through to the mainstream and out of the confines and rules of the hardcore Punk scene. The Antz played Sheffield and Doncaster numerous times and during 1980 played the Top Rank venue twice; the first one in June being accompanied by sporadic outbursts of violence from the Antz London following and saw Adam Ant try to break up the fighting himself.

 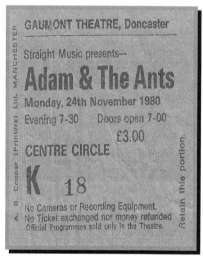

Above: Adam and the Ants played two dates at Sheffield Top Rank in 1980 including this one. Right: Ticket for a Doncaster gig later that year

Dave Spencer … "The early Adam and the Ants were quite an influence on me, especially in my song writing with Cute Pubes. That first LP had a certain style that, when I listen back to the songs I was writing at the time, is clearly in there."

Tony … "I went to see Adam and the Ants around the time before they were starting to get big. This was at the Sheffield Top Rank. They were ok but I wasn't over impressed that much. It just wasn't my style really, though their first LP Dirk wears White Sox; was pretty good. Later on I went to see the Ants offspring group Bow Wow Wow play an afternoon set at the Sheffield Limit club. I went to that gig on my own, but got mates with a couple of punk kids from Matlock. The group only had a handful of songs so played most of them two or three times. I stood right at the front... inches away from Anabella their singer. She was only the same age as me but gave it her all. I bought that tape they did 'Cassette Pet' which was only available on that format. I had also bought the 'C-30 C-60- C-90 go' single too. That was a great late punk single especially in its ideology of

258

pirate taping. Like *'don't bother buying records just tape them instead?'* That was years, even decades in front of the downloading craze."

Andrew Morton …"We would go up to the Top Rank in the afternoon and try and get our names on the guest list for that evenings gig. It usually worked."

Tony … "Another group that were always friendly with the fans were 999. They talked to us and gave us 999 stickers, badges and other promotional stuff. Sometimes a couple of us would wag school and go up to the Top Rank on an afternoon and be there when the big tour lorries with all the groups gear in would arrive. We would just hang around and try and suss out who was in charge of the road crew and then ask if they needed any help humping the gear in to the venue. They nearly always let you help out a little and then they would put your names down on that night's guest list. We managed to do this with 999, Chelsea, Undertones and some others."

Punk nights at the Top Rank could occasionally expose more than fans bargained for!

Lynne Haythorne … "While still at school, one of the gigs I went to was Siouxsie and the Banshees at the Top Rank. At this time there was quite a divide between all the different youth factions – Mods, Rockers, skins and Punks – and I remember that as we arrived at the Top Rank panic set in as the word was going around that a load of skinheads were on their way over to have a fight with everyone queuing up to get in. My boyfriend at the time pushed me over the railing to apparent safety and wearing a shocking pink mini-dress and matching tights, I ended up showing all I had got underneath to escape the potential trouble."

Joanne Orgill … "We went to the Top Rank club in Sheffield as often as we could afford to. There was a golden era when it seemed that anyone who was anyone would appear at the venue. My memory is very sketchy here – I have to rely on Helen for affirmation, but I think I saw the Damned (several times), Siouxsie and the Banshees, the Ruts, Sham 69 (where I met my first punk rock boyfriend – a Billy Idol look-alike, who apparently ended up living in a cave!!???)), the Cure, Adam and the Ants and probably a whole plethora of others. I seem to remember Thursdays and Sundays being the main gig nights but could be wrong there – very rusty memory!"

Lynne Haythorne … "There was one Stranglers gig when I had managed to get my t-shirt signed by Bass player Jean Jacques Burnel … he signed it on my left breast. Not all of the 'New Wave' stars showed their appreciation of local Punks so kindly."

Tony ... "We went to see UK Subs Sunday night at the Top Rank and they played a great set. I think it was during a song of theirs called 'World War' (I may be wrong)...anyway, the guitarist Nicky Garrett put on a great show and he topped it off during this song.

He disappeared for a good section of the song and everyone was wondering where he had gone to. Then out of nowhere (it seemed) he re-appeared from '*under the floorboards*' of the stage...the stage floorboard going flying and he was still playing his guitar. It was a great show and all the Punks were well impressed."

Above: Rotherham Punk fans at the start of the decade – 1980 – 1981 in Rotherham town centre

Mark Senior... "In the early 80's I used to go to the Saturday night disco down the polytechnic with my then punkette girlfriend Ruth,(she is now a lab technician or some such thing in York), and a load of other punks including Big John. I would also go to Mona Lisa's, Rebels etc. There were some drop dead gorgeous punkettes in Sheffield, several of whom I went out with. For some reason I hardly ever pulled at the Limit and I hated the place, they used to play too much arty farty stuff like Bauhaus and Gang of four etc and I hated the way your boots used to stick to the filthy, lager coated lino."

Andrea Deakin (Rotherham Punkette) ... "I remember the Punk nights at Rebels night club. They were great times. Anyone who was a Punk would be there. There was always this massive guy who was into Rock music, Meatloaf or whatever, anyway he would be banging on the stage with a big stick and between records he would be protesting and shouting for some real music to be put on. There was also a couple who always went and

260

they were kind of traveller hippy types. They would actually be having sex blatantly while we were all around. No one cared."

Rotherham during the start of the decade, like Sheffield, Doncaster etc, had its own Punk meeting places and sporadically there would be Punk nights at clubs and pubs around the area. The local youth club disco still being the main source of social entertainment for most young Punks, but the lure of something stronger than Tizer in a plastic cup soon loomed. One of the main meeting places for the Punk crowd and the new prototype Goth influenced Punks was the Charters Arms pub in Rotherham Town centre.

Gary Gillott (Chippie) ... "All the local Punks would meet in the Charters and loads of us would go on outings to the Retford Porterhouse to see the Punk gigs. After the gigs there, we would hang about the train station until the early hours, waiting for the next train. The staff at the station had gotten to know us all and they would light us a fire to keep us warm."

Sheffield Punks would congregate in the city centre on Saturday afternoons with bottles of cider on hand.

Mark Senior ... "I remember Saturday afternoons in the summer - drinking cider in the peace gardens. Also, around that time I used to drink in the Wapentake. A lot of my mates were rockers and apart from Martyn on the door I was the only punk who used to drink in there. I also liked rock and got on great with the hairies. I still see some of the old wap regulars like the DJ's Ken and Les, one of the bouncers (Lightning) in the Nelson over Christmas where we reminisce about old times over a few jars. My other regular boozers back then were the Museum and most of West Street. Many are the memories of braving freezing winds and pissing rain to get to the outside bog at the Museum before joining the lads in a rousing chorus of the Monkees 'Daydream believer' on the juke box! For a while quite

Above: Mark Senior

a few punks used to drink in the Brewery tap on Snig hill which was very handy for my last bus back to Grenoside!"

Helen McLaughlin ... "We used to meet up every Saturday lunchtime with the Sheffield punks next to the fish tank in The Hole In The Road and slowly we would all wander down The Moor and go into Atkinson's café and then on to Lewis Leathers and Virgin Records right at the bottom of The Moor."

Records popular with the local Punk crowd, that did not fit with the traditional Punk style, were Magazine's 'A Song from under the floorboards', Adam and the Ants 'Car trouble', the Cure's 'A forest', Human League's 'Being Boiled. Also Bill Nelson's 'Furniture music', Teardrop Explodes 'Bouncing babies' and the new more melodic and contemporary sound of Siouxsie and the Banshees with first 'Happy House' in March 1980 and then shortly afterwards 'Christine' and the album 'Kaleidoscope'.

To a varied soundtrack of Power Pop, Post-Punk and high energy Punk Rock, local young Punk fans were enjoying the last few bursts of their Punk summers!

Tony … "That summer of 1980 was, for me, the last truly great one for Punk and also for my youth, in as much as I still felt that exuberance, naivety and innocence of being a young teenager. I was knocking about with Pete Roddis still and we had also made mates with Dean Stables and Tracy Stanley, so we would hang around together a lot and listen to music and stuff. We would knock about the local woods and get up to no good a lot of the time."

Tracy Stanley … "Oh my God, I had forgotten all about those days. I remember one day that we set an old mattress afire and it got out of control and we were panicking."

Tony … "The sun seemed to be shining every day. We were listening to lots of different Punk related music. Some that spring to mind are Drones 'Can't see' (where did they pull that one from? the perfect 1980 Pop 45), the Moondogs 'Who's going to tell Mary', the Salford Jets 'who you Looking at', Revillos 'Scuba Scuba', the Donkeys 'What I want', Magazine's 'Song from under the floorboards and Joy Division's 'Love will tear us apart'. We were having some great times and laughs to a fantastic soundtrack. Soon we would all be doing our own thing and yet again it would be a case of great friends parting our separate ways."

Julian Jones … "I would always be getting bullied by the skinheads. There was one who would go to the same youth club I went to (we were both from a different school); anyway he would always give me a right chase or beat me up. He would always nick my badges and then I would see kids at school with my badges on."

Richard Chatterton … "When I had become a Punk, I always felt a little awkward with my peers who lived in Brinsworth who didn't really get it. They may have liked the music but it did not really change their lives; they carried on going to the same local, going to the football match, working (something I wasn't really into at the time) and basically staying the same. The Three Magpies was my local, which I started to venture into a little later when it became my brothers regular haunt. I always felt out of place, although there were enough people around who did like the music – especially The Jam and the upcoming Ska bands."

Meanwhile the local World War Two generation were, in the most instances, not that keen on Punk Rockers (as they would not have been no more enamoured with Rock n' Rollers and Mods in previous years). As much as we love them, they came from a different era; one that concerned the war effort and saving our great land so that future generations such as ours could enjoy that very freedom and express ourselves as we saw fit. Don't mean that they were gonna like it though. However, not all were ignorant to the revolution and the Punk Rock cause... even if it often appeared that way at times.

Tony … "Me and a couple of my Punk mates were passing by the old pensioner's bingo crowd. Now they were made of tough stuff those veterans of the 'Full house and felt tip' brigade and back in those days, they were still chain-smoking, card cheating and seriously slandering anyone not to their veteran types liking; Punks were definitely in the old guard's top ten of disgusting local wasters. As we walked past them in our tartan trousers, zip covered jackets and gravity defying heads of spikes, the mutterings of distempered disgust and annoyance were aimed at our direction. Laughing we walked by them *'Evening lasses'* we said to their shocked faces. *Blimey they can speak actual English'* was the expression written on their faces... *'but lets not detract from our put down of what we don't like'* was the attitude. Anyway, my Mum comes out of the chippy and she goes over to the Bingo storm troopers. Yes they were her mates and accomplices in the world of evening gambling. When she joined up with 'em they were still going on about the filthy bunch of Punk Rockers they had passed. My Mum turned round and recognised me and my mates and then laid straight into the gang. I could see her finger waving in their faces and wasn't sure what was being said so I left her to it. Bless her. A little embarrassing I suppose and very un – street cred but as honest and confrontational as any spiky tops outburst.

   She was fantastic with all of the many Punks who came round to our house and some virtually lived in the front room just about. How she put up with the noise and the mayhem all of that time I will never know, but all credit to her she never complained. Christ she even liked 'White Man in Hammersmith Palais' by the Clash and when one of my mates who was right into the Jam asked which record was playing in the other room, she proudly replied *It's 'Down in the Tube Station at Midnight' lad.'.* Can you beat that?"

One young Punk girl even ended up taking a very close member of her family along to see a display of Punk pantomime from the Damned.

Gill Frost … "One of the Punk bands I really got into was the Dammed and I saw them a number of times, one of them being at the Lyceum in Sheffield. Believe it or not, my mum really liked the Damned, so she came along to that concert with me, my brother and his mates. It was a bit of a worry, taking your middle aged mum to see a punk band – I mean; you wonder what people's reactions are going to be, don't you? Well, there was one or two who assumed she must just be one of the Lyceum staff, but other people were amazingly friendly and chatted to her, saying how great it was that she was into that type of music. There was no stopping her after that."

The original Punk groups had, by now, mostly lost the best part of their street credibility and for most local Punks it would be the new Punk groups that they were going along to see. Cockney Rejects fit the bill for a while during 1980.

Andrew Morton ... "The first gig the Cockney Rejects were supposed to play at the Limit was cancelled. I went up and they announced the cancellation when we were inside the venue. The group had been locked up so the gig would be re-arranged for a later date. They did end up playing that one at a later date, which was an afternoon one. They were really good too."

Above: Cockney Rejects ticket (Andy Goulty's collection)

Richard Chatterton ... "I took my youngest brother Craig, who was only eleven, to see the Rejects at the Limit. This was a matinee gig and he was still two years under the age limit."

Helen McLaughlin ..."I remember going to see the Cockney Rejects at The Limit in Sheffield one Saturday afternoon. They had all been arrested for something or other so we all marched down to the police station and caused havoc outside. I had orange glittery nail varnish on my eyes as eye shadow; it was a bugger to get off."

Jeff Turner (Cockney Rejects singer) ... "We drove on for Sheffield where we were due to play a 1.00pm matinee at the Limit club the following afternoon. I was rooming with Vince and Wellsy and at 5.00am the next morning some cunt started kicking at the door, saying, *'CID, open up.'*

I thought it was a joke; that if I opened the door I'd find one of the lads standing there with a bucket of piss. *'Fuck off'*, I said. *'We're asleep.'*

But they kept hammering. It was the CID and they nicked all three of us."

The arrests were allegedly in connection with an incident a week or two before in Walsall, when Mickey Geggus (Rejects guitarist) had done some skins over with an iron bar the morning after the Battle of Birmingham. They ended up being interrogated and subsequently grassed on by an outsider who named all who had been in the van with Mickey at the time of the alleged incident.

Jeff Turner... "We had sold out the show at the Limit club that afternoon. The owner phoned and asked the police if they'd release Mickey but they refused. Mickey had been charged with GBH, malicious wounding and causing an affray. It made the papers. The Daily Mirror called us notorious.

I had to drive back to the gig and tell the audience what had happened. I offered them their money back or the chance to use their tickets at a gig we'd rescheduled for the following Saturday if Mick got out.

264

Mick got out on bail and the following Saturday we did the gig and we started rowing with each other while we were playing, threatening to knock each other's teeth out. It was all going out over the mic. I don't know what the crowd must have thought. We went backstage. He took his guitar off. I took my shirt off and I just hit him. Then it went off into a full scale row. We both got cut, there was blood everywhere. It went on for five minutes and I was getting upped and it was just as well my mates kicked down the door and pulled us apart. When they broke in, they said they found us holding on to each other like terriers."

The bust up relieved the tension that been building up throughout the tour and Jeff and Mickey shook hands, made up and drove home. Their next visit to Sheffield would be equally as violent, but this time it would be the fans themselves who would be involved in the fighting; outside and inside the venue.

Andrew Morton … "I went to the Top Rank one too. The skins were laying into the greasers that night. This one bloke had taken a right pasting and was crawling up the road across from the Rank. They weren't a very nice lot those Sheffield skinheads. A lot of them were into glue sniffing so they were high as kites."

Paul White (Sugar) … " Me and my mate found out how to get through to the lift at the Top Rank and we went up in it, only to be met by one of the Rejects road crew who told us we had better make ourselves scarce cos if they saw us they would beat us up."

Tony … "I liked some of the Cockney Rejects records; stuff like The 'Flares and Slippers' E.P, 'I'm not a fool' and 'Bad Man', they were fantastic records, but can't say I was a proper massive fan like some of the lads around at the time. Earlier in the year some of our mates had gone to see them play the afternoon gig at the Limit Club. I don't know why we didn't go to that one as we were in Sheffield centre that afternoon? Another mate of mine Ricky had gone crackers on the Rejects and bought the LP and all the singles.
      Later in the year, me and Ricky went to see them play at the Sheffield Top Rank. When we got outside the venue, the skinheads were hammering the rockers who were on their way to a rock gig at the City hall. I think it was the Scorpions that were playing that same night. They were ambushing the Rockers as they tried to cross through the subway below the Top Rank. We saw this happening and were hoping that we wouldn't be the next in the firing line. Fortunately, we managed to get into the gig unscathed, although the Rejects set was marred by constant fighting all the way through just about. Cockney Rejects themselves were really good. They had got really accomplished as musicians and were really in their stride. I liked their attitude and stance. They certainly didn't stand for any bullshit, that's for sure. I even bought a massive tour poster, which I got signed by Jeff and Mickey.
      Earlier on outside the venue I spotted a couple of clownish type of punks. They looked plastic to me anyway. Inside I realised that these two were actually two of the support band who were called the Exploited. They were absolutely crap; the only thing to impress me was Guitarist Big John's Johnny Thunders and the Heartbreakers shirt. Even so I was ashamed to be a part of the same scene as them. Punk was almost dead even up North

now. Well for me anyway because if this was the example of what Punk Rock was now serving us up.; well count me out.

That night I was glad to get home and away from this thing called Punk Rock, which was no longer something refreshing and non conformist. It was conforming to its own straitjacketed rules and the Exploited were prime examples. Not that long after this tour the Cockney Rejects started moving into a more Rock influenced style. Who can blame them?"

There was one way of dealing with the repetitive and mindless moronity of the 'Do what a Punk should do as told by the Sunday papers brigade' - as told by this Stranglers follower.

Mark Senior … "One memorable occasion Hugh and John (Jean Jacques Burnel) debagged a bloke who'd been gobbing at them at a Sheffield City Hall gig; Cornwell rammed one of my dad's chocolate éclairs up his backside,(My dad was a baker before retiring and the band asked me for a couple of dozen éclairs for the Sheffield gig, the rest were eaten normally!) Following the Stranglers around on tour was many things but dull wasn't one of them!"

Andy Goulty … "One of the times I went to see The Stranglers at the City Hall, I was with some of the older lads up on the balcony. One kid in front of us was getting in the way and gave us some lip, so one of the older lads got a hold of him and hung him over the balcony head first. I couldn't believe it, though it was quite funny really."

Right: Rotherham Punk Dave Frost

Tony … "Around that time around Rotherham and Sheffield there was so many differing factions that had evolved out of Punk. There was the 'multi-coloured hair ten inch back combed spikes' of the Siouxsie and Toyah influenced girls, the New Punk leather jacketed dyed jet black hair gang of lads who were into Discharge and that lot, the so called Positive-Punk gang who could be seen at Killing Joke gigs, the nascent Goths who were copying the Banshees, Bauhaus, the Birthday Party and the Cure and so on. Somewhere in the middle were kids like me who liked bits of most of these styles as well as others but were gradually becoming bored with the uniformity of it all? Also as much as I loved the Jam, and some of the Mod stuff and loved a lot of the clothes – I would now be wearing Harrington's, Levis and Chelsea boots – at that time I could never have swapped the Punk style for a parka. That would just be swapping one uniform for another. It really was a confusing time for me."

The diverse book ends of the Punk scene and its offsprings could not be better exemplified than when Doncaster 'out and out' Punk band Soshal Sekurity (Yes that's how they spelt their name) played a Doncaster gig supported by Bauhaus influenced Futurist synth/guitar duo Wonder Stories. Both vied for the mixed audience's attention and both displayed the inverted snobbery of playing to an audience's expectations. In short, each one of the acts gave off the stereotype cliché-ridden images of their independent scenes; the atypical Punk band with no future v the pompous anti-Punk stance of the 1980 futurist aficionado. To many, both of these attempts were a far cry from the original spirit of Punk and its promises of change and the excitement of creating your own future. Yes those times were full of promise, but could also prove boring and confusing during its given moments.

Above: Left...me with Punk Rock cat Tommy and one eyebrow on and one off. Right: wearing original Clash 'White Riot' tour shirt playing a Woolworths guitar

Richard Chatterton ... "I started to feel a conflict inside my Punk world. Although I loved the pure Punk thrash of The Ramones etc and would go and see hardcore Punk such as Crass and the Exploited, I was more and more being drawn to the arty side of Punk. I was getting more into bands like Joy Division and Bauhaus."

Sheffield Leadmill first opened its doors for live gigs in 1980...the first groups to play there were Cabaret Voltaire and then the Dead Kennedy's on their very first UK tour.

Richard Chatterton ... "I hung out at the Limit club, but also went to the Leadmill. I saw The Fall, Cabaret Voltaire and Dead Kennedys in the venues first few weeks of opening."

Patrick Tierney ... "One of the greatest gigs was at the Leadmill; Dead Kennedy's supported by UK Decay. When they went off stage, they were completely covered in spit, but when the Dead Kennedy's came on their singer Jello Biafra said *'If anyone spits on me I will kill them'.* No one did."

Tony ... "Me and Pete went to the Leadmill in the late summer of 1980 to see Dead Kennedys play. The venue was not yet open for regular gigs and to be honest it was in a right state at that point. We had a great night though. The gig was a bit of a wild one but definitely fun. Jello Biafra was diving into the audience a lot of the time. They only had the first LP songs at that time but they all sounded great and went down well. We got our Dead Kennedys 'California uber alles' picture sleeves signed by the band afterwards. They were stood outside having a breather as it was red hot inside. Seemed like decent guys. I think they must have been the first Americans I had ever spoken to."

Helen McLaughlin (Right) ... "We went to see the Dead Kennedys at The Leadmill when it had holes in the roof and portaloos. The portaloos lasted about an hour and stopped working and it rained and rained through the holes in the roof. Jello Biafra got his willy out on stage. The whole place ended up flooded in water and wee and God knows what. We drank lager and black in the pub on the corner (we always drank lager and black - God, we were 15, we didn't know what to drink!)."

Lynne Haythorne ... "I was at the Kennedys gig too. The toilets were terrible. You went in and you could see straight outside. The whole place was in a mess. So different to how it is nowadays."

Chiz recalls another Dead Kennedy's gig at the Leadmill ... "The Dead Kennedys supported by Peter and the Test Tube Babies, Millions of Dead Cops, and our very own Mau Maus; that was one of the best gigs ever. Every band was at their best and the atmosphere was brilliant. Our mates Society's Victims turned up at a high profile gig at the Leadmill once (It could have been this one but I am not sure), anyway, they said that they were the support and just walked on stage and played... Cheeky Bleeders!"

Other gigs at the Leadmill included a rare date from Crass (who only ever played two in Sheffield), but the venue was closed down in September 1980 after its license was refused. Benefit gigs were played by Cabaret Voltaire and The Fall to raise enough money to allow it to re-open and also a grant was passed by the Sheffield City Council. Finally, after a large grant of £22,000 was given from the government Manpower services, the venue re-opened in September 1982. Almost every band that ever made it thereafter would play at the venue at some point and The Leadmill would eventually become one of the leading live venues in the country. The list of bands that have played there and gone on to bigger things is almost endless. Back in 1980, though, one of the last great big Punk concerts of the original Punk era was when The Jam returned for the 3rd time to the Sheffield Top Rank.

John Harrison ... "The Jam at Sheffield Top Rank... what an experience!"

Tony ... "I saw the tour dates months before in the NME and went crazy to get tickets to see the Jam at the Sheffield Top Rank'. Me and my mate Pete got some and a lad who was nicknamed Batty from our end, well he went with us to see them. There were quite a few familiar faces from the punk scene around that night. John Harrison, who I would later form a Mod band with was there and I recall him telling me that he had been there all day and watched the Jam sound check and hung about with them for a while. I can remember when the Jam came on Weller slipped down. He was not amused with himself over that. They were absolutely blinding that night and played loads of the 'All Mod Cons' LP and most of the singles. Me and Pete were well chuffed. Next day; Monday morning was a real come down after that gig.

In 1980 as well as listening to the Jam and the Clash (as always), I was also digging The Cure, Undertones, Gang of Four, Siouxsie and the Banshees, Damned, Joy Division, Magazine, Buzzcocks, Skids, Pinpoint, 999, the Members, Chelsea, the Photos, The Fall, the Boys, Angelic Upstarts, Girls at our best, The Sound ('Hey Day' what a classic single), the Passions etc. The Slits 'Cut' LP was also big on the turntable for me and my mate Dean (Beanz)... It was mostly a mix of the established Punk groups and the more obscure Post-Punk that was coming through on the John Peel show, which I always tried to listen to as much as I could."

Julian Jones ... "Tony used to take me round to this lad's house, who we called 'Posh Punk' and he was crackers about Cabaret Voltaire, I would get to liking some of their stuff too. At this time, and I don't know why, I would be having endless fits of laughter. I did end up quite liking the Cabs though and eventually managed to stop laughing."

Tony ... "I went to one of the John Peel road-shows and Peely walked past me and my mates, who were sprawled across the floor and I piped up and asked him if he would play some requests for us. He seemed annoyed, a bit put out, and he said he would see what he could do. He never did put any records on for us. I do not think he was that fond of Punk kids themselves. But he was a massive driving force throughout the whole period and beyond. I guess he was entitled to be so mardy when he had managed to engineer so many fantastic groups to the public's attention."

The high tide of punk was now rapidly receding, but still the younger generation showed no lack of enthusiasm for the Punk Rock experience.

Gill Frost ... "My brother started bringing other punk albums into the house. One I really loved, and still do to this day, was 'Inflammable Material' by Stiff Little Fingers and they were the first live band I went to see. That was a steep learning curve! They played at Sheffield Polytechnic and were supported by a band called The Wall. I made sure I got as near to the front as I could, as I was so excited....Big mistake. When the band came on, everyone around me started pogo-ing like mad and I couldn't help but be carried along by them.

I thought I was having fun, until I realised my feet were never actually touching the ground. I couldn't keep up with all these big blokes around me and began to fall backwards. Luckily, big brother was right behind me and grabbed me out of the way before I fell under all those big army boots and dockers. Having learned my lesson, I stood back and had the time of my life and realised I would want to go to see lots more live bands in future."

Above: Rawmarsh youth club Punkettes Joanne Frost, Julie Lee and Fiona Palmer on the dance floor

Tony ... "Around that time, say late 1980, a lot of the original Punk groups that were left were, to be blunt, fuckin' crap. I didn't get what the Stranglers were doing anymore, all that 'Men in Black' rubbish, which was all drug fuelled music and just as boring as the stuff that Punk had kicked aside. Likewise, the Damned were bringing out their prototype Goth album the Black Album with its 15-minute one full-sided track 'Curtain Call'... One of the best albums of that time, for me, was the Skids 'Absolute game'. I always loved the Skids and that was a fantastic LP. I still play that one a lot."

A new style of Punk mixed with all the cartoonish elements and slapstick of Punk was loosely termed Herbert - also being a close relative of the new Oi! Punk style - and no other group in 1980 could be better described as Herbert than Splodgenessabounds who had achieved a chart hit earlier in the year with their 'Two Pints of lager and a packet of crisp please'.

Mark Senior ... "One gig I can remember in 1980 was Splodgenessabounds at the Poly. All the feminists were there determined to cause a ruck. The support (Auntie Puss and the piss flaps) kicked things off when they asked them why they had beards and why weren't they at home cooking their husband's tea! Auntie Puss then invited *'Any boilers that need a shag can form a queue outside my dressing room'.* All hell broke loose and when Splodge came on it got even worse/better when Aileen got on stage and stripped off followed by a couple of feminists who ended up fighting with Max Splodge!"

Tony ... "I think the only so called Herbert group that I liked were the Not Sensibles with their 'I'm in love with Margaret Thatcher' single."

Late 1980 and the earlier open mindedness of the Punk movement was slowly becoming outdated and many punk fans had moved on. In the meantime, while some great Punk records were still being occasionally produced, a lot of the most interesting if not as immediate music was coming from the Post-Punk groups.

Tony ... "I did really like Gang of Four. I was first impressed with them back in mid 79 when they were on some Saturday morning pop show doing 'At home he's a tourist'. I bought quite a few of their records and went to see them at the University and they were really good; a lot different to most of the other Punk groups around."

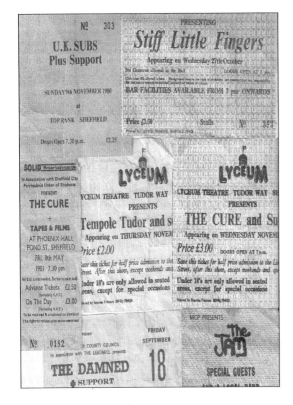

Above: Some more Gig tickets from my own collection

1980 - 1981 was also a time when many of the Punk and New wave groups began to call it a day.

Tony ... "Me and Pete went to see the Buzzcocks at the City Hall and you could tell that they were getting tired of it all. They played all the best songs but just appeared so bored. There was a load of punk kids all sat at the edge of the stage heckling for the early stuff(the venue was not at all full with mainly the area directly in front of the stage being used), and Pete Shelly was so despondent. He announced 'Orgasm Addict' as though it was just a case of going through the motions. This was Buzzcocks by numbers. In one sense, it was ok cos they did play a hell of a lot of stuff we wanted to hear, but in another sense, it was kind of sad. I have seen the Buzzcocks a few times since and they were much better and a totally different band to that night at the City Hall."

Andy Goulty ... "We were sat at the edge of the stage as Buzzcocks played. They were good, but appeared to be past caring and the hall was too big for them really."

The following year Buzzcocks were no longer and following the same path were Magazine, Skids, Subway Sect and others. X-Ray Spex, Penetration, T.R.B, the Lurkers and the Adverts had all called it a day in 1979. It was now down to a small handful of traditional Punk style groups to keep the Punk spirit burning. Groups such as The Ruts, Angelic Upstarts, Stiff Little Fingers, Cockney Rejects and UK Subs were all setting the charts alight during 1980 and all would play memorable gigs in the region. But there was also Punk's most visual rebels the Clash who always brought the crowds in when they played in Sheffield. Their last Sheffield date had been on the 'London Calling' tour, but the following year a low key gig at Sheffield's newly refurbished Lyceum theatre was pencilled in on their short autumn tour.

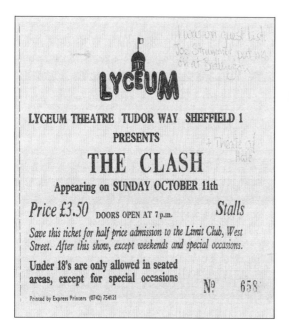

Above: Mick Jones of 'The Clash onstage at Sheffield Lyceum (from my collection and one of the photos taken by us that night)

Tony … "Me and my mate Dean got tickets for the Clash gig at the Lyceum. We went to the venue early on in the day hoping to get to see and meet the Clash. We hung around for bloody hours. We tried sneaking in to the venue to check out the sound-check but got thrown out. The car with Clash number plates was outside. I can't remember if this was Bernie Rhodes their manager's car or the bands. Anyway, one of the entourage a Rasta guy saw us hanging around and he asked us to help move some gear into the venue. Yes, here's our chance to get on the guest list we thought and yes, I am glad to say this worked.

Later on we sold our tickets to a couple of punk kids outside who didn't have any. I remember us saying we only wanted the ticket price, even though the gig was a sell out. We thought that this was sort of sticking to the punk ideal and not ripping fellow fans off. Me and Dean were quite proud of sticking to our principles. That is until we got to the front of the queue to get in and told the doormen we were on the guest list. They told us our names weren't on there and we were in shock. I can remember my heart was beating so fast and the panic was setting in. Christ what are we gonna do now? Go and find the kids we sold the tickets to? We could try to persuade em to sell em back to us? No way - they wouldn't fall for that; who would? Force em to part with em? Nah that's not right. Christ we were stuck well up the creek. *'Oi mate'*, we said to the doorman one more time, *'c'mon have another look for our names we aren't kidding yer'*. The doorman says *'Look yer not on here now sod off'*...The heart's about burst from my chest by now...it's pretty cold but I am sweating...*'Right just let us have a look ourselves at yer list'* I said. By this time we could see some of our mates behind us with their tickets and they were bleeding laughing at us. Then - and I reckon the gesture was probably to get us out of the way one way or another - the doorman shows us his guest list sheet and we see it small as anything down at the bottom...it was there in tiny scribbled biro Dean and mate. *'That's us two',* we piped up *'now come on let us in we are holding the queue up'.* Next minute we were in there...and thank God for that. Our lives would have been forever tainted with the thought that we had screwed up our chances to see a Clash gig.

The Clash that night were super. A brilliant gig yet again. 'Complete Control' was amazing... we got right at the front, it was red hot, and the atmosphere was electric. We managed to get to meet them too. Earlier in the evening, I had managed to catch Mick Jones for a quick chat. He looked so small and thin whereas on stage he always looked larger than life. Anyway, Jonesy didn't mingle with the fans after the gig but the others did. We had a great chat with Paul and Topper who were really friendly and we took some photos with them, which, apart from a couple of live shots, never turned out worse luck.

Above: Me and local Punk mate Beanz (Dean Stables)

Most people were all over Joe. He appeared quite stoned to us and he signed our shirts and then disappeared. A few years later I would get a much better chance to meet and talk to Joe Strummer. At that same gig I got mates with a punk fan called Frank from London. He needed a place to crash as he was following The Clash on tour. Anyway I put him up for the night. Thing is we were walking home from Sheffield to Rawmarsh which is a good 12 miles or so. I don't think poor old Frank realised the hike we had in front of us and as we were only in Tinsley he was asking! *'Is your place just around the corner then?'...* *'Yeah not far mate'* I told him. It couldn't have put Frank off too much as whenever he was in Sheffield to see a band he would manage to find me and scrounge a place to kip for the night.

One of the times that he was up our end, he came round to Beanz house with me: the morning after a gig. It was so funny 'cos when Beanz pulled out the plug on their old Redifusion TV, the sound was still coming through from the speaker which was from the radio that was built in with it. Frank's face was a picture. He couldn't believe it. He was like *'But you've taken the plug out and there's no electric on... how's that?'* He was totally bewildered... and then when we used to send him off home on the local bus and tell him to give the bus driver 2 pence he wouldn't believe us. *'2p for a bus journey?' It would cost me 50p down London.'* he would reply. Another thing he would say was that it was always colder up here than down South...but he was a good kid Frank. He liked the Jam too so that put him in great stead with me. He came from Walthamstow. I wonder where he is now."

The Clash played a very well received set that night at Sheffield's Lyceum venue including classics such as 'Clash City Rockers', 'Complete control', 'White Man in Hammersmith Palais', 'Janie Jones', 'Safe European Home', 'Stay Free', 'Career Opportunities', 'London's burning' and more recent, but equally much loved songs, like 'Brand New Cadillac', 'London Calling', 'Guns of Brixton', 'Somebody Got Murdered', 'Armageddon Time' and 'Working for the clampdown'.

Above: Mark Senior (Sheffield Punk and Stranglers fan)

Those other Punks of 1976 The Damned were also still doing the rounds and Sheffield was always a date almost guaranteed to be included on their tour date sheet.

Tony ... "About the third time I saw the Damned at the Sheffield Top Rank was in July 1980 – we met the band and they were quite loony as you would expect. Captain Sensible was exactly the eccentric that you imagined him to be. This was around the time when Captain Sensible would end up throwing beer all over the crowd and finish the gig naked except for his guitar strapped around him. I managed to get a tape of this gig and I can hear myself shouting for 'New Rose' on it. They also did a version of 'Pretty Vacant'. This was pretty shambolic and played in true Damned style.

I saw the Damned play loads of times; must have been at least twelve different gigs. They were always a laugh. Captain Sensible drew a moustache on me, which was funny.

274

Dave Vanian was suitably vampire-ish but once ...Rat Scabies was not friendly at all '*Why don't you Fuck off and go and catch the Captain he's a real Punk rock star*' we got from him. But I suppose he must have got sick of teenage pint-sized punk kids chasing him around only to ask him some ridiculous question when cornered. Anyway most of their gigs were a real riot."

Bryan Bell ended up being invited to an after show party ... "Yeah we got back to the hotel and I was wearing my big furry boots. The Captain was taking the piss out of em, so I say '*That's rich coming from you with that big furry mammal wrapped around yer*'. The Captain pissed himself laughing. We had a great time though, and they wanted me to go on the rest of the tour but I was working that week."

Tony ... "Yes Bryan told me about this about halfway through the Damned's set and I think at that point he was gonna go and was thinking '*bugger the job*'. He suggested me going along as well but as I said at the time '*I can't mate I've got my paper round to do in the morning*'."

Paul Clarke ... "I saw The Straps support the Damned at Sheffield Top Rank. I got the Straps' singer's autograph on my ticket and I think he was taking the piss as he wrote Jock Strap."

Tony ... "I enjoyed the Straps- their drummer was Jim Walker who was in P.I.L. He was quite friendly with us, chatting away and that. In fact, I can remember this was at the time when I was trying to start my own fanzine 'Ghetto' and I sort of tried interviewing him and other members of the band.

Above: Sheffield Punkette 'Rocka Debs' (Steve Marshall's sister and lead singer of all girl Sheffield combo 'Siren') With another 'all girl Punk group the Slits' influence

I recall them as being really down to earth type of blokes. They were asking us if we came to see many Punk bands and if we had jobs, to which we told them we were still at school.

They said they would try and get our names etched on to their next single. Their Single at the time 'I just can't take anymore' was like an early psychobilly record. I went out and bought it the following day from Sound of Music in Rotherham. They also had an album out at some point. I never got to hear that for some reason."

The results of Thatcher's Britain could be viewed on trips from out of the area by local Punk fans.

Andrew Morton ... "We went to see the Damned at Manchester Mayflower club. That was a rough venue. In fact, it was rough inside and out. There were burnt out cars around and that was the first time that I saw shops open but all boarded up with shutters down. That's a pretty common sight nowadays but back then it was not so common- not round where I lived anyway."

Myself still looking for the answers within Punk Rock in 1980

Julian Jones ... "The first group I saw was the Damned at the Top Rank. I went up on the bus with Andy Beaumont and some others and as soon as we got off the bus on Pond Street, everyone just scattered everywhere. I wasn't sure what was happening but I soon found out when the skinheads started chasing us. Earlier on, I had been in the police station all day as I had been accused of nicking some gates for a bonfire, which I hadn't done but I got arrested. I told the police *'Can I go soon cos I am going to a concert'*... *'Who you going to see?'* they said *'The Damned'* I told them...*ummm!* Their faces said it all. So yeah I had been locked up all day and then it was off to see the Damned."

Political motivation was becoming more common towards the end of the original Punk era and the region's Punks were more than ready to become militant if the situation demanded.

Helen McLaughlin ... "Demonstrations were also 'our thing'. We were 15 years old but whenever there was a demo (and there were lots!) we were there. C.N.D., Rock against Racism, Animal Liberation, anything against the Tories.
   One Saturday afternoon hundreds of people (us included of course) sat down in the dual carriageway outside Weston Park (near the children's hospital in Sheffield) and blocked the road on both sides. There was word that beagles were being forced to smoke cigarettes inside the University laboratories nearby. Whilst we caused general mayhem in
276

the road, rumour was that some of our party broke into these laboratories and liberated the beagles. Don't know if this is actually true."

Martin Hickman (Rotherham Punk fan) … "When I was a young man I was full of anger about everything then Punk came along… yeah that's for me I thought and the scene and the friends I met have stayed with me ever since. It also taught me to question things through the music. This would, later in life, lead me to becoming a campaigner on the left in the trade union movement and wider class struggle. I would say that the founding stones of my later life were carved during this exciting period."

For some Punk fans, the end was near and it was time to move on: taking the experience and influence of Punk along with them.

Julian Jones … "After that year or two of being into Punk, which really when I think about it - it was Punk that got me into music, I started listening to other stuff and doing my own thing."

Following the Adverts split a year and half since, lead singer TV Smith was back doing the rounds in Sheffield with his new band, which was taking the sound of Punk a few steps forwards.

Andrew Morton … "Tony was giving me some hassle to go and see TV Smith's Explorers at the Limit club. We ended up going and it was a really good gig. TV Smith ended up jumping into the audience during one song."

Tony … "Yeah I remember that gig and yes it was a good one. All TV's songs came across a lot better when played live. 'Looking down on London' that was great live. TV Smith was really energetic and his new songs were really good…taking the formula of the Adverts a step further. His LP was good too. Also, Andy Morton and me went to see The Cure a couple of times around that time. The first time was at the Polytechnic. We were up in the afternoon too and saw the Cure doing a photo shoot for some magazine or something. They were stood at the back of the poly across from the train station. That time the Cure were really good. They were still playing quite a bit of the first album 'Killing an Arab', 'Jumping someone else's train', 'Grinding Halt' etc. The next time we saw 'em was at the Lyceum and they were quite boring. They had changed so much in about 6 months."

Punk groups could either disappoint or surprise, and even at this later stage of the Punk era, there were some memorable Punk gigs to attend in Sheffield.

Tony ... "A few of us went to see Richard Hell and the Voidoids in Sheffield. This was quite a while afterwards, I may be wrong, but I think it was one of the first times (apart from a Elvis Costello support slot) he had played around here since the Clash tour in 77, when Richard got bottled, spat on and heckled big style. We only went as we always sort of considered guys like Richard Hell and Johnny Thunders to be top Punk guys and obviously they had been a big influence on how the punk look had come together. In retrospect Thunders was the epitome of the whole wasted junkie rock star life style. Not a massive fan of the first Richard Hell LP but I really liked the later one 'Destiny Street'. He was great live too. He still had that Punk hair style as well, whereas later on he grew his hair really long."

In the early 80's the Punk and Post-Punk generation were constantly changing and so were their hangouts.

Richard Chatterton ... "I would hang out in The Marples in Sheffield, but also the Charter Arms in Rotherham Town Centre. That place became a second home for me, when I got into Art College in 1980. It was the only place I could continue to dye my hair and go to without getting any hassle. I left college and spent a year on the Dole, hitching around to see bands and then I returned to RCAT in 1981. I hung around with Sheffield, Rotherham and Chesterfield punks and when one place was getting on my nerves I'd go to the next."

Travelling to and from gigs - needs must be met and fun could often be irresistible.

Wayne Kenyon (Doncaster Punk) ... "We used to sleep out on the train station loads of times in Leeds & Sheffield. When we used to sleep out in Leeds, we had to catch a train to Rotherham in the early hours or wait about 2 or 3 hours more for one to Donny; never had a ticket and we used to avoid the guard and then hope we made it to Rotherham where we would get a bus back to Donny. While in Rotherham we would go round to places like bread shops in the town centre and nick stuff from their delivery; milk, bread etc.

Another time when we went to see Chelsea supported by Major Accident at the Leadmill me and my mate Tommy spent the night on Sheffield train station in the waiting room with 2 punks from Derby. Me and Tommy ripped the fire guard out and used it as goal posts, then used a coke can as a ball and played football all night until the first train back to home."

Towards the end of 1980 and into 1981 the local Punk scene had changed almost beyond recognition, with fan's differing viewpoints being clearer than a year or two previously.

Nicky Booth ... "Looking back my changing attitude to punk was obviously a lot to do with simply growing older. Two or three years is an awfully long time for a teenager, so

278

what seemed vital and exciting to me at school in 1979 was being replaced by a thirst for a new and varied musical diet a couple of years later when I was at college. It was great while it lasted and I still get dewy eyed listening to the Damned's 'Smash It Up' (who'd have thought it?) but things move on."

Phil Tasker ... "I didn't get in to the second generation of punk bands, there didn't seem much point, I was more interested in how the original punk bands were developing like Siouxsie, PIL, Magazine, Wire, Cure, Talking Heads and new bands like Gang of Four and some of the fledgling electronic bands such as the Human league."

Right: Post-Punk fans Julian Jones and Lynne Haythorne with Post-Punk & 60's enthusiast Gary Davies

Tony ... "By this time I was listening to all sorts, still plenty of Punk but also lots of variations of that style. I loved the Skids and Magazine had released a fantastic run of singles that year. In addition, my two favourite groups the Jam and the Clash brought out their most ambitious works to date, which managed to stretch their abilities to the maximum and really showed the lower division Punk groups how things could be achieved.

First there was 'Sound Affects' by the Jam - which saw Paul Weller stride confidently through two sides of groundbreaking 'New Wave' song writing - and then 'Sandinista' by the Clash at the end of the year and that record was a revelation for me. I got some real stick from the hard core Punk kids who thought that the record (or what parts they had bothered to listen to), was hilarious. But, to me the record was fantastic. True, the group had lost their immediacy and it was clear now, that their Punk years were a thing of the past...but we were now into a new decade and it was time to move on! As much as I consider the golden period of the Clash was 77 – 79, 'Sandinista' opened up so many different styles of music and lots of sounds that otherwise I would probably not have gone anywhere near. There was rockabilly, reggae, dub, early traces of hip-hop, jazz, disco, folk, rock, soul and no Punk at all. The closest to the classic Clash sound was 'Somebody got murdered'."

Phil Tasker ... "I thought the Clash were ok with London Calling, a bit more challenging and experimental, but I drew the line with Sandinista, although there were some good tracks on it. Later Clash stuff on Combat Rock was more controlled and powerful and ended up quite successful, but the first two albums were the best."

Andrew Morton ... "'Sandinista' is an amazing record. There is so much on there to listen to and it was unbelievably ahead of its time. I listen to 'Magnificent Seven' nowadays, and it still sounds modern."

Dave Spencer ... "As much as I loved the Clash, 'Sandinista', at the time, was just not my cup of tea really. Yeah, it was great value for money and it certainly stretched the boundaries with music at the time, but I could see from the start that it was flawed. I didn't buy it, but I do now have it in my collection all these years later."

Tony ... "'Sandinista' changed my musical horizons once again, just as 'London Calling' had done the year before... which seemed a lifetime away at the time -

Above: Was I surrendering my love for Punk Rock?

- as so much had happened on the Punk front between 1979 and the end of 1980. My tastes had certainly broadened that is for sure.

I listened to that LP all the way through and that Christmas, 'Sandinista' was the big LP on my record deck. I realise that a lot of it was not always fully formed and that as a whole it could be considered flawed, but that was also part of its appeal. Christ, wasn't Punk all about change? There was nothing new or fresh in what most of the new Punk groups were coming out with."

Chapter Fourteen

The Blitz of 81

"I can remember taking extra toys with me to the Marples, and giving them to the punks waiting to get in who had none" - **Valerie Garvey (Sheffield Punkette)**

It had been less than four years since the Punk explosion had hit Sheffield and its lower paid cousins Rotherham and Doncaster. Back then it had been a slow developing movement with only a handful of inspired musicians grabbing the flame... aiming to set the clock back to zero and start again using the new barely scribbled Punk manifesto as their blueprint to kick down the doors of the establishment.

Above: Mark Senior and Sheffield Punks at a Sheffield Poly Disco Summer 1981

By the turn of the new decade and into 1981, the main stars of Sheffield's 'New Wave' B-movie flick had either broken up or taken a different journey on a spaceship to the stars. Sheffield's biggest stars that had landed at the advent of Punk Rock were The Human League and they were now at the brink of major stardom; although to achieve this, they had traded their style of cutting edge post – modernist dance music for a slightly sweeter taste of synthesiser Pop.

By 1980, out of the pioneering local 'New Wave' venues that had sprung up from the blitz of Punk Rock - Rotherham Windmill, Doncaster Outlook and Sheffield's Limit club - only the latter one was still open for business. The local Punk and closely related 'New Wave' community had also changed unrecognisably in comparison to its 1977 founding fathers.

Gone were the open mindedness and experimentation aspects of Punk Rock's original approach to both clothes and music. In its place came a new flavour of Punk Rocker. One who wanted to hear their Punk played fast, faster and faster... louder and even louder...a crusty studded leather jacket and a bullet belt were essential in clothing attire ideal to match the velocity of a thousand bullets being fired at one ever speeding train called 'New Punk'...It did all sound and feel very much like Heavy Metal. It was the Blitz of 1981.

Tony ... "There was still plenty of forward thinking Punk kids around, but Punk itself was starting to become stale and safe; much like the stuff it was meant to replace."

But there was still time to grab some good times before the party ended.

Wayne Kenyon ... "One of my Punk mates was Mark Burgess; He was a great lad but a bit wild. I remember him once whacking this bouncer with his bike chain cos he wouldn't let him in this club because of the way he was dressed. Another incident was really funny too. In the 'Great Rock n' Roll Swindle' there's a part where Sid Vicious slams a cake in some chick's face. Well Mark was in the chippy one night and had just got himself some fish and chips and some chick said something about the way he was dressed to which Mark's response was... well he copied old Sid didn't he...straight into her boat race. Everyone used to talk about it at the time."

Paul Smith (Sheffield Punk) ... "I remember drinking tea in Atkinson's cafe on the Moor on the top floor above the store. We would all meet there when we bunked off school. I also remember buying records from Revolution on the Gallery near the Castle Market and a punk disco night at Rebels."

Throughout the Punk era of the late 70's and into the first years of the new decade there were a scattering of local Punk groups, along with those already covered within these pages earlier. Groups such as Borstal (from Barnsley) The Spasms (from Chesterfield), Rough Copy (who supported The Damned at Sheffield Polytechnic), Repulsive Alien (from Dronfield), Mau-Maus, Media Attack, Low Life, Doncaster's The Kick-starts, Rotherham's PVC (soon to open their zips to reveal something cuter!) along with other fledgling bands formed in Youth clubs, Pub back rooms and living rooms unknown to anyone but the faithful few who attended their gigs and often one off performances.

In early 1981 small pockets of resistance on the local Punk front were to be noticed with Rotherham Punk band Cute Pubes (recently PVC), who were still taking the blueprint of the Clash and following various line ups and name changes were now ready to play their debut gig under the Cute Pubes name.

Dave Spencer recalls the gig and the influence in the band's name change ... "There was a kid at our school called Ashley Naylor who, for some unfathomable reason walked around shouting *'I DARE be a pube!'* It was just one of those meaningless, hilarious things that made kids laugh and for a while, everything had a 'Pube' attached. For a while we were going to be called Cosmic Pubes, before deciding that it sounded ridiculous. So we called ourselves Cute Pubes.

When we finally decided we were ready to play, we hired St Barnabas church hall in Broom Valley, just down the road from our school, Oakwood Comprehensive, on Saturday February 18th 1981. We picked up the keys from the caretaker, a sweet old lady who lived on Moorgate Road, the night before the gig, and - yet again - told her that we were putting on a 'disco'. She must have thought we were very enterprising. We thought she'd got senile dementia. I cannot for the life of me work out how she didn't remember us, but she didn't.

This time there was a proper P.A. This time we had a decent set. This time we were good. We even dug up an old PVC song, 'One's Got To Go', which we already treated as a quaint curio from our 'early' days, and we got the gorgeous Joanne Orgill up to sing it.

We played to a real crowd of pogo-ing punks. And apart from the light show, which was made up of those yellow flashing lights they put up around road works, we were quite professional."

Joanne Orgill ... "Of course, I did have my own, albeit very short-lived, singing career. I was guest vocalist 'for one night only' at a Cute Pubes gig at St. Barnabas church hall opposite the New Broom pub. It was a song called 'One's Gotta Go' which I shouted at a jeering, spitting, rod-giving audience, while my Mum and Auntie were outside peeking through a crack in the curtains. I don't think they were very impressed with my singing debut. One had to go - and it was me."

Above: Rotherham Punk band Cute Pubes from left to right Dominic Wood, Dave Spencer and Graham Torr's head

Dave Spencer ... "The next Cute Pubes gig was at our school youth club, where we smuggled little eleven-year old punks in through the changing room window, just like we'd seen the Clash do on Nationwide.

We then moved onto playing other youth clubs in the Rotherham area. Each gig was virtually the same; Cav's band, Fatal Noise, supported us, we'd turn up, sound check to a crowd that hated us. We played to a crowd that hated us, and then packed up quick before they kicked the fuck out of us!

The most memorable of these was Darfield youth club. Darfield was such a backwater place that Punk still hadn't got there, this was 1981 and the crowd was almost entirely made up of Soul-boys. Even though we were getting to be quite musical, by our standards, we had a difficult time. At the end of the night I overheard one of the Soulies arguing with the youth club leader, as I was carrying some gear out to the van. The Soulie was saying *'we don't have punks in Darfield Never had. Never will. We've got to beat them up!'* In the van we armed ourselves with microphone stand legs before driving off as fast as we could. As we were reaching the edge of the village, a couple of Mods from the youth club, who had actually been talking to us during the evening, followed us and were waving to us. Like complete prats we waved back to our new found friends and they promptly threw a brick at us narrowly missing the van window."

Dave Spencer was now starting to realise the confines of playing to the traditional element of the local Punk scene.

Above: Rotherham Punk group Cute Pubes – their first gig and supported by Fatal Noise...visible are Joanne Orgill on vocals and Dave Spencer on guitar

Dave Spencer ... "We had played our first gig as Cute Pubes It had been a great gig and the Punks were still enthusiastic at that point, but not too long afterwards we began to realise that a lot of Punks had moved on and we were stuck with the hardcore crowd. We would get shouts of *'That's too slow and speed it up'.* What they now wanted was pure breakneck speed Punk Rock and we were starting to learn major seventh chords and writing proper tunes."

Still, after all the hard work put into getting the band off the starting grid, they were not ready to give in just yet.

Dave Spencer ... "The next gig we played was at the Dusty Miller on Westgate in Rotherham with Sheffield band Media Attack supporting us. This time about 30 or 40

Punks had travelled from Sheffield for the gig. We started with the Kinks 'Lola'. We'd arranged the song to start softly with guitar and vocal just like the original, but we went into double time when the whole band came in. It was, in hindsight, a bit cheesy, but we wanted something to wind up the youth club crowds who seemed to hate us anyway.

This time round it worked opposite to how we had anticipated. As we started the song, there was heckling from some of the newer crowd of Sheffield punks, *'Get Off'*, *'Poofs', and 'Smoothies'*. A quite laughable reaction really 'cos as soon as we came into the song proper they all leapt to their feet as one, as if they were all one crudely assembled puppet being lifted up and thrown about. I can remember looking at our newfound fans and thinking *'Fucking idiots'*. They were leaping and falling all over the place, though, and it was what we had all wanted when we started the Cute Pubes, but when I looked down at my feet and saw Punk Rocker Chris Long looking back up at me with glazed eyes, I thought *'This is all getting a bit weird.'''*

The local hard-core Punk crowd, like the rest of the Punk loving generation of the country were now almost exclusively turned onto the real Punk. The real Punk street music of the new groups and the so-called 'Oi!' movement was now classed as the stalwart die-hard sound of Punk Rock. Some of it was good, most of it well intentioned and almost all passionate, honest and straight to the point. For a while the real punk groups would provide a healthy antidote to the shallow conservatism of the 'New Romantic' scene.

Above: Angelic Upstarts ticket

Tony … "Angelic Upstarts played at Rotherham Clifton Hall early in 1981. That was a good gig really, apart from the fighting that was part and parcel of going to see the Upstarts. If I remember correctly they played 'White Riot' that night!!"

Andrew Morton … "I had forgotten about that gig, to be honest. I can remember more about that Sandhall Park one that the Upstarts played, which was a riot as the skinheads all kicked off and there was some serious fighting going on."

Darren Twynham … "The Upstarts at Clifton Hall… great gig. We were sat on the edge of the stage at that one. Lead singer 'Mensi' was telling us all about their trip over to the Charters Arms pub just down the road. They had been over to try and down a few bottles of Newcastle Brown, them being proper Geordie lads, but were pissed off that they didn't have any."

Punk Gigs at local venues like the Clifton hall were far and few between. For some time, there had not been a venue in the area that could be depended upon to both consistently put on regular Punk groups as well as provide a meeting place for the local Punk crowd.

From the late 70's the Marples pub in Sheffield's Fitzalan square had been putting on Punk related gigs, but now became the new focal point for Punks. London had its Roxy club in 1977, whilst up North and around the area there had been a scattering of Punk venues, but none so consistently Punk from a grass roots level as Sheffield's Marples club.

Chiz ... "The Marples! We seemed to be going there every other week. As well as many top bands who played there I remember the Injectors. They were excellent and when they disappeared, the magnificent Mau Maus made the place their own. My band the Septic Psychos didn't live far away from The Mau Maus and ended up on a Pax Records compilation with them called *'Punk's dead! 'Nah mate, the smells just summat in yer underpants'.*"

Above: Injectors band photo and gig flyer

Andy Lee ..."I really enjoyed the punk scene stuff at the Marples - however brief. I remember Crass playing there to a full house (I've still got the ticket!! Dirt and Annie Anxiety were supports!) and the local bands, the Negatives, Stunt Kites and even Repulsive Alien (remember them). Yeah some good nights - at the time (for me), it made a change from the Limit and Top Rank - and the beer was a little better too."**(Sheffield forum)**

One Sheffield Punk group who did manage to impress both the hardcore element as well as jaded Punk hopefuls who were on the brink of disowning the Punk scene; unless something exciting came along to revive it...were the Injectors. They were Punk all the way through, but never took themselves too seriously so that was often a welcome antidote to the formulaic Punk (of which much was on offer).

Tony ... "The Injectors were a Sheffield Punk band. I used to go and see them a lot. They would play The Marples and other pubs around Sheffield. I saw them at The Royal once or twice and The Hallamshire Hotel and they always seemed to be playing the support slot at the Marples. I liked them more than the main groups some of the time. They never took themselves too seriously. Their singer was just like one of us. They were ok really, and for a while they kind of became our band sort of."

Sheffield Punk band the Injectors were formed in 1980 and their line up was Nick Dennif, Brothers Chris and Kevin Walker and the appropriately named Andy Marples. In true Punk fashion, they started off from scratch – not knowing which note or chord was which to begin with – but soon managed to become the token support band around the city centre supporting many of the visiting Punk groups of the period like Anti-Pasti and Angelic Upstarts and playing their own gigs at most of the venues that would have them play.

Andrew Morton ... "I saw the Injectors many a time and always thought that they played a good gig. They were just like us really and loved a laugh. You could always catch up with their singer at the bar."

During the late summer of 1981, Sheffield city council agreed to set up a fortnight of free concerts for the unemployed called 'Rock the Rates'. Tickets had to be picked up at the Poly's box office with proof of a UB40 card. The gigs included many of the best Punk and Post-Punk groups of the day including The Fall, Bow Wow Wow, the Higsons, Sheffield's very own Comsat angels and Artery, Vendino Pact, New Order, Deaf Aids, the Exploited/Abrasive wheels/Soshal Security, UK Subs and The Damned. UK Subs singer Charlie Harper, as well as playing his own gig with the Subs, was so enthused by the gigs that he returned for The Damned gig and played an impromptu guest slot playing harmonica on The Damned's 'Looking at you'. The only down side to these concerts was the sporadic outbursts of violence; most notably at the UK Subs and Damned dates.

Tony ... "Me and a varying set of mates at each one, we must have gone to almost every one of those free gigs. There was some fighting at the Damned one and I think maybe the UK Subs one as well. It was a really great idea to get this sort of thing going and there were some great nights. The only trouble was the fighting kicking off."

As well as the Punk nights at the Marples, during 1979 to 1981, Manchester's Mayflower club was a popular venue for the local Punks to go over and visit.

Andy Goulty ... "I seem to remember me and Tony going to see Vice Squad at Manchester Mayflower club. Beki Bondage was dissing Mensi from the Upstarts for some reason."

Tony ... "Once, I and my mate Andy went along to Manchester to see Anti-Pasti at the Mayflower club. We would hang around the city centre for the day – I would pick up the latest issue of 'Grinding Halt' fanzine from HMV – and later on make our way to the gig. We got on the bus from the city centre to the venue, which I think, was somewhere around the Moss Side area. The singer Martin Roper from Anti-Pasti got on the same bus as us. How punk was that? They were ok for a while. They were Clash fans like us and I think if they had been given the chance they would have gone on to better things. When they played the Marples, which was a couple of days later and the first time they had done Sheffield, we were up there in the afternoon. We showed the singer Martin around, as he didn't have a clue where anything was. We then went and watched them sound check at the Marples and chatted with the group."

Andrew Goulty ... "Yeah I remember me and Tony were up Sheffield that day and knocking about around the Marples pub. Anti Pasti turned up and the singer was starving so we took him along to the supermarket."

Anti-Pasti were amongst the many Punk groups to play the Marples during the blitz of 1981 and for a while the community spirit of Punk was being kept alive...Many local Punks looking back on those days very fondly.

Jill Ager (Rotherham Punkette) ... "I remember the Marples gigs well - and I also recall not having to bother about getting dolled up either - some colour spray and lacquer for the hair (make up took a little time), dark clothes but best of all 'the black bag'. A few chains here and there and hey presto ! a no.92 bus into town and the best nights ever."

Above: John Vernon, Neal Moxon and Phil Morley

Andrea Berry ... "During the early 80's I also went to the Marples, this is where I met my future husband Chris Long; yes sadly he did die around 16 years ago. The Marples brings back such fab memories of snakebites and dancing and jumping to music and lyrics that meant so much; I met so many interesting people."

June Graham ... "The Marples Punk gigs were great. We had some great times there and there were so many different styles. You just can't beat those days."

Phillip Wright ... "The Marples in Fitzalan Square had the infamous Artery incident when Mark Gouldthorpe climbed out of the window and onto a ledge, still singing, while passers by underneath thought it was a suicidal jumper."

Above: Dave Frost and mate

One memory from the Marples Punk era evokes a different kind of experience than those in front of the stage watching Punk groups...an eerie connection to the venues tragic past.

Claire ... "I used to go to the Marples in the seventies when it used to be the meeting place for people on stag and hen nights, we had some great times, as I remember the live bands were downstairs and the disco was upstairs but we preferred it up stairs.

I never knew when we were boogying in there what a terrible thing had happened when Sheffield was bombed (in WW2) and the Marples took a direct hit. 70 people were buried alive and most of their remains had to stay there because they couldn't get them out. If only we knew we were dancing on peoples graves, how ironic is it that I now work for Ladbrokes in the basement and sometimes the hair on the back of my neck stands up for no reason and I feel as though someone is behind me when there is no one there. The bike shop above us has said that large items have been moved off shelves etc when they have opened up in the morning. One day three full sets of biker gear was laid out in the middle of the room when the staff opened up one morning. Apart from all these strange happenings I am amazed that I am not really scared but when I have to go into the cellar I always keep my eyes closed till the light comes on just in case." **(Sheffield Forum)**

Over in Chesterfield the excitement of Punk was showing no sign of losing its appeal...but as usual, the taste for the scene did not reach everyone else!

Chiz ... "The first Punk band in Chesterfield as I recall were the Spasms and then the Chaos Bros, Septic Psychos (who did their first gig there in 1981 after spending almost two years learning to play) and young newcomers Society's Victims - so we had plenty happening in Chesterfield as well as seeing the big bands in Sheffield. The places would be packed out as would be any pub at that time that would let a local punk band play. We also did a lot of gigs with Mansfield's Riot Squad and bands started coming to Chesterfield to play at the Fusion Club, which was above the Odeon cinema (now The Winding Wheel).

We also went to the Retford Porterhouse quite a lot but there was no way back so we would sleep in cars etc. Some of the lads dropped in through the skylights at a Vice Squad gig there and landed in the dressing room with the band, who didn't mind at all. One big problem that I'm sure everyone who was a punk in the early days can relate to was that punks were fair game for attacks by anyone with a name as a 'Big Hitter' or any

289

gang who was in town that night: be it a stag night or football match and of course, the police. Even the riot in Sheffield in 82 somehow meant *'Chase the Chesterfield punks and skinheads to the train station and put the boot into any you catch!!"*

Meanwhile, upstairs at the Marples in Sheffield the idealism of Punk diverted momentarily to aiding charity and a good cause. Who says peace loving Hippies (was there ever truly such a thing?) and Punks were enemies! At one gig it was obligatory to bring a toy along that was to be given to the children's Hospice. One Punk fan was refused his Action Man by Marcus due to the toys war association. The lad went home and put the Action Man in a football kit and brought it back to gain entrance.

Tony ... "I can remember going to that gig, but I can't for the life of me remember what toy I took along or even if I did take one. I seem to recall one of my mates Barney taking something stupid along.

I can't really remember much trouble kicking off at the Marples gigs. Maybe the odd bit here and there. It was wild though...the pogoing and slam dancing were definitely hard core...but mostly everyone just went for a good time. To begin with I was really into it and there was a sense of a kind of communal spirit there and the feeling that we were achieving something, after all there really was no other real Punk place to go at the time. The Top Rank had virtually stopped putting on Punk gigs and the Limit was mainly catering for the electro crowd. The best nights were the Anti-Pasti and Vice Squad ones, but The Angelic Upstarts also put on a couple of great shows. I think I saw them about four times in 1981 and one of them was when they played the night after the Clash had played on the Sunday night. I remember telling some of the Punk lads I knew there about the Clash gig and they wouldn't believe me."

Andy Lee ... "There was never much trouble at any of the gigs. People used to say that there was some down at the bus station afterwards, but that would have happened anyway. Inside I can remember Chris Long going in the women's toilets and causing a problem but he was probably stoned and no real problem as such."

Wayne Kenyon (Doncaster Punk) ... "I was a Punk back then. I went all over to see the Punk bands of the time. I saw Stiff Little Fingers, Angelic Upstarts, Dead Kennedy's, GBH, Peter and the Test Tube Babies, the Exploited etc."

Paul Moxon (from Rotherham) ... "I can remember going to see some Punk group at the Marples and I drunk so much beer that, on the way home I threw up all over on the bus."

Valerie Garvey (Sheffield Punkette) ... "I remember doing my hair in the toilets stood next to Annie from Dirt and thinking she looked so good. That hair of hers must have taken some right back combing. My husband also remembers the fight at the Toy Dolls gig and the Mau Maus one where they were recording it for a live album. Another time I saw Beki Bondage covered in spit (Yuk) and put a blanket around her."

Tony ... "The Outcasts were good at the Marples. They had two drummers if I remember right and one was killed in a car crash. One Punk group I liked at the time was The Wall .I had seen them at Manchester's Mayflower club and supporting SLF at the Poly. We all went up to see them at the Marples and they didn't turn up."

Andrew Morton ... "I did like some of the 'Oi!' bands for a while. I went to see Infa-Riot and the 4-Skins at the Marples. They were really good. Gary Bushell was there and you could see that he was all full of himself as he (rightly so) considered that the 'Oi!' scene was his baby so to speak."

Wayne Kenyon ... "I went to the Christmas on Earth Punk festival in Leeds at the end of 1981... there was loads of Punk bands on that one and it was fantastic."

Tony ... "I bought a ticket and I didn't even bother going to the festival. I remember at the time, trying to muster up some enthusiasm for it, but it was no use... the whole idea of spending so much time watching all those Punk bands just bored the hell out of me."

Above: Nick Bolton
(Media Attack Vocalist and bass player)

During 1980 – 81, Sounds music weekly was championing the new Oi movement and its biggest fan was one of their writers - ex-fanzine writer Garry Bushell.

Tony ... "I saw Gary Bushell one of the times that Angelic Upstarts played the Marples. I was chatting to Gary for a short while at the bar. Can't really remember what we spoke about, can't have been about 'Oi!' music because I hated it."

Andrew Goulty ... "I used to go to the Monday night Marples gigs all the time. I got chatting to Gary Bushell at one of them. I cannot remember which group it was we were there to see. Most likely would have been Infa-Riot or 4-Skins."

Gary Bushell ... "The old brain cells have wiped clear a lot of those days, though I do remember going to The Marples in Sheffield to see the 4-Skins."

This particular Marples 4 Skins gig saw local Punk band Anti-Heroes play a set to a pogo frenzied hard core Punk and skinhead crowd that almost blew the roof off when the 4-Skins hit the stage. As noted by Sounds writer at the time Garry Bushell, *'Once again there were no rucks, yet still the band get labelled as a trouble band while P.I.L can go onstage and bore everyone into a riot causing ten grand's worth of damage without anyone thinking twice about booking them again.'*

Steve Haythorne ... "I never liked any of that 'Oi!' music at all, though I suppose it was a sort of natural progression from Punk in a way."

Andy Lee ... "Even though I wasn't into 'Oi!' music, we still organised gigs of every band that people asked us to put on. I organised the 'Oi! Against Racism gig myself, with four bands, which were the 4-Skins, the Business and two others... I can't think of their names now. Some of the skinheads who came to the gigs had asked to see them so we put them on. We would put on any that were asked for as long as they didn't ask for a stupid price."

Marples Punk gigs of 1981 included two each from The Exploited and Vice Squad, GBH supporting Discharge, the legendary Crass, three Anti-Pasti gigs, UK Subs, Chron Gen, Flux of Pink Indians, 1976 originals Chelsea (who at one point in their career included Doncaster bass player and B-Troop member Kevin Donaghue), Icon, a Punk & Oi! Package of Infa Riot, Blitz and Partisans... Angelic Upstarts (twice) 4-Skins and many more... a lot of these gigs would include support from The Injectors and occasionally Debar.

Left: Doncaster Punk Wayne Kenyon

Debar were a true 'get up and have a go' local all girl Punk band. They would play support regularly at the Marples and other venues around Sheffield, including a support slot with Tenpole Tudor at the Lyceum. With members dating back to the 1977 Punk scene and previous 'Shattered Life' and 'Siren' incarnations, the most recognisable Debar line up was Sue Berry, Sarah, Mandy and Rotherham Punkette Joanne Frost. They never really took themselves seriously and like many around at the time, they tasted their very own 15 minutes of Punk notoriety before disappearing into local Punk history.

The beginning of the end of the Marples Punk gigs, however, was signalled by a new surge of uncharacteristic violence; most notably at a Toy Dolls gig.

Wayne Kenyon ... "Me and 4 mates went to see The Toy Dolls at the Marples in Sheffield. There was tension in the air from the moment we walked through the doors. There had always been friction between the Donny Punks and the Sheffield skinheads; most of who were right-wing bone-heads. Into the second song of the Toy Dolls set and it kicked off big time. It was like one of those fights you see in a cowboy movie. The whole place was at it. The skins were using chairs as weapons, but the Donny Punks were giving as good as they got. I was stood right in the middle of a brawl as I felt someone pull me away. It was my mate Barney. He dragged me out just before I became a victim of a chair. Somehow we managed to avoid fighting anyone.

The room started to clear as the Donny Punks made a swift exit. I can't remember if the Sheffield skins were still in there, but what was left was mainly Sheff Punks and neutrals like us – even though we were Punks from Donny the Sheff skins didn't recognise us as such. The Promoter decided it was best to end the gig and The Toy Dolls made a token gesture of giving out free badges etc."

Martin from Sheffield remembers the end of 'The Marples' Punk nights... "I had been going there a couple of times a week at one period. Infa Riot, for some reason always used to get a big crowd. The last gig at The Marples was the Toy Dolls. One of the skinheads wrapped a stool over someone's head and that was it...no more gigs."

Left: Punkette Fiona Palmer

Andy Lee ... "The fire Limit for The Marples upstairs part was 200 people; supposedly. We had 750 at the Crass gig. The fire inspectors did turn up at one gig, started to count every one, so I ran to the fire exit, and got as many out as I could. I reckon I probably got about half of the crowd out."

Though the Marples Punk gigs escaped the full attention of the fire inspectors, the flames of the Sheffield Punk scene were starting to fade to a series of dying embers. The Blitz of 81 would soon be making way for the disjointed and ultimately failed and miserable Punk scene of the following year. In Chesterfield too, the scene was slowly starting to wind down; not due to a lack of enthusiasm, but because of a lack of a regular outlet and venue to nurture the remaining enthusiasm for the Punk Rock of the early 80's.

Chiz ... "It got harder during the early eighties for any venue to let punk bands play in Chesterfield. I remember we set up a gig with the Mau Maus, No Dead Meat (formed after the Septic Psychos merged with Society's victims) and Criminal sex (ex Chaos Bros) at an old brick dance hall in the town centre called Jimmy's (St James' Hall). It was a great night and went without any trouble. Then we were told we couldn't play there again because it was being knocked down to build a supermarket. Ten years later it was still there."

However... where a Punk has a will - a Punk will have his way...

Chiz ... "To protest about the lack of venues available we (No Dead Meat) rented a generator and played one Sunday dinner time on the top floor of the town centre multi-storey car park. It was funny because it was so foggy that the police could hear us but could not see us. From the eighth floor of the car park, we could see blue flashing lights speeding around but it was not until three quarters of the way through our set and the fog began to lift that the police spotted the silhouettes of punks around the top of the car park. It wasn't long then before they came up to put a stop to the proceedings

Eventually we got a regular venue big enough to bring some of the top punk bands to Chesterfield. It was 'The Conservative Club!!!' I know this seems extreme now but we tried everywhere else, including the Labour club and nobody would have us. We advertised it as 'The Con Club' and were treated to some very memorable gigs by Conflict, Peter and the Test Tube Babies and the Subhumans amongst others.

Above: Punk group No Dead Meat on top of the multi storey and below the police 'rooftop' invasion

The bands played upstairs so nobody saw the Tory propaganda on the walls in the club. The place was a dump as Tories were very few and far between in Chesterfield but they told us they made enough profit from beer sales on the first night of our punk gigs to redecorate! We, the promoters, (Noise ain't Dead promotions) were strictly non-profit and kept the ticket prices to around half the price of most other venues.

Any accidental profit went to the 'Hunt Sabs' or would be given back to the local punks by means of a free vegetarian buffet at some of the smaller gigs at The White Swan. Smaller bands would play at the White Swan in the centre (now a Chinese fast food restaurant). There would be a couple of bands every Tuesday so there was no need to bombard the local papers every week and fly post the town. We all knew if we turned up we would have a good night. Bands like the English Dogs, the Varukers, Disorder and The Instigators played there until the landlord moved to Torquay."

Over in Rotherham a last Punk counter-attack took place towards the end of 1981.

Paul Clarke ... "I went to quite a few gigs and some stand out for different reasons. A good one was the Punk Package tour at Rotherham Clifton hall. There was Anti-Pasti, Chron Gen and Vice Squad. I got backstage and managed to get Beki Bondage to sign the inside of my biker jacket."

Above: Rotherham Clifton Hall Punk package tour flyer and a rare original poster of the event (Poster courtesy of Alyn at Punkposters.net)

Tony ... "I got backstage at the Clifton Hall gig and managed to get a snog out of Beki Bondage. It seemed a long day. Me personally, I was bored out of my head. The most interesting bits were chatting to Glynn Barber the singer of Chron Gen and then backstage meeting Beki. There were lots of Punks there... it seemed like everyone from the local Punk community turned out for that one, but the atmosphere was dead as door-nails for me. There was a bomb scare after this Clifton Hall gig had finished. What was that all about?"

Andrea Deakin ... "Yes, bomb scares in Rotherham in the Punk era? There was no explanation either, so we never found out the reason why."

Gill Frost ... "One of my favourites of the early 80's was Vice Squad. The singer was a very attractive blonde called Beki Bondage and I really wanted to look like her. It wasn't really that easy to get leather studded miniskirts and fishnets off Rotherham market, though, so I had to make do with just listening to the music. My brother and I went to see Vice Squad; supported by another couple of bands we loved called Anti-Pasti and Chron Gen. They played at Clifton Hall and it cost just two pounds for the ticket...what a bargain!"

One particular gig was significant in showing a clear divide between Punk and its fans old and new!

Tony ... "One of the times I saw 'Chelsea' (who were one of the original 2nd wave punk groups formed in late 1976), and this particular gig was at the 'Marples'. They played a good set based on the 2 LP's worth of material they had but the punk kids in general just weren't that bothered and the crowd were not really responding that well. I popped my head round the dressing room after their set and 'Gene October'(the singer) was going crackers and throwing a right wobbler...going on about how crap all the new Punk groups were and the punk kids nowadays don't know a good punk group when they see one. He was certainly wound up about something."

Dave Spencer ... "In 1981 I saw the beginning of Punk's slow lingering death when I went along to see original 'New Wavers' 'Chelsea' play at the Marples in Fitzalan square. The crowd seemed very different from the Top Rank - less fun, more negative. Rather than leap about enthusiastically at the front, everyone clung to the bar area watching almost disdainfully. OK, this was not the classic Gene October, James Stevenson, Dave Martin, Geoff Myles and Chris Bashford line-up, but they were still good. They were still better than all the other bands playing at The Marples.

I loved Chelsea, so I was amongst the tiny throng of about 20 little punks dancing at the front. Just behind us, was this massive She-Devil of a woman who didn't seem to like us kiddies having a good time? I actually thought it was a bloke at first, but it really was a female giant. She was the drummer of the all 'girl' support band, who I think were called 'Bobar' or something like that. After a few random shoves, she singled me out (maybe because I was the skinniest, scrawniest, or specciest, or all three) and kept pushing me into a punk called Chris Long. I must have landed on him about three times when his pint spilt down him. He took his empty plastic glass and crushed it into my head. So, I walked through the dancing throng and into the tightly packed bar area. Chris Long followed me, jumped on my back, and started punching me in the face from behind. Some skinheads pulled him off me and moved me towards the bar to see if I was ok. They might have even bought me a drink. I heard later that he was taken outside and given a severe kicking for that, but perhaps we will never know, as I have heard that he died some years ago. At the time, I was really shocked, having been in trouble with Teds, Mods and Soulies, it seemed mad that punks were now attacking each other. At the end of the night 'Gene October' came out to the bar and I asked him if there was any chance of a support slot in the future and he went ballistic in a *'Who do you think you are?'* kind of way and I went home feeling quite bewildered."

A shame-inducing example of Punk's often apathetic tendencies that understandably tainted the vision of Punks like Dave Spencer towards the fast disappearing Punk ideal. Gene October must have calmed down, with the aid of some relaxing roll-ups, when he went over to Marcus Featherby's abode following the gig.

Andy Lee ... "Marcus's house was a one bedroom flat really. There were often numerous people sleeping on all the floors, especially after gigs. We may have 6 or more people coming back home with us. Various bands stayed over with us. 'Gene October' from 'Chelsea' came back and this was probably one of the best nights at our house; he talked to me all about the very early days of Punk in London, while we shared roll-ups that I re-rolled from the ashtray."

By late 1981 and certainly the following year, time was running out for Punk Rock in all of its differing guises. The breath of fresh air that had been the new Punk groups had quickly grown stale and set in its concrete 'Punk' pillbox for good. For some the hardcore sound of Discharge, Exploited etc was enough... but many local punk fans now demanded more.

The mood was changing throughout the nation and Sheffield was no exception. The Thatcher years were in full swing and the patriotic fervour of the Falklands war of 1982 disguised the widespread discontent, unemployment, anger and hopelessness of a whole generation of youth. Yet, despite this political and social unrest (and a show of real pro-active violence during the nationwide riots of summer 81) nothing really changed as the 80's progressed into a decade of fake glamour, mass consumerism and a swift clean sweep that rendered the local coal industry redundant almost overnight.

Meanwhile fringes grew longer, the Leyton Buzzards went looking for Modern Romance, shoulder pads grew bigger and wider (and that was just the lads) as a new era of Pop complacency sugar-coated the hidden frustration of our generation. The bullets and shells fired at the system during the Blitz of 1981 were running out and the last show of Punk aggression had shown its crumpled cards. Sheffield and the region would suffer much throughout the next decade and the Punk generation itself would see class division first hand. But the music would go on!

Nicky Booth ... "The next wave of punk bands such as Vice Squad, Discharge, Anti Pasti, Exploited, etc, left me a bit cold to be honest. It seemed to me that they were stuck in a very limited niche, just peddling rabble-rousing rubbish for people who just wanted to jump up and down. Some of these bands were also a bit too near the Oi movement for my liking...very unpleasant. By 1981 I was still following my favourite punk bands, but I really loved a lot of the new wave music that was permeating the airwaves by then. Industrial music was another area of interest in the early 80s, because after punk you couldn't really go back to listening to chart fodder for the masses could you?"

The new hardcore punk groups continued to bash out their metallic sounds throughout the rest of the mid 80's and the local Punk scene almost disappeared underground with its hardcore followers remaining faithful to the end. On a positive note some of the early 80's Punks did become more politically motivated; supporting causes such as CND, anti-vivisection and becoming involved in banning fox hunting.

Consequently, Punks almost became the new Hippies.

Above: Richard Chatterton – bored with the straitjacket of Punk but trying to hang on to its ideals

Tony ... "It was clear, by late 1981, that Punk was just about dead... even as far North as round here. There was no real hope in it at all for me and the music was just hammering away at a brick wall so to speak. The Marples carried on putting on Punk gigs, while the other venues in and around Sheffield virtually ignored the Punk groups. Punk was now screaming at the system but no one was listening any more. It was as though we had had our say and blown our chances... a case of *'that's yer lot now shut up and make way for Duran Duran'*...Fuck that!"

Chapter Fifteen

Where's Marcus Featherby now?

"Marcus never got the credit he deserved, he had a great hand in making the Sheffield scene at the time come alive, he gets criticised for not creating a record label like Factory in Manchester (which got money off Virgin) whilst the pair of us lived off my Giro... but we brought out many records and organised scores of gigs. AND the gigs were great, with next to no trouble in all that time" – **Andy Lee (Sheffield Punk and Marples promoter)**

Tony ... "Marcus Featherby used to make us laugh. Just the name itself was funny."

He came and he went; Marcus Featherby. No account of the Post-Punk and later Punk scene in Sheffield can ever be complete without recognising the input of an enigmatic, faithful and contradictory man called Marcus Featherby. Mention his name to any of the generation who were around during the last throes of Punk and the Post-Punk period and you would probably be met with a variety of comments that would invariably include hints of disdain, respect, disbelief, amazement, admiration and wonder.

Marcus appeared, seemingly out of nowhere, in Sheffield in 1979. His past contained a biographical CV of coming from a French aristocratic family, manager of Blondie, Mercenary in Africa, professional backgammon player, Stranglers entourage worker, Red Cross worker and civil rights worker. Or so he and others claimed! One thing is for sure however, he made a positive impact on the Sheffield music scene.

Left: Sheffield Anarchists flyer given to the author at a Marples gig

Marcus was impressed by the local Post-Punk groups such as Cabaret Voltaire, Vice Versa and Artery and strove to get these and others the recognition they deserved. He managed the Negatives, Artery, In the Nursery, Punk band Mau Maus, and Barnsley's Danse Society. Artery's first single 'Mother Moon' was paid for by Marcus and their 'Unbalanced' single(with Live tracks recorded at Rotherham's Arts centre gig in 1980) was on Aardvark records the label that also released his compilation LP 'Bouquet of Steel' featuring the cream of the best local bands. The last contribution to vinyl that Marcus was involved in was the Pax label that released records by Mau Maus, and a series of Punk compilations such as The Wargasm LP that featured Rat Scabies and Captain Sensible of the Damned, Angelic Upstarts, Poison Girls, Dead Kennedy's, Flux of Pink Indians etc.

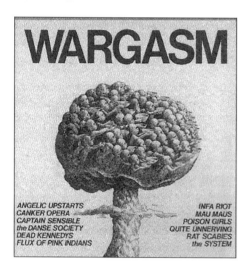

Above: One of Marcus Featherby's ventures the Wargasm LP

Martin Fry (Vice Versa/ABC singer) ... "When Marcus Featherby hit town, he set it off like a firework. He was a great catalyst. He was very threatening, a curious guy, almost a Brian Epstein man of mystery, a Svengali." **(From 'Beats working for a living' by Martin Lilleker)**

Phillip Wright ... "Marcus called me once and said that the DJ for the Negatives gig at the KGB (old Abbeydale cinema) was going to be late and could I help? So I did, never done it before, totally scared to death but muddled my way through it, Marcus said *'When The Negs (as he called them) come off stage, hold the crowd back!'* as if they were going to be mobbed like the Beatles!...Which of course they weren't.

- I had first met Marcus when he had only been in Sheffield for a few days, he told me his name was Marcus Weatherby, next time I saw him he said it was Marcus Featherby, hmmmmm....still, that was Marcus, he told me loads of names over the time I knew him. I remember the house on Whitham Road with the cats, the entire photo's and various assorted people who wandered in and out, including the Icelandic lad (Aeinaar I think his name was) who was a great chess player."

Marcus Featherby became involved with almost all of the key players in Sheffield's music scene. He was involved in duck-and-dive ventures often with many of the bands around at the time and was always willing to give a helping hand for anyone who asked, sometimes exposing some of his darker traits while doing so.

Jarvis Cocker (Pulp) ... "We'd go up there (Whitham Road – Broomhill where Marcus lived); with our latest cassette we'd done in my mother's living room. We were always trying to persuade him to put something out. He was just a dodgy bastard. I remember once being with him walking down the street and there was a Barclays bank and he said, *'right we've got to run now'.* And we had to run past the bank and go back to normal pace afterwards.

He obviously owed them money and he didn't want to be spotted through the windows. But it was one of those things – without him we wouldn't have got to play any concerts or owt so we've got to be thankful to him for that but there were lots of dodgy things about him." **(From 'Beats working for a living' by Martin Lilleker)**

Rob Dowling … "He also ripped a lot of people off. Nobody saw a penny from the Wargasm album, which he financed by putting up the house that he was renting off me. I got grief for years after that…apart from that he did do a lot for the Sheffield music scene and he discovered Artery so all is forgiven." **(From Sheffield Forum)**

Above: Local Punks and New Romantics from the Rotherham area in Skegness summer 1981 (Shaun Angell)

Tony … "I can remember Marcus being all over the place in Sheffield at that time. He also had something to do with 'Rat Records' the Punk record shop near the Leadmill. I can still see him now sat at the table at the Marples taking the money and making passing comments with the Punks as they came in. The bouncer there was a big guy nick-named Banger who never smiled. He was a work-mate of my brothers. You didn't mess with him."

As well as being involved with the Sheffield Post-Punk bands, Marcus also put his promotional skills to hand and set up a series of regular Punk gigs at Sheffield's Marples pub venue. From the late 70's to March 1984 the Marples hosted 100's of Punk gigs that included most of the gig going Punk bands of the day and even an October appearance of Velvet Underground luminary Nico.

Andy Lee … "Beki Bondage from Vice Squad and all of Chron Gen stayed at Marcus's house. Someone said somewhere that Beki did not like getting spat on, but I remember her telling me that night that she had become ill after being spat on at one particular gig. I can't blame her not liking it, I wouldn't have done either, never mind the illness.

We put on most of the Punk bands of the day; the only ones we didn't get were the ones who wanted too much money. My favourites that played there were Crass, Poison Girls, Flux of Pink Indians; but I knew them personally as well and stayed with all of them when I was down in London. Nicer people you could not have hoped to meet.

We had a bouncer at the Marples, who was the actual Pub bouncer. He would pop up a few times every hour and chat with me on the door. He was the one bouncer who never had to lay a hand on anyone. He liked Rock music but he was interested in what we were doing. Many people used to hang around the door chatting, it was a really good social space; then they would pop in to watch the bands."

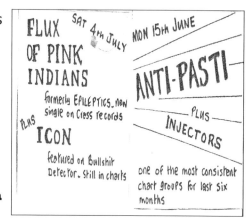

Right: Marples tickets (from Andrew Goulty's Collection)

Martin dust (Sheffield Punk) on Marcus …"Was he a nurse? Did he win a medal in the Olympics? He was a laugh and I liked his stories, it's just that one after the other it was a bit hard to take. I remember the time he told the NME that Wattie from the Exploited liked to smoke a pipe and listen to New Order, Wattie didn't even smoke."

Andy Lee … "Many things he said about Africa, America and Iceland turned out to be true. He never told me he had an Olympic medal. However after leaving school and being an excellent long distance runner, he was the only smoker who ever beat me in a race (then I became a smoker)."

It is clear that Marcus had a massive effect and influence during his time on the Sheffield scene. As a result of his managerial and promotional work many music fans have countless fantastic memories of the gigs he put on. It is also worth considering his input to local record releases too and the fact that he was greatly involved with the free gigs that the Polytechnic put on in 1981. Regardless of any criticism, Marcus and his cohort were constantly busy and helping to feed a gig hungry Sheffield Punk scene.

Andy Lee … "I was 17 and organising gigs and making posters – which we made from fluorescent wallpaper and spray cans. Marcus would organise for people to go out and stick posters up with me (I think he may have done it a couple of times). I would collect the money on the door and count it (which was useful for two people living on the poverty line) but The Marples pub itself footed the bill for the bands. If we had a good night they used to give us a fiver or something, but it was my Giro Cheque that kept me and Marcus in food every fortnight. ...he was the front man and I did all the leg work."

Tony ... "I had a Vice Squad and Chron Gen at the Marples poster. It was a yellow one with a marker pen drawing of Beki Bondage and the tour dates with Sheffield Marples encircled. I also had loads of flyers but all are long gone now."

In 1981, the Punk scene, considered to be on its last legs or worse by many, was sometimes socially at odds with the parallel Sheffield Post-Punk scene.

Above: Marples flyers from 1981

Andy Lee ... "There were many cliques in Sheffield at that time, local bands like Clock DVA etc, who used to hang about at The Bee-Hive on West Street, which was near Cabaret Voltaire's studio so I think it seemed trendy to them. They were older than me, and being so arty, and me being a Punk, they looked down on Punks. They all slagged Marcus off, because he was actually doing something (with the help of people like me). It was a great shame he never got the respect that he truly deserved."

Phillip Wright ... "Lots to say and everyone has their own opinion, but Marcus was good for the Sheffield music scene, helping galvanise the area, organizing gigs, writing reviews for music papers and setting up one of the first record labels in the city -

- (Limited Edition records, which became Aardvark Records) and being as infamous as he was famous. He arrived one winter, turned up at a gig, got chatting to people, including me and my friends, saying he had just arrived from New York via Iceland. He had a big professional camera and took loads of pictures. He said he was 29 years old, which seemed a
ncient, as we were all 16/17. We would see him at gigs and he would tell us about local bands he wanted to go and see.

Then we would start hanging round his flat at the weekend, 107 Whitham Road, and it was always full of Sheffield band members and interesting characters. He showed me a broken camera, which he claimed he had dropped when he slipped on an icy street in New York, while running for a taxi with Debbie Harry from Blondie. He had 100's of records and 1000's of photos of bands, gigs, and other people. At one point he claimed his real name was something like Dominic Duchanaakt, or at least something Dutch sounding, and that he was from a very posh family (he spoke with a very posh accent compared to us!), he said he had been a male model in the 60's, that he had run away from home, hated his step father, etc. No one really knew anything about him, and that was his appeal I guess. He was one of life's mysteries."

Andy Lee ... "Marcus actually organised the Rock on the Rates thing although the Leadmill lot took what credit they could."

Marcus Featherby; he came and he went. Mysteriously he departed from Sheffield. Rumours abound that he was on the Exploited singer Wattie's hit list for unpaid royalties. He allegedly informed no one of his destination and his whereabouts at all. He was last spotted in the dressing room of Top of the Pops in 1987. He was no longer called Marcus Featherby!

Tony ... "I had got sick of Punk and its uniformed look...the music was all the same and just did nothing for me at all. I tried to stay a part of it throughout the last few months of going to see punk groups at the Marples pub in Sheffield in a hope of getting back to the roots of it all. Although being great for a while - and the new groups did seem to mean it and offer something more earthier than the last few punk groups' LP's - it soon turned safe and monotonous.

The only records that I did really like from the Punk groups of 81 were Vice Squad's 'Resurrection' e.p (and their John Peel session was good too), the Anti-Pasti singles, Chron Gen's 2 records 'Puppets of War' e.p and 'Reality' and also the Zounds single 'Subvert' on the Crass label. Ant-Establishment were ok too. I used to have contact with one of them called Kev Gritton, and he sent me a Demo tape through and loads of group stickers. The rest of the hardcore stuff though, all sounded the same to me.

I saw just about everyone that was on the grass roots punk scene at the time... Angelic Upstarts, The Outcasts, Chron Gen, UK Subs, Charge, Vice Squad (fantastic live!), Anti-Pasti, The Wall etc and these were all great gigs. Also, there was Discharge, Crass, Mau Maus, Icon, Flux of Pink Indians and so on, but these lot were not for me. I was hanging on to it in hope really.

The Marples was, in a way, Sheffield's late punk era equivalent of London's Roxy club. Its svengali Marcus Featherby was a genuine guy who cared for the kids out there who wanted to hear live music at a pittance and who just needed to belong. The whole idea of the Marples and its Punk scene was admirable and I hear many old Punks speak of it with a misty eyed look of nostalgia. This was Punk Rock at the bottom of the pile; Proper -
304

snotty Punk Rock - with a home of its own. Me personally, I was screaming inside *'I was a Punk Rocker now get me fuckin' out of here!'"*

Dave Spencer … "One of the things that has always stuck in my mind about the Punk influence… is when a friend of ours came to see our band rehearse and he goes *'So what are your main influences then?'*… To which we replied *'well the Clash for a start'*. His reply was *'well instead of using the Clash for an influence why don't you go back and find out what their influences are!'* We did just that and started to listen to the Kinks and the Stones…but it was a bit sort of *'hush hush don't let anyone know'* sort of thing."

"Well I believe in this and it's been tested by research…that he who fucks nuns will later join the church" **(The Clash 'Death or Glory' 1979)**

Tony … "Yeah as soon as I heard those words I clicked on to the significance of them. Back in 1977, it had been *'No Elvis, Beatles or the Rolling Stones'*… now for me personally it was *'No Upstarts, Exploited and the nowhere League'*…where's the Kinks, Faces and Stones records."

The Marples era was Marcus Featherby's and the Punks of 81's heyday; Gigs almost every night, if not at that venue, then not too far away at the other Punk places to be seen at.

Above: Doncaster Punks Mark Burgess and Wayne Kenyon

Amongst the last Punk groups to play at the Marples were Angelic Upstarts and the Exploited. Around 1983 – 1984 the gigs gradually decreased to almost none and then the Punk era in and around Sheffield was almost gone. The final footnote in the legendary venue's history would be with the ironic new ownership of more recent times. Bearing in mind that the Marples pub was bombed by German Bombers during the famous Sheffield Blitz of December 1940 – leaving over 70 civilians dead and wounded – part of the actual venue is now owned by a German company that sells motorcycle accessories.

Anthony Cronshaw … "The Marples is now owned by fuckin' Jerries! What an insult to the British People that is."

Chapter Sixteen

Fall out

"Back then towards the end...it was often a case of either carrying on with Punk or – like some of the lads – move into the Mod thing" – **Dave Frost (Rotherham Punk)**

Whilst many local Punks were happy enough watching the Punk bands bang out their 3 minute anthems at the Marples, there were some that were starting to demand a little bit more for their money and felt a division between the different factions of the Sheffield scene.

Above: Julie Lee and Lynne Haythorne- contemplating what next?

Lynne Haythorne ... "Punk became stale; all the coloured hair and the image became all the same and boring. It had been great while it had lasted but I wanted something more now.

I started buying lots of second hand clothes and adapting new styles. Fiona Palmer opened her shop and I would go there. I was also influenced by Vitamin Z a local group.

They would be doing the same kind of thing with clothes. It was a new way of dressing but very much like Punk before it...Do it yourself was still a part of it."

Tony ... "Around this time, I was at a cross-road between the end of Punk and Mod. I just did not relate at all to most of the Punks that were on the scene at the time. They seemed to be moving more and more hard-core, whereas I wanted to look smarter and listen to more interesting music than just Punk Rock."

Richard Chatterton ... "I remember seeing a Sixties play which starred South Yorkshire actor Keith Barron as a young student who is drifting away from his working class roots but still doesn't quite fit into the college cognoscenti. Likewise I wanted to mix with arty (ok often pretentious people) but also mix with the 1977 style Punks but the latter would never come to the Post-Punk gigs with me, unless the bands had Punk roots like P.I.L or Siouxsie and the Banshees. This struggle I had at the time was once very evident when I wanted to stay at a party in Sheffield – the Sheffield art crowd were all there – Jarvis Cocker was sat in the kitchen (just back from college in London). I had met him a couple of times in the Limit club and interviewed him for my fanzine. Anyway, I wanted to stay and mingle, especially with the girls, but my mate Cookie, who was a die-hard old school Punk with closely shaved head wanted to go. He said he was going to walk to Shiregreen, and didn't have enough money for a taxi. It was a horrendous night, throwing it down and I had to make a choice 'should I stay or should I go'. With heavy heart I went with him. Well he was a mate."

Punk during the early 1980's may have been old hat for the fickle music press, but its main acts could still manage to impress fans.

Above: Chesterfield Punk Rockers (From Richard - Chatterton's collection)

Chris Sheridan (Chesterfield Punk) … "The guys & gals I knew invited me back to their digs for the evening and lots of alcohol was consumed and during the course of the evening someone appeared clutching tickets for the Clash Casbah tour date, at Leeds University. I managed to secure one of the tickets and stuck around for the gig. The gig, due to my intake of alcohol is a bit of a blur, but as I recall the Clash ripped through an awesome set of all the favourites to a most appreciative Yorkshire crowd. One thing that sticks in my mind was that it was an incredibly hot venue and I was convinced people were spitting on me, although I was informed it was sweat dripping from the ceiling."

Soon after this tour, the Clash would take a change of course in their career, and through a series of incidents, from the disappearance and re-emergence of Joe Strummer, the sacking of drummer Topper Headon and later guitarist and songwriter Mick Jones - to their conquest of the U.S.A; the group would lose their edge and never truly recover. The glory days of the Clash and the original Punk bands were almost over and the feel and vitality of Punk, for many of the local teenagers, was lost along with them.

Tony ... "By the early 80's there seemed to be loads of Punk kids around Rotherham and Sheffield and the groups' names on the back of their leather jackets were mostly the new Punk ones!...The Addicts, Discharge, Blitz, Exploited and the self explanatory One Way System!

Some of these new Punk groups were ok to begin with as they were taking Punk back to where it had started out. It did feel healthy again for a while, for maybe a few months at least. I mean, when you think about how distanced some of the original groups had got by this time, it was refreshing to hear some proper punk stuff again. Then after a while it soon became obvious that the new Punk groups were never going to move on. They weren't about to change at all. Most of them were happy to just play the same stuff all of the time. In fact it was just the same as Heavy Metal really. That's the road Punk went down afterwards and it goes straight to the present day when Punk and Heavy Metal are one of the same and in some cases appeal to the same crowd. I may be wrong about this, but that wasn't why I got into Punk in the first place. It was all about starting afresh and from scratch and then doing the best you could from there on. Not staying the same."

Richard Chatterton ... "In Rotherham there were a few people I would see and hang around with in The Charters pub. The ones I can remember are Alan, Dave, Nobby, Fiona, Chippy (who shared my hairstyle), Spence (great guitarist) and my best buddy for a while was Richard Davis, who was at the time an Elvis Costello look-alike. I met him at Art College and we both ended up at Sunderland Poly. Another great friend was, and still is, Dave Graham, a fellow Brinny lad – and the first youth I ever saw with dyed hair, when I came across him once whilst walking home from school. He was older than me, but a meeting on the last bus, when he would not stop going on about the band Magazine, galvanised our friendship. We still share our love of early Ultravox, Cabaret Voltaire and Bill Nelson's Red Noise."

Tony ... "One of the true legends of our lot was a kid called Barney who got into the Punk scene quite late on - but he made up for it by going the whole hog. He would have put Sid Vicious to shame. He would do absolutely anything. If we told him to do something, no matter how outrageous, then he would do it, just to impress, and for the laugh I suppose. Barney started out as plain old Mark Barnet. I went all the way through school with him and he was quite a bright lad. He never did anything wrong at all and always did his schoolwork. While we were going to Punk gigs, he would call round and buy my old scalextric track off me. He started to like Gary Numan and became a bit of a 'New Wave' kid. We got him interested in the more tasty Punk music and introduced him to the clothes and stuff. Before you knew it, he was well on his way. He dyed his hair, bought a kilt, bondage trousers, and the lot. He started to live the lifestyle 24/7. That was fine but he had a lot of making up to do and he became a kind of pet Punk Rocker for anyone who he knocked about with. Barney would go out with any lass he could get near to. He wasn't bothered if they had boyfriends either. I saw him take a right hiding, once, when he had gyrated behind a hard kid's girlfriend. This was to the conga or something and there was 7 or 8 lasses in a line and there was Barney behind them giving it some."

Andy Goulty … "Barney was legendary. He got up to things the rest of us would never do. I can remember once, when we were all hanging around the Park and this moped stopped at the traffic lights, well Barney jumped on the back of this fella on his moped and hung on there. When the lights switched he set off with Barney hanging on to him."

Andrew Morton … "Barney came up to see me once and he pulled our overflow pipe out, while he was waiting for me to come to the door. He was always polite though and would say soz!"

Dave Spencer … "Wasn't there some story about him and a dog?"

Left: the Legendary Mark Barnet alias Barney Rubble

Tony … "Barney called round with a woman's wig on and his kilt with some fish net stockings underneath. We were hanging around the local shops and the lollypop woman was there at the crossing waiting for the kids to come out of school. Barney took our dare and ran up to the lollypop woman and acting his normal crazy self swiped her lollypop stick off her and ran all over with it diving up and down and all sorts. The lollypop woman was chasing him and asking for it back and after a while she managed to get it back. We were pissing ourselves at him."

Tony … "He would call for me and my mum would say *'Daft lad's at the door'*. She would be laughing and I would go to the door and he would be stood there with a kid's pedal car around his waist, with a woman's massive wig on, and his kilt and he would be going *'Brum Brum'*. I still always laugh at him when I think of him, even now. He was proper crazy."

Andrea Deakin … "Barney came into the pub with his dog under his arm, so the landlord says *'You can come in with him, but if the dog craps, you pick it up'.* Well he sits down with us and the first thing that the dogs does is - you guessed it - shits on the floor, so Barney, totally un-phased, just picks it up with his bare hands. Then he wipes his hands down and picks up my glass to pass to me yuck! *'I'll have another drink please'.*"

Tony … "Me and Bryan Bell dyed Barney's hair. Bryan bleached it and when it was time to rinse it we took him outside on Bryan's Dads drive and we chucked buckets of water over him to rinse out the dye… Barney wasn't proud."

Andrew Morton … "If you ever took Barney to visit anyones house, that was it, they could always expect further visits from him. He would always manage to make his way to whereever you had taken him."

Tony … "He had this real hard core Punk bird and he came round to my house with her and a few other Punks. They nicked 2 of my records X-Ray Specs 'Identity' and Clash 'Cost of Living E.P'. I was bloody quick on the ball with that one. I kind of sensed that they were missing from my record boxes. Next day I went to pay him a visit. He used to live in his mum's loft- that was a right sleazy and disorganised joint, outside the window was plastered with gob too. He was leaning out of it when I got there. He wouldn't come down and he was laughing, the bastard, he knew why I was there. I got the records back and he said it was his bird who swiped 'em. Yeah and The Sex Pistols are re-forming and playing a gig in my back garden."

John Harrison … "I remember Barney. Me and Tony once took the Jam song 'To be someone' to mind and that line *'There's no more cocaine, its only ground chalk',* well we did grind some white chalk up and took it to Barney's house – he used to live up in the attic – and we sold it him telling him it was cocaine."

Above: Dave Spencer and friends, including Barney at far right

Tony … "Barney was even in an early version of the band I put together. He bought himself a bass guitar and he could maybe play a few notes. In true Punk moronity the songs would be suitably called' I'm a Brat- I'm a Moron' and other nihilistic titles.

When we were hanging around we would snowball the buses passing by the park and Barney would even jump on to the cars as they were speeding by. It's a wonder he didn't kill himself. The cops were after him once and he went on the run for a day or two, sleeping rough (this incident did involve a dog as a witness). After a few days, he emerged from the woods with a fire starting behind him and a police siren going off in the background.

He carried on with the Punk lifestyle long after it had all ended. I think he got really into U2 at one point as I can remember him going to see them live. He became more and more a crusty type. I once saw him get on the bus with a dead pheasant in his hand for his dinner. I never saw him for years. Then, one day, out of the blue, about 1994, I spotted him walking towards me. He had tracked me down and he came back for a coffee. He was on his way to go over to Europe to hang out. That was the last time I ever saw him."

Richard Chatterton ... "In Sheffield, I hung around with people who were slightly younger than me and who I guess were, also like myself, second generation Punks, who had been a little too young when Punk first hit. My best friend at this time was called Macky, from Pitsmoor, a stunning looking guy with a broad Mohawk, who used to flick a lighter under his face when it got dark to show how good looking he was.

He was very popular in the clubs we were hanging out in, and to this day I still get asked how he is, although I haven't seen him for almost twenty years since he left for London.

We would go to the Limit, the Leadmill, Rebels Punk night on Thursdays - where I made many great friends - and the Sin Bin on Commercial Street. It was around this period – 1980 to 1985 – where I would meet many friends who I still keep in contact with (albeit on an occasional basis). There was Simon Davies (Doggy), Paul Gorman, Tim Collins, Daz, Dave Millward (who I met on a trip to Nottingham's Rock City venue after he had just come out of the nick) – he was and still is Punk with trouble attracting towards him (often through no fault of his own), and also is a 100% Blade. Also there was Grant (a Gary Numan clone who is now working in a Sheffield Secondary School like myself), Twinny, Julian (Captain), and Jamie Smith (now a Techno producer and Head charge impresario). There were many others, a lot of whom I no longer see.

At Rebels and Sin Bin clubs, we used to hang out with a group of girls we nicknamed the Dread pack. Everyone looked at them when they arrived at a club or gig. There were three of them and they were all striking; with long dresses bought on the Kings Road, hair extensions and snake painted faces. We despised them – but I was chuffed to go out with two of them later on."

The rapid descent into 'mediocre Panto performance' of Punk and the increasingly grotty wallowing of the so-called New Punk was not making much of an impression on some of the seasoned 2nd generation Punks of the area.

Dave Spencer ... "It just became awful really. I was thinking *'what's all this about'*... Anti-Nowhere League and the like? That was not the Punk Rock I enjoyed and had been so fond of. About January or February 1982, the Penthouse club on Dixon Lane near the Sheffield market changed its name to Rebels and became a rock club. Thursday night, though, was punk night.

If my memory serves me well, and often it doesn't, we managed to secure the opening night gig. Maybe because we were beginning to attract a bit of a following or, for once, knew someone who worked there. In a way, it was a fantastic little place, low ceiling, and low stage in the corner near the D.J booth. It always seemed like something was about to kick off and it often did. Over the years, my memory of the gig has been distilled into a three-scene sketch.

SCENE ONE. We are on stage, playing to a decent sized crowd (for a Thursday, in February) about eight songs in I hear a strange banging and look at the rest of the band who look at the edge of the stage to my right. I quickly follow their gaze and there stands a short, hard looking monstrosity of a biker belting the stage with a pool cue (or walking stick/cane) shouting *'Play some AC/DC'*. I look at the rest of the band – what do we do? Ignore him. So we try to. 'Play some FUCKING AC/DC. A bouncer walks on and says *'that's it boys'*. As we protest, he says *'It's for your own good! Get off quick'*. So we leg it across the dance floor to the dressing room.

CUT

SCENE TWO. We are in the dressing room, laughing our heads off, having some much needed booze and congratulating each other for just surviving. *'What a weird gig that was'* etc. When the door burst open, knocking some or all of us flying, spilling drinks all over the shop and a voice shouts, *'PLAY SOME FUCKING AC/DC!'*
CUT -

SCENE THREE. Back on stage, Graham hits the riff! E/G/E/A/E/G/A. *'I want to tell you a story'* I reply. E/G/E/A/E/G/A. *'About a woman I know'* ...
FADE."

As well as trying half heartedly to please AC/DC rocker fans, Dave's Punk group Cute Pubes were trying hard to distance themselves from the restrictions of the new anarcho punks whilst still holding on to the punk ideal. They started the new year of 1982 with a new drummer. One with a fresh and welcome approach to playing Punk Rock; proving that the excitement of playing rock n' roll could still account for something.

Dave Spencer ... "Not long after the Rebels gig, our drummer, Neal Moxon decided to quit. He was always a bit of a rocker at heart and probably wondered what they hell he was doing putting up with this shit, when he probably wanted to play AC/DC anyway.

We had got to know a kid called Gary 'Chippie' Gillott, who was the drummer for a band called Spiral Vision, a dark sort of new romantic band who were doing quite well. When Chippie heard that we need a drummer he asked if he could give it a crack, but when he rehearsed with him he over complicated things and tried to play it all jazz-like. What we wanted was a punk rock Ringo. We found him in a kid called Simon Bird, not a punk at all, but a very, very, tight drummer. We auditioned him and then interviewed him, to see what he was made of, and to see if he shared our sense of humour. We were probably always bastards to him, but once we got Simon Bird in the band, we soared. He gave us space to develop and we rapidly, dramatically changed. All of a sudden, we were finger picking the guitars on some songs and putting real harmonies in others. All the influences we had been listening to were beginning to shape us, after all, we had been playing for nearly four years by this time.

The only problem was that we were playing to an audience that did not exist any more. Punk had expanded and fragmented so much by 1982 that as we were moving into 60s style garage-band psychedelia, the new punk rockers were screaming *'We're the Exploited Barmy Army! Don't try te mess!'*

Above: Cute Pubes rehearsing

Simon Bird (Rotherham musician/Cute Pubes drummer) ... "The Hallamshire Pub on West Street Sheffield was my first ever live public gig. I was just 17 and very nervous.

From 1982 onwards I was part of the music scene in Rotherham and for the first part of that decade I spent playing drums for a band that, at the time, were quite well known. They went by the name of Cute Pubes and it was my bona fide initiation in to playing live music.

Looking back, playing that gig at the Hallamshire was not unlike being drunk for the first time, but without the booze! All right, I felt a bit of an outsider and probably was, but shiver mi timbers, it got rid of any frustration I had as a teenager; so much so that when playing the track 'White Riot', Graham Torr (lead guitarist) had to violently gesture toward my head, with the butt of his guitar, to try and make me stop playing, after they had already finished the piece. Now that's what I call getting lost in the music and somehow, the crowd, mob, rabble, audience, whatever they were, I think, hated us. But I didn't care, because now I was in a punk band.

Well to call it a punk band might not have been exactly true. In my opinion, they certainly weren't anarchists and were respectful to me and what I 'stood for'. Anarchist I was not, although they did take the piss just that tiny bit too much at times but I soon found not to take it personally and that *Drummers* where usually treated that way. Anyway, my interview for the job of drummer was more like the Spanish Inquisition - all three of them (Dominic Wood, Dave Spencer and Graham Torr) lined up, sat on chairs with me, the non - descript, sat opposite. I can't remember much of the interview/ interrogation or any of the questions they fired at me, except for one, *'Can you play rock fast?'* I think their premise was to prod me from all angles to get the desired reaction. They must have got the feedback they wanted, although they were obviously still a bit dubious about me; needless to say I was recruited.

How do I see it all today? Going for the ride and as a, by-default experience-seeking teenager, I settled in to my newfound mode of transport through my late adolescence and my soul seemed to be comfortable with it. I was not a punk and the people I mixed

314

with at that time were not all punks but the ethos of punk seemed to allow you to say what you wanted when you wanted. Punk seemed to me to be the foundation of the Cute Pubes. The music of the band and the music the lads brought to my attention, during that period, has been the foundation to the way I played the drums, until I packed it all in at the age of 32. Even now, when any musical ideas run through my head, punk plays a big part in the thought process at base level, or at my first thought, so to speak. As for the pure punk way of living, for me, the desire to load raw truth into metaphorical cannon and blanket bomb everyone has never been there, but that's why I liked punk, it based itself on seeing and living the truth and that's where I base myself today in 2008."

Lynne Haythorne ... "Locally we followed a band at college called Vitamin Z. I remember the lead singer was Damien Hand and another member was Darryl De Silva. Darryl was known at college as a bit self-indulgent. Darryl is now an actor and has recently been seen on the police drama 'Out of the Blue'. We would also go to the Leadmill and Limit club and come across members of Human League, ABC and Heaven 17."

Left: Rotherham Punk girls Joanne, Fiona and June

Dave Spencer's personal love affair with Punk Rock would be a lifelong passion, but back in 1982 time and patience with the average Punk crowd was quickly running out.

Dave Spencer ... "Suddenly, we were playing to a crowd who didn't seem to have a clue. At our next gig, Simon Bird's debut, at the Hallamshire Hotel on West Street in May 1982, the audience was split in two, and in hindsight, we did as much as we could to provoke the split. A friend of ours, Fiona Palmer had recently opened a second hand clothes shop, Bad Fashions, on Kimberworth Road, in Rotherham, selling clothes to the likes of us; kids who wanted to dress a bit different, but couldn't afford the off-the-peg punk rock look. Anyway, by this time we'd done that to death already.

So when we stood outside the Hallamshire with our gear, waiting to get in, we looked a breed apart from the support band, The Plastic Toys and their mates. They were in leathers and Doc Martens and we were in kaftans and knee length suede boots.
The landlord opened the door and took a look at the lot of us and said, *'We don't have punk groups'*, and closed the door. We (Cute Pubes) knocked again until he came back and we said, *'We're not punk, we're a psychedelic rock and roll revival band'*. He looked us up and down, and dubiously, suspiciously, let us in.

Again, I have no idea how we came to be acquainted with the Plastic Toys, but they were good lads, and were right enough to us. They played harder than us, but now that we had Simon in the band, we sounded good without having to play 'hell for leather'. We were in a strange position of being ahead of the crowd, whilst being amongst the youngest people in the place. None of us were old enough to be in pub in the first place and I, being the youngest in the band, wasn't even seventeen, never mind eighteen. It felt like half the audience were at the same stage that we were in 1978, enthusiastic, but clueless and we knew it, and played up to it. We hated the new 'shit comedy' punk bands, and we were not afraid to say it. We had had a song called 'World War Three' for a year or so, and I introduced it by saying, *'This is a song called 'World War Three', which is not to be confused with the song of the same name by the Anti-Nowhere League, who are, frankly, a bit bobbar'.* Some of the dullards at the back roared a roar of disapproval and someone even shouted, *'You swore!'* We laughed our little bollocks off. No matter what they looked like, they weren't as scary as the Darfield youth club soul boys who wanted to kill us, and they definitely weren't as scary as a biker who'd beat us up with a pool cue unless we played some AC/DC. The problem was that they were the future of punk, and it was our past."

Above: Cute Pubes Dave Spencer, Simon Bird (Drums) Dominic Wood (Bass guitar) Graham Torr (guitar) at Sheffield Limit club

Punk gigs also offered Roadie work for those inclined to do so.

Spencer Summers was originally from London and was initiated into the punk scene after witnessing gigs by the Sex Pistols and Siouxsie and the Banshees. Later in 1979, he was asked by the UK Subs to work for them on the road ..."I met the Subs at a gig they played at the Marquee and singer Charlie Harper asked me to roadie for them. It just went from there and I ended up working for them for about 5 years or more. Later on, we did Retford Porterhouse and I can remember all of the fighting, some of which I was involved in as there were scabs (miners who went back to work) there."

Spencer later worked for Bad Manners, where he would roadie for them at venues up and down the country but also local venues such as Doncaster Rotters. He left London to settle up North after being divorced and settled in Maltby near Rotherham. Sadly, he now suffers from M.S but says... "Those days were fantastic and I wouldn't fuckin' swap 'em for anything; even with my illness I wouldn't swap it in exchange for those days."

Tony ... "Sod this Punk crap...I'm going to go and see Kim Wilde at the City Hall, power pop with great tunes. Ok a bit too polished on record, but live they all sounded brill. Also, Kim...she looked stunning and gorgeous, and the band included James Stephenson from Chelsea and Gen X. But, this is not to be taken too seriously. It's just that at the time I felt like I had enjoyed the Kim Wilde gig a lot more than most of the punk gigs I had been going to for the last year or so.

I was still buying Clash records and the Jam, Damned, and the few others that were left that were worth bothering with, but punk was not agEing very well for me and it had become downright boring. In fact, it was becoming like Billy Smarts Punk Rock circus.

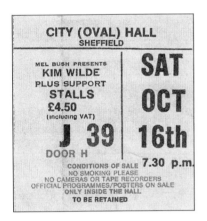

Around this time, I paid a visit to Julian Jones. He had been listening to Punk for a while and started playing drums with a mind to forming his own group. Anyway when I went round to see him, after he showed me what progress he had made learning to play the drums, he pulls out an LP by The Who and says *'Here borrow this, you will like it'.* The LP was 'My Generation' and I know it sounds so clichéd, some might say obvious; I know when I heard The Who's 'My Generation' LP, it lit a spark in me, rekindled that zest for rock n' roll again. In fact, it was a similar feeling to when I first heard the Clash first LP and the Jam 'All Mod Cons'. And that can't be a bad thing."

Punk had long since lost its sense of adventure and for the local generation, there would be new alternatives or progressions to take as Punk continued to swallow up its own conformity. Some would prefer the camaraderie and street sense of the skinhead scene, others would travel a path that would lead to Goth, that itself had been instigated by Punk era groups such as the Cure and Siouxsie and the Banshees. Or there would be the Punk influenced Psychobilly scene with groups like The Meteors, the New Psychedelia that followed the Mod Revival, the futurist New Romantics, Gary Numan worshipping Numanoids, the raincoat wearing Joy Division Post-Punk fans, Mods, Positive Punks, tribal Punk and a whole host of spin off cult styles and fashions. For most though, the euphoria and excitement of Punk was a thing of the past, only its influence and attitude remaining valid.

Julian Jones ... "For me, the New Romantic scene killed Punk off. I was never into that scene at all, I quite like some of it nowadays, like The Human League etc, but back then it was all guitars for me. By that time I was starting to play drums and guitar myself and forming a band...but yeah the Punk thing did die off around that time. It became all the Oi! kind of stuff, which I never liked."

Andrew Morton ... "What destroyed Punk for me was when it branched out into so many different things. There were too many cults and far too much rivalry going on."

Pete Roddis ... "The Punk thing sort of died out and then there was the New Romantic scene, which I went into: Unfortunately!"

Dave Frost ... "A lot of the Punks went along with the hardcore Punk stuff; and that was what I went into as well. I liked Discharge a lot and Anti-Nowhere League too. The hardcore style was the way forward with Punk for me."

Bryan Bell ... "To begin with - we were the new don't care generation. I did not actually leave the Punk movement as much as I grew up and found that the new groups that were coming through were only interested in trying to be the same. The old game of shocking people was not working any more either. Punk became boring. I wasn't going to be told what music and groups I could listen to. I thought the whole idea of it was to do what you wanted and listen to what you liked. All the rules were stifling. I was glad to have been a part of it though."

John Harrison ... "I went to see Discharge at Retford Porterhouse. This was later on, about 1980 I reckon, I went with Paul Maiden and Sugar and the gig was all glue sniffing and what have yer. I was a Mod really and thought *'This is not the scene for me anymore'.*"

Nicky Booth ... "By this time the bondage trousers had been put to one side. Oxfam shops became the big thing, and jumble sales were still a good source of top-notch clobber. We were always on the look out for good quality 1940s suits, cricket trousers, ties and shoes. Overcoats were big then too – in every sense of the word. It was, for once, kind of fashionable to be in the North too, what with Sheffield and Manchester bands making some of the most cutting edge sounds of the day. So what did I do? I moved to London."

Regardless of Punk's eventual disintegration, local Punks and musicians understandably share a common ground of fond memories of the era.

Valerie Garvey ... "Sheffield was a good place to be a Punk. You could go down town and meet up with your mates- no need to phone them- just go down to the Peace gardens or Woolworth's café. Those were the days."

Pete Cooper ... "Out of all the original Punk bands, the only ones I regret not seeing were the Sex Pistols, the original Ultravox and X-Ray Spex, although I did have a ticket for them and numerous other bands at a gig in London back in 1978 which cost me 70p. To this day I still don't know why I didn't go."

318

Paul Clarkson ... "That 3 years of the early 'New Wave' was a massive rush, certainly the first six months was like a rollercoaster."

Dave Parsons (Sham 69") ... "Yes the 3 or 4 years of Punk, and for me playing with Sham at the time was a real rollercoaster ride and it all kind of blurs into one."

Bryan Bell ... "I loved the idea of not dressing the same as anyone else and of being an individual. We were not conforming to a dress code at all. Also, I did not like every Punk band, as a lot, to me, were crap. I look back at those days as a good part of my life, meeting bands, travelling all over the country to gigs and having a really good time."

Paul Bower (2.3) ... "Punk only really lasted for about 18 months and then it was over."

Above Left: Original Punk Rocker Steve 'Smiler' Marshall in 1982
Above Right: Phil Murray of Phil Murray and the Boys from Bury at their first gig

Martin Dust ..."I still loved Soul and Motown when I was into punk, people can try and pretend it was year zero if they wish but it really wasn't, great fun though."

Anthony Cronshaw ... "That period- from 1976 to 1979; it was just unbelievable; such a fantastic time to be around in Sheffield. By 1981 my gig going days were just about over but those three years were something else. There will never be a time quite like it ever again."

Shaun Angell ... "The most notable Punk bands, for me, were the Clash and the Skids. They proved that they could develop and diversify their style and music."

Jo Callis ... "I think Punk must have affected me quite significantly, it gave me direction and new challenges. I think these movements did pretty much the same all over, brought like-minded people together for positive benefit and injected a bit of colour and vibrancy into the local culture. Also these movements presented opportunity to the people who got creatively involved; there are many leading figures in the media now who got their opening by writing fanzines, taking photos, designing clothes, making low budget films, recording and managing bands around their local scene for a hungry and growing audience. I would like to hope that the current financial recession may invoke a similar DIY, home grown ethic in modern culture, it seems to take such difficult times to inspire people to create their own ambitions."

The Punk fall out was a time of uncertainty, with many Punks not knowing which path to take next? However, the period did have plenty of focus for some disillusioned ex Punks who were determined to continue the Punk Holy Grail with renewed confidence. As the period began to pass into the rich tapestry of Rock n' Roll's history, some chose to decide to chronicle the Punk era.

Above: John Robb (Singer of respected Post-Punkers the Membranes and author of 'Punk Rock' book) larking around with mates in Rotherham' 'Hornblowers' club in the early 80's

Ex Membrane John Robb, for example, managed to successfully record the many and varied voices of the movement's original pioneers and musicians. His work managed to capture the excitement of the times in the exact words of almost all that were involved in creating the many flavours of 70's Punk Rock in the UK. The Author visited Rotherham on numerous occasions and is good friends with some of our own local Punk influenced generation. For others, the way ahead was to step out of their plastic trousers and mohair jumpers and into something sharper!

Punk's influence could not be ignored and would inspire creativity, but with a realisation that the visuals of Punk needed to be left behind to begin afresh.

320

Tony ... "For me personally, Punk was always about being pro-active; Getting involved in something. Being creative in whatever way you could. My European studies project at school was even about Punk in Europe. I always felt the need to be changing and not staying the same. I was pro-active in my teens; in so much as I would be writing Punk poetry and later lyrics. I would be drawing stuff, making badges, adapting clothes and thinking of new ideas in art lessons: Almost always-rejecting authority of all manners. What did the older generation know that was of use to me?

I would learn to play the guitar and form a punk band (which later became Mod band The Way) and try my hand at fanzine writing. Anything went as long as you were trying to do something. Later when I had left school, I was determined to form my own group. Most of my early attempts might have eventually resulted in amounting to very little, but at least I was doing something and trying. That is the thing about Punk now. It is all the same. It's just another cult thing like the Teds were back then; there are no more new ideas coming out. It is just a nostalgia circus as well. I would hate to think that future generations will only think of Punks as Mohicans, safety pins, coloured hair and leather jackets. The look and style of Punk rapidly became tiresome for me in the early 80's, but at heart, I never let go of its effect on me and its idealism is still with me. This book being an example I would hope."

Above: John Harrison

John Harrison ... "They were superb times. It was a fantastic time to be around. I loved it and I will never forget those days but it was such a relief to get out of the Punk clothes and into a sharp smart Mod suit. In 1979, I was still a punk at heart but I could see where it was going and I wanted to look neat and smart. Just like my heroes the Jam."

The Punk Rock explosion created many varying facets of music and popular culture: inspiring the best part of a whole generation to create new talent and ideals that would spread in a thousand directions. From fanzines, photography, clothes design, poetry and even comedy via the Young Ones, the influence was wide reaching and knew no acceptable boundaries. Sheffield and the locality were no exception.

However, the early 80's would prove to be more commonly known for the steel city as being the home of the sound of the synthesiser being played to an industrial background by the likes of the Human League.

As Punk either became stilted in its conformity, or bravely managed to stretch the confines of its three chord wonders, in Sheffield the era of Post-Punk was upon us and a new progression of music fans would emerge. From Blitz kids, futurists, Punk-Funkers, Goths, electro kids, Positive Punks and Mods, the new era had arrived and for a while, anything seemed possible!

Chapter Seventeen

They must be Tourists

"With Post-Punk, Punk didn't die; it just got even more interesting" – **Richard Chatterton (Rotherham Punk and Post-Punk fan)**

Tom Cleary ... "I first heard Joy Division at the Limit, the same night some drunken guy with his arm in a cast wanted to take me on, but my mate dragged me out. Probably a wise move, but I was not happy."

Mark Senior ... "I loved punk but also got into rock and metal when most of my contemporary punks were getting into miserable stuff like Joy division and Bauhaus."

Tony ... "The down side of Punk for me? Well for a movement that was created ideally to break all of the existing rules, within a short period of time it had invented and enforced so many of its own rules. That's why a lot of the Post-Punk music seemed to be such a healthy antidote to Punk for a while. There were some really good records out. I liked a lot of it, most of it from hearing it on the John Peel show. Stuff like Gang of Four, Girls at our Best, Magazine, The Fall and Wire. There was also the poppy indie type of groups such as the Fire Engines, TV-21; Josef K etc... some of these would turn up supporting groups like the Undertones and the like. I also had a lot of respect for the Sheffield groups and that scene back then."

Left: Human League's Phil Oakey... one of Sheffield's true musical Pioneers of the Punk and Post-Punk generation

Richard Chatterton ... "The Limit club deserves a book by itself. Some superb gigs I saw there: Killing Joke, Fad Gadget, Punilux, Teardrops, and Disease etc. The Gents toilets always flooded out. I also got thrown out of the Limit once and knocked myself unconscious when attempting a somersault."

As the 70's were coming to an end many saw Punk as being on its last legs whilst the Post-Punk spirit being very much alive... especially up North. In Sheffield, there was the local group scene that was directly influenced by the Punk ideal but not using the music as their main starting point. 'Disco wrecked Rotherham'... while still desperately trying to fight on (with a few keeping the Punk cause alive), did have a hit and miss live music scene with gigs at the Arts centre. Vena Cava played there on the 2nd of May 1980, the Negatives, Uncool dance band, Artery and Pulp amongst others also playing gigs there within the same year. But it was the industrial grey steel blitzed city of Sheffield that was mostly providing the Post-Punk nucleus of musicians.

Fuelled by Punk's uncompromising non-conformist attitude and the wave of energy that swept aside the old guard, the clutch of Sheffield's small crowd of musicians-to-be were, by the late 70's, desperately trying to achieve a scene of their own. Mostly it did not involve guitars to the fore. Groups like Vice Versa (soon to be A.B.C), Cabaret Voltaire, I'm so Hollow, They Must Be Russians, and The Human League were gradually developing their own individual approach, albeit, often in an unconventional and recognisably unorthodox way. But this was Sheffield's idea of doing things and often refreshingly so.

Phil Oakey (Human League singer) ... "The Sheffield scene at the moment is amazing. There's an incredible number of bands. Sheffield is the most graffiti'd city I know....walk down the street and you'll see the name of a new band sprayed on the wall every day. And it's not just confined to electronic bands. There's just a lot of talent." **(Taken from NME September 9th 1978)**

Simon Eyre ... "We used to regularly see Human League, Clock DVA, Heaven17, the Extras and the Push at The Limit on West Street, The University and the Broadfield and there was always a good sized crowd out to see them."

The path of the Human League and their tribe would now meet up with ex Rezillo Jo Callis.

Jo Callis ... "I began to get involved on the songwriting front with the Human League, with Bob Last being their manager and pretty much mine also. I welcomed the change of scene and exploration into another musical genre; that of Electro Pop! The League had recently parted company with half the group; Ian Marsh and Martin Ware (who went on to form Heaven 17 / BEF) and needed some new input and a slightly more 'commercial' (hate that word) boost to their song writing direction, so after Suzanne, Joanne and Ian (Burden) I 'slipped in' quite nicely."

Paul Bower ... "Following Punk there was a lot of new music and bands coming through-The Human League, Cabaret Voltaire (who had been around for a long time, but were just getting noticed). ABC came out of the end of the tail end of the Punk thing. They had been called Vice Versa and Martin Fry had run his own fanzine 'Modern Drugs' before eventually they came together to form ABC."

Martin Fry ... "We grew up seeing the Sex Pistols, the Clash, the Jam and Subway sect, but our generation wanted to do something entirely different." **(Record Collector magazine December 2008)**

Cheryl (from Sheffield) … "I saw The Human League in 1978 at the Top Rank supporting the Stranglers. I remember them playing a cover of 'Bridge over troubled water' with synthesizers; I'd never heard anything like it before. Not sure if the punk audience appreciated it at the time!!! I worked next door to Thornberry hospital where Phil worked; it was quite weird to see him on the no 60 bus the next day."

Lynne Freeman … "At the Crazy Daisy there would be Phil Oakey with his curtain of hair, leaning lazily against the door at the bottom of the stairs in a Bryan Ferry/Roxy Music kind of way; this was before he met the girls and formed the Human league."

Throughout the whole Punk period and the final days of the 70's, there had been a small but consistent type of Punk fan. One who would rather listen to David Bowie, Ultravox, Kraftwerk, and The Human League etc than the Damned, Sham 69 or Angelic Upstarts. Some of these music fans had been initially excited by the first wave of the Punk groups in 1977, but soon became tired of the monotony of a lot of the sound of Punk Rock. As usual, down in the South (but also crucially in Birmingham too) the beginnings of a new movement were starting to gel together. First in clubs like 'Billy's' and then 'Blitz' (the first name that would be attached to the new scene would be 'Blitz Kids'). Former Punk fan and Rich Kid Rusty Egan along with his Generation X roadie friend Steve Strange were two active participants in this new scene, contributing greatly to its groundbreaking club culture.

Further north and in places like Leeds and Sheffield this new antidote to the negativity of Punk was also starting to come together. The new scene was now being termed 'New Romantic' or 'Futurist'. Soon there would be a regular gathering of like-minded music and fashion conscious fans at clubs like Sheffield's Crazy Daisy and a little later the electro nights at The Limit club on West Street. Even later on, Rotherham would hold its own electro nights at its Windmill club - which a few years earlier had been a notable Punk Rock venue. It was inevitable that it wouldn't be long before the local music scene would see its own versions of the 'New Romantic' groups emerge.

Rotherham Punk Rocker Paul Clarkson, a student who had travelled and studied in Nottingham and London, now started to notice a shift in style with the more adventurous fashion conscious Punk fans.

Paul Clarkson … "I'd always gone to clubs as I knew most of the people that ran them. First it was Billy's wine bar (which became Blitz). Steve Strange took over the place on Tuesday evenings. We would all travel down there on the tube – looking quite odd and getting plenty of stares – my crowd and then girlfriend were part of the fashion scene and I guess you could say were the so called 'in crowd' of the time. We were always getting to know when things were kicking off.

By now, I had a Billy Idol style haircut and was wearing black leather jodhpurs. To begin with, the New Romantic crowd would consist of about 40 people milling around outside the club. Steve Strange would sit inside at the front of the club and nod and motion to the doorman to let certain people in; if you didn't look good enough, you didn't get in… simple as that. Brilliant concept! There was never any danger of a punch up 'cos everyone just wanted to pose. The other clubs were 'Club for Heroes' on Baker Street…

which was Steve Strange again... and there was Kilt in Soho, I think Robert Elms did that one. Also the Palace (great big place on three floors like an old cinema...top private bar and lots of celebrities there), Chris Sullivan's Wag club on Wardour Street, Hell in Covent garden and others. The music would vary from each club but a lot of it was Bowie, Spandau Ballet, Iggy Pop, Kraftwerk etc."

Sue Lowday ... "Rex Davis was the guy in the Kites group who first spotted the New Romantics. I was not impressed with his descriptions of the style. Soon we took it all on, and before we knew it we had the baggy shirt sleeves and pirates' trousers. I had visited my sister in London in early 1978 and we went to see one of the first screenings of Derek Jarmans' film Jubilee, so I had my first glimpse of Adam Ant there. It is quite a gritty film and so I was not impressed but later on when he had camped up the image, I thought it a laugh and joined in the 'knowingly self conscious' dressing up."

The New Romantic scene was now also starting to appeal to local Punk fans that were... either tired of Punks rules and inverted conformity or...simply saw the colour and Romance of this new movement as a sign to simply move on.

Above: Blitz kids including a young Boy George whose early career would include a job as onstage dancer at a Bow Wow Wow gig at Sheffield Polytechnic in September 1981 and an early Sheffield Leadmill date with Culture Club

Tracy Stanley ... "When I was 16 things were starting to change in the area and the New Romantic vibe was coming through. I was a dedicated Punk (or so I thought) but I really liked Ultravox, so decided to go and see them at Sheffield City Hall. I was wearing a bright red mini to match my bright red spiky hair and red pointed ankle boots with black elastic on the sides (which I had bought from Rebinas in Sheffield, which was a fantastic shoe shop where all the hip people went). I recall walking in late and the lights were on full with New Romantics wearing a variation of trench coats, full theatrical make up, ruffles, frills and knickerbockers. Ultravox blew my mind that night – they could actually play – and I was hooked."

Nicky Booth ... "I was at Art College in Rotherham in the early 80s when Sheffield suddenly found itself on the musical map. The Human League were at the top of the charts, ABC were being romantic and Cabaret Voltaire were being subversive. For me punk was losing its appeal by this point, probably because there was so much other exciting stuff bubbling under. Cabaret Voltaire were particularly interesting. They were a bit punk in their DIY ethos, but the music, if you can call it that wasn't like anything else.

326

New found sounds were collaged with electronic pulses; snippets of soundtracks culled from underground movies were spliced into dissonant walls of sound. Was it music? Was it art? I still loved the Stranglers, but the Cabs were becoming a new obsession."

Shaun Angell … "I was hugely influenced, in the late 70's and early 80's, by the outgoing Punk scene and the following 'New Wave'/Futurist bands that were arriving on the scene. I personally loved the sounds of bands like Spandau Ballet, Duran Duran, Kraftwerk and obviously the local Sheffield bands Human League and Heaven 17. It was something very different; a sign of the times perhaps – and also a rival to the recent great Mod revival of 1979."

Left: New Romantic Ivor Hillman Pictured with his cousin Richard Jobson of The Skids

Ivor Hillman … "At the end of the 70's a new scene was developing that took my eye, it was the emergence of the New Romantic scene. Kilts, Ballet shoes, frilly shirts and make up; this was for me. Now I really would be noticed, I started listening to bands like Spandau Ballet, Visage and Duran Duran and the lipstick became easier and easier to apply. Not surprisingly, the old bus rides became even harder than back in the Punk days. *'Poof'* was the usual shout from the hairy arsed miners of Rawmarsh, but I could take it and used the flamboyant style to my advantage. I formed my first band Spiral Vision (whom later became just Vision), then breaking away to form My Pierrot Dolls. We were the talk of the town; 4 blokes in make up caused quite a stir in little old Rotherham."

Pete Cooper … "Vision… well I joined before we even had a name. There was Ivor on vocals, Andy Beaumont on keyboards, a drummer ,saxophonist and bass player who I cant remember the names of .After a couple of months me Andy and Ivor recruited Chip on drums and Pete Jackson on keyboards and became Spiral Visions then shortened it to Vision. That lasted about 6 months then Ivor left to join My Pierrot Dolls. We then recruited Colleen Allen on vocals and she remained for approx 12 months and numerous gigs.

After Colleen left, Russ Park became the vocalist so the line up was now Russ on vocals, myself on guitar, Andy and Pete on keyboards and chip on drums. The first single was recorded with this line up for the ep 'Danse Macabre'. About 2 months after this I decided to quit and joined another local group 3D Fiction; 'Vision' ironically got signed to the label just after my departure then shortly had the hit 'Lucifer's Friend', still that's life. I carried on in 3D Fiction for about a year then left due to musical differences."

Above: Local New Romantics fronted by Punkette Julie Lee at the Spiral Vision show at Rawmarsh youth club May 1981

Vision guitarist Gary Steadman had previously played in New Romantic favourites Classix Nouveau - themselves an offshoot of Punk band X-Ray Specs. Their early line up also included future My Pierrot Doll singer Ivor Hillman, but it was the aforementioned line up that was around when they recorded and released their first single 'Lucifer's Friend' in 1981 on PRT records.

'Love Dance' was their belated follow up in 1983 and a stripped down version of the group continued throughout the whole New Romantic era and onwards into the New Pop phase.

Nicky Booth ... "Around this time I got to know the local band Spiral Visions, later shortened to Vision. They recorded an EP and asked me and a couple of friends to design the sleeve, so we secretly made full use of the dark room at college and came up with a fashionably sombre image of the band peering out of the windows of a derelict building as was the vogue at the time. As I was still handy with a sewing machine I ended up making one or two stage outfits for Andy Beaumont, their strangely coiffured keyboard player. Later they managed to get themselves a manager and some sort of record deal at which point we were drafted in to do the sleeve for what I think was their first proper single, 'Lucifer's Friend'. The cover wasn't that great, they wanted images of the band so we had to suppress our creative urges, but we came up with a nice airbrushed band logo though. We only charged a measly £50 for quite a lot of work, but when I rang their manager to ask for the money he threatened to break my legs...He was a lovely bloke! I understand that the single went to Number 1 in Italy. Around this time a few of us started mucking about with synthesizers and guitars ourselves, but we were hopeless and disorganised despite our enthusiasm so it never came to anything. It didn't stop me dreaming though."

Sadly Vision singer Russell passed away and their 15 minutes of fame was an appearance on local TV programme Calendar, along with an extra helping of cult status as their less than a handful of singles attained popularity amongst fans of the era across Europe.

The dream was swiftly turning into reality for the Human League as they moved from the alternative charts into the larger scheme of things that is the music biz! But the change in instruments promoted a bit of a dilemma for one member.

Jo Callis ... "Ha! -The Human League is the only Band I've ever been in where I didn't break a sweat on stage. That always stuck in my mind. I guess I was a bit tied to a keyboard in The League, and I like to move about a bit. There was also the fact that although reasonably competent with the guitar, my weapon of choice, I was rubbish on keyboards, and still am.

My favourite times though were probably when the sex the drugs and the 'electro' rock and roll combined together in joyous Technicolor indulgence and jubilant celebration. Even taking the rough with the smooth, those years were by and large good to me."

Tony ... "I was never a massive fan of the New Romantic scene. Of course I did like a lot of the music. I had the first few O.M.D singles, Simple Minds, Visage singles, all the Ultravox LP'S with John Foxx as singer and even Spandau Ballet's 'Cut a long story short' and 'Chant no.1'. I also loved B-Movie. I could see where the New Romantics were coming from. It was a credible attempt to provide some colour to the violence and urban decay of Thatcherite Britain and also gave a good kick in the balls to the narrow mindedness of a lot of Punk. Quite a few of my old Punk mates had succumbed to it, but it was never for me. Even so I take my hat off to some of the lads for the clothes they wore. They did still have the power to shock and, in some cases offend, and that was not a bad thing in itself. I took my girlfriend to see Spiral Vision when they played at Rawmarsh youth club. It was as much of a case of 'having somewhere to take her', as actually wanting to see the group. I can't remember too much of that night anyway."

Sue Lowday ... "Everybody dressed up at the Art College in those days, the canteen was the place to look at what everybody was wearing, mostly hunted down in junk shops, jumble sales, Laurence Corner in London. I think the only outfit that I really got comments about was when I bought a boiler suit from Milletts, that didn't go down too well for some reason, can't think why?"

The New Romantic scene did not always impress Punk fans –

Andrew Morton ... "Some of the kids who had been into Punk got into the New Romantic thing and they just looked atrocious."

Bryan Bell ... "I had been a fan of O.M.D for quite a while, so when I was up at the pub and kids were starting to go on about them, I would be saying *yes they are good have you heard 'Electricity' or 'Messages' ?*. They would go *'what!'* I also didn't mind some of Cabaret Voltaire's records and I had both the Kraftwerk albums from way back."

Steve Haythorne ... "I did like The Human League and also later on ABC – their 'Lexicon of Love' LP was great, but I didn't like Duran Duran and that kind of New Romantic style. I suppose it was indicative of the times really; style over substance."

Pete Cooper ... "True, I had been a member of Vision, and I also saw Classix Nouveaux, Duran Duran, Japan, Blancmange and A Flock of Seagulls, but as for being a New Romantic I was still a punk at heart so I didn't really get too involved."

Tony ... "I never saw The Human League at all. Me and Pete almost went to the Top Rank concert they played. I think this was about April 1980 when their 'Holiday' e.p was released. Phil Oakey was at the Siouxsie and the Banshees gig at the Top Rank that I went to. We were stood right at the side of him. Later on some of my mates who had been Punks, were now into the Futurist/New Romantic scene, they were raving on all about it. I did end up buying the first two Human League LP's, but that was a bit later on. Funnily enough years later I bought a load of singles from a Rotherham second hand record shop 'Back track' and lots of them had belonged to Phil Oakey. Most of them still had his name on them. (I assumed they weren't hooky). There was loads of different styles of music, hardly any of it being synthesiser sort of records."

Nevertheless, the emerging 'New Romantic' style (and synthesiser sound) was still popular amongst many of the local Post-Punk generation.

Steve Cowens (Sheffield author) ... "At 15 or 16 I got into the piss – poorly named New Romantic scene and started going to clubs like the Crazy Daisy on High Street and The Limit Club on West Street. I stopped well fuckin' short of putting make up on like a lot of lads did who were into the scene. I'd dance the night away flicking my stupidly overgrown fringe to the latest tunes like Visage 'Fade To Grey', Spandau Ballet's 'To Cut a long Story Short' and Kraftwerk's 'The Model'. The Crazy Daisy had a bad reputation for trouble and my Dad warned me about going to the club." **(From 'Steel City' by Steve Cowens and Anthony Cronshaw)**

The attraction of the scene, for some ex Punks, could be the glamour of the futurist acts themselves, or not surprisingly the 'to be expected involvement' of the fairer sex.

Pete Roddis ... "I got into the New Romantic scene, well basically cos all the Punk girls were moving that way and I was always interested in what the girls were up to, if you know what I mean! I would go all over during those times. The Crazy Daisy club in Sheffield was a regular one. I would go and see some of the groups too. The Human League was one and I also saw Ultravox at the City Hall and they were really good. It was so much different to Punk, there was obviously more money involved in it and the show that Ultravox put on was fantastic. They could afford all the lighting and all that so it was far more glamorous and more of a show in a sense."

Tracy Stanley ... "The weekend after I had been initiated into the New Romantic scene at the Ultravox concert, I was off to Leeds to a shop called X Clothes, which was an extremely trendy clothes shop for Punks and New Romantics. I went there for an ex-army trench coat, which was a mile too big, but if you pulled the belt in really tight, it served its purpose.

My sister Sharon had been a silver service waitress and had this really frilly uniform, but she was a good few dress sizes more than me, so with money short and a look to capture I cut it up and made two dresses with high ruffled collars and frilled cuffs, what a transformation!

With a pair of silky gloves and my Mother's pill box hat, I was now a fully fledged New Romantic; quickly switching from the sounds of Punk to Duran Duran, Visage, The Human League, Simple Minds, Japan, Depeche Mode to name but a few. I was also going to various gigs at the City Hall and the Lyceum, which had just been refurbished."

New Romantic fun at the Rotherham Art Centre

For local fan Shaun Angell, a chance *out of the blue* led to a memorable live concert by New Romantic favourites Roxy Music across the Pennines in Manchester.

Shaun Angel ... "1980 was a top year for music and fashion. Two concerts I attended were memorable for different reasons. One being The Skids one mentioned earlier and the other was Roxy Music. In the summer of that year I travelled to the Manchester Apollo to see Roxy Music. I only really went cos an older girl – whose boyfriend couldn't make it asked me to go with her instead – well it'd be rude not to have gone wouldn't it .I couldn't take my eyes off her as she swayed to Bryan Ferry's cool tunes. When she asked me later if I enjoyed it, I said *'Oh yes! The concert wasn't bad either."*

Shaun shares some teenage fashion ventures from the 'New Romantic' era.

Shaun Angell ... "From 1978 – 1980, I often made the short journey from my Rotherham home on the old X92 bus service to Leeds, where I would spend all my spare money on the latest gear including baggy trousers, Mohair jumpers, trench coats, winkle picker shoes and double breasted shirts from a popular shop at the time called X Clothes; scary to think that its 30 years ago.

About the same time, I was just getting into the football scene and fashion, music and looking good on the terraces always went hand in glove. 1979/80 saw me having a daft haircut called 'The Wedge'. Back then, me and the mates all thought that we looked cool, but looking back now, wearing dungarees, and looking like you'd got a mushroom on your head wasn't the best decision I ever made. But we didn't give a fuck cos we were making a statement and loved it!"

Tony ... "My only concession to the Futurist scene - clothes wise at least - was buying some of those Bowie shirts or fireman shirts as they were sometimes called and wearing them when I went to see Simple Minds a couple of times."

The sounds and fashions of Post-Punk and early Futurism were often to be seen on the football terraces. The Casual look too, had been knocking around for a few years, now gaining more recognition with a mix of the styles and sounds of 1980. The big crossover group at that period were Simple Minds (who famously split their 1977 Punk group Johnny and the Self Abusers on their first singles release). The stadium rock and pomp of 1985 was half a decade away but their futurist dance sound could be heard in a different kind of stadium ... and amidst an ever increasingly volatile social climate.

Shaun Angell ... "In May 1980 I travelled to Hampden Park in Glasgow for the old firm game 'Rangers' v 'Celtic'. This was a football match, but also a cup final and a tribal gathering of two groups of people with completely different identities; Protestant Rangers against Catholic Celtic. One month previously, I had bought tickets to see Simple Minds who were to play at Ford Green in Leeds. But the concert was cancelled after the Irish centre in Leeds was attacked by soccer hooligans who said that by *'bringing the group to the city'*, they were helping to raise funds for the IRA from a supposedly sympathetic Jim Kerr the lead singer. These were never more than rumours, but when I got the chance to go to the match a few weeks later I couldn't resist.

The band had released a classic 'New Wave' sound called 'I travel' and it was booming out before the match kick off. Celtic fans in the crowd were bouncing up and down, Rangers fans responding by burning an Irish tri colour. It was mayhem but I loved every minute of it. At this time, and certainly the following year '1981', music, fashion, football and violence went hand in glove and it was no coincidence that the country as a whole was rapidly descending into anarchy and chaos with unemployment, race riots, industrial unrest and crime going through the roof."

Meanwhile Sheffield's Human League had signed with Virgin records, released their 'Holiday 80' e.p in April and received a name check from The Undertones in the lyrics of their 'My Perfect Cousin' single... *'His mother bought him a synthesiser – got the Human League in to advise her – Now he's making lots of noise – playing along with the art school boys'*. Not exactly pleasing the League (they stated that only one member had actually been to art school) the poetic sarcasm was merely a speck in the river Don compared to their internal tensions that were becoming more and more significant as 1980 wore on. In November of that year The Human League split into two groups; one of which was Heaven 17 (joined by Glenn Gregory) whilst the others (Phil Oakey and Adrian Wright) continued with their hard earned name and welcomed on board ex Rezillo and Rotherham lodger Jo Callis along with Sheffield lasses Joanne Catherall and Susan Sulley who were recruited on the dance floor of The Crazy Daisy. The classic pop era Human League was complete.

The sounds of The Human League and many other contemporary futurist sound
heard (amongst the flavours of other styles of music) at local clubs of the area: v
fashion and clothes became a focal point – sometimes for more than obvious re

Shaun Angell … "Two of the most popular venues from the 'New Romantic' time, we.
The Crazy Daisy in Sheffield and Charades in Rotherham. Where else – on a Saturday
afternoon – could you go before the match and listen to Gary Numan, Depeche Mode,
John Foxx and Tenpole Tudor while sporting wedge haircuts and wearing trench coats,
Baggy Johns and yachting pumps and yet be universally accepted!

   The 'Daisy' would be packed with strangely dressed people (some smoking or sniffing
illegal substances) gyrating their bodies to this wonderful music. Likewise, on Friday
nights 'The Charades' was just as fantastic...one of the great things about that place was
walking up the stairs behind all the birds in their short tartan skirts...superb! I've never
known a place where all the lads would trip over themselves to let all the women in first."

One of the groups on the New Romantic scene that local disillusioned ex Punks like Pete
Roddis, Tracey Stanley and futurist and Punk fan Shaun Angell followed were local
Rotherham group My Pierrot Dolls.

   Futurist group My Pierrot Dolls were formed in 1981 by ex Spiral Vision member Ivor
Hillman. Ivor had been an early Punk fan amongst a very small crowd of like-minded New
Wavers who lived in the Rotherham suburb of Rawmarsh. Becoming disillusioned by the
constraints of Punk, and initially influenced by his cousin Richard Jobson of The Skids
and their early forays into 'new musik', Ivor soon turned to the new sounds coming
through during the last few months of the 70's and the early days of 1980. The new
Futurist scene offered an alternative to the greyness of Post-Punk and the nihilism of
contemporary Punk and as a result he wanted to play a part in the burgeoning movement.

   Ivor played many local concerts with his new group; all helping them to build up a keen
and loyal local following. Future Pulp star Jarvis Cocker went along to some of their
concerts and can be seen in the background of a fan's photograph taken at a Rotherham
Art centre date.

   Following a constantly changing line up and a single 'End of an Era', that the group
themselves were disappointed with, the group settled down to a steady line up of Ivor
Hillman: vocals, his brother Ian Hillman on synthesiser, Barry Thurman: Bass guitar,
John Airton: guitar and on drums Howard Daniels (who had previously played with The
Skeletal Family).

Over in Doncaster a kind of 'Futuristic' package line up played the town in March 1981.
Bottom of the bill were future pop stars Blancmange (who were likened to Joy Division at
the time) on a show that also included popular 'New Romantic' act Classix Nouveaux,
Naked Lunch and Post-Punk evangelists Theatre of Hate... a group who, the audience of
Futurists, Numanoids, Adam Ant highwaymen and a mix of Blitz kids and Punks, gave a
fair appreciation to ...but seemed to prefer the DJ's post-set choice of Ultravox's 'Quiet
Men'; which filled the dance floor after Theatre of Hate left the stage. Back to Sheffield and
a unexpected pair of guests arrived on the Limit club dance floor one night in early 1981.

Timothy Green … "We didn't go to the Limit that often, but my best memory of it was
popping in there after seeing Kraftwerk at Sheffield City Hall, for a disco. This was in 1981

nd the disco was playing a sort of Bowie/indie/early New Romantic style. After a short while, a couple of coolly dressed guys popped in, and had a dance for a few numbers. It was Wolfgang Flür and Karl Bartos from Kraftwerk. We heard that they regularly went clubbing after playing in a new city."

Above: My Pierrot Dolls fans from Rotherham with at the far left ex Punk Rockers Pete Roddis and Tracy Stanley...also Kraftwerk ticket(Lynne Haythorne)

The New Romantic scene, like Punk itself, also had its D.I.Y approach to clothes, with similar ventures (as Punk had taken previously) now being set out on by its scenesters.

Lynne Haythorne ... "When the 'New Romantics' came onto the scene I was at college and it seemed like a general progression musically and fashion wise. People began scouting charity shops and jumble sales for clothes of the past to adapt and bring up to date."

Veteran local Punk musician Dave Spencer did not share the vision of the 'New Romantic' dream, but was also feeling the much-felt emptiness of the Post-Punk fall out.

Dave Spencer ... "In July we (Cute Pubes) played at the Limit. It seemed like a lifetime since we'd last been there to see the Skids, but now we were finally there! It was a Thursday night and we were supporting Rotherham's 'New Romantics', Spiral Vision. When we arrived, the first surprise of the night was that they had renamed themselves simply as Vision.

We'd been vaguely aware of them as they went in our local pub in Rotherham, the Charter Arms. They had recently replaced their singer, Colleen Allen with the proto-Goth Russell Bonnell. I can't really remember that much of them before this gig but we must have seen 'em play, because the whole gig sticks in my mind as being a real shock as far as how naff the new image was. Whereas we had a new song called 'War Hero' about

seeing the traumatised soldiers coming home to hollow glory at the end of the Falklands conflict, which had ended a couple of weeks before, they had songs like 'Pagan Ritual', (Chorus: *it was a ritual, a pagan ritual*) and their new single 'Lucifer's Friend'. They played in front of a white sheet with Satan's head on a pentangle. To us it was so crass and cheesy. We had a great gig, followed by a great giggle at this silly music. Surely nobody in their right mind would fall for this ...Welcome to the 1980s proper! But people did fall for it and we started to feel like we were in a kind of limbo - We didn't have the maturity to see that we could forge our own path -

Above: New Romantics (Tracey Stanley & Shaun Angell are both at the far right of the photo) at a My Pierrot Dolls Concert at Rotherham Art Centre with a young looking Jarvis Cocker and an early Pulp line up in the background

- we could only see ourselves in terms of what had gone before, and what other people were doing."

The local New Romantic's were also beginning to realise that underneath the glossy sheen of the image (and all the genuine effort to look great), that the facade was being exposed and last orders were being called for many of the genuine originators of the local scene.

Tracy Stanley ... "I do recall when dancing the night away to the sounds of Roxy Music and Soft Cell at Tiffany's. Someone asked me if I was a waitress. I nearly died I had gone to all that trouble adapting our Shaz's uniform and some shit had sussed me out. So from that night on my trench coat stayed firmly shut. Later I grew my hair into a lob sided bob and was altogether more demure much to my parents' delight."

Darren Twynham ... "Yeah, I got into the new Romantic thing for a while too. I was listening to Spandau Ballet, Ultravox and after seeing them support Hazel O' Connor in 1980 Duran Duran. It filled the gap left by punk for a while."

Punk Rock reared its ugly old barnet again in this story... as Punk stalwarts UK Subs once more pogo into the picture as My Pierrot Dolls singer Ivor recalls a story from later in their career.

Above left: Local 'New Romantics' and Punk fans at Rawmarsh youth club
Above Right: My Pierrot Dolls Ivor Hillman singing

Ivor Hillman ... "We were supporting the UK Subs at the Sheffield Leadmill in 1985. Anyway, we got there early and did our ound – check through the support band's P.A, which sounded wazzy; but we were the support band after all!

It got to 7.30 and there was no sign of the Subs. The promoter came down and said quickly *'Looks like you're headlining – the Subs don't look like turning up'.* We hurried upstairs and did a quick soundcheck through the main P.A and it sounded awesome! The promoter then came into the dressing room and gave us 2 crates of Budweiser...Yes we've made it!

About 8.30, there was a commotion upstairs and Charlie Harper and the UK Subs had all turned up. Our dressing room door opened and in came the promoter again with *'Sorry guys, the Subs are here- you're back to being support.'* He then took out 5 bottles of 'Bud'- one for each member of our band and took the rest up to the Subs...Shit !!!

After splitting, My Pierrot Dolls attained a cult following and a compilation album of past recordings was released in 2004. Ivor Hillman still continues to perform to this day.

The New Romantic scene had hit its apex around mid 1981 - and soon became just as jaded as its other musical predecessors; paving the way for the 1980's decadence and pompous hierarchy that was the 'New Pop' years. The local Futurist scene never really took off with the expected impact it initially promised to stimulate and encourage. For a short while, it had evolved into a scene of colour, dressing up and a Post-Modernist mix of the outlandishness and originality of early Punk, Bowie-ism mixed with the glamour of 1950's film stars... all set to a soundtrack of electro dance music with a spoonful of funk and contemporary soul. Many of the local Punks (and some Soul boys) took on board the change and welcomed the new era of Dandyism and dressing up that the New Romantics offered. Ultimately, though it would never provoke the same-life changing epiphanies that Punk had given our generation.

Above: My Pierrot Dolls during their later line up ... 2nd Photo - Vision members and fans ...singer Andrew Beaumont at the right with fan June Graham and drummer Gary Gillott with fan Julie Lee in the background.

For Sheffield, the Electro boom was the direct follow up to the Futurists and would continue throughout the 80's: its much-loved home being the Limit club. Like Punk before it though, the New Romantic scene (and Sheffield and the locality was no exception) there was a time limit to its shelf life. As The Human League continued their journey to Pop stardom and ABC fired their Poisoned arrows into a Lexicon of Love, the remaining main players of the scene traded avant-garde clothing and Kraftwerk LP's for the lure of dollars and expensive promotional videos in the Bahamas. Or the other option...to continue working 9 – 5 ... the one that most of the era's dreamers, fans, trend setters and innovators were now faced with.

Riding the storm and Glamour of the Duran Duran years, the remainder of the local Post-Punk groups continued to strive forwards. The years 1980 to 1984 was also a time fondly remembered by some of the musicians of the local Post-Punk scene.

Simon Hinkler of Sheffield band Artery... "That era was a phenomenal time for music in Britain, and the Sheffield area had its own particular slant and attitude... with very diverse bands emerging. Personally, I look back on it as having been the very best of times, and a time when I did my apprenticeship as a musician."

Jo Callis ... "In Sheffield at that time, we used to go to the Roxy/Bowie night in Wendy's (I think it was called) every Wednesday and sometimes at weekends, and there seemed to be a lot of gigs and events at the University that seemed to be open to all. We'd often sink a few pints in The Pig and Whistle beforehand."

And also much appreciated by the music fans themselves.

Phillip Wright ... "Sheffield pretty much invented the music that became known as Post-Punk. While cities up and down the UK had clones of the Pistols and the Clash, Sheffield never really did. The closest was a band called The Stunt Kites, who were pretty good, I saw them a few times, but most bands were moving in a totally different direction to the rest of the UK, bands like Artery, The Human League, Clock DVA, Cabaret Voltaire etc were considered experimental. Artery gigs started off low key (you can hear me shout 'Heinz!' on one of their live recordings, from Rotherham Arts College from memory!) but soon they became 'the' gig to be seen at, more like musical events than gigs. Original singer Mick Fiddler moved from vocals to guitar and violin, Mark Gouldthorpe took over on vocals and looked like he needed to be in a strait jacket. Garry Wilson on drums always moved his head from left to right like a clockwork toy, Neil McKenzie on bass had a really good sound, similar to Jean Jacques from the Stranglers. Simon Hinkler was on keyboards. I have all their early singles and was convinced they would make it big nationally; John Peel was a big fan. I was delighted a few years ago when my daughter bought me two Artery compilation CD's for Christmas. Best Artery song ever... 'Afterwards'. Of course it was through my following Artery that I met Marcus Featherby."

During the Punk fall out, as the Post-Punk era had been kicking in, Sheffield Punk group 2.3 were trying out a new sound with new musicians brought along to help try and accomplish the new approach.

Simon Eyre ... "I did a recording session with 2.3 just as a session guitarist with my mate Jeremy Meek on bass. It was just the 4 of us, Paul Bower, Hayden Boyes Weston, me and Jez. It was kind of the second incarnation of 2.3; Paul wanted to add a bit more of a groove to the band so he got us in cos of our more funky background. I remember it turned out pretty good. 'Modern Man' was one of the songs; me and Jez sang backing vocals on that one. Paul was great, I loved his lyrics."

A funky side to Punk had already emerged with groups like Scritti Politi, Gang of Four (whose 'Entertainment' LP would be a massive influence over the ensuing years) The Pop Group and Punk's most primitive maestros The Slits.

Tony ... "Pete Roddis bought that single Slits 'In the Beginning there was Rhythm' on one side and the other was The Pop Group. We weren't quite sure what to make of it at first but we knew there was something interesting going on."

The following year, the classic and much sampled 'Papas got a brand new Pigbag' by Pigbag was released – being massive in the clubs and on its second shot becoming a chart hit. Even the New Romantic crowd would start to spread their funky wings with Spandau Ballet's 'Chant number 1'. Clearly, Post-Punk did have its interesting moments and in parallel to this, Sheffield itself was moving along with its own scene.

Post-Punk era groups that could be found playing around Sheffield and Doncaster (and all the places in-between) were - amongst others - Veiled Threat, In The Nursery, B- Troop (from Doncaster), Vendino Pact, Pulp, Chakk, The Danse Society (from Barnsley) and They Must be Russians. As well as these, and the veterans of the scene such as Comsat Angels, The Human League and Cabaret Voltaire, there were always plenty more just around the corner who wanted a shot at making their mark.

Simon Eyre ... "The Thompson Twins used to gig at The Broadfield on Abbeydale Road well before any chart success; they were a loud, punky guitar band with a really unusual sound. Also the Comsat Angels, or Radio Earth as they were then known - they were a Jazz Rock band of real musos, playing Chick Corea/Mahavishnu Orchestra type stuff. Both these bands transformed into something completely different to make a bid for commercial success."

Michael Day ... "Pulp I loved of course, in fact I played a gig with my second band supporting Pulp and Jarvis was always a great guy."

Pulp had been playing, with an ever-shifting line up, since the Punk days of 1978, Jarvis Cocker being a fan of both the original Punk groups and the following Post-Punk fall out. Their first official gig was at Rotherham Arts Centre on July 5th 1980, which was a last minute chance option presented to them by a certain Marcus Featherby. Jarvis addressed the Rotherham crowd (a mix of local Punks, students and the curious) with *'Are you ready to rock Rotherham?'* From that moment on, despite more setbacks than most groups could normally expect – and certainly more than their fair share of members (they could possibly give Mark E Smith's The Fall a run for their money on that stake), Pulp would be around on the Sheffield scene for many years; the nationwide music world eventually catching up with them around the time of Britpop. Jarvis Cocker, like that other Cocker from Sheffield 'Joe', is as synonymous with Sheffield as steel itself and continues to perform sell-out concerts to this day.

Meanwhile back in the grey toned days of Sheffield back in the early 80's, young music fans were still searching for the next new thing to take over where Punk had left off.

Timo from Sheffield recalls the Sheffield Post-Punk scene on West Street in the early 80's ... "I saw many, many bands at the Limit club in the early 80's. From 'The Future' (a mixture of later Human League and Clock DVA personnel in white boiler suits) to the B-52's. I also recall, as a Blade (Sheffield united fan), that the club was regarded by Owls (Sheffield Wednesday fans) as being their territory.
    I also remember the nights at the George with great affection. I played there myself, as well as watching Clock DVA, I'm so Hollow (Rod Leigh was a mate of mine and later

collaborator in 'Workforce'), Artery etc. The DJ was Disco John, and everybody who was connected to Sheffield music seemed to go. Martin Russian of NMX fanzine (the then bible of the indie scene) was always there taking photos of the bands onstage. I remember the night The Naked Pygmy Voles (an experimental 'noise' band) supported Clock DVA. I have never seen so many punters crammed into the top room of a pub in my life. The atmosphere was great, and I don't recall a single bad incident. Very, very happy days."

Tony ... "I wasn't heavily into the Sheffield scene as such. I would be up Sheffield a lot of the time and would notice all the flyers all over the city or in the record shops like 'Rare and Racy' etc. I would go and see some of the groups play. To be honest I always had a lot of respect for the Sheffield groups as they always had a go and didn't take their cues from the London groups or anywhere else. It was a very interesting time for Sheffield groups and their music. It was always different, often a healthy alternative to some of the Punk groups I was going to see, and the way most of the groups revelled in the greyness and the industrial aspect of the city, it always made me laugh. In a respectful way - that is."

Jo Callis ... "We used to go and see The Cabs (Cabaret Voltaire) and Comsat Angels and no doubt various others, I remember us turning up late to a Depeche Mode gig at the Uni and they were just finishing their set. I was liking a mix of stuff at the time, Rock, Glam and Soul still as well as hard Funk, Bowie of course and Leftish Field Electro and Dance stuff, Quality Disco & R n' B like Chic, KC and The Sunshine Band, I still liked a bit of Punk, Dolls, Thunders etc. I even had a wee Rockabilly spell and was a total Gene Vincent nutter."

A figure from Sheffield's colourful past reappeared back into the life of Philip Wright during the early 80's.

Phillip Wright ... "When I met Liz (my wife) I saw less and less of Marcus (Featherby), he had started working with Scottish punk band, the Exploited and started a new label called Pax Records. Then... he turned up at my wedding in 1983, camera in hand, taking pictures (I wanted to look like Martin Fry of ABC and had an electric blue shiny wedding suit made to measure!). He was always charming, often chain-smoked and told outrageous stories, which never sounded true but occasionally he would pull out some photo's which seemed to back up what he had said. He came for dinner one night not long after I was married and then he just disappeared. I didn't see him for about five years and then came home from work one night and he was there. A mate of mine, Mark, had run into him and told him I had moved house and they just turned up. Marcus was called something else by that point, I think he said he was James Stratford-Barratt and he was working at the BBC on cookery programs, which was funny as when he lived at Whitham Road he lived on baked beans on toast! That was the last I saw of him.

At one point, when I was dressing like a Mod, he gave me an American G.I's Mac, which was very cool and looked great, much better than wearing a Parka. I am not sure where he is now and I am not sure that I, or anybody else for that matter, ever knew who he really was."

Now, but only momentarily for the author, a glimpse of a new positive hope arrived with one particular gig at Sheffield's Polytechnic.

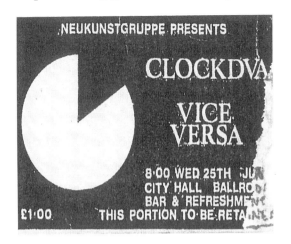

Tony ... "February 1982 and I went, along with my best mate at the time Dean, to see Theatre of Hate at Sheffield Poly. We had already seen them play at the Limit Club and also supporting the Clash, but this particular gig was the one. The place was quite full and there was an excitement and tension in the air, a feeling that something new was being created.

Theatre of Hate came on and they played a fantastic set. The crowd consisted of a lot of the Harrow Punks who had been followers of the early Adam and the Ants. They were pretty hardcore and they were doing the slam dance and shoving all over. The atmosphere was fantastic and captured a feeling of Punk but in a new form."

Sheffield ex Punks such as Michael Day were now enjoying the decadent and fun filled nights in West Street's Limit club, which had managed to ride the storm of the Punk era and continue to highlight almost all of the best new music coming through during the Post-Punk days; including reggae.

Michael Day ... "There were so many bands that it all seems to blur together and some of the gigs were packed and others were sparsely attended. I also worked behind the bar for a while at the Limit pulling the Tuesday, Wednesday and Thursday night shifts (9 p.m. – 2 a.m.) Tuesday's were reggae nights and so I saw Steel Pulse, Black Uhuru, Sly and Robbie and all kinds of other fantastic reggae bands on those nights... Wednesday was students and nurses (half price drinks) and Thursday seemed to be odd band night and really quiet while everyone warmed up for the weekend or you would get the occasional stag party or hen party in there by mistake.

It was during this time that I got to know the bouncers a lot better and realized that although they were animals when called on, overall they were nice guys, I used to take a taxi home with Andrew Dunraven and he was a good bloke. One of my funniest bar stories was on a Wednesday night, everyone was always bladdered because even watered down beer in enough quantity will have an effect and I was working the main bar. One of the taps (press once for a half, twice for a pint) was stuck which worked out ok for the regular *'10 pints of lager please mate'* orders, but in order to turn it off you had to put your finger over the spout which in turn caused enough back pressure to shut off the valve.

While performing this delicate operation one night, I managed to spray the entire line of people at the bar which most took extremely well except for the one guy shaped like a bowling ball who was not amused, he called me a few choice words and despite my offer of a free drink appeared ready to come over the bar at me. Now the floor of the bar was higher than the club floor, most likely to make the bar staff look bigger but this guy was drunk and on a mission so I pressed the little buzzer under the bar that signalled the bouncers in the lobby that we needed help (this was used anytime trouble broke out in the club), I saw the main doors open and something akin to the parting of the red sea as the bouncers moved quickly to where I was and as I casually pointed at this guy he disappeared as if on a rope and was promptly taken outside, no doubt to meet the parking meter conveniently installed outside the front door.

I also remember those big bass speakers up near the main stage and how every once in a while someone would fall asleep in them because they were so drunk."

Above: Some of my Concert tickets from 1980-82

Later era Punks such as Wayne Kenyon from Doncaster became tired of the Punk scene and evolved into skinheads; although becoming a different type of skinhead than those who had been terrorising the young Punk fans of Sheffield. Post-Punk and the many associated cults were not for Wayne, however.

Wayne Kenyon ... "I was a Punk at school from 1981 to around March 1984; then I turned skinhead. Why? Well I always saw the Punk movement as being working class and I thought it was becoming very fake and full of poseurs. I hated the way it was all going

342

Goth. Goth was not for me, it was more suited to college kids playing at being rebels before they went into their jobs in banks and became Thatcher's Yuppies. For fuck's sake I was a miner at Broddy pit at 16 years old but left because I wanted to spend more time with my Punk band and going to gigs. I didn't want to spend my youth underground for 8 hours a day, even if the pay was good.

I was into bands like the Redskins and the Burial and also remember local Mod band The Way who were also influenced by the Redskins at the time and I thought were awesome. I was also into Ska and bands like Madness.

Yes I was a skinhead, but I was never a fascist. The skinhead scene was split right down the middle with fascists and left wing skins. A lot of people regard all skinheads as being fascist, but that's just all media crap. It was always a good story to write about Nazi skins whilst socialist's skins just didn't have the headline grabbing effect that the Nazi ones had."

There were also individuals out there who would be both influenced by the local Post-Punk scene, whilst still retaining their original tastes in music.

Duncan Payne had been an avid fan of Soul, including the classic Northern scene but also the 70's Philly style. During the late 70's to mid 80's he lived in Sheffield and was soon to be an avid gig-goer on the Sheffield Post-Punk scene. Here he recalls those days...

"Come secondary school most of my friends had been into metal or punk whilst my thirst for Soul would seemingly never be quenched as I sought out recordings from the present and the dim and distant past, as recommended by the fortnightly bible known as Blues & Soul. 1979 brought about a change. The current Soul scene was stagnant, disco was dead. And my best mate Steve, who had always been fluid in his musical tastes, decided to become a Mod on the back of the Ska revival. Not content with just buying the latest 2-Tone releases he also sought some of the late 60s Ska material, Prince Buster et al, and force-fed me a diet of the stuff. Suddenly my horizons were opening and I was no longer quite so blinkered in my outlook.

It wasn't Steve who opened my eyes to what was happening right under my very nose, however. It was fate. Having screwed up my GCE's big style, I stayed on at sixth form to do retakes and attempt to take 3 'A' levels as well. Fuck that for a lark! After working like a twat for a term I decided that if I was going to work I might as well get paid for it. And so I said goodbye to mainstream education and hello to the form of slave labour more commonly known as retail.

Within days of working on Fargate at a branch of a nationally known retailer I had been befriended by a colleague who was heavily into music. He talked about bands who I had at best vaguely heard of but more often than not I was completely ignorant. But, more interestingly, there was a never ending supply of colorful characters who would visit the store and single out Dave. And soon I found out why. Dave was in a band. And these visitors were either in bands themselves or just completely mental about the local music scene."

Gary Davies (Rotherham Musician) ... "I was never that interested in any particular genres back then or where the music that I liked actually fitted in. To me the Clash weren't strictly a Punk band as such. I saw them more as a rock n' roll band with reggae influences. With Punk, or more particularly the Post-Punk music, I was more into music that sounded kind of different. I liked Joy Division and I can clearly recall myself and Julian Jones, who at the time I was trying to form a group with, being very keen on 'Metal Box' by P.I.L."

Michael Day ... "The Sheffield Scene was great for someone like me, always a different band to see every night and you could rely on a decent crowd as all the bands appeared to support each other, and I think we must have passed the same few pounds around for years! Local bands I really enjoyed: Cabaret Voltaire whom I saw at NOWSOC which was mostly a bunch of pretentious jackasses, but this put the Cabs in my heart forever."

Duncan Payne ..."Ah yes; the local music scene. You see, there was something happening at Sheffield at that time that I had hitherto been blissfully unaware of. But now, with my new found open mindedness to music, and with my new friend Dave to guide me I was ready for a whole new world.

My dabblings in the local scene lasted only for about 18 months and I was a bit of a part-timer at it, forever being tempted back by Detroit 45s, but at least I got to see something that was a little bit special. My premier focus of attention between early 1981 and the summer of 82 was New Model Soldier (who to be different inserted an umlaut above the M). They were Dave Kerley's band, Parsons Cross' finest. They played all the main venues in Sheffield, most notably the Hallamshire, the Royal, George IV and the Leadmill and through Kerley I got to see the likes of Artery, The Mirror Crack'd, Mark Mywurdz, Chakk and, of course, Pulp - who actually supported NMS on several occasions.

Jarvis Cocker and Dave Kerley were not exactly greatest mates but they had a healthy respect for each other's music. Indeed, it seemed that all the bands on the scene took an interest in each other regardless of musical differences. 'Cocker' would often be seen at a New Model Soldier gig when not supporting them and also at the shop. My impressions of Cocker and his group were that they would have little hope of success despite them getting played on 'John Peel'. Indeed, to a degree I was right because, Cocker apart, the Pulp line-ups had broken up and regenerated numerous times before they made it big. Cocker, however, was articulate and highly intelligent but remarkably shy for a 'front man', yet his vulnerability and humour made him a huge hit with the female members of staff at the shop.

By this time, the world had gone crazy over the Human League and maybe Oakey himself believed the hype. I saw them play the Lyceum at the height of 'Dare'-mania but I always preferred their earlier material, particularly the 'Reproduction' album. Dave Kurley was more biting with his observation of the Human League; The Human Leg? Only good for standing on....'

Kurley, like Oakey, had an ego and he was likeable with it. He had warmth and great humour. But although humour often transcended into his lyrics it was generally of the dark variety. Kerley had a love of Python but he also adored Stephen King and Steven

Spielberg. As a result he did not so much as write songs as put stories to music and given his influences, horror and fantasy were well to the fore.

Night moves

TONIGHT
The Stranglers/Taxi Girl — Lyceum, Tudor Way, Sheffield.
Clint Eastwood-General Saint — Sheffield University.
Vic Goddard and the Subway Sect — Retford Porterhouse.

SUNDAY
Injectors/Debar/Society's Victims — George IV, Infirmary Road, Sheffield.

MONDAY
Orchestral Manoeuvres in the Dark/Random Hold — Sheffield City Hall.
Blue Orchids/Tsi Tsa — Marples, Fitzalan Square, Sheffield.
New Model Soldier/Blim — Hallamshire, West Street, Sheffield.
Flying Alphonso Brothers/Mugshots — Maze, Bar 2, Sheffield University.

TUESDAY
The Slits (cancelled) — Lyceum.
Vice Squad/Chron Gen — Marples.
Vital/Mark Mywords — Sheffield Polytechnic (Totley site).

WEDNESDAY
John Holt — Top Rank Suite, Sheffield.
Hot Gossip — Lyceum.
Red Zoo/Mirror Crack'd — Royal, Abbeydale Road, Sheffield.
Gordon Beck/Alan Holdsworth 4 — George IV.
Black Mariah — Rebels Nightclub, Dixon lane, Sheffield.

THURSDAY
They Must Be Russians — Marples.
TV21/Animal Magnet — Limit Club, West Street, Sheffield.
Mirror Crack'd — Big Tree, Chesterfield Road, Woodseats, Sheffield.
Department S — Sheffield University.
Renegade — Penguin, Mason Lathes Road, Shiregreen, Sheffield.
Eta School — Hallamshire.
Mr. Sloane (formerly Ketham Island) — Red Lion, Heeley, Sheffield.
Stax — Rebels Nightclub.
Mugshots — Travellers Rest, Main Street, Rotherham.

FRIDAY
Eurythmics — Sheffield Polytechnic.
Wager/Vena Cava — Rotherham Arts Centre.
Fallen Angel — Clifton Hall, Rotherham.
Maximum Joy/The Balloons — Retford Porterhouse.

New Model Soldier were a three piece and, probably unique at the time, as they did not have a drummer. The rhythm came from the guitar, bass and keyboards. If I remember rightly the other guys were called Paul and Miggsy, with Paul doubling up on keyboards and guitar. The sound they created was sometimes mournful, frequently sinister yet always fresh. Two of my favourite tunes 'Foster Kenzie' (A little knowledge is a dangerous thing, Foster Kenzie is a dangerous man) and 'An Air of Resentment' (An air of resentment hangs around, Waiting to be breathed, No cooperation clogs my lungs, No express relief) were typical of NMS at their best and were frequently played in their sets. Both songs appeared on a four-track EP released in July 1981 which was financed by the trio. Sadly, they were ripped off and the sound quality was dreadful, pressed as it was onto recycled vinyl. A truer way to appreciate NMS was to catch them live. Watching Kerley on stage was intriguing. Statuesque whilst singing he would transform into a whirling dervish during instrumental passages, something which added to the whole nightmarish atmosphere of surrealism, horror and fantasy. The crowd, seemingly made up of Goths, ex Punks and art students, would generally chill appreciatively. Far too uncool to cheer or applaud, they registered their approval by returning time and again to see the band perform."

Meanwhile over at the Limit club...

Michael Day ... "Vice Versa's Steve Singleton was always in the limit with his weird little dance moves that kind of looked like Ian Curtis pogoing and he would shake the blond hair while dancing to the most obscure Talking heads song he could get Paul to play, his brother Simon was also a limit regular. Paul Unwin (the DJ) at the Limit was good enough to support the local talent and Clock DVA's '4 hours' was a regular song as was 'Nag Nag Nag' by the Cabs (I believe he even played 'Western Mantra' on a particularly slow night which was about a 25 minute pre-trance type record – it wasn't well received by the townies!). The Human League were also represented with 'Being boiled' and 'Circus of death' getting plenty of action although the later stuff was a little too poppy for the Limit."

While the Limit Club and the other live music and Disco filled habitats of Sheffield's West Street and its neighbouring junctures, were entertaining the young drinkers, Electro fans and hip scenesters, the time was approaching for Sheffield to be noticed as a place where *'things are happening'*.

Duncan Payne … "By this point the national music press had caught onto the exploding Sheffield scene and New Musical Express caught up with Kerley and gave NMS a rave write up. It was only later that it transpired that the whole thing had been a mistake and that the journalist should have been interviewing Bradford newcomers 'New Model Army'. Obviously they didn't know the difference down south between Bradford and Sheffield. After all they are only 45 miles apart. And as far as Kerley was concerned it was good publicity and to my mind it was well deserved.

With Sheffield becoming *the* place for music Bath University staged a gig showcasing some of Sheffield's top underground acts early in 1982. New Model Soldier was one of the headline acts, along with Pulp. Yet this was about as good as it got for Kerley and the band. I caught them at what turned out to be their final gig, at the Leadmill a few months later. By now elements of percussion had been added to their sound, something which seemed to detract from the essence of NMS. But apart from that, Kerley seemed to be on a downer at the time, probably frustrated at the lack of any tangible success coming his way. He would never have sold out but he felt that the band deserved greater recognition for their talents.

I first became acutely aware of his growing frustration and desire to rebel a few months earlier. Working in the ultra conservative environment which so cramped his style he virtually signed his own letter of resignation by bleaching his naturally brown hair and dyeing his fringe bright pink. The result of this was that the shop manager banished him to work in the stockroom and promised to make his life as difficult as possible. Kerley saw the funny side of riling the boss so, but the novelty soon wore off and he left his job after a few months.

There was something clearly not right between the members of the band that night at the Leadmill. The set was cut short and Kerley stormed off to the dressing room, resurfacing later to tell anyone who wanted to listen that the band was finished. Few did listen. The fact was that although people who saw NMS play appreciated what they did they were hardly going to mourn the passing of one group when there was so much diversity and talent to be seen in the city almost every day of the week.

I did not see Dave Kerley at all after he left his job. That is until about six years later when I bumped into him outside a bookstore on Barkers Pool. Exchanging pleasantries I asked him what he was doing at the time. *'I'm thinking of becoming an actor,'* he replied; Once a performer always a performer. But I've never heard of his whereabouts since."

The Post-Punk period had a wealth of venues to put gigs on, but apart from the dreary City Hall, there was nowhere big enough to put on the groups who had played the live circuit for so long. The Top Rank gigs were becoming fewer as the decade wore on, but in 1981 the Lyceum venue – which had previously been a theatre and nowadays has reverted back to one – was re-opened. Many of the breaking bands of the Post-Punk era played there, including a slightly struggling U2 (whose biggest rivals at the time were Sheffield's very own Comsat Angels), Simple Minds, Orange Juice, Bow Wow Wow etc.

346

This period saw Sheffield become one of the countrys most respected cities for homegrown musical talent. Human League's 'Dare' and its number one single 'Don't you want me' had helped to put the city on the musical map and then there was the enormous success of ABC and their 'Lexicon of Love' LP.

Sheffield's very own Cabaret Voltaire had been around from well before, and during the whole Punk explosion, performing their version of what Punk should sound like with the singles 'Do the Mussolini head kick' and 'Nag Nag Nag', and now they were at the forefront of the City's music scene.

Tony … "In January 1981 I went to see Cabaret Voltaire play with The Fall at Sheffield University. They were interesting to say the very least with their slide shows and all those strange sounds they produced. Can't say that it converted me as such, but I always kept an eye upon what they were doing from then on – buying some of their LP's along the way. I could see that there was much more to them than the couple of singles I had of them: the 'Nag Nag Nag' single and 'Silent Command' e.p. I went to see them a couple more times that year, one of the dates was at the Sheffield Polytechnic and it was one of those free ones. The main group from Sheffield that I went to see were Artery; there was a period in 1981 when I went to see them play a lot. They kind of filled the gap left by Punk for a while."

Above: Artery's Simon Hinkler at the Limit, a Pulp sharing Marples gig flyer and Mick Fidler at Rotherham Arts Centre (Simon Hinkler)

Artery were formed from the ashes of Sheffield Punk band 'The' and were led by charismatic lead singer Mark Gouldthorpe with Neil McKenzie on bass guitar, Mick Fidler on guitar and saxophone, Gary Wilson Drums and Simon Hinkler on keyboards, piano and guitar. They played gigs extensively around Sheffield and the area at venues such as the Broadfield and The Marples, and ventured further afield with gigs in London and eventually playing their own nationwide full tour dates.

Shifts of line up occurred, but Artery soldiered on and proved to be one of the most inventive – certainly amongst the most intense – of all the Sheffield Post-Punk bands of the early 80's. Their group history includes being attacked by Hell's angels (who took a dislike to Mick Fidler wearing a dress), singer Mark Gouldthorpe climbing out of the

Marples window and onto the outside ledge and playing Deep Purple's 'Smoke on the Water' to a disinterested Rotherham Clifton Hall crowd. Future Pulp star Jarvis Cocker was a regular attendee at their gigs as was most of the Sheffield scene itself. Artery did transform their songs to vinyl with a clutch of singles and LP's, but they were best experienced live. Unfortunately, their train never truly stopped at the station and their final gig was played at the Leadmill in 1985, though uniquely Mick Fidler sang while Mark Gouldthorpe observed from the audience.

Artery are now back, alive and well and performing again on a irregular basis and sound as fresh and exciting as they ever did; evoking the Post-Punk sound for a new and old generation of Sheffield music fans. Going back to the very start of the 1980's Simon Hinkler recalls his first performance with the band.

Simon Hinkler of Artery ... "The Rotherham Arts Centre show was my first ever Artery gig. I had joined a week or so earlier, so there had not been many rehearsals, and I only played on a handful of songs on the night. At the time, there was a sense of the band shifting up a gear. They'd had their first single out, and the Sheffield compilation album 'Bouquet of Steel' was just being released, with Artery's 'The Slide' as the opening track. I think for these reasons, it was decided to record the 'Rotherham Arts Centre' show, particularly in order to capture some of the older songs which the band would probably never be playing again."

Tony ... "I saw Artery play loads of times. At places like the Poly, University and the Marples. They usually delivered a great performance and after seeing them I would encourage some of my mates to go to the next gig as well. I went to that one where the singer Mark Gouldthorpe climbed onto the ledge outside of the venue looking down over Fitzalen square. I was not quite sure what was going on, but then that was usually the case with Artery. Their gigs were quite intense. I can remember one of their gigs at Sheffield Poly and they started playing some new songs, which didn't go down very well. The group got quite pissed off.; but when they played some of their better-known songs like 'Unbalanced' and 'Toy Town' the audience geared up. Singer Mark Goldthorpe announced during the encore *'if this doesn't make you dance, nothing will'*."

Simon Hinkler ... "I remember the hall at Rotherham Arts centre was not full, and much of the audience were sitting on the banks of seats at the back of the hall, with some people on the floor in front. I remember being very nervous, sitting on a lone chair at the side of the stage, waiting to make my first appearance with the band.

There were so many great Artery gigs, but unfortunately, the Rotherham Arts centre was not one of them. I suppose there was a degree of nervousness among the band about the show being recorded (by the input Studio chaps) but also the audiences in the smaller towns and cities outside of Sheffield were always more reserved. I only recall playing in Rotherham twice – the other time was in one of those 'upstairs in a pub venues'. I forget the name. Oh and that night I was hanging out with an Icelandic guy called Einar who was a big Artery fan. He later went on to be in The Sugarcubes... (Yes The Sugarcubes were definitely influenced by Artery)."

Formed in November 1981 from the ashes of Sheffield bands Scarborough Antelopes and Short Circuit, TSI-TSA were another local set of talented musicians who gigged just about every venue in the area, and although receiving record company interest, never achieved the recognition and rewards that should have been due to them. The original line up was Robert 'Dingo' Dowling on vocals and rhythm guitar, Michael 'Daisy' Day on Vocals, Jonathon Wills on bass, Mick Hercun on guitar and drummer Mark Whitham.

Sharing a rehearsal room with fellow Sheffield band the Negatives and enjoying a hectic social life of nights at the Limit club and every other bar between West Street's Hallamshire Hotel and the Saddle, TSI-TSA certainly knew how to have a great time and make some pretty accomplished music along with it. Songs like 'Billinghams Island', 'Feeling like a whisper', 'Swimming' and 'Mobilization'(an old Scarborough Antelopes cover) showed influences of U2, Echo and the Bunnymen, Sheffield's own Comsat Angels and a love of the Clash, Buzzcocks and Talking Heads (They often covered 'Psycho Killer).

Michael Day ... "Dingo's flair for writing was immediately evident and he sounded much more art school than his roots over at Gleadless Valley, and so the clever, sometimes pretentious lyrics flowed easily."

Even so, TSI-TSA never took themselves more seriously than the nightlife and fun that supported their music's existence. They left a legacy of first-rate songs that still resonate today,

Above: Rob 'Dingo' Dowling and Michael Day (TSI-TSA)

capturing a period in Sheffield's music scene, when its Punk inspired generation took it upon themselves to pick up instruments, write some great songs and enjoy their 15 minutes of fame.

Sheffield's Limit Club in the early 80's was a social 'must be there' for many of the local music fans (and musicians), but the place was always unpredictable and throughout its history, from the Punk days right up to its closure, violence and crime was frequently a part of the occasion; though generally most of it was not maliciously intended (football rivalry aside).

Michael Day ... "Many fights obviously involved young ladies and the concept that if you had danced near one of them, they were close to being your girlfriend and this inevitably led to hurt feelings, a few more pints and then punching the successful suitor. I suspect that a lot of the girls at the Limit knew they could provoke this kind of reaction and some must have got off on it.

Night moves

SATURDAY
The Flying Bears/Empty Bed Blues Band . . . Chaucer School, Parson Cross, Sheffield.
The Bootleg Beatles . . . Retford Porterhous.
Shiva . . . Brimington Tavern, Chesterfield.

SUNDAY
Insight/The Ya-Yas . . . Hallamshire Hotel, West Street, Sheffield.
Satanic Rites . . . George IV, Infirmary Road, Sheffield.
The Battlefield Band . . . Rotherham Arts Centre.
Paul and Chris Stockton . . . Highcliffe Folk Club, Greystones Road, Sheffield.
Badger in the Bag . . . Red Lion Folk Club, High Street, Wath.

MONDAY
The Mirror Crack'd/Mark Miwurdx . . . The Maze, Bar 2, Sheffield University.
Alyx . . . The Penguin, Mason Lathe Road, Shiregreen, Sheffield.
Child's Play . . . Creswell Social Centre.
Kirlian Lens . . . Coach and Horses, Doncaster.
Paul Metters . . . Nailmakers Arms Folk Club, Backmoor Road, Norton, Sheffield.

TUESDAY
Freddie McGregor . . . Sheffield City Hall (cancelled).
Spiral Vision/Tsi-Tsa . . . The Limit Club, West Street, Sheffield.
The Mix . . . The Mill, Halfway, Sheffield.
Pencil Stripes . . . The Bluebell, Hackenthorpe, Sheffield.

WEDNESDAY
The Process/Bass-Tone-Trap . . . Sheffield Polytechnic.
Blue Rondo a la Turk . . . Romeo's and Juliet's, Bank Street, Sheffield.
Mrs Beech . . . The Royal, Abbeydale Road, Sheffield.
Chude and the Crimson Flame/Workshop . . . Norfolk Comprehensive School, Sheffield.

THURSDAY
Johnny Thunders . . . The Limit Club.
Haze . . . The Penguin, Sheffield.
The Mix . . . Red Lion, Heeley, Sheffield.
Yellow Lines . . . Hallamshire Hotel.
Phoenix Rising . . . George IV.

I myself managed to date a few girls from there (date being a pretty loose term) and even managed to close the deal a few times. One particular night I had taken my treasured Ford Escort and parked it in the elevated parking lot near the City Hall.

Leaving with my young lady du jour, I intended to impress her with a ride home followed by a few minutes action on her parents couch. Sadly, when I reached my car, someone was sitting in it with the engine running and as I approached the door, he floored the accelerator propelling the car through the fence, dropping about 6 feet to the rear of the City Hall and then smashed it into the back of the City Hall building, jumped out and ran off. One look at the ford escort shaped rust imprint below the broken fence told me all I needed to know about the state of the car and sure enough the sub frame was cracked. I took my date home in a tow truck which did not score any points in the getting laid department."

There would also be incidents that really could have only happened at the Limit Club, and although not ethically or morally correct to laugh at; all the same this story of Michael Day's is hilarious if imagined in the context of the times and the inebriation involved.

Michael Day ... "Another funny or not story involved an evening when a young guy in a wheelchair came to the Limit – it wasn't exactly wheelchair accessible so the bouncers carried him down the steps. He was wearing a John Travolta type white suit and promptly started drinking and spinning his wheelchair on the dance floor. Lots of girls gave him the sympathy dance and he looked to be doing all right until one of the Limit's famous fights broke out. He was caught in the midst of a huge brawl and the girls had disappeared leaving him to the luck of the draw. As one big lad lost his balance, the wheelchair bound chap was tipped out of his chair and onto the dance floor where he proceeded to skilfully dodge the flying boots

and blows. When the fight cleared however, he was left like a fish out of water struggling to get back in his wheelchair, his white suit was now the colour of the Limit dance floor – black, and none of the girls would go near him as he had a Limit odour about him and was filthy. Looking back it wasn't funny but it was a surreal moment and not surprisingly that young man was never seen in the Limit again."

350

Andrea Berry ... "There was something about the Stella in The Limit Club too. It made you drunk much faster than anywhere else but it wasn't a normal kind of drunk, I'm sure they put chemical alcohol in brown carbonated water!"

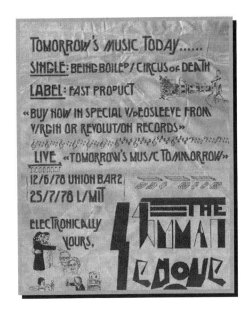

Phillip Wright ... "The Limit always played great music and was where I spent every Saturday night from 1978 to about 1983. In 1981, I met my wife to be in there, I had seen her and her friends on West Street before and we had sort of smiled at each other a few times, she also was a big Jam fan like me and liked Punk/new wave music.

I had gone from wearing a leather bike jacket in my early Punk days to wearing a Mod suit, and then just normal stuff, and always used to hang around the stage area with my mates. I remember Mick McLean on the door, and Andy Dunraven and Louis, plus some lad called Ivan and a really evil looking bloke called (I think) Mick Cricher who ended up in prison for manslaughter.

The main thing was, of course, the music, and even today, if I hear a certain record I will think to myself 'Limit record'. These would include 'I Got you' by Split Enz, 'Tainted Love' by Soft Cell, 'About the Weather' by Magazine, 'Transmission' by Joy Division, 'Furniture Music' by Red Noise, 'Life In Tokyo' by Japan, 'Boys Cry' by Original Mirrors, 'Into the Valley' by the Skids, anything by the Jam. The DJ (Paul 'Legs' Unwin) used to play 'Sunday Papers' by Joe Jackson and say into the microphone *'if this isn't number one next week I want to know why'.* he said it every week but it never got to number one! But the one record that above all others, to me, is The Limit record of all time is 'Quiet Life' by Japan. I only have to hear the opening keyboards and I am once again back in the sweaty, dark, but totally fantastic, Limit Club!!!!"

The Limit did however; start to lose its charm and appeal during its later days.

Andrea Berry ... "Towards the end the Limit went down hill completely. It might have always lacked in the decor department but it had a relaxed atmosphere, then all of a sudden, it was full of violence and became an unsafe place to go - unless you wanted someone to stick a broken bottle in your face. I think the fights were the main reason it closed down, they couldn't run a business with only a handful of customers who wanted to kill each other!"

Phillip Wright ... "When the Barracudas played, they got an encore then tried to get back on stage but for some reason the bouncers had heard enough and wouldn't let them!"

Seventies Punks like Richard Chatterton, who had always been fond of the left field of the Punk movement, were now conjuring up their enthusiasm for the Steel city's Post-Punk music.

Above: Barracudas at the Limit (Courtesy of Sheffield History site)

Richard Chatterton ... "I was always in awe of people who I met who were in bands. I was close friends with Vena Cava (later 'St Christopher'), who I met at Rotherham Arts Centre. They went on to get record of the week from Martin Lilleker in the Sheffield Star.

This was no mean feat as at that time Sheffield's electronic music age was at its peak, with The Human League, Cabaret Voltaire, ABC, Heaven 17 and the Comsat Angels all making the steel city proud. St Christopher never made the big time but I still have all of their records. Recently I saw Dave Kerley, who I had not seen for 25 years or more. He had fronted New Model Soldier who had supported St Christopher and I was excited to tell him that I still had his single: although I can't play it, as I no longer have a record player. '*Oh you were my hero back then*' I told him; '*And still are.*"

As much as the wide-ranging scope of Post-Punk was an influence in the formation of Sheffield bands, the younger teenagers who had been challenged by the Punk ideal still wanted to achieve their aims with something less intricate than the intellectually expected style of early 80's Post-Punk idealism. Yes, Punk as a musical form may have ultimately disappointed a lot of this generation, but that did not stop them from wanting to have a bash at it themselves.

Tony ... "I had been writing lyrics for some time - from way back in the middle of Punk. Most of them were very naïve to say the least, lots of angry rants against the system etc. In 1978, I made my first attempt at a 'New Wave' group. We were called The Autos - what a crap name - and there was me and a couple of mates with kids' guitars and a bontempi organ: fucking atrocious. Our first song was called 'The Tramps' (remember that one Andy?). Then a few years later came the next stab at the idea including a line up that including Mark Barnet (also known as Barney Rubble and a host of other names including Stan) on bass guitar and a mate called Rick on drums. We named our band Voxx. We wrote all sorts of crap Punk stuff and would rehearse at the drummer's house for full weekends until one day I picked a bird up and when I took her back to his house he pulled a knife on me. That was the end of that bit of fun."

Paul White (Sugar) ... "I used to go to this pub called the Queens Hotel in Rawmarsh, and I can remember hearing this Punk band rehearsing upstairs."

Tony ... "Yes that was the next failed Punk group I had started up, which was called Terminal Daze. That was myself on guitar, Paul Clarke on bass and Dean Stables singing, and I think he also had a guitar as well...there was no drummer in that one. I was playing an old Woolworths guitar. We were trying to do versions of Clash songs from the Clash songbook that I had. Fortunately, we never recorded anything. I can remember Sugar coming up once to see what the racket was."

Above: Local Punks John Vernon and Phil Morley

The early 1980's had offered many flavours of music and choices of fashion, many having a direct link to the Punk explosion. To some of the local music fans it was a case of picking the best of what was available, which could mean diversity and quantity minus the excitement and immediacy of Punk Rock.

Tony ... "Around this time me and Julian Jones wrote a song called 'Rearrange'. I wrote the lyrics and he did the chords on my guitar. I sung it and we put it down on a cassette. It was about making a fresh start away from the confines of Punk. I still have the lyrics for that one and it sounded quite good all considering."

Julian Jones ... "Yeah, I remember that one... it was later on about 1981- 82 and by that time Punk was finished really. I was into lots of different types of music by then."

Dave Spencer ... "It was ironic that even though we didn't get into punk until 1978, we were then moaning about 'Johnny-come-lately's' in 1982. Ironic also that we were complaining about the narrow-mindedness of the punk crowd whilst being unable to see ourselves as being anything but a 'PUNK' band. In rehearsals we were coming up with better and better songs but we were getting so pissed off with the situation of the disappearing punk scene and the vacuous nonsense that replaced it that we started to turn on each other. Christ knows what we argued about, but after a while, that's all we seemed to do.

So we split up in November 1982...The Jam split up the next week...The Clash sacked Mick Jones in 1983 and basically it all ended there and then...The Damned lost Captain Sensible and turned professional then disappeared entirely. All the bands that we loved seemed to be fading away. It was like the beginning of a new 'dark age'. So everyone tried to find something to fill the void. Even though we were only together for a little over two years, we managed to get in the studio on half a dozen occasions and left a 'legacy'

of 17 tracks, which show how quickly we grew and how tragic it was that we packed it in just as we were beginning to really shine.

Graham Torr started a heavy metal band. I tried and failed to start a new band with a mish-mash of hardcore punks and 'not at all punks', which inevitably failed, before starting a band called The Filth and The Fury, with Dom and Simon out of the Cute Pubes. We were basically Cute Pubes-lite. Dominic and I also started an acoustic band, which came to nothing. Eventually, Dom and I went our separate ways and in 1985, I started a band called Springheel'd Jack.

Apparently, there had been at least one band before us who were called Springheeld'd Jack and I can think of two that came after us.

Right: 70's Punk Richard - Chatterton during the early 80's

We were the Rotherham-based band who were together from 1985 to 1992. I had started to get into Buffalo Springfield and the Loving Spoonful and wanted to play something a bit different, but with my own unavoidable punky-edge. This is what I tried to do with Springheel'd Jack. Unfortunately, none of my band mates had heard of Buffalo Springfield or the Loving Spoonful or any of the other stuff I was forcing down their necks and in retrospect, I was trying to knock square pegs into holes. I used to say that our sound was Crosby, Stills and Clash. In my dreams."

Tony … "1981- 1982 - I was still going to lots of gigs. Killing Joke, The Cure, Pulp, Spizz Energi, The Fall, Big Country, London Cowboys (Ex Pistol/Rich Kid Glen Matlock's much-ignored group). I managed to have a brief chat with Glen 'a real Sex Pistol' at the bar before their set - and many others. I used to like Orange Juice and Aztec Camera and the Smiths (who I was a big fan of in their early days). They were all really talented from the start, but the way they were held up as the 'New Brightest Hope for Pop' was just plain stupid to say the least. I stopped even reading most of the music weeklies for a while. They were just a load of Bollocks really."

Above: A self-designed promo ad for 'Voxx' and myself (1982)

But there were still groups that were only a few steps removed from Punk that still managed to excite some Punks.

David McKendry …"The Cramps at the Limit club - crazy! Lux with a microphone stuck down his throat! And a large area of ceiling tiles brought down around the stage area! Christ they were loud, only time I have ever winced in pain, had to resort to sticking toilet paper in my ears."

And the few pioneers left from the class of 76 were still doing the rounds, in this instance managing to excite and overwhelm an overjoyed fan.

Gill Frost … "I had moved my attentions to Siouxsie and the Banshees. God, I adored that band and still love Siouxsie Sioux to this day. I couldn't control myself when I got tickets to see them play at Sheffield City Hall; I was in my first year at sixth form college, so it must have been about 1985 or 86 and, as usual, I went with my big brother. That concert stands out as one of the best I have ever seen and it was the first time I experienced getting all-emotional at seeing a band play live. Siouxsie gave it her absolute all and, during the encore, she was on her hands and knees, crawling around on stage, as though she hadn't got an ounce of strength left in her. Embarrassing as it is, I had tears running down my face. When we got outside afterwards, my big, six feet five brother turned to me and asked if I'd felt funny during the gig. When I asked what he meant, he confessed that he'd felt at the end as if he wanted to cry. Ha! It wasn't just me then."

There was also a new Glam style that was mixed into a recipe of Punk, Metal, Pop and good old fashioned Rock n' Roll. The step sideways to check it out was not uncommon.

**Above; Lords of the New Church playing at Sheffield Leadmill
Photos taken by me**

Paul Clarke ... "Lords of the New Church (Punk super group with Brian James of The Damned, Stiv Bators of Dead Boys, Kermit from Sham 69 and the drummer out of The Barracudas), well, they were on the tube and I thought they were the best band ever. They were my band. Tony painted me their first album cover on the back of my leather jacket. I thought it was superb, a real one off. I loved it."

Tony ... "We saw Lords of the New Church at the Limit club early on and then the Leadmill. For a while they seemed like the last great hope for Punk and Rock n' Roll, but like much of the music I was into around that time, I became bored of them, even selling all of their records as well. We also went to see Hanoi Rocks quite early on in their career

356

at Sheffield Dingwalls. Not usually my cup of tea at all, but I had bought their 'Oriental Beat' LP and surprisingly I enjoyed it. So off we went to see them and it was a cracking night. The drummer was Razzle and he died not long after. I think it was in a car crash? I think Barney was with our lot that night. Me and Barney used to go round and nick people's pints when they weren't looking."

Whilst some local Punks chose to relieve their boredom by various means of escapism and embrace the misinterpreted 'No Future' slogan of the Pistols from a few years previously, one local Punk inspired Punk girl decided to get up and do something. She decided to open up her own clothes shop... you could call it Punk enterprise!

NEW LINE IN OLD FASHIONS

OUT-OF-WORK school leaver Fiona Palmer, aged 17, was fed up sitting around with nothing to do, so she decided to start up in business.

Now her fashion shop, selling secondhand Forties to Sixties clothing is booming and is a mecca for trendy youngsters.

Fiona, of Bawtry Road, Brinsworth, Rotherham, buys her clothing from fleamarkets and jumble sales for selling at her shmp in Kimberworth Road.

Said Fiona: "I had been out of work a year and was fed up of having nothing to do.

"The shop has really caught on. There is a terrific interest. Unemployed youngsters and students are among my main customers.

"What they particularly look for are flared dresses and skirts from the Sixties and stiletto-heeled shoes."

Fiona at her secondhand clothing shop.

Fiona Palmer in her newly-opened shop on Kimberworth Road, selling clothes from the 50's and 60's. F.4613P.

Fashion shop with a difference

Above: Fiona Palmer and her clothes shop venture

Rotherham Punkette Fiona Palmer (who also sang on the Siouxsie-esque track 'Dream world' for a one-day only studio venture with Cute Pubes members) now grabbed the spirit of Positive-Punk and began to cater for the alternative fashions that were now appealing to a wider scope of Post-Punk era teenagers. Kids who had just left school or college and wanted to simply look different. Her shop in Kimberworth near Rotherham mainly catered for unemployed Punks, futurists and sixties-obsessed kids looking for an alternative to the high street shops of the nearby towns and Sheffield city centre.

Buying her stock from local flea markets and jumble sales, Fiona also kitted out local groups such as Cute Pubes along with the more tuned-in students of the area. Punk idealism still thrived in the region in 1982 after all...Whilst bargain-hunting Punks and their many offspring cults were checking out Fiona's clothes emporium, the lure of the continent was on the cards for one lot of local Punks...

In May 1982, a trip to Calais (courtesy of Rotherham Arts College) was made by a bunch of local Punks and New Romantics. Local Punks June Graham, Joanne Frost (Debar guitarist), Pete Jackson, Lynne Haythorne, Rizard!, Paul Maiden and Julie Lee – displaying an assortment of various multi coloured hair styles – travelled there by ferry, along with New Romantic group 'Vision' members Andrew Beaumont and Gary Gillott; himself more of a Punk at heart than New Romantic.

Lynne Haythorne … "The trip to Calais was organised through RCAT, unsure of the purpose, however for us it was alcohol and humour filled. We visited Soho on the way and struck up a deal with bouncers to enter a sex shop and view a film. We didn't generate that much attention in London as (anything goes I suppose). However, the ferry to and around Calais was a different matter. People stared and appeared intimidated as we commenced drinking at 8am and we became louder and more boisterous.

Rotherham Punks take a trip to Soho in London... Left to right June Graham, Joanne Frost, Lynne Haythorne, Richard and Paul Maiden

- Getting off the ferry, we jumped at the chance to spend the afternoon in the Stella houses. The rest is a blur."

Gary Gillott (Chippie) … "Andrew Beaumont I think was the main one who got it organised for us. The first thing that we did when we got over there was go straight to this Stella bar that was just out of port. It was full of English people in there and we got the kind of *'Oh here come the punky types'* sort of look and attitude from them. So we all got sloshed in this little bar. That's probably why I can't remember much more I suppose."

Some Rotherham Punk and Post-Punk fans would move away and find the Punk ideology still intact in other parts of the country.

Richard Chatterton … "In 1982 I moved to Sunderland for three years, where I studied Fine Art and continued to see great bands, hanging around with like minded art students and local Punks. Inspired by the fanzine created by my still close friend Russell Dunbar called 'Acts of Defiance', I Xeroxed my own entitled 'Wonder Stories' which ran for just two issues. I did manage to interview Pulp, Richard Hell (twice), Icicle Works, Flesh for Lulu and Brigandage (the latter being part of the ill – fated 'Positive-Punk' movement). Sunderland became another of my retreats and I got to know a few local mackems – Russ's brother Mike, Alf (who sadly recently died), John, Raf, Hud, and John Collinson Paul (then Thomma), Gerry, Jim Tate. I saw gigs and went to clubs in Newcastle and Sunderland, the best being 'The Drum Club' in Sunderland and 'The Bunker' a co-operative venue set up by some of my friends which printed fanzines, had its own rehearsal space and was a place for local bands to play. The venue still exists today."

Above: Rotherham Post – Punkers with the odd New Romantic on a 'Calais' Punk generation export trip.

Original 1st and 2nd generation Punk Rockers of the locality were now either coming to the end of their particular journey's across the musical map and hanging up their bondage strides -

Bryan Bell ... "The very last gig I ever went to was The Cocteau Twins at the City Hall about 1983."

Tony ... "The last Punk gig of the original era I went to was, I think, the Damned at Sheffield Dingwalls. I can't remember going to any more at all after that."

- Or were being drawn towards other musical pastures! There was plenty of spin off cult scenes and genres to emerge from the ashes of Punk back in the early to mid 80's; one of which would, in later years, become instantly recognisable in its style of dress and focus on all things dark – Goth.

Andy Morton ... "There was a period after Punk that I kind of got into the Goth thing, going to see Sisters of Mercy, Fields of the Nephilm, The Mission etc."

Goth started as a kind of hybrid of various aspects of the Punk and Post-Punk style, fashion and music. Originally, almost an actual subsidiary of Punk itself, where Punks had moved away from the traditional Punk fare and succumbed to the darker sounds and look of groups such as Siouxsie and the Banshees, UK Decay, Bauhaus and The Cure. Soon though, the Goth clans would develop their own style and scene after attaching themselves - to an assortment of different groups.

By 1985, Goths were a mix of ex Punks, disgruntled New Romantics, and bored students and even on very rare occasions, fans of the latter day Mod scene. Goth aside, some Punk fans would continue to spread their musical wings into other genres but still keep taking a peek at the Punk scene's last gunslingers in town.

Andrew Morton ... "After my brief flirtation with Goth, I continued going to gigs (and do to this day). I saw The Ramones quite a few times as well as 999 – who I saw at a Punk festival with the Lurkers and Sham 69. I also went to see The Mission, P.I.L and lots more gigs. I went to see Joe Strummer each time that he played Sheffield and also Mick Jones in Big Audio Dynamite; including one of their early gigs at the Leadmill."

Gill Frost ... "The last time I saw the Damned was with my husband, my sister and her partner. They were still writing new material, so played old and new songs but it was great, as always. After the concert, I got Captain Sensible's autograph, while my husband went over to Dave Vanian to get his. It's worth mentioning that Dave Vanian was across the road sitting in a car at the time, while his heavily pregnant other half, who was also in the band, was outside the vehicle throwing up. I'm not sure I'd have had the guts to approach them at such a 'delicate' time, but my hubby came up trumps, coming back with a long-awaited autograph."

Tony ... "I saw Bauhaus at Sheffield Top Rank in 1983 and it was one of the worst gigs I ever saw. I was absolutely bored out of my head. I was certainly no fan of Goth that's for sure; the last Siouxsie record I bought was 'Spellbound' in 1981."

Dave Spencer … "Killing Joke were a big deal for us. They were taking the punk energy in new directions and were fantastic live, with Jaz Coleman being one of the best front men ever - frighteningly charismatic. We saw them at the Lyceum and the Leadmill."

The early 1980's continued to see the local Punk generation take many different paths. Whilst a few still attended the Punk gigs that were by now quite thin on the ground in Sheffield, others would take a step sideways and draw inspiration from the Positive-Punk groups that were coming through during 1982. Brigandage, Sisters of Mercy and Theatre of Hate along with Southern Death Cult being some of the groups that were being tagged with this new alternative to the No Future concept of contemporary 1980's Punk. This was Positive-Punk during a less than positive era!

Richard Chatterton … "We went down South to see the Danse Society. I went with Simon from Penistone. There was a Barnsley entourage travelling down by coach. One guy organised a general knowledge quiz, which I thought was very un-Punk. We caught our first glimpse of Ian Astbury of Southern Death Cult - who were also playing - in a chippie before hand. The Barnsley crew stormed the floor when Danse Society took to the stage, which I thought was great. Nomad Punkess Aileen had said that she hated Danse Society's lead singer and then she cuddled him all the way home."

Above: Paul Clarke and me (1982)

Julian Jones … "After Punk I liked groups like P.I.L and the more progressive stuff. Then me and Gary started to listen to lots of sixties music and formed our first real group Alternative Route."

Gary Davies … "Through meeting my closest friend Julian Jones was forged a very turbulent yet exciting, and unknown to us at the time, a life-long friendship with music. What came out of that intrigue and youthful excitement was our very first band Alternative Route that we formed in 1980 – 81.

The line-up consisted of me as songwriter and guitarist, Julian Jones songwriter and drums, Andrew 'Pretty Boy' Pashley lead vocals and last but not least the diminutive and priceless entity of John Atkin on Bass. Our influences were an eclectic mix ranging from well crafted songs of Burt Bacharach, The Beatles, the Stones and The Kinks through to 70,s rock bands in Deep Purple, Led Zeppelin and obviously the music of the current time to include Punk, Post-Punk and New Wave."

Alternative Route played, along with their own songs, covers of the Who, Kinks and other sixties groups songs. They were the first stepping-stone for Julian and Gary who between them moved onto a succession of Local groups (Turn the Key, Maxine and Lazy Dollies and others) before Julian finally settled upon becoming a solo recording artist. He is one of Sheffield's most talented and respected musicians. Fellow 'Route' member Gary Davies also continued with his love of music and song writing and performs to this day: playing gigs locally and nationally.

Gary Davies ... "Alternative Route, for me, was the most exciting time when everything was brand new and the naivety was still there with a fresh approach all of the time.

Whenever Julian and me get together, we often have a giggle about those times. Back then, we were really the babies of the contemporary music scene but we did manage to mix many of our influences with the sounds of Post-Punk in an attempt to create something new. This was the foundation for Alternative Route's sound which then provided the learning curve for many years to follow."

Shaun Angell ... "As the 80's progressed, I started getting into another craze that was enveloping the youth of the time... 'the football or Soccer casual' scene. Gone were the outrageous clothes to be replaced by a new sportier look. Music by the Jam, the Clash, Dexys Midnight-

Above: Gary Davies, Julian Jones & Nicky Booth

- Runners and Haircut 100 were the frequently played tunes. One era had ended, another had just begun."

John Harrison ... "I just wanted to play in my own band. The Punks had paved the way and I wanted my own shot at it."

Many former local Punks had long since discarded their bondage trousers for the New Romantic look whilst others were riding the parallel style of Futurism. Some tried to keep the street ethos of Punk alive by going for the sounds of the new Punk movement with skinhead favoured Oi! music and fashion. However, a considerable other element had been taking a step backwards to the mid 1960's for new inspiration. The Mod Revival came and went, taking its fashion victims along with it, but the real Mods never went away.

Chapter Eighteen

The New Mods

"Yes, I am a Mod and I was at Margate. I'm not ashamed of it – I wasn't the only one. I joined in a few of the fights. It was a laugh. I haven't enjoyed myself so much in a long time. It was great – the beach was like a battlefield. It was like we were taking over the country" - **From the rear sleeve of 'White Riot' single by The Clash.**

Phillip Wright ... "As the Punk scene started to become much more mainstream, and more of a fashion, me and my mates switched to wearing suits and ties like The Jam."

Above: Sheffield Mod Darren Gray on his 1965 'Lambretta 150' in 1979

The Sixties Mod scene in Sheffield and Rotherham had been a short-lived but memorable experience with an extremely healthy dose of quality live music provided by the many top class acts and groups that played at 'The Mojo' club in Sheffield – Small Faces, Ike and Tina Turner, The Who, Georgie Fame and the Blue Flames, Inez and Charlie Foxx, Spencer Davis group etc, as well as the occasional home grown Soul group.

The other main clubs were the 'Esquire' (now the Leadmill) and The Black Cat club but many others existed throughout the decade. Rotherham too had its own venue for the Mod acts to play. Simply named The Mod club the venue hosted gigs from Joe Cocker, Them (with Van Morrison) and an early incarnation of David Bowie's Mod group the Mannish Boys.

The towns other Mod venue was The 21 Club situated on Moorgate and this managed to book, amongst others, Cliff Bennett and the Rebel Rousers.

Katrine from Rotherham was a Mod in the sixties and recalls some of her experiences of the local Mod scene of the time...

Katrine ... "I never intended to become a mod but the alternative was being a Rocker and not liking the clothes, music or motor bikes I didn't have much option. So progressing from Sunday night dancing at a venue which was above the Odeon on Corporation street, I started going to the Baths Hall on Sheffield Road, there I was fortunate to see many bands including 'Them' singing 'Here comes the night' and The Gaylords later to become Marmalade (not so great!).

Clifton Hall was always good, in my memory it was huge and took ages to walk round to see who was there, I went just before it was demolished and it seemed tiny! I frequented the LBJ club, which was somewhere near Masborough and this was always a popular event. The Assembly Rooms was also good. My favourite place though was the Pendulum, which was at the top of Moorgate. This was always a good night and the music I loved At this time I was working as a Saturday girl in Saxon shoes in Rotherham (THE place to get your shoes) so every Saturday morning I got there early to choose the shoes I would be purchasing for that night ! All my Saturday money went on this! All our coats were worn long (I still like this style now!) with often something very short underneath, famous words *you will catch your death in that*! I don't remember ever getting a taxi; you caught the last bus or walked. If you were lucky, some nice person with a scooter would take you home!"

The local Sixties Mod scene soon gave way to Flower Power and a gradual progression towards serious Rock followed by Prog-Rock, which is where we came into the story at the start of this book. The Seventies Mod scene, however, had sprung out of Punk and although very much influenced by the original Sixties version, would mould its own style and taste to the whole concept of Modernism. It would be a good few more years before the region saw a true resurgence of the original Mod style and outlook with its extreme attention to detail. The new Mod bands mostly used the same venues as their spiky haired uncles. In addition, many local ex Punks were amongst the many now turning to Mod for a scene of their own.

Punk itself had hardly even started when the very first inklings of a Mod Revival were to be seen. Apart from the regular scooter clubs, who had been around for years- some even dating back to the original 60's Mods, there were the school blazer and skinny tie wearing 'New Wave kids' who looked to The Jam and the streamlined/slim detailed side of the Punk look. Some of these Punk kids would gradually rid themselves of their safety pins and plastic trousers and keep their tennis shoes, suit jackets and straight legged jeans to develop a new look. They already had the haircut, just about (see Paul Weller and his variations on the short Mod cut that was very popular with many of the Punk kids), now they would become 'The New Mods'.

Tony ... "The real surprise for me was that I ended up going backwards to go forwards. I was sick of contemporary music and found myself falling in love with the whole sixties Mod thing. The Who, Small Faces, The Action, The Creation, The Kinks and others were a massive influence and in particular sixties black American R n' B and Soul. I had liked some aspects of the Mod Revival that was just coming to an end by then but I never completely endeared myself to it. Much of it was lazy and not really, that sharp. Even so I knew some very smartly dressed Mods who had been into it well before the 'Quadrophenia' hype."

Punk had been their initiation for many but there was also another influence on the Mod Revival which had itself been a direct descendant of the original Mod scene; Northern Soul.

Ian Brown (Stone Roses) ... "I used to go Northern Soul all-nighters in Rotherham and Doncaster. I was very into it, I was. All through the night till late in the morning."
(From 'Stone Roses' by John Robb)

In 1978, the NME had run a feature on the Northern Soul scene in Sheffield and its new converts at the Kay Gee Bee club in the city. Favourite tunes being spun were Tim Tam and the Turn ons 'Wait a minute', Wynder K Frogg's 'Green Door' and Dobie Gray's 'Out on the Floor'. The feature's writer noted that the kids now attending these Northern nights would most certainly have never even heard of Punk luminaries such as Joe Strummer or Jimmy Pursey; they lived a separate existence, far removed from the rock press and the Punk explosion. Theirs was an intimate and secret existence of nocturnal gatherings in clubs that were known only to the people on the scene; a world of chasing the dream of attaining that elusive rare soul 45 on some obscure American indie label, of dancing until the early hours and living for the weekend.

This was an almost identical lifestyle to the Mods of the sixties (clothing attire excepted) and would eventually intertwine with the next generation of Mods that were already starting to emerge. However, to begin with the new Mods would be associated with a different style that could be quite easily be adopted by ex Punks - many of the Mod revival's earliest champions being the Punk kids who had become tired of the nihilism and constraints of their Punk scene.

Tony ... "Throughout the first half of 1979, there was a sense that the Punk scene was giving way to the Mod thing, but for me personally at the time, I didn't really feel any conflict between the two scenes. I suppose that was due to my total intoxication with the Jam."

A notable factor in the Sheffield part of the Mod Revival was when The Jam played two nights at the Sheffield University in spring 1979. The meeting of two youth scenes was in clear evidence that night.

Bryan Bell ... "When we went to see the Jam at Sheffield University we met up with Graham Fellows' (Jilted John) sister. That night she was proud of her multi coloured hair. This was around the time that the Jam had started to attract a bigger Mod following; this gig was one of the two that the Jam played on two consecutive nights in May 1979. Funny thing was that none of the punks were fighting and the mods didn't bother us, but some of the mods themselves were fighting with each other."

Nick Orme ... "'All Mod Cons' had come out at the end of 78 and that was it − 'In the City' was fab, but me and my mates weren't that keen or sure about 'The Modern world'. Anyway, we just had to go and see the Jam again. Of all places, the following May, they were booked to play Sheffield University at the lower refactory...which was a right shit hole.

COPYRIGHT: Virginia Turbett/Redferns/MUSICPICTURES.COM

On the night, it was quite full with a scattering of indifferent student hippies amongst the Mods and Punks; in this place that was like stepping back in time where nothing seemed quite right about the place...pillars all set in the wrong place and the bar miles away. That night the Jam exceeded our expectations and the crowd went wild from the off. Christ this was May 1979 and what a time to be alive. A couple of my mates − poor sods − they ended up getting trampled on by the mob of Jam fans that were jumping up and down trying to emulate Paul and Bruce's flying leaps...but hey! They saw the funny side of it. I know everyone else who was there felt the same as us...you could see it on their faces...there was something in the air; an indefinable experience that you just can't replicate. I am just so glad that I saw the Jam there that night. It was something special right in the middle of a golden era."

Above: Paul Weller of the Jam onstage at Sheffield University May 1979

The Jam were interviewed by Garry Bushell for Sounds magazine whilst playing their two May 1979 Sheffield University dates. Following a discussion in the Sheffield hotel they were staying at, in which Weller enthused about new Mod band The Chords, and admired the spirit and unity of the then burgeoning mod revival, he also remarked that the scene would most likely go the same way as punk itself once the record companies get hold of the scene and the competition started between the groups...

Paul Weller ... "The general consensus is it'll be all over by August....I'll still be wearing me mohair suit in ten years time." **(From Garry Bushell's interview with The Jam at Sheffield University in May 1979)**

In the feature, Gary Bushell also wondered if Paul's unwillingness to align himself to the mod movement was for fear of putting the punks off.

Phillip Wright ... "The 1979 Jam tour was at the other Students building, Weston Bank, now called The Foundry or something like that. They played two nights there, and of course, we went to both. In fact, they usually seemed to play two nights in Sheffield after that and always got a huge crowd. The second time I met the Jam was at the Top Rank when we blagged our way in to the sound check by helping carry the gear.

The third, (and last) was the final time they ever played the Top Rank when we talked to the roadies and asked if we could stick around after the gig. My wife (girlfriend at the time) was with me and she was so excited at meeting them. Paul Weller was talking to me about a recent tour of Japan and how the audience sat in silence and just politely clapped and how weird it all was. My wife (Liz) was surprised that Paul Weller was only about 5ft 9, when he looked so tall on stage."

Gary Bushell's feature continued ... "On arriving at the Sheffield venue Yorkshire accents are mocked by Bruce Foxton, whilst Paul considers that the stage seems bigger than the actual hall. Later as the Jam charge on to the stage Bushell watches them from the balcony as Weller hollers *'this is the Modern World'* and the audience erupts to the power chords of the Jam classic. The crowd dance, pogo, crush each other, faint, punch fists and fingers at the band through an energy injected euphoric set. Songs played that night included 'Mr Clean', 'Away from the numbers', 'Strange Town', 'Tube station', 'A Bomb in Wardour street', 'Butterfly Collector', 'Standards', 'Bricks and Mortar', 'Heatwave' and a finale of 'David Watts."

Some of the London mods who had travelled up for both nights didn't consider the gig as tight as the recent Paris gigs but Bushell thought it was the best gig he had seen all year.

To be expected, but not needed, there was the inevitable culture clash between the new Mods and their Punk ancestors and the Jam (and often their fans) were always stuck in the middle from 1979 onwards.

Tony ... "There was a nasty scrap between two of my mates... a real clash of New wave cultures. Pete was my best mate at the time and John Harrison was a Mod (and later to be another really good mate of mine... playing in the band with me etc)... it was really my fault I have to admit now. Me and Pete were on the bus and John and another Mod were on too. When we got off at our stop I dared Pete to spit on the bus window where they were sat, and Pete being never one to turn down a dare did just that...the gob was running all down the windowpane of the bus where John was sat and it just looked like it was actually all over him. His face showed very little amusement I can say. Me and Pete were nervously laughing as we went up the hill back to my house.

As we turned the corner, John and his mate were running up the bottom of my street, shouting and gesturing, jeering etc. They were after our blood. Shit we thought we have done it now with our stupid dares. We managed to get indoors and laugh at them through the front bay window of my Mum's front room...our HQ so to speak. Oh well we had survived to run another day. We put some Jam records on and laughed it off.

Come the Monday night youth club and as soon as we got there we were out-numbered by all the local Mod wannabees and skinheads who were all 'giving it some' saying that we were going to get beat up. We certainly believed them anyway. John came in to the hall. He was wearing a Harrington jacket, sta-prest trousers, Fred Perry polo shirt and Jam shoes... but there was something different to the parka wearing mod of only two days previously. Instead of the spiky Paul Weller Mod haircut, John now had the skinhead. And he looked well hard too.

That night, Pete and I put up with all the usual stuff that kids come out with when there's going to be some trouble. We listened to all the threats, insults, jeers, questions and also stood at the side of the dance floor while newly cropped John and one of his mates did a mock grapple to some ska music...as if demonstrating what lay in store for us. As it happened, it was Pete who they were going to be gunning for. It was him that they laid the blame with as he had actually done the gobbing. The plans were now being laid out for a post youth club square down at the bottom of the road. Pete wasn't scared. He never backed down from anything so he decided he was going to give it his best shot. John was two years older than us and had a bit of a reputation but there was no way that Pete was going to run away and back down. He managed to keep his cool all the way through.

The gangs were building up...the lasses getting their buzz out of the testosterone vibes being displayed. The tribe mentality was never clearer but ultimately mixed up. Here was a genuine battle to the last between a Punk Rocker and a Mod. *'Get yer tickets at the bottom gates'.* It's a Rawmarsh exclusive. The scrap started just up the road from the school and round one saw Pete and John really lay into each other... fists flying all over and the cracks and thuds of punches connecting with bone and muscle were non-stop. The crowd of Mods, skinheads and local kids were 99% against Pete and me...only future My Pierrot Doll member Ian Hillman (himself sporting a skinhead crop at the time) was on our side.

The fight stopped and they both caught a breather. After a while, everyone moved up to a different location and then they squared up to each other once more. John was spitting blood and Pete had hurt his knuckles quite bad. They stared at each other like two prizefighters and then John said *'If we start again and I say stop, will you stop?'*... To which Pete replied *'No fuckin' way'.* John stood there for a while and then decided enough was enough. Pete walked away...the fight done with. He was followed by another older Mod who obviously wasn't happy with the outcome, but he was stopped by another lad who made it clear that it had been a fair fight and it was finished with. Pete went in...the crowd dispersed, I got some verbal off some of the lads and a few threats but I ignored 'em and everyone went home. Later when John and I became really good friends, we would sometimes talk about that night. I always felt bad about it... but we were young and stupid. I never saw a Mod and a Punk fight each other like that again ...Christ why should they. We were all in the same boat. It was quite sad to see really and I was partly to blame."

Pete Roddis … "You would always be getting the Mods coming up to us, saying that The Jam were Mod. They didn't realise they had come out of the Punk thing at all."

Bryan Bell … "All Mod Cons also stands for All Modern Conveniences' as well. The Mods picked up on the Mod connection only. To me, personally the Mods belonged to the sixties any way."

In August, 'Sounds' magazine featured a five page special on the Mod revival. The feature spoke to young Mods and also did a run – through of all the Mod bands of the time. Along with the more well-known Mod bands such as Purple Hearts, Secret Affair etc were lesser known ones such as Speedball, 007, Fixations, Sta-prest, Crooks, Chicane, Beggar and an all girl vocal group named The Look. The scene was now set for another youth scene… one to replace Punk but welcoming onboard one of that very scene's finest groups.

Above: Sheffield Mods in 1979 (Phillip Wright)

The Jam were rapidly becoming the main flag-bearers for the splintering 'New Wave' scene and by 1979 were only equalled by the Clash. Many punk fans from the Sheffield and Rotherham area saw that the times were changing and, put off by the orthodox approach to Punk being offered by many of the current Punk bands, were moving more to the Mod style. Whilst many local Punk fans would fully embrace the oncoming Mod Revival, some would prefer to continue to hold on to their punk roots but still embracing groups like the Jam and a select few of the best of the new Mod groups.

Tony … "At the time, about mid 1979, I was wearing Jam shoes, had my hair like Weller and wore tight fitting sports tops and Fred Perry polo shirts, but I still considered myself a punk. I bought a pair of so-called Mod trousers out of the back pages of the NME from The Cavern clothes shop. They were advertised as being the same as the ones that they made for The Jam. I never had any problems, at the time, with mixing my influences as I always thought that the side of punk that I was attracted to in the first place, was very Mod influenced anyway. The early Clash looked very Mod in a garage band sort of style. They were often described as a Mod group in their first features in the music papers. Also, music wise they had that Kinks and Who influence all through their songs. '1977' their

369

'White Riot' b-side is a direct link to the Kinks 'All day and all of the night', and tracks such as 'Clash City Rockers' and 'Guns on the roof' were virtually remakes of 'I Can't Explain'.

I used to like some of the mod groups at the time. The main ones were Purple Hearts (previously punk group the Sockets) and the Chords. Some of the groups like the Jolt, who were a 2nd division punk group with a sixties influence, they were later considered Mod but they had been around for ages. Another Mod group were the local group the Negatives. I never managed to get to hear them, back then, but I can remember them playing gigs at the time."

Nick Orme … "I went along to the Secret Affair gig at the Polytechnic in 1979 which was a great gig and they played a fantastic set, but the night was spoilt by the National Front skinheads turning up and the group scarpered and opted out of doing an encore."

Many of the 'New Mods' had arrived on the doorstep of the Mod Revival via Punk, but some other local Mods had also stepped in from the Soul Boy scene and were not that empathetic with the Punks.

Dave Spencer … "Life back then for a young Punk was becoming a bit more dangerous. The number of Punks that had grown to 40 (at our school at least) was slowly beginning to dwindle, as the Punks started to become Mods.

Above: unashamedly capitalist marketing aimed at the 'In Crowd' of early 1980.

These kids weren't anything to worry about, as they'd only just stopped spiking their hair so were sort of neutral. The Mods to be wary of were the Soulies who became Mods. They were generally older than us and had never been punks and were about to enjoy the thrills of punk-bashing.

We used to go to a disco at St Cuthbert's Methodist church hall in between The Stag roundabout and The Brecks roundabout. This disco wasn't attached to any particular school, so there was an element of danger even before the Mod/Punk/Soulie rivalry was taken into account. The first couple of nights that I went to, seemed to pass off peacefully enough, but after a while older Mods used to come along. One night, a group of Mods, some of them grown men, were working their way round the hall, grabbing whatever little punk rocker was on his own and giving them a good hiding. We didn't stand a chance, so, I

370

grabbed a punk rocker myself, either Cav or Dom – can't remember which, pushed him through the fire escape and said, *'Let's go'* and legged it."

For local music fan Steve Haythorne, things had come full circle with the mod revival. He had seen the end of the original sixties Mod era as a young child when as he recalls *'Parkas back then were not seen as being very cool'*, and had admired the coolness of the Mods look. Steve became a Northern Soul fan during the early 70's and throughout his flirtations with Glam Rock, Prog-Rock and Punk, he had never given up the torch for his much-loved soul music. Now, with the Mod Revival, he would become a Mod, dress smart again and get out the records of his youth club days.

Steve Haythorne ... "Yes I came into the Mod scene through the back door with Northern Soul, and now started to buy Ben Sherman's, loafers and smart trousers. I personally thought that the Mod Revival was great, though in the back of my mind I always was troubled by the thought that it was quite sad in some respects that here we were taking an older style and making it our own.

I liked the 2-Tone stuff a lot and bought every single record on that label. Loved the Specials and the rest; I saw UB40 when they were good and we used to go the Limit club now and again. The best nights were the Wednesday Reggae nights. All the West Indian community would be in there and the place would reek of ganga. One of the nights, me and my mate were the only two white faces in there."

Bryan Bell ... "A couple of us wandered into the Limit Club one night late on just by chance and the Bodysnatchers were playing. The place was full of Mods but we didn't get any hassle from 'em...I knew most of them anyway as a lot of 'em were old Punk mates who had moved into Mod."

It would be Punk's smartest dressed combo that would influence many Mod influenced Punk fans.

Phillip Wright ... "I had a made to measure black mohair suit like the original Jam wore, made by an old tailor on London Road. The following year I had a light grey one made at 'March the Tailor' on the Moor. Four button grey jacket, two ticket pockets on both sides and lots of buttons at the cuff. I paid weekly for that suit; a bloke came round and collected a quid a week or something daft. Some lads I knew went to a tailor somewhere in the markets in Rotherham; he had made loads of baggy trousers for the Northern soul lads for years. I was lucky enough that my older brother, Dave, had some Ben Sherman's left over from the early 70's that still looked good and fitted me."

John Harrison ... "It was always the Jam for me, but I was also into a lot of the ska music that was around. I liked Madness and The Selecter. I also liked Secret Affair and Purple Hearts for a while."

Tony ... "By mid to late summer 1979 I had dropped the Mod-influenced style that I had seen as part of the New Wave Punk kind of look- obviously very much influenced by 'The

Jam'. My outlook was not one based on this new Mod Revival thing. I had started off with Punk and still had plenty of faith in it at that point. I still liked some parts of this new Mod thing but a lot of it was just so plastic. It would improve when the poseurs had moved on and the hype had died down.

Above: Sheffield Mod Philip Wright and friends 1979.

By this time, there were a bunch of Mods who were going to our youth club: and I had a lot of respect for them. They were a year or two older than us and were really smart. We would have some great conversations with them and they would be saying that they had a lot of time for Punk but they only wanted to look smart now and listen to soul and black music. They were also into some of the Northern soul as well, though not all of it. Not long after, the sheep following 2-Tone-loving scruffy type of Mods were 'jumping on the bandwagon'. These were the sort who thought being a Mod was wearing a parka covered in beer mats and badges, listening to Madness and the Specials only and fighting with Punks. I never got into any trouble with this lot but got chased a few times and had a knife pulled on me."

Some may say that 'Quadrophenia' was part of the ruining of the ill fated Mod revival, and whilst there is much truth in this, there can be no doubting that the film also made a huge impact on the Punk and Post- Punk generation of the region. In the ensuing years, the film has gained almost legendary Youth cult/movie status with each generation that passes taking time out to watch and absorb.

The original choices for playing the part of Jimmy in the film 'Quadrophenia' were two of Punk's most recognisable faces Johnny Rotten and Jimmy Pursey. Both auditioned for the role, Rotten becoming reluctant to commit to the part and 'Pursey' feeling that he could fit the role quite well. Ultimately, neither would be in any way associated with the film and it would forever be remembered for Phil Daniels' fantastic portrayal. The film needed plenty of extras and one choice was made to include members of Barnsley 'Vikings scooter club' who were recruited for two weeks filming in 1978 for the beach fight scenes. Whilst enjoying the privilege of being a part of the film, the lads from Barnsley were not overall impressed with the local Brighton population's indifference to them and especially their accents...resulting in Barnsley Mod Steve Orridge's retort of... *"The girls here fook me off."*

Of the two thousand extras used from the film, the Mods were drawn mainly from the North and the Rockers from the South. In hindsight, it springs to mind, that this must have been a conscious effort made by the director Franc Roddam in order to create an authentic rivalry between the two youth factions. Also, as this was 1978 there were a lot of Punks used during filming, much to the disgust of some of the scooter clubs involved. Actor Mark Wingett (later in The Bill) famously turned up for his audition wearing a dog collar and full Punk attire.

The commitment to the Mod cause by the scooter clubs was evident throughout the many conversations from the Northern Mods. They even planned to pass the faith on to their offspring. Here are some quotes from the time that were made whilst filming.

Kevin Lawn (Barnsley Mod) ... "I've got a little girl of two and I'll make her a Mod when she grows up. She sits on my scooter now. She loves it. And my brother, e's 30 and still a Mod."

The distaste for Rockers and Bikers was also clearly genuine.

Kevin Lawn ... "Look at a lad on a scooter, ow' good he is. Then just look at that one on a bike – you can't go out dressed up on a bike."

Steve Haythorne ... "I knew some of the lads in the Barnsley Vikings scooter club and I remember one of them not being able to make it to the 'Quadrophenia' shooting and he never forgave himself. For years afterwards, and I presume to this day, whenever he watches the film he has a tear in his eye and thinks *'I could have been in that'.*"

These Northern Mods displayed a more ardent zest towards their scooters, much more than the original sixties Mods; who mostly used them as a means of transport and commonly would not even know how to fix one if one did happen to break down. They spoke of a love of scooters and held a knowledge of its parts that would rival any mechanic. These new Mods would eventually grow into that other offshoot of Mod – the scooter boys. Meanwhile back in the late 70's, as in Punk before it, young teenagers were aiming to be a part of this new style of Mod.

Steve Parlett (Rotherham Mod) ... "I got into Mod at the age of 11 (in 79/80), when a friend of mine at school brought a tape of his older brothers to school in Wath. It had the Specials, Selecter, and Madness etc on it, but it also had Secret Affair, the Purple Hearts, and the Chords on it, and I was hooked. I went through a 'This is England' style conversion from slightly flared high waisters and a German helmet haircut, to a rainbow range of Fred Perry tops (first one black with yellow trim, then sky blue, burgundy, red with navy trim, lemon etc), numerous pairs of tonic trousers, and penny or tasselled loafers (with the obligatory white socks). I got heavily into the Jam, and at this time all my school mates were into the same thing, although at the time we all interchanged a mod look with a rude boy look - tonics and perries and loafers, suits and brogues, parkas and crombies. The gang around that time was Tom Redfern, Lee Hanson, Mick Taylor (who went all Style Council and became a poet later) and Steve Clegg. We would scour old shoe shops for dead stock loafers; in particular, a shop in Wombwell became the Holy Grail as the owner had kept tons of mod-style loafers from the first time around! We also started knocking round with Bobber and Carney (Paul) from Swinton."

Stuart Hardman was a young teenager from near Barnsley in 1979 and soon became seriously interested in the Mod scene. He recalls ... "The summer of 1979, the film Quadrophenia was out in the cinemas, scooters were zipping about all over the place, parkas were been worn at school, I was just about to start my second year at senior school.

By that September we had probably missed the best of the Mod revival around here in South Yorkshire, the Mods Mayday album had been recorded with the then cream of the crop of the bands on the scene. Bits and pieces had filtered through to us before we finished our first year at the school, but I seem to remember things came through a bit slower, I was more aware really by September of 79. Seeing the likes of Secret Affair, Madness, The Jam, Selecter, the Chords, the Lambrettas and The Specials on Top of The Pops, everything seemed be to awash with black and white, and the green of parkas."

Steve Parlett ... "I remember thinking the 79 mod revival and 2-Tone thing was great, but I think it was the Jam that got me looking back at the original mod scene and the music ('Heatwave' on 'Setting Sons' LP for example) and also reading of Weller's obsession with Steve Marriott. So I started to collect old Tamla and Soul/R&B records and honed up on the Small Faces before going though a whole British R&B phase (Them, Stones, Alexis Korner, Cyril Davis etc).

In our early teens our world pretty much revolved around the local youth club on Festival Road, where the boys would beg the DJ for some mod stuff to be put on, and if we were lucky we'd get 30 minutes of our stuff and go crazy on the dance floor, with Tom Redfern busting my nose on at least one occasion during a particularly frenetic 'My Generation'! I remember being particularly impressed too with a Soul boy from West Melton who would give it the big northern soul bit to 'Out on the Floor' by Dobie Gray."

Nick Orme ... "After Punk, it was the next great thing. I loved The Jam throughout Punk anyway, but when the Mod thing came along, I embraced it with open arms. It was all about youth and being young anyway."

374

By this time in Sheffield and the suburbs, both Mods and Skinheads were both enjoying 2-Tone.

Anthony Cronshaw ... "2-Tone and the Mod Revival proved to be more popular with our crowd than Punk, and the Skinhead fashion, combined with the Mod movement pushed itself to the forefront in the city of Sheffield."

Sheffield soon saw many of the new Mod and 2-Tone groups playing the very same venues that the Punk groups had, and still were playing. The March of the Mods tour, which was Mod's equivalent to the Punk Anarchy tour, saw Purple Hearts, Secret Affair and Back to Zero play at the Limit Club on 28th August. That same month Merton Parkas played there and in September Small Hours and the Chords also performed their sets to enthusiastic Mod audiences. Others to play the city were Back to Zero, Teenbeats, and regular appearances from the Specials, Madness and the Selecter, the latter supported by The Beat played 'The Limit club' in September 1979.
 The two bands played to a mixed crowd of Punks, Mods and skinheads who were skanking in unison to the ska of The Selector by the end of their set. By the end of the year, the Limit Club saw return gigs from Purple Hearts and Merton Parkas whilst Secret Affair supported by Squire played at the Polytechnic on Wednesday 5th of December.

Andrea Berry ... "The Beat were a great band! But I did have to pretend not to like them as I was a punk."

Beat singer/guitarist Dave Wakeling surprised everyone when, instead of disappearing backstage afterwards, he came and mingled with the fans - drinking pints and chatting along with them.

Nick Orme ... "The Specials at the Limit Club was a great experience...as anyone who ever went to the place will tell you – the stage was so small as well as the venue itself – so to see all the members of the group on there playing away and skanking to their ska sounds was such a sight. It brings a smile to my face just thinking about 'em."

Tony ... "When we saw The Piranhas supporting the Jam...they played 'Tom Hark' which was just in the charts at the time, and the place was a mass of Mods, Punks, skinheads and rude boys giving it their all to the song. There was a sense of unity for the whole 3 or 4 minutes of that song."

Yes! For a short while, the Mod and 2-Tone scene in the region was awash with the same youthful exuberance of Punk.

Nick Orme ... "The 2-Tone and Mod/ska thing really took me over and diverted me away from Punk...I still went along to some Punk gigs and liked the music and I always loved the Jam but when the 2-Tone came in it was great. I still love it now."

Phillip Wright ... "As with Punk before it, the Limit club always had great bands on. The Specials played there when they were still called Special AKA. I chatted to them after the gig and they gave me a black and white checked badge, which said 'Special AKA - Rude Boys' which I still have. Madness played there shortly after, they came on to 'One Step Beyond', and musically they were very tight. A few weeks later it was The Beat supporting The Selecter and I met Dave Wakeling (Beat singer) in the Limit toilets (!) and he grabbed me while Selecter were playing and pulled me up on stage and we were both dancing about. Not long after that The Limit had an official Mod Night, every week and bands like the Chords and the Purple Hearts played there, along with The Killermeters from Huddersfield, who were really good. The DJ played all the usual records you would expect."

Some Punks, however, would have varying views and experiences of the Mod revival.

Steve Lloyd … "I never saw the point in the Mod revival; to me it didn't seem like a natural movement at all and was the same as with the Rockabilly thing that came out, just rehashing something old. Punk was new but this wasn't. I did like the 2-Tone groups though. I saw 'The Specials' and enjoyed them."

Andrea Berry … "I remember seeing Bad Manners live at the Sheffield Show in Hillsborough Park. It was horrible.

Secret Affair at Limit club (Phillip Wright)

'Buster Bloodvessel' was spitting all over when he sang - I'm glad I wasn't in the front row!"

David McKendry …"After the punk scene died down, we had to put up with bloody 2-tone."

Then the inevitable clash of styles and culture would arise once more...

Patrick Tierney … "The most threatening atmosphere I ever experienced at a gig was at the Top Rank on the Specials/Madness/Selecter tour. The music was brilliant, but the weekend mods didn't want us there."

376

Pete Cooper … "One evening on the John Peel show I heard 'Gangsters' by the Specials'. What a song that was. I went to see them play live, although I don't think I was appreciated by the rest of the crowd, but nevertheless I escaped intact."

Phillip Wright … "Mods V Skins - Yes this weird rivalry broke out. This was weird because original skinheads were mods who didn't want to be longhaired hippies. The mods and skins sort of blurred in the early 70's to become suede heads (although that name might be a media creation) and with the Crombie overcoats, I guess Madness were a suede head band. Skinheads chasing mods about in town on a Saturday afternoon

was just like watching the Punks and Teddy Boys from a few years before. We never saw too much trouble but one night when we came out of KGB on Abbeydale Road, after a Mod/Ska/Soul night, a huge gang of skinheads were milling about and one threw a bottle at us, we didn't hang about as we were heavily outnumbered."

Tony … "Once around late 79, me and Pete Roddis were in the Hole in the Road in Sheffield and it was jam – packed with Mods and Rude Boys. At that time, we were kind of

Sheffield Mods with Phillip Wright (Centre)

having some respect for the more cooler and stylish Mods and Rudies – basically us being influenced by the Clash and the Jam and what their influences were.

The Mod crowd here this day could not have been more representative of the other side of Mod that we weren't that keen on. They were bolstering themselves up and starting their *'We are the Mods'* chanting - Parkas and targets galore. In one big tribal gathering of this Punk revived Mod thing, the masses of Mods were as one (eh! where's the individualism now?). Then by pure chance, from the top end of the hole in the road at one of the many entrances, came two gigantic denim clad Rockers… marching down like big footed yetis. The Mods absolutely scarpered in all directions, knocking down anyone in their path. A hundred or so of 'em and two Rockers minding their own business had spooked 'em. I mean what would Jimmy in 'Quadrophenia' have said to them had he seen that happen?"

Thankfully, there was a very much cooler kind of Mod...

Darren Gray (Sheffield Mod) ... "I was 17 in 1980 and had recently discovered the Jam and Northern Soul. I recall attending Clifton Hall in Rotherham and watching in awe at the great Mod dancers chucking talc on the floor."

Over in Sheffield, the only real Mod band that was active during the 1979 Revival was a group who had sprung out of Punk and were called the Negatives. The three piece Punk influenced Negatives formed in 1978, and had appeared with two tracks on the local compilation LP 'New Wave from the heart'.

They were originally Brad Martini – Bass guitar, Fraser Charlesworth – Guitar and piano and singing Drummer Pete Eason, later joined by Steve Wilmot on drums. They were then managed by Marcus Featherby and in 1979 moved away from Punk and evolved into the Mod band they are mostly remembered as.

Jarvis Cocker... "By the time I got to see the Negatives, they had gone full on Mod, which was probably Marcus's instigation. He was such a chancer, I guess, that as soon as he got a whiff of something being a bit successful, he'd go like -

Above: Sheffield Mod Band the Negatives

- The Negatives are a bit of a pop band, let's make them Mod because Mod is happening now,' and would kind of fuck 'em up in the process."**(From 'Beats Working for a living' by Martin Lilleker)**

Purple Hearts vocalist Bob Manton recalls a Limit Club outing when the Negatives supported the Hearts.

Bob Manton (Purple Hearts singer) ... "All I can remember is that a band called (I think) The Negatives supported us, they were local and had a single out called 'Electric'... something? I got way too drunk and sang the end bit of 'I've Been Away' backwards."

The first Negatives' single was 'Electric Waltz'/ 'Money Talk' and it was released on Featherby's own Limited Edition label. Named Single of the week by the NME in early 1980 and tipped for great things by local fanzines and the music press, 'The Negatives' were yet another local band that ultimately missed the boat. They played a gig at

378

Rotherham Clifton Hall and after being wrongly advertised as a Sheffield rock band the gig was poorly attended.

One ill-fated promotional set up was to play a gig at K and D records in the old Hole in the Road. This was met with fighting, mods filling the whole area and the news that the police were on their way. Another incident saw them banned from one Sheffield venue for a brick being thrown through a window and indifference towards their door policy of charging 40p for Punks, £1 for Hippies and free entry to Mods. It seemed that everything that they tried always fell through and despite trying their hardest to break through and appeal to Sheffield's Mods; they ultimately gave up and abandoned the Mod image.

By September 1979, the Mod Revival was in full swing all across the country and Sheffield and Rotherham was no exception. On a Saturday afternoon in Sheffield city centre there would be crowds of Mods gathering around the Moor area. Often there would be some trouble but not very often would it be anything serious.

In Rotherham town centre at the weekends the Mods would meet up at the Whitehall café and other cafes around town. They could be found drinking coffee and popping pills and chatting excitedly about the latest ska and rare soul 45's they had been buying and where the best local tailors and best Mod clothes were to be found.

Above: Pauline Black of Selecter at Sheffield Limit club (Phillip Wright)

Tony … "I can remember loads of parties I went to and there would always be Mods there. Sometimes there would be a bit of trouble kick off but most of the time everyone would just get pissed and mess about. I used to borrow my Jam shoes to a lad at school called Russ and he would wear them to the Mod do's in Rotherham and bring them back to me the day after at school. I very rarely wore them at that point."

John Harrison … "We used to go to the 'Birdcage' in Hoyland a lot. I went out with a lass at the time called Dawn, and she was into the Mod scene. Her dad was the verger at Greasborough church. A lot of Mod music got played there and a fair few Mods went. We also went to the Mod nights at the Assembly Rooms and Clifton Hall in Rotherham."

The lure of the so called 'Mod Mecca' of London's Carnaby Street' proved to be anything but that description for many young Mods who ventured there in the late 70's.

Phillip Wright ... "I went to London to buy a suit from Carnaby Street with my mate Deano (who now lives in Poland and still has a scooter!), I was so disappointed, Carnaby Street looked like a street at the seaside, full of cheap stuff. The suit was not great either, so I decided to get them made after that. I did buy a pork pie hat from X-clothes in Leeds. If I ever saw a cool shirt, I would just have Liz sew the buttons on the collar so it looked like a Ben Sherman. The new mods all started wearing white socks I decided to wear red ones, just to be different. We also started wearing cravats at one point! Me and Liz went to London and I bought some cool loafers from Sloane Square in the sale."

Early in 1980, the start of the new decade, Rotherham Clifton Hall booked Mod band the Lambrettas to play (at that point they were in the charts with their version of old Mod favourite The Coasters 'Poison Ivy'). Although not taken that seriously by the hard-core Mods, The Lambrettas did corner their own little part of the Mod Revival and earned their fifteen minutes of fame playing venues like the Clifton Hall to enthusiastic Mod audiences. Local Mod John Harrison went to the concert and recalls the experience of that night and another profound one from the time.

John Harrison ... "Yeah I went to see the Lambrettas at Clifton Hall. It's a long time ago so I can't remember that much but it was quite a good night with plenty of Mods there. I went with my mate Paul. It was also around this time, when I was into the Mod scene, that I took some magic mushrooms; it was the second time I had taken them but it was also the last time. I was with Paul and we were in the Rotherham Library café as I had taken them. I remember when they started to kick in and take effect. I looked at Paul's eyes and they were shaped like targets. Then it got worse as I looked out of the window and saw a Westlers hot dog van go flying by. I started to hallucinate all sorts of things and I *'thought this is not the thing for me.'* We went outside and we walked arm in arm, Paul had not taken any I don't think, so he was reassuring me sort of. I bet we looked a right pair; I know I felt a right state. Anyway, that was it for me, never again, chuffing hell I had thought that they would be something that was supposed to make me laugh and I certainly wasn't laughing. Nah not for me, I would stick to my booze from now on."

Dexys Midnight Runners played Sheffield Polytechnic in March, the Top Rank on 15th June 1980 and the day after at Doncaster Rotters also making time for a date in Barnsley, as did The Killermeters. Mod was massive around Sheffield and the area for a good year or so, but it was 2-Tone that really impressed the punk generation the most.

Nick Orme ... "I saw the 2-Tone tour with the Specials, Madness and Selecter at the Top Rank... that was a fantastic night. It all seemed to be fitting into place with that gig; top class performances from all of the groups too."

With 2-Tone and the re-emergence in popularity of ska, Rude boys sprang up all over Sheffield and Saturday afternoons in Sheffield city centre would be awash with crombies, pork pie hats, sta-prest trousers and ox blood brogues.

Meanwhile over in Rotherham...the Advertiser's entertainment pages ads appeared for Mod nights at The Assembly Rooms; one of which proclaimed a night of entertainment that offered 'Mods – 1960's meet Mod's 1980 – complete with Mods DJ Contest to find Rotherham's best Mod DJ'. A prize of £10 in cash was waiting for the winner. As a matter of interest, the entry fee was 70p before 8pm and 90p afterwards.

John Harrison ... "I would go to The Assembly Rooms too; I had some fantastic nights there; the birds were bloody lovely, all those short skirts and stuff – it really did it for a young lad like myself. The music was great too."

But even greater things came to those who were patient enough to wait for the Jam's first appearance in the steel city for almost a year and a half.

John Harrison ... "When I went to see the Jam on the 'Sound Affects' tour we went up in the afternoon and got in for the sound check. Weller was pretty arrogant (laughs). One guy asked him what America was like to which Paul replied *'Same as fuckin' last time'*. I can remember thinking ... Arrogant bastard, but that was part of how he was. It was part of what his appeal was. Rick Buckler, on the other hand gave me a full pack of fags when I was talking to him.

Later on after the gig, we were coming out of the Top Rank and going for the last train. We had to go through the old bus station. This was probably the only time I came up against any aggravation. There were two mates and me and all of a sudden, we came across this lot of skinheads. We had to turn tail, everyman for himself. We ran back to the Top Rank, where everything was packed up just about, and the bouncers were at the door. They asked us *'What's up?'.' Have yer seen these lot?* (laughs), *they are gonna kick our heads in'* we said. So they let us in. Thank God."

Mods and Jam fans always had a healthy respect for Paul Weller, whether they liked his music or not; regardless most self respecting Mods would admire his taste in clothes and style...going to great lengths to emulate his clothes attire...or style of shoes.

Phillip Wright ... "True story this... One day we had seen pictures of the Jam in these sort of stripy shoes and I was wondering where you got them from, when my mate Neil Kitson (A massive Jam fan and now a famous photographer) said *'they are like bowling shoes, like when you wear when you play 10 pin bowling'* so I thought, *'cool!'* The next Saturday lunchtime I went up to Firth Park bowling alley in a pair of crappy old shoes, paid my money to play, swapped my shoes for the bowling shoes and just walked back out. I met my mates on Fargate in the afternoon and they were stunned. We were all wearing cycling shirts at the time - that was another part of the fashion. Most of the Mod wannabees just wore the parkas and stuff; we just tried to be cool and wore authentic mod gear and anything that Paul Weller wore."

Trips to the coast, often by the traditional Mod method of transport (the scooter) were also a commonplace during the Mod revival days. Russ Weaver (later a member of Revolver one of Rotherham's Mods favourite sixties styled bands) recalls his experience of one such trip to the coast back in those days. Minus his scooter, the trip almost ended up being a trip to the local infirmary.

Russ Weaver (Rotherham Mod/musician) ... "My memories are quite vague about the Mod revival of the late seventies and early eighties (probably due to the excess amount of alcohol consumed).

I remember though one day, aged 18 going to Skegness with my then girlfriend Shannon Finch. I think it was a Bank holiday or certainly a weekend. After getting off the Gordon's coach in our Mod parkas and bowling shoes we headed towards the sea front of Skegness. We were both perplexed to why there were so many police in Skegness (I mean Skegness was certainly not known for being the crime capital of the UK).

Above: Darren Gray in 1979

We walked around the corner of one street and it all too suddenly became apparent... We walked straight in front of a marching army of skinheads. Luckily the march was so large that it was policed, but that didn't stop hundreds of knuckleheaded skinheads baying for our blood. The police managed to stop most of them but I got a few elbows and punches as they walked passed. Anyway the first horde walked by and about 40 un-escorted stragglers followed...we then cowered behind a wall only centimetres away from the marauding thugs...hearing their gruff voices stating how they were going to tear the mods heads off. Needless to say our day trip turned into a day of the best hide and seek I've ever played."

Punk and skinhead veteran (not counting his many years on the terraces following the Owls) Anthony Cronshaw came across the local Sheffield Mods by accident and ended up being involved in accommodating them for their own Mod night.

Anthony Cronshaw ... "Myself and a friend called Martin decided to try our hand at the old mobile disco malarkey and through another mate we managed to get a gig at the Woodbourne boozer near Attercliffe. It was a Thursday evening and after we'd set up bright and early waiting for the punters to arrive, we imagined that we'd be serving up the usual chart dross. What a surprise we had when a load of Mods turned up, some on scooters, but all looking the business with their hair, clothes and attitude. To say we were a bit short on their material was an understatement, but we muddled through and explained the situation to some of the lads we knew who did the football, mind you there is only so many times you can play 'My Generation'.

The following week though we were ready after we'd begged, borrowed and stole a vast array of vinyl that included such classics as 'Wade in the Water' by Ramsay Lewis trio, Louie Louie' by The Kingsmen and Booker T's legendary 'Green Onions' plus a fair sample of Motown and Soul Classic's. British groups including the Small Faces, Kinks and The Who provided some excellent 45's along with the modern generation that included The Jam, Lambrettas and the ever-popular Secret Affair. Week after week and month after month the place was rammed to bursting point; we did get the odd Skinhead wanting a bit of Oi! But we never seemed to have any so we would throw in the odd Ska classic from yesteryear. But it was the Mods that were paying the wages and even when we did gigs around town we would always invite them along if they fancied it because it gave us another excuse to play the sounds of a bygone era.

The room upstairs used to shake like mad and I was expecting the ceiling to go through at anytime, the place was as hot as a sauna sometimes but it never bothered me because Mart did all the driving and I always had a cool lager to hand. Like they say all good things come to an end and in his wisdom, the landlord decided that the upstairs room needed a facelift so the Mods needed to find a new home. This they did when the Staniforth Arms provided a suitable replacement... but myself and Martin decided to play one last Thursday at the Woodbourne and we all partied into the early hours."

Like Punk Rock before it, soon; the new Mod scene itself would prove to be just as much of a disappointment to some and just a new uniform for the fashion followers. Original Punk Rockers would often sample the new Mod revival and take on board some of its influences, especially clothes wise, but soon realise the shallowness of some of its appeal.

Phillip Wright ... "By 1979 I was dressing like the Jam and not wearing my leather jacket or combat trousers anymore. All the Jam fans were the same, we all knew each other and would hang out a lot together. The big problems arrived with the launch of the movie 'Quadrophenia'. That, coupled with the 2-Tone record bands taking off into the charts meant that once again, a small movement became a mainstream fashion. In the early days, you could see Mod type bands at the Limit. I remember a group of lads from Huddersfield called The Killermeters, who were pretty good, amongst others, and you would see a few lads in the audience in mod suits, but all of a sudden you could not walk up The Moor on a Saturday afternoon for seeing gangs of lads in Parkas, having pitched battles with bikers every so often, and young kids walking up Fargate singing '*we are the mods*'. It was time to leave that scene behind, not the music, just the fashion."

Timothy Green ... "In 1979 I developed a mild interest in the '2-Tone' scene and started to wear my jeans without turn ups and buy Harrington jackets etc. I went to Barnsley Town Hall to see Secret Affair and The Purple Hearts and the place was full of ageing Northern Soul fans who had arrived on their scooters.

The Purple Hearts were ok and Secret Affair were late cos of filming on Top of the Pops'. I recall Purple Hearts group members coming to the front of the stage to some of the unconvinced Northern Soulies. I myself got a hard time from the Soulies. After the groups had played the DJ played lots of Northern Soul classics and the Soulies started doing their thing and dancing."

Julian Jones ... "The thing is back then; there was all the division between Mods, Punks etc. I used to like the Specials and I had to play them in secret. I went to see them at Herringthorpe when they played there. Later on, I was into The Who, Kinks etc, which is strange really cos I did it the wrong way round – the Punk stuff and then the Sixties stuff. The band I formed Alternative Route would play lots of that kind of stuff."

1980 had passed and the local Mods descended upon the coastal town of Scarborough for the 1981 May Bank Holiday; resulting in a déjà vu scenario of a repeat of the 1964 Mods beach riots. Photos of Mods in police cages - including a small number of local Sheffield area Mods - were plastered all over the Daily papers with inside pages of rhetoric that lambasted the Mods with cries of decency being spoilt yet again by these *'sawdust little Caesars'*. After that, the Mod Revival was dead in the water. The true Mods would return to their underground roots and nurture their cause within its own exclusive little world.

During that same red-hot and tension filled summer, with rioting going on in many of the major cities of the country, the youth of Sheffield and Rotherham (like everywhere else) were restless, bored and itching to have their say. The idea to organise an important outdoor concert was brought to fruition, in a hope to help ease the tension and bring together- rather than segregate and divide - all the local youth tribes of the area. The location for the concert was at Rotherham's Herringthorpe leisure centres playing fields. The Headlining act was the Specials: The date Saturday June 27th 1981.

Tony ... "Me and my mate Andy were coming back from one of our late jaunts from Manchester the day the Specials played at Herringthorpe playing fields. We arrived back in Sheffield about early lunchtime and we headed for the no.69 bus stop. We paid our fares (2p anywhere back in those days) and went up to the upper deck of the bus. We couldn't believe our eyes when we saw that there must have been about 20 skinheads sat up there. They were soon joined by another large bunch of them, now cramming the upper deck area and just about filling up down below. *'This is it'* we thought *'Get ready for it. Would they just beat us up there and then, wait until we tried to get off the bus, or even worse throw us out the top window or something. 'Christ! , it's been a good life up* *to yet'* we nervously concluded. But unbelievably, they just looked at us, didn't say a word and continued chatting with each other. These were the core of the Sheffield Skinhead scene and there we were on the no.69 bus with them heading for Rotherham. Perhaps they were saving all their energy for the Battle of Herringthorpe playing fields?"

Martin Ridgeway was a 12-year-old 2-Tone and Mod fan and remembers ..."I was on one of the lad's shoulders so that I could see what was going on. I seem to remember that a lot of the trouble started with the flat tops, or Teds, throwing bottles and things at the group."

Lynne Rollinson (Rotherham Mod and ska fan) ... "Remembering July 1981 when the Specials came to Rotherham of all places, they played at Herringthorpe playing fields. It was more of a battle with Rotherham v Sheffield skins but with a musical score in the background."

Jimmy Mathison (Rotherham Skinhead) ... "I was at the Specials gig. I think I must have been one of the hooligans. That day all the Sheffield Skins came along, there was all the Rotherham lot, and it was a case of them against us. It soon kicked off with the Rotherham skins against the Sheffield skins."

John Harrison ... "I went to the Specials Herringthorpe gig. There were plenty of beer tents and it was a free event so that was a good start. The Specials were good, but all the scrapping spoilt it. Terry Hall was trying to get the Sheffield and Rotherham skinheads to calm down, but it just wasn't happening. Soon the cops were there and they were starting to make arrests, but still the fighting went on. I think, that by about 5pm all the scrapping and everything had calmed down. Me and my mate Andrew (who was also a Mod) ended up going to town for a night out."

Julian McKenzie (Sheffield 2-Tone fan and author of 'Tonight Mathew 'I'm going to be a rude boy') ... "I can remember the Specials at Herringthorpe just as if it was yesterday. I can remember the scrapping in Rotherham bus station and being chased all the way out of town right up to the Tinsley cooling towers by a bunch of the Rotherham skins."

Andrew Morton ... "The Specials gig at Herringthorpe was a real riot. I went with my mate Clarkey and all was well during UB40's set (who were supporting), there was loads of Skinheads and I never had realised that there were so many Rotherham skinheads until that day. Anyway, as well as the Rotherham ones there was the Sheffield lot, who had arrived in droves. When the Specials came on, it all kicked off between the two factions - scrapping, pushing and shoving, the whole crowd going back and forth in one brawling and fighting mass. It was no good at all, the Specials only played two or three numbers and then they were off. The Hallam DJ's who were there were constantly on the PA calling for calm and saying that *the Specials want to come back on and we want them to come back on, but the fighting has got to stop first*. Eventually it was organised for the Sheffield no.69 buses to come over to the playing fields and the police got as many of the Sheffield skins on to them as they could."

Helen McLaughlin … "We went to see the Specials at Rotherham Playing Fields down near where the cricket pavilion was. The Sheffield punks came over. It was great although I can't remember why it happened. Afterwards we all went back to Sheffield to another of our haunts (along with the Howard Hotel) Sheffield Poly (near the bus station) and had some more lager and black."

Lynne Rollinson … "In 1981 we went to see the Madness 2-Tone film 'Take it or leave it' and afterwards we were all walking back to Pond Street bus station, the eight of us - trying to attempt the Madness shuffle."

It would not be long after the notorious Rotherham gig that the Specials split and the glory days of 2-Tone, and certainly its counterpart the Mod Revival, would be over. Pauline Black had left the Selecter in May and now the remaining Mod groups were either splitting or jettisoning their Parkas, suits and Mod image in a bid to disassociate them-selves from what the music press were now condemning as a fad. Groups like Secret Affair and the Chords and their attempts to make serious new bodies of work were largely dismissed or practically ignored by the Post-Punk snobbery of the times. Local Mods were also dwindling and now was the time to see who the fashion followers had been. The final blow was delivered in late 1982 when it was announced that Paul Weller had decided to end The Jam.

John Harrison … "It was a shock to hear the news. The Jam had meant so much to me over the years and now they would be gone. It was kind of an empty feeling; but thinking back it was not unlike Weller to come up with such surprises. I suppose we have to be thankful really that they didn't carry on and on like all the other groups. What the Jam had back then, for us fans, was something special and it still goes on inside. A Jam fan is always a Jam fan."

Phillip Wright … "I saw the Jam on every single tour, from their first 'In the City' tour in 1977 during my Punk days right to the very end; usually multiple times on most tours. Some mates and me would also take time off school or work (call in sick) and then hang about outside the Top Rank and when the band arrived, we offered to help the roadies to carry the gear in. Once we had lugged the gear in, we always stayed behind and listened to the sound check. We used to take our picture sleeves (singles and albums) and get them autographed, still have them to this day of course! I introduced my future wife to Paul Weller after one gig as she loved him; made me look like the hero!"

Above: The Jam concert tickets from the author's collection and a Paul Weller top ten from 1979

Stewart Hardman ... "I remember watching the first ever episode of The Tube in 1982 and The Jam were on. They had a load of Birmingham Mods on the show as well and I remember being aware of people who were into the same thing as myself (1980- 81 had been quiet for Mod).So here I was on a real high and the Jam about to appear on the telly and then Paul Weller announces live that the band would be breaking up at the end of the year. So mixed emotions were felt that night to say the least. Even now, watching footage from that show, I can still be transported back to that night and the way I felt. The feeling that the whole Mod thing for me would be over was overwhelming and I was distraught."

Tony ... "I went to the two nights that the Jam played at the Sheffield Top Rank in March 1982. They were absolutely fantastic. Coming on with 'Strange Town' the atmosphere was out of this world. These two gigs were the last time I saw the Jam; but what a memory."

John Harrison ... "I gave all my 'Jam' memorabilia away – I had posters, signed stuff, badges, cuttings the lot, even a letter from 'Weller' himself – but I gave it to this local lass called Sue who was crackers about Paul Weller and the Jam."

Tony ... "The Jam had always been there for me; right through the Punk era and beyond. It was a special time, but it had to end sometime. Yes I respected Weller for splitting The Jam. It book-ended the whole Punk era for me and it saved them from becoming another tired old act doing the rounds. Those 'Jam' days mean something and the music lives on; it will never die."

Steve Haythorne ... "I was well into the Mod Revival scene, but it was all over in a flash."

Tony ... "The thing with the Mod Revival was that it was too Punk influenced. Most of the groups involved had been Punk groups previously, which is all good and well, but it dragged it down a bit. In retrospect, there really was not enough rhythm and blues in there, apart from Nine Below Zero and the Little Roosters and as much as I did like some of the Mod groups that had come out of Punk, ultimately it was often just a case of Punks in Parkas!"

John Harrison (Left) ... "I had some fantastic times during the Mod Revival days, lots of great Mod nights at the clubs and venues around the area, some right laughs too. I was wearing some really sharp suits and it felt great to look smart. So yeah, they were great times, but it really was the end for me with that particular era of Mod when the Jam called it a day. I remained a Mod, but the heart and soul of Mod had gone. I was now thinking about having a real crack at it myself. I just needed to get myself a bass guitar and some other like minded people to join in with."

The gauntlet was down, The Mod Revival had failed and the Jam were now gone, so who was going to take the crown of being the UK's leading band for the Mod generation? Who could justify the title of being such a band? The Mod revival bands had simply faded away. Only the Specials could have possibly gained the Jam's mantle, and they had dissolved before them. It looked like the choices were either to accept the so called 'New Pop' that was fast approaching as the 80's nosedived into its musical and fashion zenith...hello Kajagoogoo haaaaaaaaaaaa – the pain! Or soldier on with the scattered remains of the experimental and progressive - but often dull and disjointed - Post-Punk scene. You could continue to carry the clarion call of *we are the Mods we are the Mods we are we are we are the Mods* with no group to identify with. Or alternatively, you could start your own group instead.

Chapter Nineteen

The New Breed

"Eventually Mod was like a very mainstream fashion and the last few bands that played at the Limit Club were mediocre. Luckily the mod craze passed over and me and my mates were still wearing our mod clothes while everyone else was rushing to become a new romantic. It was like 'our scene' again, normal service had been resumed" – **Phillip Wright (Sheffield Mod)**

Tony ... "I had been playing guitar for some time now, well in a fashion anyway. I knew some basic chords and could make a row that's for sure. I had formed a couple of Punk groups that were to be honest atrocious. I knew I had to keep soldiering on though and no matter what I wasn't going to have any lessons. I wanted to develop my own style with my own influences.

I had known John Harrison from the Punk days and then his involvement in the Mod Revival. He was also a mate of local Punk Bryan Bell who I also knew. We would meet up at a local pub about mid 1982 and have a few beers and chat about getting a group together. Myself and John, quickly came to realise that we had much the same ideas and aims, so we formed a group. There was only the two of us to begin with. I showed John some bass lines I had written and he picked

Above: John Harrison and myself – founding members of The Way in 1982

up really fast. We then started to write our own songs as well as doing covers of The Who, Kinks and Tamla Motown standards. We were called Control at first, with us both having a crack at singing. We then got a rehearsal room up at Rawmarsh comp and it all sort of snowballed from there.

We were both massive Weller fans and John had been a Mod since 1979. I had shed my Punk look and was wearing Mod clothes too. We would be wearing Ben Sherman button down's, Pop art shirts, lots of Fred Perry's, sta-prest trousers, boating jackets and suits. Going along to The Assembly Rooms and Clifton Hall in Rotherham, we searched for a drummer to complete our line up and become a proper band, but to no avail. I noticed that the Mod scene was now quite an underground thing, but I found it far more healthier than the over exposed Mod Revival.

At that time I was starting to buy loads of old sixties soul records. First it was the Tamla stuff, followed by all the Stax and Atlantic label records. We were big fans of Otis Redding, Eddie Floyd, and the Miracles etc. I was also buying more obscure soul records as well. I would be all over the place, searching the record shops for Mod stuff. Rotherham market had a decent stall on Saturday afternoons. Then there were all the second hand record shops in Sheffield. It was like old times again - amassing heaps of vinyl and finding out new sounds and records. The thing is, a lot of the Punk generation couldn't understand the move from Punk into Mod, well I never really had a problem with it. I saw both of them kind of intertwined; they were both about being young and having short hair, wearing streamline clothing – with narrow lapels etc - and listening to raw energetic music. When Punk became boring and created its own rules, I found the whole idea of being a Mod totally refreshing. I mean what else was there?"

The musical influences had changed very much for Punk generation Mods who were now digging the black sounds of sixties American R&B. But it could be hard to find others with similar tastes in music and clothes.

Tony … "Me and John used to go to a local working mens club for a few pints and we would sit at the front and laugh at the club bands that were on. It's a wonder we didn't get a right hiding; anyway the resident drummer there, he was good-humoured and he would laugh at us taking the piss really. He knew we didn't mean any harm I suppose. Well, we got talking to him at the bar and after buying him a pint, he told us about this kid from Mexborough he had been teaching drums. His name was Ian Deakin and in no time at all, he was with us and we were now a three piece just like the Jam. Pow!!

We played our first gigs at the Rawmarsh youth club where we rehearsed. They went down quite well. We were called Reaction at that point. We put posters up all over Rawmarsh for the first few gigs we did. Throughout 1983 - 84 we kept on writing songs and rehearsing them. We were all Mods."

Mod groups formed were often, if not always, springing up with unshakable Punk influences; to begin with anyway.

Phillip Wright … "I taught myself a few chords when I was 14, then Big Jon decided he wanted to be a drummer and his brother Tim wanted to be a singer, so we called ourselves "Urban Youth" and told everyone we were a punk band. At this point we had no instruments! By the time, I was 16 I left school, started work, and bought my first electric guitar, 65 quid (a lot of money back then) from Musical Sounds on London Road. Jon got a drum kit and we started practising in a room at Herdings Youth club. Just doing covers, Jam, Buzzcocks, Clash, etc. We went through a load of names without ever playing live, Far Removed, The Switch, before settling on The Bloc. Mainly because it sounded different and it was what Pete Townshend, of The Who had used to describe being out of his head on speed and stuff, 'being blocked'. It was through the youth club (and the legendary Ted Jenkins) that we got our first gig. It was at an international Festival that was being held in Sheffield and a band was needed to play at the Crucible in the studio (there is a small theatre alongside the main Crucible theatre called The Studio). We were told we needed to have an 'international' flavour, so we decided to do some Clash style reggae along with our own Jam/Undertones inspired punk pop. We drafted in a bass player called Tony, who played bass in an afro Caribbean church on Sunday mornings and brought in a lad called Steve Meyers to play guitar alongside me.

We played about 6 songs to an audience of around 50 people, then for an encore we did 'My Generation' all jumping about and acting crazy; Great fun. Our second gig was a laugh but not at the time. We played at the Arbour Thorne pub, turned up in our Jam suits only to find out it was a biker's pub! I thought we were going to be lynched but once we got going the crowd were ok. Our bass player, Juggerz, named after his jug ears decided not to show up so we had no bassist, we must have sounded awful but we somehow pulled it off.

Above: Phillip Wright – guitarist with the Bloc and later the Prams

Tim went to Uni after that and I was drafted into a band called the Prams, who were from Rotherham, a sort of Post-Punk band, the bassist was called Simon Lee Ellis, he was a really cool guy, the drummer was a girl called Caroline and the singer was a real character called John. We had about four practices at a practice room down at West Bar, near the main police station, then one night the place got broken into and my guitar was nicked, leaving me in a real bad state, so I had to leave, without ever gigging with them, while I tried to save up some money for another guitar."

Tony … "When we started out playing, and even well into our Mod era, we would still play Clash songs whilst rehearsing. 'Police and Thieves' was one that we would often do.

In early 1985, Terry Sutton a Mod from Mexborough joined The Way on vocals and lead guitar. The line up was now complete and we started to write more new songs, rehearse like hell and soon we were looking for gigs to play. Our first ones were, yet again, at the Rawmarsh Youth Club. They were always a good warm up type of gig. Then we moved on to play gigs in Mexborough, where we did our first interview with local Mod fanzine 'Target'."

Above: Back to the old Rawmarsh youth club, an old Punk haunt, which by 1984- 85 was a regular warm up gig for The Way

As local groups like The Way were starting to play gigs and get noticed, a new breed of younger Mods was turning on to the style. Rotherham became a formidable haven for young Mods who were thirsty for the Mod way of life: the black music that was a crucial part of it, the clothes, and the haircuts and if possible their very own group to follow and identify with. Other groups popular with the local Mods were Makin' Time (with future 'Charlatan' Martin Blunt) the Prisoners, the Rage, the Scene, Direct Hits and the Gents.

The Gents had started out as a Heavy Metal band and later turned to ska and popular mod cover versions for their sets. They played consistently around the area, often at Mod promoted events, and released an LP of their own material in 1985.

Stewart Hardman … "Another chance find was in the local press, when on a bored Saturday just before I was just about to leave school in 1983, I saw a picture of this band, all dressed in very Mod looking clothes. In the write up below, it mentioned their

392

influences, being 60's music and the Jam, and, I had to read it a few times, they mentioned that word MOD. That was it, the band was the Gents, and they were all local to Doncaster not far from me, as I lived in a little village halfway between both Barnsley and Doncaster. The end of the article was to promote a new single and a concert, and this was to take place about a mile from my parents' house. I had to go, this was a sign. Well indeed I did go, and went on to see the band well over 100 times over the next 8 or 9 years until they split up: Even getting to the point on knowing the band and the management quite well by the end. I did a big piece on the band when they split, in a Modzine that I used to write for about 5 years. In the meantime, had a new band to get into, and this was a local band, I could actually get to see them play, unlike with The Jam, whom I never had the chance to see.

At this first Gents gig, I met up a few more like-minded people, in among a load of normal looking types. I had given up the chance to go to my school leaving party for this gig, and a good thing I did, for I had taken my first tentative steps to taking an active part on the Mod scene, as opposed to just listening to the music at home. The amount of times I got told off both at home and school for writing the names of bands or the word Mod on any available piece of paper or blackboard, this now started to make it feel real.

I'd found a record in a record shop in Barnsley one Saturday, the band, Squire, Get Smart was the album, I couldn't believe it when I saw it, here was the band that I had read about a couple of years before so I couldn't wait to get home to play the record. Well I did and loved it. I contacted their fan club, and got a couple of singles and LP's from them, along with letters from the main man of the band Anthony Meynell, in which he would tell me about new plans for the band etc, all were handwritten too (this being before the days of word processors). I still have these to this very day.

Another major turning point, occurred when I got a flyer sent through from the Gents fan club in May or June 1985, about an all dayer at The Clifton Hall in Rotherham, with them playing live along with two other bands, but the main thing was a Mod all dayer. I just had to go, fate had passed my path again and given me this chance, as up to that point I still had never been to a real out and out Mod event, they had always been too far away to get to. I remember getting my parents to drop me off near, (but not too close to the venue).

They parked up and spent the afternoon in Rotherham Park, saying that they would wait for me, it was midday to five pm event... So I remember walking through the park, and I just couldn't believe my eyes when I saw the halls, all these mods walking about, and mod girls with their bob haircuts and mini skirts amidst a sea of black and white. WHOAA, I was just totally taken aback, where had all these fellow Mods suddenly appeared from? That moment my heart missed more than a beat, it was, in the words of Secret Affair – literally dancing."

The other local Mod band, apart from The Way and The Gents were another Rotherham band called Revolver, but it was a visiting London band that the local Mods held most dearly to their hearts.

Steve Emmerson (Chesterfield Mod) ... "My fave Mod band has to be the Prisoners; the best band ever, they were awesome in the Mod era and should have gone on to better things. They never made a bad record. I must also mention the Gents, Makin' Time, the Moment and the Scene (they were an excellent Mod band)."

As with the Punk scene, it wasn't long before the area had its own fanzines. These new Mod fanzines such as 'Generation X', 'Target', and 'Immediate Reaction' would give the

Above: Gents flyer

local Mods all the latest news on the local scene, with upcoming gigs, club nights, new Mod attire as well as run downs of favourite Mod records. One such fanzine was called 'Beyond all limits'- previously 'First Impressions'- and was run by Sheffield Mod man about town 'Bell'

In issue no.4 of 'Beyond all Limits' (published in 1985) the editorial piece speaks about the divide between the local Mods... *"Most of the older Mods like the older stuff like Small Faces, Them and Yardbirds- whilst 'The younger Mods, on the other hand, like more of the modern stuff like Direct Hits, the Rage, the Untouchables, and the amazingly fantastic Makin' Time. They also like a percentage of Northern Soul, just like most Mods all over the country."*

In the fanzine there are three local Modernist societies listed; Generation X run by James Blonde, The Reaction by Tom Redfern and 'City Limits' run by the fanzine's writer himself.

Stewart Hardman ... "At the Mod do I went to at Rotherham Clifton Hall in June I saw stalls selling records and fanzines etc. I quickly snapped up singles by the Scene, the Moment and the Rage, plus fanzines with names like 'In the Crowd', 'Face to Face' and others. I started to write my own fanzine, buoyed on by all the others that I had bought. So 'Have a Good time' was born. All my time was spent sat at a typewriter and cutting and pasting the first few issues together, getting interviews with bands etc."

Young Mods did not always share the fondness that some other Mods had for live bands. Instead they were searching for the purer Mod ethos and for a while the local venues of Rotherham provided them with a common ground with what seemed like a new generation of Mod inclined lads and lasses.

Martin Ridgeway (Rotherham Mod) ... "I have quite a few recollections from about 1982 onwards. I remember Paul Critchlow organising a lot of the early Rotherham Mod do's. The bouncer on the door at the Assembly rooms knew me and my mate Dave, who both being underage at the time 13 – 14, he used to let us in if we bought him a pint.

Occasionally we did not get served and would spend most of the night running the gauntlet and hiding from big Col the doorman.

I also recall being confused around that period as there seemed to be dividing factions between the Mods. Musically at the time, I was only digging' sixties soul, anything Hammond organ fuelled and also the likes of the Small Faces with a little fondness for the 2-Tone stuff. That I know now was the divide - the revivalist boys and the traditionalists.

Left: issues 4 and 6 of Sheffield Mod fanzine 'Beyond all Limits'

I had already started having clothes tailored at that point and I recall an incident when this oik came up to me at my local youth club, parka fully patched and badged, and he asked me what kind of Mod I was because I wasn't dancing to 'David Watts' by The Jam. I didn't even know what the record was and did not recognise it as being Mod in any way. Likewise, when we used to attend the Clifton Hall nights, more often than not, when the bands came on, quite a few of us used to hit the bar because we didn't get what they were playing. Naïve maybe, but it certainly wasn't our cup of tea."

Steve Parlett ... "As we got older, styles changed, and lots of my crew went all New Romantic, but I stuck to my guns and pretty much ploughed my own furrow. I started making regular trips to Rotherham town centre, and as well as occasional skirmishes with the skins in the Market, became firm friends with lots of other like-minded people from around Rotherham - Critch from Rawmarsh, Roy Mason, Gaz Mason from East Herringthorpe, Big Dave from Rawmarsh, James Hamilton and Wayne Dearman.

It must have been around this time that we started going to the various gigs being put on in town. The Way at Clifton Hall was memorable for me - I was still in a dark 3 button suit with a short Weller style haircut, white socks and loafers with a skinny tie (as were most of our mates) but during the gig I noticed a small number of guys who really knocked me out in terms of their different style. They had tailored trousers on, with buttons at the hem, one had stepped bottoms on his trousers with frogmouth pockets, and they wore either very high-collared button-down shorts with pleat-back and button, or Gabicci style Italian knitwear, with smart college boy crop haircuts. They were slagging off the music and only came alive when the DJ started spinning soul records and when they started to dance - again, I was mesmerised.

I then made it my business to become like these cool cats and moved towards a bespoke style, with a soul/R&B focus. We used George Kristofferson (from Leeds) from his Rotherham market stall initially for tailoring - he was great at accommodating our various foibles - buttons at the hem, V-cuts, steps, various ticket pocket variations, vent lengths etc. Had a lovely midnight blue one from him, along with a not so nice mid-blue, and some brown Prince of Wales trousers.

The most memorable Rotherham suit I ever saw was a full navy tartan one that Roy Mason had made - you could see him in it from 3 miles away!"

Mark Ellis (Mod DJ from Leeds) ... "One of the nights in Rotherham, we were all trying to find somewhere to sleep and we noticed an extremely loud pair of check pants approaching us and realising it was Roy we jumped out to greet him and the shock on his face was a picture.."

Whilst most self respecting local Mods would usually attain their Mod attire from a mix of mail order casual wear - Local tailors for their suits and even the commercial catalogues for Fred Perry Polo shirts, Bowling shoes and occasionally Ben Sherman Button downs amongst many other sources (some of which would often be kept secret for fear of others copying) - there was always shops like 'Pulse' in Sheffield that was aimed at the Commercial side of Mod fashion. It had previously been a big Punk hang out and stocked a good range of vinyl during the late 70's, but now it was tempting aspiring 1960's obsessed kids to buy all the Mod related look from their enterprise.

Above: Rotherham Mod Roy Mason & a Mansfield Modette mate

Tony ..."Yes 'Pulse' was very posey that's for sure. You would walk in - it was actually shaped like a cavern - and you would be presented with all the usual crap like the target patches, Northern soul patches and badges, dodgy Parkas and Boaters and the like. But, having said that, if you looked beyond all that, there was usually a small but really good percentage of decent button down shirts. I would buy lots of my shirts from there on a

Saturday afternoon; all the Paisley ones, Pop art styles and polka dots, pinstripes and also occasionally I managed to get my hands on some decent Italian style knit wears. I had some nice 'Small Faces' types of shirts and cardigans."

Yet again, as in the Punk days, the local charity shops would soon become a unique source of clothes. Many local Mods -some of whom had been doing the same back in the Punk days - would manage to trace some cool vintage clothes. Mods are like Magpies and can usually suss out what's best and where it's located. With this cool instinct for clothes, Charity shops would be on most of their hit lists on Saturday afternoons, as well as the local market, along with any other source of 'gear' available.

Above: Local Mods Steve Parlett and Rad

John Harrison ..."Back in 1979 you could get some really good Fred Perry shirts from Caprice. Rotherham Market was quite good for Mod clothes, to be honest. There was a guy at the top of the market who had his own stall and I would buy trousers and jackets from him. All of the Mods would go to that stall. You could also buy Jam shoes from a different stall. Other than that, I would buy my clothes from the catalogues that were around. I bought my boating blazer from a catalogue and you could also get bowling shoes. Well it was weekly payments so it was easier to kit yourself out that way."

Phillip Wright ... "We raided charity shops for mod suits, or sometimes a lad on the estate would be lucky enough to have a dad who had been a mod and had a couple of suits in the loft. I used to go down to the shoe stalls on the outdoor market next to Castle and Sheaf Market on a Friday morning before work, I was lucky enough over time to get a great pair of loafers, a pair of brogues and a pair of Doc Marten shoes for a few quid a pair."

Stewart Hardman ... "I got my first suit from The Cavern (a Carnaby street based Mod clothes shop that was also in Doncaster), it was a grey 3 button suit for £50. Armed with this and a suit carrier and a couple of button down shirts, I made my first tentative steps to a Mod rally. Not so much 'Quadrophenia' as we had no scooters so we went by train. At York train station, we were met by loads more Mods, in fact a few carriages of the train seemed to be packed with a sea of green parkas."

Steve Emmerson ... "Our mod lot used to wear stuff from the second hand shops, suits, cardi's, shirts, ties, shoes etc. We couldn't afford the new stuff...we always had parkas and were always smart at the Rotherham do's wearing loafers, desert boots, Fred Perry's etc...just anything mod or related really."

Above: Pulse 'Sixties' Boutique and record shop

Steve Parlett ... "Around this time we were using Colin Starsmore of Darnall as tailor to the stars! ... A lovely fella and great tailor. Saturdays were spent having fittings at Colin's and in Sheffield centre going to Spin City to buy 60s soul and R&B 45s, and catching up with Bell and the crew at an Italian cafe off Division St."

Stewart Hardman continues his tale of first venturing to a Mod weekender ..."In Scarborough, we managed to find a B&B willing to take 5 teenage blokes in one go, and we made our way to the dinner time do down Huntris Row. We got there to the sight of two thirds of the road being full of scooters adorned with lights and mirrors, the little hairs at the back of my neck started to tingle at the sight.

That night we were treat to a venue on three levels, from the Lemon Tree club in the cellar, up to a couple of rooms above the pub the Salisbury Arms. I saw the first gig up there by a new band by the name of the Clique. They were 3 guys from London and one from Belgium. The other lads I had come down with all went home on Sunday, but I stayed on and alone I went down to the Scooter competition held on Marine Parade, which was on the sea front. Again it was a fantastic sight to behold. I didn't know which way to look for all the scooters. That afternoon was followed by another great night time event, this time the Gents playing.

Having to go to that event on my own I was very nervous, but I made a lot of good friends that weekend, quite a few of which I still see to this day, and not all from my local area. Over the next 20 years and over, I have made friends from as far away as America, Spain, Italy, Germany, France, Australia, Japan, Sweden and a whole host of different countries."

Above: Steve Parlett and his Mod posse in Doncaster train station and Scarborough

Tony ..."The Scarborough Mod weekends were always worth the trip. Back in the 80's it was very 'Mod only' orientated, but gradually as time went on it became a mix of Mod and swinging sixties styles."

John Harrison ... "I went to Scarborough with my mate Andrew, who knew these skinheads from Mexborough who had a caravan there, so we went in the van with 'em. On the way, we got stopped by the cops and they checked us for drugs. They didn't find any; as they had been hidden well. When we got to Scarborough, it was full of Mods and scooters everywhere. We went to the night dos and there was some trouble on the dance floor, but nothing major. The skinheads stopped all week, but Andrew and me were only there for the weekend so we caught the train home. It was a great weekend though."

By the mid 1980's, Mod had become a very much underground scene that was riding the storm of the new pop years.

Stewart Hardman ... "There were a couple of very lean years during the 80's, pretty horrible from a personal point of view to be a Mod when all around was all very 80's New pop, Spandau Ballet/ Human League, electro pop. I was chased around Doncaster in early 1985, by a load of Skinheads; I still have a dent in my head after getting a boot to the head one day."

The mid 80's local Mod scene was never better than in 1985 ...when most of the recognised Mod bands would play in Rotherham as well as local bands playing the more clued-in venues. Mod fanzines were being produced with the true D.I.Y ethic that had earlier been exemplified by the Punk writers and there was usually somewhere to buy good clobber and, most importantly, somewhere to go wearing it. The fashionably unsure Quadrophenia obsessed Mods of 1979 were long since 'out of sight', but how long would this new generation of Mods keep hold of the flame?

Steve Emmerson ... "The Rotherham Mod do's. I went there many times. It was always a great place for gigs/events and all-dayers. I saw many good bands there. I saw The Prisoners, Small World, the Rage, the Moment, the Cynics, Direct Hits, Yeh Yeh, the Theme, the Boss, the Gents (although some questioned if they were actually a Mod band but they were great live) and The Way."

Left: Mods on the dance floor at a Scarborough Mod weekend (from my collection)

Stewart Hardman ... "By getting a regular subscription with the Phoenix list (which did have its distractors but was a great way of keeping in touch with the Mod scene), I was made aware of a series of local Mod gigs and do's in Rotherham. The course of approx 2 years of gigs would go down into the history banks of all who attended. I saw the likes of The Moment, the Direct Hits (both of these twice), Small World, the Rage, The Way and more; The gigs happening every few months or so."

Tony ... "The Way built up a great Mod following around the Rotherham area. This was a time when Mod faves like The Prisoners, Long Tall Shorty, Small Hours, The Rage (ex Purple Hearts),The Cynics, and The Untouchables etc - were playing the Mod events around the Rotherham area and it was quite an exciting time. I have to say, though, that I hardly ever listened to the other Mod bands even when I went to the do's. My time was taken up with listening to Soul and R&B and writing songs as well as playing gigs and fitting in some quality drinking time."

Steve Emmerson ..."I liked The Way. They were a good band and perfect to start any Mod event. They were raw but talented; very powerful with a Jam style but you could also hear where their other influences were coming from. They always went down really well with all the Mods that I knew and saw at the Rotherham do's. I did have a 3-track demo tape, which was also good stuff, but sadly I cannot find it nowadays. I am hoping Tony and the band will bring them out on CD in some way in the future."

Above: Mod John Harrison

John Harrison ... "One of my favourite songs that we played was 'Days like Tomorrow' which we did plan to be a single...but unfortunately that never happened."

Tony ... "We played a great gig at Conisborough station hotel. It was for a Doncaster Rovers presentation night and we played two sets and were paid in beer money. This they came to regret after all of us in the band, our sound guy and all our girlfriends, were slowly supping the bar dry. The bar staff started refusing us the free beer. Anyway, the two sets went down great, despite the fact that the only Mods there were ourselves and the ones we had brought along with us. We did a storming version of 'Louie Louie'."

Ian Deakin (Mexborough Mod/Drummer with the Way) ... "I can't even remember playing that gig. I can remember being there but not playing at all. I can still remember though, that we got paid in beer and I think John just about supped em dry."

Tony ... "In May we recorded our first demos in a Doncaster studio. We were there all day. It was boring, but at least we got our songs down on tape. A couple of weeks later we gave a copy of our Demo tape to Paul Weller after a Style Council gig. When I got home that day after recording the demo tape, it was all over the papers about the Clash busking tour. They did Leeds and I remember thinking I should have been there but my commitment was to the Mod band I was in and this was our way forward. The Clash were almost a part of our history now and they weren't even finished yet."

Rawmarsh Baths Hall is long gone now, but it did have a very worthy history for dances in the sixties and was even chosen to host the Beatles on one of their earliest tours, BUT THE VENUE'S PROMOTER TURNED THEM DOWN (OUCH!!)...The venue did salvage some of their sense and in the same decade chose to book the Pretty Things and Cliff Bennett and the Rebel Rousers amongst others. Following the heyday of the Sixties, the venue (which as its name suggests also doubled up as a swimming baths), was open for hire; usually for weddings and similar social functions. When the Mod revival kicked in around the area, it wasn't long before Mod nights were starting to be held there. One of those Mod nights included two sets from The Way.

Tony ... "We used to go to Rawmarsh Baths when the Mod nights were on and ended up playing a gig there as well. As usual with most of our gigs, things started off ok but soon descended into chaos."

John Harrison ... "It was mayhem that night; one of the bouncers had it in for one of the lads who was with us and they were going to fight but as the bloke pulled his fist back he whacked Tony's then girlfriend and knocked her out. It all kicked off from there and ended up spreading outside and the cops turning up."

Tony ... "During all the trouble I saw John grab hold of the takings, which were in a green cash box we had. I didn't realise what happened until the next day when I had flashbacks of what I saw. It was quite funny really."

John Harrison ... "I shared the money out for the four of us. It was a case of some for Tony, a quid for Terry; ten bob for Ian and oh a few quid in the back pocket for me. It was total mayhem so it was like 'cash from chaos' so to speak."

Tony ... "No one got paid, the DJ, the bouncers, the sound engineer, the roadies; they all ended up donating their services for free - unwittingly of course."

Sadly, there would be losses to be endured within local Mod circles.

Tony ... "One of the Mod lads who followed us around was a local lad called Darren Marsden. He was 14 and was a great lad - very enthusiastic, exuberant and always having a great time. He would be calling around and wanting to listen to music and raving on about the latest sounds he had come across. He was at the Rawmarsh baths do and some other ones. Sadly, he had a weak heart and some rare problem that meant he would have to have an operation when he was 16. I got to know him very well and really liked him. He was a proper fan of The Way. When he was almost 16 he had the dreaded operation and he never came round. Apparently there was never much chance of it being successful and he knew it as well. I still think about him from time to time and think of how his life was cut so short. There was another Mod kid called Paul from Mexborough, who used to come to our rehearsals... and he also sadly passed away when he caught meningitis at the age of something like 15 or 16."

Steve Parlett ... "The 1983 to 85 period saw us attending numerous mod do's and weekenders. Scarborough Mod Rally, where we all stayed at Gaz Mason's auntie's B&B

and where we first hooked up with the Sheffield crew (Rad, Bell, Damien etc). We saw the Rage, Yeh-Yeh, the Way-out, the Threads, the Gents, Direct Hits, the Prisoners, the Moment etc, numerous times. We also travelled a lot to Mansfield, Derby, Stoke, to a variety of mod do's, and began attending the Attic Club at the Queens Head Attercliffe, with Sean Phillips and Nik Parry DJing, and we also started to cut our own teeth DJing.

Our weekends got further and further away, attending all-nighters in Stoke, Coventry (Hip Citizens, very cool bunch) and even Gloucester one weekend, where we also got an hour's slot (me and Rad) in the early hours. Major tracks at the time were 'Keep an Eye on Love' by Ernestine Anderson, 'Sh'Mon' by Mr Dynamite, 'Wack Wack' by the Young-Holt trio, 'Hey you little boogaloo' by chubby Checker, 'Shake Shake Shake' by Jackie Wilson etc."

The Way from left to right: John Harrison, Ian Deakin, Tony Beesley and Terry Sutton (first picture at left)

John Harrison … "When I look back on my Mod days… obviously the best times were when I was playing with The Way. I sometimes think nowadays – though – that if we had have carried on me and Tony would probably not have been around now. I know I certainly wouldn't have been alive. The temptations would have been too much and who knows what we would have got into and how we would have ended up. Yes, it all happened for a reason really and the ending was quicker than I would have imagined but good or bad it was all worth it."

Tony …"The high point, for me and I think probably for the rest of the band, was when we played at the Mod Rally in Scarborough in June 1985. We went down there in the back of Terry's dad's transit van with all the gear in the back with us. When we got there, we soon got chatting to the Mods who seemed to be all over the town. We got our gear into the venue, which was the Salisbury Hotel on Huntris Row. Then we downed a few pints in the bar followed by an interview with a Mod fanzine and having our photographs taken outside with our guitars. I have no idea what we said in that interview whatsoever and I never saw the finished article.

By the evening, when we came back to the venue from the B&B, there were loads of Mods queuing up outside the place. We got into the venue and soaked up the atmosphere. The place filled up pretty quick and the Mods were starting to dance to the soul and R&B that was playing. John was a little nervous but downed a few pints to take the edge off. We were itching to get on stage and do our thing. We weren't sure how we would come across or if we would get a positive reaction at all. Ian set the tape running and we got up there and played our set - the best one we ever did - and we were soon buzzing and bouncing off the very receptive and enthusiastic Mod crowd.

Above: flyer, news piece and ticket for The Way Mod events

We did some of our own songs like 'Walk it Talk it', which was a very Mod R&B one, and also some choice Mod cover versions like 'Heatwave', 'Sweet Soul Music' and the two biggies Small Faces 'All or Nothing' and The Who's 'I can't Explain'. These went down a storm. The Mods that night loved us and the atmosphere was electric and we got to do two encores. 'Yeh Yeh' went on after us.

After the gig we felt on top of the world. We carried on drinking until the early hours. John and Terry were well pissed and vandalised the Tory club's sign on the way back to the B&B. The next day me and Ian went and had some snaps taken on the beach and posed alongside some of the scooters. Looking back that gig was one of the best experiences of my life and it's something that I will never forget. We had reached our peak now and it was up to us to keep up the pace. Unfortunately, we messed it all up some months later."

John Harrison ... "That Scarborough gig was the high point for me. It was unbelievable. What an experience and so much better than the Rotherham Live Aid event that we did."

Ian Deakin ... "I do remember that gig and yes it was one of the best. I really enjoyed it. John showed his appreciation by wrecking something to do with the conservative club down Huntris Row. He could get quite violent at times especially after too much to drink and where politics were concerned. He would go off on rants every now and again. But he was a great kid really and I always liked him: funny bloke as well."

Above: Rotherham Mods Carny and Steve Parlett and at right Steve DJing (both at Rotherham Assembly Rooms)

Rotherham Clifton Hall, as well as hosting Northern soul nights – one of which the legendary Soul music pioneer Dave Godin attended, was still holding many memorable Mod event nights as did the other Mod venue just down the road the Assembly Rooms.

Mark Ellis ... "The Prisoners at the Assembly Rooms. Summer 85...Thatcher in full flower and yes the Mod scene...Countdown label compilations, mod societies, almighty ding dongs with the casuals, skinheads, psychobillies, train-spotters (it happened), poodle-haired metal-heads, scooter-boys, rugger fans or anyone else who so loved Mods ! I remember it well. Rotherham was and still is a large rough and ready township, situated somewhere between Sheffield, Barnsley and the Twilight Zone - the writing was on the wall in some respects.

Standing outside the Assembly Rooms in Rotherham after running the gauntlet of taunting, jeering 'fat knacker' townies and the atmosphere was electric. Hipster clad, very cool looking girls, smart modernist chaps and a whole bunch of Brian Jones look-alike 'psychedelics' (the first time I'd clocked this style) and every person looked a million dollars.

Essentially, this was my first sojourn to a major Mod event with a high Mod count and just remembering the sheer ice cool on display that night brings it all back, the passion and audacity of the whole thing - smack dab in the middle of what had to be the most culturally devoid decade.

Into the 'cavernous' interior of the Assembly Rooms and you couldn't move for people 'shooting the breeze' with each other and then there was the dancing! The dancing supplied by the Mods in the 80's was, to be quite honest, utterly fantastic and this night introduced me to some of the best dance moves I have ever set eyes on. 'Wack da doo doo doo de doo doo Wack Wack' – my introduction to The Young Holt trio's 'Wack Wack' 45. Nifty jazz and niftier dancing – hipshake, windmill, turn on a sixpence.

However, it was the bands we had come for and they did not disappoint. Blistering! This word will suffice Graham Day and the boys ripping the paint off the walls with the best set I had ever seen. The Direct Hits also gave it some in an equally superb set. Now memory has decided to squint its eyes a bit and detailed synopsis of the set lists of both bands is kind of impossible to conjure up. But it's the whole sense of that evening that shoots back into clarity... a sense that something big was afoot. The Mod scene was really starting to rev up back then.

Amongst the fray, mutterings that the local football casuals were waiting outside, beating the hell out of anybody that didn't fit their bill...us! This added to the excitement in the Assembly Rooms...our heads were spinning. Outside – let's face the music. But the police were there, mopping up, a couple of vans full of natives baying for our blood."

Steve Emmerson ... "The best nights were at the Assembly Rooms. That was a great venue and the sound was always fantastic and always a good atmosphere between all the Mods and the band members with good stalls, merchandise, fanzines, demo tapes, badges, flyers, singles etc. All the Mods were a friendly bunch and they would talk about scooters and the mod scene all day long. I always felt at home at those events."

Martin Ridgeway ... "Me and a small crowd of Mods would always walk out of the hall when the bands came on. No disrespect to them but we never had any time for them. As a result I missed out on The Prisoners who I love nowadays."

Tony … "The Assembly Rooms nights were great, but there was always that element of the Rotherham locality who wanted to spoil things. Once though, I can remember it was some of the Mods themselves that were having a go with each other. I think some Mods from down South had come up and there was some of that North v South hostility kicking off."

Andy Bull (editor of 'Immediate Reaction' fanzine and Chesterfield Mod) … "The Mod do's in Rotherham were one of the best things about the 80's Mod scene, mainly because they revolved around live music which was something that the obsession with 60's cool in the mid 80's eventually seemed to kill off. The Prisoners, Small World, Makin' Time and the Direct Hits were all top draws at the time and they all played Rotherham. During this time Rotherham actually eclipsed Sheffield and Leeds for its Mod events."

Steve Emmerson … "The only time I had a problem going to the Rotherham Mod do's was at an all-dayer event and we were offered, well nearly forced to pay out for some drugs. We were picked on as we were younger Mods aged 15 to 16, but some of the older Rotherham Mods took care of us."

As in the Punk era, the status of being part of a Youth cult would always carry the burden of impending violence around the corner.

Above: Mods (including Steve Parlett. Lisa and Dom Bassett at a Makin'Time gig in Mansfield)

David (Sheffield Mod) … "I regularly got smacked in Sheffield in the early 80's around the Castle and Sheaf markets, by the skins. I also had run- ins with the casuals, who were a different lot each weekend, depending on which team was at home! Around this period, I also attended many do's in Rotherham."

Steve Parlett … "Without wanting to glamorise violence, one extremely memorable evening was at a Makin' Time gig in Mansfield. We all liked the Rhythm & Soul slant of the band (and the singer - keyboard player Fay Hallam in particular), plus Dom Bassett (who had wowed us at the Blackpool Mod Rally in the Winter Gardens) was DJing. So this time I booked a 52 seater bus, with attendees from all over Rotherham and Sheffield (including the afore mentioned Parry and Philips). I remember what I was wearing - cream button down and tan tailored trousers with brown basket weave shoes to arrive, then I changed into a brand-new dark gold tailored mohair suit for the main evening. I remember the first track we hit the dance floor to was 'Country Fool' by the Showmen, with me and Rad kicking it off.

Fairly early on, some football lads arrived (Sheffield United on the way home from an away game) and I spotted one of them (all of 25 years of age) threatening a mod kid of no more than 15 - I sidled over and told him that if he wanted trouble he should start on men not boys! He laughed it off, shook my hand and said *'Sorry mate, you're right, we're all mates here we just came to see the band - no problem'*). The whole gig then went off without a hitch, the band was great and the DJ kept us all happy with a great mix of dance floor soul and R&B.

As we were leaving (with a couple of bottles of Pils each for the way home!), we got just outside the venue, waiting to round up all the people on the bus, when up walk two of these casuals and they ask *'who wants to have a Worksop Blade then?'.* Me and Carney (Wednesday fan!) looked at each other, handed our bottles to my then girlfriend Maria, and piled in. Then all hell broke loose. It was mayhem, wave after wave of this lot kept coming forward, and me and Carney were knocking them down like 9 pins. It was when I got a drum stick over the head from some muscle bound gimp in a vest and blonde highlights that I really saw red, and we all went mental. At one stage, Dom Bassett himself was out in the car park, swinging a chair around at any casual he could reach, and we gave them a proper good Yorkshire hiding. As the Police started to arrive in numerous vans, I turned to face the next one, only to find a bloke who must have been at least 6 foot 7 - I couldn't even reach his face to punch him! I decided it was time to depart and spun on my heels only for him to grab the collar of my suit jacket and rip the back out of it as I legged it (brand new suit remember!).

I made it onto our bus, seeing lots of friends with black eyes, plenty of claret knocking about but pretty upbeat (must have been the adrenaline). All of a sudden, the afore-mentioned gorilla got on the bus, and started coming towards the back for me. He got about half way, when a policeman with an Alsatian boarded the bus... he grabbed the casual by the shoulder, but he swung an arm out to hit the copper - this resulted in the copper rolling up his dog lead into a nice thick metal slug and whacking him across the face with it - blood and teeth everywhere. He soon got off the bus quietly. No mods were taken by the Police and we made our way back to Rotherham. When I got in, I was sat in the kitchen, my mum and dad arrived back from a 2-week holiday abroad to find me with a rag of a suit, a broken watch, missing id bracelet, a broken tooth and dirt all over me. My mum screamed, but my dad just said *'Did you win?'* and I said *'Absolutely'*, and he told me to go to bed. Happy days!"

Steve Emmerson ... "We were chased a few times by skins and casuals as we went to or from our mini bus, some casuals we chased back, but we mainly stayed out of trouble, it wasn't too bad a place to go. One time at the Assembly Rooms, I was doing an interview with Jeff Shadbolt of the Rage for my fanzine The Enthusiast and a few bricks came through the windows -

Above: Steve Parlett, Carny and a fellow Mod celebrate their Victory over the Casuals

- But no-one was hurt, not really any serious trouble as there was always a good turn out at Rotherham and plenty of mods to look after the younger ones."

Martin Ridgeway ... "I used to go and buy Mod records from Andy's record shop in the Castle market in Sheffield and there would be all the skinheads hanging around there. I had to pass them each week I went there but I never got any hassle from them. They would eventually give me a nod of respect. They did once get hold of another skinhead and I heard a sickening thud as the guy went down. I thought that now they were buzzing from the violence that they might decide to turn on me when I went back out but I got out ok. I guess I must have been one of the lucky ones."

Around this time an old provincial vendetta was re-awoken in the divide between skinheads and mid 80's Punks when Doncaster Skinhead band Skin-Deep played their first gig at Rotherham Assembly Rooms. Lead singer of Skin-Deep Wayne Kenyon recalls.

Wayne Kenyon ... "Two years or so after being at the Toy Dolls Sheffield skins v Donny Punks brawl, I played my first gig with my band Skin-Deep at the Assembly rooms. Again it was attended by both Sheff skins and Donny Punks and again chairs were used as weapons, 10 getting broken and 13 windows smashed. To this day, I still don't know if the hatred between the two factions was because the Sheffield skins were right wing or if it was just a Donny v Sheffield thing, probably cos the skins were right wing... I guess."

The friction between the many diverse youth cultures did not begin and end with skinheads and Punks or Mods and Skinheads.

Martin Ridgeway ... "Me and my mate Dave were up Sheffield once and we got chased by Hip Hoppers (there's a first)...I managed to hide in a shop for a while, which was, of all things a photo frame shop, how long can a teenage Mod pretend to browse in a photo frame shop I ask? Anyway, a young kid grassed on me, so I had to leg it again; I did manage to get away and onto the bus back to town. Dave had got split up from me, and we ended up on the same bus out of Rotherham, him with a right shiner."

Clearly, trouble dished out with a Doc Marten boot was easy to come by; but it was during the mid 80's that another youth cult came along that would dispense physical violence and hostile indifference towards the local Mods. The Casuals had actually been around for some time, especially in Liverpool and later Manchester, parading their new clothing attire on the football terraces and were considered by some to be an indirect descendant from the Mods (through their avid and obsessive taste and zest for clothes). Netherthless, the affiliation ended there and for the casuals they mostly showed minimum respect and even less violent restraint towards their opposing youth cult 'the Mods'.

Rotherham Mod **Dave Gooderham** (later to become a style conscious skinhead) recalls ... "It was always the casuals that had it in for us...we were always getting chased or belted by them. Once we got chased across the Grange golf course on the way to a do and if they weren't edging up to us in cars with fuckin' baseball bats, they would be sneering at us through the window of the Sound of Music record shop in town. I remember though, that after so long me and my mate Martin decided that we had had enough of them.

We were in the record shop looking through the records and yet again there they were glaring at us and mimicking us and giving it some *'C'mon then ...C'mon out then!' 'Not again'* I remember thinking *'I'm sick of this'.* Anyway, this was one time that my mate Martin flipped and he came back with *'Yeah C'mon then...C'mon inside if yer want some!'*...So in they came and he went straight for the first one 'Bang!' he gave him a right punch and they were scrapping all over the shop. The others came in and we gave 'em a right run for their money. After that we didn't seem to get that much trouble from the local casuals. We had just had enough of it, but we had taken our fair fuckin' share of beatings I can tell you."

410

Andy Bull was a Mod from nearby Chesterfield and was regularly in Sheffield … "I think that Sheffield in the 80's was a terrible place to visit, but a good place to pick up clobber, whether it be 'Harrington's' in the castle market where you had to run the gauntlet of skinheads, or the casuals on a Saturday. It's a bastard when a city has 2 football clubs – you never get a Saturday off.

On one occasion, I was with my nephew Tony Smith who used to edit 'Suede head times' fanzine. I was in the usual get-up, but definitely no parka! Even if you wore one, you left it at home for trips into the steel city. Tony was wearing a sky blue Harrington, half mast sta – prest trousers, red socks, loafers, and we ran into the usual skinhead crew(1980's unemployment meant there was a skinhead guard at the Castle Market every day). Expecting the worst, I was ready to be on my toes, but surprisingly all we got was a look up and down from them and an almost grudging nod of approval.

The run-ins with the Casuals were the worst. We ran into the ICF on the train one day, which happened to be when that Casual programme was being filmed around 83/84 time. One of our lads got his jeans 'stanleyed'. Strangely though, within a few weeks that same lad became obsessed with football hooliganism and along with his brother became two of the main lads in the notorious 'Chesterfield Bastard squad' as did many Mod mates of mine from that era."

Martin Ridgeway … "I had a run in with the trendies once or twice. One in particular I remember was after I had seen my girlfriend at the time off on her bus in Rotherham bus station and I clocked a gang of them giving me the eye. As I set off they quickly made their pursuit and I ended up legging it out of the bus station and headed off in the direction of Rawmarsh.

Above: Local Mods at a Mod night at the Queen's head in Attercliffe

I ran like hell with the blokes chasing me as hard as they could. Knackered and out of breath with my adrenalin surging and heart almost bursting, I managed to get into the pub 'The Comedian' at the edge of St.Anne's road. I went to the bar and ordered a coke and took small sips of it as I waited to see if they had seen me go in there. As I glanced around and saw all the pub's regulars looking at me, I saw that along each window of the place there was a face looking in. Yes they had seen me and were not giving up. I could see that they had weapons as well and I was not impressed at all. The feeling was unreal. How do I get out of this one?

A few of the regular blokes who were in there, who would be in their mid to late 30's about, well they came up to me and asked what was up. So I told them and their reply was *'Don't worry about that lot son, we'll sort them out for you'.* They did that alright and the trendies (or casuals) scarpered. The regulars said that it was alright to go now and I would be ok. I waited a while in trepidation, supped my coke and then ventured out. The feeling was still there as I stepped outside. *'Are they still hanging around and hiding?'* Anyway they weren't and I got home ok, but I will never forget that feeling I had of being in that kind of predicament."

Steve Parlett ... "We had regular scraps with casuals around this time, in Rotherham town centre and also at home in Wath, where we would battle the Wombwell Casuals near to Cortonwood Colliery. Looking back, I can understand Paolo Hewitt's assertion that Casual was the latest iteration of mod - I'm standing there in a cream Harrington, button-down shirt under a crew neck jumper, with some sta-prest trousers and loafers fighting a bloke wearing a Chipie button down shirt and Benetton crew neck, Farah slacks, moc-croc slip-ons and a Burberry golf jacket! The similarities are striking; it was just the wedge haircut and the football angle that was so different!"

Dave Gooderham ... "I knocked about with some of the skinheads for a while. They wore their braces and a union jack t-shirt and went out with the intention of belting anyone...no questions asked. I wasn't having any of that, so when I became a skin, I made sure that I went to the original skinhead style for my influence."

Meanwhile, skinheads of nearby Doncaster were making the traditional Mod and skinhead Bank holiday visits to the coast. This time it would be Skegness that was to experience the interruption to seaside frivolities and the opposition would be the casuals.

Wayne Kenyon (Doncaster skinhead and member of Skin-Deep) ... "August bank holiday Monday 1985... Me, Mik and Andy got on a coach for Skeggy. On the coach we met 4 other skinheads, Sparks, Kaz, Chris and Kev all from Donny.
   We arrived in Skeggy and went straight to the festival boozer, which was packed, with hundreds of skinheads from all over the north and midlands. We got drinks and sat on the grass outside. I had never seen as many skinheads in one place at one time. Apparently the year before there had been even more and a lot of trouble.
   While sat on the grass, a group of about 30 casuals/trendies came past to check out our numbers; the skins became a little bit aggressive and the casuals took flight except for one black youth who stood and gave a sieg heil salute to the skinheads. This was a big mistake as around 15 skins gave him a right old kicking. In fact an ambulance had to come and take him away and I believe he was only stopped from being killed when a few

skins took pity and stopped others from beating him anymore. Me and my mates did not take part in the beating. Mob violence against an individual was not our way.

In fact, we were a little sickened by it. Closing time came and the landlord tried to get people to leave...No chance!! The police were called and as they tried to enter the pub they were greeted by a hail of glasses and bottles. Eventually after the pub refused to serve any more drinks the room began to empty. The first place approx 1000 skinheads headed for was the beach. Straight down the beach watching families sit in amazement at what they were seeing. Along the beach to the pier, which has amusements etc, the place got trashed. By now the police were onto what was going on. Police dogs were biting people and I saw several skins with their jeans torn by dog bites including girls. Then we were met with hundreds of casuals, football lads all out for a fight, all intoxicated. Needless to say, the casuals got many a kicking.

Above: Skinheads (including Doncaster Skinhead Wayne Kenyon; 2nd from the left in the foreground at Skegness August Bank Holiday 1985 (taken from Wayne Kenyon's collection)

The time came for us to get back to the coach, Oh dear, we had to leave the safety of the mob and head back alone. How were we gonna get back without bumping into the huge casual gang. We planned a route through the backstreets... On the way a guy was digging his garden, Chris decided that a part of the guy's fence would make an excellent weapon so he started to break off part of the wooden fence. The guy looked up and seeing several skinheads said nothing.

Eventually we made it to the coach. Sat on there; the main group of casuals spotted us and surrounded the coach... They were beckoning us to get off... We were not crazy...

We said *'get on if you want a fight.'* In the aisle of the coach, it would have been just about even. For some reason they didn't get on... then after about 5 minutes of banter the main group of skinheads appeared out of the blue and we pissed ourselves as the casuals took flight, some getting caught and getting another kicking. We stood on the coach and cheered them on... regretting that we had to go home early because of coach times. Sparks never made it back to the coach; he had been arrested earlier in the day and was safely locked up in the police cells.

A year later, we went again... This time prepared with gum shields (yes fuckin' gum shields, ha ha). There were only about 200 skins there this year. The festival pub stopped skinheads from going in; in fact, it may have been closed. We all met at a pub under the pier. As we left, the pub this time the police got wise and surrounded us and gave us an escort to the train station where they kept us for most of the day. The next year we did not bother to go at all, as we thought the numbers would be even lower... I wrote a song for my band Skin-Deep called 'Skinhead bank holiday Monday' but it never made it to the album. Mik from the band is now in Babyshambles."

Above: Doncaster anti-racist skinhead band Skin-deep led by Wayne Kenyon

Skin-Deep were a greatly under-rated 1980's skinhead band from Doncaster. With a positively anti-racist stance and a love of ska, Street Punk and classy pop with a message, their influences were - to begin with the Cockney Rejects - but soon made way for a sound that paid respect to mid 80's agit-indie pop such as the early Housemartins and Redskins amongst others. They played locally and at scooter rallies and recorded one album 'More than Skin-deep' that included outstanding tracks such as 'Our own way', 'I won't be fooled' and the cross- breed sound of Madness and Bad Manners on a diet of Georgie Fame of 'Come into my parlour'. They also had a track 'My life's fine' featured on 'The Sound of Oi! Compilation LP. Like many local groups of the Punk era before them, fame and full recognition sadly eluded them, but not through the lack of trying.

Meanwhile back in 1985, local mods and skinheads were mixing in 'one time' opposing circles.

Dave Gooderham … "I went down to Carnaby Street one year and it was full of Punks, but I got on well with them and we all got chatting…they were telling us all the best places and stuff."

Jamie Kennedy (Skinhead from Swinton near Rotherham) … "During the early to mid 80's I was going to the local youth club. I noticed a group of lads who were older than me and they looked very smart. They were also looking quite menacing with their ox blood DM's, short-cropped hair and jeans topped off with long black crombies with cravats in the top left hand pockets. Alongside these were another group wearing smart shoes (mainly black and white striped bowling shoes) and U.S army issue green parkas.

These two groups would dance together to a selection of cool sounds that I was keen to hear more of. I noticed that they were dancing different to each other but having fun anyway; I wanted to join in. I made the decision that I would opt for the skinhead look; besides the hair would be no problem to get sorted. Speaking to the eldest of the skins, my questions went along the lines of *'Where do I get the clothes and the music?'*. Rich (my new skinhead mate) supplied me with some badges, 2 tapes of cool ska tracks and some pointers of where and how to get started. I remember my Dad was real chuffed that I had made a choice of wanting to dress smart. My next port of call was a trip to Donny to get my Crombie and DM's. Although I was a lot younger than the skinheads, I would hang around with them, having great times at local do's (they would venture much further afield). We always hung around with the Mods as well, having some great times and getting on really well with them. Some of my other mates soon started getting into the Mod style and dressing the part too. I found myself digging their look as well, and before long the DM's were being exchanged for bowling shoes, Levi's for sta-prest trousers and the crombie for a parka. I did keep the short skinhead hairstyle though. Things were still fine with the local skins, but whenever us Mods went out of town, we always seemed to have run-ins with the other skins.

It's strange as I am not sure what we would be classed as really; we were somewhere between Mods and Skinheads, taking influences and styles from both looks. Most importantly, it was cool and still is. From then on I never settled into either and remain somewhere in-between with a mix of skinhead and Mod."

The mid 80's; and the vague fashion based stylings of the Mod revival were long gone. The next generation of Mods coming through were becoming more stylised, more self-conscious in their original 1960's roots and influences and certainly paid more attention to detail than the old 'Quadrophenia' crowd. As with the Punk scene not so long before it, the Mod scene of the late 80's could also prove to be too stifling and pastures anew were sought; albeit with a taste of Mod cuisine still remaining edible.

Tony … "By that time,1987, I was still a Mod but I had moved on to a more European style of mod – very much influenced by the Style Council and Paul Weller's kind of Italian style look. I would be wearing penny loafers, Prince of Wales trousers, Polo tops, white

Levis, bold striped button downs, my hair varying from the classic short spiky Mod cut to the long fringe and soul boy wedge style and I would also wear some subtle bits of bloke's jewellery to top the look off. I was still loving all the Sixties Soul/R&B stuff along with the Small Faces etc, but also moving ahead with stuff like contemporary jazz and funk. There were some top class records out at the time like ones from Black Britain, Tommy Chase, and James Taylor Quartet etc. I suppose it was a diversion from the classic Mod style and also to get away from the more narrow-minded Mods who were aplenty at the time.

   Me and some of the lads saw the Style Council a few times in Sheffield. The first time was when Tracie Young was supporting; she was later to join my own group The Way after I had left. A couple of times some of us got to meet Paul Weller and he was pretty cool and not how you would expect. I got chatting to him about the band I was in. His interest suddenly stepped up a few gears when I mentioned that we were planning on incorporating a Hammond organ into the line up. I can remember at one of these backstage meetings that he had a Polaroid camera wrapped around his neck. Mind you he did have a little difficulty understanding our broad Yorkshire accents."

Some punk music fans still managed to take a look at what was happening on the local Mod gig front.

Andrew Morton … "I saw the Style Council on the 'Our Favourite shop' tour in 1985. They were quite good. Over the years I have began to appreciate Weller's work with The Jam more than back in the day. Around the same time in 1985 I also went to see the Untouchables supported by Makin' Time' in Sheffield, and the year before that The Redskins."

Tony … "A lot of Weller's work with the Style Council is very much under-rated, although there is some stuff from then that I never listen to at all. He certainly seemed to wind up both the Punk and Mod lots who had been so into the Jam."

Steve Haythorne … "I was more of a Style Council man than The Jam to be honest. It was more soulful and the songs really did take you places. I mean 'Paris Match' that is a fantastic song. I love Paul Weller's songwriting."

However, some local long time fans of Weller and The Jam were becoming tired of the diverse and multi layered tapestry of 'Paul Weller's increasingly eclectic song writing.

John Harrison … "I liked the Style Council for the first couple of years. I was into what Weller was trying to do, but through their last couple of years, I wasn't too keen on a lot of their stuff."

And as Mods and ex-Punks alike were starting to show some disdain towards one of Punk's greatest songwriters, the author's own group itself was heading on a downward spiral.

Tony ... "After the 1985 Scarborough Mod rally, The Way went on a bit of a downer. We played a handful of local gigs but it was never the same. We did the Rotherham Live Aid gig at Herringthorpe playing fields and the usual local gigs.

One gig we played in Mexborough we ended up putting our guitars down and giving the audience some abuse. John called them a bunch of wankers and we had to get out of town fast. It was quite funny though. We did interviews with the local papers and some photo shoots and me and Terry started writing some new material. It was now becoming obvious, though, that the two of us no longer shared the same vision of what we wanted the band to be. I was interested in going more Soul/R&B and after listening to a lot of Stax and also Dexys records I wanted to add a horn section etc. Terry was more interested in staying as we were and honing in on our Jam influences. After a blazing backstage row before a gig at Rotherham Arts centre, and a few more stunted rehearsals me and John decided to split from the band.

We started our own thing going whilst Terry and Ian carried on with The Way. The new sound and line up never materialised for us and after auditioning lots of musicians, John returned to The Way...I soldered on writing new songs and trying out girl singers, jazz drummers, funk bass players and so on, eventually briefly returning to The Way myself (which didn't work out anyway) and I decided to call it a day and start up a fanzine. In a local paper it was announced that The Way was now without Tony Beesley. Well, I had formed that band but those days were behind me now so good luck to them, I thought. I always kept in contact with them anyway and went on many boozed up nights with drummer Ian."

The Way played gigs at Rotherham Assembly Rooms and other Mod places to be, before adding Paul Weller Respond label protégé Tracie Young - who had sang on the last Jam single 'Beat Surrender' and the first 'Style Council' single 'Speak like a child' - to the line up on backing vocals. This line up appeared on the local TV Calendar programme performing one of Terry's finest songs 'The Torch'- a mid tempo blue eyed soul belter.

They ventured to London for interviews, set up on the back of a truck outside the Leadmill when The Housemartins were playing there, recorded more demo tapes, made a second appearance on TV and were reviewed in the NME. John Harrison was prompted to leave shortly before and was replaced by John White (later to become a highly respected session player with artists such as Groove Armada amongst others). Ironically a horn section was added in 1987. After many brave attempts at hitting the big time The Way went their separate ways. Terry went on to record many top quality songs with varying line ups and name changes, whilst Ian played drums for a later line-up of Dave Spencer's

Spring Heel'd Jack. Terry and Ian still occasionally play in inter-changeable line-ups of Bands.

Rotherham Clifton Hall no longer exists as a building and after demolition, is now a car park. Many felt at the time, including a fair proportion of the Northern Soul crowd that were regulars there, that the Council allegedly went ahead with getting rid of the venue because it was starting to be seen as being on the verge of becoming the next big venue of the North. The Northern Soul scene, and its close relation the Mod scene, were seen to be connected to drug taking and other ill repute passtimes and this would not be allowed to happen. The Assembly Rooms no longer exists either.

Steve Haythorne … "I went to the very last Clifton Hall night, which would have been a Northern Soul night. Great night, I am sure, but all I can really recall from it was that one of the lads was in a state and we had to take him home; too much drugs I suppose."

Gill Frost … "I was gutted when they pulled Clifton Hall down to make it into a car park."

Above: Local Live events ads (taken from the Rotherham Advertiser)

There was another connection to the Mod scene and one that evolved from it and became known as the scooter scene. Developing an obsession for scooters and a mix of Punk, ska and Mod sounds, scooter boys were usually comprised of ex Mods and skinheads who would form scooter clubs and arrange rallies and events for their club and its members. They continue to thrive to this day and are always adding new members and taking great pride in their scooters.

Gary (from the Rotherham scooter scene) … "Punk just passed me by; I just closed my eyes and waited while it had finished really. Then there was the Mod thing, along with the scooter scene, and this was more my thing. The music and scooters, the whole scene with its regular events was much more my cup of tea."

Vanessa Sorrell … "I went out with a scooter boy/Mod in the mid 80's. As well as attending a couple of Mod nights at Clifton Hall, I went on one or two scooter rallies, the one I can remember most is when we went down to Margate. It was funny cos there we were expecting a weekend away and being put up somewhere…well we were put up in a

418

tent. There were loads of us in tents and it was freezing. The music played at the night do's was less Mod than the later ones I went to. You would hear Housemartins and that kind of stuff...maybe some soul, but it was definitely more of a scooter boy thing rather than a proper Mod event."

Tony ... "I may be sticking my neck out here, but I have always felt that the true difference between a scooterist and a real Mod is that a scooterist worships his scooter, whilst a Mod worships his wardrobe."

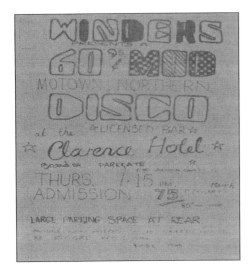

Steve Parlett ... "I have to say though, that I never got into the scootering thing, it was always the clothes and the music for me."

The Mod scene itself also continues healthily to this day, forever evolving and changing. Over the last 20 years its style and outlook have been adopted by the media and fashion world with various degrees of success. The Mod look will always be regarded as the ultimate in Cool and its participants will pass on their knowledge to future generations of Mods for years to come.

The scene in and around Sheffield still thrives in an underground club scene that assimilates the many influences that Mod has taken on board over the years. As the Punk era generation of Mods from Sheffield and the area begin to 'fade-away' there will always be a new bunch of wide-eyed Mod kids out there ready to step in.

Chapter Twenty

The Way Forward

"Whether you liked the music or not, Punk booted down the door and paved the way for everything interesting that has happened in music since" – **Nicky Booth (Rotherham Punk)**

Anthony Cronshaw … "In 1980 I was coming to the end of the road with the gigs and the gig scene. The Mod nights I DJ'd at were probably my last involvement with the local music scene that I'd first enjoyed back at those Bowie/Roxy nights in the mid 70's … followed by Punk in the Daisy, all the numerous gigs around the area, the arrival of The Limit and the ever popular West Street area plus the Marples, from 1976 to 1982.

Because of the lack of a job, I pissed off to Jersey and by the time, I returned I just stopped doing the city and went back to spending my time in suburbia. But, at least I had been a part of the youth culture that had swept the nation and Sheffield was also part of that. It also allowed me to travel the country for four years and looking back the highlights are endless. Amongst many great experiences were; seeing the Sex Pistols and the Clash in their prime, touring with Sham 69 (trouble and all), meeting lots of new friends and keeping them to this day. I believe the music lovers of the area enjoyed the greatest era ever. There were the dodgy fashions that I (and others) adopted along the way, but most of all it was about being part of the movement that led the way for the generations that followed and leaving the option open for them to grab the Punk ideal."

From 1977 to 1985 the Punk generation and all of its offshoots (the many sideshows and cults that came out of Punk like Oi!, New Romantics, Positive Punk, Psychobilly, Goth, New Punk, Anarcho-Punk, Power pop and a whole host of others) had seen a vibrant and mostly healthy music scene of live gigs and the associated social lifestyle of being a part of it all. A whole generation of teenagers in Sheffield, Doncaster and Rotherham and all the surrounding suburbs had simply put 'had the time of their lives'. This generation had experienced all the trials, highs and lows of growing up with a soundtrack that may never be matched.

Paul Clarkson … "Some of my fave Punk moments? Well, seeing the Clash with the stuka background, place packed out and everyone buzzing. Also seeing them at the Hyde Park gig. Sham 69 at Sandpipers club (the low roof had so many holes in it after all the pogoing and the club looked a total wreck when the lights went back on), the first few seconds of hearing 'Anarchy in the UK', oh and of course must not forget the Punkettes with their make up, outfits and bleached hair etc…WOW!"

Graham Torr ... "Eventually, people and fashions move on as they have to but as with everything else in my life since, I remember feeling sad for a while and was reluctant to move with it. (There's no fucking way I was gonna wear a Parka in July!!). So in a slow transition into digging the Ramones or Motorhead...I grew the hair and moved on too.

I'll never forget that shit though and still play my 'Bollocks' album...and now, having put this to paper, I miss my old friends. Hopefully, music made the man eh?!"

Tony ... "The best times for me, looking back, were the early days; when me and my best mates were only just discovering Punk and personally I didn't have a clue what it was really all about to begin with. I would buy allsorts of crap thinking it was Punk Rock and so did my mates. I remember when Dire Straits 'Sultans of Swing' came out and one of the gang bought it thinking it would be Punk cos of the new wave sounding name. We pissed ourselves laughing when we played it!

Nevertheless, they were the best times and that discovery and everything being new was all a part of it. We were young and, I suppose very impressionable, and Punk just happened to hit us exactly at the right time. I used to wish I had been older and been able to go to all those early Punk gigs, and although yes I would have loved that, I really wouldn't change one thing in hindsight. It all happened in perfect sequence for me..."

June Graham ... "The Punk era was, for me, just unbelievable. That time could never be bettered. It was just such a great time to be growing up. I often think about it and I can hear the influence in a lot of music nowadays."

Paul Clarkson ... "After Punk I listened to, apart from the obvious progression of Paul Weller, The Clash, Iggy Pop, Lou Reed, Buzzcocks, The Jam, Undertones (all of which are on my ipod), it was The Smiths, New Order, some of the 2-tone stuff and bits of Oasis, Blur, Pulp etc. I still like some of the stuff I had liked before Punk like Jimi Hendrix, The Who and Bob Marley. I guess, though, that Punk was the defining influence on me and nothing after that ever really truly hooked me."

Richard Chatterton ... "Nowadays I listen to lots of different stuff; 60's Psychedelia, proto-Punk, reggae and Indie but most of it has a link to the Punk, Post-Punk and electronic bands of 76 – 79. Modern bands have the sound but few have the edge, the urgency or the spirit of rebellion and defiance.

Punk did steer me away from a conformist life and opened my eyes to possibilities that you can really DO IT YOURSELF and you don't have to follow the crowd. I have a mortgage; have to sometimes wear a tie. I have various teaching jobs at a few schools and colleges and also do commissions trying not to be pinned down – I guess I still try to stick to the Punk manifesto."

Simon Eyre ... "The 70s was an amazing time for music. The punk revolution affected everybody, bands were forming left right and centre and they had a massive amount of influences to choose from, from Kraftwerk to The Pistols, there was real excitement. They were special times musically and I don't think things have ever been as diverse and exciting since."

Nicky Booth ... "I was only 18 when I went to Camberwell School of Art in 1983 - and it was fantastic to be in London. I went to see lots of bands – The Stranglers and the Cabs (obviously), but my tastes were broadening so I went to see people like Laurie Anderson and Durutti Column too. I saw The Smiths at a free gig on the South Bank around this time. They were huge, and I quite liked them, but really, they were a bit too mainstream for my tastes. Instead I was getting into a lot of so called Industrial music, and as such became an avid follower of bands such as Nurse With Wound, Hirsche Nicht Aufs Sofa, Die Krupps and Laibach – the latter being my current favourite. Their gigs are always a sight to behold. Are they really fascists or is it some sort of parody? Whatever the case, they are deadly serious in their delivery. I remember reading a review in the Guardian of a 2003 gig that I saw, the last line of which read *'Laibach have been on the go for 30 years and in all that time they haven't cracked a smile once. Marvellous!'* I quite agree."

Chiz ... "There is no after punk for me and I'm afraid nothing much has ever stirred me as much since. The odd songs come and go like a couple of Kaiser Chiefs songs and a bit of Arctic Monkeys but nothing I'd rave on about. I went to see Alice Cooper at the Sheffield Arena once and was enjoying it until I saw the rip off prices of the merchandise and that reminded me why the whole punk movement shits all over everything else.

One big difference is that I like ska now and can enjoy a dance to the Specials etc whereas back in the day the animosity between us and the 'fashion followers' (because that is what most of them were) created a mental barrier where the music couldn't come through. I also managed a ska band from Chesterfield called Lord Skaman and the Magnificent Seven in the early nineties."

Gill Frost ... "Those were the days. I used to love going into the Sound of Music record shop, which used to be at the top end of Rotherham's inside market, and seeing what they had to offer. You would never have been able to go into Woolworths and buy an album by Crass, but you could always rely on the Sound of Music to stock records for those of us with less average musical tastes. It was so exciting if you not only found something by a band you loved, but it was on coloured vinyl as well!"

Tony ... "One other thing about Punk was that the older generation, and I am speaking often about people in their early twenties even, well they just didn't get it at all. They really could not understand what it was that we were getting out of it all. Of course that was often when that very ignorance fucked them off and exploded into violence. The Punk days were not all that easy in that sense... but that's the way it was!"

There was a sad ending to the career of Barnsley's X-Rippers who reformed in 2002 as singer Phil Taylor recalls –

Phil Taylor (X-Rippers) ... "Earlier I did say that our 1981 split was for the best but when Brent and Rots met by chance in the summer of 2002 Brent asked if we fancied getting the band back together for one last gig, two weeks later the band were franticly rehearsing and on the 6th September 2002 at their old stomping ground The Portcullis now known as the Arches... the X-Rippers Brent, Munk, Rots and Brains preformed to a

300 strong crowd. After this gig we realised we had a Punk Debt to 1978 and started on the circuit again and once more the gigs came fast and furious playing with bands like 999, the Lurkers, Vibrators, and we are regulars at the Wasted festivals, also going over to Germany with Splodge.

The band recruited Big Al to help Munk out in 2004 and this made the songs fresher and fuller. Unknown to us Monk was seriously ill and slowly went downhill. He was diagnosed with terminal pancreatic cancer and passed away in March 2005. Munk was the founder of our band with his flamboyant guitar playing and cheeky grin: he stripped the old songs of their darkness and resurrected them as we play them today.

The last words in this part of our story are for Munk - he was an inspiration for all of us in the X-Rippers and we made a pact after his sad passing we would carry on and play our hearts out at every gig. We are still playing today and I believe Munk would be proud of what we have achieved. We all miss him as a band member and a bloody good mate."

The X-Rippers continue to play to this day.

Paul Clarkson ... "Punk informed my life to the point of me saying *'Oh well, fuck it!'* to some things. This is harder to do as you get older and have more responsibilities and a mortgage and job etc, but still nowadays if it says *'don't do that'* I will do it or try to do it a bit differently. I am now a lecturer in typography, graphic design and advertising so I can still push some of the concepts of Punk, but in different ways, to a whole new generation. I can be subversive, but from the inside and in a positive way, not necessarily damaging but still challenging."

Helen McLaughlin ... "I had some pink plastic ankle boots that I bought from Western Jean Company on Fargate. I loved those ankle boots and wore them everywhere. My sister is 5 ½ years younger than me and I think was completely embarrassed by me at the time, however some of her friends from then have said *'you were so cool, I really admired you'* and *'I really wanted to be like you and I remember your pink boots!'* I don't actually think this was true at the time somehow but things have turned full circle now and how we were and what we did seems cool again now. We had about two absolutely mad, fantastic years at the peak of it all. I am proud of us, what we did and the fun we had. I loved it all."

Phil Tasker (Vice Squad singer) ... "It (Punk) only really lasted for a couple of years at the most in its purest form but it was like an intensely burning flame, especially being a teenager at the time. As for what happened to Vice Squad members, Roger and Clive joined Shytots for a while... then Roger went to Art College. Clive went to London and currently fronts a Punk tribute band called Scam 69! Chris went down South and became an accountant and I joined a band which came out of the ashes of the Basking Sharks who were an electronic band during 81 – 86.I then became guitarist in Degree 33 an industrial techno band from 91 - 96 producing original material using sound and video."

Phillip Wright ... "They say that the music and records that you like in your teenage years stay with you for the rest of your life, so for me it starts with Bolan and Bowie and ends with the Jam (I was 20 in 1982) . To be a teenager when the punk stuff exploded was incredible, great new bands were appearing in the NME week after week; I bought so many singles and albums and went to gigs almost weekly. No wonder I was always skint. For a time, until it became mainstream, it was something that was 'owned' by the people that were part of it. Outsiders couldn't get in. We were all brought together by a love of a style of music (first Punk, then the Jam, then Mod) and we had our own clubs that catered for us, we didn't go to the usual mainstream clubs like Romeo and Juliet's, we went to the Limit, etc... We knew, and hung around with, people in local bands, we would congregate on Fargate on a Saturday afternoon, and we would do the same route week after week, starting at Virgin records at the bottom of the moor. We would look at people and see what they were wearing, buy records, buy clothes. I really can't help but smile when I think about it all."

Nick Orme ... "What can I say? The whole era from Punk through to Mod and 2-Tone was a fantastic time to be alive. Afterwards there was a big come down...personally I thought the rest of the 1980's were shit."

Steve Parlett ... "In 87 I went to university in Salford, which was very difficult financially, and I did not have the means to keep up with the tailoring, record-buying etc, so I gradually left the 'Mod look' behind. However, to this day (and I'm now 40) I'm still obsessed with 60s R&B, Soul, Jazz and the 79 sound, and probably 4000 of my 6000 tracks on my Ipod are this kind of music. I've also gone back to Fred Perry jumpers, button down shirts and Bass Weejun loafers so it's still very much within me!"

Tracy Stanley ... "I feel so privileged to have been around to be a part of the Punk and New Romantic scenes because there has not been anything like them since. Although the fashions have come and gone from those days, I am proud to say I was a Punk and a New Romantic first time around. To me it felt like a natural progression in going from one to the other, as it still involved weird clothes and even weirder make-up. I still love to play music from that era and it always brings back strong memories and takes me right back to that time."

Shaun Angell ... "Musically, fashion wise and socially... I would say that the period from 1979 to 1982 was the best time of my life. Leaving school, getting my first job, my first pint and my first fuck! Things do not come any better do they?"

Julian Jones ... "I look back on those Punk days as a kind of weird sort of daft period in time. But they were great times. I never got on with all the Oi! stuff and the Exploited, Discharge and all that side of it. But the thing is people look back now and that's what they think Punk was, and it wasn't."

Steve Haythorne ... "I never really fully embraced the Punk thing as such. I liked what I thought were the best from it - the Clash, Elvis Costello, Devo, Magazine and Ian Dury but not a lot of it. I suppose I flirted with it for a couple of years and then it was back to my beloved Soul music, which is what I listen to now."

Joanne Orgill ... "Although I have a fairly dodgy memory about Rotherham's punk scene, I have someone who can give me a jolt every now and then. After a schoolgirl crush (I thought he looked like Elvis Costello – he had the whole geek look going on) and twenty odd years down the line, I managed to hook my own Cute Pube. David Spencer and I are married. We have our own mini punk rocker and a punketta. Two Rotherham punk rockers done well!!"

Michael Day ... "I moved to San Francisco in 1987 and have lived here ever since. I was known as Daisy back then by all. (Day = Daisy – go figure)."

Wayne Kenyon (Punk/skinhead and member of Doncaster skinhead band Skin-Deep) ... "When you think about skinheads and shaved heads now, it doesn't really seem like anything different. But go back to the late 70's and early 80's and it was very extreme to shave your head. Nowadays, every bloke on the street, just about, has their head shaved, but back then it was only Skinheads who did it. You stood out a mile back in the day with your head shaved and wearing Doc Martens, Ben Sherman's and Levis etc. Back then, we had to go to London just to find a shop that sold proper Ben Sherman's; now you can buy them in catalogues and all over the place. How times change."

Patrick Tierney ... "I know punk was meant to destroy and lay waste all the bloated bands like E.L.P., Pink Floyd, the ludicrously over-rated (to this day) Led Zeppelin and so on, but it could be argued that punk re-energised some of these bands. The Who and Rolling Stones released their best albums for years during this time – 'Who Are You' and 'Some Girls' respectively, so it wasn't totally one way."

Darren Gray ... "The music, clothes, and Mod ideals have formed the basis of my adult life which I adhere to today. My total love of black soul music with the rebelliousness and creativity of British youth will stay with me 'till I kick it'."

Dave Burkinshaw ... "There is still plenty of good music out there but I don't think it will ever be the same as the first time Punk came around. I still get my old Punk records out every now and again and turn the volume up, you ought to see the wife's face. Luckily, I have managed to pass my music taste onto my son and daughter as they like a lot of my old stuff."

Shaun Angell ... "Back in the day, we had space invader machines, youth clubs, the Crazy Daisy and Charades club. We made our own entertainment and the nightlife (and indeed the day life) were so much better then. No mobile phones, no computers and no stupid fuckin' reality shows. We did not need them did we? Our reality was going out Friday night, Saturday afternoon – and if you were not nicked at the footie match – it was back out Saturday night.

Anyone who is over 40 plus now, will tell you that the late 70's to early 80's was a magical time to be young. The young un's of today aren't happy unless they are doing a line of coke and then knifing some poor cunt in the back...what's that all about then? Just playing at being plastic gangsters, selling drugs and carrying weapons...what a load of bollocks!"

Andrew Morton ... "The Punk days will always be with me. I can't remember all of it and every group I went to see, but I wouldn't swap those times for anything."

Paul Clarke ... "The funny thing is: when I speak about those days (and the things we used to get up to) with people who were not around at the time, they don't believe me. Their attitude is kind of *'Yeah sure' what ever you say!* But we all know what it was like along with all the great gigs, music and laughs and that's the most important."

Tony ... "After Punk and then my band The Way I was a little lost really. I tried forming other bands but to no avail. The chemistry was never there with any of the musicians I rehearsed with. I even went and auditioned for a club band (the horror) in Barnsley but fortunately I gave it a miss; I wasn't too keen on playing Bruce Springsteen numbers. I had a bash at producing my own fanzine called Populist Blues in 1986, which focussed on the local music scene. I interviewed quite a few local bands including Springheel'd Jack, T- Dive, and even my old band The Way. The fanzine was successful but ran at a financial loss so I knocked that in the head.

Throughout the following years, music was always still very important to me and I ventured into many genres and scenes. I would buy Indie singles and see loads of bands at the Leadmill, listen to contemporary Funk and Soul, get prematurely excited with the early 90's 'New Wave of New Wave' movement that spawned 'Britpop' of which I was also a massive fan, checking out early gigs by the likes of Oasis, Blur, Elastica, Supergrass etc. In the late 80's to 1991, I became involved in the House music scene and would buy heaps of imported 12"ers from Warp records. I went to House nights at the Leadmill and some of the other clubs in Sheffield at the time. For a while, it was fresh and exciting but became boring after about a year. Throughout all of this time, I was still a massive fan of black music and in particular, my R&B and soul records collection that I still had from the Mod days and was still adding to... and still continue to do so.

In the very early days of the 90's Paul Weller reappeared on the music scene playing solo sets around the country under the guise of The Paul Weller Movement. I went to a low attended gig of his at Sheffield University around this time and picked up his first single 'Into Tomorrow' which was a real return to form for him. I continued to follow Weller and his music and do so to this day, seeing some fantastic gigs around Sheffield and Doncaster at venues like the Leadmill, City Hall, Don Valley stadium, Octagon centre and Doncaster Dome. I suppose the Mod influence and style would always be with me no matter what. The look and image had always been with me despite trying out other scenes, the detail and taste is part of my genetic make up and it just won't go away. Looking back even when I was a Punk there was a Mod hiding away in me trying to get out."

Some Punks of our generation chose their favourites of the era to follow and even on occasion, become friends with during the mid 1980's. Sheffield Stranglers fan Mark Senior continued to remain intoxicated with the sound of the men in black and followed the group on tour around the UK and Europe - enjoying many memorable meetings with the Stranglers. Mark moved to Germany, with fond memories of those days and being part of the Sheffield Punk scene of the late 70's and early 80's and whenever the sounds of 'Black and White', 'the Raven' or 'la Folie' grace a stage... Mark won't be far away.

The original local Punk scene most likely began with that Sex Pistols and Clash Black Swan gig back in July 1976 and quite probably died with the Marples' last dying breaths. It was certainly dead long before the Clash lingered to their dishonourable end following their abysmal 'Cut the Crap' record of late 1985. The Punk scene, along with its accompanying Post-Punk after shocks lasted the best part of a decade and what a decade it had been. But as Sheffield Punk and Post-Punk pioneers '2.3' proclaimed on their first and only vinyl outing back at the start of 1978 ... where to now?

The way forward now would be a long and varied after-shock of trying to recreate those turbulent days of Youth, energy, excitement and euphoria. Always casting a glance backward to those days and taking its idealism and unavoidable influence along, the Punk generation of the region branched off into a thousand directions to do their own thing. The 1980's saw the rise of the Indie scene that had been a direct journey out of Post-Punk. The die-hard Punk groups carried on as though the scene had never changed

Above: Dedicated Stranglers fan Mark Senior with Stranglers bassist Jean Jacques Burnel

- and along the way would attract many new generations of young Punk kids, many of whom may not have been born in 1977. Electro music reigned in Sheffield for a good while and the steel city's biggest export The Human League achieved the fame they had been chasing for so long. Cabaret Voltaire, one of the most respected groups to ever come out of the North also continued to inspire and influence contemporary music, most notably the new sounds that the serious side of dance music was aspiring to.

In 1985 House music and then its own massive array of spin off genres, most notably Acid House and techno was just around the corner. Once more Sheffield would be a big part of a new genre of music that its youth would become immersed in with rampant enthusiasm. Some of the earliest 'House' nights were held at Sheffield Leadmill and later on the city gave birth to first 'Fon' and then 'Warp records' and all of its wide reaching scopes of presenting Dance music to the new generation of teenagers after a scene of their own. The Acid House scene would include in its ranks many old local Punk Rockers who were still searching for that vibe they had experienced from Punk and would now be dropping an E and embracing a whole new culture that would partly shape the future of the whole of the country's youth and its future generations.

Punk's idealism and influence would be incorporated into every aspect of the media and the accompanying varied cults and fashions to emerge over the years. Its profound influence - locally as well as nationally - would remain with almost everyone who had tasted its dangerous excitement. Local groups such as Phil Murray and the Boys from Bury, Springheel'd Jack and much later on Arctic Monkeys and many others would always cast a nod in the direction of Punk for their main sources of inspiration.

As well as musicians, Punk also gave a lot of its affected teenagers the confidence to achieve so much more in their twenties, thirties and onwards. The notion of Punk being about no future and a blueprint of nihilistic negativeness has been shot to pieces by the many stories of self-achievement that many of the local Punk generation aspired to. In a strange twist of fate, considering Punk's anti-authoritarian stance, a considerable few have chosen to work within the education and teaching system. Many move within media circles and at least one is now a Professor! Musicians, authors, businessmen, accountants, journalists, computer experts, firemen, policemen, teachers, Political activists and animal rights campaigners and so on. Punk helped inspire and give the confidence to the local Punk generation to become all of these varied and nationally representative - dare we say - careerists. 'Our Generation', like all of those before and after it, has now been absorbed into the standard fabric of society. We rebelled, we stuck two fingers up to it, we voiced our dissent and our disappointment with it and then we became a part of it. Our only consolation is that now we have the chance to infiltrate from within.

Gill Frost … "Over the years, I've been to loads and loads of gigs, far too many to remember. I still go to them now and I don't think anything can compare with seeing a live band, especially if it's a band you love. If I can feel my body vibrating because it's so loud… then so much the better. And I'm very pleased to say that there are plenty of young punks and Goths still around to keep the tradition going."

Pete Roddis … "Nowadays I go along to see Punk groups again (Pete put his New Romantic days behind him long ago as simply an unfortunate phase and has now returned back to his Punk loving roots)… I also love going to the 'Rebellion' Punk festivals in Blackpool and others in Newcastle. I often go along on my own but soon get chatting to fellow old Punks and have a few beers with them chatting about the old days and music and stuff. I have had some great conversations with some of the group members too. TV Smith of the Adverts is a really nice fella. There's always plenty to see and enjoy and I have some great times at these and the Punk gigs I go to."

As for the local Mod scene… it was given a breath of fresh air and revived back to life by Britpop and the region was blessed with a clutch of venues that accommodated the Mods. Venues like Browns club and The Travellers pub in Rotherham in the mid 90's and The Washington pub in Sheffield later on along with the Sheffield City Hall's ballroom event Brighton Beach which began as a very Mod orientated monthly event but in later days lost its Mod crowd to an increasingly Student lot. 'The Pow Wow' club was launched in 2005 in Sheffield and continues to this day. Other Mod clubs like 'Touched by the hand of Mod', 'Mod for it' and briefly the authors very own 'Back to the Roots' nights showed that the

Mod scene was still very much alive. As for Punk itself, it just soldiers on as resilient as ever: Rotherham itself rapidly re-gaining a healthy live groups scene with many name Punk groups playing venues in the town. Sheffield and Doncaster also continue to thrive and if you scratch beneath the surface, there are some young local 'New Generation' Punk bands around worth catching live.

Tony ... "In June 2008 legendary workhorse Punk band UK Subs played Rotherham at the No.10 club supported by Riot Squad and locals Phil Murray and the boys from Bury. The venue was packed with Punk rock kids of all ages- Some old guys from the old scene and a mix of hardcore punks with Mohawks, bleached hair and leather jackets. The groups all went down well and pogoing and slam dancing got going - especially during the Subs set. I smiled all the way through the Subs set. It reminded me of the old days and yes, it was fun!

Earlier on, I had a great chat with UK Subs front man Charlie Harper. I have to say that he looked bloody good and had aged great - all considering. The Punk Rock life style has obviously been good for Charlie Harper. We chatted about the Punk scene and comparing the present scene to the original one, we both agreed that back then there were so many different sounding bands, whereas now there is a set style of Punk that knows all the right chords and has the energy but not necessarily the originality."

Charlie Harper ... "The thing is with the Punk groups back in the late 70's, you had all these groups that all sounded so different. No one sounded like each others band. The Jam had their own style and so did the others like Wire, Siouxsie and the Banshees, the Clash, Buzzcocks and so on. Now Punk is pretty much all the same. I do like a lot of it but it's not got the originality of the original groups."

When asked about the many gigs UK Subs have played in Sheffield and the area, Charlie can only remember snippets.

Charlie Harper ... "I know we have played so many times up here but after so many years it's hard to remember them all. I cannot even remember playing the Limit Club at all, but I can remember playing the Marples when it was the 'bring a toy along' night, and bits of other gigs. I also used to come up on the train to watch some other Punk groups play in Sheffield. I came up to see the Damned at the Poly on one of those free gigs that were on at the time. I remember coming up on the train and I got chatting to that guy with the long fringe - what was his name? Phil Oakey. Yeah we had a good chat about music.

There was one gig and I think it was in Sheffield where for some reason; the promoter had got these really small monitors set up. I said to him *'they are gonna get nicked'* they were so small and guess what they did get nicked!"

Tony ... "We chatted about what music we both liked and Charlie and I share a liking for sixties American garage bands and old rhythm and blues."

430

Charlie Harper ... "I listen to all sorts really. I like stuff like The Sonics and Sam the Sham and the Pharaohs 'Woolly Bully' that's a classic, same with 'Louie Louie' by The Kingsmen. I also like Iggy Pop as well."

Tony ... "I asked Charlie if he remembers having his Iggy Pop 'Metallic k.o' t-shirt? I told him one of my mates nicked it off him to which he laughed and said that happened a lot. Charlie does think that the punk crowd up here, both back then and now, is a lot more genuine than down in London and often less poseur-ish. This is something a lot of the groups have commented on and is a great testament to the character of our local music fans.

The UK Subs played a cracking set that night. They played many of their old classics and some more recent ones. I enjoyed them - probably much more than the last few times I saw them back in 1981 at the Leadmill and Marples etc. If any band is still carrying the torch for Punk Rock in the 21st century then it surely is the UK Subs. What did Stiff Little Fingers say *'Punk may be dead but we are still dying?'* That is still the case.

Rotherham and Sheffield and Doncaster all have their Punk Scenes still going and yeah it's not changing so much and some of the groups do mostly play 'punk by numbers', but the kids love it, the old punks occasionally come back to the fold and its still good fun. Nothing wrong with that... not really what Punk started out to be, but ideals and movements always fall out somewhere along the line. It is only to be expected, though, that everyone has their own opinions of what it all meant and when it lost its appeal and subsided.

For me personally, the original Punk scene died as soon as it started to try too hard to be Punk and being afraid to take risks. In some ways 'Wire' were the perfect Punk group... always moving ahead with modernist ideals but still keeping their music minimal. Punk as an ideology? Well it's still around today isn't it."

A couple of months following the UK Subs gig Eddie and the Hot Rods also played in Rotherham at the Blues Café, and they too turned in a solid set including classics like 'Do Anything you wanna do', 'Quit this town', 'Telephone Girl' and The Who's 'Kids are alright' as well as some impressive new numbers. Lead singer Barrie Masters, like Charlie Harper has aged remarkably well and after their two fantastic sets, he chatted to fans reminiscing about the bands 30 plus years career. It seemed a little surreal sat chatting and having a beer with Barrie when I think back to all those years ago; watching the Hot Rods performing 'Do anything you wanna do' on the Marc Bolan show."

Phil Tasker ... "Punk was a time when people were more individual, you could think more about what you wore and be more creative, also kids were being encouraged to question authority and I think it was the last true youth rebellion before we all got sucked back in to the commercial machine. I still use those punk principles today if I can, question what the government and the fat cats want us to do and stop being manipulated by those with the power! The trouble is there are kids now who have been tamed by the system and I don't think we will ever see the like of the punk movement again."

Martin Clarke … "I loved those days. I was 21 in 1977 and those 3 or 4 years were just unbelievable; the excitement, the tension and those amazing 3 minute songs."

Paul Bower … "It would be wrong to look back on those times with rose tinted glasses as there was a lot of violence going on, what with the National Front etc, and also there was a lot of competition between the bands in Sheffield. You can't just think of it as some kind of Golden time really as not everyone was in it just for the music. There was a lot of motivation for the money and to be famous. For a brief period it was healthy and then it became stale."

Tony … "For some time I felt a bitterness and disappointment with Punk and in particular with the Clash. I had really believed in the Clash and Punk and firmly expected things to change for our generation. Punk Rock had motivated me and I expected a life ahead with the same sort of excitement and vibrancy that I had felt during that era. Was I naive or what? The big come down was as bad as that for me though… I never wanted a 9-5 job, a mortgage and a holiday in the sun once a year with a box at the end of it.

For a year or two my disappointment with Punk and rock in general resulted in me not playing a single white boy's music on my turntable at all. Not one single guitar-strumming rocker got even close to my deck…only a stream of funk and R&B and soul through my soul boy 'anti-rock' phase of the mid 80's.

Later on, and especially after meeting Joe Strummer, I started to realise the truth…that we had laid far too much faith in mere musicians. Why should we expect them to have all the answers? And lead the way? Now I realise how much the Clash, Weller and a handful of musicians and poets gave us. The music was enough really, the rest is up to us! I am no longer pissed off about the Punk thing."

Dave Spencer … "Punk became less and less relevant as the years went by. I went to see the old bands (like the Damned & 999 and UK Subs) and the new bands as they came along, but no one ever tickled my fancy.

I ended up getting into Bob Dylan. Once upon a time I would have called him the original Hippy, but now I see him more as the original punk. Or that might have been Elvis Presley or John Lennon? My attitude to the whole experience now, is that the kids of our generation were given a choice (A lucky break, perhaps?). We were presented with the most exciting music that we had ever heard and we leapt at the chance to be a part of it. Some people in the Deep South would have chased Elvis out of town in 1954 for being a dirty hillbilly. Some would have chosen Acker Bilk over the Beatles in 1963 and some folkies would have thought that Bob Dylan was 'Judas' just for daring to play electric music in 1966. Some would have kicked the shit out of anyone just for admitting to liking this Day-Glo, adrenalin-fuelled monster that was Punk Rock. And some of us realised how lucky we were and took the kicking if we had to."

Nicky Booth … "I am in my 40's now, with a wife, two kids and a mortgage. My choice of clothes is a little more sober, but I still think of 'bum flaps' quite fondly. The development of technology means that I can now make music at home with my computer and several synthesizers. Like many middle aged dads I still dream of being a rock star –

432

but after several years I am still working on that difficult first album. One of the nice things about my job at Museums Sheffield is that it occasionally brings me into contact with people who are/were involved in the Sheffield music scene. For example, I worked on a sound installation with Martyn Ware (Heaven 17, ex Human League) a few years ago, and I also got to meet one of my all time heroes, Richard H Kirk (Cabaret Voltaire) a while ago too. I tried explaining to my wife that it would be like her meeting Elvis Presley, but she didn't seem to get it. Pioneers of electronic music are pretty low on her agenda obviously. It made my year though.

My passion for underground music definitely stems from the shock of hearing punk as a spotty youth. Why settle for the mainstream when you can scratch the surface and find all sorts of weird and wonderful stuff lurking below? Punk was a necessary kick up the arse and it shook *everything* up, not just the music scene. There hasn't been a revolution like it before or since and I was glad to be there when it happened."

Above: Nicky Booth at right meets one of his Punk era heroes Richard H. Kirk of Cabaret Voltaire in 2005

Rezillo and ex Human Leaguer Jo Callis rekindled old memories whilst going along to see his old human friends.

Jo Callis … "Fay, Eugene and myself went to see the Human League in the Glasgow Carling Academy a year or so ago (Dec 07 I think) and I was surprised to find myself having quite an emotional moment during the Encore of 'Together In Electric Dreams', my bottom lip was quivering, my eyes were welling up! It was as if Phil was singing it to me, but I guess we did have our Electric Dream together, and to some extent, we still have. I love old Phil."

Jo Callis is now officially, once more, a Rezillo and continues to perform with the group playing regularly at venues such as the Corporation in Sheffield where they played a fantastic 'time defying' energetic set in February 2009. At this gig, they performed the whole of their classic 1978 LP 'Can't stand the Rezillos' for the final time. Their 'download only' single 'Number one Boy' of the same period also ranks amongst the very best of Rezillos pop.

Tony ... "In 2000 my Mum passed away. Whilst clearing out her house, I came across my old Sex Pistols 'Anarchy in the UK' Tour t-shirt. It was visibly very old and torn, and I could see that my dear old Mum, at some point had been using it to wipe up some varnish or something, which was typical of my Mum. It reminded me of all those years ago when I managed to get on the guest list at a Clash concert; after meeting and chatting to all of the Clash at various points, I had managed to get all of their autographs on my first album Clash t-shirt. To be perfectly honest, I was never one of the autograph pestering fans – the whole idea of Punk was to break down the barriers between the groups and us etc, and I had sold my Jam autographed ticket for £3(for beer money), a long time since – but the Clash autographs on that t-shirt, well that was something really special. I wore it with great pride for a few weeks or so, and then one day the unthinkable happened. *'Tony, I have washed your t-shirt and its come up blooming' lovely in the wash'* my Mum proudly proclaimed. *'What t-shirt ?'* was my reply to which I was given a full display, right in front of my bewildered eyes, of my prized, cherished and much loved Clash first album cover t-shirt - all bright and sparkling clean - minus any signs of any Clash autographs. I am ashamed to say that I went crackers and wrecked the dining room table and then pissed off with the ultimate mug on. My Mum didn't speak to me for days, but forever more she had a great tale to tell of when she did the ultimate act of washing the Clash out of my clothing!

I had a good look at that 'Anarchy' shirt, remembering all those Punk memories of living in that house. All those days of mates coming and going, doing my mate Pete's hair with food colouring before going to see The Clash and staining the carpet, me and him cutting each others hair (Yes that's how D.I.Y it was!). Writing Punk poetry and all those years of listening to the music and setting off on those eventful journeys to the Punk concerts, sometimes not knowing that some of us were going to get a belting when we got there! Not all those days were memorable in good ways; they could also be very violent and tense! Also - the early days of The Way when me and John Harrison had started writing our first songs for our group, wearing my first Mod suit ready for a night out, the laughs, the low times with no money and the many changes that we faced growing up there. I picked up the 'Anarchy' t-shirt and along with some other Punk memorabilia, I uncharacteristically threw them in the bin – the memories are firmly entrenched in my mind anyway."

Some years after the Punk explosion a chance meeting resulted in a true life defining experience, that brought around full circle, the journey through Punk Rock that the author had lived through. The follow up chapter would prove to be even more poignant in 2002.

Tony ... "In 1989, my old group The Way managed to get a support slot with Joe Strummer and his Latino Rockabilly War in Doncaster. The next night I went to see them play at Sheffield Leadmill. The set included many Clash classics including 'London Calling', 'Brand New Cadillac', 'I fought the Law' etc, and I took quite a lot of photographs of Joe and the group. Not surprisingly, I bumped into numerous old mates from the Punk days, and after the gig I got chatting with Terry of The Way (they had supported Strummer the night before in Doncaster). He led the way down the stairs to the Leadmill backstage area, where Joe and the group and the rest of the entourage were all hanging around. I managed to get some photos taken with Joe Strummer, which I was pleased about; but the best part was to come, when we all got invited back to the after show party at the hotel.

Above: Joe Strummer plays the Sheffield Leadmill (taken by myself)

We hit the hotel bar and the whole lot of us gathered around a couple of seated areas, different little parties ganging up together. Also there, was Alex Cox the director of the films 'Sid and Nancy', 'Repo Man' and 'Straight to Hell' etc. The party was in full swing. After an hour or so, some of us moved up to one of the upstairs rooms. There was myself, Terry and his girlfriend, my girlfriend of the time, roadies, guitarist Zander Schlos and the rest of Joe's group, as well as Joe himself. Again, we all paired up into small gangs of nattering, boozing but happy folks. I made sure I was in Joe's gang: the last gang in town!

Sharing a reefer and passing around the cases of Holsten Pils, Joe Strummer and myself chatted away for what seemed like hours. We talked about the Clash and their gigs in Sheffield (the fight with Mick at the Top Rank included), how the first Clash LP had affected me, how I hated the last Clash LP, ('*Yeah but there were 2 decent songs on there- 'This is England' and 'North v South'* Joe said in its defence, but Joe mostly agreed with me that 'Cut the Crap' was well- CRAP). We talked about my attempts at fanzine writing and Joe invited me to London to have a crack at it. We talked about the Punk era and the groups from the period and our mutual respect for the much-maligned Clash triple LP 'Sandinista'. As a matter of fact, we did talk for hours and never once did Joe show any disinterest. He was genuinely interested in what I and others had to say.

Joe Strummer was a hero of mine, in an age when we really shouldn't have been looking for heroes: but there were not many around and lo and behold, Joe was the one for many of our Punk Rock generation. Along with Paul Weller, Strummer influenced my teenage years - the pair of 'em with their poetry and music - and though I never would have admitted it at the time, yes they really were my heroes!

While we were chatting, Joe said to me *'Every day we are learning something new and each time it's something that we didn't know or realise the day before or even a few minutes since'.* That is what I found exciting about Punk (and the Clash with their ever-changing direction). That the next day there would be something new out there to listen to and find out about, especially listening to the John Peel show. That is what Punk and the Post-Punk period was all about for me and the

Above; Joe Strummer and me backstage Sheffield Leadmill

- moment that it all became the same and a set style then it died... I never expected to hear what would happen that Christmas of 2002 though.

In the early morning hours, around 4am, I left Joe's after-show party after shaking Joe's hand. Sometime later, I saw Strummer with the Mescaleros supporting The Who; playing many of those old Clash classics, along with some new quality songs. A couple of years later I switched on the teletext and saw a headline that truly made me stop in my tracks. It said Clash guitarist dies of heart attack. Shock! A massive jolt to the system as I read the heartbreaking news that Joe Strummer was no longer with us. It just would not sink in. My wife at the time was perplexed as to why I was so affected. You just cannot explain it to someone who does not understand. That Christmas of 2002, I mourned the loss of Joe Strummer just as if I had lost a close member of my family. I secluded myself from people. I could not get through to anyone why I felt this way.

When we lost Joe Strummer, who (like us all) was certainly never a man without flaws and contradictions, we – the Punk generation died a little. We realised our fallibilities, our weaknesses and our mortality. Above all, amongst the many legions of old Clash fans, we all felt that the world was now a different place without Joe Strummer- and maybe it is.

The world has changed so much for us all. Major terrorism and the shrinking of the world through mass-communication have surely turned the world upside down from those days in the late 70's when the local Punk generation first held up its cards.

Then, in hindsight, when you think about it: Joe Strummer's passing at the age of 50, it was not so much a sign of our generation's last breaths of true relevance and importance, but actually a symbolic gesture that now was the time for us to stand aside, to make way for the new. Let the kids have Punk and its many offspring scenes (along with the ever-evolving Mod scene) for themselves. It's up to them now what they do with it. We will still come back now and again to have a look at what's going on - as long as we are welcome, that is.

The passing of Joe Strummer and many others from 'Our Punk generation' simply book-ended our era. In Sheffield, Rotherham, Doncaster, Barnsley, Chesterfield, Leeds, Manchester, London, Belfast and a whole host of cities around the country and to an extent, the world; our reign had come to an end. Nothing lasts forever: but didn't we have a fine time. 'Our Generation'... the Children of the Revolution. Yes that was our story."

Acknowledgments

I would like to thank first everyone who has read this book. I hope that you have very much enjoyed it. It has been a real pleasure in writing and researching and has brought back many long forgotten memories for myself and also for many of the people who have kindly contributed. In no exact particular order I am in great debt to all of the following people

Dave Spencer (for true enthusiasm, immense help, moral support, inspiration and the usual telepathic understanding of how our twin minds work...and also for being as obsessed by the subject as myself and producing a front cover that really does the biz!)

Anthony Cronshaw- Sheffield author and lifelong Owls fan (for much inspiration, invaluable help and encouragement – often over a few well earned pints!)

Pete Roddis (for the great friendship and irreplaceable memories we shared)

John Harrison (for the many laughs, ideas and empathy – a fantastic fella)

Paul Bower - Gun-Rubber (Sheffield's first Punk fanzine) and '2.3' singer/guitarist (for his patience, time and interest and being amongst the first to contribute, along with permission to use quotes and front cover images from Gun Rubber fanzine)

Andrew Morton (for help, friendship and inspiration)

Paul Jespersen (for proofing)

Darren Twynham (a great mate)

Paul Clarke (were we that daft?)

Julian Jones (a fantastic help and a walking diary of contacts)

Phillip Wright (fantastic source and a mine of info on Punk and Mod in Sheffield)

Wayne Kenyon (for CD's, kind use of music, photos, words, encouragement and a never ending willingness to help out)

And still in no particular order but due as much appreciation -

Dizzy Holmes at Detour records, Pete Hill, Stuart Bates, Simon Hinkler (Artery), Nicky Booth, Paul Hutley (The Diks), Morg - who runs Doncaster Punk web site www.hallcross.co.uk/donnypunx/index.htm Paul Kelly – fantastic bloke - who also runs a superb Punk web site Punk Domain at http://www.punkdomain.com , Bryan Bell(one of the first Punk Rockers I ever saw), Bob Gray (original Jam keyboard player), Helen McLaughlin, Joanne Orgill, Steve Wright(who runs the Radio Stars website), Martin Gordon (Radio Stars), Andy Lee, Graham Torr, Duncan Payne, Nick Orme, Richard Chatterton, Tony Harvey, D.Muscroft, Rob Saripo(and a thanks to his wife Anne Saripo

439

for her kind help), Phil Udell, Ric Hobson, Dave Walker and the Mod Culture web site, Mark Ellis, Chiz (Riot Squad singer), Ian Robertson, Paul Clarkson, Pete Cooper, Sue Lowday, Lynne Freeman, Spencer Summers, Steve 'Smiler' Marshall, TV Smith (The Adverts) for very kind recollections and patience, Polystyrene (X-Ray Specs) for prompt replies and title for Chapter six , Simon Currie, Jim Darnill, Steve Haythorne (a fantastic conversationalist and a mine of info),Tracy Stanley, Sheffield forum website, Sheffield History website, Black Market Clash website, Stewart Hardman, Gary Robinson, Barry Thurman, Barrie Masters(Eddie and the Hot Rods) for a fantastic conversation, Rob (Dingo) Dowling, Jo Callis (Rezillos and Human League), Andrew Goulty (another great friend), Russ Weaver, Gary, Phil Tasker (Vice Squad singer) for invaluable help and photos, Andrea Berry, Big Dave Gooderham, Phil Taylor and all the X-Rippers from Barnsley, Jill Ager, Shaun Angell, Ian Clayton, Jeff Turner and Mickey Geggus of 'The Cockney Rejects', Steve Mardy, Timo, Steven Doidge, Ivor Hillman (My Pierrot Dolls), Knox (Vibrators), Martin Hickman, Dave Burkinshaw, Honest John Plain (The Boys), Robert Armitage (for help with promotion and flyers), Marsha Armitage (for the interest and belief), Simon Potter of 'Print on Demand', Mick Hill the promoter at no.10 club in Rotherham, Chelle, Paul Sharpe (Vice Squad photography), Simon, Bob Manton (Purple Hearts), Steve Metcalfe who runs the Boys website at http://www.theboys.co.uk/, Andy Bull, Martin Ridgeway, Gary (Chippie) Gillott, Paul White (Sugar), Michael Day, Gary Davies, June Graham, Tom Cleary, Charlie Harper (UK Subs), Valerie Garvey, Arturo Bassick (The Lurkers, Pinpoint, 999) a super geezer and one of the last true Punk Rockers, Fiona Palmer, Steve Parkin, Pete Weston, Sally Burton, Nick Ward, Barry Bartle. Vicky Beard, Lorna, Jen Jones, Sophie and all the team at Parkgate WH Smiths, Bill Noakes (Northern Maps), Alyn from www.punkrockposters.net, **Margaret at** Sound of Music record shop, Circles record shop amongst many others who provided all those records to listen to and then buy.

Lots of extra thanks to Lynne Haythorne, Phillip Wright, Steve Parlett, Richard Chatterton, Steve Marshall, Phil Tasker, Andy Goulty and Andrew Morton for the use of their personal photos, memorabilia, Simon Hinkler for Artery photos and Paul Marko (author of The Roxy London WC 2) for advice and help...

Visit the official website at
www.ourgenerationpunkandmod.co.uk

For kind permission

"Identity it's the crisis can't you see" from the song "Identity" by X-Ray Spex composed by Marianne Elliott-Said...Published by Maxwood Music Ltd
Used by kind permission.

For fantastic reference, photos, use of quotes and inspiration 'Beats working for a living' by Martin Lilleker

Eve Wood of Sheffield vision website for kind help and contacts (to purchase the DVD 'Made in Sheffield' and the book ''Beats working for a living' visit www.sheffieldvision.com

'Cockney Reject' by Jeff Turner and Gary Bushell (Cheers Gary and Jeff for the quotes)

A big thanks to Rotherham Public Library for kind use of their archives section Rotherham Advertiser and Doug Melloy for invaluable articles, photographs and information. Sheffield Star for kind use of articles.
New Musical Express, Sounds, Record Mirror, Melody Maker, Smash Hits, Record Collector (lots of print fingered hours were spent trawling through the 100's of yellowing but fact filled back issues of all these mags).

If I have missed anyone, I am Sorry and I promise to buy you a Pint if you remind me the next time I see you...All effort has been made to contact everyone involved in this book regarding any quotes and articles of artistic and photographic status. If you see anything that needs correcting or acknowledging please do not hesitate to contact me and all future re-prints of this work will be amended to accommodate.

Most of all the biggest and kindest thanks go to my fiancée Vanessa for massive encouragement, patience and interest, Catriona and my youngest son Sean for technical help and my eldest son Dean for true faith in my endeavour and help with formatting etc

Without all of you, this book would have been impossible.

A MASSIVE

THANKS TO EVERYONE

Gone but not forgotten

John Simon Ritchie (Sid Vicious) 1957 - 1979
Joe Strummer 1952 – 2002
Russell Bonnell (Vision)
John Lake (Extras singer)
Nick Sanderson (Clock dva)
John Mcgeoch (Magazine)
Jack Airport (X-Ray Specs)
Joey, Johnny and Dee Dee Ramone
Jez Bird (Lambrettas)
Darren Marsden 1970 To 1986
Munk (X-Rippers)
Tracie O'Keefe
Howard Pick up (The Adverts)
Paul Fox (Ruts)
Malcolm Owen (Ruts)
Ian Curtis (Joy Division)
Paul Raven (Neon Hearts/Killing Joke)
Vaughn Toulouse (Department S)
Ian Williams
Mikey Dread

And in Memory of my Mum and Dad … If only you knew?

Recommended reading

Beats working' for a living (Martin Lilleker)
Not like a proper job (John Firminger and Martin Lilleker)
Take me to the Limit (Neil Anderson)
Cockney Reject (Jeff Turner with Gary Bushell)
Rip it up and start again. Post-Punk 1978 – 1984 (Simon Reynolds)
Steve Diggles' Harmony in my head (Terry Rawlings)
The Secret life of a teenage Punk Rocker (Andy Blade)
God's lonely men: The Lurkers (Pete 'Esso' Haynes)
Soul Rebels – Dexys Midnight Runners (Richard White)
Joe Strummer and the legend of the Clash (Kris Needs)
Sniffin' glue: the essential Punk accessory (Mark Perry)
No one is Innocent (Alan Parker)
London's Burning (Dave Thompson)
The Roxy London WC2 a Punk history (Paul Marko)
Babylon's Burning: from Punk to Grunge (Clinton Heylin)
England's dreaming (Jon Savage)
This is a Modern life (Enamel Veguren)
Soul Stylists (Paolo Hewitt)
Mod a very British Phenomenon (Terry Rawlings)
The Modfather (David Lines)
Redemption song: the definitive biography of Joe Strummer (Chris Salewitz)
Paul Weller My ever changing Moods (John Reed)